Research Anthology on Convergence of Blockchain, Internet of Things, and Security

Information Resources Management Association
USA

Volume I

Published in the United States of America by
IGI Global
Information Science Reference (an imprint of IGI Global)
701 E. Chocolate Avenue
Hershey PA, USA 17033
Tel: 717-533-8845
Fax: 717-533-8661
E-mail: cust@igi-global.com
Web site: http://www.igi-global.com

Library of Congress Cataloging-in-Publication Data

Names: Information Resources Management Association. editor.
Title: Research anthology on convergence of blockchain, internet of things,
    and security / Information Resources Management Association, editor.
Description: Hershey, PA : Information Science Reference, [2023] | Includes
    bibliographical references and index. | Summary: "This reference book
    describes the implementation of blockchain and IoT technologies to
    better protect personal and organizational data as well as enhance
    overall security, while explaining the tools, applications, and emerging
    innovations in security and the ways in which they are enhanced by
    blockchain and IoT"-- Provided by publisher.
Identifiers: LCCN 2022030165 (print) | LCCN 2022030166 (ebook) | ISBN
    9781668471326 (h/c) | ISBN 9781668471333 (eISBN)
Subjects: LCSH: Blockchains (Databases) | Computer networks--Security
    measures. | Internet of things. | Convergence (Telecommunication)
Classification: LCC QA76.9.B56 R474 2023 (print) | LCC QA76.9.B56 (ebook)
    | DDC 005.74--dc23/eng/20220815
LC record available at https://lccn.loc.gov/2022030165
LC ebook record available at https://lccn.loc.gov/2022030166

British Cataloguing in Publication Data
A Cataloguing in Publication record for this book is available from the British Library.

For electronic access to this publication, please contact: eresources@igi-global.com.

Editor-in-Chief

Mehdi Khosrow-Pour, DBA
Information Resources Management Association, USA

Associate Editors

Steve Clarke, *University of Hull, UK*
Murray E. Jennex, *San Diego State University, USA*
Ari-Veikko Anttiroiko, *University of Tampere, Finland*

Editorial Advisory Board

Sherif Kamel, *American University in Cairo, Egypt*
In Lee, *Western Illinois University, USA*
Jerzy Kisielnicki, *Warsaw University, Poland*
Amar Gupta, *Arizona University, USA*
Craig van Slyke, *University of Central Florida, USA*
John Wang, *Montclair State University, USA*
Vishanth Weerakkody, *Brunel University, UK*

List of Contributors

Table of Contents

Section 2
Development and Design Methodologies

Section 5
Organizational and Social Implications

Section 6
Managerial Impact

Section 7
Critical Issues and Challenges

Preface

Security on the internet has never been more crucial as today an increasing number of businesses and industries conduct their vital processes online. In order to protect information and data, further study on emerging technologies, such as blockchain and the internet of things, is critical to ensure companies and individuals feel secure online and best practices are continuously updated.

Staying informed of the most up-to-date research trends and findings is of the utmost importance. That is why IGI Global is pleased to offer this three-volume reference collection of reprinted IGI Global book chapters and journal articles that have been handpicked by senior editorial staff. This collection will shed light on critical issues related to the trends, techniques, and uses of various applications by providing both broad and detailed perspectives on cutting-edge theories and developments. This collection is designed to act as a single reference source on conceptual, methodological, technical, and managerial issues, as well as to provide insight into emerging trends and future opportunities within the field.

The *Research Anthology on Convergence of Blockchain, Internet of Things, and Security* is organized into seven distinct sections that provide comprehensive coverage of important topics. The sections are:

1. Fundamental Concepts and Theories;
2. Development and Design Methodologies;
3. Tools and Technologies;
4. Utilization and Applications;
5. Organizational and Social Implications;
6. Managerial Impact; and
7. Critical Issues and Challenges.

The following paragraphs provide a summary of what to expect from this invaluable reference tool.

Section 1, "Fundamental Concepts and Theories," serves as a foundation for this extensive reference tool by addressing crucial theories essential to understanding the concepts and uses of blockchain, the internet of things, and security in multidisciplinary settings. Opening this reference book is the chapter "A Holistic View on Blockchain and Its Issues" by Profs. Mohd Azeem Faizi Noor, Saba Khanum, and Manzoor Ansari from Jamia Millia Islamia, India and Prof. Taushif Anwar from Pondicherry University, India, which covers a holistic overview of blockchain and argues about basic operations, 51% attack, scalability issue, Fork, Sharding, Lightening, etc. This first section ends with the chapter "Application of Technology in Healthcare: Tackling COVID-19 Challenge – The Integration of Blockchain and Internet of Things" by Ms. Andreia Robert Lopes from Hovione Farmaciencia, Portugal and Profs. Ana Sofia Dias and Bebiana Sá-Moura of ISEG, Lisbon School of Economics and Management, Portugal, which discusses IoT and blockchain technologies, focusing on their main characteristics, integration benefits, and limitations as well as identifying the challenges that need to be addressed.

Section 2, "Development and Design Methodologies," presents in-depth coverage of the design and development of blockchain and internet of things technologies for their use in security across different industries. This section starts with "Blockchain-Enabled Secure Internet of Things" by Prof. Vinod Kumar from Madanapalle Institute of Technology and Science, India and Prof. Gotam Singh Lalotra of Government Degree College for Women, India, which discusses the blockchain-enabled secure internet of things (IoT). This section ends with "SEF4CPSIoT Software Engineering Framework for Cyber-Physical and IoT Systems" by Prof. Muthu Ramachandran from Leeds Beckett University, UK, which proposes a systematic software engineering framework for CPS and IoT systems as well as a comprehensive requirements engineering framework for CPS-IoT applications which can also be specified using BPMN modeling and simulation to verify and validate CPS-IoT requirements with smart contracts.

Section 3, "Tools and Technologies," explores the tools and technologies used to implement blockchain and the internet of things for facilitating secure operations. This section begins with "Blockchain for Industrial Internet of Things (IIoT)" by Prof. Rinki Sharma from Ramaiah University of Applied Sciences, India, which presents the importance of blockchain in the industrial internet of things paradigm, its role in the different industrial internet of things applications, challenges involved, and possible solutions to overcome the challenges and open research issues. This section ends with the chapter "Cyber Security and Cyber Resilience for the Australian E-Health Records: A Blockchain Solution" by Profs. Shailesh Palekar, Nagarajan Venkatachalam, and Peadar O'Connor from Queensland University of Technology, Australia, which explores how blockchain can be a single digital option that can address both cybersecurity and cyber resilience needs of electronic health records.

Section 4, "Utilization and Applications," describes how blockchain and the internet of things are used and applied in diverse industries for various security applications, such as security. The opening chapter in this section, "Perspectives of Blockchain in Cybersecurity: Applications and Future Developments," by Profs. Muath A. Obaidat and Joseph Brown from City University of New York, USA, aims to provide a neutral overview of why blockchain has risen as a popular pivot in cybersecurity, its current applications in this field, and an evaluation of what the future holds for this technology given both its limitations and advantages. The closing chapter in this section, "Advanced Cyber Security and Internet of Things for Digital Transformations of the Indian Healthcare Sector," by Profs. Esha Jain and Jonika Lamba from The NorthCap University, India, reviews the need for cybersecurity amid digital transformation with the help of emerging technologies and focuses on the application and incorporation of blockchain and the internet of things (IoT) to ensure cybersecurity in the well-being of the business.

Section 5, "Organizational and Social Implications," includes chapters discussing the impact of blockchain and the internet of things on society including how they can be utilized for security purposes across industries. The chapter "Blockchain Technology for IoT: An Information Security Perspective" by Prof. Karthikeyan P. from Thiagarajar College of Engineering, India; Prof. Sasikumar R. of K. Ramakrishnan College of Engineering, India; and Prof. Thangavel M. from Siksha 'O' Anusandhan (Deemed), India presents a detailed investigation of various IoT applications with blockchain implementation. The closing chapter, "Blockchain and IoT Integration in Dairy Production to Survive the COVID-19 Situation in Sri Lanka," by Profs. ruwandi Madhunamali and K. P. N. Jayasena from Sabaragamuwa University of Sri Lanka, Sri Lanka, proposes a dairy production system integration with blockchain and IoT.

Section 6, "Managerial Impact," considers how blockchain and internet of things technologies can be utilized within secure business and management. The opening chapter, "Applying Blockchain Security for Agricultural Supply Chain Management," by Prof. Teresa Edgar from the University of Houston, USA and Profs. Amarsinh V. Vidhate, Chitra Ramesh Saraf, Mrunal Anil Wani, and Sweta Siddarth

Waghmare of Ramrao Adik Institute of Technology, India, provides an overview of blockchain technology and its potential in developing a secure and reliable agriculture supply chain management. The closing chapter, "Blockchain and IoT-Based Diary Supply Chain Management System for Sri Lanka," by Profs. K. Pubudu Nuwnthika Jayasena and Poddivila Marage Nimasha Ruwandi Madhunamali from Sabaragamuwa University of Sri Lanka, Sri Lanka, investigates how blockchain technology can be used in today's food supply chains to deliver greater traceability of assets.

Section 7, "Critical Issues and Challenges," presents coverage of academic and research perspectives on the challenges of using blockchain and the internet of things for various security applications across industries. Starting this section is "A Comprehensive Review of the Security and Privacy Issues in Blockchain Technologies" by Prof. N. Pradeep from Bapuji Institute of Engineering and Technology, India; Prof. Renjith V. Ravi of MEA Engineering College, India; Prof. Mangesh Manikrao Ghonge from Sandip Foundation's Institute of Technology and Research Centre, India; and Prof. Ramchandra Mangrulkar of Dwarkadas J. Sanghvi College of Engineering, India, which covers blockchain's security and privacy issues as well as the impact they've had on various trends and applications. The closing chapter, "Blockchain With IoT and AI: A Review of Agriculture and Healthcare," by Prof. Pushpa Singh from KIET Group of Institutions, Delhi-NCR, India and Prof. Narendra Singh of GL Bajaj Insitute of Management and Research, India, studies the literature, formulates the research question, and summarizes the contribution of blockchain application, particularly targeting AI and IoT in agriculture and healthcare sectors.

Although the primary organization of the contents in this multi-volume work is based on its seven sections, offering a progression of coverage of the important concepts, methodologies, technologies, applications, social issues, and emerging trends, the reader can also identify specific contents by utilizing the extensive indexing system listed at the end of each volume. As a comprehensive collection of research on the latest findings related to blockchain, the internet of things, and security, the *Research Anthology on Convergence of Blockchain, Internet of Things, and Security* provides business leaders and executives, IT managers, computer scientists, hospital administrators, security professionals, law enforcement, students and faculty of higher education, librarians, researchers, and academicians with a complete understanding of the applications and impacts of blockchain and the internet of things. Given the vast number of issues concerning usage, failure, success, strategies, and applications of blockchain and internet of things technologies, the *Research Anthology on Convergence of Blockchain, Internet of Things, and Security* encompasses the most pertinent research on the applications, impacts, uses, and development of blockchain and the internet of things.

Section 1
Fundamental Concepts and Theories

Chapter 1
A Holistic View on Blockchain and Its Issues

Mohd Azeem Faizi Noor
https://orcid.org/0000-0002-8257-4985
Jamia Millia Islamia, India

Saba Khanum
Jamia Millia Islamia, India

Taushif Anwar
https://orcid.org/0000-0002-6937-7258
Pondicherry University, India

Manzoor Ansari
Jamia Millia Islamia, India

ABSTRACT

Blockchain, the technology behind most popular cryptocurrency Bitcoin and Ethereum, has attracted wide attention recently. It is the most emerging technology that has changed the financial and non-financial transaction system. It is omnipresent. Currently, this technology is enforcing banks, industries, and countries to adopt it in their financial, industrial, and government section. Earlier, it solved the centralize and double-spending problems successfully. In this chapter, the authors present a study of blockchain security issues and its challenges as well. They divided the whole chapter into two parts. The primer part covers a holistic overview of blockchain followed by the later section that argues about basic operations, 51% attack, scalability issue, Fork, Sharding, Lightening, etc. Finally, they mention an intro about its adaptation (financial or non-financial) in our 24/7 life and collaboration with fields like IoT.

DOI: 10.4018/978-1-6684-7132-6.ch001

INTRODUCTION

Blockchain is a neoteric technology that promises to shift routine activities from central parties to the actual users (decentral parties). It is seen as significantly for making systems more transparent and de-centralised, an innovation through peer-to-peer architecture and cryptographic methods that should make middle intermediaries unnecessary and empowered individuals. All entries in the ledger are immutable. Blockchain advantages force businesses, banks, and various other fields towards decentralization. Also, the potential of blockchain is far beyond and higher than any buzz and it will change society by enabling trust among them.

Decentralization has various positive aspects over centralized and distributed systems. The centralized system has central dependency which affects the overall system if the central hub fails. To get rid of the dependency on single-point failure different nodes are empowered and made self-dependent. These participants or nodes of the system participate and work collectively to share, verify and build trust in the overall system (Yli-Huumo,Ko,Choi, Park, & Scotlander, 2016).

The objective of the research to explore various aspects of blockchain. We have tried to cover holistic view by encompassing vital sections of blockchain like different consensus mechanism, issues, and challenges in detail.

The Chapter is divided into four major sections. first section introduces the basic characters along with the difference with relative terms. Second sections shed light on working, types, and consensus mechanism. Third section issues and challenges in detail. And lastly, issues are mentioned specific to blockchain applications.

1.1. Characteristics of Blockchain

a). **Trust:** One of the main characteristics of blockchain, which is mainly invoked by decentralization architecture of the system. The trust factor means not trusting anyone in the system. It eradicates the role of the third party from the system and only the involved user has the power to move their asset and makes the system transparent. The evolution of the internet has failed to solve the trust factor but blockchain does successfully.

b). **Shared and Public:** In order to ensure transparency, the ledger is kept public. Every stakeholder has a copy of the ledger. Manipulation in the ledger transaction can be easily identified. A change in the single entry will change the hash of not only the current block but also changes the hash of the previous block. For example, in the Banking system, the complete ledger is maintained by banks or government bodies and kept privately. Now due to blockchain this ledger does not involve any bank or government authorities. All entries are kept public and any peer can directly connect to the ledger and check the validity of transactions.

c). **Peer verification:** Firstly, the new user's identity is verified using an authenticated process. Once the node becomes part of the system, it has access to viewing the blockchain. Any transaction initiated is checked and verified by another peer node in the transaction and then only added to the ledger. After all, the participants have been empowered to check the verification of the transaction as the distributed ledger of the system is shared among all.

d). **Immutability:** The transactions or data saved in blockchain remains unaltered and indelible. This feature of blockchain makes the system incredible. Blockchain, instead of relying on the central authority ensures the transaction with the help of peer nodes. The process of verification includes the mining process and the validity of the transaction is done by every peer node. If the transaction is not approved by the majority of peer users, the transaction is not added to the ledger. Once the transaction is added in the block, no one has the authority to manipulate, alter, delete or update the transaction.

e). **Decentralization and democratic:** The concept of decentralization is to make the system independent. It means the whole network is not controlled by any governing authority. The group of nodes itself regulates the network. So, blockchain users can directly access relevant data from the web and store their assets. This asset can be anything viz. cryptocurrency, important documents, contracts, or any other digital asset. Decentralization gives power to the common person on their assets. Moreover, no need to worry about single-point failure and data security. Data is not maintained by a single hub, every node in the network is having the ledger copy. This deficit the system from total breakdown. Lastly, the system runs on the specific algorithms which control scams and fraud in the system.

f). **Redundancy:** The ledger is with everyone who is authorized to use the system. This characteristic of blockchain has increased the availability and trust among all unknown participants. As a result, no single point failure can exist.

g). **Enhanced Security:** In blockchain there is no third-party control. So, no one can change the information stored on the ledger. This feature enhances the security power which is achieved through "cryptography". Cryptography includes encryption through complex mathematics algorithms like SHA256, HMAC etc. that helps to secure the network from attacks. Every information in the block is first hashed and then saved into the ledger. Every block data is hashed and linked with data in the previous block. This makes all blocks in the chain and hence named "Blockchain". A change in the current block will change the hash of the previous blocks. It is very difficult for an attacker to change the hashes of all the blocks of the blockchain. So, Changing or tampering in data using Hash IDs become quiets impossible

h). **Consensus:** This feature is extremely important for the smooth functioning of the blockchain. It is the core part of any blockchain architecture. Every blockchain is having a consensus mechanism viz. PoW (Proof of Work), PoS (Proof of Stake), DPoS (Delegated Proof of Security) etc.

1.2 How Blockchain is Different From Various Terms

As with any new technology, there is an enormous amount of hype and misinformation. The same incident happens with blockchain and various misinformation and misunderstanding lead to confusion among users and they fail to differentiate the terminology related to blockchain. Figure 2 shows how various terms are related to blockchain.

1.2.1. Bitcoin

Word Bitcoin got popularity before the word blockchain and most people are not able to differentiate between both terms. Bitcoin is the first application implemented over the blockchain framework. Cryptocurrencies are created on the top of blockchain and Bitcoin is one of the cryptocurrency (Vujičić, Jagodić, & Ranđić, 2018). Bitcoin cannot work without blockchain. Ethereum is another example of cryptocurrency that works on the top of the blockchain.

1.2.2. Cryptocurrency

S. Nakamoto proposed a framework for peer-to-peer exchanges of currency (Nakamoto, 2008). His goal was to invent a decentralised digital cash system. The by-product of this system was Cryptocurrency. Even Nakamoto missed this term significantly.

Jan Lansky (2018), defines six conditions for a system that will be considered as cryptocurrency:

1. It does not need a middle authority such as a bank or state.
2. It keeps track of cryptocurrency units with respective owners.
3. The system should define the process of creating new cryptocurrency and ownership of these created units.
4. One can prove exclusively cryptographically ownership of cryptocurrency units.
5. The cryptographic unit will be changed after performing transactions. Such transaction records can be proved by an entity by declaring the current ownership of these units.
6. If two apart transactions are instructed for the same cryptographic units at the same time then at most one of them will take place.

Thus, cryptocurrency is the token based on the idea of Distributed Ledger and this facility is provided through blockchain. Cryptocurrency is referred to as a digital currency platform whereas blockchain is applied to store the transactions record. So, both are interrelated but have different roles.

1.2.3. Cryptography

Bitcoin transactions are backed by Cryptography and blockchain record cryptography-based Bitcoin transactions (Crosby, Nachiappan, Pattanayak, Verma, & Kalyanaraman, 2016). The Bitcoin protocol uses public-key cryptography for cryptographic hash functions and digital signatures (Gaurav, Kumar, Kumar, & Thakur 2020). The elliptic curve cryptography, which is asymmetric in nature, is a cryptographic algorithm used in Bitcoin (Lu, 2018). Compared to the RSA algorithm, it requires less computation with a smaller key size and provides more protection.

So, the cryptography algorithm is used for the transaction in financial blockchain and it is not blockchain rather it is a more security mechanism.

1.2.4. Linked List

Blockchain is like the linked list with some differences. Blockchain is the chain of blocks. These blocks are interconnected like nodes are connected in the linked list. Every block has a link with the previous block with a hash function whereas Linked list uses pointers for the same. Linked List is a linear way of arranging and storing records or data whereas blockchain follows Merkle Tree to store all the info related to the transaction. Data manipulation and tampering are nearly impossible in blockchain whereas linked lists permit such activities. Blockchain follows the only structure of Linked list which is accompanied by the hash function, mining, and consensus protocols (Gupta & Sadoghi, 2018).

1.2.5. Distributed Ledger Technology

DLT is an automated system that records the transactions with their details in a distributed fashion across several sites. DLT has no central authorities, unlike traditional databases (Alketbi, Nasir, & Talib, 2018). DLT has different types based on usability. Some of them are DAG, Tempo, Holochain etc. blockchain is one of them which is most popular. Some of the well-known cryptocurrencies that use blockchain DLT are Ethereum, Bitcoin, Dash, Dogecoin etc.

Conclusively, blockchain is a subset and type of DLT. All blockchains are DLT but all the DLTs are not blockchain.

Figure 1. Visualization of various terms related to Blockchain

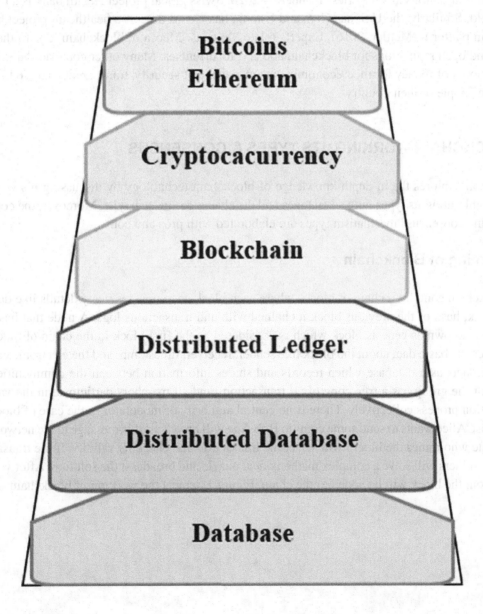

1.3. Current Trends and Practices

Now blockchain has worldwide recognition and a lot of research work has been done in recent years and it is still a hot topic for researchers throughout the world. This is only possible because blockchain is currently being used in different fields with great success. HealthCare, e-voting, Land- registration, Assets- registrations, securing supply chains of goods etc are some real-life examples of using blockchain. These applications encompass decentralization, immunity and transparency that makes it unparallel from other technologies.

The United Kingdom, Denmark, Honduras, Australia, Saudi Arabia, Switzerland, and many others have taken footstep to unleash the hidden capabilities of blockchain technology. Estonia is the first country that implements blockchain-based e-voting. Dubai, the city of future, aims to adopt blockchain in all their transactions in a paperless manner by 2020. Swiss global project Health bank is a milestone in this field. Similarly, the U.S. has Gem and Estonia has Guard time as a healthcare project based on blockchain platform (Mettler, 2016). Experts relate Malta as 'Mecca of blockchain' due to their unrestricted and open regulations for blockchain and cryptocurrencies. Many other countries have invested a huge amount of money for their economy, data management security, transparency and to build trust within the people of their country.

2. BLOCKCHAIN WORKING, ITS TYPES & CONSENSUS

This section explores the in-depth knowledge of blockchain technology by discussing it's working in detail. Highlighting its types with advantages and disadvantages in each type. Moreover, the core of the blockchain "consensus" mechanism types are elaborated with pros and cons.

2.1 Working of Blockchain

The blockchain contains a chain of blocks where each block encompasses many details like data, hash of the block, hash of the previous block it chained with and transactions logs. A node that has no parent block is known as genesis block which is considered as the first block in the chain of blocks. The node stores the basic data about the block like sender, receiver, timestamp, and the electronic cash. The blockchain acts as a database which records and shares information between the communities. Each member of the group has a true copy of all transactions and all members participate in the validation and updation process collectively. There is no central authority or moderator in the case of blockchain.

Suppose Alice wants to send some coins to Bob. She will broadcast this message to the network. Now Miner (one who mines the block) will select the transaction and check its validity. If the transaction is valid then miners will solve a complex mathematical puzzle and broadcast the solution. After validating the solution, the block will be added to the chain. Figure 1 depicts the working of blockchain.

Figure 2. Working of Blockchain technology (Nadeem, Rizwan, Ahmad, & Manzoor,2019).

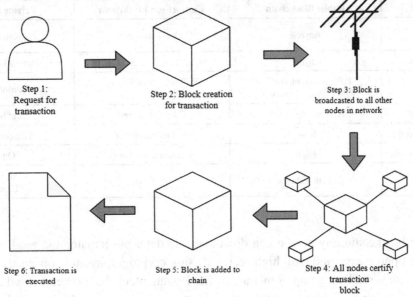

2.2. Types of Blockchain

Blockchain can be categorized based on the application type (financial or non-financial), evolution type (1.0 Bitcoin, 2.0 Ethereum, 3.0 EOS). There are three kinds of blockchain (Table 1) on Usability basis:

a.) *Public Blockchain*: Anyone can join the network after the verification and validation process. Everyone has access to the whole ledger. Every peer has equal rights, nobody can empower other peers. The first blockchain, Bitcoin, introduced by Satoshi Nakamoto was public and open for all. The direct transfer of cryptocurrency takes place between the peer nodes. Having empowered nodes, this public blockchain has many benefits but at the same time, if any way any theft occurs in the system the peer node can-not claim anywhere.

b.) *Consortium Blockchain*: In this type of blockchain the peers are empowered with equal rights but there are some regulators which help in making the decision. This is the most talked and promising blockchain according to researchers.

c.) *Private Blockchain*: This blockchain is more like a centralized system. Certain stakeholders have all the access. Not everyone can become the part of the blockchain and hence only involved stakeholders have the right to access the ledger. The consensus is different as used in the public and consortium blockchain. Decision-making power is with certain owners like previously with banks.

Table 1. Blockchain Types

Characteristics	Public Blockchain	Consortium Blockchain	Private Blockchain
Read Permission	Anyone	Known users	Known users
Write Access	Anyone	Multi-selected organisation	Single organisation
Consensus	PoW (Proof of Work), PoS (Proof of Stake)	PoW (Proof of Work), PoS (Proof of Stake)	PoA (Proof of Authority)
Immutability	Almost impossible	Could be altered	Could be tampered
Transaction Speed	Slow	Lighter and faster	Lighter and faster
Energy Consumption	High	Comparatively low	Quiet low
Examples	Bitcoin, Ethereum	Ripple, R3	Multichain, Blockstack

With public blockchain any person can download the data, participate, and read the data. Public blockchains are open source and with high security using cryptography and consensus protocol. Consortium blockchain is run by a group of members. The Private blockchain is centralised in nature where a user needs permission to join or leave the group. Companies who wanted to create their own currencies started using this type of blockchain. Additionally, these blockchains differ in transfer rate, node rights and usage range. Examples of public blockchain include Bitcoin, Ethereum, private types include Multichain and Blockstack and consortium blockchain include Ripple and R3.

2.3. Different Consensus Mechanism

Consensus Mechanism is the protocol for legitimate transactions which is added to the blockchain. Through this protocol, the blockchain network agrees on a transaction globally. Different consensus mechanism is used by the different types of cryptocurrencies. For example, Proof of Work (PoS) used by Bitcoin, Ethereum, Proof of Stake (PoS) used by Peercoin, Ethereum (maybe in future), Delegated Proof Of Stake (DPOS)used by EOS, Bitshares, Practical Byzantine Fault Tolerance (PBFT) by Hyperledger etc. Table 2 highlights the comparison among them.

a)   Proof of Work (PoW)

PoW is suggested by Satoshi Nakamoto which is considered as a first blockchain consensus mechanism. The consensus process is recognised as mining and the involved nodes are recognised as a miner. Miners mine the block. Miners bundle the transaction from mempool as Block and check the accuracy of all transactions within the block. Now they try to solve a difficult mathematical puzzle that needs huge computational power. This puzzle is difficult to solve but easy to verify. It can be solved through the 'trial and error' method. Random value of nonce is adjusted to get the required hash value. The first one to solve this puzzle will publish the hash value of the block and will get block rewards along with fee reward for it. This block will be appended in the chain.

PoW requires a lot of resources which is unsustainable and not feasible in the future. So many block-chains are moving to new or different consensus algorithms.

b)   Proof of Stake (PoS)

It is an environmental friendly approach as it does not solve a highly complex puzzle like PoW. Therefore, it consumes very less electricity to verify the transactions. It is a randomized process that selects validators for verifying the transactions. The validators are like miners who produce the blocks. The validators have to deposit their tokens for a certain amount of time to become eligible for produc-ing blocks. The validators who deposited higher stake had the highest chance to validate a block. On completing the process Validators will get rewarded for their work.

It has a major disadvantage. As the rich validators will have more chance to validate the block so rich validators will become richer and rest validators don't get enough chance to validate the block and win rewards.

c)   Delegate Proof of Stake (DPOS)

This is a very fast consensus and implemented in EOS popularly. This process introduces a new word 'Delegate' or 'witness'. Delegate can be a person or organisation who will produce blocks. The user stake their coin to vote for particular delegates. Higher the stake, higher will be the weight of the vote. Several delegates are selected based on the percentage of their votes. Now, they will get a chance to produce new blocks in a round-robin manner and get rewarded for their work. This reward will be distributed among their respective electors proportional to their tokens as a vote.

d)   Practical Byzantine Fault Tolerance (PBFT)

This consensus mechanism is designed as a 'fault-tolerance' algorithm that works in the asynchronous and distributed system. This network reaches consensus even when some of the malicious components propagate wrong information or fail to respond. This algorithm ensures correct information to flow among the nodes and mitigating malicious nodes' effects. It can tolerate malicious nodes if their number is less than one-third of the total nodes.

All nodes in this network are ordered in sequence. One of them is selected as leader or primary node and the rest are referred to as backup nodes. The primary node gets a message from the client and broadcasts it to the backup nodes. Now, backup nodes will send a message to each other including the primary node. Each node ensures that they get 2F+1 (F = max no of the faulty nodes) valid 'Prepare messages' including themselves. Finally, Primary and backup nodes reach on an agreement and reply back to the client. If the client receives F+1 replies from different nodes with the same results then it is considered a successful reply.

Table 2. A comparison among Consensus Algorithm

Property	PoW	PoS	DPoS	PBFT
Resource Consumption	High	Low	Very Low	Very Low
Nature	Decentralize	Decentralize	Centralize	Decentralize
Type	Permission-less	Permission-less	Permission-less	Permissioned
Throughput	Low <10 tps	Average <20 tps	High >5000tps	High >1000 tps
Tolerated Power	<50% Computing Power	< 50% Stake	<50% Validators	<33.33% Malicious replica
Transaction Fee	High	Low	Low	Very Low
Example	Bitcoin	DoS	EOS	Hyperledger

3. CHALLENGES AND ISSUES OF BLOCKCHAIN

3.1. 51% Attack

51% attack refers to an attack on a blockchain in which a group of miners controls more than 50% of the network's mining hash rate or computing power (Chanti, Anwar, Chithralekha, & Uma 2020). This will prevent any new transaction to occur and to reverse the transaction. 51% attack can further cause double spending problems. The attackers surely were not able to create new coins but would compromise the security of the blockchain (Apostolaki, 2017).

The Dangers of a Mining Monopoly

The objective of Bitcoin (underline technology -- Blockchain) is to run a distributed ledger that powers permission-less peer-to-peer transactions. A 51% attack is not dangerous only that it can create a double-spend which causes a merchant to lose money, but rather it can finish the entire system. With a majority of sustained hash power, an invader can continuously (or periodically) invoke a blockchain reorganization which disturbs the reliability of the network. At the extreme, they can mine empty blocks forever and only lengthen the chain on their own blocks, shutting all others out and causing the chain to be totally impractical.

3.1.1 Previous Approaches to the Problem

- Invalidating blocks: This logical approach is used by miners to invalidate fishy looking blocks. The process of invalidation invokes a clean break and the chain extends to null or void block.
- The Threshold Paradox: Now, the vital part is to decide which block behaviour is suspicious and when to invalidate? Setting time limit (threshold) could be one option, but soon the time limit theory is discarded as due to network and propagation issues half of the block could be considered in invalidating zone. The paradoxical aspect is no matter how the big-time limit is set; the fault line does not withhold with the time limit.

- Block re-org depth ("automatic checkpoints"): Keep in check using block height and forbidden beyond re-orgs. This method also not able to fulfil the expectation. As any block deeper than blocks could be valid or invalid because of the threshold timing problem.
- Nakamoto Consensus and the Byzantine General's Problem: "Nakamoto Consensus" is the original consensus used in the first application (Bitcoin) of blockchain. The beauty of the original proof-of-work lies in identifying the correct version of the ledger.

Byzantine general's problem describes a group of generals who want to attack a city but is not able to coordinate their attack. In Bitcoin, each solved block as a "general" that the rest of the army can follow. Doing the work thus designates a miner as having a turn to play the role of general. It is been realized that the genius of using proof of work as a distributed time-stamping mechanism is very difficult to tamper with.

3.1.2. Some Solution to - The Problem

i) *Non-fully distributed solutions*: - If we consider a simple solution not to allow reorgs > 6 blocks, then a 6-block reorganisation, that comes at the same time as a new block could divide the chain. Though, it would be simple for attentive miners to sense the split and reset it. But, this action can't be fully automated and it requires human intervention and coordination among honest miners. This can work as a practical matter, but this is not a wholly distributed solution.

ii) *Non-distributed solution*: - It allows a group of reliable pools (3 out of 5 signatures) to invalidate a block. This could be completed in a way where nodes must observe the re-org taking place; the pools can't arbitrarily direct the chain.

iii) *Middle Ground*: - It would be possible to get some penalty in the middle, 20, 30, 50%... and this could create a race condition, but only at a shallow reorg depth. The race would soon be over, and just as important, an attacker could not fool honest nodes into battling each other because they would each see a similar penalty.

3.2. Finality

It is an affirmation, that all the committed blocks in the blockchain will not be revoked again if wrong data is input in the blockchain. As the transaction once added to the blockchain could not be altered. Finality falls back to Nakamoto Consensus. When the race ends and the longest chain proof of work overtakes the attacker chain eventually (no matter how long), it is finalized in the purest sense. The 51% attack is discussed by satoshi in his first white paper, elaborates that blockchain characteristics can be overtaken by attaining 51% of the computation power. To ensure the proper functioning of blockchain finality become vital. There are three types of finality in the blockchain

1). Probabilistic Finality
2). Absolute Finality
3). Economic finality

In the *probabilistic finality*, chained-based protocols are used. Bitcoin's Nakamoto consensus is an example of probabilistic finality, where it is recommended to wait for at least 6 blocks to confirm a transaction. This ensures the less likelihood of revert of transaction. In the case of *absolute finality*, a transaction is confirmed by PBFT-based protocols viz. Tendermint. A list of validators approves the transaction. *Economic finality* applies monetarily cost for a block to be reverted. This type of finality is opted by Casper FFG.

According to Eric Brewer's CAP theorem, in case of partition, a distributed system can preserve either consistency or availability. Consistency ensures the correct state of the system which can be attained through probabilistic finality and availability is favoured by absolute finality.

3.3. Scalability

Scalability is one of the main rooted issue related to blockchain. The researchers are trying to solve the scalability issue from its initial stage. The scalability defines the number of transactions per second. The very first application of blockchain is Bitcoin that offers maximum 6-7 transactions per second (tps) and 2nd application is Ethereum that offers 20 tps which is very low as compared to other application's transactions. For example, Visa handles 1667 tps, PayPal process 170 tps etc (Conti, Kumar, Lal, & Ruj, 2018).

Scalability depends on many factors such as block size, network latency, Consensus algorithm, complex calculations etc. With the advancement of these factors, we have to compromise with security and tend more towards centralisation. Each factor has its own cons and pros. Scalability depends on many factors such as block size, network latency, Consensus algorithm, complex calculations etc. With the advancement of these factors, we have to compromise with security and it tends more towards centralisation. Now, we will discuss block size and median confirmation time that play a big role for scalability issue.

3.3.1 Block Size

Nakamoto suggested 1 MB Block size for Bitcoin. These Blocks contain numerous transactions. Generally, a Block contains approximately 1500-3500 transactions, given the 1 MB limit. It varies with the size of transaction details. Miners take 10 minutes to generate a new block (Conti et al, 2018). Let's consider some cases with block size to increase the scalability.

First one is to increase block size upto tolerable limit that will acquire more number of transactions. In this case, all nodes need to perform all the required calculations. Due to increase in size, it will be harder for the node to process all transactions. To verify the transactions, miners need more advanced resources and it will filter the less equipped miners and will empower the more equipped miners. Thus, it will lead to more centralisation. Also, it results, threat over security like 51% attack.

The second case is to increase the block size up to infinity. This case is the worst situation. For miners, it will be very difficult to process the transactions and resources can't be enough for it. The final case is to increase block size narrowly. It will amass a bit more transactions but it is not an optimal and feasible solution.

Another case is that we have several blockchain and run the different applications on different blockchain, i.e. no need to run all computation on a single blockchain rather distributes it. This approach distributed the load of single blockchain into many of them. So, it increases the performance but will do bargaining with Security. This approach will distribute the hash power in different blockchain and to avoid from 51% attack we need a large chain that should have all hashing power with it. So, scattering the hash may lead to security.

3.3.1.2 Median Confirmation Time: Another Reason for Scalability

This is one more reason that delays the transaction and generating the block. Median Confirmation Time is the duration of time that the user must wait as the transaction accepted into a mined block. It happens due to the lower transaction fee. The more transaction fee, the more chance to be accepted for the mining. Currently (on 19-05-2020) 71,141,960 bytes is the aggregate size of transactions that are waiting to be confirmed and this is known as Mempool size.

To solve the scalability issue many approaches had been done and some new techniques and methods are introduced. Sharding and Lightning Network are the methods that tried to solve the scalability issue. Now, we will have a look over it.

3.3.2 Sharding

Sharding is a database concept to make it more efficient. In blockchain, Sharding splits the overhead of computation among multiple groups of shards/nodes. These shards keep a part of blockchain and not complete blockchain information. These shards work in parallel to increase efficiency that allows the network to enhance the scalability. Sharding based projects are Ethereum, Zilliqa, and Carding to get scalability solution. However, Sharding is still unproven technology in term of blockchain (Moubarak, Filiol, & Chamoun,2018).

3.3.2.2. Lightning Network

This technique is also called off-chain approach. In this network, no need to keep each record on blockchain rather it adds another layer on the top of blockchain and creates a payment channel between any two parties on that extra layer.

These two parties need to create a multi-signature wallet and they can access it with their private keys. At least one of them must deposit some amount of cryptocurrency into that wallet. After every payment, the amount will be deducted from the wallet if both do signing with their private keys. They can do any number of transactions on this channel. They can use this channel as long as they need. Anyone of them can close the channel. After closing, the latest balance sheet of wallet that was signed by both parties will be broadcast to the network. Miners will check balance sheet and if found everything right, will release the funds to the respective parties. This will be considered as a single transaction on blockchain. So in this way, the Lightning Network can reduce the load on blockchain (Poon, Dryja, 2016).

The above discussion concludes that Satoshi Nakamoto proposed 1 MB limited block size in 2008. James A. Donald, First-person who interact on a forum with Satoshi Nakamoto, commented: "the way I understand your proposal, it does not seem to scale to the required size." After a decade, scalability is still a serious issue for Bitcoin and other cryptocurrencies. The experts are trying to get an optimal and permanent solution but still not achieved. Block size and security are a trade-off. Many latest implementations are yet unproven.

Scalability Trilemma (figure 3) says that there is a trade-off between three important properties: decentralization, scalability, and security. Blockchain can have at most two of them (Tssandor, 2019).

Figure 3. The Scalability Trilemma: - Satisfying all three at the same time is difficult.

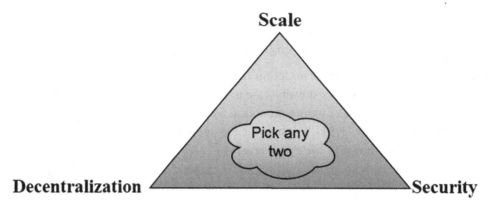

3.4 Fork

There are basically two types of fork, Soft fork and Hard fork. Any update in the chain that also supports previously blocks in the chain is termed as soft fork while an update that does not support previous blocks and make another chain is termed as Hard fork. Figure 4 illustrates both concepts. The user need not to upgrade the node on soft fork as it is compatible with the earlier version while Hard fork is must to update as it is not compatible with the earlier version. The hard fork is the result of the disagreement between the experts or users. Hard fork disturbs the harmony among users (Hamida, Brousmiche, Levard, & Thea, 2017).

Many researchers are not happy with the restricted block size of the blockchain. They want to increase it. To achieve it, they did hard fork over blockchain and named it as Bitcoin Cash (BCH) in August 2017 with 8MB block size (Figure 5). Later, in May 2018, it fourfold and become 32 MB. As a result, it can process 61 tps. The worrying point is that it will generate 4.5 GB per day which need huge storage space and resources will be out of financial reach for common miners. Eventually, it will face the risk of centralisation.

Figure 4. Soft Fork and Hard Fork

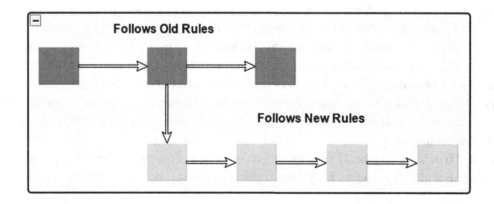

Figure 5. BCH Fork (at block 478558)

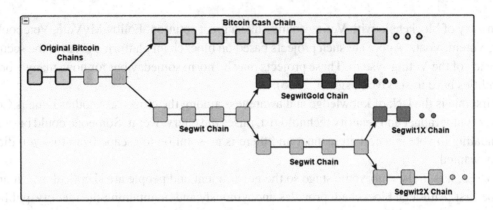

Segregated Witness (SegWit) is the result of soft fork. This protocol code was released in 2015 and updated on Bitcoin in August 2017. Initially, Bitcoin was suffering from a bug called transaction malleability. This bug mutates scriptSig in such a way that changes the transaction identifier (txid) but not the signature and content. Signature is known as witness. The SegWit fixes this bug. It keeps digital signature details outside and moved to the extended block while calculating the txid of the transaction data. So if an attacker tries to change the ScriptSig, it will not affect txid. The signature takes more than 50% of the transaction data. If we omit signature, we can process more number of transactions within a block. After implementing SegWit the max block size is about 4MB that results in a better throughput (Conti et al, 2018; Wuille, 2019).

3.5. Lack of Standardization

The numbers of users are increasing with the popularity of blockchain. Consequently, we have thousands of blockchain projects on different platforms with coding languages, consensus mechanism, protocols, and standards. So, it is a matter of concern on how these projects can interact with each other. Lack of interoperability creates problems for users and investors. The user must make n account for n platform. The ideal solution is to make a single account for n platforms. Standardization can unite the enterprises to collaborate on application development and consensus mechanism.

4. DISCUSSING BLOCKCHAIN ISSUES ON SPECIFIC APPLICATIONS

There exist various financial and non-financial applications of blockchain that hints how the blockchain taking over the world. BFSI, FX, FinTech, etc. from financial category to Healthcare, Land Registry, Identification from the non-financial category, it's all about the domination of blockchain applications. In the beginning, Banks and other sectors were skeptical about adapting blockchain but the scenario is now changed with time. Nowadays many financial and non-financial organizations and individuals are investing their resources in blockchain-based applications. However, such applications are facing various issues due to many reasons like infrastructure, lack of knowledge, fund, etc. In this section, some issues and challenges of basic financial and non-financial application will be discussed.

4.1. Voting System

The chemistry of blockchain with Voting sounds like a great solution. FollowMyVote, Votebook, Vote-Watcher, Votem, Voatz, Agora are such projects based on blockchain platforms to solve the security and transparency of the Voting system. These projects may be norm someday but for now, many worries and vulnerabilities have to survive (Osgood, 2016).

The first one is the lack of knowledge and awareness among the citizens. Another issue is Coercion. M Green, cryptographer and security technologist, raises the query over it. Someone could be convinced by intimidating to vote in a certain manner and there is no solution to escape from that you did not do what they wanted.

Next issue, it is in the embryonic stage so the government and people are skeptical over it and don't want to be first. Although blockchain provides anonymously and maintaining the identity, public confidence and trust are necessary elements for blockchain-Enabled Voting's success. Due to its open-source voting platform nature, anybody can audit his recorded vote.

4.2. Healthcare

Healthcare is another non-financial application of blockchain. Gem Health Network, Guardtime, health-bank, healthureum are some major and nascent projects related to health based on blockchain. The primer issue is the financial crisis. The healthcare expenses grow uninterruptedly and Hospitals and clinics are not getting an adequate amount of fund to maintain the infrastructure and quality services. Many hospitals and clinics are not able to start or afford such advanced technology's features.

Such projects are worldwide and can be accessed from anywhere. The barrier is the law made by individual country. Some countries are favouring it and some are on the other side. The main concern is health providers and hospitals follow several regulations and laws. These regulations and laws should be supportive for the privacy of the patients (Mettler, 2016; Ahram, T., Sargolzaei, Sargolzaei, Daniels, & Amaba,2017).To access the health record, the patient uses a private key. If a person met an accident unfortunately and he is unconscious or in coma state then how the clinicians will come to know his health records.

The drug counterfeit issue is at its peak. According to a report, Pharmaceutical enterprises bear $200 million due to counterfeit drugs worldwide. A jillion of people died due to counterfeit drugs each year globally. Blockchain can reduce these fatalities with a great margin. Now a question pops up, why government and pharmaceutical enterprises are apathetic towards the adoption of blockchain?

4.3. Supply Chain

Despite the Supply chain is the natural application of blockchain still it is not in use too much. The supply chain has the potential to bring a new market and dominate the market. There exist thousands of e-services and they have their tied delivery services. Blockchain can be a boon for them.

Similarly, blockchain can track the food and diet and can analyse the effects of the diet. This analysis can bring reasons for illness. Which food she/he took before getting unwell, it can be known through the use of food tracking (Niranjanamurthy, Nithya, & Jagannatha, 2018). Additionally, it can also be noticed the nourishment and effect of diet on the patient.

The monger or salesman can track their products and they come to know who is using their products. Based on various such information, they can take the decision and can build their market. The consumer can verify the authenticity of the product directly. For example, recently, Nestlé has launched open blockchain to track the milk. Similarly, many other companies also launched their blockchain platform to track their products. Nevertheless, it is not in practice at the mass level.

4.4. Banking

The Financial industry has a well-established infrastructure already and it is a grand challenge for the cooperate world to switch on blockchain. No doubt, it will reduce the cost by a big margin (Nakamoto, 2008) and provide enough security but it needs skilled employees and new infrastructure. It needs an adequate amount of money to set up the initial blockchain infrastructure. While applying it on legacy systems, it still faces some challenges. Due to the new infrastructure, the maintenance value is high. It will take some time to adapt to the new environment. Many financial organisations have skeptical about its adoption. However, if they have long planned then obviously adoption of blockchain is more fruitful (Zheng, Xie, Dai, Chen, & Wang, 2017).

Although there are abundant benefits of blockchain in financial applications, there exist some barricade and challenges as well. These challenges need to be addressed before implementing globally. These challenges include security, scalability, interoperability, cost, efficiency etc.

4.5 Regulations and Governance

Many countries consider blockchain as important assets for their country and some countries don't. The economy of countries relies on a set of policies and regulations. The regulations vary with country. Japan was the first nation to use Bitcoin as cryptocurrency and presently about 2k cryptocurrencies are in the market. In contrary to it, the business of cryptocurrencies is considered illegal in many countries. Conclusively, rules and regulations of the individual country are denying the adoption of blockchain globally (Conti et al, 2018).

Because of the lack of standard rules and regulations, scams and market manipulation have been commonplace in the crypto world. As a result, we have myriad scams like Ponzi scheme, BitKRX, Mt. Gox etc., which stole millions from investors (Conti et al, 2018; Lansky, 2018). And, investors neither claim to website owner nor the government.

4.7. Blockchain Integrations With IoT

Blockchain and Internet of things both are significant fields and amalgamation of both are opening a huge number of possibilities for the future. In this direction IOTA, a new blockchain IoT based platform is introduced. IOTA has the capability to overcome the blockchain drawbacks. Scalability and low-cost communication between the different things/nodes of the internet is done by maintaining a common ledger. Low cost communication among the things enhances and gives an insight into the bright future of blockchain Internet of things platforms.

Interoperability among the node persists a major drawback in the field of blockchain and internet of things. Progressive work is carried by a lot of researchers to overcome these drawbacks. (Makhdoom, Abolhasan, Abbas, & Ni, 2018). The advancement of new technologies has made a huge leap in recent decades. It brings about a drastic change in every phase of human life that is capable of intelligent tasks. Blockchain and internet of things (IoT) both are disruptive technologies that have received a lot of attention from industrial, academic and financial technologies (Shrestha & Kim, 2019).

In the centralized IoT system, there is a risk of loss of privacy of sensitive information because centralized servers can access plain text data from various IoT devices. There is a huge interest in implementing blockchain to the IoT system to ensure the privacy of IoT data and the decentralized access model (Reyna, Martín, Chen, Soler & Díaz, 2018). Blockchain technology is used to retrieve information and store this information in blocks from different IoT devices to ensure transparency among global users (Rathee, Sharma, Kumar & Iqbal, 2019). In the last decade, numerous security techniques and approaches have been highlighted. Blockchain plays an important role in the securing of many IoT applications (Minoli & Occhiogrosso,2018).

The decentralized architecture of the Blockchain-based IoT system can offer security and many other benefits. The benefits of the integration of IoT with Blockchain are Data Integrity, Transparency, Security, Decentralization, Autonomy, Identity Management, Immutability, Resilience, Anonymity and Cost Reduction. The Internet of things (IoT) systems suffer mainly from security aspects. Blockchain plays an imperative role in mitigating the challenges associated with security. Using smart contacts Blockchain can easily handle and monitor the security aspects of IoT systems.

5. CONCLUSION

This chapter explains the basic knowledge of blockchain, 51% and scalability issues. Next, it describe the adaptation issues in specific application of blockchain. Blockchain encompasses a huge number of possibilities and possesses a very bright future. The use cases of this field are countless and the way it is been adapted by other technologies and industries is hyperphysical. This technology has the potential to do miracles in future. There are an ample amount of opportunities blockchain offers but at the same time, it suffers from various challenges and limitations such as scalability, security, and privacy, compliance and governance issues. These issues and challenges need to be thoroughly explored and addressed.

REFERENCES

Ahram, T., Sargolzaei, A., Sargolzaei, S., Daniels, J., & Amaba, B. (2017, June). Blockchain technology innovations. In 2017 IEEE Technology & Engineering Management Conference (TEMSCON) (pp. 137-141). IEEE. doi:10.1109/TEMSCON.2017.7998367

Alketbi, A., Nasir, Q., & Talib, M. A. (2018, February). Blockchain for government services—Use cases, security benefits and challenges. In 2018 15th Learning and Technology Conference (L&T) (pp. 112-119). IEEE.

Apostolaki, M., Zohar, A., & Vanbever, L. (2017, May). Hijacking bitcoin: Routing attacks on cryptocurrencies. In 2017 IEEE Symposium on Security and Privacy (SP) (pp. 375-392). IEEE. doi:10.1109/SP.2017.29

Chanti, S., Anwar, T., Chithralekha, T., & Uma, V. (2020). Global Naming and Storage System Using Blockchain. In Transforming Businesses With Bitcoin Mining and Blockchain Applications (pp. 146–165). IGI Global. doi:10.4018/978-1-7998-0186-3.ch008

Conti, M., Kumar, E. S., Lal, C., & Ruj, S. (2018). A survey on security and privacy issues of bitcoin. *IEEE Communications Surveys and Tutorials*, 20(4), 3416–3452. doi:10.1109/COMST.2018.2842460

Crosby, M., Nachiappan, Pattanayak, P., Verma, S., & Kalyanaraman, V. (2016). Blockchain technology: Beyond bitcoin. *Applied Innovation Review*, 2(6-10), 71.

Gaurav, A. B., Kumar, P., Kumar, V., & Thakur, R. S. (2020). Conceptual Insights in Blockchain Technology: Security and Applications. In Transforming Businesses With Bitcoin Mining and Blockchain Applications (pp. 221-233). IGI Global.

Gupta, S., & Sadoghi, M. (2018). Blockchain transaction processing. In Encyclopedia of big data technologies, (pp. 1–11). doi:10.1007/978-3-319-63962-8_333-1

Hamida, E. B., Brousmiche, K. L., Levard, H., & Thea, E. (2017, July). Blockchain for enterprise: overview, opportunities and challenges. Academic Press.

Lansky, J. (2018). Possible state approaches to cryptocurrencies. *Journal of Systems Integration*, 9(1), 19–31. doi:10.20470/jsi.v9i1.335

Lu, Y. (2018). Blockchain: A survey on functions, applications and open issues. *Journal of Industrial Integration and Management*, 3(04), 1850015. doi:10.1142/S242486221850015X

Makhdoom, I., Abolhasan, M., Abbas, H., & Ni, W. (2018). Blockchain's adoption in IoT: The challenges, and a way forward. *Journal of Network and Computer Applications*.

Mettler, M. (2016, September). Blockchain technology in healthcare: The revolution starts here. In 2016 IEEE 18th International Conference on e-Health Networking, Applications and Services (Healthcom) (pp. 1-3). IEEE.

Minoli, D., & Occhiogrosso, B. (2018). Blockchain mechanisms for IoT security. Internet of Things, 1-2, 1–13. doi:10.1016/j.iot.2018.05.002

Moubarak, J., Filiol, E., & Chamoun, M. (2018, April). On blockchain security and relevant attacks. In 2018 IEEE Middle East and North Africa Communications Conference (MENACOMM) (pp. 1-6). IEEE. doi:10.1109/MENACOMM.2018.8371010

Nadeem, S., Rizwan, M., Ahmad, F., & Manzoor, J. (2019). Securing Cognitive Radio Vehicular Ad Hoc Network with Fog Node based Distributed Blockchain Cloud Architecture. *International Journal of Advanced Computer Science and Applications*, 10(1), 288–295. doi:10.14569/IJACSA.2019.0100138

Nakamoto, S. (2008). Bitcoin: A peer-to-peer electronic cash system. Retrieved from https://bitcoin.org/bitcoin.pdf

Niranjanamurthy, M., Nithya, B. N., & Jagannatha, S. (2018). Analysis of Blockchain technology: Pros, cons and SWOT. *Cluster Computing*, ●●●, 1–15.

Osgood, R. (2016). The future of democracy: Blockchain voting. COMP116: Information Security, 1-21.

Poon, J., & Dryja, T. (2016). *The bitcoin lightning network: Scalable off-chain instant payments.* Academic Press.

Rathee, G., Sharma, A., Kumar, R., & Iqbal, R. (2019). A Secure Communicating Things Network Framework for Industrial IoT using Blockchain Technology. *Ad Hoc Networks*, *94*, 94. doi:10.1016/j. adhoc.2019.101933

Reyna, A., Martín, C., Chen, J., Soler, E., & Díaz, M. (2018). On blockchain and its integration with IoT. Challenges and opportunities. *Future Generation Computer Systems*, *88*, 173–190. doi:10.1016/j. future.2018.05.046

Shrestha, R., & Kim, S. (2019). Integration of IoT with blockchain and homomorphic encryption: Challenging issues and opportunities. Role of Blockchain Technology in IoT Applications, 115, 293–331. doi:10.1016/bs.adcom.2019.06.002

Tssandor (.2019). Retrieved 24 July 2019, from https://steemit.com/blockchain/@tssandor/a-gentle-introduction-to-blockchain-scalability-part-i

Vujičić, D., Jagodić, D., & Ranđić, S. (2018). *Blockchain technology, bitcoin, and Ethereum: A brief overview. In 2018 17th International Symposium Infoteh-Jahorina (INFOTEH).* IEEE., doi:10.1109/ INFOTEH.2018.8345547.

Wuille, P. (2019). Segregated-witness-and-its-impact-on-scalability. Retrieved 24 July 2019, from https:// diyhpl.us/wiki/transcripts/scalingbitcoin/hong-kong/segregated-witness-and-its-impact-on-scalability/

Yli-Huumo, J., Ko, D., Choi, S., Park, S., & Smolander, K. (2016). Where is current research on blockchain technology?—A systematic review. *PLoS One*, *11*(10), e0163477. doi:10.1371/journal. pone.0163477 PubMed

Zheng, Z., Xie, S., Dai, H., Chen, X., & Wang, H. (2017, June). An overview of blockchain technology: Architecture, consensus, and future trends. In 2017 IEEE International Congress on Big Data (BigData Congress) (pp. 557-564). IEEE. doi:10.1109/BigDataCongress.2017.85

This research was previously published in Blockchain Applications in IoT Security; pages 21-44, copyright year 2021 by Information Science Reference (an imprint of IGI Global).

Chapter 2
Concept of Blockchain Technology and Its Emergence

Padmavathi U.
National Institute of Technology, Puducherry, India

Narendran Rajagopalan
National Institute of Technology, Puducherry, India

ABSTRACT

Blockchain refers to a distributed ledger technology that helps people to regulate and manage their information without any intermediaries. This technology emerges as a promising panacea for authentication and authorization with potential for use in every possible domain including financial, manufacturing, educational institutions, etc. Blockchain has its birth through the concept of Bitcoin, a digital cryptocurrency by Satoshi Nakamoto, called as Blockchain 1.0. Blockchain 2.0 came into existence in 2014 with Ethereum and smart contracts. The challenges such as scalability, interoperability, sustainability, and governance led to the next generation of Blockchain also called as IOTA, a blockchainless cryptocurrency for the internet of things runs on the top of their own ledger called Tangle, which is immune towards quantum computers. This disruptive technology evolved to provide cross chain support and more security through Blockchain 4.0. Finally, the chapter concludes by discussing the various applications of this technology and its advantages and security issues.

EMERGENCE OF BLOCKCHAIN

Blockchain, the underlying technology behind cryptocurrencies has its origin that stem from a problem of verifying timestamp digitally in the late 1980s and early 1990s. In 1990, Haber & Stornetta published a paper titled 'How to Timestamp a digital Document'. In this paper, they proposed to create a hash chain by linking the issued timestamps together so that the documents get prevented from being either forward dated or back dated. Later in 1992, the concept of Merkle Trees was added to this design by Haber, Stornetta and Dave Bayer. Merkle trees helped to improve the efficiency of the system by collecting several time-stamped documents into a cryptographically secured chain of blocks. Each

DOI: 10.4018/978-1-6684-7132-6.ch002

record in this chain is connected to the one before it. This helps the newest record to know the history of entire chain. Then, Wei Dai one of the noted researchers, introduced the concept of b-money which is used to create money through solving computational puzzles and decentralized consensus. But this proposal lacks implementation details. (Blockchain, an emerging technology for the future - Data Driven Investor - Medium n.d.)(The Exponential Guide to Blockchain - Singularity University n.d.)(History of blockchain | Technology | ICAEW n.d.)

(A brief history in the evolution of blockchain technology platforms - By n.d.)In 2005, a concept called "Reusable Proof of Work" (RPoW) was introduced by Hal Finney, a cryptographic activist. This concept combined the ideas of both b-money and computationally difficult Hashcash puzzle by Adam Back for the creation of cryptocurrency. RPoW registers the ownership of tokens on a trusted server. These servers allow the users to check the correctness and integrity of users which in turn helps to solve double spending problem. (History of Blockchain | Binance Academy n.d.)

In 2008, a mysterious white paper titled "Bitcoin: A peer to peer Electronic Cash system", by visionary Satoshi Nakamoto gives birth to the concept of Blockchain. In this paper, Nakamoto combined cryptography, computer science and game theory to describe the digital cash "Bitcoin". This helps the participant to transact from one account to another account without the help of intermediaries such as central authority or bank. (A Brief History of Blockchain: Blockchain Basics Book from ConsenSys Academy n.d.) The following timeline table gives a brief explanation on the emergence of blockchain.

Table 1. Timeline for the Emergence of Blockchain

Year	Emergence of Blockchain
1990	Stuart Haber & Stornetta introduced timestamping a digital document so that they could not be tampered.
1992	The concept of Merkle trees was proposed to collect several documents in one block.
2000	The theory and idea of cryptographic secured chains was proposed by Stefen Konst
2005	Hal Finney introduced "Reusable Proof of Work" (RPoW) that helps users to solve double spending problem in the creation of cryptocurrencies.
2008	Satoshi Nakamoto Proposed Bitcoin, a digital currency which makes use of Blockchain as the underlying concept.

Concept of Blockchain

As the world needs more modernization and digitization, everyone is ready to accept and adapt new technologies(Blockchain Technology Explained: Introduction, Meaning, and Applications - By n.d.). Blockchain, a new disruptive technology was introduced with its very first modern application termed Bitcoin. The term Blockchain is simply defined as the chain of blocks containing encrypted information stored on a decentralized distributed network. This blossoming technology impacts various industries miraculously and its application grows numerously.

Blockchain, a shared ledger in which all the data are recorded digitally has a common history and is available to all the participants in the network. This eliminates any fraudulent activity or duplication of transactions(Blockchain Technology for the Transportation Industry: Where the Future Starts n.d.).

A blockchain is a chain of blocks. Each block contains encrypted information and hashed pointers to previous block, making it difficult to retroactively alter without modifying the entire chain (What's inside a Block on the Blockchain? n.d.). The first block is called genesis block. Every block contains two components. They are

Block Header
Block Body

Block Header

It is a bunch of metadata about the block. The various components present in the block header is

Version: The Block version number
Hash of the previous block: Used to make connection between the blocks
Merkle root: The hash of all the transactions inside the block
Time: Timestamp of the block
Target or difficulty: A value used to regulate blocks
Nonce: An arbitrary number used once to solve cryptographic puzzle.

The Block header looks as follows

Figure 1. Block Header in Blockchain(What Is Hashing? [Step-by-Step Guide-Under Hood Of Blockchain] n.d.)

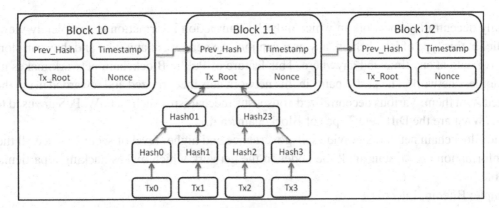

Block Body

It contains all the transactions the are confirmed in the block. Each transaction contains a set of entries and one transaction header which references to other entries in the transaction. Every entry in transaction is identified by its unique ID.

How Does Blockchain Work?

1.   A transaction must occur.
2.   The transaction must be verified.
3.   The transaction must be stored in a block.
4.   The block must be given a hash. After hashing, the block can be added to the blockchain.

For example, suppose if we want to add a purchase transaction to the blockchain, then it could be done as follows. Initially a purchase has to be made. After the purchase is made, the transaction details such as transaction time, amount and participants has to be verified. The verified transaction is now stored in the block. Then, the block is given is a unique hash and is added to the blockchain(Blockchain: Everything You Need to Know n.d.).

Types and Versions of Blockchain

More types of Blockchains are required in order to solve problems such as reliability on huge servers, need for trusted parties, cost effective transaction processing and so on. In General, there are three different types of Blockchain(6 Essential Blockchain Technology Concepts You Need To Know n.d.). They are

1.   Public Blockchain
2.   Private Blockchain
3.   Federated or Consortium Blockchain

Public Blockchain

It is a fully decentralized network in which only the transaction information is completely viewable to the public. In this type of Blockchain, any user can join the network at any time and they can store, send and receive data at any time and anywhere. This feature of Public Blockchain network makes it call as Permissionless network. The participants in this network gets incentivized and rewarded using the token associated with them. Various decentralized consensus mechanisms such as PoW, PoS are used to make decisions(What are the Different Types of Blockchain? n.d.).

Public Blockchain networks provide self-governance and higher level of security since all the transaction information are present in all the nodes in the network which makes hacking a particular node impossible.

Example: Bitcoin, Litecoin.

Private Blockchain

Private Blockchain usually called Permissioned Blockchain are used within an organization in which the participants need consent in order to join the network. Private Blockchains are more centralized and the transactions are private. The enterprises that want to collaborate and share data can make use of private blockchains since it provides more efficiency and faster transactions. The code in this type of blockchain is precisely private and hidden which results in eliminating decentralization and disintermediation(3

Types of Blockchain Explained - HedgeTrade Blog n.d.). Here, the central-in-charge helps to achieve consensus by giving the mining rights to anyone in the network.

Example: Bankchain.

Consortium or Federated Blockchain

A hybrid model between public and private Blockchain in which a number of approved users have control over the network. The term consortium is defined as the group of companies or the group of representative individuals who come together to make decisions for the best benefit of the whole network. The consortium blockchain allows only a few selected predetermined parties to verify transactions and to participate in the consensus process instead of allowing any user in the network in case of public blockchain and a single organization in case of private blockchain(The Different Types of Blockchains - ALTCOIN MAGAZINE - Medium n.d.).

Example: r3, EWF

In a nutshell, we can conclude that Public Blockchain is a good option where openness and censorship resistance is needed and Private and Consortium Blockchain fits where privacy and control is required.

Blockchain Version

Figure 2. Versions of Blockchain(ICO InterValue - World's First Practical Blockchain 4.0 Project — Steemit n.d.)

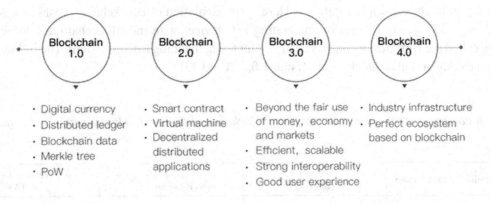

Blockchain 1.0

Blockchain born with the concept of Bitcoin(Blockchain Version - Javatpoint n.d.). Blockchain 1.0 represents the application of Distributed Ledger Technology over cryptocurrencies for transfer of values and to confirm transactions. Bitcoin, developed as a decentralized, peer-to-peer digital cash system comes as a result of 20 years of research in cryptocurrency and 40 years of research in cryptography. A core breakthrough in computer science comes as a long-standing solution to the issues associated with digital cash. With bitcoin, users are able to receive funds in digital wallets immediately without waiting for days for transfers. Blockchain currencies assures that any transaction can be sourced and completed directly without the involvement of any third parties intermediary.

Blockchain 2.0

In order to overcome the issues such as wasteful mining, lack of network scalability that come with the concept of Bitcoin, one visionary named Vitalik Buterin extends this concept beyond currency and proposed a platform called 'smart contracts' where the developer's community can build distributed applications (DApps) for the Blockchain network. Smart Contracts are small computer programs that are deployed on the Blockchain are usually triggered by events. These smart contracts can perform tasks automatically which in turn eliminates the need to manage time consuming and costly manual business processes. A most prominent example is the Ethereum Blockchain network. It is impossible to tamper or hack smart contracts. It reduces the cost of verification, execution and allows transparent definition overcoming moral hazard problems. This version of Blockchain successfully processes a high number of transactions than version 1.0.

Blockchain 3.0

Many new technologies such as NEO, IOTA and EOS want to improve the capabilities of Blockchain 1.0 and Blockchain 2.0. This gives birth to Blockchain 3.0 which focuses to address the issues associated with the previous versions. For this, Blockchain 3.0 makes use of different protocols, techniques and frameworks. It avoids centralized architecture and employs decentralized storage and communication. The scalability problem that persisted from the first generation to second generation of blockchain is resolved in this version using the concept called Tangle. Various features that distinguishes Blockchain 3.0 from previous versions are high scalability, interoperability, adaptability and sustainability(Blockchain: 1.0, 2.0, 3.0 and Future n.d.)(The Future is Here – The Evolution of Blockchain - Toshi Times n.d.).

Blockchain 3.0 mainly focuses on integrating IoT devices with the Blockchain technology. IOTA generally called the Blockless chain was designed for the demanding IoT ecosystem. The following table 2 shows the comparison of blockchain version 1.0, 2.0 and 3.0

Table 2. A comparison on various attributes of Blockchain 1.0, 2.0, 3.0(Padmavathi and Rajagopalan 2019)

Attributes\Blockchain version	Version 1.0 (Bitcoin)	Version 2.0 (Ethereum)	Version 3.0 (IOTA)
Mining	Miners	Miners	Each node
Speed	7 TPS	15 to 20 TPS	Increases as the number of nodes increases.
Language	Stack based	Turing Complete	Turing Complete
Hashing Technique	SHA-256	Ethash	Curl
Reason	Created as an alternative to regular money	Is developed as a platform which facilitiates peer-to-peer contract applications	Is designed as a communication protocolfor IoT
Data Structure	Linked List	Linked list	DAG
Block validation time	10 minutes	14 to 15 seconds	No blocks
Vulnerability	Vulnerable to brute force attacks and quantum computers	Vulnerable to quantum computers	Quantum resistant

Blockchain 4.0

In addition to scalability and safety issues, Blockchain 3.0 lacks business level infrastructure. So, it could not be used for real world business. Moreover, the DApp developers have to work a lot in designing and programming, since everything has to be started from the scratch and there is no service-oriented framework on the base-layer ledger. The next generation of Blockchain is designed in such a way that it tries to solve the problems associated with Blockchain 3.0(What is blockchain 4.0? - Quora n.d.)(TOP Network: The Harbinger of Blockchain 4.0 Era - TOP Network - Medium n.d.).

Blockchain 4.0, a nascent technology brings about lower costs and shorter development cycles, encouraging companies to make use of this technology. In the history of blockchain evolution, Blockchain 4.0 will be the business-accommodating superior public chain that can execute various use cases and applications.

Here are some of the highlights of various Blockchain 4,0 projects

Seele

* Aims to provide unity in the Blockchain platform.
* It enables users to perform cross chain communication.
* Matrix Proof-of-Work Consensus Algorithm.
* On-chain and off-chain sharing.
* Heterogeneous Forest Network.
* Value Internet.
* 2000+ TPS.

Top Network

* Completely Permissionless
* 2-layer sharding, 2-layer lattice DAG, 3-layer network.
* PBFT-DPoS consensus algorithm
* Upto 300,000 TPS

Multiversum

* SQL-based phrase structure
* Proof-of-Integrity consensus algorithm
* Upto 6400 TPS

Metahash

* Provides reliable and quick transactions of any assets
* Multiple Proof-of-Stack consensus algorithm
* 100,000 TPS

InterValue

* Creates infrastructure for Blockchain 4.0
* HashNet Datastructure
* Counterattack to quantum attacks
* Both turing and non-turing language
* 2-layer consensus based on interaction of HashNet and BA-VRF acknowledgement mechanism.
* Upto 1 M TPS

Integrating IoT devices with Blockchain

According to various research reports, there are about 5 billion IoT connected devices today which is predicted to increase up to 50 billion devices by 2022. The IoT devices plays an important role in changing the current world to smart world. As the number of IoT devices continues to proliferate, data verification, transaction verification, access control all become vital. Further, the security breaches of IoT increases due to the gathering of data from different devices at one place, remote control of devices by hackers, managing the devices, lack of ability to find compromised nodes, leakage of sensitive data and other activities. It is an arduous task to overcome the security issues faced by IoT devices(Leading Blockchain Integration With IoT Devices for Enhanced Security n.d.)(Blockchain IoT: How Will Blockchain Be Integrated Into the Growing Internet-of-Things? n.d.). The problems and security issues with IoT devices could be unlocked if IoT devices becomes decentralized.

Many security experts believe that Blockchain could be the silver bullet needed by the IoT devices to solve its issues. Blockchain when integrated with IoT could improve security and distributed processing power of IoT devices and also solves the problem of cloud-based data monopoly(Blockchain Applications in Internet of Things (IoT) Explained n.d.). Further, the blockchain is able to track and process the massive flow of data that pours from myriad of IoT devices. Blockchain and IoT is viewed as a perfect match since blockchain could solve many of the issues associated with IoT devices.

Even though many of the issues of IoT devices are solved by rapidly accelerating Blockchain technology, the convergence of these two blossoming technologies suffer from certain problems. Since the IoT devices are designed to be light weight and have low processing power, the integration of Blockchain in these devices poses a problem. Also, associated with Blockchain is the scalability issue and sky rocketing fees. So, many companies took convergence of these technologies on their many agenda and starts working on it.

(Elsts, Mitskas, and Oikonomou 2018)IOTA, the Blockchainless cryptocurrency for the Internet of Things is especially being designed for the integration of IoT devices with Blockchain technology. It is a quantum resistant Directed Acyclic Graph (DAG) which works on the top of their own ledger called Tangle. In this graph, nodes are the IOTA transactions and the validation corresponds to edges. Each transaction must validate two other transactions before joining the network. For validation, Proof-of-Work mechanism is used. IOTA is designed to provide zero fee transactions and unique verification process which is able to solve the scalability issues of Blockchain.

DAG differs from other blockchain in such a way that DAG works on 'horizontal' scheme and blockchain is based on 'vertical' scheme and also there are no miners and blocks in DAG, hence the name blocklesschain(Blockchain 3.0 and COTI - Next Generation Technology Without Mining? n.d.). The nature of graph is acyclic and also flows in a specific direction. The transactions in IOTA is not duplicated and there is no wait time for the blocks to be confirmed which in turns reduces the sky rocketing transaction fees. Even though, IOTA tries to be a perfect solution, there exists communication overhead of integrating IoT devices with IOTA blockchain.

Applications of Blockchain

It has become apparent the Blockchain technology has broken shackles and its application stack grows continuously from cryptocurrency to digital identity in the Internet-of-Things and entered mainstream business operations across industries(Top 10 Blockchain Technology Applications Explained In-Depth n.d.)(20 Real-World Uses for Blockchain Technology | The Motley Fool n.d.)(Blockchain Applications That Are Changing The World | Edureka n.d.).

The following are some of the real-world applications of Blockchain.

1. Finance
2. HealthCare
3. Land Registry
4. Insurance
5. Digital Voting
6. Global Trade
7. Copyright and royalty protection
8. Inheritance
9. Drug traceability
10. Government
11. Supply chain monitoring

Banking

The banking sector is prone to errors and frauds, since it involves handling of money and highly dependent manual networks. More than 40 percent of the financial bodies suffer from heavy economic crimes annually. In order to keep money safe and secure, the financial institutes require mediators in large amount. The involvement of mediators lead to an increase in expenses and an increase in manual processes which in turn increase errors and frauds. Blockchain technology comes as a solution to these issues and helps improve banking services by allowing only authorized participants to access the data. It keeps a log of all the logging transactions thus preventing errors and frauds. The major areas in which Blockchain helps the banking sector is in making faster cross border payments, cheaper KYC and trade finance(Blockchain and Finance: Two Peas in a Pod - Blockgeeks n.d.)(How is Blockchain Revolutionizing Banking and Financial Markets - By n.d.).

Healthcare

Patient data which plays a critical role in Healthcare sector is scattered across different departments in the Hospital. Because of this, the data is not easily accessible at the time of need. In addition, the patient has to waste some time in collecting these data. In order to resolve these issues, Healthcare could be equipped with Blockchain Technology. When Health data is stored on Blockchain technology, it becomes available and accessible to the health care providers as well as patients at any time and at any place.

Land Registry

Land registry involves the transfer of ownership of a land from seller to buyer. Since this process is handled on paper, it leads to many frauds and confusion. Blockchain aims to give crystal clear view of legal ownership by providing 100% computer-based solution instead of paper-based titles.

Insurance

Existing insurance claim processes have high complexity and are more fraudulent. It takes a long time period for the customers to claim their insurance. Blockchain could help solve these issues and also make the process easier. Using this technology, the payers are able to collect the required information automatically and the customers are able to get their claims without any delays.

Digital Voting

Even a single vote can change the fate of a country. Voting plays a critical role in the future of a country. Blockchain technology, if combined with voting could make the voting process transparent and its immutability property make to truly count the votes.

Global Trade

Global trade refers to Exchange of goods, capital and services across different countries. About one-fifth of the cost of transportation is mainly spent on trade documentation. This is because different systems are involved for processing different transactions between various supply chain participants. This cost could be reduced with the help of Blockchain technology, because all the information that needs to documented are stored on blockchain and is shared by everyone in the network.

Wills or Inheritance

The wills documented on a paper may sometimes go into wrong hands and could be used illegally. This could be avoided by storing the wills digitally on a Blockchain network. With the help of smart contracts, the wills become crystal-clear and legally binding without leaving any space for frauds.

Copyright and Royalty Protection

In this growing world of internet access, it is mandatory to have copyright and ownership laws on our digital contents. Real time and transparent royalty protection could be provided with the help of blockchain technology. It ensures the artists and the creator of the content to get their fair share on purchase of their content by others.

Drug Traceability

The problem of counterfeit drugs leads to millions of deaths every year all over the world. Blockchain technology proves itself as a solution to this problem by tracing the drugs from the point of their origin as raw products till it reaches consumers as end-product. The tracking of drugs is done based on their serial and/or batch numbers which in turns ensures that the process is transparent and the consumers get the right deal.

Monitor Supply Chain

It is the process of viewing the performance of the product from the place of its origin till it reaches the retailer. Blockchain helps doing this process in a secure and shared manner. If anybody wants to alter the product on its way to the customer, Blockchain easily identifies and reports it to the producer before the product reaches the customer.

Government

Government sector which work in siloes faces a lot of data transactional challenges. Blockchain technology boasts the power to transform these challenges and enable management of data in an easier and better way. Because of the use of Blockchain technology, the data becomes transparent and monitoring and auditing the transactions become an easier job.

Advantages of Blockchain

The various advantages that are associated with blockchain are as follows: (The Top Advantages Of Blockchain For Businesses n.d.)(5 Big Advantages of Blockchain, and 1 Reason to Be Very Worried | The Motley Fool n.d.)(Top five blockchain benefits transforming your industry - Blockchain Pulse: IBM Blockchain Blog n.d.)(Advantages and Disadvantages Of Blockchain Technology - DataFlair n.d.) (Blockchain Applications and Its Future - By Roger James n.d.)

1. Decentralization

   The lack of central data storage in Blockchain is an exciting feature of this technology that avoids running massive data centers for verifying transactions. It also ensures that, the entire network could not get compromised even if it falls into the hands of wrong persons.

2. Reduced Transaction Costs

   The business-to-business transactions and peer-to-peer transactions that take place in Blockchain network allows for verification and completion without the involvement of middleman. This reduces cost to both users as well as to the businesses over time.

3.   Efficiency

Completing a transaction using traditional paper work processes is exhausting and consumes a large amount of time and man power. Moreover, there are chances for human errors. Blockchain technology helps us to complete the process faster by streamlining and automating transactions. Further, the participants in the network need not maintain multiple documents. Instead, the same single digital ledger is shared by everyone in the network making establishment of trust easier.

4.   Traceability

Monitoring and tracing supply chain of a product from its origin is a complex and tedious process. But, with Blockchain, the tracking of ledger along the chain from its point of origin is made easier. This helps us to learn where a product come from and also helps to locate and correct any problems that come in the path of the product.

5.   Security

Blockchain technology offers high level of security, since all the transactions are added to the blockchain only after maximum trust verification and also every participant in the network is given a unique identity key linked with their account. In addition, the data ledgers are protected using cryptography and the ledgers are dependent on the adjacent block to complete this cryptography process. Further, the transactions are recorded in the chronological order making the blockchain timestamped. This makes tougher for the hacker to hack or disturb the chain.

6.   Faster Processing

In case of traditional banks, it takes lot of time even days to months to initiate and process transactions. This is because the financial institutions across the world are open at different time zones and are functional only during week days. But, after the invention of Blockchain technology, which works 24 hours a day, seven days a week, the processing of transactions is done more quickly. That is, the process gets completed within few minutes or few seconds.

Security Issues in Blockchain Technology

1.   Majority Attack (51% Attack)
2.   Social Engineering Attacks
3.   Software flaws
4.   Malware
5.   Eclipse attacks

51 Percent Attacks

If more than 50 percent of a blockchain's computing power is produced by a hacker, then it is called as 51 percent attack. In this attack, a lie could become a truth if it is said by more than half of the nodes present in the network. Here, the hackers assume control of the entire network and double-spend coins preventing others from creating blocks and transactions. This type of attack was first highlighted by Satoshi Nakamoto in Bitcoin. Smaller Blockchains have high level of risk suffering from this attack(What are Blockchain's Issues and Limitations? - CoinDesk n.d.)(5 Blockchain Problems: Security, Privacy, Legal, Regulatory, and Ethical Issues - Blocks Decoded n.d.).

Social Engineering Attacks

This type of attack is almost very common in all fields. Its main goal is to fetch the private key or login information of the user. Phishing is one of the most popular social engineering attacks. In phishing, a malicious actor sends the victim a mail or a message or sets up a website or social media and asks you to send your credentials immediately. If we give all our credentials to them, then it would be highly impossible to stop them from clearing our account.

Social engineering attacks could be prevented by not sending our credentials or private leys to any malicious actors and by making the participants of the blockchain network to be aware of such kind of attacks.

Software Flaws

Blockchains have proven themselves to be resilient to almost all types of attacks, but it is inevitable that Decentralized Applications (DApps) built on top of them suffer from bugs. A report said that, over $24 million was lost in the blockchain network because of software bugs. To prevent such types of flaws, the software used by the blockchain network must undergo rigorous testing and review.

Malware

There are many types of malware that could cause security issues to the blockchain network. It could range from any malicious crypto mining software to code that could shut down a company's server. The most popular malware associated with blockchain network is cryptojacking. It mainly deals with cryptocurrency. In this, the computer's resources are taken over by unauthorized persons referred as cryptojackers. It leads to performance issues and increased electricity usage. It paves way for other hostile codes and a loss of multi million dollars to victims. Through vigilance, we could stop malware from its performance.

Eclipse Attacks

This attack happens in decentralized network in which the aim of the attacker is to eclipse a specific node or a specific set of nodes from the entire network. It could simply be defined as monopolizing a node's connection from others so that the victim node does not receive any information from any nodes other than the attacking nodes. The malicious actors exploit the victim nodes in such a way that the victim nodes receive information only from the malicious nodes believing the incorrect state of the blockchain. Eclipse attack could also be used to attack the whole blockchain network by hijacking the mining powers of eclipsed nodes. The attacker by this way can easily gain enough support from the victim nodes and establish a fork to the true ledger. The occurrence of eclipse attacks depends on factors such as data structure of the network, number of connections per user and the unique IP addresses assigned per node. (What is an Eclipse Attack? | Radix DLT - Decentralized Ledger Technology n.d.)

CONCLUSION

This chapter concludes that, Blockchain a hotly debated topic could be the probable solution for many of the problems and loopholes faced by the current technologies. This ground breaking technology bridges the gap in current technology and ensures safety of our personal information. The various types and versions of blockchain are discussed. The chapter also concludes that, if IoT and Blockchain are integrated, they could be called as a perfect match made in heaven that would help the users in handling large amounts of data, allocate and distribute processing power, improve connectivity globally and efficiently. A few of the interesting real-world applications of Blockchain are discussed. But still, there exists a lot more applications like immutable data back-up, distributed cloud storage, equity trading and so on. Even though blockchain inherent several advantages and security features, that makes the Blockchain records resistant to attacks, there still do exists some security risks that must be recognized and mitigated in order to make the future of Blockchain bright.

REFERENCES

Real-World Uses for Blockchain Technology. (n.d.). https://www.fool.com/investing/2018/04/11/20-real-world-uses-for-blockchain-technology.aspx

Types of Blockchain Explained. (n.d.). https://hedgetrade.com/3-types-of-blockchain-explained/

Big Advantages of Blockchain, and 1 Reason to Be Very Worried. (n.d.). https://www.fool.com/investing/2017/12/11/5-big-advantages-of-blockchain-and-1-reason-to-be.aspx

Problems, B. Security, Privacy, Legal, Regulatory, and Ethical Issues - Blocks Decoded. (n.d.). https://blocksdecoded.com/blockchain-issues-security-privacy-legal-regulatory-ethical/

EssentialB. T. C. Y. N. T. K. (n.d.). https://tradeix.com/essential-blockchain-technology-concepts/

A Brief History in the Evolution of Blockchain Technology Platforms. (n.d.). https://hackernoon.com/a-brief-history-in-the-evolution-of-blockchain-technology-platforms-1bb2bad8960a

A Brief History of Blockchain: Blockchain Basics Book from ConsenSys Academy. (n.d.). https://consensys.net/academy/blockchain-basics-book/brief-history-of-blockchain/

Advantages and Disadvantages Of Blockchain Technology. (n.d.). https://data-flair.training/blogs/advantages-and-disadvantages-of-blockchain/

Blockchain: 1.0, 2.0, 3.0 and Future. (n.d.). https://www.linkedin.com/pulse/blockchain-10-20-30-future-marian-marik-danko

Blockchain 3.0 and COTI - Next Generation Technology Without Mining? (n.d.). https://www.forbes.com/sites/geraldfenech/2018/11/23/blockchain-3-0-and-coti-next-generation-technology-without-mining/#7719151f4ce4

Blockchain, an Emerging Technology for the Future - Data Driven Investor. (n.d.). https://medium.com/datadriveninvestor/blockchain-an-emerging-technology-for-the-future-b7856af83175

Blockchain and Finance: Two Peas in a Pod. (n.d.). https://blockgeeks.com/guides/blockchain-and-finance/

ApplicationsB.FutureI. (n.d.). https://hackernoon.com/blockchain-applications-and-its-future-f42fee305873

Blockchain Applications in Internet of Things (IoT) Explained. (n.d.). https://www.blockchaintechnologies.com/applications/internet-of-things-iot/

Changing, B. A. T. A. The World. (n.d.). https://www.edureka.co/blog/blockchain-applications/

Blockchain: Everything You Need to Know. (n.d.). https://www.investopedia.com/terms/b/blockchain.asp

Blockchain IoT: How Will Blockchain Be Integrated Into the Growing Internet-of-Things? (n.d.). https://businesstown.com/blockchain-iot-be-integrated-into-the-growing-internet-of-things/

Explained, B. T. Introduction, Meaning, and Applications. (n.d.). https://hackernoon.com/blockchain-technology-explained-introduction-meaning-and-applications-edbd6759a2b2

Technology, B., & the Transportation Industry. Where the Future Starts. (n.d.). https://enterprise-info.trimble.com/blockchain-technology#applications

VersionB. (n.d.). https://www.javatpoint.com/blockchain-version

Elsts, Mitskas, &Oikonomou. (2018). Distributed Ledger Technology and the Internet of Things: A Feasibility Study. doi:10.1145/nnnnnnn.nnnnnnn

History of Blockchain. (n.d.). https://academy.binance.com/blockchain/history-of-blockchain

History of Blockchain. (n.d.). https://www.icaew.com/technical/technology/blockchain/blockchain-articles/what-is-blockchain/history

BankingH. I. B. R.MarketsF. (n.d.). https://hackernoon.com/how-is-blockchain-revolutionizing-banking-and-financial-markets-9241df07c18b

ICO InterValue - World's First Practical Blockchain 4.0 Project. (n.d.). https://steemit.com/blockchain/@sergeyklimenok/ico-intervalue-world-s-first-practical-blockchain-4-0-project

Leading Blockchain Integration With IoT Devices for Enhanced Security. (n.d.). https://www.forbes.com/sites/geraldfenech/2019/01/22/leading-blockchain-integration-with-iot-devices-for-enhanced-security/#52f4d0a031bf

Padmavathi, U., & Rajagopalan, N. (2019). A Research on Impact of Blockchain in Healthcare. *International Journal of Innovative Technology and Exploring Engineering*, *8*(9), 35–40.

The Different Types of Blockchains. (n.d.). https://medium.com/altcoin-magazine/the-different-types-of-blockchains-456968398559

The Exponential Guide to Blockchain. (n.d.). https://su.org/resources/exponential-guides/the-exponential-guide-to-blockchain/

The Future Is Here – The Evolution of Blockchain. (n.d.). https://toshitimes.com/the-future-is-here-the-evolution-of-blockchain/

The Top Advantages Of Blockchain For Businesses. (n.d.). https://www.smartdatacollective.com/top-advantages-blockchain-for-businesses/

Top 10 Blockchain Technology Applications Explained In-Depth. (n.d.). https://www.blockchaintechnologies.com/applications/

Top Five Blockchain Benefits Transforming Your Industry. (n.d.). https://www.ibm.com/blogs/blockchain/2018/02/top-five-blockchain-benefits-transforming-your-industry/

Network, T. O. P. The Harbinger of Blockchain 4.0 Era. (n.d.). https://medium.com/top-network/top-network-the-harbinger-of-blockchain-4-0-era-84137d572f60

What Are Blockchain's Issues and Limitations? (n.d.). https://www.coindesk.com/information/blockchains-issues-limitations

What Are the Different Types of Blockchain? (n.d.). https://dragonchain.com/blog/differences-between-public-private-blockchains

What Is an Eclipse Attack? (n.d.). https://www.radixdlt.com/post/what-is-an-eclipse-attack/

BlockchainW. I. 4.0? (n.d.). https://www.quora.com/What-is-blockchain-4-0

HashingW. I. (n.d.). https://blockgeeks.com/guides/what-is-hashing/

What's inside a Block on the Blockchain? (n.d.). https://learnmeabitcoin.com/guide/blocks

This research was previously published in Blockchain Applications in IoT Security; pages 1-20, copyright year 2021 by Information Science Reference (an imprint of IGI Global).

Chapter 3
Introduction of Blockchain and Usage of Blockchain in Internet of Things

Chandrasekar Ravi

National Institute of Technology Puducherry, India

Praveensankar Manimaran

(iD) https://orcid.org/0000-0003-3614-5722

National Institute of Technology Puducherry, India

ABSTRACT

Since the advent of the web, the number of users who started using the internet for everyday purpose has increased tremendously. Most of the common purposes are to access their data whenever they want and wherever they want. So many companies have started providing these services to normal users. These companies store huge volume of data in the data centers. So protecting the integrity of the data is the main responsibility of these companies. Blockchain is one of the trending solutions that gives storage immutability to the users. This chapter starts with the working of blockchain and smart contracts and advantages and disadvantages of blockchain and smart contracts and then goes on to explain how blockchain can be integrated into the internet of things (IOT). This chapter ends with an architecture based on the proof-of-concept for access management, which is blockchain-based fully distributed architecture.

INTRODUCTION

Blockchain is a peer to peer network which is distributed among the untrustworthy peers and the untrustworthy peers can interact with each other. The interactions will be verified using some form of cryptographic mechanisms. Blockchain enables applications to run in a decentralized manner without any need for centralized authority. Blockchain makes it possible to do transactions between trustless parties without the need for centralized authorities (Christidis & Devetsikiotis, 2016). Blockchain uses cryptographic techniques to provide authentication functionality to peers. Smart contracts have been

DOI: 10.4018/978-1-6684-7132-6.ch003

defined as "self-executing scripts" and usually smart contracts will be stored on the blockchain which can provide automated workflows in the network.

BLOCKCHAIN

Blockchain is similar to the database which is distributed among the peers participating in the network and the network structure it forms is peer to peer network so there is no need of centralized entity. Blockchain is a digital decentralized ledger (Novo, 2018). Blockchains are important because they provide a safe and secure way for people to make any type of transaction without having to trust anyone. Blocks in a blockchain can be thought of as a sheet of paper. Blocks, just like paper, can hold any type of data on them. The first block in the blockchain is called genesis block. The genesis block will be initialized when the blockchain network starts for the first time. The second block will have the transactions and the cryptographic hash value of the first block. Next blocks will follow the same.

Each block(other than genesis block) will include the hash value of the preceding blocks. This will form a linked list in which the node is a block. It is shown in Figure 1. Each block will have id associated with it. Each node will hold a copy of the blockchain. Each node can be used by a single user or more than one user. Bitcoin introduced blockchain architecture to solve the double-spending problem (Nakamoto, 2008).

Figure 1. Blockchain structure

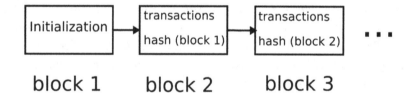

Since different peers will have the same copy of the blockchain, each peer will try to create the next block for the blockchain. Once the peers created a new block, the new block will be broadcasted to all other peers in the network. If two peers have created two different blocks then the latest and the longest block will be chosen as the next block. This process is called forks. The discarded block is called orphan blocks. Based on the total difficulty of blockchain, the longest block is chosen.

Each user will have a pair of a private key and public key (Hellman, 2002). Using those keys the user can access the blockchain. Transactions will be signed by the peers using the peer's private key. Once the transaction is signed and verified it will be included in the block. Once a transaction is added to the block it will be broadcasted to the other peers or users in the blockchain. Peers can validate the transactions by using the creators public key. After the validation and verification of transactions, the transaction will be ordered based on consensus mechanism and the transactions will be packed into a block and it will be broadcasted to the other peers in the network.

Blocks contain a set of transactions. Each transaction transfers the values from one entity to another entity. Pool miners are solo miners who mine the blocks. Mining operation bundles the set of transactions into blocks. Miners are chosen based on the consensus(proof-of-work in the case of bitcoin) mechanism. Once the miners finished mining they will be rewarded with transaction fees which is usually some amount of bitcoin in the bitcoin network. In the Proof-of-work(POW) approach difficulty level is increased after a certain amount of blocks mined. To avoid the double-spending issue, all the peers in the blockchain network will verify the transactions. Each peer will get an update from the network and it will verify the block by checking the validity of the transactions and previous block hash. Then the peer will append the block to its local blockchain. Each peer will have a set of rules for validating transactions. Using these rules the peer nodes can validate the transactions.

Properties of the Blockchain Technology

- Rules are determined by decentralized peers. Peers can decide the consensus algorithm. Peers can determine the properties of the blockchain network.
- All the peers can see and verify the transactions which had occurred in the blockchain network. Since all the peers can see the transaction non-repudiation is enforced. Public key cryptography is used for verifying the transaction.
- All the peers in the blockchain network will hold the copy of the blockchain ledger. Since all the peers hold the ledger even if one or more peers are compromised the remaining peers can preserve the integrity of the data.
- Transactions are validated by the peers chosen based on the decentralized consensus mechanism.
- Ledger is tamper-proof. Since all the peers will have the ledger to modify the data more than half of the peers should be compromised.

Types of Blockchain Network

The first type of blockchain network is a public blockchain network. Any node can participate in the public blockchain provided it has a valid private key-public key pair from the authorized certificate authority. Any node can participate in the consensus mechanism. The second type of blockchain network is private blockchain network. It is mostly used by the organizations where the transactions are business to business and only the authorized entities can participate in the transaction.

Advantages of Blockchain Technology

Blockchain is fully distributed peer to peer network where no central authority is used. Since it uses consensus algorithm to choose the node for mining the next block to modify the data the consensus mechanism has to be compromised. So it preserves the integrity of the data. Once a node created a block or added transaction to the block it can be verified by any node in the network. So even though the nodes are not trustworthy it can't fake the transactions. So it allows the interactions between non-trusting parties.

Techniques to Preserve Blockchain for Users

Use unique public key for each transaction. Since each transaction uses the unique public key the miner can always verify the block contents using the miner's private key. In private blockchain, if entities involved are competitors of each other use different network so that it can control the entities participating in the network.

CONSENSUS

It is an agreement between two or more agents. When transactions are added to the block, the order of these transactions is very important. All the nodes should agree on some common order then only it can be added to the block. In Proof-of-Work(POW) to add each block to the network, the node should solve a computationally hard cryptographic problem. In Proof of Stake(POS), only those peers who stake the specified amount of cryptocurrency can participate in the mining operation. If consensus is not maintained different nodes will have different states of the blockchain. To maintain consistency in the blockchain network distributed consensus algorithm is needed. Order of the transactions for the next block will be decided by the validating nodes. Whichever order is supported by the majority of the nodes that order will be chosen. In a public blockchain network, this will lead to "Sybil attack" (Douceur, 2002). Because a single malicious entity can use multiple ids and influence voting.

If a single entity uses multiple identities it can take over the network. Bitcoin solves this problem by using a computationally expensive mining operation. Bitcoin uses a consensus mechanism called proof-of-work. Proof of stake is used in ethereum. Private blockchain networks don't need computationally expensive consensus mechanisms because all the nodes are trustworthy. Practical Byzantine Fault Tolerance(PBFT) (Castro & Liskov, 1999) is used in most of the private blockchain networks. The main property of the PBFT is that it will be assumed that at least two-thirds of the nodes are honest and the remaining nodes can be faulty (n). So It will need at least 3n +1 nodes. In Juno blockchain network ("Juno", 2019) Tangaroa algorithm is used. " unique nodes list " is used in Ripple (Armknecht, Karame, Mandal, Youssef, & Zenner, 2015).

ASSETS

Assets can be represented in the table as digital assets. Each peer will use the public key for its identification. Transactions are used to modify the asset. Assets are introduced by some special transaction by a node or set of nodes which can be used only for this purpose. In private blockchain whichever node configures the blockchain network can create assets. That node can give permission for asset creation to other nodes also. All the nodes in the system should agree on how the assets are generated and how the assets are exchanged.

SMART CONTRACTS

The definition of Smart Contract is given as "computerized transaction protocol that executes the terms of contract" (Szabo, 1997) by Nick Szabo. In most of the blockchain implementations, smart contracts will be stored along with the data in the blockchain network itself (Christidis & Devetsikiotis, 2016). When two parties are doing a transaction smart contract can be used to reduce the need for a trusted middleman.

Smart Contract Properties and Usage

- Business logic can be expressed using smart contracts.
- Smart should be ready for all possible inputs.
- Smart Contracts are deterministic.
- All peers can see the code of the smart contract.
- The behavior of smart contracts should always be predictable.

EXISTING BLOCKCHAIN TECHNOLOGIES

Bitcoin

It is a cryptocurrency. It uses public-key cryptography and Proof-of-Work(POW) consensus mechanism. The transactions will be verified using the POW algorithm. A new block is created every 10 mins. When someone receives bitcoin it is recorded as UTXO (unspent transaction outputs). UTXO contains the bitcoin amount and locking script which can be used to send cryptocurrency from the amount.The minimum amount of cryptocurrency that can be sent is called "satoshi".

Ethereum

It is designed by Vitalik Buterin (Wood, 2014)."Ether" the cryptocurrency used in ethereum. Smart contracts on ethereum can be programmed using the programming language called "solidity".It uses the "Proof of Stake" consensus mechanism. Block creation time is 12 approximately seconds.

Hyperledger Fabric

It is a private blockchain (Androulaki et al., 2018) which is mainly used for business to business applications. It uses practical byzantine fault tolerance consensus mechanism.

USAGE OF BLOCKCHAIN IN IOT

In the manufacturing industry, the current centralized model has a high maintenance cost. Using blockchain software updates can be distributed so that even after the support for the device is stopped, the device can receive updates from the peers. A smart contract can be used to control and monitor the distribution process autonomously. The peers who supply the software update can bill the other peers which need the software update if the blockchain network supports cryptocurrency.

FileCoin (Benet & Greco, 2018) can be used to rent the disk space of the user. EtherApis ("EtherAPIs", 2019) can be used to bill the devices which need the API services.

CHALLENGES OF USING BLOCKCHAIN IN IOT

- high latency - since all the nodes should have updated copy of the ledger it will take a lot of time for a transaction to be propagated throughout the whole blockchain network.
- low throughput - only one block can be mined at a time it won't be efficient if there are more number of blocks to be mined at the same time.
- Confidentiality of the data - Since all the nodes can look at the transaction the privacy of the user is compromised. To enforce the confidentiality the data should be encrypted with the user's private key before adding it to the blockchain.
- Verifying the identity of the miners - since any node can become the miner it would be troublesome if the attackers took control of more than half of the mining nodes. So to solve this issue the number of nodes should be more in such a way that it would be impossible to take control of more than half of the nodes.
- Regulations - It is a very new technology. The government doesn't have any regulations in place to handle all the situations.

BLOCKCHAIN IN IOT SECURITY

IBM is providing blockchain services in the supply chain domain so that it can efficiently track items when they are moving from source to destination. In IBM Watson IOT platform (Kaul, 2016) selected IOT data can be added to a private blockchain network. IOT devises data is converted into the format given by the blockchain network. The data can be accessed and supplied by the user's of the network and they can verify the integrity of transactions. In IBM Watson IOT platform the users of the blockchain are mostly business partners who are using the IOT services.

Provence uses blockchain to provide trust between parties when they are using supply chain. Filament uses in-house built wireless sensors called "Taps" which can communicate with computers within 16 km. Taps create a mesh network in which blockchain is used to store the identification of devices. It uses smart contracts for communication using blockchain-backed identities because of that it doesn't rely on cloud services. Foxconn Technology, Robert Bosch, Cisco, Bank of New York Mellon and some other companies have formed a ground which focuses on securing IOT using blockchain technologies. IOT devises firmware and other important software's hash values can be stored in private or public blockchain. No one other than authenticated users can perform software updates on those devices. Before performing updates the software's integrity can be verified. IP spoofing and IP address forgery attacks can be prevented by using Identity and access control systems which are based on the blockchain technology. IOT security can be improved by using identity systems and access control systems which are based on the blockchain technology (Kshetri, 2017).

ADVANTAGES OF BLOCKCHAIN OVER CLOUD IN IOT

In the cloud model, most operations are performed in the servers in the cloud. Those servers identify and authenticate IOT devices. In the cloud model, the cost is very high. That is the biggest constraint when the cloud model is integrated into IOT. In 2016 every day 5.5 million new devices (Van Der Meulen, 2015) were connected to the IOT network, estimated by Gartner. Each node in the IOT network is vulnerable to various attacks which can compromise the whole IOT network (Banafa, 2016). Most prominent attacks in IOT are stealing the sensor data, modifying the sensor data, taking control of the IOT devices and DDOS attacks. Smart water meters can be used to monitor the water usage and alert users of any water leakage. But hackers can use this information to determine whether the user is at home or not. If there is no water usage for some specified period, then the hacker will determine that the user/consumer is not at the home. Centralized cloud models are susceptible to manipulation if the cloud service provider wants to modify something or remove some data to reduce the cost. Int 2014 in the city of Flint, Michigan flint authorities altered sample data taken by researchers to analyze the lead level in the drinking water.

In the Bitcoin network, the message exchanges between the nodes can be compared to the financial transactions. Messages are exchanged by smart contracts. Smart contracts ensure that messages are sent by the valid sender. This technology can eliminate another crisis as same as above. Blockchain eliminates the need for centralized authority which maintains the IOT network so it can save cost. By using decentralized architecture server downtime can be removed. The integrity of the data in the blockchain is preserved by using cryptographic keys and digital signature.

BLOCKCHAIN FOR SUPPLY CHAIN SECURITY IN IOT

Using blockchain the product can be traced from fully functional product to raw materials used. If some part is defective the products which are having the defective part are identified and tracked and the replacement for those parts can be done quickly and efficiently. If any of those products is compromised because of some security breach, those products can be traced back and security updates can be sent to only those products. Internet-connected cameras by Hangzhou Xiongmai Technologies recalled its products which are affected by Mirai malware (Antonakakis et al., 2017). If blockchain-based supply is used it would have become so easy to trace the users who are using vulnerable cameras and provide software updates or replacement to those users.

BLOCKCHAIN FOR ACCESS CONTROL IN IOT

Centralized access control systems are well suited for the traditional human-machine internet-based communication systems. In IOT devices are mobile (Sun & Ansari, 2016) and may be handled by different "management communities" from time to time. So centralized access control systems won't work for these type of systems. In IOT devices' battery,CPU and storage are limited. When devices are querying the access management system very frequently and the devices' access control system needs frequent updates centralized architecture will fail.

Advantages of Decentralized Access Control System

- Devices can be grouped into clusters. Each cluster can have separate access control policies.
- In centralized system access control, managers use sleep pattern to save energy. In this approach even if one system is sleeping another node can take care of the access control management.

- Multiple managers can also be possible.
- This approach is highly scalable.

The implementation uses a single smart contract. Blockchain stores and distributes access control information. So all the nodes will have a copy of the access control details. IOT devices are size constrained so it won't be able to have a copy of the blockchain.so "management hub" will act as an intermediary between IOT devices and blockchain. In this system, all the functionalities will be defined in the smart contract itself. To manage the smart contract, special nodes called "managers" will be used.

Decentralized Access Control Architecture

The blockchain-based decentralized access control system is shown in Figure 2 (Novo, 2018). Its components are explained to subsequent sections.

IOT Network

It allows communication between devices which are constrained in terms of power. All IOT devices would have a public key. The IOT devices are not part of the blockchain.

Managers

The permission for all the IOT devices will be controlled by the managers. The managers won't store the blockchain and won't participate in the mining operations. So these are lightweight nodes. So even one or a group of IOT devices can take the role of managers. Or some kind of edge devices can be used for this purpose. Managers can interact with the blockchain network only when it is required. All the IOT devices should be under manager's control. One or more IOT devices can be under a single manager. More than one manager can manage a single IOT device. Manager can specify access control permission for all the IOT devices it managers.

Figure 2. Blockchain based access control

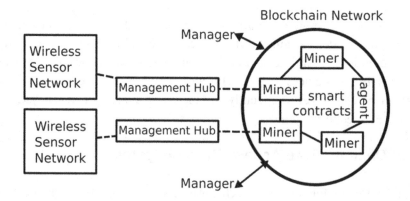

Agent Node

The smart contract is defined and deployed in the blockchain by the agent nodes. The smart contract will have an address and once the smart contract is accepted in the blockchain network, the address of the smart contract will be returned to the agent node.

Smart Contract

Transaction triggers the operations defined by the smart contract. Only managers can modify the smart contract. The smart contract controls all the operations are being performed in the blockchain network.

Blockchain Network

A private blockchain is used in this system. Any node can access the values in the blockchain network. But adding data in the blockchain network will be done by a specified set of nodes. Special miner nodes will perform the transactions in the blockchain.

Management Hubs

Management hub acts as an interface between the IOT device and block network(miner). It converts the message from the COAP format to JSON format. A single management hub can manage one or more wireless sensor networks. A single miner can have a connection with one or more management hubs. constrained devices can't become management hubs because it needs to process a huge number of simultaneous requests at once. IOT device should know the location of the management hub and management hubs should be able to verify IOT devices.

Interfaces Provided by the System

Smart Contract

Each manager will have set of a public keys. Each IOT device will have a set of public keys.
Policy p(s,t.r) - an IOT device 's' have access for resource 'r' of IOT device 't'
Functionalities provided by the smart contract is given below:

- RegisterManager (public key of manager): Registers new manager
- RegisterDevice: Registers an IOT device
- AddManagertoDevice: for IOT device it sets a manager
- RemoveManagerFromDevice: from IOT device it removes a manager. (manager can only self remove itself no other option)
- AddAccessControl: Add access control policies for a device by its manger
- DeregisterManager: Removes a manager(self removal)
- DeregisterDevice: Removes a device(done by any of its manager)
- RemovePermission: Remove IOT device access for a resource held by another IOT device
- QueryManager: Returns list of devices managed by a manager
- QueryPermission: Returns access control permissions for an IOT device

Management Hub

It will be used to query whether an IOT device can access a resource held by another IOT device.

System Workflow

There are 4 phases:

- Blockchain network initialization
- Registration of the nodes
- Defining access policies
- Discovering policies

Blockchain Network Initialization

Blockchain network is created for the access management system. Once the network is created then the smart contract will be deployed on the blockchain by the agent node and the address of the smart contract will be returned to that agent node. All managers will use this address to register itself as managers and to define access policies for a set of IOT devices it manages(this address is hard-coded in the managers and management hubs). The management hub will look for the miner node and it will connect to the closest miner node. All the management hubs will have set IOT devices associated with it.

Registration of the Nodes

Any node can be registered as a manager. Manager node can register IOT devices for which it can define access policies. A manager can manage any number of nodes. If an IOT device wants to register under a manger then it can verify the authenticity of the manager.

Management of the Nodes

Multiple managers can control the same IOT device. Managers can remove itself for an IOT device under its control. Only the manager can add another manager to the IOT device it manages. But it can't remove other managers.

Defining Access Control Policies

Managers can define access control policies for IOT devices it manages. Access control policy specifies which resource can be accessed by which IOT device. Each policy may have an expiry time.

Updating Access Control Policies

Manager can delete and modify the policy at any time.

Resource Request

If any device wants to access the resource of the other device it will query the management hub for this information. Management hub will query the miner which then queries the blockchain(it doesn't perform any transaction) and returns the answer to that query. Once the management hub gets the answer, it will pass the answer to the IOT device which asked for access permission details.

Limitations

Miners need to be paid for maintaining the blockchain network running.so it will increase the cost for the users who are using the blockchain. Since all the nodes should have updated content it will the processing time is very high. (12s for each transaction)(only the manager node will do the transaction. Management hub will not perform any transaction).

CONCLUSION

This chapter has briefly explained the concept of blockchain technology and the way the smart contract is used to control the blockchain. Origin of the blockchain technology has also been explained along with the use of blockchain technology. This chapter then has explained how blockchain can be integrated into IOT and what is the security issues it solves in IOT and about the performance penalty that the system incurs because of the addition of blockchain in IOT. This chapter has finally ended with a decentralized access control system which solves some of the problems the centralized access control system faces because of the huge growth of a number of IOT devices.

REFERENCES

Androulaki, E., Barger, A., Bortnikov, V., Cachin, C., Christidis, K., De Caro, A., ... Muralidharan, S. (2018, April). Hyperledger fabric: a distributed operating system for permissioned blockchains. In *Proceedings of the Thirteenth EuroSys Conference* (p. 30). ACM. 10.1145/3190508.3190538

Antonakakis, M., April, T., Bailey, M., Bernhard, M., Bursztein, E., Cochran, J., . . . Kumar, D. (2017). Understanding the mirai botnet. In *26th USENIX Security Symposium (USENIX Security 17)* (pp. 1093-1110). USENIX.

Armknecht, F., Karame, G. O., Mandal, A., Youssef, F., & Zenner, E. (2015, August). Ripple: Overview and outlook. In *International Conference on Trust and Trustworthy Computing*(pp. 163-180). Springer. 10.1007/978-3-319-22846-4_10

Banafa, A. (2016). *A secure model of IoT with Blockchain*. OpenMind.

Benet, J., & Greco, N. (2018). *Filecoin: A decentralized storage network*. Protoc. Labs.

Castro, M., & Liskov, B. (1999, February). *Practical Byzantine fault tolerance* (Vol. 99). OSDI.

Christidis, K., & Devetsikiotis, M. (2016). Blockchains and smart contracts for the internet of things. *IEEE Access: Practical Innovations, Open Solutions, 4,* 2292–2303. doi:10.1109/ACCESS.2016.2566339

Douceur, J. R. (2002, March). The sybil attack. In *International workshop on peer-to-peer systems* (pp. 251-260). Springer. 10.1007/3-540-45748-8_24

EtherAPIs: Decentralized Anonymous Trustless APIs. (2019). Retrieved from https://etherapis.io/

Hellman, M. E. (2002). An overview of public key cryptography. *IEEE Communications Magazine, 40*(5), 42–49. doi:10.1109/MCOM.2002.1006971

Juno: Smart Contracts Running on a BFT Hardened Raft. (2019). Retrieved from https://github.com/kadena-io/juno

Kaul, A. (2016). *IBM Watson IoT and its integration with blockchain.* Academic Press.

Kshetri, N. (2017). Can blockchain strengthen the internet of things? *IT Professional, 19*(4), 68–72. doi:10.1109/MITP.2017.3051335

Nakamoto, S. (2008). *Bitcoin: A peer-to-peer electronic cash system.* Retrieved from http://bitcoin. org/bitcoin. pdf

Novo, O. (2018). Blockchain meets IoT: An architecture for scalable access management in IoT. *IEEE Internet of Things Journal, 5*(2), 1184–1195. doi:10.1109/JIOT.2018.2812239

Sun, X., & Ansari, N. (2016). EdgeIoT: Mobile edge computing for the Internet of Things. *IEEE Communications Magazine, 54*(12), 22–29. doi:10.1109/MCOM.2016.1600492CM

Szabo, N. (1997). The idea of smart contracts. *Nick Szabo's Papers and Concise Tutorials, 6.*

Van Der Meulen, R. (2015). Gartner says 6.4 billion connected 'things' will be in use in 2016, up 30 percent from 2015. Gartner.

Wood, G. (2014). Ethereum: A secure decentralised generalised transaction ledger. *Ethereum project yellow paper, 151,* 1-32.

This research was previously published in Transforming Businesses With Bitcoin Mining and Blockchain Applications; pages 1-15, copyright year 2020 by Business Science Reference (an imprint of IGI Global).

Chapter 4
A Novel Survey on Blockchain for Internet of Things

Jay Kumar Jain
Sagar Institute of Research and Technology, India

Varsha Jain
Bansal Institute of Science and Technology, Bhopal, India

ABSTRACT

Internet of things (IoT) is ready to change human life and release tremendous financial benefits. It may be that lack of information security and the belief of the current IoT are actually restricting its selection. Blockchain changes in an appropriated and secure record holds reliable records of information in various areas and possibly resolves information security concerns in the IoT system. This chapter presents a thorough review on the existing blockchain progress with an accent on IoT applications. The authors first give an overview of blockchain architecture including blockchain technologies and key characteristics of blockchain. The authors then discuss the blockchain for the internet of things including blockchain for IoT: technologies. Furthermore, they list some challenges and problems that will hinder blockchain development and summarize some existing approaches for solving these problems. Some possible future directions are also discussed. Future research bearings are ordered for a viable mix of blockchains in the IoT system.

INTRODUCTION

A blockchain is a decentralized, distributed database that is used to maintain a continuous growing list of records, which is called a block. This is a digital ledger of records which is shown in a network to capture transactions between different parties. For use as a distributed ledger, a blockchain is autonomously managed by a peer-to-peer network, which adheres to a protocol for inter-node communication and validates new blocks and after its creation includes all transactions. Each block contains a cryptographic hash of the past block, a timestamp, and exchange information. All members like businesses or people, utilizing the common database are "hubs" associated with the blockchain each keeping up an indistinguishable

DOI: 10.4018/978-1-6684-7132-6.ch004

duplicate of the record. Each section into a blockchain is an exchange and all these exchanges show a trade of significant worth among members (i.e., an advanced resource that demonstrate rights, commitments or proprietorship). By and by, a wide range of sorts of blockchains are being developed and tried. Nonetheless, most blockchains pursue this essential system and approach. When one member needs to make an exchange with another, the various hubs in the system speak with one another utilizing a predecided component to watch that the new exchange is legitimate.

This mechanism is referred to as an assent calculation. When a transaction has been acknowledged by the system, all duplicates of the record are refreshed with the new data. Different exchanges are generally joined into a "hinder" that is attached to the record. Each square contains data that alludes back to past squares and along these lines all squares in the steel together in the dispersed indistinguishable duplicates. Taking an interest hub can include new, time-stepped exchanges, however, members can't erase or adjust the passages once they have been approved and acknowledged by the system. On the off chance that a hub changed a past square, it would not synchronize with the remainder of the system and would be prohibited from the blockchain. A legitimately working blockchain is in this manner changeless in spite of coming up short on a focal head.

Blockchain Architecture

According to Lee KuoChuen, D. et al. (2015), Blockchain is a series of blocks, which carries a complete list of transaction records like a traditional public ledger. Figure 1 outlines the case of a blockchain. Each block indicates the immediately previous block via a reference that is fundamentally a hash value of the previous block known as parent block. According to Buterin, et al. (2014) it is worth noting that uncle blocks (offspring of the block's predecessor) hashes will likewise be stored in ethereum blockchain. The initial block of a blockchain is known as genesis block which has no parent block. The author then presents the block structure in section 2.1, digital signature working in section 2.2. Additionally, authors also give a precise of blockchain key attributes in section 2.3. Also, Blockchain taxonomy is shown in section 2.4.

Figure 1. Sequence of blocks.

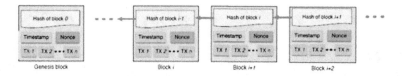

Block

A block comprises of the block header and the block body as mentioned in Figure 2. In particular, the block header includes:

1. Block version: implies which set of block validation rules to pursue.
2. Parent block hash: it is 256-bit hash values that indicate to the previous block.
3. Merkle tree root hash: the hash value of all the transactions in the block.

4. Timestamp: current timestamp as seconds since 1970-01-01T00:00 UTC.
5. nBits: current hashing target in a minimal format.
6. Nonce: a 4-byte field, which usually starts with 0 and increases for every hash computation.

The block body is made out of a transaction counter and transactions. The maximum transaction that a block can contain relies upon the block size and the measure of each transaction. Blockchain utilizes an asymmetric cryptography mechanism to validate the authentication of transactions. An asymmetric cryptography-based digital signature is used in an unfaithful situation. Author next quicky explains digital signature.

Figure 2. Block Structure

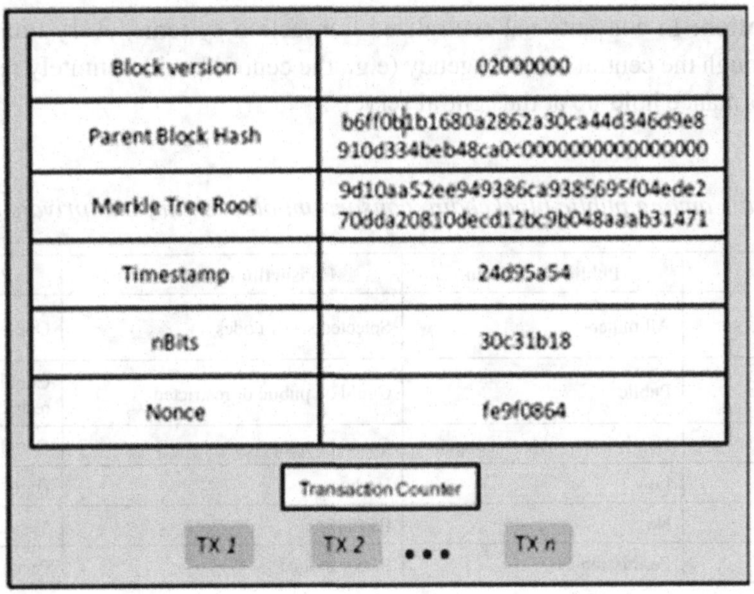

Block version	02000000
Parent Block Hash	b6ff0b1b1680a2862a30ca44d346d9e8 910d334beb48ca0c0000000000000000
Merkle Tree Root	9d10aa52ee949386ca9385695f04ede2 70dda20810decd12bc9b048aaab31471
Timestamp	24d95a54
nBits	30c31b18
Nonce	fe9f0864

Transaction Counter

TX 1   TX 2 • • •   TX n

Digital Signature

Each user holds a set of the private key and public key. The private key is used to sign a transaction. The digital signed transactions are spread all over the entire network and afterward are accessed by public keys, which are shown to everyone in the network. Figure 3 shows an example of a digital signature used in blockchain. The classic digital signature includes two phases: the signing phase and the verification phase. Take Figure 3 for instance again. When a user Alice wants to sign a transaction, Firstly she generates a hash value obtained from the transaction. Then she encrypts the hash value by utilizing her private key and is included transfer to another user Bob the encrypted hash with the original data. Bob verifies the received transaction by comparing the decrypted hash (by using Alice's public key) and the hash value generated from the received data by the same hash function as Alice's. The typical digital signature algorithms utilized in blockchains incorporate elliptic curve digital signature algorithm (ECDSA) defined by Johnson et al. (2001).

Figure 3. Digital signature used in Blockchain

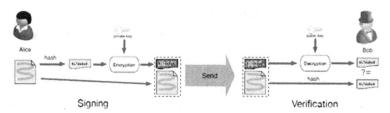

Key Characteristics of Blockchain

Precisely, blockchain has the following key properties:

- **Decentralization:** In conventional centralized transaction systems, every transaction should be validated through the central trusted agency (e.g., the central bank) definitely resulting in the cost and the performance hold-up at the central servers.

Table 1. Differentiate among public blockchain, consortium blockchain, and private blockchain

Property	Public blockchain	Consortium blockchain	Private blockchain
Consensus Determination	All miners	Selected set of nodes	One organization
Read permission	Public	Could be public or restricted	Could be public or restricted
Immutability	Nearly impossible to tamper	Could be tampered	Could be tampered
Efficiency	Low	High	High
Centralized	No	Partial	Yes
Consensus process	Permissionless	Permissioned	Permissioned

Differently, a transaction in the blockchain network can be regulated in between any two peers (P2P) without the authentication by the central agency. In this manner, blockchain can considerably diminish the server costs (including both development and operation cost) and reduce the performance bottlenecks at the central server.

- **Persistency:** Since every transaction spreading over the network should be verified and recorded in blocks distributed in the entire network, it is nearly impossible to tamper. Additionally, each broadcasted block will be approved by other nodes and transactions will be checked. So any falsification will be diagnosed easily.
- **Anonymity:** Each user can interact with the blockchain network using a generated address. Further, a user will generate multiple addresses to avoid identity exposure. There is no longer any central party keeping users' private information. This mechanism preserves a definite amount of privacy on the transactions included in the blockchain. Note that blockchain cannot ensure the ideal privacy preservation due to the constitutional constraint.

- **Auditability:** Since all the transactions on the blockchain is verified and recorded with a time-stamp, users can easily validate and trace the previous records by accessing any node in the distributed network. In Bitcoin blockchain, every transaction can be detected to previous transactions iteratively. It enhances the traceability and the transparency of the data stored in the blockchain.

Taxonomy of Blockchain Systems

Current blockchain systems can be roughly classified into three types: public blockchain, private blockchain and consortium blockchain. Buterin et al. (2015) compare all the three types of blockchain from different perspectives. The comparison is shown in Table 1.

- **Consensus Determination**: In the public blockchain, every node can participate in the consensus process. And the selected group of nodes are responsible for validating the block in consortium blockchain. As for the private chain, it is fully managed by one organization who can determine the final consensus.
- **Read Permission**: Transactions in a public blockchain are visible to the public while the read permission rely on a private blockchain or a consortium blockchain. The consortium or the organization can umpire whether the stored information is public or restricted.
- **Immutability**: Since transactions are stored in multiple nodes in the distributed network, therefore, it is certainly impossible to tamper the public blockchain. However, if most of the consortium or the ruling organization wants to tamper the blockchain, then the consortium blockchain or private blockchain can be reversed or tampered.
- **Efficiency**: It takes enough time to propagate transactions and blocks because there are a huge number of nodes on the public blockchain network. Taking network safety into consideration, limitation on the public blockchain will be much more severe. Hence, transaction throughput is restricted and the latency is high. With fewer validators, consortium blockchain and private blockchain can be much efficient.
- **Centralized**: The chief difference in between the three types of blockchains is that public blockchain is decentralized, consortium blockchain is partially centralized and private blockchain is fully centralized as it is governed by a single group.
- **Consensus Process**: Everyone in the globe can join the consensus process of the public blockchain. Apart from public blockchain, both consortium blockchain and private blockchain are permissioned. One node should be certificated to join the consensus process in consortium or private blockchain.

Since public blockchain is exposed to the world, it can mesmerize many users. The communities are .also very active. Several public blockchains emerge day by day. As for consortium blockchain, it can be applied to several business applications. Currently Hyperledger (2015), Hyperledger is evolving business consortium blockchain frameworks. Ethereum also has provided tools for constructing consortium blockchains. As for private blockchain, there are still a few companies applying it for efficiency and auditability.

EXISTING BLOCKCHAIN TECHNOLOGIES

Blockchain furnished decentralized data storage service with a tamper-resistant ledger having blocks chained in serial in distributed networks. It can record and secure transactions or transactional events with cryptography. The first Blockchain was suggested by Satoshi Nakamoto et al. (2008) and implemented in 2009 as the sanction technique for the proliferating cryptocurrency-Bitcoin (2007).

The data is recorded in a secure and distributed manner in the blockchain. The fundamental unit of records in Blockchain is the transaction. Every time a new transaction is generated, it is broadcast to the whole Blockchain network. Nodes receiving the transaction can validate the transaction by verifying the signature attached to the transaction, and mine validated transactions into cryptographically secured blocks. Such nodes are called block miners (or miners for short). To permit a miner to construct a block, a consensus problem required to be solved in a distributed way. The miners that manage to resolve the consensus problem broadcast their new blocks into the network. Upon the receipt of a new block, the miners yet to be able to resolve the consensus problem append the block to their own chains of blocks locally maintained at the miners, after all the transactions enclosed in the block are validate and the block is also proven to provide the right answer to the consensus problem. The new block consists of a link to the previous block in the chains, just by exploiting cryptographic means. All miners can synchronize their chains on a general basis, and specific terms are defined to ensure the consistent ledger shared among the distributed network, e.g., Bitcoin Blockchain keeps the longest chain only, in the case where there is discrepancy into the chains. In the following, few more detailed descriptions are given on these key components of Blockchain, i.e., the data structure, the consensus protocol, smart contracts and the security analysis on Blockchain.

BLOCKCHAIN FOR THE INTERNET OF THINGS

As described in ITU Report, (2015), the Internet of Things (IoT) refers to the network of many physical objects (20 billion by 2020, according to Gartner et al. (2016) which are given with Internet connection. Those devices acquire information about the surrounding environment, and they communicate with each other and with software systems by the Internet. As a result of such rich interaction, they also generate a large amount of data, in turn, usable to enable dependent services.

Instead of the benefits provided by these services, critical privacy issues may arise. It is because the connected devices (the things) spread sensitive personal data and disclose the behaviors and preferences of their owners. People's privacy is definitely at risk when such sensitive data are directed by centralized companies, which can make an illegal use of them: as a matter of fact, Edward Snowden's revelations showed that people's data stored by Internet and telecommunication companies have been exploited within a mass surveillance program, i.e, the PRISM program.

To prevent this situation, the goal of our research is to encourage a decentralized and private by- design IoT, where privacy is ensured by the technical design of the systems. Authors believe that this can be accomplished by adopting Peer-to-Peer (P2P) systems. In particular, the blockchain could be very helpful in constructing such privacy preserving IoT. S. Nakamoto et al. (2009) said the blockchain is a P2P ledger, initially used in the Bitcoincryptocurrency for economic transactions.

It is tamper-proof and consists only authentic information; additionally, since it is P2P, it is not handled by any single centralized entity. Because of these reasons, cryptocurrencies are just one of the possible applications of all this technology.

A private-by-design IoT could be fostered by the merging of the blockchain and a P2P storage system. Sensitive data generated and exchanged among IoT devices are stored in such a storage system, whose P2P nature could guarantee privacy, robustness, and absence of single points of failure. Including with this storage system, the blockchain has the basic role to register and authenticate all operations performed on IoT devices data. Every operation on data (creation, modification, deletion) is registered in the blockchain: this could guarantee that any abuse on data can be detected. Moreover, access policies can be specified and enforced by the blockchain, preventing unauthorized operations on data. In this system, people are not required to entrust IoT data generated by their devices to centralized companies: data could be securely stored in different peers, and the blockchain could ensure their authenticity and prevent unauthorized access.

Limitations of IoT Security

M. Pticek et al. (2016) said that IoT network prevails with its ability to interconnect several devices possessing multiple sensing and computing abilities with little human interventions. Sensing and actuating devices form heterogeneous IoT networks to provide several applications. Typical IoT applications consist of smart home, smart transport, eHealth and smart grid discussed by C. Perera et al. (2014).

A typical IoT architecture includes Perception, Networking, Service, and Interface Layers, from bottom to top. The Perception layer also called the sensor layer in other IoT architectures summarized in, contain sensors and actuators collecting and processing environmental information to execute functions, such as querying temperature, location, motion, acceleration. The perception layer is an indispensable part of a variation of IoT applications. Multiple types of end devices can be adopted in the perception layer to bridge the physical world and the digital world. Classic end devices include Radio- Frequency Identification (RFID), wireless sensors and actuators, Near Field Communications (NFC), and mobile phones. For example, the RFID tag is a small microchip linked to an antenna. By attaching RFID tags to objects, the object can be identified, tracked, and monitored during logistics, retailing, and supply chain. The Networking layer is responsible for connecting other smart things, network devices, and servers. The Service layer constructs and manages specific services to meet the IoT application requirements. The Interface layer facilitates data use interactions with objects for certain applications.

BLOCKCHAINFOR IOT: APPLICATIONS

IoT networks are data-centric, where data are uploaded by a huge number of end devices. This makes both data and devices be the prey of potential attacks on IoT. Sensory data in an IoT system can be personal or sensitive, e.g., medical IoT; or from national applications, e.g., the IoT-based smart grid proposed by W.L. Chin et al. (2017) and nuclear factory by R. Langner et al. (2011). The integrity and privacy of the data are important. Blockchain is believed to hold the key to fix security, data integrity and reliability concerns in the IoT network. Provided ensured data integrity, Blockchain has drawn a lot of attention for multiple IoT applications (e.g., supply chain management defined by K. Korpela et al. (2017) and smart city by K. Biswas et al. (2016)), beyond the cryptocurrency. Blockchain technologies handle security risks on both aspects of sensory data and end-devices.

The correctness of sensory data. The data in Blockchain powered IoT networks can be separated into Blockchain-related data, e.g., account, balance and transaction fee, and IoT-related data, e.g., sensory data. The Blockchain-related data can be validated based on previous transactions, e.g., the expense must be fewer than the balance of an account, as done in other typical Blockchain applications. The IoT-related data are secured by signatures in a transactional fashion, which guarantees that only the messages sent by the authorized IoT devices are recorded and exploited. On the other hand, the correctness of IoT-related data can be ensured by the Oracle service which gives an authenticated data feed. The backward-linked hashed structure to increase the trustworthiness of sensory data recorded in IoT-Blockchain ledgers. Malicious functionality of IoT devices. The malicious behaviors of end devices in IoT-Blockchain can be summarized as the following three types: (1) sending transactions with false signatures, which can be detected, punished and rejected by the Blockchain system; or (2) sending transactions with invalid data but correct signatures, which can be removed by false data detection algorithms and punishing the transactions source nodes; or (3) consuming resources, e.g., DoS, which can be prevented by transaction fee mechanisms.

BLOCKCHAIN FOR IOT: TECHNOLOGIES

In this section, authors describe typical technologies of Blockchains which can be used in IoT applications. Firstly, they present three categories of current Blockchain networks and map IoT applications into suitable Blockchain categories. After that the core function of Blockchain, namely, the consensus protocol, is analyzed from two key points, followed by representing Blockchain projects compared in the suitability in IoT applications. Based on access controls of the Blockchain networks, the state-of-the-art Blockchains can be classified into public Blockchain, private Blockchain, and hybrid Blockchain which mixes of the former two.

- **Public Blockchain:** The main class of Blockchain is public Blockchain in which, with no access control, any uncertified, untrustworthy node can read and record transactions, and take part in mining blocks and contributing to Blockchain. Designed for open access to public distributed networks, public Blockchains can give strong scalability. However, preserving the consistent records of public Blockchain becomes increasingly tough, as the network scales up, and would compromise the block creation rate of public Blockchain consequently. This is due to the fact that, without access control, public networks do not have strict control policy on the identification and certification of any participants according to V. Buterin et al. (2015), and therefore the executed consensus protocols have to scarify the block creation rate for security. Specifically, PoW and PoX are normally used in public Blockchain as consensus protocols, achieving lower block generation rate compared with PBFT algorithm utilized in private Blockchain, which will be analyzed in detail later in this section. Current public Blockchain projects, containing Bitcoin and Ethereum, also specify the openness and capacity-limited attributes. Public Blockchain is best suited for the IoT applications with open access or flexible peers at a large scale, such as VANET and supply chain.

- **Private Blockchain:** Another well-known class of Blockchain is private Blockchain which resides in closed proprietary networks with stringent access control and read/write permission, as well as participant identification and certification. Private Blockchains can meet the privacy needs and has been increasingly drawing attention from financial institutions. The proprietary networks, on which private Blockchains operate, can be efficient for high speed and low latency. For instance, high speed of up to tens of thousands of transactions every second can be achieved in private Blockchains. Private Blockchain acquires BFT protocols, i.e., PBFT and its variability, as consensus protocols, which give higher capacity with restricted access control. The access control given by private Blockchain further protects IoT applications from external adversaries. In general, private Blockchain is best suited for IoT applications with the small scale of miners, because of both the high communication complexity and overhead of BFT protocols. When the network size goes beyond twenty, the capacity of private Blockchain exponentially slows down. Apart from multiple BFT consensus protocols, private Blockchain can use other efficient consensus protocols, e.g., Paxos and Raft, in response to particular types of failures, e.g., crash failures and fail-stop failures.
- **Hybrid Blockchain:** Another category of Blockchain is hybrid Blockchain which was proposed to leverage the advantages of public and private Blockchains, to be more specific, the block create rate of private Blockchain and the scalability of public Blockchain. Another recent example of hybrid Blockchain is ByzCoin which dynamically forms hash power-proportionate consensus groups to gather recently-successful block miners. Communication trees can be employed to optimize transaction commitment and verification under normal operation. More examples of hybrid Blockchain consist a resilience optimal Byzantine consensus algorithm that Crain et al. proposed for consortium Blockchain which relies on neither a leader nor a signature or randomization. The proposed consensus protocol companies reducing multivariate Byzantine consensus to binary Byzantine consensus satisfying a validity property. The property is that, if all the non-faulty processes propose a similar value, no other value can be decided. The hybrid Blockchain is attractive to IoT applications due to the complexity and heterogeneity of IoT networks. A hierarchical Blockchain structure was introduced for the smart home applications, where a private Blockchain, maintained by resourceful ''miners'', runs at each home and public Blockchain runs on the ''miner'' network.

BLOCKCHAIN SOLUTIONS FOR IOT SECURITY

Blockchain technology has been showcased by industry and research community as a disruptive technology that is ready to play a major role in overseeing, controlling, and most importantly securing IoT devices. This section discusses how blockchain can be a key enabling technology for providing practical security solutions to today's challenging IoT security problems. Firstly, the section gives a concise background about blockchain, and after that outlines open research IoT security problems and challenges which blockchain may give solutions for. Also, the section gives the literature of blockchain-based solutions for IoT security problems.

Background

A blockchain is basically a decentralized, distributed, shared, and immutable database ledger that stores registry of assets and transactions throughout a peer-to-peer (P2P) network. It contains chained blocks of data that have been timestamped and verified by miners. The blockchain works on elliptic curve cryptography (ECC) and SHA-256 hashing to give solid cryptographic proof for data authentication and integrity discussed by A.M. Antonopoulos et al. (2014). Fundamentally, the block data consists of a list of all transactions and a hash to the previous block. The blockchain has a full history of all transactions and gives a cross-border global distributed trust.

Trusted Third Parties (TTP) or centralized authorities and services can be disrupted, compromised or hacked. They can also misbehave and become immortal in the future, despite the fact that they are trustworthy now. In the blockchain, each transaction in the shared public ledger is validated by a majority consensus of miner nodes which are actively incorporated in verifying and validating transactions. In a bitcoin network, miners validate the block by calculating a hash with leading zeros to meet the difficulty target. Once transactions are verified and validated by consensus, block data are immutable, i.e. data can never be erased or modified. Blockchain can be built as (1) permissioned (or private) network that can be prohibited to a specific group of participants, or (2) permission-less or public network which is open for anyone to join in. Permission blockchains outfit more privacy and better access control Fig. 4 illustrate a typical design structure of a Blockchain. The design structure is mainly composed of the block header and the block body which consists of a list of transactions. The block header consists of multiple fields, one of which is a version number to track software of protocol upgrades. Also, the header consists of a timestamp, block size, and the number of transactions. Merkle root field showcases the hash value of the current block. Merkle tree hashing is commonly used in distributed systems and P2P networks for efficient data verification. The nonce field is used for the proof-of-work algorithm, and it is the trial counter value that created the hash with leading zeros. The difficulty target enumerates the number of leading zeros and is used to keep the blocktime approximately 10 min for BitInfoCharts, Block - Bitcoin Wiki, (2016) and Ethereum Average BlockTime Chart, (2016). The difficulty target is adjustable periodically and is grown (with more leading zeros) as the computation power of hardware grows over time. The blocktime is set by design to account for the propagation time of blocks to reach every miner, and for every miner to reach a consensus.

Figure 4. Blockchain design structure showing chained blocks with header and body fields

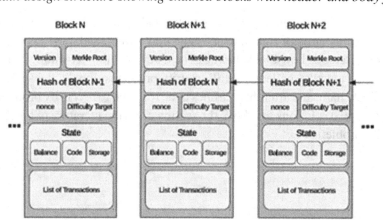

Bitcoin is one of the first and the most famous applications that execute on the top of blockchain infrastructure. In general, the bitcoin blockchain has been the underlying platform and technology of several of today's most popular cryptocurrencies. However, with the advent of the Ethereum blockchain, which enacts smart contracts, the potential use of space for blockchain has become endless. Ethereum blockchain was introduced and opened for use to the public in July 2015. Subsequently, similar smart-contract blockchain platforms have lately emerged. Those consist of Linux-Foundation (2017), C. Kuhlman (2016), Stellar, Stellar network overview, (2014), Ripple, Ripple network, (2013) and Tendermint [2017]. In contrast to bitcoin blockchain which is primarily used for digital currency transactions, Ethereum blockchain has the potential to store records and more importantly run smart contracts. The term smart contracts were first introduced by Nick Szabo in 1994. A smart contract is basically a computerized transaction protocol that runs the terms of the contract. In the simplistic definition, smart contracts are programs written by users to be uploaded and run on the blockchain. The scripting or programming language for smart contracts is known as Solidarity which is a JavaScript-like language.

Ethereum Blockchain provides EVM (Ethereum Virtual Machines) which are basically the miner nodes. These nodes are able to provide cryptographically tamper-proof trustworthy execution and enforcement of these programs or contracts. Ethereum supports its own digital currency which is known as Ether. As in bitcoin, in Ethereum, users can send coins to each other using normal transactions which get recorded on the ledger, and for such transactions, there is no requirement for a blockchain state in bitcoin.

However, for Ethereum to assist smart contract execution, a blockchain state is used. A smart contract consists of its own account and address, and associated with it is its own executable code and balance of Ether coins. The storage is perceptual and holds the code to be executed on the EVM nodes. EVM storage is relatively costly, and for a large storage to be uploaded to the blockchain, another remote decentralized data store like BitTorrent, IPFS, or Swarm can be used. The smart contracts, however, can hold a validation hash of such remotely stored data. The possible use cases and applications of smart-contract blockchain applications are vast and endless, extending from cryptocurrency and trading to autonomous machine-to-machine transactions, from supply chain and asset tracking to automated access control and sharing, and from digital identity and voting to certification, management, and governance of records, data, or items discussed by J. Mattila et al. (2016). Based on blockchains, commercial deployments are increasing rapidly. For instance, Safeshare releases (2016) have offered insurance solution using blockchain based on bitcoin. Similarly, as per linux foundation, (2017), IBM has launched its blockchain framework using Hyperledger Fabric platform. The framework supports the development of blockchain applications, and in contrast to other frameworks, it does not need cryptocurrency. The IBM blockchain is being used commercially into banks, supply chain systems, and cargo shipping companies.

Potential Blockchain Solutions

In the context of IoT, blockchain depends on smart contracts is expected to play a noteworthy role in managing, controlling, and most importantly securing IoT devices. In this section, authors discuss and summarize a few of the intrinsic features of blockchain that can be immensely useful for IoT in general, and IoT security in particular. Address Space. Blockchain has a 160-bit address space, instead of IPv6 address space which consists 128-bit address space according to A.M. Antonopoulos et al. (2014). A blockchain address is 20 bytes or a 160-bit hash of the public key created by ECDSA (Elliptic Curve Digital Signature Algorithm). With the 160-bit address, blockchain can generate and allocate addresses offline for around 1.46*1048 IoT devices. The probability of address collision is approximately 1048, which is considered adequately safe to provide a GUID (Global Unique Identifier) which requires no registration or uniqueness verification when assigning and allocating an address to an IoT device. With blockchain, centralized authority and governance, like that of the Internet Assigned Numbers Authority (IANA), is removed. Currently, IANA oversees the allocation of global IPv4 and IPv6 addresses, Furthermore, blockchain gives 4.3 billion addresses more than IPv6, therefore making blockchain a more scalable solution for IoT than IPv6.

Lastly, it is worth noting that several IoT devices are constrained in memory and computation capacity, and therefore will be unfit to run an IPv6 stack.

Identity of Things (IDoT) and Governance. Identity and Access Management (IAM) for IoT must address various challenging issues in an efficient, safe, and reliable manner. One primary challenging issues deal with ownership and identity relationships of IoT devices. Ownership of a device changes during the lifetime of the device from the manufacturer, supplier, retailer, and consumer proposed by I. Friese et al. (2014). The consumer ownership of an IoT device can be changed or revoked, if the device gets resold, decommissioned, or compromised. Managing of attributes and relationships of an IoT device is another challenge. Attributes of a device can be consist of the manufacturer, make, type, serial number, deployment GPS coordinates, location, etc. Aside from attributes, capabilities, and features, IoT devices have relationships. IoT relationships may consist of the device to- human, device-to-device, or device-to-service. An IoT device relationships can be deployed by, used by, shipped by, sold by, upgraded by, fixed by, sold by, etc.

Blockchain has the capability to solve these challenges effectively, securely, and efficiently. Blockchain has been used widely for giving trustworthy and authorized identity registration, ownership tracking and monitoring of products, goods, and assets. According to P. Otte et al. (2017), approaches like Trust Chain are proposed to enable trusted transactions using blockchain while providing the integrity of the transactions in a distributed environment. IoT devices are no exception. Blockchain can be used to register and give identity to connected IoT devices, with a set of parameters and complex relationships that can be uploaded and stored on the blockchain distributed ledger.

Blockchain also gives trustworthy decentralized management, governance, and tracking at every point in the supply chain and lifecycle of an IoT device, as portrayed in Fig. 5. The supply chain can incorporate multiple players such as factory, vendor, supplier, distributor, shipper, installer, owner, repairer, re-installed, etc. As shown in Fig. 5, key pairs can be changed and re-issued at many points during the

Figure 5. IoT device lifecycle security management

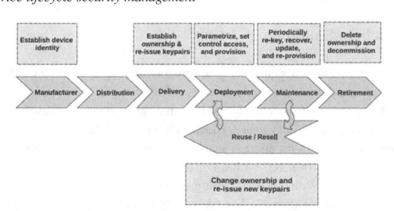

lifecycle of an IoT device. Issuance of key pairs can be done firstly by the manufacturer, then by the owner, periodically after deployment.

Data Authentication and Integrity, By design, data transmitted by IoT devices connected to the blockchain network will always be cryptographically proofed and signed by the real sender that holds a unique public key and GUID, and thereby ensuring authentication and integrity of transmitted data. Additionally, each transaction made to or by an IoT device is recorded on the blockchain distributed ledger and can be tracked securely.

Authentication, Authorization, and Privacy, Blockchain smart contracts have the capability to provide decentralized authentication rules and logic to be able to provide single and multiparty authentication to an IoT Device.

Information Authentication and Integrity, By structure, information transmitted by IoT gadgets associated with the blockchain system will dependably be cryptographically sealed and marked by the genuine sender that holds an interesting open key and GUID, and in this manner guaranteeing confirmation and trustworthiness of transmitted information. Also, every exchange made to or by an IoT gadget are recorded on the blockchain circulated record and can be followed safely.

Validation, Authorization, and Privacy, Blockchain shrewd contracts have the capacity to give a decentralized verification tenets and rationale to have the capacity to give single and multiparty validation to an IoT Device.

Likewise, smart contracts can provide a more efficient authorization access rules to connected IoT devices with much less complexity when compared with traditional authorization protocols like Role Based Access Management (RBAC), OAuth 2.0, OpenID, OMA DM, and LWM2M. These protocols are used these days for IoT device authentication widely, authorization, and management. Moreover, data privacy can be also ensured by utilizing smart contracts which set the access rules, conditions, and time to allow certain individual or group of users or machines to own, control, or have access to data at rest or in transit. The smart contracts can spell out also who has the right to update, upgrade, patch the IoT software or hardware, reset the IoT device, provision of new key pairs, initiate a service or repair request, change ownership, and provision or re-provision of the device.

Secure Communications. IoT application communication protocols as those of HTTP, MQTT, CoAP, or XMPP, or even protocols related with routing as those of RPL and 6LoWPAN, are not secure by design. Such protocols must be wrapped inside the other security protocols such as DTLS or TLS for messaging and application protocols to provide secure communication. In the same way, for routing, IPSec is typically used to give security for RPL and 6LoWPAN protocols. DTLS, TLS, IPSec, or even the light-weight TinyTLS protocols are heavy and complex in terms of computation and memory prerequisites, and complicated with centralized management and governance of key management and distributions using the famous protocol of PKI. With blockchain, key management and distribution are totally removed, as each IoT device would have his own unique GUID and asymmetric key pair once installed and connected to the blockchain network. This will lead also to significant simplification of other security protocols as that of DTLS, with no need to handle and exchange PKI certificates at the handshake stage in case of DTLS or TLS (or IKE in case of IPSec) to negotiate the cipher suite parameters for encryption and hashing and to establish the master and session keys. Therefore, lightweight security protocols that would fit and stratify the needs for the compute and memory resources of IoT devices become more feasible.

Blockchain and IoT Related Work

In the article, research work on IoT security and blockchain is reserved, with most of the work being focused on leveraging blockchain technology to benefit IoT in general. M. Conoscenti et al. (2016) have classified 18 use cases of blockchain, out of which four cases are for IoT. The four use case categories for IoT consist of an immutable log of events and management of access control to data proposed by G. Zyskind et al. (2015), trading of collected IoT data by Y. Zhang et al. (2015) and D. Wörner et al. (2014), and symmetric and asymmetric key management for IoT devices by L. Axon et al. (2015) and C. Fromknecht et al. (2014). I. Friese et al. (2014) have laid out the issues and challenges for the identity in IoT. These challenges primarily incorporate ownership and identity relationships, authentication and authorization, governance of data and privacy. In Section 5.1, the authors discussed how blockchain can be a key enabler for resolving these challenges.

A. Bahga et al. (2016) proposed a blockchain-based framework for industrial IoT (or IIoT). The framework enables IIoT devices to communicate with the cloud and the blockchain network both. Each IIoT device is furnished with the single-board computer (SBC) having control and communication interface capabilities for both cloud and the Ethereum blockchain. IIoT devices are intended to deliver data to the cloud for storage and analysis, and send/receive transactions to other devices on the blockchain network, and also to trigger executions of smart contracts. As a proof of concept, the authors designed a simple platform using the Arduino Uno board and Ethereum smart contracts and discuss briefly how the platform can be used for machine maintenance and smart diagnostics.

The applications of blockchain smart contracts to IoT are reviewed by Christidis et al. (2016). The authors discussed how smart contracts of blockchain can facilitate and bloster the autonomous workflow and the sharing of services among IoT devices, as proposed by V. Pureswaran et al. (2014). However, the authors contend how IoT can benefit from blockchain networks in aspects regarding billing, e-trading, shipping and supply chain management. Furthermore, they discuss a scenario where blockchain can facilitate the buying and selling of energy automatically among IoT device like smart meters.

Smart contracts can be utilized to set user-defined criteria for energy trading. The authors likewise discuss another scenario for asset tracking of container shipment using smart contracts and IoT.

POSSIBLE FUTURE DIRECTIONS

Blockchain has showcased its potential in industry and academia. Authors describe possible future directions with respect to four areas: blockchain testing, stop the tendency to centralization, big data analytics, and blockchain application.

This section presents future directions in optimizing security, scalability, and capacity of Blockchain for future large-scale high-capacity IoT applications. The design of Blockchain for IoT application would also adapt to the specific attributes of IoT networks, such as immense scale, inherent partitioning incomplete network connectivity, non-trivial topology, non-zero propagation delay, heterogeneous data, and limited device memory.

- **Blockchain Testing:** Recently multiple kinds of blockchains appear and more than 700 digital currencies are listed in up to now. However, few developers might falsify their blockchain performance to attract investors driven by the huge profit. Besides that, when users want to merge blockchain into business, they have to know which blockchain meets their requirements. So blockchain testing mechanism required to be set up to test different blockchains. Blockchain testing could be separated into two phases: the standardization phase and the testing phase. In the standardization phase, all aspects have to be made and agreed. When a blockchain is introduced, it could be tested with the agreed criteria to valid if the blockchain works fine as developers claim. As for the testing phase, blockchain testing required to be performed with various criteria. For instance, a user who is in charge of online retail business cares about the throughput of the blockchain, so the examination requires to test the normal time from a user send a transaction to the transaction is packed into the blockchain, capacity for a blockchain block and etc.

- **Stop the Tendency to Centralization:** Blockchain is built as a decentralized system. However, there is a trend that miners are centralized in the mining pool. Up to now, the top 5 mining pools together own larger than 51% of the total hash power in the Bitcoin network. Aside from this, selfish mining strategy showcased that pools with over 25% of total computing power could get more revenue than a fair share. Rational miners would be mesmerized into the selfish pool and finally, the pool could easily exceed 51% of the total power. As the blockchain is not intended to serve a couple of organizations, some methods ought to be proposed to solve this problem.

- **Big Data Analytics:** Blockchain could be well integrated with big data. Here, authors roughly categorized the blend into two types: data management and data analytics. With respect to data management, blockchain could be utilized to store valuable data as it is distributed and secure. Blockchain could also guarantee that the data is original. For instance, if blockchain is used to keep the patient's health information, the information could not be altered and it is hard to steal that private information. When it comes to data analytics, transactions on the blockchain could be used for big data analytics. For instance, user trading patterns might be extracted. Users can predict their potential partners' trading behaviors with the analysis.

- **Blockchain Applications:** Currently most blockchains are utilized in the financial domain, an ever increasing number of applications for different fields are appearing. Traditional industries could take blockchain into consideration and apply blockchain into their fields to improve their systems. For instance, user reputations could be stored on the blockchain. At the same instance, the up-and-coming industry could make use of blockchain to improve performance. For example, Arcade City, a ridesharing startup gives an offer of an open commercial center where riders connect directly with drivers by leveraging blockchain technology. A smart contract is a computerized transaction protocol that runs the terms of a contract. It has been proposed for a long time and now this idea is designed with blockchain. In the blockchain, a smart contract is a code segment that could be run by miners automatically. The smart contract has transformative potential in multiple fields like financial services and IoT.

CONCLUSION

Blockchain has showcased the capability to change the traditional industry with its key features: decentralization, firmness, privacy, and audit. In this chapter, the author presents a described outline on blockchain for IoT. Authors first review blockchain progress including the blockchain creation and the key properties of the blockchain. Some possible future titles are proposed in the same way. Nowadays, block-based apps are bouncing, and authors want to later lead exams at the top of blockchain-based applications. Blockchains and IoT were given the signal of research bearings to improve the range, security, and adaptability of the blockchains for the powerful reconciliation of the future of progress.

REFERENCES

All-In-Bits. (2017). *Introduction to tendermint.* Retrieved from https://tendermint.com/intro

Antonopoulos, A. M. (2014). Mastering Bitcoin: Unlocking Digital Crypto-Currencies. O'Reilly Media, Inc. Retrieved from https://bitcoin.org/en/

Axon, L. (2015). *Privacy-awareness in Blockchain-based PKI.* Tech. Rep. Retrieved from https://ora.ox.ac.uk/objects/uuid:f8377b69-599b-4cae-8df0-f0cded53e63b/datastreams/ATTACHMENT01

Bahga, A., & Madisetti, V. K. (2016). *Blockchain platform for industrial Internet of Things.* Tech. Rep. Retrieved from http://file.scirp.org/pdf/JSEA_2016102814012798.pdf

Biswas, K., & Muthukkumarasamy, V. (2016). Securing smart cities using blockchain technology. *Proc. 18th IEEE Int. Conf. High Performance Comput. Commun.; 14th IEEE Int. Conf. Smart City; 2nd IEEE Int. Conf. Data Sci. Syst., HPCC/SmartCity/DSS'16,* 1392–1393. 10.1109/HPCC-SmartCity-DSS.2016.0198

BitInfoCharts. (2016). *Block - BitcoinWiki.* Retrieved from https://en.bitcoin.it/wiki/Block

Buterin, V. (2014). *A next-generation smart contract and decentralized application platform.* White Paper.

Buterin, V. (2015). *On public and private blockchains.* Retrieved from https://blog.ethereum.org/2015/08/07/on-public-and-private-blockchains/

Buterin, V. (2015). On public and private blockchains. *Ethereum Blog.* Retrieved from https: //blog.ethereum.org/2015/08/07/on-public-and-private-blockchains/

Chin, W. L., Li, W., & Chen, H. H. (2017). Energy big data security threats in IoT-based smart grid communications. *IEEE Communications Magazine, 55*(10), 70–75. doi:10.1109/MCOM.2017.1700154

Christidis, K., & Devetsikiotis, M. (2016). Blockchains and smart contracts for the Internet of Things. *IEEE Access: Practical Innovations, Open Solutions, 4,* 2292–2303. doi:10.1109/ACCESS.2016.2566339

Conoscenti, M., Vetro, A., & Martin, J. C. D. (2016). Blockchain for the Internet of Things: A systematic literature Review. *The 3rd International Symposium onInternet of Things: Systems, Management, and Security, IOTSMS-2016.* 10.1109/AICCSA.2016.7945805

EconoTimes. (2016). *Safeshare releases first blockchain insurance solution for sharing economy.* Retrieved from https://www.econotimes.com/SafeShare-Releases-First-Blockchain-Insurance-Solution-For-Sharing-Economy-181326

EtherScan. (2016). *Ethereum Average Block Time Chart.* Retrieved from https://etherscan.io/chart/blocktime

Friese, I., Heuer, J., & Kong, N. (2014). Challenges from the Identities of Things: Introduction of the Identities of Things discussion group within Kantara initiative. *2014 IEEE World Forum on Internet of Things (WF-IoT),* 1–4. 10.1109/WF-IoT.2014.6803106

Fromknecht, C., Velicanu, D., & Yakoubov, S. (2014). *CertCoin: A namecoin based decentralized authentication system*. Retrieved from https://courses.csail.mit.edu/ 6.857/2014/files/19-fromknecht-velicann-yakoubov-certcoin.pdf

Hyperledger Project. (2015). Retrieved from https://www.hyperledger.org/

IBM. (2017). *IBM blockchain based on hyperledger fabric from the linux foundation*. Retrieved from https://www.ibm.com/blockchain/hyperledger.html

International Telecommunication Union. (2015). *Measuring the Information Society Report*. International Telecommunication Union (ITU).

Johnson, D., Menezes, A., & Vanstone, S. (2001). The elliptic curve digital signature algorithm (ecdsa). *International Journal of Information Security*, *1*(1), 36–63. doi:10.1007102070100002

Korpela, K., Hallikas, J., & Dahlberg, T. (2017). Digital supply chain transformation toward Blockchain integration. *Proc. 50th Hawaii Int. Conf. Syst. Sci.* 10.24251/HICSS.2017.506

Kuhlman. (2016). *What is eris?* Retrieved from https://monax.io/2016/04/03/wtf-is-eris/

Langner, R. (2011). Stuxnet: Dissecting a cyberwarfare weapon. *IEEE Security and Privacy*, *9*(3), 49–51. doi:10.1109/MSP.2011.67

Lee KuoChuen, D. (Ed.). (2015). *Handbook of Digital Currency*. Elsevier. Retrieved from http://EconPapers.repec.org/RePEc:eee:monogr:9780128021170

Linux-Foundation. (2017). *Blockchain technologies for business*. Retrieved from https://www.hyperledger.org/

Mattila, J. (2016). *The blockchain phenomenon: The disruptive potential of distributed consensu architectures*. ETLA working papers: ElinkeinoelämänTutkimuslaitos, Research Institute of the Finnish Economy. Retrieved from https: //books.google.com.pk/books?id=StNQnQAACAAJ

Nakamoto, S. (2009). *Bitcoin: A peer-to-peer electronic cash system*. Available: https://bitcoin.org/bitcoin.pdf

Nakamoto, S. (2008). *Bitcoin: A peer-to-peer electronic cash system*. Retrieved from https: //bitcoin.org/bitcoin.pdf

Otte, M., de Vos, M., & Pouwelse, J. (2017). TrustChain: A Sybil-resistant scalable blockchain. *Future Generation Computer Systems*. doi:10.1016/j.future.2017.08.048

Perera, C., Zaslavsky, A., Christen, P., & Georgakopoulos, D. (2014). Context aware computing for the internet of things: A survey. *IEEE Communications Surveys and Tutorials*, *16*(1), 414–454. doi:10.1109/SURV.2013.042313.00197

Pticek, M., Podobnik, V., & Jezic, G. (2016). Beyond the internet of things: The social networking of machines. *International Journal of Distributed Sensor Networks*, *12*(6), 8178417. doi:10.1155/2016/8178417

Pureswaran, V., & Brody, P. (2014). *Device Democracy - Saving the future of the Internet of Things*. IBM. Retrieved from http://www-01.ibm.com/common/ssi/cgibin/ssialias?htmlfid=GBE03620USEN

Ripple. (2013). *Ripple network*. Retrieved from https://ripple.com/network

Stellar. (2014). *Stellar network overview*. Retrieved from https://www.stellar.org/developers/guides/get-started/

The-Bitcoin-Foundation. (2014). *How does Bitcoin work?* Retrieved from https://bitcoin.org/en/how-it-works

Wörner, D., & von Bomhard, T. (2014). When your sensor earns money: Exchanging data for cash with bitcoin. In *Proceedings of the 2014 ACM International Joint Conference on Pervasive and Ubiquitous Computing: Adjunct Publication, UbiComp '14 Adjunct.* ACM.10.1145/2638728.2638786

Zhang, Y., & Wen, J. (2015). An IoT electric business model based on the protocol of bitcoin. *2015 18th International Conference on Intelligence in Next Generation Networks*, 184–191. 10.1109/ICIN.2015.7073830

Zyskind, G., Nathan, O., & Pentland, A. (2015). *Enigma: decentralized computation platform with guaranteed privacy*. Retrieved from http://enigma.media.mit.edu/ enigma~full.pdf

This research was previously published in Transforming Businesses With Bitcoin Mining and Blockchain Applications; pages 68-90, copyright year 2020 by Business Science Reference (an imprint of IGI Global).

Chapter 5
Security Aspects of the Internet of Things

Dominik Hromada
FBM, Brno University of Technology, Czech Republic

Rogério Luís de C. Costa
(iD) https://orcid.org/0000-0003-2306-7585
CIC, Polytechnic of Leiria, Portugal

Leonel Santos
(iD) https://orcid.org/0000-0002-6883-7996
CIIC, ESTG, Polytechnic of Leiria, Portugal

Carlos Rabadão
(iD) https://orcid.org/0000-0001-7332-4397
CIIC, ESTG, Polytechnic of Leiria, Portugal

ABSTRACT

The Internet of Things (IoT) comprises the interconnection of a wide range of different devices, from Smart Bluetooth speakers to humidity sensors. The great variety of devices enables applications in several contexts, including Smart Cities and Smart Industry. IoT devices collect and process a large amount of data on machines and the environment and even monitor people's activities. Due to their characteristics and architecture, IoT devices and networks are potential targets for cyberattacks. Indeed, cyberattacks can lead to malfunctions of the IoT environment and access and misuse of private data. This chapter addresses security concerns in the IoT ecosystem. It identifies common threats for each of IoT layers and presents advantages, challenges, and limitations of promising countermeasures based on new technologies and strategies, like Blockchain and Machine Learning. It also contains a more in-depth discussion on Intrusion Detection Systems (IDS) for IoT, a promising solution for cybersecurity in IoT ecosystems.

DOI: 10.4018/978-1-6684-7132-6.ch005

I. INTRODUCTION

Internet of Things (IoT) as a term was used for the first time in 1999 by Kevin Ashton, a British technology pioneer (Farooq, Waseem, Khairi, & Mazhar, 2015). He defines IoT as the system of physical objects in the world that connects to the internet via a sensor. This ecosystem is full of intelligent machines interacting with each other, with objects, environments, and infrastructures. This new technology has impacted the whole population from everyday people's lives to industry solutions, helping people to work smarter and efficiently, and giving them more control over monitored environments, objects, and infrastructures.

In several market areas, IoT became an essential part of business activities, e.g., providing real-time data about operation activities or measuring the performance of supply chain machines and logistic operations. The data collected by IoT devices can be analyzed later, and provide decision-makers with invaluable insights into their processes with the help of Business Intelligence (BI) to make business processes even more efficient, faster, environmentally friendly, and less expensive. Therefore, IoT opened new opportunities for data analysis and knowledge discovery (Gubbi, Buyya, Marusic, & Palaniswami, 2013). Main IoT applications areas include transportation and logistics, Smart Healthcare, Smart Environments, and City Information Modeling (Ullah, Ahmad, Ahmad, Ata-ur-Rehman, & Junaid, 2019).

On the other hand, the data collected are a double-edged sword. It may be a significant help, but also a threat to people's privacy and security, as their activity can be monitored everywhere and anytime (Neisse et al., 2015). Also, poorly secured devices may lead to attacks on other systems and lead to personal information leaks and misuses due to unauthorized access.

Some of the main security concerns in the context of IoT are related to basic processes (for example, identification, authentication, and access control), data integrity, data confidentiality, data privacy, and data availability (Sicari, Rizzardi, Grieco, & Coen-Porisini, 2015; Farooq et al., 2015). But the layered architecture of IoT is also subject to several attacks and threats, each of them being most common in or targeted to a specific layer (Weyrich & Ebert, 2016; Swamy, Jadhav, & Kulkarni, 2017).

Some of the *traditional* security countermeasures (e.g., the use of security protocols, authentication controls, and privacy by design) may fit in the IoT context. But the new solutions for IoT security include the use of Fog Computing, Blockchain Technology, Edge computing, and Machine Learning-based techniques (Baouya, Chehida, Bensalem, & Bozga, 2020; Ozay, Esnaola, Yarman Vural, Kulkarni, & Poor, 2016).

The use of Intrusion Detection Systems (IDS) in IoT networks is subject to some additional challenges. Deep packet inspection (DPI) and stateful packet inspection (SPI) are computationally expensive and not adequate for the IoT network. An alternative solution in IoT ecosystems may go through an IDS based on IP flow analysis. Additional challenges related to an efficient IDS for IoT networks include aspects related to chosen incident detection methodology, the IDS implementation strategy, and IDS's intrusion detection capabilities.

In the following section, we present the main aspects related to the IoT processing cycle. Then, Section III presents the main security concerns in the IoT context. The IoT layered architecture and the most common threats of each layer are described in Section IV. Section V discusses some current countermeasures based on *nontraditional* solutions and Section V presents open issues and future directions. Finally, Section VII concludes the chapter.

II. ASPECTS OF IOT NETWORK PROCESSING CYCLE

The IoT opened several new opportunities in a wide range of applications. Figure 1 presents the main components of a processing cycle in the IoT.

A. Recognition

All the involved objects in the network must have unique identification and must be recognized accordingly. That means that two entities present in the network cannot have a similar identification representation. Hence, the two main components of successful recognition are addressing and naming. Each entity is assigned a particular address and name, where their combination is unique for it. The allocating address task uses IPv6 as the number addressing scheme of 128 bits. The naming process can use several methods, such as IP-based codes, electronic products codes (EPC), and ubiquitous codes (Al-Fuqaha, Guizani, Mohammadi, Aledhari, & Ayyash, 2015).

Figure 1. Processing cycle in IoT networks

B. Obtaining

IoT obtains and collects data from different devices via sensing utilities, such as RFID (radio-frequency indicators) tags, actuators, wearables, etc. These data are further transported via gateways and stored in areas such as cloud storage (Sehrawat & Gill, 2019).

C. Conveyance

Responsibilities of reference of information from one point to another are assigned to ensure data transportation, which is essential for the proper functioning of IoT. In other words, all the communication, including messages, conversations, files, and other data, is transmitted through this component, which uses specific protocols, such as z-wave, Zigbee and 6LoWPAN (Low power Wireless Personal Area Networks) (AlSarawi, Anbar, Alieyan, & Alzubaidi, 2017).

D. Processing

The data collected via sensors are then processed with the help of a variety of operating systems, such as Android and TinyOs, using a range of hardware platforms like Intel Galileo and Audrino (Basha & S A K, 2016).

E. Assistance

IoT applications can provide several types of assistance. The most helpful is the assistance related to identity. The next is the assistance associated with data aggregation, which can be done without any communication channel, and unifies different technologies in a single application. The following assistance deals with the aggregated information to perform task decisions and actions needed. The fourth assistance is the ability to be omnipresent that provides the services of IoT ubiquitously without the strictness of time and location (Gigli & Koo, 2011).

F. Connotation

The whole cycle ends with this component, which acts as the brain of the IoT process. All the devices can get the response as all the data and decisions are connoted here (Basha & S A K, 2016).

III. IOT SECURITY CONCERNS

The use of IoT devices has an unmediated impact on users' lives, hence high priority to the security measures must be given together with well-defined security guidelines consisting of new systems and protocols to ensure that the possible threats related to security and privacy will be limited. Specifically, the processes of authentication, integrity, data confidentiality, and data privacy are among the main elements of IoT security (Farooq et al., 2015). Other important concerns include identification, trust and access control (Sicari et al., 2015), and data availability (Atzori, Iera, & Morabito, 2010).

A. Identification

The identification process is crucial for the network to decide whether the smart device can be trusted or not. Serious threats may arise from permitting an intruder to enter the secured network (Sicari et al., 2015). Despite this fact, we must prevail a system that can detect these possible security threats but is still able to provide its device identity to other qualified devices. Therefore, devices interacting with their users must know their identity and can distinguish them too (Atzori et al., 2010).

B. Authentication

In the case of IoT, authentication is quite challenging as it usually requires appropriate authentication infrastructures and servers to be secure, such as two-factor authentication. As in IoT passive utilities are used, such as RFID tags or sensor nodes, the standard procedures commonly used in other IT sectors cannot be used, as these passive utilities cannot exchange too many messages with the authentication servers (Atzori et al., 2010), (Farooq et al., 2015), (Sicari et al., 2015).

C. Data Integrity

The data transmission can be disrupted by plenty of factors that cannot be controlled by the nodes involved. For example, data changes during transmission, server outages, or electromagnetic interference (Riahi Sfar, Natalizio, Challal, & Chtourou, 2018). Hence, data integrity is preserved with the help of common surveillance methods to protect the data transmitted from cyberattacks and to avoid external interference during the communication itself. For this purpose, methods like checksums and cyclic redundancy checks (CRC) are used to guarantee data accuracy and reliability with the help of error detection mechanisms (Sicari et al., 2015), (Atzori et al., 2010).

D. Trust

Trust is a very broad term covering many disciplines beyond security, hence it is more difficult to be established (Atzori et al., 2010). Nitti et al. (Nitti, Girau, & Atzori, 2014) conducted a study that had as main objective to explore how users accept the IoT objects around them. Interestingly, 43% of respondents say they are worried about their data, therefore are afraid to use the IoT utilities. 18% think that IoT objects used are not operational and 8% believe they are not reliable. Users are concerned with the fact that they cannot always determine when, whether, and to whom the personal information could and could not be exposed (Riahi Sfar et al., 2018). It is believed that as soon as the users gain certainty that the IoT objects are secured enough by the manufacturer and their data cannot be misused, the IoT technologies will be most likely better adopted by their users (Sicari et al., 2015).

E. Data Confidentiality

User is secured by data confidentiality which ensures that confidential information is trusted. This process is done by various mechanisms to prevent any exposure against the user's will. These security mechanisms ensure data privacy work with the help of data encryption, two stage authentication, and biometric authentication mechanisms which protect data from unauthorized access. In the case of IoT devices, these mechanisms ensure that sensor networks maintain their sensor nodes hidden from unauthorized neighboring nodes as well as their communication from unauthorized readers (Farooq et al., 2015).

F. Access Control

Access control is associated with permissions in the usage of resources that are assigned to different entities connected to the IoT network. These permissions specify whether the user is granted access and the user's authorizations to perform specified tasks. Access Control List (ACL) is used to specify a device used and the user's access level. Here the administrator of the network must be careful with access granting as a mistake can result in serious threats (Riahi Sfar et al., 2018).

G. Data Privacy

In the IoT environment, the amount of data collected and stored is rapidly increasing and users cannot be sure that this data will be used only for the purposes they gave consent to or will not be misused in the nearest future. Hence, protecting stored data has the same priority as securing its transmission. The IoT environment is full of devices, readers, sensors, and applications that might collect data on multiple levels that together can expose user's habits, their actual or most common locations, where the user lives and goes to work, does shopping, or even their diet via smart fridges. As nowadays we can evaluate many aggregated data with the help of Business Intelligence, the data leak may result from useful insight from market sectors to unwanted surveillance by the cyber attacker or even the government. As data are stored on centered cloud services and they are not anonymous and collected all the time, their privacy should be given high priority (Farooq et al., 2015; Gubbi et al., 2013; Riahi Sfar et al., 2018).

H. Data Availability

IoT gathers, analyses, and provides data to its users. Data availability ensures that the data is provided to its user when needed without necessary delays. This state is supposed to be maintained even under unfavorable conditions, such as cyberattacks, by implementing appropriate secure measurements, such as firewalls preventing denial of service attack (DoS) or its advanced version - distributed denial of service attack (DDoS). Moreover, this should be facilitated by the corresponding hardware infrastructure which is supposed to be well secured as well. In the case of data loss prevention, data should be sufficiently backed up, which helps to ensure system components replication in the case of system failure, providing reliability and availability (Atzori et al., 2010).

IV. IOT SECURITY AND LAYERS ARCHITECTURE

Internet of Things can be broadly defined in four layers. Going top-down, it begins with the *application layer*, followed by the *middleware layer* (or *data processing layer*) (Sikder, Petracca, Aksu, Jaeger, & Uluagac, 2018) and by the *network layer* (also known as *transport layer*). The *perception layer* (or *sensing layer*) is the last one. Figure 2 represents this layered architecture.

The first two layers represent the utilization of data in the application, the following two where data are captured (Weyrich & Ebert, 2016). Some authors (e.g., Antão, Pinto, Reis, & Gonçalves, 2018) refer to a *business layer* as a layer above the application layer, which is supposed to manage the whole IoT system, including applications, business models, and users' privacy. Discussing such a business layer is out of the scope of this chapter.

Each IoT layer has its objectives and characteristics and may suffer distinct types of threats. Figure 3 presents some of the most common threats of each layer. In the following, we identify the main components of each layer and the threats which may occur on the layer.

Figure 2. IoT Layers and Components (Adapted from Sikder, Petracca, Aksu, Jaeger, & Uluagac, 2018)

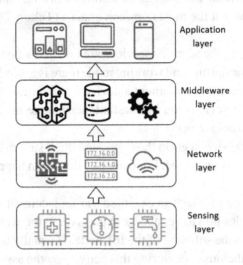

Figure 3. Common threats in IoT layers

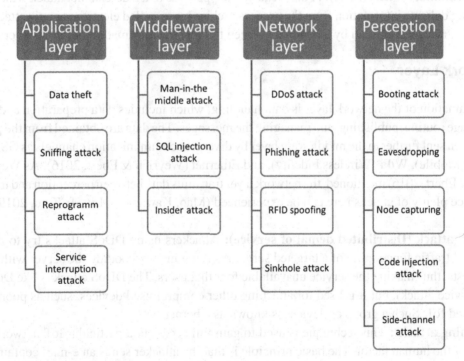

A. Perception Layer

The perception layer represents the physical layer of IoT and is responsible for data collection and its transmission. Utilities working on this layer include sensors (e.g., camera sensors, temperature sensors, chemical sensors, detection sensors, and humidity sensors), and wireless sensors networks (WSNs), global positioning systems (GPS), RFID systems, and electronic data interfaces (EDI). Hence, this layer provides most of the data collection. The attacks on utilities working on this layer are mainly aimed at the sensors. In the following, we list the most common attacks (Tukur, Thakker, & Awan, 2019).

1) **Booting attack:** Usually, all the security services are enabled when a device is in working mode. But between the booting, or startup, and working mode there is a window when the security services are not fully enabled. Hence, at this moment a device is vulnerable to possible attacks. Moreover, edge devices due to power savings are in constant sleep-wake modes. Therefore, they are more likely to be vulnerable to these attacks.

2) **Eavesdropping:** An interloper can get in the communication stream between nodes within a closed network to listen to the data transmitted. For example, this often happens with poorly secured baby cameras, smart TVs, etc.

3) **Node capturing:** This type of attack is executed via replacement of the original node with the intruder's one which enables him to get access to parts or, in the worst case, to the entire network.

4) **Code injection attack:** As the software of the IoT nodes is usually updated OTA (over the air), the opportunity to inject a malicious code during this activity by the assailer might give him unauthorized access to the system, which can lead to the execution of unwanted actions.

5) **Side-channel attacks (SCA):** A data leak can happen due to a side-channel attack which involves gaining delicate information from the processor chips by so-called electromagnetic attacks, timing attacks, radiation emitted by a computer screen to view the information before its encryption.

B. Network Layer

The main function of the network layer is data handling, which includes data preparation and transmission, message routing, publishing, and managing the messages. The data are obtained from the perception layer and then sent further to the middleware layer by divergent communication channels as GSM (Global System for Mobile), WiFi (Wireless Fidelity), and Ethernet (Weyrich & Ebert, 2016). As Weyrich et al. (Weyrich & Ebert, 2016) mentioned, the network layer transmits data between perception and middleware layers, hence plenty of attacks here can be experienced (Mao, Kawamoto, Liu, & Kato, 2019).

1) **DDoS attack (Distributed denial of service):** Attackers using DDoS attacks try to disrupt the normal traffic functioning of a targeted server resulting in overflooding the server with unwanted requests, thus making the service unavailable for other users. The DDoS attack is like DoS (Denial of service attack), but it is used for attacking other compromised devices, such as poorly secured infected IoT. Such a group of devices is known as a botnet.

2) **Phishing attacks:** This technique is used to gain full access to a particular IoT network with the help of the human factor. The basic principle is that the attacker sends an e-mail containing a link to some page that requires the user to enter his credentials, in most cases e-mail and password. Either for registration into a fake internet game, where the user can win a prize, or into a page that looks like a login page of a social network or online payment service website (e.g. PayPal), asking for the user's credentials. As this e-mail is sent to thousands of e-mail addresses, the attacker relies on somebody entering his credentials. As users usually have only one password and e-mail for all their accounts, after this action the attacker can gain access to all their sensitive data, including full access to a particular IoT network.

3) **RFID spoofing and cloning:** Even though RFID tags use plenty of security measures, such as different operational frequencies and different protocols, they can still be compromised. First, they can be cloned, which is a process of duplication of the original RFID tag. Therefore, they can be used for spoofing, which means to use a cloned RFID tag to gain access somewhere. Hence, it is used in access or asset management operations.

4) **Sinkhole attack:** It is a type of routing attack where false routing details are forwarded to nodes in a network causing a huge amount of network traffic. The attack is initiated from a compromised node that has been compromised by the attacker which infiltrated into the network. Besides false routing attacks, this can be used to issue a variety of other attacks.

C. Middleware Layer

This layer provides software utilities that make the communication between IoT components possible by data filtering, analysis of data semantic, management, and discovery of the device and access control (Weyrich & Ebert, 2016). Hence, the middleware layer has two main tasks. The first one is confirming the authenticity of the user, and the second is data transfer. The main tasks of this layer (Hu, Zhang, & Wen, 2011) are listed below.

1) **Man-in-The-Middle attack:** In this type of attack, the perpetrator pretends to be the legitimate user of an IoT system being in between the communication of two users who are communicating within their network with each other. As their communication goes through the cyber attacker, he can interact with both participating sides, impersonates them both trying to gain access to the information they are trying to send to each other. Thus, the perpetrator can control and manipulate the conversation.

2) **SQL injection attack:** A very serious threat to any system may result in unauthorized access, confidential data loss or even exploiting the whole network or individual machines. An intruder inserts a particular malicious SQL statement in the vulnerable web applications, which are connected to the backend databases, resulting in their compromising.

3) **Insider attack:** During this attack, the cyber attacker appears to be an authentic member of the network. Hence, it is very difficult to identify attacks like these. The perpetrator can be a present or former member with access to the details of the system resulting in the ability to launch different types of attacks within the network. Hence, it is very important to keep ACL up to date at any time.

D. Application Layer

The application layer is the topmost one in this architecture responsible for providing services and establishing the sets of protocols used for messages passing at the application layer. It is the interface bridge between the IoT devices and the network. For instance, the end IoT device is a computer with a browser as an application layer using protocols such as HTTP, HTTPS, DNS, SMTP, and FTP. This layer can be further divided into two sub-layers (Weyrich & Ebert, 2016):

- **Application service sub-layer:** Its main function is to span the connection between the end-user and applications; hence it is over the application layer of IoT.

- **Data management sub-layer:** Tasks performed by this sub-layer include machine-to-machine (M2M) services, Quality of Service (QoS), data process, and directory services. As this layer is in this architecture considered as the final one where the end-user has a direct connection to, plenty of threats are possible to occur.

    1) **Data theft:** The data which are collected by IoT devices with their sensors are most vulnerable while in transit. Intruders can steal the data easily and misuse them for personal use or resell it to another person if proper security protocols are not applied and followed.

    2) **Sniffing attack:** If the data packets are poorly encrypted or without encryption at all, they can be caught, and sensitive data can be extracted with the use of sniffers during its transmission.

    3) **Reprogram attacks:** If the IoT device's programming process is not secured, an intruder can remotely reprogram the IoT device easily resulting in making another infected device in his growing botnet, misusing collected data, etc.

    4) **Service interruption attack:** Due to artificially making the services of an application's network too busy to access to the legitimate users, the network becomes unavailable resulting in its significant slowdown or denial of service.

V. COUNTERMEASURES

The whole IoT ecosystem contains three major elements: users, hardware, and software. Hence, to ensure a secure environment within a network, designers and developers must focus on all of the elements involved. Focusing on the users and their behavior within the network can give the designers and developers valuable insights, and enable them to understand better the problems of the whole system, resulting in the enhancement of overall IoT security, and protecting users' privacy and minimizing their risks by educating them to be more aware of their surroundings. Furthermore, to observe how the users interact with the system can be useful to implement appropriate security countermeasures. Some of the *traditional* countermeasures include security protocols, single sign-on, access, and authentication controls, security awareness, establishing trust and privacy by design (Ogonji, Okeyo, & Wafula, 2020).

In this section, we present some new technologies, strategies, and architectures that have gained popularity over the years for being very helpful in enhancing security, including Fog Computing, Blockchain Technology, Edge computing, and Machine learning (Baouya et al., 2020; Ozay et al., 2016). We also present the main challenges related to the creation of an Intrusion Detection System (IDS) for IoT.

A. Fog Computing

Internet of Things and cloud computing are powerful technologies that can work together. IoT facilitates utilizing and incorporating smart applications and cloud computing provides needed space and functionalities that can help manage, store and process the data (Rahman et al., 2019). As IoT gathers a lot of data in real-time using all sorts of devices, services, and technologies, there is a need for storage of this gathered data for possible future analyses and processing. Hence, the cooperation between both technologies has become a beneficial solution which leads to better efficiency in organization and security of the stored data. As the technologies evolve, the attacks and threats become more sophisticated as well. Hence, it was found that cloud computing itself lacks some features. Therefore, the fog computing was introduced to aid the drawbacks of cloud computing itself and make it more efficient and secure.

The basic principle of fog computing is that the fog extends the cloud enabling it to be closer to the things which interact with IoT data. The fog can be described as an additional layer between the end nodes and the cloud. It provides additional detection, invalidation, and reporting of malicious activities. The fog works as a smaller inner cloud within the big cloud, and, thus, the fog also provides isolation from the major cloud to be infected and deals with the security incidents on its own.

Figure 4 represents how the fog can extend the cloud. Devices with computing, network connectivity, and storage, known as fog nodes, can be deployed anywhere with a network connection, such as in a vehicle, water reservoir, or traffic systems. Examples are switches, routers, embedded servers, and video surveillance cameras.

Figure 4. The Fog extends the Cloud closer to the devices producing data

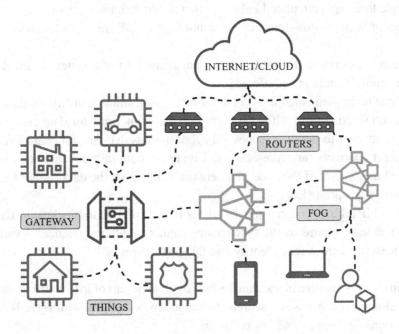

The major advantages of fog computing for IoT security are:

- Whenever the IoT system is attacked, this attack must go through the fog layer where it can be identified and mitigated. This layer acts as a middleman between the end-user and the cloud.
- As the data is stored in the fog rather than on the devices, the risk of attacks to a great extent has been reduced. Moreover, as the fog is a smaller unit than the cloud unit, it can identify these issues faster and react accordingly preventing the broader part of the network to be compromised.
- Fog computing facilitates discovering malicious activities, such as malware, by being able to red flag them when a problem appears.
- As fog computing is a relatively closed unit, the information transmitted is transported within the fog network rather than through the whole network, if possible. Hence, the chances of eavesdropping are minimized as the network traffic is reduced (Rahman et al., 2019).

This solution also presents some challenges and limitations such as the guarantee of privacy between the fog and IoT devices, the software update capabilities of IoT devices need to handle remote security updates, and the scalability and efficiency of IoT solutions need to be designed to overcome the limitations of resource constrained IoT devices.

B. Blockchain Technology Security Solution

From a security point of view, the IoT applications and platforms lack the security feature in the decentralization of information collected as all data are stored on a centralized cloud. Hence, this issue may be solved by implementing blockchain technology into the centralized cloud system (Kshetri, 2017). Moreover, blockchain technology prevents data duplicity, sensors' data tracking, and offers safe data transfer. With the help of various cryptography techniques, continuously growing blocks containing lists of records are made forming a circulated ledger known as blockchain.

The advantages of implementing blockchain technology in IoT are:

- As blockchain is a distributed system, when a particular part of a system is attacked and its security fails, the entire system is not affected.
- Blockchain can be implemented in every layer of IoT as a suitable utility for data transport.
- Being a decentralized system with cryptographic hash functions for data encryption, it is much harder for the attacker to perform successful cyber theft as data are not centralized on one cloud.
- Based on smart contracts (as represented in Figure 5), data in blockchain can be only accessed by authorized users. Even if the node in a network is infected, the data cannot be read as they are encrypted with appropriate keys.
- IP spoofing and IP address forgery attacks are more difficult due to blockchain-based identity and access management systems as the blockchains cannot be altered. Hence, devices can't be connected to a network using a fake identity and fake signatures.

As presented in the previous list, blockchain technology can be part of IoT security solutions. However, blockchain technology in itself poses research challenges to be tackled with regards to its scalability, efficiency, arbitration/regulations, and key collision.

Some examples of challenges and limitations in this field are blockchain vulnerabilities, such as the consensus mechanism depending upon the miner's hashing power can be compromised, and the private keys with limited randomness, which attackers exploit to compromise the blockchain accounts.

C. Edge Computing Security Solutions

Edge computing takes the storage of data and computation much closer to the location of use, thus saving the bandwidth of the network and improving response time (Sodhro, Pirbhulal, & de Albuquerque, 2019). It is very similar to fog computing, but the main difference is that fog computing processes data within a fog node or IoT gateway situated within LAN, whereas edge computing processes the data on the devices or sensors themselves without transferring them. Figure 6 represents the main differences between fog and edge computing.

Figure 5. Smart contracts

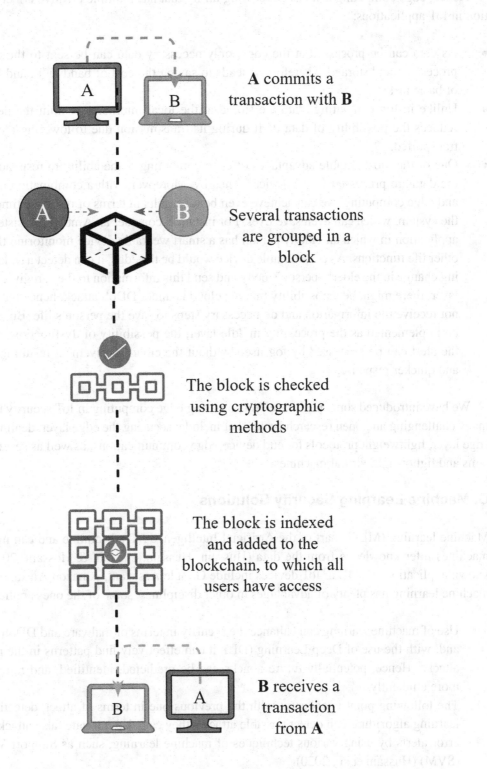

A commits a transaction with **B**

Several transactions are grouped in a block

The block is checked using cryptographic methods

The block is indexed and added to the blockchain, to which all users have access

B receives a transaction from A

Hence, edge computing is a fast-processing utility that has multiple positive effects of implementation in IoT applications:

- As data can be processed at the edge, only necessary data can be sent to the cloud for further processing and storage. Therefore, it leads to saving the cost of bandwidth and faster processing of basic tasks.
- Unlike in fog computing, data are stored at the local internet or within the device itself. This reduces the possibility of data theft during its transmission due to lowering the amount of data transported.
- One of the most notable advantages of edge computing is the ability to respond very quickly as the data are processed in the device or nearby. Moreover, with a combination of fog computing and edge computing, we can achieve even better results in terms of response time and security of the system, which can even save lives. For instance, consider an Ambient Assisted Living (AAL) application in which an elderly person has a smart wearable device monitoring their heart rate or other life functions. As the wearable device would be the edge, it can detect a sudden life-threatening change in the elderly person's body and send this information to the caregiver. Without the fog layer, there might be a possibility that the cloud is under DDoS attack, hence the caregiver would not receive the information and do necessary steps to save the person's life. But as the fog would be implemented as the processing middle layer, the possibility of dysfunction is lowered, hence the alert can be processed by fog itself without the cloud involvement resulting in a convenient and quicker response.

We have introduced some positive effects on using edge computing in IoT security but there are still many challenging and open research issues that include: securing the edge layer, dealing with untrusted edge layer, lightweight protocols for end device-edge communications, as well as secure operating systems and lightweight virtual machines.

D. Machine Learning Security Solutions

Machine learning (ML) is part of the Artificial Intelligence (AI) discipline and can make devices and machines infer knowledge from the data (Hussain, Hussain, Hassan, & Hossain, 2020). Some well-known applications of ML in IoT devices include Google Assistant, Amazon Alexa, or Apple Siri. As machine learning has plenty of advantages in other disciplines, some of the ones applicable for IoT are:

- Use of machine learning can enhance the security in terms of malware and DDoS attack detection and, with the use of Deep Learning (DL), it can effectively find patterns in the previously made attacks. Hence, potentially future attacks can be predicted, identified, and mitigated faster and more efficiently.
- The following point is coherent with the previous one in terms of attack detection. As machine learning algorithms can detect possible attacks, they can also mitigate false attack alerts and false error alerts by using various techniques of machine learning, such as Support Vector Machines (SVM) (Hussain et al., 2020).
- Utilization of machine learning properties can lead to cost and energy consumption reduction, improvement of customer care, and efficiency.

ML algorithms could be used to improve the IoT security domain, although they have some limitations in the IoT environment, such as scalability, complexity, latency, compatibility, and vulnerability. Learning efficiency, response time, automatic feature selection and parameter tuning strategies are also challenging in such context.

Figure 6. Data process within network

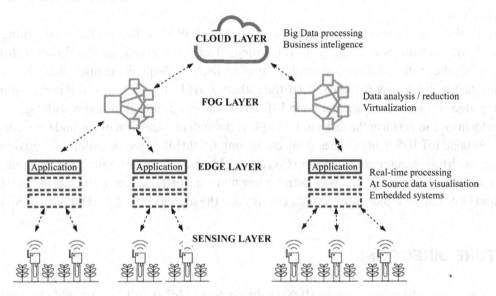

E. Intrusion Detection Systems

Conventional intrusion detection systems use techniques based on packet capture and analysis to detect intrusions or attacks. *Deep packed inspection* (DPI) techniques scan packet headers and examine the content in the application data field, looking for any evidence of attack (Abuadlla, Kvascev, Gajin, & Jovanovic, 2014). However, the use of DPI-type IDS is impractical for high-speed connections and inspection is not possible when the contents of the packet data field are encrypted (Husak, Velan, & Vykopal, 2015). In *stateful packet inspection* (SPI) techniques, the semantics of the protocol are checked and any record outside the defined is considered an intrusion or anomaly. However, this technique is oriented towards known protocols and does not affect unknown protocols. Also, it does very little when it comes to malicious code as it does not analyze the payload of packages. Finally, both techniques are computationally expensive and can create a bottleneck in the network (Koch, 2011; Liao, Lin, Lin, & Tung, 2013).

Considering the limitations of techniques based on packet analysis, DPI, and SPI, and considering the less computational and resource requirements of the approach based on flow analysis, an alternative solution against intrusions and attacks in IoT ecosystems may be using an IDS based on IP flow analysis (Santos, Rabadão, & Gonçalves, 2019). This type of IDS has as a strong point in its favor: the lower need for computational resources to operate, as they only analyze the flow records that contain aggregated information from packet headers, reducing the amount of data that needs to be processed. In this way, they can provide an answer almost in real-time, low implementation cost, fewer privacy concerns, and that can be used with traffic consisting of packages that have their encrypted payload. A weakness of these IDS is the difficulty in detecting some attacks using only information from the packet header, so many of the known attacks are not detected. When compared to IDS based on packet detection, with the cryptographically unprotected payload, the detection of network attacks hidden in the packet payload is not as accurate as packet-based detection. However, the increasing use of end-to-end encryption in distributed applications, such as web portals, mobile applications, and e-mails, has left limited space for the application of payload-based intrusion detection systems and opens the way for the IDS based on flow analysis.

Recently, there has been a huge increase in research on IDS for IoT, especially concerning the application of ML techniques (especially deep learning) (Dutta & Granjal, 2020). However, ML-based techniques face the challenge of the low availability of realistic, high-quality datasets that contain diverse attacks for the IoT. In Dutta & Granjal (2020), the authors also identify a strong effort in the optimization of existing algorithms for implementation in IoT, and in the development of nodes with high computational performance to perform the tasks of IDS in IoT, through the adoption of fog and edge computing. Implementing an IoT IDS using edge and fog computing would allow the detection of intrusions in IoT ecosystems with less resource consumption. (Chaabouni, Mosbah, Zemmari, Sauvignac, & Faruki, 2019). However, most of the existing proposals detect a low number of attacks and focus mostly on attacks on routing and DoS and, less frequently, on attacks related to the source of the data (Dutta & Granjal, 2020).

VI. FUTURE DIRECTIONS

The use of Intrusion Detection Systems (IDS) in the context of IoT is still an open and promising issue. Despite considerable progress in the development of IDS solutions designed specifically for IoT ecosystems, existing solutions still have numerous limitations. Also, some solutions require considerable computational overhead or modification of the software of IoT devices that, in an environment of limited computational resources, turns out to be a weakness.

Regarding the detection methodology, and although there is no consensus on which of the methodologies will be the most appropriate, the solutions that use the methodology based on anomalies are the ones that consume more computational and energy resources, while the methodologies based on signatures or specifications are the ones that require fewer resources. However, anomaly-based detection is the one most often proposed in studies, in part because of its potential to detect unknown attacks. For this, it is necessary to develop, analyze and compare lighter and optimized anomaly detection algorithms, mainly based on ML (especially deep learning) for IoT networks (Dutta & Granjal, 2020).

Also, integration of detection techniques based on rules, anomalies, and specifications should be used, to avoid their weaknesses and obtain their benefits. To this end, it will be necessary to dedicate greater effort to the refinement of this integration, namely by improving the modeling of the behavior of IoT ecosystems to allow a better definition and parameterization of network parameters to detect intrusions (Cervantes, Poplade, Nogueira, & Santos, 2015; Bostani & Sheikhan, 2017; Fu, Yan, Cao, Kone, & Cao, 2017).

At the level of the IDS implementation strategy, given the computational limitations of the IoT devices and the privacy and confidentiality requirements of the information collected, the solution may include the exploration of hybrid detection solutions, using edge and fog computing (Chaabouni et al., 2019). This approach will allow decision making close to the perception layer, improving the privacy and confidentiality issues of the information collected and minimizing the need for necessary network resources between the perception layer and the cloud, making use of the computing power of the cloud, during the training phase of machine learning algorithms.

Regarding the intrusion detection capability, the existing solutions are limited concerning the diversity of attacks they detect. Most of the intrusions detected are located at the perception layer of the IoT architecture, at the DoS level, and at the network layer, at the level of routing attacks, possibly due to the use of existing generalist datasets, which do not represent the particularities of IoT systems and applications, leaving other types of intrusions, internal and external, and from other layers, without specific solutions for some IoT protocols. Although some works propose datasets more suited to the reality of IoT (e.g. (Moustafa & Slay, 2015; Sivanathan et al., 2017; Bezerra et al., 2018; Verma & Ranga, 2019)), there is a need to intensify this work, in the sense of creating public datasets that include the different IoT protocols and their threats/attacks, to be able to develop IDS solutions adapted to the diversity of threats to which the IoT ecosystems are subject.

These datasets, specifically suitable for IoT, must be public and serve as a reference for the validation of solutions proposed by the scientific community, and must be properly labeled and support a wide variety of attacks and protocols used in IoT ecosystems. In this way, it will be possible to improve the IDS validation strategy, as it will be possible to compare, in a clear, practical, and convenient way, the different IDS developed.

At the level of IoT technologies and protocols, the vast majority only cover perceptual layer protocols such as 6LoWPAN and RPL, which means support, interoperability, and expandability with other technologies and protocols, used at the network layer or application, are not addressed in the analyzed proposals.

Besides, only a few solutions refer to aspects or features related to the privacy of network traffic and the management of the communication of internal messages and IDS alerts. This is an important topic, because if the internal messages between the various components of an IDS or the intrusion alert messages are intercepted and tampered with it will result in the loss of the reliability and effectiveness of the IDS.

Finally, it should be noted that most solutions presented make use of packet capture, and respective payloads, to develop their intrusion detection processes. Intrusion detection solutions based on the analysis of IP traffic flows can be considered, reduce the use of resources, such as the processing and storage of network packets, which is especially important when using devices with limited resources at the computational level.

VII. CONCLUSION

In this chapter, the authors identified the main security aspects of the Internet of Things. and identified possible attacks, threats, and vulnerabilities of IoT.

The authors characterized the IoT in terms of its processing cycle. Then, the authors identified the processes and features that are the most common security concerns in IoT networks, namely identification, authentication, data integrity, trust, data confidentiality, access control, data privacy, and data availability. The authors described the IoT layers and architecture, and the attacks and threats that are the most common for each layer.

Then, the authors presented a set of countermeasures based on new technologies, strategies, and architectures to enhance IoT security, namely security solutions based on Fog and Edge Computing,

Blockchain Technology, Machine learning, and Intrusion Detection Systems (IDS) for IoT. Each of such solutions has its advantages and application challenges, but the limitations of resource constrained IoT devices impose constraints on the scalability and efficiency of most proposed IoT cybersecurity solutions.

The IDS for IoT is the authors' main research direction in terms of countermeasures for IoT. Such IDS should use lighter and optimized anomaly detection algorithms, mainly based on machine learning. Also, integrating detection techniques based on rules, anomalies, and specifications would increase the IDS efficiency. Computational limitations of the IoT devices and privacy and confidentiality requirements of collected data lead to hybrid solutions, which use Edge and Fog computing.

Datasets specifically suitable for IoT must be created and turned public to serve as a reference for the validation of proposed solutions. Such datasets must be labeled and support a wide variety of attacks and protocols used in IoT ecosystems. Also, the use of intrusion detection solutions based on the analysis of IP traffic flows can be considered, reducing the use of resources, such as the processing and storage of network packets, which is especially important when using devices with limited resources at the computational level.

As future work, the authors intend to advance the study of IDS for IoT, mainly with the application of machine learning techniques in this context. The authors also plan to prepare data sets of the IoT context for benchmarking solutions of the literature.

ACKNOWLEDGMENT

This work was partially funded by National Funds through the FCT (Foundation for Science and Technology) in the context of the project UIDB/04524/2020.

REFERENCES

Abuadlla, Y., Kvascev, G., Gajin, S., & Jovanovic, Z. (2014). Flow-based anomaly intrusion detection system using two neural network stages. *Computer Science and Information Systems*, *11*(2), 601–622.

Al-Fuqaha, A., Guizani, M., Mohammadi, M., Aledhari, M., & Ayyash, M. (2015). Internet of Things: A survey on enabling technologies, protocols, and applications. *IEEE Communications Surveys and Tutorials*, *17*(4), 2347–2376. doi:10.1109/COMST. 2015.2444095

Al-Sarawi, S., Anbar, M., Alieyan, K., & Alzubaidi, M. (2017). Internet of Things (IoT) communication protocols: Review. In *2017 8th International Conference on Information Technology (ICIT)* (pp. 685-690). doi: 10.1109/ICITECH.2017.8079928

Antao, L., Pinto, R., Reis, J. P., & Gonçalves, G. (2018).˜ Requirements for testing and validating the industrial Internet of Things. In *2018 IEEE International Conference on Software Testing, Verification and Validation Workshops (ICSTW)* (p. 110-115). doi: 10.1109/ICSTW.2018.00036

Atzori, L., Iera, A., & Morabito, G. (2010). 10). The Internet of Things: A survey. *Computer Networks*, 2787–2805. doi:10.1016/j.comnet.2010.05.010

Baouya, A., Chehida, S., Bensalem, S., & Bozga, M. (2020). Fog computing and blockchain for massive IoT deployment. In *2020 9th Mediterranean Conference on Embedded Computing (MECO)* (p. 14). doi: 10.1109/MECO49872.2020.9134098

Basha, S., & S. A. K., J. (2016, 03). An intelligent door system using raspberry pi and amazon web services IoT. *International Journal of Engineering Trends and Technology, 33,* 84-89. doi:10.14445/22315381/ IJETT-V33P217

Bezerra, V. H., da Costa, V. G. T., Martins, R. A., Junior, S. B., Miani, R. S., & Zarpelao, B. B. (2018). Providing IoT host-based datasets for intrusion detection research. In Anais do XVIII Simpósio Brasileiro em Segurança da Informação e de Sistemas Computacionais (pp. 15–28). Academic Press.

Bostani, H., & Sheikhan, M. (2017). Hybrid of anomaly-based and specification-based IDS for Internet of Things using Unsupervised OPF based on Map-Reduce Approach. *Computer Communications, 98,* 52–71.

Cervantes, C., Poplade, D., Nogueira, M., & Santos, A. (2015). Detection of sinkhole attacks for supporting secure routing on 6LoWPAN for Internet of Things. In *2015 IFIP/IEEE International Symposium on Integrated Network Management* (pp. 606– 611). IEEE.

Chaabouni, N., Mosbah, M., Zemmari, A., Sauvignac, C., & Faruki, P. (2019). Network intrusion detection for IoT security based on learning techniques. *IEEE Communications Surveys and Tutorials, 21*(3), 2671–2701.

Dutta, M., & Granjal, J. (2020). Towards a secure Internet of Things: A comprehensive study of second line defense mechanisms. *IEEE Access: Practical Innovations, Open Solutions, 8,* 127272–127312.

Farooq, M., Waseem, M., Khairi, A., & Mazhar, P. (2015). 02). A critical analysis on the security concerns of Internet of Things (IoT). *International Journal of Computers and Applications, 111,* 1–6.

Fu, Y., Yan, Z., Cao, J., Kone, O., & Cao, X. (2017). An automata-based intrusion detection method for Internet of Things. *Mobile Information Systems, 2017.*

Gigli, M., & Koo, S. (2011). 01). Internet of Things: Services and applications categorization abstract. *Adv. Internet of Things, 1,* 27–31. doi:10.4236/ait.2011.12004

Gubbi, J., Buyya, R., Marusic, S., & Palaniswami, M. (2013). Internet of Things (IoT): A vision, architectural elements, and future directions. *Future Generation Computer Systems, 29*(7), 1645–1660. doi:10.1016/j.future.2013.01.010

Hu, C., Zhang, J., & Wen, Q. (2011). An identity-based personal location system with protected privacy in IoT. In *2011 4th IEEE International Conference on Broadband Network and Multimedia Technology* (pp. 192-195). doi: 10.1109/ICBNMT.2011. 6155923

Husak, M., Velan, P., & Vykopal, J. (2015). Security monitoring of HTTP traffic using extended flows. In *2015 10th International Conference on Availability, Reliability and Security* (pp. 258–265). Academic Press.

Hussain, F., Hussain, R., Hassan, S. A., & Hossain, E. (2020). Machine learning in IoT security: Current solutions and future challenges. *IEEE Communications Surveys and Tutorials, 22*(3), 16861721. doi:10.1109/COMST.2020.2986444

Koch, R. (2011). Towards next-generation intrusion detection. In *2011 3rd International Conference on Cyber Conflict* (pp. 1–18). Academic Press.

Kshetri, N. (2017). Can blockchain strengthen the Internet of Things? *IT Professional, 19*(4), 68–72. doi:10.1109/MITP.2017.3051335

Liao, H.-J., Lin, C.-H. R., Lin, Y.-C., & Tung, K.-Y. (2013). Intrusion detection system: A comprehensive review. *Journal of Network and Computer Applications, 36*(1), 16–24.

Mao, B., Kawamoto, Y., Liu, J., & Kato, N. (2019). Harvesting and threat aware security configuration strategy for IEEE 802.15.4 based IoT networks. *IEEE Communications Letters, 23*(11), 2130–2134. doi:10.1109/LCOMM.2019.2932988

Moustafa, N., & Slay, J. (2015). UNSW-NB15: a comprehensive data set for network intrusion detection systems (UNSW-NB15 network data set). In 2015 Military Communications and Information Systems Conference (pp. 1–6). Academic Press.

Neisse, R., Steri, G., Baldini, G., Tragos, E., Nai Fovino, I., & Botterman, M. (2015). *Dynamic context-aware scalable and trust-based IoT security, privacy framework*. River Publishers.

Nitti, M., Girau, R., & Atzori, L. (2014). Trustworthiness management in the social Internet of Things. *IEEE Transactions on Knowledge and Data Engineering, 26*(5), 1253–1266. doi:10.1109/TKDE.2013.105

Ogonji, M. M., Okeyo, G., & Wafula, J. M. (2020). A survey on privacy and security of Internet of Things. *Computer Science Review, 38*, 100312. doi:10.1016/j.cosrev.2020.100312

Ozay, M., Esnaola, I., Yarman Vural, F. T., Kulkarni, S. R., & Poor, H. V. (2016). Machine learn-ing methods for attack detection in the smart grid. *IEEE Transactions on Neural Networks and Learning Systems, 27*(8), 1773–1786. doi:10.1109/TNNLS.2015.2404803

Rahman, M. A., Rashid, M. M., Hossain, M. S., Hassanain, E., Alhamid, M. F., & Guizani, M. (2019). Blockchain and IoT-based cognitive edge framework for sharing economy services in a smart city. *IEEE Access: Practical Innovations, Open Solutions, 7*, 18611–18621. doi:10.1109/ ACCESS.2019.2896065

Riahi Sfar, A., Natalizio, E., Challal, Y., & Chtourou, Z. (2018). A roadmap for security challenges in the Internet of Things. *Digital Communications and Networks, 4*(2), 118–137. doi:10.1016/j.dcan.2017.04.003

Santos, L., Rabadão, C., & Gonçalves, R. (2019). Flow monitoring system for IoT networks. In *World conference on information systems and technologies* (pp. 420–430). Academic Press.

Sehrawat, D., & Gill, N. S. (2019). Smart sensors: Analysis of different types of IoT sensors. In *2019 3rd International Conference on Trends in Electronics and Informatics* (pp. 523-528). doi: 10.1109/ ICOEI.2019.8862778

Sicari, S., Rizzardi, A., Grieco, L., & Coen-Porisini, A. (2015). Security, privacy and trust in Internet of Things: The road ahead. *Computer Networks, 76*, 146–164. doi:10.1016/j.comnet. 2014.11.008

Sikder, A. K., Petracca, G., Aksu, H., Jaeger, T., & Uluagac, S. (2018). *A survey on sensor-based threats to internet-of-things (IoT) devices and applications.* arXiv preprint arXiv:1802.02041.

Sivanathan, A., Sherratt, D., Gharakheili, H. H., Radford, A., Wijenayake, C., Vishwanath, A., & Sivaraman, V. (2017). Characterizing and classifying IoT traffic in smart cities and campuses. In *2017 IEEE Conference on Computer Communications Workshops (Infocom Wkshps)* (pp. 559–564). IEEE.

Sodhro, A. H., Pirbhulal, S., & de Albuquerque, V. H. C. (2019). Artificial intelligence-driven mechanism for edge computing-based industrial applications. *IEEE Transactions on Industrial Informatics, 15*(7), 4235–4243. doi:10.1109/TII. 2019.2902878

Swamy, S. N., Jadhav, D., & Kulkarni, N. (2017). Security threats in the application layer in IoT applications. In *2017 International Conference on I-SMAC (IoT in social, mobile, analytics and cloud) (I-SMAC)* (p. 477-480). doi: 10.1109/I-SMAC.2017. 8058395

Tukur, Y. M., Thakker, D., & Awan, I. (2019). Ethereum blockchain-based solution to insider threats on perception layer of IoT systems. In *2019 IEEE Global Conference on Internet of Things (GCIoT)* (p. 1-6). doi: 10.1109/GCIoT47977.2019.9058395

Ullah, Z., Ahmad, S., & Ahmad, M. Ata-ur-Rehman, & Junaid, M. (2019). A preview on Internet of Things (IoT) and its applications. In *2019 2nd International Conference on Computing, Mathematics and Engineering Technologies (iCoMet)* (p. 1-6). doi: 10.1109/ICOMET.2019.8673468

Verma, A., & Ranga, V. (2019). Evaluation of network intrusion detection systems for rpl based 6LoW-PAN networks in IoT. *Wireless Personal Communications, 108*(3), 1571–1594.

Weyrich, M., & Ebert, C. (2016). Reference architectures for the Internet of Things. *IEEE Software, 33*(1), 112–116. doi:10.1109/MS.2016.20

This research was previously published in IoT Protocols and Applications for Improving Industry, Environment, and Society; pages 207-233, copyright year 2021 by Engineering Science Reference (an imprint of IGI Global).

Chapter 6
A Study on Data Sharing Using Blockchain System and Its Challenges and Applications

Santosh Kumar Smmarwar
National Institute of Technology, Raipur, India

Govind P. Gupta
iD https://orcid.org/0000-0002-0456-1572
National Institute of Technology, Raipur, India

Sanjay Kumar
National Institute of Technology, Raipur, India

ABSTRACT

Blockchain since 2009 has been gaining more popularity in various fields to use in numerous applications to overcome the security issues such as privacy, transparency, and mutability of data in the process of data sharing. Process of data sharing has many addressed and unaddressed challenges such as information encryption and decryption, data authentication, storage security, latency time, transfer speed of data, detecting malicious nodes, prevent the computer system from attacks, trust in the sharing process. In this chapter, the authors have reviewed the data sharing paper based on blockchain technology and presented the analysis of various techniques used in the information sharing process. The comprehensive analysis is categorizing in the following areas like incentive mechanism-based work, IoT-based data sharing, healthcare data sharing, and internet of vehicle data sharing using blockchain.

DOI: 10.4018/978-1-6684-7132-6.ch006

INTRODUCTION

In the recent era of Big Data development with the advancement in information and communication technology the rate of growing data and digital resources has been grown exponentially. Storing these data has become important for customer and business organizations (Feng et al., 2019). One of the ways to control the growth rate of data to reduce the same information creation is through the data sharing process in various organizations such as health care, academic, financial sector, etc. Data sharing has many uses in various fields such as healthcare, the internet of things, smart devices, and internet of vehicles, supply chains, and logistic networks. In data sharing, secure data sharing is necessary to achieve security goals like confidentiality, integrity, availability, authentication, transparency, and privacy of the data. These problems can be overcome by using blockchain technology in making data sharing transparent, immutable, decentralized storage, integrity protected, and confidentiality. The feature of transparency and immutability of blockchain made it most popular to deploy or integrate into secure data sharing. Blockchain technology is based on the three pillars that are distributed ledger, peer-to-peer communication, and consensus protocol. These are the core of this technology that makes it more secure and transparent (McGhin et al., 2019). In this survey study, we have reviewed the blockchain used data sharing papers and analyses various methods used by the early researcher for secure data sharing to resolve the privacy concern by using some cryptographic techniques.

OUR CONTRIBUTION

In this research paper we have reviewed the work of data sharing using blockchain technology, to get a research trends of various security mechanism used in blockchain for information sharing. We found that in our study most of the author described comprehensive overview of secure data sharing by proposed method such as incentive mechanism, privacy preserving scheme, dynamic data access control policy, secret sharing schemes and some attribute based encryption technique. In this paper we demonstrated the summary of existing work and methods used in blockchain to secure data sharing. Shown existing work, pros and cons of early research work in areas of healthcare data sharing and IoT device-based data sharing, incentive-based data sharing and various industrial application.

MOTIVATION

As mentioned above security challenges faced by centralized authority such as single point of failure may lead to the collapse of all data, high sharing cost, reduce manual verification (Goyal et al., 2018), reduce wastage of time, brings transparency and immutability in the system encourage us to work on secure data sharing among the peer to peer or decentralize environment by integrating blockchain technology and smart contact functionality (Mohanta et al., 2019). Since the inception of blockchain technology came into existence these have brought some potential solutions that may be overcome by using blockchain in various emerging fields of information technology.

OVERVIEW OF BLOCKCHAIN TECHNOLOGY

Blockchain is distributed ledger technology initially developed for cryptocurrency purposes like bitcoin by an unknown person named Satoshi Nakamoto in 2009(Feng et al., 2019), (McGhin et al., 2019). It is a decentralized system of digital ledger stored the synchronized copy of data. The blockchain system is based on asymmetric cryptography where two keys, a public key for device identification and a private key for signing transactions used (Goyal et al., 2018),. Blockchain is a chain of the block, each block linked to the next block via hash value in chronological order. Blockchain is supported by a combination of three technologies that are distributed ledger technology, peer-to-peer network, and consensus protocol among all nodes (Mohanta et al., 2019). In decentralized, ledger block is added through consensus mechanism among nodes in the blockchain network. There is some of the popular consensus protocol used in blockchain mining as proof of work (POW), Proof of stake (PoS), and Practical Byzantine Fault Tolerance (PBFT) protocol. This is the most popular technology in recent times used by industry and academia nowadays. It has the characteristics of transparency, immutability, decentralization, anonymity (Hasselgren et al., 2019). The simple blockchain diagram has depicted below where every block is added from its previous block through hash value in a chronological way.

Figure 1. Structure of blockchain

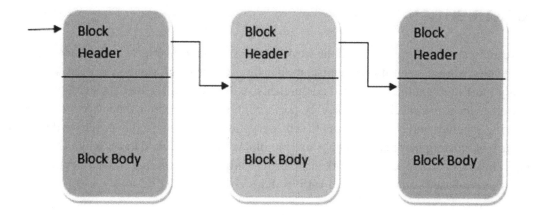

CLASSIFICATION OF BLOCKCHAIN

- **Public Blockchain**: Public blockchain is decentralizing networks to have more security. In this, ledgers are visible to all users who are connected to public networks. Anyone is free to join the network and add a block to the ledger (Xu et al., 2017). The most frequently used example is bitcoin and ethereum.
- **Private Blockchain:** In a private blockchain only selected nodes are allowed to join the network and add the data to the digital ledger. This allows anyone to view the ledger of data for example hyperledger fabric (Dinh et al., 2017).

- **Consortium Blockchain**: It is a combination of a group of the organization located at a different location (Dib et al., 2018). Only predefined organizations communicate, verify, and append-only transactions to the distributed digital ledger (Gai et al., 2019).

PROPERTIES OF BLOCKCHAIN

There are the following properties of blockchain technology that make it a powerful system to use in various fields as a solution (Liu et al, 2019).

- **Autonomous**: Autonomous property of blockchain makes it free from third party's control. Anyone can enter into the network verify and append transactions to the blockchain database.
- **Distributed**: in this, once the block confirms by all the peer's entities by some proof of mechanism then it is added only to the ledger. It works based on peer-to-peer infrastructure.
- **Immutability**: Immutability means no modification is possible in the block, once the block happened to the ledger. It would reflect all nodes in the global ledger.
- **Decentralize**: decentralization property makes the elimination of third parties involved in processing the transaction, reduces the cost, time and brings transparency among the nodes.
- **Anonymity**: this property hides the user identity in the blockchain network so that no node in the network trusts other nodes or its peer node.

Figure 2. Generalize diagram of blockchain applications

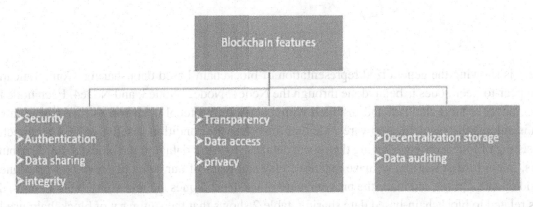

APPLICATION OF BLOCKCHAIN IN DATA SHARING

Blockchain technology has potential industrial application in many fields such healthcare industry, smart transportation, finance sectors, E-governance, food supply chain and many more in data sharing to brings the transparency, immutability, traceability and integrity as well. Blockhain technology can be useful in reducing the cost of production by using integrated smart contract facility and eliminates the central control of data. In healthcare sector it may provide the secure access of data sharing with greater transparency among different hospital globally to provide quick treatment to the patients. The finance sector can be achieved with less number fraudulent activities by using blockchain in transactional process. In smart transportation blockchain can support transparent, secure tracking of vehicles and brings transparency in insurance work to prevent illegal claim. The E-governance sector suffered from lack of transparency, so it also has wide applicability in this sector to provide secure authentication, data privacy and prevent fake data auditing. Similarly for other sectors also blockchain has various industrial application in terms of transparence, security, decentralization storage, integrity and immutability (Dubovitskaya et al., 2020).

THE ARCHITECTURE OF BLOCKCHAIN IN DATA SHARING

Figure 3. Simple architecture of blockchain data sharing

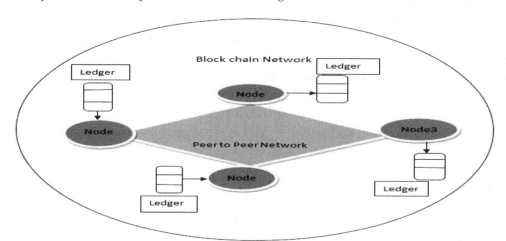

Figure 3 is showing the generalized representation of blockchain-based data sharing. Communication among peer-to-peer nodes is being done through the Node1, Node2, Node3, and Node4. Each node has its own ledger to store the data and installed with a software protocol is known as the smart contract which is automatic executable software code that runs after the condition is satisfied. The architecture is consisting of four users each having their local database to share data into the blockchains distributed ledgers. In the further section, we have mentioned the summary of our study of previous work done in the field of data sharing and made the pros and cons of used techniques in their work. Table 1 shows that papers related to blockchain-based data sharing, table 2 shows that the summary of blockchain used in the healthcare domain, table 3 indicates that blockchain is used in IoT data sharing.

LITERATURE SURVEY

In this survey of data sharing based on a blockchain platform, we have comprehensively reviewed papers on data sharing based on cloud data computing, Internet of Things (IoT), healthcare data, internet of vehicles, and blockchain-based platform for secure data sharing.

SURVEY BASED ON INCENTIVE MECHANISM

In paper (Bhaskaran et al., 2018) the work of the author has based on a user-associated consent-driven mechanism, in which a double-blind data-sharing approach is used for KYC (know your customer) validation using a blockchain system for banking institutions. This provides the dynamic access control of data sharing. It reduces the time and cost of manual verification. It has some drawbacks such as scalability issues, limited storage, and low transactional throughput.

In the paper (Shrestha et al., 2018) author proposed a decentralized data sharing framework based on blockchain for incentivizing data owners with digital tokens, author introduced blockchain with a smart contract concept for incentivizing participants in sharing their data and reward digital tokens. This approach of data sharing allows only the interested data seekers and ensures the data owner of misusing their data by illegal users. In this model, the author brought the escrow service to manage the user with legal obligations. The proposed framework is designed with due care of transparency, access control policy and specifies the purpose of data sharing. In paper (Naz et al., 2019) author focused on data authenticity and data quality during the process of information sharing. To achieve this author used the Shamir's secret sharing encryption technique and the online review system of Watson analyzer to identify the fake reviews. The advantage of this work is no leakage of hashed information, lowest computation time in encryption.

In paper (Wang et al., 2019) also author proposed an incentive scheme that discussed boosting blockchain-based IoT data sharing of the historical block. In this work, the author used the coin-locking strategy and micro-payment system to speed up the transmitting process. To ensure the security of data Shamir's secret sharing scheme played a great role. This proposed work can identify the malicious or dishonest nature of the sharing nodes. Although this system is efficient it has some high bandwidth cost limitations.

In the paper (Xuan et al., 2020) author presented an incentive mechanism for secure data sharing. This incentive method is based on evolutionary game theory which encourages participants to share their data securely and establish trust among the user who wants to share data to the blockchain-based secure platform. In addition to the game, theory the author applied the evolutionarily stable strategy and symmetric game theory to predict the most trustable sharing node among the various participants. However, this method has some limitations of data size and quality of data obtains by the recipient.

SURVEY BASED ON ACCESS CONTROL AND ENCRYPTION METHOD

In (Wang et al., 2017) author addressed the problem of conventional resource sharing in government departments such as efficiency, reliability, and security. These issues could be solved by the emerging blockchain technology. In this work, the author proposed the blockchain concept on government information, asset detail, resource sharing system to improve its reliability and security through the features of transparency, immutability, and traceability, and decentralization network of blockchain. This technology reduces the cost of implementation of sharing process than the traditional approach. However, this technology needs to be enhanced for the large scalable network in government setup and optimize the efficiency as well as the performance of the system. The work (Gupta & Gupta, 2017) has been discussed about the web application threats and vulnerabilities that may cause the major disruption in using the web application among various organizations. The proposed work concerns the potential security flaws and measures the threat.

In paper (Nakasumi et al., 2017) author presented the solution to solve the problem of double marginalization and information inconsistency in supply chain management. This system uses blockchain and homomorphic encryption techniques to provide transparency, immutability, traceability to user data. In this system author also added legal and authentic regulatory decisions of collecting data, storing, and sharing sensitive information. With the use of blockchain technology at supply chain it minimizes complex problem such as capacity risk in supply chain and improves the supply chain efficiency. It also increases the demand forecasting of consumers up to some extent. In the future, this solution needs to be bringing some incentive mechanism to handle the capacity risk and encourage users in sharing information.

In paper (Zhang et al., 2018) author focused on the privacy threat of data stored on the cloud due to the lack of processing power and storage capacity of IoT devices. To overcome these threats of data stealing and security author proposed architecture combined with the functionality of privacy preservation and authorized fine-grained user control access. In this work author used two types of method that is the attribute-based signature (ABS) and ciphertext-policy attribute-based encryption (CP-ABE). The ABS is used to provide fine-grained access control that identifies users or devices and attribute of signature instead of other signature schemes like ECDSA (Elliptic curve digital signature algorithm).

In the paper (Wang et al., 2018), the author discussed issues in existing data sharing models such as transparency and traceability methods. To improve these issues author presented the blockchain technology as a new data-sharing scheme. In which the author introduced the concept of the double-chain structure of blockchain, these double structure concepts differentiate between original data storage and transaction data. The first structure is responsible for storing original data and the second is for transaction data. To make reliable and safe sharing author used the proxy re-encryption technique.

In (Rawat et al., 2018) author presented the information sharing framework for cybersecurity infrastructure to prevent, detect, and respond to cyber attackers. The Cyberspace world is facing the ongoing challenge of safeguard confidential information and critical assets from potential future attacks. The proposed architecture known as ishare uses blockchain technology to share cyber threat information securely, reliably, and transparently among multiple organizations. The ishare framework is captured constantly high-resolution cyber-attack information to prevent IT resources from being compromised by an attacker. The proposed framework aimed at providing the procedure of transaction in ishare, cyber-attack detection and sharing information, deploying cyber-defense solutions and updates. To analyzes, the proposed framework author used the one-way-attack, two-way attack, and Stackelberg game for cyber-attack and defense analysis approach for security performance.

In (Cash et al., 2018) author presented a two-tier blockchain model consist of permission and permission-less blockchain to analyze the computing power of proof of work consensus algorithm and Proof of Authority protocol algorithm on ethereum platform. The environment used in work is Mac OS and Ubuntu Linux operating system. the result analysis shows the better performance of PoA algorithm on permissioned blockchain in term of constant or no change in block count on both operating systems when the number of nodes increases. In permission, blockchain required less computation power for consensus algorithm than permission-less. However, the less computation of permissioned blockchain may possess the threat of malicious users due to its less computing power required by consensus protocol. So this needs to establish reliable and strong trust among nodes.

In paper (Wang et al., 2019) author addressed the problem of data sharing flexibility where some of the public-key encryption with access control (PEAC) schemes are not able to control the encryption easily on both sides by the data owner. So in this work author proposed the functional broadcast encryption (FBE) to control the file-based encryption and receiver-based encryption simultaneously. This FBE technique can share the set of the file to a group of users. FBE is an expansion of the PEAC scheme. It is more efficient, flexible, feasible in terms of technically, economically and cloud storage performance while PEAC has storage overhead costs.

In (Shrestha et al., 2019) author has shown the concern over online services used by a user in the travel domain, addressed the privacy concern of user's data collected by travel agencies. In this paper, the author proposed the framework of user-controlled privacy-preserving to user's data while using online services of hotel booking systems through blockchain technology. This model is developed on a multichain framework to control the user profile data like name, nationality, birth date, contact phone number, address of the user, and purpose of travel. The multichain framework relies on the public key encryption technique. Multichain is used to restrict access to data by authorized users only. Multichain is a kind of private blockchain to maintain the privacy and access policy of data

In (Wu et al., 2019) author presented the efficient, effective, and user-controlled privacy-preserving traceable attribute-based encryption scheme in blockchain environment to protect the data integrity and non-repudiation of transactions. The data-sharing environment poses some security threats of cracking the secret key and leakage of sensitive information in a distributed environment, so to prevent these challenges author proposed the pre-encryption technology to improve the efficiency of attribute-based encryption (ABE), this pre-encryption technique does the necessary pre-calculation before the message to be encrypted is well known. The attribute bloom filter (ABF) is used in this scheme to determine the existence of an attribute or element in the set and hide the attributes in an anonymous access control scheme. To prevent the cracking of the secret key author combined the user's signature and the main master secret key of Attribute Authority in the user's master secret key.

In (Samuel et al., 2019) author presented the privacy and security concern to achieve efficient services by service providers in data sharing. Because huge data is generated by multiple smart home appliances that possess privacy and security threats and lacking fair data sharing which reduces the transparent participation of users. so given the author of the above issue proposed a fair data sharing scheme to encourage user participation based on their reputation score by using the PageRank mechanism in this work, the Pagerank mechanism provides the authenticity of node and adds block into the ledger.

In paper (Eltayieb et al., 2020) author has pointed out the drawback of the traditional cloud storage system of data sharing that poses the service availability, centralize information database, high running operational cost, and privacy concerns. To come out of this concern author proposed the integrated concept of blockchain consists of attribute-based encryption to make the secure cloud environment for information exchange. In this survey work, the concept of a smart contract is used to provide storage efficiency in the cloud atmosphere. In this work, the author achieved the confidentiality and integrity of data by using the concept of a secret sharing scheme and access tree.

In (Rahman et al., 2020) author proposed a framework based on Accountable cross-border data sharing, in this work author, presented a global cloud platform connected to the security gateway of different regions that allows data sharing among different countries securely. This framework has the feature of penalty for misbehaving nodes or entities in the sharing process. The authenticity of data is verified by the Elliptic curve digital signature algorithm. The framework consisted of three entities such as data sender, data receiver, and any entity or party. This platform allows the sharing based on the under relaxed trust assumption on sender and receiver. The author in (Sumathi, & Sangeetha, 2020) provides the concepts of blockchain in banking system to make efficient and secure storage with distributed ledger property of blockchain. Author highlights the risk of data center failure can be overcome by using decentralize system of blockchain and it provides the immutability in data modification. The author in (Mohan, & Gladston, 2020) proposed the work for cloud data auditing with help of merkle tree and blockchain to maintain the integrity, transparency and immutability. The blockchain store transaction in distributed form, so that it is difficult to modify the data by unauthorized users.

SURVEY BASED ON HEALTHCARE DATA SHARING SCHEME

In the paper (Amofa et al., 2018) author has shown challenges for health information exchanges and the inability to control the data once has been transmitted such as privacy and integrity. The problem of data access control discourages the participants from sharing the health data. For this author proposed a blockchain-based system framework for secure control and sharing data among different hospitals. This is done by pairing-based user-generated acceptable use policies by using the smart contract. This framework minimizes the threat to data after sharing. In this work, the author used the cryptographic key method and smart contract to define the access level of a person's data. By this approach, the author reduced the financial cost of managing data, improve the efficiency of accessing health data, provide secure distribution of data, and has low latency. However, this proposed model has scalability problems.

In (Guo et al., 2018) author address, the issues of authenticity of electronic health record (EHR) placed inside on blockchain. So to prove the validity or authenticity of EHR, the author presented the secured attribute-based ensured signature scheme with more than one authority. In this scheme, the secret pseudorandom function seeds are used among the multiple entities that prevent the collision attack. The computational bilinear Diffie-Hellman technique is used to achieve no modification and complete privacy, the integrity of attribute signer. The ABS is secure in the random oracle model. This scheme improves the performance and cost of medical data sharing among many authorities. The prime objective of the ABS scheme is to prove the validity of EHR data.

In (Wang et al., 2018) author presented the framework of a secure cloud-assisted EHR system by using Attribute cryptosystem along with blockchain to reach confidentiality, integrity, authentication, and fine-grained access control of data. This model integrates attribute-based encryption followed by identity-based encryption (IBE) to encrypt the patient secret data. The identity-based signature (IBS) is used to provide the digital signature for the authenticity of EHR data. This scheme combined all the techniques into a single one to achieve different functionality this known as attribute-based/identity-based encryption and signature(C-AB/IB-ES). Cloud storage provides fast transmission, file sharing, data storing space, minimum cost, and efficient access.

In paper (Thwin et al., 2018) author analyzed the personal health record system (PHR) in regards to blockchain properties that may arise the concern of privacy, integrity as well as confidentiality due to the transparency property of blockchain. The author also described some of the other issues of blockchain such as concern of storage, privacy aspect, user consent revocation, model performance, energy cost, and scalability. To resolve some of the above-mentioned problems such as on-chain data privacy; limited storage author used the Shamir's secret sharing data scheme by using the concept of proxy re-encryption technique to ensure the privacy concern of PHR. the authenticity is ensured by verified signature before storing data on the blockchain and all the data are inclusive with the signature of gateway server on the blockchain. This model also considered the availability of data by storing only meta-data on blockchain nodes and privacy concerns by using a fine-grained access control policy. In this access control policy, the encryption is done only by the data owner by using proxy re-encryption and the keys are known to the gateway server.

In paper (Liu et al., 2018) author focused on the concern regarding privacy and security of files stored on the cloud server. For this author used ciphertext-policy attribute-based encryption (CP-ABE). The CP-ABE provides a secure access control policy to a user, a secure decentralized environment, and provide user-friendly service. The confidentiality of data and efficiency of the model are guaranteed by the symmetrical encryption algorithm. The secure access control is provided by the CP-ABE technique and with an access tree structure. It also ensures anti-collision attack and data integrity by using the crypto-graphic hash value. This model has the advantage of the higher efficiency with symmetrical encryption for files as well as CP-ABE fork, increased reliability, data security, and integrity. However, the model has some limitation like computation time increase as the number of attribute increase in the policy.

In paper (Theodouli et al., 2018) author has pointed out the concern regarding privacy and security needs in healthcare data sharing. For this concern author presented the potential use of blockchain to address these issues through the smart contract feature of blockchain technology. The smart contract further categorizes into three contracts for different functions such as registry contract for users regis-try, patient data smart contract contains the hashed data of health information and permission contract for access control of data. This work aimed at private data sharing and access permission of healthcare information. The blockchain-based architecture has achieved the security goal while sharing healthcare information such as integrity, user identity and provides accountability and auditing. However, this architecture is not suitable for the large-scale network.

In (Liu et al., 2019) author aimed at the nature of medical data privacy and sensitivity during sharing and provides a protection scheme for patient data. In this scheme, the author used private blockchain to address the security and privacy concern. The private blockchain is more secure than the public block-chain to ensure the security of electronic health records. This blockchain-based scheme satisfies security requirements such as transparency, tamper proofness, immutability. In this system for mutual authen-tication and generating session key author used the symptom matching algorithm for communication of two same type disease patients about their illness in future. In this work, the Author used delegated proof of stake (DPoS) mechanism to prevent dishonest nodes participation in the data sharing process.

In (Wang et al., 2019) author has shown the security threat to cloud-based stored medical data such as privacy and security issues. In this regard author used blockchain technology as a solution to provide data privacy and security to cloud-based stored information. The cloud manages for storing the EHR ciphertext and hybrid blockchain contain the indexes of electronic health record (EHR). The framework proposed is reliable, secure, and effective efficient privacy-preserving EHR sharing protocol by using the searchable encryption and conditional proxy re-encryption technique. This framework uses the proof of authority consensus protocol as the authenticity of the nodes in the decentralized network that is consortium blockchain. The cryptographic primitives such as bilinear map, public-key encryption with conjunctive keyword search technique, and conditional proxy re-encryption are implemented on ethereum blockchain platform.

In (Nguyen et al., 2019) author discuss the concern of storage security of electronic health records(EHR) on mobile-based cloud environment that having the security and privacy concern while sharing informa-tion among patients, healthcare providers, and third party. Given the above issues, the author presented a novel EHRs sharing model which integrates blockchain ledger and decentralizes interplanetary file system (IPFS) with mobile cloud network. To provide secure access control and EHR sharing to medical data we use the smart contract. In this model proof of concept, the mechanism is used to provide decentralized access control of EHR data sharing on mobile cloud framework to analyze the proposed scheme. The advantage of this model is to provide the minimum network latency and data security as compared to other existing information-sharing models and it is feasible for various e-health applications.

The work (Gupta et al., 2021) proposed the blockchain based secure concept for healthcare by using the cloud assisted system and make the data sharing efficient by using the attribute based encryption method. The proposed method is computationally efficient and storage efficient as well as robust.

SURVEY BASED ON IOT DATA SHARING

In (Liu et al., 2018) author discussed the issues related to collecting high-quality data from IoT mobile terminals and how securely share these data among mobile terminals, prevent device failure and communication failure. To overcome these above challenges, blockchain technology is proposed for data sharing and data collection efficiently. In this paper author combined ethereum platform with deep reinforcement learning to make an efficient, secure environment for data sharing and exchange. Reinforcement learning facilitates the collection of a large amount of data while blockchain provides reliability, security, and efficiently sharing data. Ethereum node stores the data and creates a private blockchain to share data. This private network has two nodes named mining node and non-mining node. The mining node checks the validity of blocks and adds them into the ledger while the non-mining node is used as receiving and broadcasting e data sharing among nodes. The objective of this proposed system is to support the mobile terminal to sense surrounding personal of interest devices to gain an edge in higher data collection, geographic transparency, impartiality, and minimum power consumption. After the simulation test, this scheme is feasible to higher security, reliability, and anti-collusion to DoS, DDoS in data sharing. However, this system is not extendable to every blockchain node and executes multiple tasks at the same time on each mobile terminal.

In paper (Si et al., 2018) author proposed the lightweight IoT information sharing security framework by using decentralize platform. The author used the double chain model that combines the data blockchain and transaction, which protects source data storage and is responsible for storing the indexes of transaction data respectively. The double-chain concept is used to maintain data consistency and avoid tampering with IoT data. The practical Byzantine fault-tolerant consensus mechanism increases the registration efficiency of nodes, higher the transactional throughput and privacy of sharing data by using the partial blind signature method. In This paper author used the dynamic game method which provides the cooperation among the node and detect the malicious behavior of a node, this dynamic game method find out the state of an unauthorized node and estimate the reputation value by using PageRanker algorithm, higher reputation value provides trust in sharing the data. The loss of private keys is secured by secret sharing.

In (Pham et al., 2019) author addressed the issues of time and cost in data collection from sensor devices in IoT environments for intelligent systems. These data collections also have security challenges like data leakage, privacy, and integrity. This author proposed the blockchain-based architecture which ensures integrity, authorization, confidentiality, and transparency in the data sharing process. The data collection is being done through the IoT gateway. After receiving data the IoT gateway encrypts these data and stores them at off-chain storage, asymmetric encryption technique used on ethereum blockchain ensuring data security and integrity to overcome these security issues. So that to get higher transaction speed and provides reliable service availability. However, this has scalability concerns to include large peers at the network.

In (Hofman et al., 2019) author addressed the demand of customers in manufacturer, retailer, and supplier like food security and safety, sustainability. For this author proposed a methodological approach in a complex organization such as supply chain and logistic network for development and deployment of data sharing by using the blockchain technology with smart contract. This approach of data sharing in supply chain and logistic networks use blockchain technology to reduce the implementation time in commodity trading in the supply chain. In this work, the technology used by the author is distributed ledger technology that creates data sharing reference model for supply and logistic network, informatics principles as a Turing machine, ontologies

In the paper (Cech et al., 2019) author discussed the creation of a huge amount of data from IoT devices and sensor nodes, collecting and securely sharing these data is the biggest challenge. The author developed an expanded fog computing model with the integration of blockchain to share sensor data among fog computing nodes. The new model is known as HCL-BaFog (Hypriot Cluster Lab) to collect data and provide secure sharing of information to other fog nodes. The proof of concept that usages the total virtualize function of the blockchain platform to ensure fairness in data sharing and the round-robin block creation schedule method. The feasibility of the data-sharing model is tested by a testbed of Raspberry Pi SBC (single board computer). This model uses the multichain framework to enhance the performance of fog computing nodes and enable trust among peer nodes. However, this proposed scheme is platform-dependent on the behavior of blockchain.

In (Lu et al., 2019) author address, the potential threat of data sharing that is data leakage and the security of the network. given the author of the above issue presented the blockchain-based secure file sharing model among different parties, Then introduced the information-sharing problem at machine learning problems by bringing privacy secured federated learning. To maintain privacy this model uses sharing model of machine learning instead of actual data. The blockchain-based collaborative architecture is used to reduce the risk of data leakage in sharing the data among multiple entities. Federated learning uses the concept of differential privacy to more strengthen data security. The normalized weighted graph is used to generate the structure data instead of unstructured. The proof of training quality algorithm converts the data-sharing problem in model sharing, this protects the privacy of the data owner. The purpose of federated learning provides training to a data model that may provide correct responses for information sharing request entities. This federated model used various machine learning algorithms such as a random tree, random forest.

In (Manzoor et al., 2019) author discussed the issues of cloud-based data sharing centralize system which requires third-party services to pay some fee for services. To overcome these scalability and trust issues blockchain technology is used as a solution in IoT data sharing that uses the proxy re-encryption technique to facilitate secured data transmission and visibility only to the data owner and intended user into the blockchain network. The data is stored on the distributed cloud after passing through the encryption process. The secure sharing is performed by a smart contract between the data owner and the data requester. The whole framework is implemented on the ethereum virtualize platform to increase the performance, reliability as well security features. The proposed architecture consists of four entity includes IoT devices, data users, cloud-enabled service providers, and blockchain platforms. From the security point of view, the author applied a certificate-based proxy re-encryption (CP-PRE) scheme that consists of seven polynomial-time algorithms. The feasibility of the model is shown on permissioned ethereum blockchain with the sensor of devices and cloud server for storing data. However this system is not scalable to distributed cloud storage, so this will be the future enhancement of this proposed system.

In (Liang et al., 2019) author addresses the issues of previous data transmission techniques such as low security, the higher management cost of data, lack of proper monitoring in the industrial Internet of Things. These concerns may lead to tampering of data, unauthorized access in IoT devices. This decreases the quality, consistency, and efficiency of quality data. In the view of above issues, the author presented a secure blockchain-enabled data transmission model for the Industrial Internet of Things, which using the dynamic secret sharing technique to provide secure transmission. The dynamic secret sharing protects the private key. Key-value of private and public key sign the intelligent data transaction as well as prove its validity of own transaction. In this paper author secured the data transmission by blockchain sharing model that protects the decentralized system from attack. This model used the docker virtualization technique for creating the power blockchain network sharing model. The experiment shows that this model has achieved high security and efficient reliability, improves the transmission rate and packet receiving rate. However this model needs a lot of enhancement in the future to introduce power blockchain in large scalable networks, needs to remove data redundancies in the file storage system.

The paper (Stergiou et al., 2020) is related to provide the security and management of big data in fog based environment for 6G wireless networks. This work provides the secure and efficient platform for using internet and sharing information as well as provide scalability for large big data.

SUMMARY OF EXISTING WORK ON DATA SHARING WITH BLOCKCHAIN

See Table 1

SECURITY CHALLENGES OF BLOCKCHAIN SYSTEM

- **Performance and scalability:** These are the significant feature of blockchain in terms of processing information. The performance depends upon the task the nodes perform like authentication, verification, running the consensus mechanism, and maintained the synchronized copy of the transaction to the global digital ledger (Croman et al., 2016). Another concern of blockchain is scalability when several users increase in the network the computational overhead also increased (Kosba et al., 2016).
- **Storage capacity and privacy:** As the blockchain is based on the decentralization concept to provide secure storage and access to transactions or data, store information on the ledger and maintain privacy among users for various services is the biggest challenge. The concern of decentralized systems is leakage of the public and private key used for encryption and decryption, limited storage capacity such as IoT devices (Xie et al., 2019). This needs to be improved in future work.
- **Energy consumption:** energy consumption is also associated with the above-mentioned issues. It may happen when more users are connected to network or IoT environment in solving puzzles the consensus algorithm like PoW requires hard computational resources in the mining process to overcome these energy constraints many researchers presented the energy-efficient algorithm such as proof of stake (PoS), delegated proof of stake (DpoS), practical byzantine fault tolerance (PBFT), etc.(Xie et al., 2019).

Table 1. Comparison of existing papers on blockchain-based data sharing

Reference	Focused area	Method	Pros	Cons	Tools
Xu et al., 2017	Fine-grained access control and privacy preservation	Bilinear pairing method ABS CP-ABE	Privacy-preserving User control Data access policy	The limited computational power of IoT devices	Hyper ledger Pairing based and GNU library
Dinh et al., 2017	Focused on attribute-based signcryption scheme and confidentiality and access control	Bilinear mapping function Secret data sharing scheme Access tree method	Establish trust Lowest keysize and signcryption cost Computation and communication overhead overcome	Risk of DDoS attack	VC++ PBC library
Goyal et al., 2018	KYC validation using blockchain	Double-blind data sharing	Provide dynamic access control of data Reduce manual verification, time, and cost	Not scalable limited storage Slow transaction speed	Hyper ledger fabric Private network blockchain
Feng et al., 2019	Data sharing incentive mechanism	Evolutionary game theory Evolutionary stable strategy Symmetric Property of the game theory	Enhanced user participation	Data size and data quality limitations	Ethereum network MATLAB
McGhin et al., 2019	Proposed incentive schemes for boosting IoT data sharing	Coin-locking strategy Shamir's secret sharing scheme	Identification of malicious nodes behavior The enhanced motivation of nodes to share data	High bandwidth cost Slow data sharing.	Ethereum framework Microsoft Azure
Mohanta et al., 2019	Data authentication and data quality	Shamir's secret sharing Online review system RSA algorithm	Data integrity Less computation time in encryption	Not scalable	Ethereum network
Gai et al., 2019	Focused on encryption scheme to control simultaneous data sharing of data to a group of users.	Functional broadcast encryption Probabilistic polynomial-time algorithm(PPT)	FBE is storage efficient FBE is feasible in terms of technically and economically	Obsfucation program is not efficient in practical applications	C language

Table 2. Comparison based on healthcare data sharing

Reference	Focused area	Method	Pros	Cons	Tools
Fukumitsu et al., 2017	Secure cloud file sharing	CP-ABE, Access tree structure, ECB model, Symmetric encryption algorithm	Increased reliability of data security and integrity,	Encryption time increased with file size increase	Ethereum network and JPBC library
Wang et al., 2017	Health care data sharing using blockchain	Blockchain with smart contract	Provide auditing and accountability,Automatic workflow	Not scalable	Private blockchain
Wang et al., 2019	Medical data sharing and protection scheme	Delegated proof of stake	Better security performance	Low throughput and scalable	Private blockchain
Shrestha et al., 2019	Proposed secret data-sharing model for PHR	Proxy re-encryption, AFGH algorithm	Privacy of on-chain data Improved storage capacity	Energy consumption Not Scalable	Ethereum network
Rahman et al., 2020	Based on personal health data and sharing framework	Cryptographic key and smart contract	Reduce the financial cost of managing data, Low latency,	Not scalable	Ethereum VM

Table 3. Comparison based on IoT data sharing

Reference	Focused area	Method	Pros	Cons	Tools
Shrestha et al., 2018	Data sharing in supply chain and logistic network	Distributed ledger technology, Turing machine, ontologies	Reduce implementation time in commodity trading in the supply chain	scalability	Ethereum and DLT
Zhang et al., 2018	Proposed expanded fog computing model by integrating blockchain to share sensor data.	Proof of concept, PKI method, Round-robin block creation schedule method	Huge data processing capability to advance IoT applications	The proposed scheme is platform-dependent on blockchain	Private blockchain Fog computing, Multichain framework
Bhaskaran et al., 2018	Enhancing security in IoT devices data sharing	Blockchain and smart contract	Ensured data integrity and security, Ensure service availability	Not scalable	Ethereum TestNet Truffle framework
Naz et al., 2019	Incentive mechanism with on-chain and off-chain data that creates trust	DQDA algorithm, EM algorithm, Marginal social welfare greedy auction(MSWG)	Trust in sharing of off-chain data, Data quality is high at low cost	Not suitable for higher energy consumption devices.	Consortium blockchain
Eltayieb et al., 2020	secure data sharing among internet of vehicle by using blockchain	The fair blind signature scheme, Multi-signature and threshold mechanism, Threshold secret sharing scheme	Provide security and privacy of vehicle, Communication and storage cost-efficient	High computational complexity	Ethereum, Linux, MIRACL library

Table 4. System configuration of experimental environment

Reference	OS	CPU	Memory	Tools
Xu et al., 2017	Ubuntu 16.04	Intel (R) core(TM) i7-6700 CPU @ 3.4 GHz	3 GB RAM	• Go-ethereum • nodeJs • truffle
Dinh et al., 2017	Windows 10, 64 bit	Intel i5-7400, 3.00 GHz CPU	4 GB RAM	• VC++ 6.0 • PBC Library
Feng et al., 2019	Windows 7, 64 bit	Intel i5-3470 cpu@ 3.2GHz	4GB RAM	• MATLAB 6.5.0.1809139 release 13
Mohanta et al., 2019	64 bit OS and X64 based processor	Intel (R) core(TM) M3-7430 CPU @ 1.61 GHz	8 GB RAM	• Ethereum • Solidity • Vs code • Ganache • metamask
Gai et al., 2019	windows 10	Intel 2 core 8 i7-8565 CPU, 1.8 GHz & 1.99GHz	8 GB RAM	• C language

CONCLUSION

Recently blockchain has gained a lot of recognition because of its features such as transparency, immutability, decentralized environment, peer-to-peer node communication, and distributed ledger. It can be used in diverse fields like the internet of things, healthcare, cloud storage, supply chain, smart cities, etc. It is accompanied by transparency to the ledger's data and transactions. In this survey, we have summarized the existing work based on data sharing techniques using blockchain platforms in areas of IoT, healthcare, and the internet of vehicles. Most of the authors proposed the security model that provides an incentive mechanism for secure data sharing by using different Cryptographic algorithm and achieved the protection of data up to some extent of security goal. However, there is still some hidden security threat and challenges that need to improve more accurately in future work like scalability, energy consumption, privacy and security of decentralize storage as well as integration of blockchain for fog computing to provide better security, data integrity at fog layer, as fog layer help to provide better services with low latency and to utilize full bandwidth.

REFERENCES

Amofa, S., Sifah, E. B., Kwame, O. B., Abla, S., Xia, Q., Gee, J. C., & Gao, J. (2018, September). A blockchain-based architecture framework for secure sharing of personal health data. In *2018 IEEE 20th International Conference on e-Health Networking, Applications and Services (Healthcom)* (pp. 1-6). IEEE. 10.1109/HealthCom.2018.8531160

Bhaskaran, K., Ilfrich, P., Liffman, D., Vecchiola, C., Jayachandran, P., Kumar, A., ... Teo, E. G. (2018, April). Double-blind consent-driven data sharing on blockchain. In *2018 IEEE International Conference on Cloud Engineering (IC2E)* (pp. 385-391). IEEE. 10.1109/IC2E.2018.00073

Cash, M., & Bassiouni, M. (2018, September). Two-tier permission-ed and permission-less blockchain for secure data sharing. In *2018 IEEE International Conference on Smart Cloud (SmartCloud)* (pp. 138-144). IEEE. 10.1109/SmartCloud.2018.00031

Cech, H. L., Großmann, M., & Krieger, U. R. (2019, June). A fog computing architecture to share sensor data by means of blockchain functionality. In *2019 IEEE International Conference on Fog Computing (ICFC)* (pp. 31-40). IEEE. 10.1109/ICFC.2019.00013

Croman, K., Decker, C., Eyal, I., Gencer, A. E., Juels, A., Kosba, A., & Song, D. (2016, February). On scaling decentralized blockchains. In *International conference on financial cryptography and data security* (pp. 106-125). Springer.

Dib, O., Brousmiche, K. L., Durand, A., Thea, E., & Hamida, E. B. (2018). Consortium blockchains: Overview, applications and challenges. *International Journal on Advances in Telecommunications, 11*(1-2).

Dinh, T. T. A., Wang, J., Chen, G., Liu, R., Ooi, B. C., & Tan, K. L. (2017, May). Blockbench: A framework for analyzing private blockchains. In *Proceedings of the 2017 ACM International Conference on Management of Data* (pp. 1085-1100). 10.1145/3035918.3064033

Dubovitskaya, A., Novotny, P., Xu, Z., & Wang, F. (2020). Applications of blockchain technology for data-sharing in oncology: Results from a systematic literature review. *Oncology*, *98*(6), 403–411. doi:10.1159/000504325 PMID:31794967

Eltayieb, N., Elhabob, R., Hassan, A., & Li, F. (2020). A blockchain-based attribute-based signcryption scheme to secure data sharing in the cloud. *Journal of Systems Architecture*, *102*, 101653. doi:10.1016/j.sysarc.2019.101653

Feng, Q., He, D., Zeadally, S., Khan, M. K., & Kumar, N. (2019). A survey on privacy protection in blockchain system. *Journal of Network and Computer Applications*, *126*, 45–58. doi:10.1016/j.jnca.2018.10.020

Gai, K., Wu, Y., Zhu, L., Qiu, M., & Shen, M. (2019). Privacy-preserving energy trading using consortium blockchain in smart grid. *IEEE Transactions on Industrial Informatics*, *15*(6), 3548–3558. doi:10.1109/TII.2019.2893433

Goyal, S. (2018). *The History of Blockchain Technology: Must Know Timeline*. Academic Press.

Guo, R., Shi, H., Zhao, Q., & Zheng, D. (2018). Secure attribute-based signature scheme with multiple authorities for blockchain in electronic health records systems. *IEEE Access: Practical Innovations, Open Solutions*, *6*, 11676–11686. doi:10.1109/ACCESS.2018.2801266

Gupta, B. B., Li, K. C., Leung, V. C., Psannis, K. E., & Yamaguchi, S. (2021). Blockchain-assisted secure fine-grained searchable encryption for a cloud-based healthcare cyber-physical system. *IEEE/CAA Journal of Automatica Sinica*.

Gupta, S., & Gupta, B. B. (2017). Detection, avoidance, and attack pattern mechanisms in modern web application vulnerabilities: Present and future challenges. *International Journal of Cloud Applications and Computing*, *7*(3), 1–43. doi:10.4018/IJCAC.2017070101

Hasselgren, A., Kralevska, K., Gligoroski, D., Pedersen, S. A., & Faxvaag, A. (2019). Blockchain in healthcare and health sciences–a scoping review. *International Journal of Medical Informatics*, 104040. PMID:31865055

Hofman, W. J. (2019). A Methodological Approach for Development and Deployment of Data Sharing in Complex Organizational Supply and Logistics Networks with Blockchain Technology. *IFAC-PapersOnLine*, *52*(3), 55–60. doi:10.1016/j.ifacol.2019.06.010

Kosba, A., Miller, A., Shi, E., Wen, Z., & Papamanthou, C. (2016, May). Hawk: The blockchain model of cryptography and privacy-preserving smart contracts. In *2016 IEEE symposium on security and privacy (SP)* (pp. 839-858). IEEE.

Liang, W., Tang, M., Long, J., Peng, X., Xu, J., & Li, K. C. (2019). A secure fabric blockchain-based data transmission technique for industrial Internet-of-Things. *IEEE Transactions on Industrial Informatics*, *15*(6), 3582–3592. doi:10.1109/TII.2019.2907092

Liu, C. H., Lin, Q., & Wen, S. (2018). Blockchain-enabled data collection and sharing for industrial IoT with deep reinforcement learning. *IEEE Transactions on Industrial Informatics*, *15*(6), 3516–3526. doi:10.1109/TII.2018.2890203

Liu, X., Wang, Z., Jin, C., Li, F., & Li, G. (2019). A Blockchain-Based Medical Data Sharing and Protection Scheme. *IEEE Access: Practical Innovations, Open Solutions, 7*, 118943–118953. doi:10.1109/ACCESS.2019.2937685

Liu, Y., Zhang, J., & Gao, Q. (2018, October). A Blockchain-Based Secure Cloud Files Sharing Scheme with Fine-Grained Access Control. In *2018 International Conference on Networking and Network Applications (NaNA)* (pp. 277-283). IEEE. 10.1109/NANA.2018.8648778

Lu, Y., Huang, X., Dai, Y., Maharjan, S., & Zhang, Y. (2019). Blockchain and Federated Learning for Privacy-preserved Data Sharing in Industrial IoT. *IEEE Transactions on Industrial Informatics.*

Manzoor, A., Liyanage, M., Braeke, A., Kanhere, S. S., & Ylianttila, M. (2019, May). Blockchain based proxy re-encryption scheme for secure IoT data sharing. In *2019 IEEE International Conference on Blockchain and Cryptocurrency (ICBC)* (pp. 99-103). IEEE. 10.1109/BLOC.2019.8751336

McGhin, T., Choo, K. K. R., Liu, C. Z., & He, D. (2019). Blockchain in healthcare applications: Research challenges and opportunities. *Journal of Network and Computer Applications, 135,* 62–75. doi:10.1016/j.jnca.2019.02.027

Mohan, A. P., & Gladston, A. (2020). Merkle tree and Blockchain-based cloud data auditing. *International Journal of Cloud Applications and Computing, 10*(3), 54–66. doi:10.4018/IJCAC.2020070103

Mohanta, B. K., Jena, D., Panda, S. S., & Sobhanayak, S. (2019). Blockchain Technology: A Survey on Applications and Security Privacy Challenges. *Internet of Things,* 100107.

Nakasumi, M. (2017, July). Information sharing for supply chain management based on block chain technology. In *2017 IEEE 19th Conference on Business Informatics (CBI)* (Vol. 1, pp. 140-149). IEEE. 10.1109/CBI.2017.56

Naz, M., Al-zahrani, F. A., Khalid, R., Javaid, N., Qamar, A. M., Afzal, M. K., & Shafiq, M. (2019). A Secure Data Sharing Platform Using Blockchain and Interplanetary File System. *Sustainability, 11*(24), 7054. doi:10.3390u11247054

Nguyen, D. C., Pathirana, P. N., Ding, M., & Seneviratne, A. (2019). Blockchain for secure EHRs sharing of mobile cloud based e-Health systems. *IEEE Access: Practical Innovations, Open Solutions, 7,* 66792–66806. doi:10.1109/ACCESS.2019.2917555

Pham, H. A., Le, T. K., & Le, T. V. (2019, September). Enhanced Security of IoT Data Sharing Management by Smart Contracts and Blockchain. In *2019 19th International Symposium on Communications and Information Technologies (ISCIT)* (pp. 398-403). IEEE. 10.1109/ISCIT.2019.8905219

Rahman, M. S., Al Omar, A., Bhuiyan, M. Z. A., Basu, A., Kiyomoto, S., & Wang, G. (2020). Accountable cross-border data sharing using blockchain under relaxed trust assumption. *IEEE Transactions on Engineering Management.*

Rawat, D. B., Njilla, L., Kwiat, K., & Kamhoua, C. (2018, March). iShare: Blockchain-based privacy-aware multi-agent information sharing games for cybersecurity. In *2018 International Conference on Computing, Networking and Communications (ICNC)* (pp. 425-431). IEEE. 10.1109/ICCNC.2018.8390264

Samuel, O., Javaid, N., Awais, M., Ahmed, Z., Imran, M., & Guizani, M. (2019, July). A blockchain model for fair data sharing in deregulated smart grids. In *IEEE Global Communications Conference (GLOBCOM 2019)*. 10.1109/GLOBECOM38437.2019.9013372

Shrestha, A. K., Deters, R., & Vassileva, J. (2019). *User-controlled privacy-preserving user profile data sharing based on blockchain.* arXiv preprint arXiv:1909.05028.

Shrestha, A. K., & Vassileva, J. (2018, June). Blockchain-based research data sharing framework for incentivizing the data owners. In *International Conference on Blockchain* (pp. 259-266). Springer. 10.1007/978-3-319-94478-4_19

Si, H., Sun, C., Li, Y., Qiao, H., & Shi, L. (2019). IoT information sharing security mechanism based on blockchain technology. *Future Generation Computer Systems, 101*, 1028–1040. doi:10.1016/j.future.2019.07.036

Stergiou, C. L., Psannis, K. E., & Gupta, B. B. (2020). IoT-based big data secure management in the fog over a 6G wireless network. *IEEE Internet of Things Journal, 8*(7), 5164–5171. doi:10.1109/JIOT.2020.3033131

Sumathi, M., & Sangeetha, S. (2020). Blockchain based sensitive attribute storage and access monitoring in banking system. *International Journal of Cloud Applications and Computing, 10*(2), 77–92. doi:10.4018/IJCAC.2020040105

Theodouli, A., Arakliotis, S., Moschou, K., Votis, K., & Tzovaras, D. (2018, August). On the design of a Blockchain-based system to facilitate Healthcare Data Sharing. In *2018 17th IEEE International Conference on Trust, Security And Privacy In Computing And Communications/12th IEEE International Conference On Big Data Science And Engineering (TrustCom/BigDataSE)* (pp. 1374-1379). IEEE. 10.1109/TrustCom/BigDataSE.2018.00190

Thwin, T. T., & Vasupongayya, S. (2018, August). Blockchain based secret-data sharing model for personal health record system. In *2018 5th International Conference on Advanced Informatics: Concept Theory and Applications (ICAICTA)* (pp. 196-201). IEEE. 10.1109/ICAICTA.2018.8541296

Wang, H., & Song, Y. (2018). Secure cloud-based EHR system using attribute-based cryptosystem and blockchain. *Journal of Medical Systems, 42*(8), 152. doi:10.100710916-018-0994-6 PMID:29974270

Wang, H., Zhang, Y., Chen, K., Sui, G., Zhao, Y., & Huang, X. (2019). Functional broadcast encryption with applications to data sharing for cloud storage. *Information Sciences, 502*, 109–124. doi:10.1016/j.ins.2019.06.028

Wang, L., Liu, W., & Han, X. (2017, December). Blockchain-based government information resource sharing. In *2017 IEEE 23rd International Conference on Parallel and Distributed Systems (ICPADS)* (pp. 804-809). IEEE. 10.1109/ICPADS.2017.00112

Wang, Y., Zhang, A., Zhang, P., & Wang, H. (2019). Cloud-Assisted EHR Sharing With Security and Privacy Preservation via Consortium Blockchain. *IEEE Access: Practical Innovations, Open Solutions, 7*, 136704–136719. doi:10.1109/ACCESS.2019.2943153

Wang, Z., Tian, Y., & Zhu, J. (2018, August). Data sharing and tracing scheme based on blockchain. In *2018 8th International Conference on Logistics, Informatics and Service Sciences (LISS)* (pp. 1-6). IEEE. 10.1109/LISS.2018.8593225

Wang, Z., & Wu, Q. (2019, October). Incentive for Historical Block Data Sharing in Blockchain. In *2019 IEEE 10th Annual Information Technology, Electronics and Mobile Communication Conference (IEMCON)* (pp. 0913-0919). IEEE. 10.1109/IEMCON.2019.8936209

Wu, A., Zhang, Y., Zheng, X., Guo, R., Zhao, Q., & Zheng, D. (2019). Efficient and privacy-preserving traceable attribute-based encryption in blockchain. *Annales des Télécommunications*, *74*(7-8), 401–411. doi:10.100712243-018-00699-y

Xie, J., Tang, H., Huang, T., Yu, F. R., Xie, R., Liu, J., & Liu, Y. (2019). A survey of blockchain technology applied to smart cities: Research issues and challenges. *IEEE Communications Surveys and Tutorials*, *21*(3), 2794–2830. doi:10.1109/COMST.2019.2899617

Xu, L., Shah, N., Chen, L., Diallo, N., Gao, Z., Lu, Y., & Shi, W. (2017, April). Enabling the sharing economy: Privacy respecting contract based on public blockchain. In *Proceedings of the ACM Workshop on Blockchain, Cryptocurrencies and Contracts* (pp. 15-21). 10.1145/3055518.3055527

Xuan, S., Zheng, L., Chung, I., Wang, W., Man, D., Du, X., & Guizani, M. (2020). An incentive mechanism for data sharing based on blockchain with smart contracts. *Computers & Electrical Engineering*, *83*, 106587. doi:10.1016/j.compeleceng.2020.106587

Zhang, Y., He, D., & Choo, K. K. R. (2018). BaDS: Blockchain-based architecture for data sharing with ABS and CP-ABE in IoT. *Wireless Communications and Mobile Computing*, *2018*, 2018. doi:10.1155/2018/2783658

This research was previously published in Advances in Malware and Data-Driven Network Security; pages 199-218, copyright year 2022 by Information Science Reference (an imprint of IGI Global).

Chapter 7
Application of Technology in Healthcare:
Tackling COVID–19 Challenge – The Integration of Blockchain and Internet of Things

Andreia Robert Lopes
Hovione Farmaciencia, Portugal

Ana Sofia Dias
ISEG, Lisbon School of Economics and Management, Portugal

Bebiana Sá-Moura
ISEG, Lisbon School of Economics and Management, Portugal

ABSTRACT

The COVID-19 pandemic has disrupted healthcare worldwide and laid several fundamental problems that will have to be tackled to ensure high-quality healthcare services. This pandemic has represented an unparalleled challenge for healthcare systems and poses an opportunity to innovate and implement new solutions. Digital transformation within healthcare organizations has started and is reshaping healthcare. Technologies such as blockchain and IoT can bring about a revolution in healthcare and help solve many of the problems associated with healthcare systems that the COVID-19 crisis has exacerbated. In this chapter, IoT and blockchain technologies were discussed, focusing on their main characteristics, integration benefits, and limitations, identifying the challenges to be addressed soon. The authors further explored its potential in describing concrete cases and possible applications for healthcare in general and specifically for COVID-19.

DOI: 10.4018/978-1-6684-7132-6.ch007

INTRODUCTION

Coronaviruses are a large family of viruses that can cause mild to severe respiratory tract infections in humans. In 2002 and 2012, with SARS (Severe acute respiratory syndrome) and with MERS (Middle East Respiratory Coronavirus), respectively, the world had the first glimpse of the potential impact of this family of viruses. In the first crisis, the SARS-CoV virus capacity of human-to-human transmission, the lack of preparation within hospitals for infection control, and international air travel enabled global dissemination of this pathogenic agent. SARS-CoV was initially detected in Guangdong province in China in late 2002, and it constituted the first known significant pandemic caused by a coronavirus, with 8,096 cases and 774 deaths reported in over 30 countries in five continents (Cheng et al., 2007). MERS-CoV was isolated from a patient who died in Saudi Arabia in September 2012, and since then, there have been multiple outbreaks that have amounted to 2564 conðrmed cases of the Middle East respiratory syndrome 881 associated deaths. It has been reported in 27 countries, although most cases (80%) have been in Saudi Arabia. One of the most striking features is that this virus seems to have a case-fatality ratio of almost 35% (Al-Omari et al., 2019).

However, the worst was yet to come. In late 2019, in Wuhan in China, an initial outbreak of a new virus spread rapidly to other areas of China (Chahrour et al., 2020). In a few weeks, this virus had spread to other countries, and as of 1st February 2020, the World Health Organization (WHO) declared CO-VID-19 a Public Health Emergency of International Concern, and on 11th March 2020, the Coronavirus SARS-CoV-2 outbreak was declared a worldwide pandemic. As of January 2021, the virus has spread globally, with 89,416,559 confirmed cases of COVID-19, including 1,935,028 deaths. For the first time in history, a health crisis shut down the entire planet. Lockdowns and mobility restrictions imposed to control the spread of the virus and alleviate pressure on strained health care systems worldwide have had an enormous impact on economic growth and pushed millions of people into unemployment and poverty. The novel coronavirus pandemic has revealed deep underlying problems in health care systems across the world, and political, and healthcare authorities should swiftly address its impact in the longer term. Dealing with the impact of this health crisis, working on disease surveillance and prevention of new similar threats, and reconfiguring healthcare systems enabling them to deliver the best care while handling potential new crises are vital areas that must be tackled.

The COVID-19 challenge has undoubtedly been a catalyst for change. COVID-19 has dramatically accelerated digitalization and the adoption of new technology. This chapter aims to explore how blockchain combined with IoT could have played an essential role throughout the COVID-19 crisis in the healthcare system and pinpoint possible future applications.

BACKGROUND

Internet of Things (IoT)

The Internet of Things (IoT) is the real result of an applied principle: if you connect every tangible "thing" to the Internet, you create a network of shared data components.

Internet of Things refers to the ubiquitous network of interconnected objects capable of information storage and exchange using embedded sensors, actuators, and other devices. The IoT is a revolutionary technology which facilitates data-driven decision making by monitoring and managing objects in real-time. According to Kevin Ashton, the then executive director of the Auto-ID Center, he coined the term *"Internet of Things"* in 1999 while working on a presentation for Procter & Gamble in the context of RFID (Radio-Frequency Identification) supply chains (*RFID JOURNAL* l, n.d.).

The meaning of IoT is connecting systems and devices that, until now, have not been connected. The IoT is made up of things or devices connected by the internet that can take in information and talk to each other, sharing information back and forth. The connected things use sensors to absorb the information. The sensors input data into a large, intelligent system comprised of smaller smart systems.

The data is obtained through devices, vehicles or patients and are sent via protocols, i.e. communication channels, such as MQTT, Rest API, Coap or Custom, to a Cloud, and are stored in a database or they are received by an application that records and works on the same data.

The expanded definition of IoT is the upgrade of mobile, home and embedded applications to become part of a network of connected physical devices that all have sensors that both import and export data. The devices, using embedded sensors, gather data about the environment in which they are operating and how they are being used. The sensors are integrated into every physical device, from electrical appliances (fridges, stoves, furnaces), to lights (home lighting, traffic lights, car lights), to smartphones and tablets to barcodes on non-electrical items (pill bottles, boxes). The devices then share the data in real time about their operational state through the Cloud to an IoT platform where there is a universal language by which all IoT devices communicate. The gathered data is then dumped, or integrated, and data analytics is performed. Data analytics is drawing valuable insights and information from masses of raw data. Data analytics is now mostly automated, with algorithms performed by Artificial Intelligence (AI) software that clean, sort, and generally make sense of the vast amounts of data that IoT devices provide. With a far higher capacity for computation than humans, Internet of Things technologies can analyze enormous amounts of data in seconds. Valuable information and insights are then pulled from the data without the aid of human beings. The information is then shared with human users and other IoT devices. The Internet of Things leads to better healthcare outcomes, more efficient manufacturing, optimization of energy production and consumption, more effective use of natural resources and lowered waste production in addition to a host of other benefits. In terms of advantages of using IoT, it allows a dynamic control of the industries, an improvement in the relationship between people and technology and essentially an easy access to data.

Regarding data privacy, the concern with the protection of data stored on the internet is increasing, and therefore it is necessary to have control of the legal and regulatory part, technical control by the open-source, social ethic and Market Self- Regulation.

IoT and Healthcare Market

The internet of things is also described as a network of physical devices that uses connectivity to enable the exchange of data. In addition, in healthcare field, IoT is used for data collection, analysis for research, and monitoring electronic health records which contains personally identifiable information, protected health information, and for other machine-generated healthcare data. Further, IoT applications in healthcare facilitate important tasks such as improving patient outcomes and taking some burden off health practitioners. IoT enabled devices to have made remote monitoring in the healthcare sector possible, unleashing the potential to keep patients safe and healthy, and empowering physicians to deliver superlative care.

IoT Healthcare market can be broadly divided into three components - Medical devices, Systems & software, and Services. Software & system segment dominates global IoT Healthcare market. Some of the leading technologies facilitating integration of IoT in healthcare domain are RFID, mHealth, Telemedicine and Bluetooth Low Energy. Growth of the market is fueled by increasing prevalence of chronic diseases, rising number of geriatric populations globally and higher efficiency provided by use of IoT in healthcare. Other factors such as availability of high-speed internet and favorable government regulatory policies are also expected to boost market growth. However, certain limitations of IoT in healthcare segment poses challenges to industry growth. Some of these are lack of interoperability, privacy and security concerns and lack of regulatory oversight.

Companies operating in the segment, both medical device manufacturers and IT companies are developing innovative products and services such as, Cognitive solution to diabetes management by Medtronic and IBM, Medical data exchange by Cisco and Philips Medical dispensing service, amongst others.

The growing of IoT in healthcare segment is anticipated due to the use of technologically advanced medical devices. Adoption of IoT services in healthcare leads to introduction of technologically advanced connected medical devices which help in remote patient monitoring and clinical care in general. Furthermore, it provides new possibilities for personalized healthcare with the use of leading healthcare applications such as Health tracker apps, Healthcare wearable, Telemonitoring and smart homes, Electronic health records, etc. The next decade may well see a revolution in the treatment and diagnosis of disease. The IoT has opened up a world of possibilities in medicine: when connected to the internet, ordinary medical devices can collect invaluable additional data, give extra insight into symptoms and trends, enable remote care, and generally give patients more control over their lives and treatment.

The global internet of things in healthcare market was valued at $113.75 billion in 2019 and is expected to reach $332.67 billion by 2027, registering a CAGR of 13.20% from 2020 to 2027. The major factors that contribute toward the growth of the internet of things in healthcare market include technological advancements, rising incidence rates of chronic diseases such as COPD, genetic diseases, respiratory diseases, and others, better accessibility to high-speed internet, implementation of favorable government regulatory policies. Furthermore, growing demand for cost-effective treatment and disease management, increased adoption of smart devices and wearables, increasing interest in self-health measurement, and reduced healthcare cost with advanced and cost effectives IoT in healthcare products and solutions. Moreover, rising interest of the startup companies in IoT healthcare industry such as MedAngelONE, Amiko, SWORD health, and Aira, is expected to boost the market growth. However, factors such as high costs associated with IoT infrastructure development, data privacy and security issues, lack of awareness among public in developing regions, and limited technical knowledge are expected to impede the market growth. Various factors such as government initiatives to support IoT platform, improvement in healthcare infrastructure in developing countries, and high R&D spending are expected to boost the market growth.

The pandemic has caused change in providers willingness to implement IoT solutions which helped in diagnosing the virus using internet of things. Furthermore, IoT technology is playing a growing role in helping authorities to prevent the further spread of COVID-19, while also treating those that have been infected. IoT, specifically and especially when combined with other transformative technologies such as Cloud and Artificial intelligence (AI). This led to wide range of applications of IoT in healthcare during this crisis. For instance, in 2020, patients and staff at a field hospital in Wuhan, China, wore bracelets and rings synced with an AI. This platform from CloudMinds the Beijing-based operator of cloud-based systems for intelligent robots to provide constant monitoring of vital signs, including temperature, heart rate, and blood oxygen levels during Covid-19 pandemic (Chamola et al., 2020). In addition, in India, the mobile application named as aarogya setu app, launched by the Union Health ministry on April 2, 2020 which helps users identify whether they are at a risk of COVID-19 infection (Nagori, 2021). Therefore, Covid-19 has uplifted the demand of internet of things in healthcare market and provides opportunities for the manufacturers in various applications in the healthcare domain during the forecast period.

The segmentation of the internet of things in healthcare market is performed based on application, component, end user, and region. Based on component, the market is segmented into devices, system & software and services (Table 1). The devices segment is further segmented into implantable sensor devices, wearable sensor devices, and other sensor devices. System & software segment are further categorized into network layer, database layer, and analytics layer. Moreover, services segment covers architecture, consulting, and application development services. Based on application, the market is segmented into patient monitoring, clinical operation & workflow optimization, connected imaging, fitness & wellness measurement, and drug development. Based on end user, global internet of things in healthcare market is segmented into healthcare providers, patients, healthcare payers, research laboratories of pharmaceutical & biotechnology companies, and government authorities. The market has been analyzed across four regions namely North America, Europe, Asia-Pacific, and LAMEA (Figure1).

In 2019, North America accounted for a major share of the internet of things in healthcare market size and is expected to continue this trend owing to rapid technological advancements, increasing investments from top players, supportive governmental rules, rise in prevalence of chronic disease patient population and increase in demand for cost effective disease treatment. However, Asia-Pacific is expected to witness growth at significant rate during the forecast period, by registering a CAGR of 17.40%. This is mainly due to rapidly changing healthcare infrastructure in the developing countries such as India and China, large patient population, rising public awareness, and increasing healthcare spending.

Figure 1. Iot in healthcare market by region.
Adapted from (Telugunta & Choudhary, 2020)

The service segment held the major market share of internet of things in healthcare in 2019, owing to growing demand for uninterrupted data flows to boost the efficiency of the medical systems, enhance security, and improve informed decision-making in real-time. However, the devices segment is estimated to be the fastest growing segment in the global internet of things in healthcare market during forecast period owing to the advancements of the wearable sensor devices, implanted sensor devices and other stationary devices. Among these devices, wearable device is the highest growing devices market. This is attributed to a surge in awareness to adopt the wearable devices, an increase in trend of self-monitoring and analysis health data. In addition, medical wearable devices can also help measure information such as blood pressure, cholesterol, blood sugar, and others, which resulted in a boost in the growth of the devices market during the forecast period.

The global internet of things in healthcare market is highly competitive, and prominent players have adopted various strategies for garnering maximum market share. These include collaboration, product launch, partnership, and acquisition. Major players operating in the market include Apple Inc., Cisco Systems Inc., GE Healthcare Ltd., Google (Alphabet), International Business Machines Corporation, Medtronic PLC, Microsoft Corporation, Proteus Digital Health, Koninklijke Philips N.V., QUALCOMM Incorporated, and Abbott Laboratories

By application, the patient monitoring segment is accounted for the highest revenue generator in 2019, owing to as patient monitoring enables data from devices to be collected and made available to healthcare professionals in real-time. Internet of Things in Healthcare services segment holds a dominant position in 2019 (Telugunta & Choudhary, 2020).

Table 1. Iot in healthcare market segmentation.

Application	Component	End User
Patient Monitoring	Sensor devices: - Implantable - Wearable - Others	Healthcare Providers
Clinical Operation and Workflow Optimization	Systems and Software: - Network Layer - Database Layer - Analytics Layer	Patients
Clinical Imaging	Services: - Architecture (system integration) - Consulting - Application Development	Healthcare Payers
Fitness and Wellness Measurement		Research Laboratories
Drug Development		Government Authority

Adapted from (Telugunta & Choudhary, 2020)

Blockchain

The first time a concept like blockchain was introduced was in 1991, when Stuart Haber and W. S. Stornetta (Haber & Stornetta, 1991) described a cryptographically secured chain of blocks for time stamping digital documents. Later, in 2000 Stefan Konst introduced his theory of cryptographic secured chains and identified strategies for its implementation (Konst & Wätjen, 2000). But the most important contribution to blockchain, came only in 2008, in a white paper written by Satoshi Nakamoto, a person or group of people, whose identity is still not known. Nakamoto introduced Bitcoin, a peer-to-peer electronic cash system that allowed for two parties to make a transaction overcoming the need for a trusted third party (Nakamoto, 2008). In January 2009, Nakamoto mined the first block of bitcoin and some days later, the first transaction took place: a man called Hal Finney received 10 bitcoins from Nakamoto. Later, in 2013, Vitalik Buterin introduced in a white paper, a new blockchain-based distributed computing platform, Ethereum, that featured a scripting functionality, called smart contract (Buterin, 2014). Blockchain and Bitcoin are concepts that are intertwined and often have been mistaken as the same, but in fact Blockchain is the technology behind Bitcoin, and its impact has surpassed Bitcoin and other cryptocurrencies and has affirmed itself as a groundbreaking technology far reaching into very different domains. Blockchain 1.0 was in fact focused on transactions, blockchain 2.0 initiated in 2013 with Ethereum and smart contracts and includes different applications in the financial area. In the last few years, the introduction of different platforms that aim to overcome the problems of Bitcoin and Ethereum, these are already part of Blockchain 3.0 and aim for global utilization of the technology. Blockchain can be defined as a decentralized database structured in blocks, each containing a certain amount of information and distributed through a chain (the ledger), and hence the name Blockchain. It is an immutable and distributed ledger that ensures data integrity (Nakamoto, 2008).

A block consists of two parts: the block header and the block body. The block header includes a block version, a parent block hash, a merkle root, a timestamp, bits and nonce. The block body is where the information about the transaction is stored. The information is organized in a Merkle tree, that is a binary tree containing cryptographic hashes, that enables all the information to be verified extremely efficiently and rapidly (Merkle, 1990) by producing an overall fingerprint of the transaction that occurred in the blockchain. In very simple terms, the Merkle Tree takes an enormous number of transaction IDs and runs them through a mathematical process that results in one 64-character code, which is called the Merkle Root, that is present at the Block Header also reducing the amount of data that has to be maintained for verification purposes (Figure 2).

Figure 2. Blockchain structure.
Adapted from (Liang, 2020)

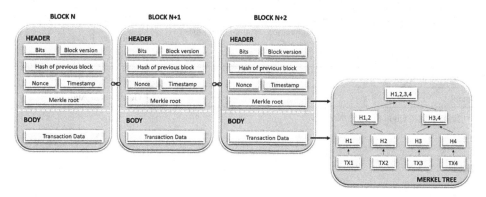

To achieve its goals, blockchain relies heavily on cryptography. In fact, the digital signatures based on asymmetric encryption are the ones used in blockchain networks. The utilization of public key cryptosystems for digital signatures was first suggested by Diffie and Hellman (Diffie & Hellman, 1976). Blockchain uses public key cryptosystems; in fact, every node of the network receives two different sets of keys: a public and a private key. Before a node initiates the transaction, it signs it with its own private key. The other nodes in the network will be then able to verify the authenticity of the transaction by using the public key.

Another key feature of the blockchain is the Hash function, which is the process of taking an input string of any length and turning it into a cryptographic fixed output. The hash function is deterministic which means that it should originate the exact same hash for the same message. The primary identifier of a block is its cryptographic hash, which works like a digital fingerprint. Ideal hashing functions should have the following properties:

- **Pre-Image Resistance:** one important aspect of secure cryptographic hash functions is that they are one-way, which means that no algorithm can produce the original input. It is very hard for a hash value to be decoded since all possible combinations will have to be tried before that, which poses a computational problem that is hard to solve. This feature provides a layer of security to any transaction.
- **Collision Resistance:** that means that it should be hard to find two different inputs that originate the same hash. Majority of current cryptographic hash functions are designed to be collision resistant, but that does not mean that they in fact are; collisions occur but they are typically very hard to find.
- **Second Pre-Image Resistance:** refers to the property in which it is computationally infeasible to find any second input that has the same output as a given input.

The peer-to-peer network is also essential for blockchain technology. This network involves a large number of computers, and each of these peers performs a specific task within the network to facilitate the activities of the blockchain eliminating problems related to the vulnerability of centralized servers while using different cryptographic methods to ensure the security of the network.

Blockchain miners are special nodes in that network that are responsible for securing and validating transactions. Mining is the process by which new transactions records (blocks) are added to the ledger (the blockchain). This process is intentionally designed to be challenging and resource-intensive and the miner that solves that complex mathematical puzzle is rewarded. The miner presents the new block that must be verified by the other nodes of the network and only if they reach a consensus the block is added.

In summary, someone requests a transaction that online is represented as a block. The block is broadcasted through a P2P network consisting of different nodes. These nodes are responsible for validating the transaction in a process called mining. The first miner to validate the new block is rewarded and the block is added to the blockchain which provides an unalterable, transparent record of all transactions. The transaction is then completed.

Blockchain has the following key features that are summarized below:

- **Decentralization:** this is one key feature of blockchain but also one of its main advantages. In conventional centralized systems the transaction needs to be validated by a central authority, in blockchain the validation is through the P2P network which means that both system and the data are resistant to technical failures and malicious attacks, and since the network includes sometimes thousands of nodes and each node has a local copy of the ledger there is no single point of failure.
- **Trustless System:** in blockchain there is no need for a central authority to validate the transaction. Moreover, the different nodes don´t need to trust one another. In fact, by distributing the transaction across the ledger and relying on a consensus to ensure its validity, blockchain overcomes the need for a trustworthy environment. By cutting the intermediaries it also reduces the costs and transaction fees.
- **Transparency and Immutability:** Each transaction is recorded on the Blockchain and is available to every node in a public network making it a transparent system. Since each block is linked to the previous one through the hash function, any attempt to change the content will affect all the other subsequent blocks that are replicated over different nodes, making it almost tamper-proof.

- **Traceability:** The distributed and transparent nature of the blockchain allows for it to be easily traced back to its origin. Every block header has a timestamp which records the time when the block is created. Nodes can therefore verify and trace the origin of the previous blocks.
- **Non-Repudiation:** Every transaction is cryptographically signed with a private key and since the private key is specific for its owner, the transaction cannot be denied by its initiator.
- **Anonymity:** Every node or user can interact with the network using a self-generated address that keeps the identity of the participant protected, overcoming the need for a central party to have users´ information.

Blockchain and Healthcare Market

Blockchain is already changing our lives from the way all citizens make transactions, manage assets, vote, and even listen to music to the way it is transforming financial institutions, companies and governments, among others. Likewise, blockchain also has the potential to completely change the landscape of healthcare.

The WHO (World Health Organization) Constitution states that "…the highest attainable standard of health as a fundamental right of every human being". Access to affordable and efficient healthcare services is essential for human wellbeing and it is a driver of long-term economic growth as well as societal development. The healthcare industry is one of the fastest-growing industries despite still being characterized as old-fashioned, overly complex, and impenetrable, mostly due to an inefficient and outdated infrastructure.

The European healthcare systems are currently facing several challenges associated with population aging. In fact, the costs associated with delivering healthcare rise faster than the GDP of each one of the European countries, which is not sustainable in the long run. Moreover, the current pandemic is adding pressure to an already pressured system which will have consequences in years to come.

It is of the utmost importance to identify and implement solutions that will strengthen healthcare systems, contributing to their sustainability with the goal of promoting better health of the citizens. Government, consumers, payers, providers will have to reimagine how care is delivered and leverage technology to reduce cost while improving or maintaining quality of the services.

Blockchain presents itself as one interesting technology that can help face some of these challenges. While the adoption of blockchain in the healthcare industry was slow in comparison to other industries, this has steadily been changing. In fact, according to a new research study published by Global Market Insights, Inc, global Blockchain Technology in Healthcare market is set to reach a value of USD 1,636.7 million by 2025 (Bhutani & Wadhwani, 2017). Its impact in the industry is widespread and its applications will only increase in the next few years. Figure 3 highlights some examples of possible application of blockchain in different domains of healthcare.

One example of this utilization of blockchain in healthcare is its role in the improvement of medical record management. New technological solutions are essential to improving patients care while reducing associated costs. Current healthcare information systems have serious problems and challenges which include fragmented patient data, centralized systems that can be used as single points of attack, and the lack of patient-oriented services.

Figure 3. Overview of applications of blockchain in the healthcare sector
(Weinberg, 2019)

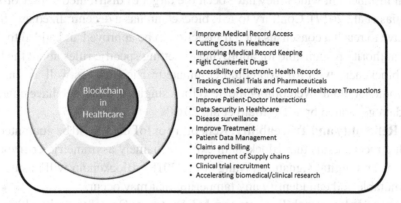

One important step towards improving healthcare has been the introduction of electronic health records (EHR) which enables doctors to easily store, view, share, and update patient records (Shuaib et al., 2019). EHRs may include very different formats of files, including images, videos, text among others that pertain to clinical data (laboratory results, imaging data and even measurements of vital signs) but also billing information and other general details that when handled incorrectly can cause very serious issues. Costs associated with EHR adoption, implementation, and maintenance of technological infrastructure necessary as well as concerns about privacy and security have been identified as problematic (Menachemi & Collum, 2011).

Moreover, data generated in healthcare settings is growing rapidly, with healthcare data suffering from various challenges, including interoperability between systems and fragmented data. In fact, patients go to different healthcare facilities and there must be exchange of the medical records, which is often hindered by different EHR systems used between institutions.

Although the EHRs are individual, patients do not control the EHRs themselves, where they are stored nor who has access to them and therefore, they are regarded with some suspicion. Generally, within institutions, the EHRs are stored in a centralized infrastructure, which by itself constitutes a risk (McDermott et al., 2019).

Blockchain has the potential to transform healthcare and help solve some of these issues by making electronic health records more efficient, secure and intermediate free. Blockchain will empower the patients to take initiative and be at the center of decision regarding their health and what happens to their data Due to its nature and for the reasons explained in previous sections, blockchain will increase system security, data privacy and security as well as improving interoperability of health data .

Blockchain for Internet of Things (BIoT) and Healthcare Market

As previously described in this chapter both Blockchain and Internet of Things are highly disruptive technologies that if integrated can open an infinite number of new possibilities. The integration of blockchain technology is often seen as the solution for the privacy and reliability concerns of Internet of Things but there are several other benefits associated with this integration:

1. **Improving Security:** The IoT devices are very easily compromised, and in fact in the past there have been several instances in which they have been the target of distributed denial-of-service (DDoS) attacks (Kolias et al., 2017). Contrary to IoT, blockchain has a decentralized architecture in which the nodes have to reach a consensus for a transaction to be approved and added to the ledger, there is no single authority responsible for approving or setting specific rules about the transactions. By combining blockchain with IoT you could eliminate traffic flows as well as single point failure, but also it would facilitate overcoming the need for a single institution to have control over the vast amount of data generated by IoT (Atlam et al., 2018).

2. **Increasing Reliability and Traceability:** Reliability of IoT data could be guaranteed by the several cryptographic mechanisms that Blockchain exploits, namely asymmetric encryption algorithms, hash functions and digital signature (Wang et al., 2018). Blockchain will ensure that data in the chain is immutable and can identify any tampering that may occur.

3. **Enhancement of Interoperability between IoT Systems:** One of the critical issues in IoT is that the different proprietary IoT platforms and systems are still not interoperable (Noura et al., 2019). Blockchain can improve the interoperability of these systems by converting the heterogeneous data from different devices and extracting, processing, transforming, and storing the data into a blockchain.

4. **Reducing Costs:** Blockchain utilizes a peer-to-peer structure without need for a central point of control, which reduces business expenses. The existing IoT solutions are expensive due to this centralized architecture which requires high infrastructure and maintenance costs.

5. **Accelerated Data Change:** The smart contracts are another relevant feature of Blockchain, that could record and manage all IoT interactions, which could be used to accelerate data exchange and enable processes between IoTs while removing the middleman. The contract clauses can be embedded in smart contracts and they are executed automatically when the specified conditions are satisfied (Viriyasitavat et al., 2019).

Reflecting about all the benefits of Blockchain and IoT (BIoT), the areas that can be apply and take advantage of this technology are infinite. BIoT has already been applied in several areas like food industry, pharmaceutical industry, healthcare, etc. It can help increase data legitimacy or reliability and provide distributed identity, authentication, and authorization mechanisms without the need for central authorities (Reyna et al., 2018).

Practical Applications

This section aims to describe some practical applications of Blockchain of Internet of Things (BIoT) in Healthcare helping face the challenges and make people and healthcare professionals life´s better.

Remote Healthcare Systems

The increase of the elderly population worldwide translates into a series of healthcare concerns, mostly related with the increase of chronic diseases every year. The senior patients visit the doctor routinely to be diagnosed and receive treatment. Besides that, when the senior patients don't stay hospitalized, they need help at home from healthcare professionals that work in the community. Therefore, remote healthcare has become extremely important. With this technology and new medical devices, patients can be monitored for a long period of time, increasing their quality of life and gaining more autonomy.

The devices that compose the remote health system are a combination of IoT and wearable technology because they are efficient and convenient. The patient wears several different physiologically sensible sensors that can be worn or implanted to measure vital signs in real life, such as blood pressure, heart rate and temperature(Pham et al., 2018). This data is sent to a centralized server, usually through a mobile phone, who collects and sends the sensor data. Healthcare professionals can access and analyze this information, preventing the need for face-to-face appointments, which is more convenient to the patient.

However, all of this is based on IoT which leads to several questions and concerns about security and privacy of data specially because the IoT architecture could be a target for non-expected hacking attacks. This can be dangerous because health information is one of the most sensitive types of data. The privacy of this data must be maintained while the EHR needs to be manageable by the healthcare teams and the patient itself.

Since the number of medical devices capable of monitoring the patient (IoT devices) has increased in the last couple of years, the privacy and security of patients is becoming an increased concern topic. To protect personal data, this BIoT project uses blockchain-based smart contracts for managing patient's information and medical devices (Pham et al., 2018). Some projects used the Ethereum protocol to create a remote healthcare system that integrates healthcare professionals and patients. This system provides a connection between the medical devices and its sensors, that generates the information about the patient's health, and directly stores the information on blockchain. Because of that, the system reduces the size of the blockchain as well as saving the amount of coins needed for transactions. This fact is especially interesting because abnormal data from the patients' sensors can trigger an emergency contact to the doctor and hospital for immediate treatment which in some cases could be lifesaving.

The author of the project already tested it with a verified smart contract on Ethereum Protocol on an experiment environment with real devices, and it works well at small scale (Luan Pham, 2018).

So, to summarize this application of BIoT in Remote Healthcare, the authors propose several changes to improve the remote system:

1. **To ensure the privacy and security of patient data:** Using a smart contract.
2. **A processing mechanism that filters the data from sensors before writing to blockchain**: Alerts the healthcare providers about abnormal data collected.
3. **With a highly secure system based in blockchain technology**: A GPS was incorporated to locate the patient in an emergency situation (Pham et al., 2018).

BIoT and Pharmaceutical Supply Chain (PSC)

Enyinda & Tolliver defined the Pharmaceutical Supply Chain (PSC) as a channel by which medicines have been shipped at the appropriate place and at the proper time (Enyinda & Tolliver, 2009).

Current PSC present numerous challenges as:

*   Rapid demand changes in the market, fierce competition that puts pressure on margins of the products.
*   Extensive supply chains increase the risks of data manipulation (too many suppliers for example).

- Ineffective supply chain risk management: the lack of monitoring or not having the right tools to do it.
- Lack of end-to-end visibility.
- Obsolescence of technologies.

Additionally, the pharmaceutical market faces the challenge of counterfeit pharmaceutical products. According to around 30% of the total medicine sold in Africa, Asia, and Latin America is counterfeit which could have major implications in citizens´ health and lives and a huge economic impact for the pharmaceutical industry. In fact, according to the same organization, the counterfeit market represents 200 billion dollars per year. Therefore, pharma companies and distributors are looking for new solutions that could improve supply chain security and traceability and therefore tackle this major issue (Jamil et al., 2019)Implementing electronic records based on blockchain technology will increase the traceability and auditability of pharmaceutical products.

When analyzing these challenges, it is important to understand the solutions that BIoT offers to this entire process. In a practical way, many things can be done to improve the supply chain. In terms of traceability, (the ability to monitor events and metadata associated with a product), blockchain technology can bring auditability, a full audit trail of data, creating a record of all the traces of the product. On compliance, (the standards and controls provide the evidence that regulatory conditions are met), blockchain brings immutability when all the operations are time and place proof, with only one source of data. Pharmaceutical companies are increasingly under pressure with regulatory issues, so this particular area is crucial to the system. On flexibility, (the ability to adapt to events or issues, without significantly increasing operational costs), blockchain offers smart contracts, a way to track data in real time along the supply chain. And at last, on stakeholder management, (an effective governance in place to enable communication, risk, reduction and trust among the involved parties), blockchain provides disintermediation, enable peer-to-peer interactions based on digital signatures (Kehoe et al., 2017)

But implementing BIoT is difficult because it is such a disruptive innovation, and the different stakeholders have to make the effort to invest in human and financial resources to implement BIoT. The investment must be made along the supply chain, from the raw material suppliers to the hospitals but also pharmacies to ensure that the product that the consumer is buying is in the best possible conditions.

Some practical examples of strategies that companies are adopting to improve the process, include:

- Using a "sealed" smart device to authenticate the goods. This sealed devices uniquely identify the object on which they are attached.
- If it's not possible to attach sensors to the good itself, it can be put on the packaging to track the goods through the supply chain.
- In the healthcare industry supply chain could be helpful to track and secure medical supplies. Combining IoT sensors with blockchain, to collect and capture information will help certifying the authenticity, and viability of the supplies through the entire supply chain and will help detect potential frauds and manipulations (Laurent, 2017).

Overall, the major advantages of the BIoT are: ensuring that all the stakeholders are at the same level, and through decentralization increase security and reliability. It's a chain that brings more trust to all of the participants, with real time information updates. Integrated blockchain-IoT can enable trust, transparency and visibility by tracking the material from the origin to end customers (Laurent, 2017).

Our country's healthcare system, hospital and primary health care, is not yet prepared to implement such a new technology because they don't have the human or financial resources needed to do it.

BIoT on Clinical Trials Research

According to a study by Tufts Center for the Study of Drug Development, it costs more than $2.6 billion to bring a drug to market and the clinical development is an important part of those costs (DiMasi et al., 2016).

Clinical trials are notoriously complex and expensive and serious challenges must be overcome to ensure their success. These challenges include patient recruitment and retention, rising costs to meet regulatory policies, monitoring complexity and issues related to data privacy and security. Moreover, data is typically obtained exclusively at clinical settings and real-world data is missing, often skewering results.

The utilization of IoT in clinical trials is still in its early stage. The Asthma Mobile Health Study was a good example of how a clinical research observational study was performed using a smartphone. It was a study that involved 7,593 participants from across the United States. Tasks such as recruitment, consent, and enrollment, that are generally resource intensive and costly were conducted remotely via smartphone. The platform that was developed for the study enabled the collection of clinical, environmental, and passive biometric data providing important findings on asthma care and research (Chan et al., 2017). Similarly, the mPower, was a clinical observational study about Parkinson disease conducted solely through an app interface in a phone. Enrolled subjects were requested to answer questions but also perform specific tasks that were recorded by the sensors in the phone. This app enabled the collection and monitoring of information about the daily changes in Parkinson´s disease symptom severity as well as potentially assessing the effect of medication (Bot et al., 2016). Although the utilization of IoT in the recruitment as well as in the long distancing monitoring in real life, is very interesting, one important challenge to overcome, that is highlighted by (Chan et al., 2017), is data security which could potentially be tackled by the blockchain technology. Collecting and analyzing real-world evidence is fundamental for phase IV studies, to understand the long-term efficacy of drugs, track possible non-expected effects on patients' health and wellbeing or even identify new therapeutic indications, likewise the integration of blockchain and IoT could be key for this activity.

Clinical trial research could profit from blockchain main benefits, namely transparency, immutability, disintermediation, auditability, and trust. Even though, the advantages are obvious there are very few examples in which the blockchain technology has been used by the pharmaceutical industry in clinical trials, which might be due to lack of regulatory instructions or a clear position on the matter from the responsible agencies, in addition to a general lack of knowledge about the technology which hinders its acceptance.

Blockchain could help in the recruitment of patients and their engagement which is a key success factor for clinical trials. It could be used for the patient to give consent to participate in the trial, archiving the informed consent through cryptographic validation in an unalterable and transparent way, that upon any change to the trial protocol needs to be accepted and validated again by the patient (Benchoufi et al., 2018). Data integrity and provenance are key in clinical trials. Sponsors and clinical sites must prove the origin and integrity of all the data to the regulatory agencies which can be ensured by blockchain. Data management is key to ensure the success of the clinical trial and blockchain has been proposed to improve software systems used for clinical data management. Multiple projects exist in that realm, namely: Medvault, Gem Health Network, BitHealth, among others (Omar et al., 2020).

One example of the integration of the two technologies is the solution offered by InnoME, Essentim and Cryptowerk that enables IoT data acquisition and allows for easy blockchain-based digital notarization. The solution can be used to collect important raw data using sensors in combination with measurement equipment, to ensure the integrity of clinical trial data from IoT devices, to detect changes to any data set being able to trace it back to the origin, to track all drugs used in clinical trials according to regulatory agencies demands, and to instantly verify the identity and experience of all the clinical research staff involved in the study (Cryptowerk, 2018). .).

Another example of a combination of IoT and Blockchain is the digital health application proposed by Angeletti et al, that confers a secure way to control the flow of personal data in the recruitment of participants for clinical trials. Blockchain technology is employed to guarantee that all personal data is only shared with the right stakeholders when the subject is enrolled in the clinical trial, ensuring privacy and confidentiality. Moreover, they use IoT devices potentially at the subject´s homes to collect relevant data that can be used in clinical trial recruitment process, to pre-screen for suitable candidates that match the inclusion criteria (Angeletti et al., 2017).

There are no magic bullets that will solve the clinical development challenges, but technology will certainly play a part. IoT is used widely in Healthcare, for example in remote monitoring, but not so often in clinical development. On the other hand, the potential of Blockchain for clinical trials is recognized but very few examples of real application exist. The combination of these technologies can open new avenues and contribute, for the successful, timely and cost-efficient implementation of clinical trials therefore accelerating the discovery of new innovative therapies that can change people´s lives.

SOLUTIONS AND RECOMMENDATIONS

In this section the authors explore how BIoT could have been used during the COVID-19 pandemics, to address a lot of the problems in the healthcare industry and how it can be used in its aftermath.

Remote Healthcare System on COVID-19

The SARS-CoV-2 pandemic is a real-life example about the importance of collecting patient's information because data is the key to fully comprehend the disease, the dissemination, and the consequences of the infection. But sharing the information worldwide must avoid breaking national and international data sharing regulations. Patients' privacy is mandatory and a major concern. However, detailed information such as blood oxygen level, heart rate and medication doses can be gathered by integrating medical devices (Medical IoT).

Having a decentralized process with blockchain could help and solve the privacy and security issues. Like the example before, blockchain supports real-time data sharing. And uploading the medical devices data remotely directly to a blockchain based system, can eliminate data forging and mutation, maintaining the trust in the numbers, improving the trust between stakeholders and protecting patient's privacy (Kalla et al., 2020).

In recent times, the outbreak of several viral infections across the world, including Ebola and Zika virus, have raised attention to a potential global health threat. Globalization enables spreading of infectious diseases (Chattu et al., 2019). Unfortunately, these examples were just a glimpse of what was yet to come. In late 2019, a new coronavirus started spreading in Wuhan in China. The SARS-CoV-2 epidemic has changed the global landscape and its impact is yet to be fully understood. This global pandemic crisis has highlighted the importance of effective and reactive surveillance mechanisms. It is of the utmost importance to spot the threat early and immediately report it to the health authorities to start preventive measurements. National health systems are ultimately responsible for the surveillance of infectious diseases, but these tasks are spread through many independent agencies, which then report back to a centralized information system. The process is slow, inefficient, and complex. Blockchain and IoT could help these independent agencies to collect, access and manage surveillance data and receive it in real time in a secure way enabling a faster and more informed response.

BIoT on PSC in COVID-19

In a previous chapter, the authors described that blockchain and IoT technology can be used to deal with many problems and gaps on PSC. With the COVID-19 pandemic, many of these issues became even more obvious. During this pandemic crisis, the world has watched healthcare systems struggle with shortage of pharmaceuticals, personal protective equipment, medical devices, and medical supplies. The rapid escalation in demand meant traditional procurement processes were no longer suitable; identifying new vendors and swiftly reallocating the supplies was essential. But instead of finding innovative solutions, countries, states, hospitals ended up fighting each other for the supplies and in many cases overpaying for them (Mirchandani, 2020).

Moreover, many factories had to interrupt or decrease their production activities, in some cases because of the lockdown, in others because they were simply not prepared (equipped and designed) to the "new normal" of social distancing and using protective equipment. The import and export of goods suffered a big impact and caused the disruption of global supply and demand.

The complexity and fragmentation of the conventional supply chains could be tackled with blockchain and IoT. Blockchain has the capacity to connect pharmaceutical suppliers and customers, while maintaining a secure record of each transaction which protects every party and ensures transparency and immutability across supply chains. It was proposed to increase the use of technology to improve forecasting, to reduce the complexity of the distribution system, and to utilize the resources effectively (Kumar & Pundir, 2020). Also, Blockchain can increase trust among stakeholders, because they can build the supply chain together, and not just be dependent on each other. That is the major difference with a blockchain implementation. It supports auditability, provenance, and transparency, based on smart contracts with high level of access restrictions and automation (Kalla et al., 2020).

COVID-19 is having a huge impact in majority of companies, nevertheless some are more resilient, adapting, and able to tackle this issue. It all depends on how companies prepare for the unknown. The BIoT and new digital technologies can improve the communication between stakeholders, anticipate disruptions and reconfigure themselves appropriately to mitigate major impacts.

According to Kumar and Pundir there are benefits of implement BIoT in a traditional PCS changing some of the standards in this area (Table 2).

Table 2. Benefits of integrating blockchain-IoT in supply chain

Activity in PSC	Blockchain	IoT	Benefits
Manufacturing the product	Registration of product with unique id and generation of a new block with product ID in the blockchain network	Product ID is scanned and transferred to the cloud	Transparency, Trust, Product details and Data security
Transported to distributor/ warehouse	Generation of smart contract block, Verification of manufacturer's contract, generation of transaction ID, product id and block ID verification	Path tracking and product ID verification GPS and smart devices (camera,sensors, temperature control, etc.) enabled track	Visibility,Traceabilit y,Reliability, Quality tracking,Transparency, Trust, Immutability
Received at distribution center warehouse	Verification of contract of the supplier, transaction ID, product ID, and block ID	Track the location of the product and update the specified quantity (information is stored in the cloud)	
Distribution center/ warehouse to retailers /hospitals	Enabled the verification of product ID and order ID	Helps in continuous tracking of products till it reaches to the final customers	

Source: (Kumar & Pundir, 2020)

BIoT on Clinical Trials: The COVID-19 Impact

COVID-19 pandemics might be a driver for the implementation of new technologies in clinical trials. This pandemic has represented an unparalleled challenge for clinical research but also poses an opportunity to innovate and implement new solutions that will enable fast, simple and cost-effective clinical development up to the standards expected by the regulatory agencies while having the patients´ interest at heart.

In the past few months, COVID-19 pandemic has disrupted the healthcare industry and the clinical trials are no exception. Since the beginning of 2019, thousands of clinical trials were either put on hold or experienced delays, as clinical sites were often overwhelmed with COVID-19 patients and resources were scarce (van Dorn, 2020). Moreover, the COVID-19 posed a risk for those patients that were enrolled in these trials and had to frequently visit the clinical sites, which was especially serious since many of these patients are already populations at risk. Many patients have discontinued participation and others are less likely to participate in any ongoing trials. These challenges will most likely persist till effective vaccines are widely available and therefore new strategies will have to be implemented to overcome this situation, in fact according to FDA Guidance on the Conduct of Clinical Trials of Medical Products during COVID-19 Pandemic, alternative methods for safety assessments could be implemented when necessary and feasible, which could include virtual visits, remote monitoring, and the use of electronic data sources (Fda & Cder, 2020). The use of mobile devices, smartphones, wearables, and IoT technology can produce real time, high quality data overcoming possible errors associated with human data collection while blockchain would ensure its integrity and security. Moreover, IoT would enable continuous monitoring, generating larger data pools which can be used to better assess the efficacy of a drug, its potential side effects, as well as its overall impact on patient's quality of life.

Related to COVID-19 research, there are currently 4274 clinical trials registered in ClinicalTrials.gov. In less than one year, researchers have identified and characterized a novel virus, developed diagnostics tools, proposed treatment protocols, and tested the efficacy of therapies and vaccines in clinical trials. Similarly, to other therapeutic areas, IoT in combination with Blockchain could also play an important role in these clinical trials by enabling virtual patient recruitment, consent, and data collection. Despite the hard times, valuable lessons have been learned on clinical development, pinpointing the main obstacles to overcome, and developing and implementing new strategies to streamline the process.

FUTURE RESEARCH DIRECTIONS

Blockchain technology can be applied to all industries (Makridakis & Christodoulou, 2019). And can be completely disruptive in so many ways for the business. It's not a surprise that many startups are using Blockchain to solve many of the company's issues.

However, BIoT is still is its early stage and the future brings challenges that need to be overcome. Some of these include:

- **Scalability:** the large number of nodes of IoT can be a difficulty, since blockchain scales poorly as the number of nodes in the network increases.
- **Processing Power and Time:** blockchain encryption algorithms required a high demand computing power. And some of the IoT devices do not have the computer power necessary to run these algorithms.
- **Storage**: Blockchain eliminates the need for a central server because it stores all transactions in a decentralized way, storing the data from the ledger in the system nodes. The distributed ledger will increase in size as time passes. Many IoT devices don't have a large storage capacity.
- **Lack of Skills:** Blockchain is a new technology and very few people have profound knowledge and experience with it. On the other hand, IoT devices exist everywhere. Therefore, efficient and productive integration of blockchain and IoT is only possible when experts of the different areas are more knowledgeable about the advantages and pitfalls of each.
- **Legal and Compliance**: Blockchain permits to connect different people from different places without having any legal or compliance code to follow, and this can be a serious issue to manufacture and services providers. This can be a barrier to implementing blockchain in many businesses.
- **Naming and Discovery**: Blockchain and IoT are two separate technologies that were not created with integration as main purpose, which means that nodes were not meant to find each other in the network (Atlam et al., 2018).

According to Makridakis and Christodoulou, the future of blockchain can move in two directions. The first will include all the applications requiring decentralized and super secured networks like smart contracts. In the future, there will be no alternative than to use blockchain with all these applications. The other direction is the use of blockchain with AI that when combined can substantially add value. Blockchain and AI can be used synergistically to improve the safety of big data and decentralizing who holds it. Now big data is centralized and owned almost exclusively by Google or Facebook. By using IoT and AI, people could preserve their own data and choose how and for who their information would be available. "At least, Blockchain and AI can cooperate on cybersecurity by combining AI and blockchain together to create a double shield against cyberattacks by training ML algorithms to automate real-time threat detection and to continuously learn about the behavior of attackers, while decentralized blockchains can minimize the inherent vulnerability of centralized databases" (Makridakis & Christodoulou, 2019).

Data Privacy

The explosion of IoT adoption is bound to threat its user´s privacy and pose significant data protection risks. The IoT devices constantly collect and share a lot of information that includes personal data, location, health data, users activities, amongst others, which means that data protection is a must have feature in all IoT systems. In healthcare, ensuring patients data privacy and security is of the utmost importance.

In this context and at the European level, the General Data Protection Regulation (GDPR), has been adopted on 14 April 2016, and came into force on the 25th of May 2018. This legislation set new rules that aim to facilitate the free movement of personal data between the EU's various Member States but also to protect and regulate data privacy. GDPR applies to any organization that holds or processes data of EU citizens. According to Article 5, the principles for personal data are: lawfulness, fairness and transparency, purpose limitation, data minimization, accuracy, storage limitation and accountability. GDPR includes a specific part dedicated to health data; it states that personal data concerning health should include all data pertaining health status (mental or physical) of an individual, in the past, present and future, as well as genetic and biometric data regardless of its source. Much of this data is nowadays obtained through technology, including IoT devices (*General Data Protection Regulation (GDPR) – Official Legal Text*, n.d.).

Some of the major issues about IoT according to the GDPR are transparency, consent, privacy. Companies are required to give customers or patients full access to their own personal data, specify how personal data is collected and used and offer clear opt-out options, and when it happens report data breaches (*Ethical IoT: GDPR, Personal Data, and Maintaining Consumer Trust*, n.d.). Importantly, users must provide consent and it needs to be informed, freely given, specific, and it requires an affirmative action. IoT companies must ensure that their devices strictly collect only the data that is necessary for fulfilling the relevant purpose, fulfilling the GDPR's principles of data minimization and purpose limitation. Moreover, they must ensure the right to be forgotten, meaning the IoT device must erase all data that it holds about an individual when requested to do so for example upon consent withdrawal (El-Mousa, 2018).

Although the application of blockchain to IoT could help manage some of these issues, for example consent could be achieved using smart contracts (Kouzinopoulos et al., 2018) and blockchain would be essential to provide security and privacy, blockchain is not devoid of challenges in what concerns to GDPR. The first one is accountability; GDPR assumes that there is a data controller, a natural or legal person, public authority, agency or other body, that must be able to demonstrate compliance with GDPR, but blockchains are distributed databases, so the allocation of responsibility and accountability is complex. The other challenge relates to the fact that according to GDPR data can be modified or erased when required to comply with legal requirements and can only be stored for a limited period of time except for public interest, scientific or historical research purposes or statistical purposes, but the information stored in Blockchain is immutable and perpetual as a way of ensuring integrity of the data (*Blockchain and the General Data Protection Regulation Can Distributed Ledgers Be Squared with European Data Protection Law?*, n.d.).

GDPR has been introduced only recently, and emerging technologies might not have been taken in account when developing it. But COVID-19 has pushed forward these new technologies, including blockchain and IoT, as part of solutions to tackle a lot of the pandemic associated challenges, therefore the authors consider that there needs to be further clarification by the lawmakers in order to accommodate the societal demand for innovation and unlock the full potential of the technologies while ensuring the privacy of citizens data.

CONCLUSION

In this paper, the authors reflected on the importance of blockchain and IoT technologies in the health-care system, focusing on its application or possible future applications during the COVID-19 crisis and its aftermath. These two technologies were not created to be used together and are used separately in the healthcare industry to tackle different issues. The IoT industry has been on the market for some decades now, and the number of medical devices that allow data collection and interconnection remotely increases exponentially every year. Nevertheless, the security problems due to the IoT architecture must be handled to ensure better privacy and security. Blockchain technology will help overcome these issues associated with IoT. The three cases explored in this article demonstrate the potential of integrating these two technologies in the healthcare sector. As the world faces COVID-19 pandemics consequences, it is of the utmost importance to understand how Blockchain for Internet of Things (BIoT) could make industries more resilient and help the public health systems cut costs while delivering the best care.

REFERENCES

Al-Omari, A., Rabaan, A. A., Salih, S., Al-Tawfiq, J. A., & Memish, Z. A. (2019). MERS coronavirus outbreak: Implications for emerging viral infections. *Diagnostic Microbiology and Infectious Disease*, 93(3), 265–285. Advance online publication. doi:10.1016/j.diagmicrobio.2018.10.011 PMID:30413355

Angeletti, F., Chatzigiannakis, I., & Vitaletti, A. (2017). The role of blockchain and IoT in recruiting participants for digital clinical trials. *2017 25th International Conference on Software, Telecommunications and Computer Networks (SoftCOM)*, 1–5. 10.23919/SOFTCOM.2017.8115590

Atlam, H. F., Alenezi, A., Alassafi, M. O., & Wills, G. B. (2018). Blockchain with Internet of Things: Benefits, Challenges, and Future Directions. *International Journal of Intelligent Systems and Applications*, 10(6), 40–48. doi:10.5815/ijisa.2018.06.05

Benchoufi, M., Porcher, R., & Ravaud, P. (2018). Blockchain protocols in clinical trials: Transparency and traceability of consent. *F1000 Research*, 6, 66. doi:10.12688/f1000research.10531.5 PMID:29167732

Bhutani, A., & Wadhwani, P. (2017). *Blockchain Technology Market 2019-2025 | Global Report*. https://www.gminsights.com/industry-analysis/blockchain-technology-market

Blockchain and the General Data Protection Regulation Can distributed ledgers be squared with European data protection law? (n.d.). doi:10.2861/535

Bot, B. M., Suver, C., Neto, E. C., Kellen, M., Klein, A., Bare, C., Doerr, M., Pratap, A., Wilbanks, J., Dorsey, E. R., Friend, S. H., & Trister, A. D. (2016). The mPower study, Parkinson disease mobile data collected using ResearchKit. *Scientific Data*, 3(1), 160011. Advance online publication. doi:10.1038data.2016.11 PMID:26938265

Buterin, V. (2014). *A next generation smart contract & decentralized application platform.* Academic Press.

Chahrour, M., Assi, S., Bejjani, M., Nasrallah, A. A., Salhab, H., Fares, M. Y., & Khachfe, H. H. (2020). A Bibliometric Analysis of COVID-19 Research Activity: A Call for Increased Output. *Cureus.* Advance online publication. doi:10.7759/cureus.7357 PMID:32328369

Chamola, V., Hassija, V., Gupta, V., & Guizani, M. (2020). A Comprehensive Review of the COVID-19 Pandemic and the Role of IoT, Drones, AI, Blockchain, and 5G in Managing its Impact. *IEEE Access: Practical Innovations, Open Solutions, 8*, 90225–90265. Advance online publication. doi:10.1109/AC-CESS.2020.2992341

Chan, Y. F. Y., Wang, P., Rogers, L., Tignor, N., Zweig, M., Hershman, S. G., Genes, N., Scott, E. R., Krock, E., Badgeley, M., Edgar, R., Violante, S., Wright, R., Powell, C. A., Dudley, J. T., & Schadt, E. E. (2017). The Asthma Mobile Health Study, a large-scale clinical observational study using ResearchKit. *Nature Biotechnology, 35*(4), 354–362. doi:10.1038/nbt.3826 PMID:28288104

Chattu, V. K., Nanda, A., Chattu, S. K., Kadri, S. M., & Knight, A. W. (2019). The emerging role of blockchain technology applications in routine disease surveillance systems to strengthen global health security. In Big Data and Cognitive Computing (Vol. 3, Issue 2, pp. 1–10). MDPI AG. doi:10.3390/bdcc3020025

Cheng, V. C. C., Lau, S. K. P., Woo, P. C. Y., & Yuen, K. Y. (2007). Severe Acute Respiratory Syndrome Coronavirus as an Agent of Emerging and Reemerging Infection. *Clinical Microbiology Reviews, 20*(4), 660–694. Advance online publication. doi:10.1128/CMR.00023-07 PMID:17934078

Cryptowerk. (2018). *Using Blockchains and IoT to Record Clinical Trial Data.* Retrieved January 22, 2021, from https://cryptowerk.com/blockchains-iot-clinical-trial-data

Diffie, W., & Hellman, M. (1976). New directions in cryptography. *IEEE Transactions on Information Theory, 22*(6), 644–654. doi:10.1109/TIT.1976.1055638

DiMasi, J. A., Grabowski, H. G., & Hansen, R. W. (2016). Innovation in the pharmaceutical industry: New estimates of R&D costs. *Journal of Health Economics, 47*, 20–33. doi:10.1016/j.jhealeco.2016.01.012 PMID:26928437

El-Mousa, F. (2018). *GDPR Privacy Implications for the Internet of Things.* https://www.researchgate.net/publication/331991225

Enyinda, C. I., & Tolliver, D. (2009). Taking Counterfeits out of the Pharmaceutical Supply Chain in Nigeria: Leveraging Multilayer Mitigation Approach. *Journal of African Business, 10*(2), 218–234. Advance online publication. doi:10.1080/15228910903187957

Ethical IoT, GDPR, Personal Data, and Maintaining Consumer Trust. (n.d.). Retrieved April 17, 2021, from https://www.aeris.com/news/post/ethical-iot-gdpr-personal-data-and-maintaining-consumer-trust/

FDA & CDER. (2020). *Conduct of Clinical Trials of Medical Products During the COVID-19 Public Health Emergency Guidance for Industry, Investigators, and Institutional Review Boards Preface Public Comment.* https://www.fda.gov/regulatory-

General Data Protection Regulation (GDPR) – Official Legal Text. (n.d.). Retrieved April 17, 2021, from https://gdpr-info.eu/

Haber, S., & Stornetta, W. S. (1991). How to Time-Stamp a Digital Document. In *LNCS* (Vol. 537). Springer-Verlag.

Jamil, F., Hang, L., Kim, K., & Kim, D. (2019). A Novel Medical Blockchain Model for Drug Supply Chain Integrity Management in a Smart Hospital. *Electronics (Basel)*, *8*(5), 505. doi:10.3390/electronics8050505

Kalla, A., Hewa, T., Mishra, R. A., Ylianttila, M., & Liyanage, M. (2020). The Role of Blockchain to Fight Against COVID-19. *IEEE Engineering Management Review*, *48*(3), 85–96. Advance online publication. doi:10.1109/EMR.2020.3014052

Kehoe, L., O'Connell, N., Andrzejewski, D., Gindner, K., & Dalal, D. (2017). *When two chains combine Supply chain meets blockchain*. https://www2.deloitte.com/tr/en/pages/technology/articles/when-two-chains-combine.html

Kolias, C., Kambourakis, G., Stavrou, A., & Voas, J. (2017). DDoS in the IoT: Mirai and other botnets. *Computer*, *50*(7), 80–84. doi:10.1109/MC.2017.201

Konst, S., & Wätjen, D. (2000). *Sichere Log-Dateien auf Grundlage kryptographisch verketteter Einträge*. http://publikationsserver.tu-braunschweig.de/get/64933

Kouzinopoulos, C. S., Giannoutakis, K. M., Votis, K., Tzovaras, D., Collen, A., Nijdam, N. A., Konstantas, D., Spathoulas, G., Pandey, P., & Katsikas, S. (2018, September 14). Implementing a Forms of Consent Smart Contract on an IoT-based Blockchain to promote user trust. *2018 IEEE (SMC) International Conference on Innovations in Intelligent Systems and Applications, INISTA 2018*. 10.1109/INISTA.2018.8466268

Krawiec, R. J., Housman, D., White, M., Filipova, M., Quarre, F., Barr, D., Nesbitt, A., Fedosova, K., Killmeyer, J., Israel, A., & Tsai, L. (2017). *Blockchain: Opportunities for Health Care*. Academic Press.

Kumar, S., & Pundir, A. K. (2020). *Blockchain–Internet of things (IoT) Enabled Pharmaceutical Supply Chain for COVID-19*. Academic Press.

Laurent, P. (2017). *Continuous interconnected supply chain Using Blockchain & Internet-of-Things in supply chain traceability*. Academic Press.

Liang, Y. C. (2020). Blockchain for dynamic spectrum management. In *Signals and Communication Technology* (pp. 121–146). Springer. doi:10.1007/978-981-15-0776-2_5

Makridakis, S., & Christodoulou, K. (2019). Blockchain: Current challenges and future prospects/applications. In Future Internet (Vol. 11, Issue 12). MDPI AG. doi:10.3390/fi11120258

McDermott, D. S., Kamerer, J. L., & Birk, A. T. (2019). Electronic Health Records- A Literature Review of Cyber Threats and Security Measures. *International Journal of Cyber Research and Education*, *1*(2), 42–49. doi:10.4018/IJCRE.2019070104

Menachemi, N., & Collum. (2011). Benefits and drawbacks of electronic health record systems. *Risk Management and Healthcare Policy*, *47*, 47. Advance online publication. doi:10.2147/RMHP.S12985 PMID:22312227

Merkle, R. C. (1990). *One Way Hash Functions and DES.*, doi:10.1007/0-387-34805-0_40

Mirchandani, P. (2020). Health Care Supply Chains: COVID-19 Challenges and Pressing Actions. In Annals of internal medicine (Vol. 173, Issue 4, pp. 300–301). NLM (Medline). doi:10.7326/M20-1326

Nagori, V. (2021). "Aarogya Setu": The mobile application that monitors and mitigates the risks of COVID-19 pandemic spread in India. *Journal of Information Technology Teaching Cases*. doi:10.1177/2043886920985863

Nakamoto, S. (2008). *Bitcoin: A Peer-to-Peer Electronic Cash System*. www.bitcoin.org

Noura, M., Atiquzzaman, M., & Gaedke, M. (2019). Interoperability in Internet of Things: Taxonomies and Open Challenges. *Mobile Networks and Applications*, *24*(3), 796–809. doi:10.100711036-018-1089-9

Omar, I. A., Jayaraman, R., Salah, K., Yaqoob, I., & Ellahham, S. (2020). Applications of Blockchain Technology in Clinical Trials: Review and Open Challenges. *Arabian Journal for Science and Engineering*. Advance online publication. doi:10.100713369-020-04989-3

Pham, H. L., Tran, T. H., & Nakashima, Y. (2018, December). A Secure Remote Healthcare System for Hospital Using Blockchain Smart Contract. *2018 IEEE Globecom Workshops (GC Wkshps)*. doi:10.1109/GLOCOMW.2018.8644164

Piscini, E., Dalton, D., & Kehoe, L. (2017). *Blockchain & Cyber Security. Let's Discuss*. https://www2.deloitte.com/tr/en/pages/technology-media-and-telecommunications/articles/blockchain-and-cyber.html

Reyna, A., Martín, C., Chen, J., Soler, E., & Díaz, M. (2018). On blockchain and its integration with IoT. Challenges and opportunities. *Future Generation Computer Systems*, *88*, 173–190. Advance online publication. doi:10.1016/j.future.2018.05.046

RFID Journal. (n.d.). Retrieved January 22, 2021, from https://www.rfidjournal.com/

Telugunta, R., & Choudhary, S. (2020). *Internet of Things (IOT) in Healthcare Market Size, and Growth 2027*. https://www.alliedmarketresearch.com/iot-healthcare-market

van Dorn, A. (2020). COVID-19 and readjusting clinical trials. *Lancet*, *396*(10250), 523–524. doi:10.1016/S0140-6736(20)31787-6 PMID:32828180

Viriyasitavat, W., da Xu, L., Bi, Z., & Pungpapong, V. (2019). Blockchain and Internet of Things for Modern Business Process in Digital Economy—The State of the Art. *IEEE Transactions on Computational Social Systems*, *6*(6), 1420–1432. doi:10.1109/TCSS.2019.2919325

Wang, H., Zheng, Z., Xie, S., Dai, H. N., & Chen, X. (2018). Blockchain challenges and opportunities: A survey. *International Journal of Web and Grid Services*, *14*(4), 352. doi:10.1504/IJWGS.2018.10016848

Weinberg, B. (2019). *14 Major Real Use Cases of Blockchain in Healthcare | OpenLedger Insights*. https://openledger.info/insights/blockchain-healthcare-use-cases/

Zimprich, S. (2019). *Data Protection and Blockchain - Security & Trust in Digital Services - Issues - dotmagazine*. https://www.dotmagazine.online/issues/security-trust-in-digital-services/data-protection-and-blockchain

KEY TERMS AND DEFINITIONS

Block: Blocks are records, which together form a blockchain. Each block contains a record of a transaction that is locked in chronological order and secured using cryptography. Each block contains, among other things, a record of recent transactions, and a reference to the block that came immediately before it.

Blockchain of Internet of Things: The integration of the two technologies. Blockchain will help solve some of the security issues typically associated with Internet of Things.

Blockchain Technology: Decentralized, distributed ledger that records transactions, tracks assets and builds trust.

Clinical Trial: A research study in which one or more human subjects are prospectively assigned to one or more interventions (which may include placebo or other control) to evaluate the effects of those interventions on health-related biomedical or behavioral outcomes.

COVID-19: Coronavirus disease is an infectious disease caused by a newly discovered coronavirus SARS-COV-2. The first case was detected in Wuhan, in China and quickly spread to a worldwide pandemic.

Internet of Things: Ubiquitous network of interconnected objects capable of information storage and exchange using embedded sensors, actuators, and other devices.

Pharmaceutical Supply Chain: A channel by which medicines have been shipped in the right quantity, with acceptable quality, at the appropriate place and costumers and at the proper time, and with optimum cost to be consistent with health system's objectives.

This research was previously published in Political and Economic Implications of Blockchain Technology in Business and Healthcare; pages 194-217, copyright year 2021 by Business Science Reference (an imprint of IGI Global).

Section 2
Development and Design Methodologies

Chapter 8
Blockchain–Enabled Secure Internet of Things

Vinod Kumar

iD https://orcid.org/0000-0002-3495-2320

Madanapalle Institute of Technology and Science, India

Gotam Singh Lalotra

Government Degree College for Women, Kathua, India

ABSTRACT

This century is the time of ubiquitous, smart, and intelligent devices. These devices have a wide variety of applications in different fields like business, manufacturing, healthcare, retail, education, security, transportation, etc. Internet of things is now becoming the inexorable part of the all these fields. But security has always been a major concern in embracing these technologies. The blockchain technology is the next frontier for securing the internet of things. It will play a pivotal role to secure the communication in internet of things ecosystem. This chapter discusses the blockchain-enabled secure internet of things (IoT).

1. INTRODUCTION

IoT is an internet technology connecting devices, machines and tools to the internet by means of wireless technologies. IoT is the one of the greatest phenomena of this century.

"According to Gartner research, The Internet of Things (IoT) is the network of physical objects that contain embedded technology to communicate and sense or interact with their internal states or the external environment." (Gartner, 2019)

IoT is offering new opportunities and providing a competitive advantage for businesses markets. It touches everything—not just the data, but how, when, where and why you collect it. The things connected to internet are changing due to the technologies that have created internet of Things. The services are being offered by devices on the edge of network without the human intervention at different levels

DOI: 10.4018/978-1-6684-7132-6.ch008

As the data generation and analysis is indispensable to the IoT, Managing and handling information throughout its life cycle is a multifaceted exercise because data have to pass through many administrative boundaries. A serious thought is to be given for protection of data in its entire life cycle.

Considering IoT as system-of-system is a good practice as the different physical and technological components are involved in actually make up an IoT ecosystem. Providing business value to any organisation is not an easy task as the architect of these systems. The enterprise architects aim for designing integrated solutions which include Protocol, applications, transport, edge devices and analytical competencies for fully functional IoT system. With the increase of complexities, the challenges are posed to keep IoT secure without affecting the other system. (Internet of things beyond-bitcoin, 2019)

The security of data is vital as claimed by International Data Corporation (IDC) that 90% of organizations that implement the IoT have to suffer an IoT-based breach of back-end IT systems in the upcoming couple of years.

2. BACKGROUND

A blockchain is a distributed ledger that maintains a growing number of data records and transactions. As transactions are related to network participants, they are documented in blocks. They are arranged in the right sequence and assigned a record timestamp when they are added. It is a decentralised technology with the removal of intermediaries the tedious inconvenient banking process can be bypassed which is cost and time efficient. Cryptographic algorithms support the blockchain technology which ensure the prevention of data distortion and ensure high security. The intermediate block on the database cannot be replaces as every block has a hash to the previous block. A block can be extended but cannot be changed.

Generally, Blockchain Technology can be categorised in two core types- public blockchain and private blockchain. (Z Zheng, *et* al. 2017)

* In a **public** blockchain, everyone can read or write data. Some public blockchains limit the access to just reading or writing. Bitcoin, for example, uses an approach where anyone can write.
* In a **private** blockchain, all the participants are well known and trusted. This is useful when the blockchain is used between companies that belong to the same legal mother entity.

2.1. The Problem with the Current Centralized Model

The existing IoT ecosystems rely on centralized, brokered communication models also known as the server/client paradigm. All devices are identified, authenticated and connected through cloud servers that support huge processing and storage capacities. Connection between devices has to be established through the internet, whatsoever the distance in-between is.

While this model has connected generic computing devices for many years, and will support small-scale IoT networks for years to come, but will not cater the need of growing huge IoT ecosystems of future.

Current IoT solutions faces many challenges because the networking equipments, large server farms and centralised clouds involves very high expenditure for infrastructure development and their maintenance. As the IoT devices grow to billions consequently it will involve a large amount of investment.

Cloud servers will remain a bottleneck and point of failure for the entire network, even if the economic engineering and economic challenges are overcome. No single platform to support IoT. Diversity of ownership of devices and the assisting cloud infrastructure makes machine-to machine (M2M) communication difficult.

2.2. Decentralizing IoT Networks

To have more reliable network a decentralized network is solution to the above discussed challenges. A standardised peer-to-peer communication architecture for handling billions of transactions among the devices will reduce the cost significantly by distributing the load of computation and storage across the billions of devices.

Nevertheless, peer- to-peer communication will solves its own issues the principal issue is the security. IoT security is not just about the protection of sensitive data. The solutions offered have to maintain the security and privacy that propose some form of validation and consensus for transactions to prevent hoaxing and theft.

The decentralized approach have to support three fundamental functions:

- Peer-to-peer messaging
- Distributed file sharing
- Autonomous device coordination

The schematic diagram of decentralized approach for IOT system is shown in fig. 1.

Figure 1. Decentralized approach in IOT (Datafloq, 2019)

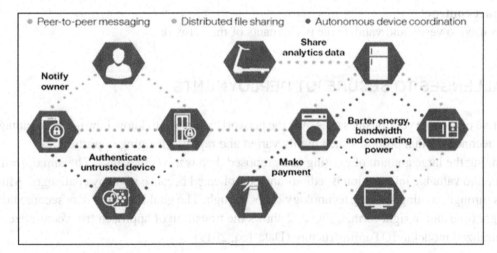

3. THE BLOCKCHAIN APPROACH

Blockchain the "distributed ledger" that support bitcoin has cropped up as an object of deep interest in the technical industry. This technology proposes a way of recording transaction that is secure, transparent, auditable and efficient; as such, it inherent the possibility of disrupting industries and enabling new business modes. The technology is young and changing very fast. To avoid troublemaking surprises decision makes across the industries and business should focus to investigate the application of technology. (A. B. Gaurav, et al., 2020)

The main components in Blockchain technology are listed here-

* **Network of Nodes**

    The transactions made on a blockchain network are collectively maintained by the nodes of the network and are checked by a protocol. 'Mining' adds the new transaction to the ledger and the other node on the network verify the proof of work.

* **Consensus**

    Consensus proposes the proof of work (PoW) and verifies the action in the networks.

* **Cryptography**

    It makes hard for unauthorized users to access or tamper Data bound by a crypto mechanism.

* **Shared ledger**

    The ledger is made publicly available and is incorruptible which is updated every time a transaction is made.

* **Distributed database system**

    The database is composed of blocks of information and is copied to every node of the system. Every block has a list of transactions, a timestamp and the information which links to the previous block.

* **Smart contract**

    It is used to verify and validate the participants of the network.

4. CHALLENGES TO SECURE IOT DEPLOYMENTS

Irrespective of the role your business has over the network, you need to know how to get advantage from this new technology that proposes such highly varied and rapidly changing opportunities.

Managing the large amount of existing and proposed data is a complex task. The aim of turning the huge data into valuable information is tedious and complicated because of many challenges. Mitigating IoT risks through existing security technology is not enough. The goal is to have data secure at the right place, right time and in right format. Figure 2 shows the transition of approach from centralized model to decentralized model in IOT infrastructure (Datafloq, 2019)

a.   Dealing with the Challenges and Threats

It is anticipated that more businesses will deploy security solutions for protection of IoT devices and services in future. As the number of online devices shall be increasing the organisation involved in the business have to broaden their scope of security.

Businesses have to adopt security as per the capabilities and risk associated with the devices involved. Business Intelligence presumes that spending on security solutions of IoT devices to increase five times in the next four years

b.   The Optimum Platform

Providing solutions to the IoT need unparallel collaboration, coordination and connectivity for each piece in the system. Though it is possible, but cost and time parameters make it difficult, until and unless new approach is applied.

Figure 2. Transition from centralized model to decentralized model

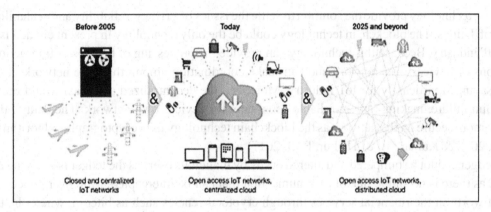

5. IS BLOCKCHAIN THE ANSWER TO IOT SECURITY?

Security is the ongoing issue for IoT. The huge market offers the ample amount of risk for device hacking in the unregulated market. We are talking of smart cars and smart homes, then the individual's privacy and security is a real concern. The data that is collected, processed and passed among IoT device over network the security becoming a huge concern (V. Kumar, et al., 2017).

Among many security recommendations for IoT devices, like biometric, two factor authorization one of the potential answer is blockchain IoT security. Blockchain is quite familiar for bitcoin and Ethereum, offering solution for the security of IoT. It provides protection against data tempering, locking access to Internet of Things devices and allowing compromised devices to be shut down in an IoT network. Hyundai has recently backed HDAC (Hyundai Digital Access Currency) a start-up specifically designed for IoT security. It has help creating a permissioned private network.

"Some of the distinguishing characteristics of the HDAC are as follows (a) PoW mining algorithm which lessens mining monopolization (b) Three minute blocks (c) Has a private/public/permissioned blockchain" @ ecurrencyholder.

Thomas Hardjono, Chief Technology Officer of MIT Connection Science advised there is need of infrastructure development for managing devices and data access. He proposed a blockchain based IoT framework known as ChainAnchor in one of his publication. The proposed framework handles device security by activation and security layers supported by manufacturers, data providers and third parties.

The layer of access in this framework keeps away the unauthorised devices or bad actors from the network. It also contains cases for safely selling and removing devices from blockchain.

There are many issues apart from the blockchain IoT security like the issue of processing power. Many IoT devices lack the power required. The present blockchains are unable to control if a group of miners control more than 50% of the network's mining hash rate. The wide spread network of nodes in a blockchain make it very difficult, but the processing power of an IoT blockchain at home can easily hacked.

Yes the IoT security definitely continue to evolve as regulations to their development. But the possibility of security system of a blockchain IoT security hold the great potential in present scenario.

6. THE BLOCKCHAIN AND IOT

Blockchain technology provide the solution to settle the issues of Privacy, reliability and scalability in the Internet of Things. The blockchain technology could be the only technology in present era that is needed by the IoT industry. Because this technology can provide the processing of billions of transaction, trace the billions of devices over network and can make coordination among the large network of devices, thereby saving significantly for IoT industry. Moreover, the decentralized approach would remove the single point failure, making a more reliable ecosystem for devices over network. The data of the users would be more secure on the network as the blockchain technology uses cryptographic algorithm. (Choi, S. et. al., 2018 & Kumar, V., & Thakur, R. S. 2017)

The ledger cannot be tampered and altered easily by malicious users as the ledger is not lying at single location, as there is no single line of communication that can be intercepted. Moreover, blockchain has proven it worth in the financial services through cryptocurrencies such as bitcoin, where the trustless peer-to-peer messaging is made possible without the intervention of third party.

It not surprising that blockchain technology has been embraced quickly by the enterprise IoT technologies. This is all because of the capabilities like decentralized, trustless and autonomous that has made it a fundamental element of IoT solutions.

Fig.3 describes the universal digital ledger in distributed transaction ledger for various IOT Transactions (Datafloq, 2019)

The blockchain can create an indisputable record of the past of smart devices over the IoT network. There is no centralized control or authority required for the functioning of autonomous devices. This results in the opening of the doors to a series of IoT set-ups that were really difficult, or even beyond imagination to implement.

Implementing the blockchain to the maximum capabilities, IoT solutions can empower trustless and secure messaging among devices in an IoT network. The message is treated as financial transaction in a bitcoin network in this framework. The smart contracts are used for the message exchange after the agreement between the two parties.

This condition can provide the control from distant location, in order to control the flow of water based on the conditions in the crop, the communication can directly be established with the irrigation system. On the similar lines data exchange can make adjustment based on the weather conditions in different fields.

Figure 3. Distributed transaction ledger for various IOT Transactions (Datafloq, 2019)

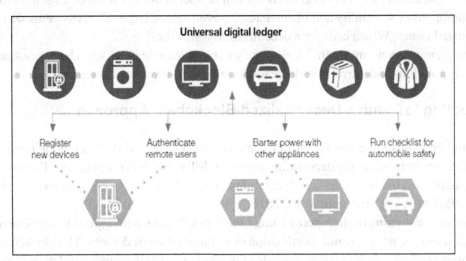

Implementing the blockchain will make true autonomous smart devices capable of financial exchanges and data transfers without the intervention of centralized party. The blockchain provides this autonomy because nodes in the network verify and validate the transactions of their own without depending on centralized authority

In this context, the smart devices can be imagined to place orders for repairing its parts without the intervention of human or third party. Likewise, smart vehicles will be able to deliver a complete report about the replacement of most important part after arriving at a workshop.

One of the most exciting competencies of the blockchain is the capability to maintain an exact trusted and decentralized ledger of all transactions in a network. This ability is necessary to assist many agreements and regulatory requirements of industrial IoT applications without relying on centralized authority.

7. RESOLVING IOT SECURITY ISSUES WITH BLOCKCHAIN TECHNOLOGY

7.1 The Problems of a Centralized IoT Network

The present IoT ecosystem is the centralized model. In this model the different devices are connected, recognized and verified through cloud services that provide high computation and storage capabilities. The internet is the fundamental requirement for information passage. A very high cost in term of infrastructure and maintenance of integrate IoT solutions is involved in the centralized model. (Zhao, S., et al., 2019).

The number of IoT devices is also one of the important issue to be undertaken. The cost involved when the number of internet connected devices reaches to millions, the communication channels will also be increased, resulting in the issue of scalability, economics and engineering.

Even if these issues are resolved one more issue is the cloud services which can disturb the entire network. Henceforth, IoT devices security will be even more difficult.

Applying centralized model to small sized IoT can be successful in saving cost because there would not be the problems of scalability and maintenance. Nevertheless, large IoT ecosystems will encounter these associated issues. Which calls for a decentralized framework.

Different areas of economy are investing largely in blockchain technology. The various countries of the world, corporations and universities have found reasons to invest in this technology.

7.2 Protecting IoT With a Decentralized Blockchain Approach

The most important emerging trend is the unification of blockchain and the Internet of Things. To solve the most of the security issues the decentralization of an IoT network is the solution. Though the decentralization, autonomy, trustworthiness and scalability potentially make it a component of the overall IoT ecosystem. (Bahga, A., & Madisetti, V. K., 2016).

When we are considering the Internet of Things, the Blockchain technology can be implemented for the successful connection, tracking, and coordination of millions of smart devices. The blockchain technology investment by the IoT industry can guarantee the appropriate management of data at various levels.

The integration of Blockchain technology into IoT networks can offer more security and privacy because this technology is based on cryptographic algorithms. The transactions are recorded orderly and carefully by which the connected devices history can be recorded.

Merging this with the fact that there is no need of central authority for the implementation of blockchain technology you will see the integration potentials and benefits are really limitless.

7.3 Two Basic Setups

There are two main schemes for using blockchain technology for providing IoT network security. In first scheme, a company integrates its connected devices to get and transmit data, then it connects them to a blockchain network. This technology smart devices exchange messages, make order and complete transactions. In the second scheme, the Ethereum smart contacts are employed by a company for automation of the process. This provides endless and safe exchanges of messages between connected devices like blockchain based financial transactions.

8. CONCLUSION

The implementation of a blockchain technology decentralized approach to an entire IoT network can help in different ways to secure the IOT infrastructure. It will guarantee proper security by ensuring the privacy and protection of data at all levels. In addition, blockchain technology can help resolve scalability issues and provide an effective functioning of the system and can solve the economic issues of the world.

REFERENCES

Bahga, A., & Madisetti, V. K. (2016). Blockchain platform for industrial internet of things. *Journal of Software Engineering and Applications*, *9*(10), 533–546. doi:10.4236/jsea.2016.910036

Choi, S. S., Burm, J. W., Sung, W., Jang, J. W., & Reo, Y. J. (2018). A blockchain-based secure Iot control scheme. In *2018 International Conference on Advances in Computing and Communication Engineering (ICACCE)* (pp. 74-78). IEEE. 10.1109/ICACCE.2018.8441717

Datafloq. (n.d.). https://datafloq.com/read/securing-internet-of-things-iot-with-blockchain/2228

Gartner Research. (n.d.). https://www.gartner.com/it-glossary/internet-of-things/

Gaurav, A. B., Kumar, P., Kumar, V., & Thakur, R. S. (2020). Conceptual Insights in Blockchain Technology: Security and Applications. In Transforming Businesses with Bitcoin Mining and Blockchain Applications (pp. 221-233). IGI Global.

Internet of things beyond-bitcoin. (n.d.). https://www.cio.com/article/3027522/internet-of-things/beyond-bitcoin-can-the-blockchain-power-industrial-iot.html

Kumar & Thakur. (2017). A brief Investigation on Data Security Tools and Techniques for Big Data. *International Journal of Engineering Science Invention*, 6(9), 20–27.

Kumar, V., & Thakur, R. S. (2017). Jaccard Similarity based Mining for High Utility Webpage Sets from Weblog Database. *International Journal of Intelligent Engineering and Systems*, 10(6), 211–220. doi:10.22266/ijies2017.1231.23

Zhao, S., Li, S., & Yao, Y. (2019). Blockchain enabled industrial Internet of Things technology. *IEEE Transactions on Computational Social Systems*, 6(6), 1442–1453. doi:10.1109/TCSS.2019.2924054

Zheng, Z., Xie, S., Dai, H., Chen, X., & Wang, H. (2017). An Overview of Blockchain Technology: Architecture, Consensus, and Future Trends. *2017 IEEE International Congress on Big Data (BigData Congress)*, 557–564.

KEY TERMS AND DEFINITIONS

Block: It is a container data structure which contain series of transactions. Each transaction within a block is digitally signed and encrypted and verified by the peer node of blockchain network.

Blockchain: It is a decentralized computation and information sharing platform that enables multiple authoritative domains, who don't trust each other, to cooperate, coordinate and collaborate in a rational decision-making process.

Internet of Things: Internet technology connecting devices, machines and tools to the internet by means of wireless technologies.

Private Blockchain: All the participants are known and trusted. This is useful when the blockchain is used between companies that belong to the same legal mother entity.

Public Blockchain: Everyone can read or write data. Some public blockchains limit the access to just reading or writing. Bitcoin, for example, uses an approach where anyone can write.

This research was previously published in Blockchain Applications in IoT Security; pages 45-55, copyright year 2021 by Information Science Reference (an imprint of IGI Global).

Chapter 9
Consequent Formation in Security With Blockchain in Digital Transformation

Shanthi Makka

🆔 https://orcid.org/0000-0002-0387-3160
Birla Institute of Technology, Ranchi, India

Gagandeep Arora
ITS Engineering College, India

B. B. Sagar
Birla Institute of Technology, Mesra, India

ABSTRACT

Blockchain technology makes use of a centralized, peer-to-peer (P2P) network of databases, also called nodes, to validate and record digital transactions between individual users located anywhere across the globe. These transactions often take place through the exchange of cryptocurrencies such as bitcoins, Ethereum, and Ripple, etc. The security and transparency that is inherently present in digital transactions place blockchain technology in high demand across various industrial applications. Each node updates its database in real-time as and when transactions occur. The transaction gets authorized only when a majority of the nodes in the network validate the transaction. Once the verification is complete, a block, consisting of hash and keys, is generated for each new transaction and is linked to previous transactions in every database. Every node updates its database with the new block. A hacker would have to break down every node in the system to commit fraud. Blockchain could play a major role in maintaining the cyber security of digital transactions in the future.

DOI: 10.4018/978-1-6684-7132-6.ch009

INTRODUCTION

This chapter deals with how Blockchain Technology guarantees security in digital transformation. Blockchain technology create consume of a centralized, peer-to-peer (P2P) collaborate of databases is called nodes, to validate and record digital transactions between individual users located anywhere across the globe. These transactions often take place through the exchange of Cryptocurrencies such as bit-coins, Ethereum and ripple etc. A Cryptocurrency (or crypto currency) is a integral advantage outline to pursue as a midway of trade that benefit powerful cryptography to protect commercial transactions, force the establishment of further units, and confirm the dispatch of credit.

The security and transparency that is in inherently present in the digital transactions place Blockchain technology in high demand across various industrial applications. Each node updates its database in real-time as and when transactions occur. The validation of transaction is depends upon the criteria that majority of nodes in network gives approval. Once the verification is completed the hash address and keys will be generated for the new transaction and further it linked to previous nodes in database and all nodes in network will get updated with this new block of values. If any hacker wants to commit any fraud activity he or she has to breakdown all the nodes in network and all the nodes are located globally and it is visible to everyone in the network would increase difficulty to commit fraud Blockchain could hit a considerable act in maintaining cyber security of digital bond in the future.

WHAT IS BLOCKCHAIN?

Blockchain is an open-source, scattered ledger proficient of reporting and accumulate facts that is then achieve by unique crypto graphical designs. This unique and innovative design makes Blockchain a safe space for data and the data cannot be deleted, modified, manipulated, or misused in any way. Another crucial form of Blockchain technology is that it is consensus-oriented which further reduces the possibility of data being manipulated or misused. Its design is such that a large number of computers (nodes) are connected over a network.

So, whenever the Authors wish to enumerate a transaction to a Blockchain, The Authors must clarify or clarify a mathematical test, the outputs of which are communal with every machine linked to the network. Only when all other computers on the network reciprocally acknowledge with the output, then only user can the add transactions to the chain. Moreover, in Blockchain, data is never gathered (Yaga, D., et al., 2019) at one peculiar location, which makes cybercriminals to access the data all most impossible.

Blockchain is, hence, the first technology that expedites the pass on of digital proprietorship in a decentralized manner. All these aspects make Blockchain so imploring to the capitalist of the technical world. As the name proposes, the Blockchain framework is made up of various 'blocks,' each of which contains the transaction data, a timestamp, and the link (cryptographic hash) to the previous block. A Blockchain is a collection of documents that are known as blocks. These blocks of records are covered and obtain by cryptography. Blocks in database (Lindman, J., 2017) connect stable and include information from other blocks, deal data, and time space.

Figure 1. Blockchain Technology
(https://blockgeeks.com/wpcontent/uploads/2016/09/blockchaintech.jpg)

Figure 2. Data Protection using Blockchain
(https://i.pinimg.com/originals/61/4a/68/614a68c360a0e91f84972b1ff6247325.jpg)

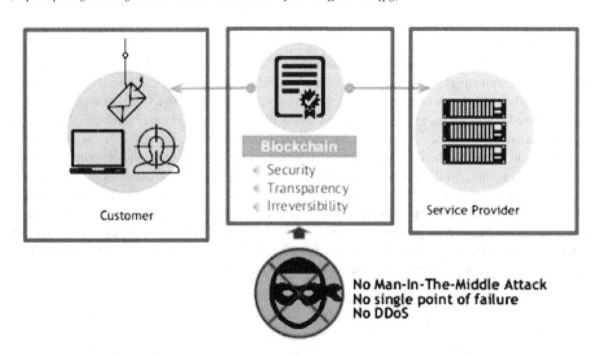

A Blockchain preserve the data from adaption. It also transcript bonds between two distinct affairs that allocate as a ledger. These ledgers are unchangeable. There's no distinct bit where these analog credit can be form or incensed. Blockchain technology is being worn in a collection of methods containing Bitcoin, Economic, Technology, Healthcare, and Insurance industries as a way to guard cyber data. They are augmenting in reputation because you can install any digital asset or transaction into a Blockchain. It doesn't matter what corporation you're a part of.

LITERATURE REVIEW

The Literature survey is presented in the form of table.

HOW BLOCKCHAIN WORKS

The Blockchain is very popular as the fundamental technology of Bitcoin. Essentially it purposes a peer-to-peer structure of computers to approve transactions (Peters, G. W., et al., 2016). Blockchain is a data structure to design and receive delivered ledger of transactions amidst a chain of computers. It permits customer to generate and confirm transactions instantly without a central power. The Blockchain technology can be classified into two divisions, one is Public Blockchain and other one is Private Blockchain.

Public Blockchain

A public Blockchain network or license less Blockchain system of connections is entirely open-ended and anybody amenable to perform in this gentle of grid can play without any consent. This is the dominant divergence among private and public Blockchain network. Anybody can battle in the formal network, execute the confer protocol, and conserve the trivial open public ledger. The benefit of Public Blockchain is greater defended than private network. But, it gives less secrecy and enormous computation potential and intensity is necessary, less ecological.

Private Blockchain

A Private Blockchain Network deserves an proposal to aid in the network. The confirmation of the challenge must be accomplished either by network discoverer or by the order determined by the author of the network. Permissions Blockchain Network puts restriction to the entry of participant and allows only the kind of participant that is required in the network. The Advantages of Public Blockchain is expanded isolation and Environmentally safe, as less computation competence is prescribed to conclude the harmony as in the case of Public Network. But, it is less protective as distinguished to public network.

Table 1. Literature Survey

Authors	Year of publication	Title	Name of the Journal /Conference	Findings
Hawlitschek, F., Notheisen, B.,& Teubner, T.	2018	The limits of trust-free systems: A literature review on blockchain technology and trust in the sharing economy.	Electronic commerce research and applications, 29, 50-63.	The Authors discussed about how the adversity of approaches may be determine and investigate the future of blockchain technology for diffuse the concern of faith in the sharing economy. Through the literature review Authors found that: The perception of reliance varies extensively between the background of blockchain and the sharing economy, Blockchain technology is to some degree appropriate to redeem faith in platform providers, and that trust-free systems are barely conveyable to sharing economy communications and will essentially confide on the expansion of credible combination for blockchain-based sharing economy ecosystems.
Seebacher, S., & Schüritz, R.	2017	Blockchain technology as an enabler of service systems: A structured literature review.	In International Conference on Exploring Services Science (pp. 12-23). Springer, Cham.	The blockchain technology is mainly focused on peer-to-peer network; facultative concert among different parties and service system is selected as unit analysis to observe its capacity. Authors have recognized a group of attributes that guarantees trust and Fragmentation, promoting the creation and strategy of a service system.
Karafiloski, E., & Mishev, A.	2017	Blockchain solutions for big data challenges: A literature review.	In IEEE EUROCON 2017-17th International Conference on Smart Technologies (pp. 763-768). IEEE.	Blockchain Technology gives great significance when we search for efficient way to store, manage, and process Big Data. Authors' demonstrated possible ways about decentralized mainframe of private data, digital property resolution, communication with IoT and public institutions' amend are having compelling force on how Big Data may develop. In this paper Authors discussed about various Big Data areas that can be entrust by the Blockchain technology.
Calvaresi, D., Dubovitskaya, A., Calbimonte, J. P., Taveter, K., & Schumacher, M.	2018	Multi-agent systems and blockchain: Results from a systematic literature review.	In International Conference on Practical Applications of Agents and Multi-Agent Systems (pp. 110-126). Springer, Cham.	Intended to provide a broad overview in application concerns and Authors evaluate impetus, hunches, necessity, durability, and constraints granted in the present state of the art. Moreover, explaining the expected disputes and advances their perception on how MAS and BCT could be connected in various application aspects.
Brandão, A., São Mamede, H., & Gonçalves, R.	2018	Systematic review of the literature, research on blockchain technology as support to the trust model proposed applied to smart places.	In World Conference on Information Systems and Technologies (pp. 1163-1174). Springer, Cham.	The agile places are exposed with perverted or compose data, with the deceitful combination of new tools, and tools with firmware versions uncertain. These possibilities damage with the expanding capacity and variety of data, tools, framework, and end users linked to the Web. The systematic study of the article is picked 190 documents, which deals with the increasing interest on the theme of Blockchain technology with 14 publications in 2014 to about 100 already in 2017. The articles focused on the areas bitcoin (about 40%), IoT (about 30%), financial (about 15%), cryptocurrencies, electronic government (about 12%), smart contracts, smart cities, Business (with about 10% each) and health (about 5%).

continues on following page

Table 1. Continued

Authors	Year of publication	Title	Name of the Journal /Conference	Findings
Zhang, N., Zhong, S., & Tian, L.	2017	Using Blockchain to Protect Personal Privacy in the Scenario of Online Taxi-hailing.	International Journal of Computers, Communications & Control, 12(6).	The Authors have make use of permanent decentralized and Ability of the blockchain to suggest a blockchain based personal authenticated security protocol, which employs Online taxi-accost as the application scenario.
Jaffe, C., Mata, C., & Kamvar, S. *International Symposium on Wearable Computers* (pp. 81-84). ACM.	2017	Motivating urban cycling through a blockchain-based financial incentives system. In *Proceeding s of the 2017 ACM*	International Joint Conference on Pervasive and Ubiquitous Computing and Proceedings of the 2017 ACM	This thesis explains a Blockchain based financial catalyst system where closets can influence their bustle and district data to collect financial rectification from industries that would like to sponsor closet activity.
Bazin, R., Schaub, A., Hasan, O., & Brunie, L.	2017	Self-reported verifiable reputation with rater privacy.	In IFIP International Conference on Trust Management (pp. 180-195). Springer, Cham.	The Authors designed a new reputed system, which is decentralized, secured, and efficient and can be applicable to practical context. Through his reputation system user's can easily obtain the accurate reputation score of the service provided within a constant amount of time. User can also provide their feedback without their own credentials.
Król, M., Reñé, S., Ascigil, O., & Psaras, I.	2018	ChainSoft: Collaborative software development using smart contracts.	In CRYBLOCK 2018-Proceedings of the 1st Workshop on Cryptocurrencies and Blockchains for Distributed Systems, Part of MobiSys 2018 (pp. 1-6). ACM.	Authors presented ChainSoft - a podium for deploy software advancement and self-moving remittance amid parties that mistrust each other, by means of blockchain technology. ChainSoft permits any developer to built software and comply software, involves automatic code authentication and accomplish users' appropriate behavior. They invented a tool for their system using Ethereum Smart Contracts and Github/Travis CI and present first decision examining its protection and deep control cost.
Choi, Jindae; Shin, Sungjung. Choi, J., & Shin, S.	2016	Propose of smart place IoT systems for strengthen security of the smart grid environment.	International Information Institute (Tokyo). Information, 19(5), 1509.	Authors designed a new model for security verification as previous step operation maintenance of smart place IoT environment. Power energy catch benefit of ICT blend technology.
Barbosa, L. S.	2017	Digital governance for sustainable development.	In Conference on e-Business, e-Services and e-Society (pp. 85-93). Springer, Cham.	Authors demonstrated the effect of digital revolution of administration structure as a mechanism to improve continual evolution and more broad associations, in the resolve of the United Nations 2030 Agenda. Three primary disputes are inscribed: the inquiry of *scope*, *adherence* of software foundation, and the system to accomplish more limpid and *liable* public academy.
O'Dair, M., & Beaven, Z.	2017	The networked record industry: How blockchain technology could transform the record industry.	Strategic Change, 26(5), 471-480.	Blockchain technology may have reframing promising for those music industries correlate with listed music, and for the suitability of music progress. While forecast of extensive fragmentation may have been abortive, blockchain technology does present to have the capability to convert the act of third affair and to make musicians' course more feasible. Blockchains could advance the efficiency and opportunity of ownership data, expedite near-imperative repayments for authority, and necessarily boost the clarity of the key chain.

Figure 3. Transaction using Blockchain
(https://dzone.com/storage/temp/7930704-blockchain-workflow.png)

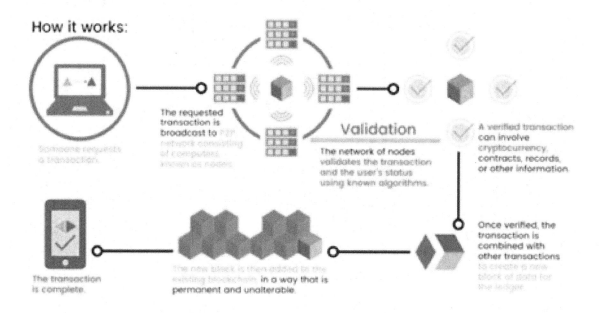

BLOCKCHAIN ARCHITECTURE

When working with Blockchain technology, it is needless to say that, you must possess a thorough understanding of Blockchain and its innate architecture. User has to competent with concepts such as Cryptography, Hash address generation, distributed ledger technology, consensus, decentralized consensus, smart contracts, and authorized computing, and many more. This first step is crucial to building a strong foundational knowledge in Blockchain technology.

Technical Architecture And A High Level View of Blockchain

Basically the Structure of Blockchain subsists of several of knobs, avouch has a provincial model of a **ledger**. In outmost scenario in the network, the knobs pertains distinct framework. The nodes broadcast with each other in authorize to obtain reconciliation on the essence of the ledger and do not depend upon a main authority to integrate and substantiate transactions. The method of obtaining this license is called consensus, and there are multiple algorithms have been constructed for this purpose. Customers dispatch their request for the transaction to the Blockchain to fulfill the working of the chain is constructed to implement. Formerly a transaction is finished, a file of the transaction is combined to one or more of the ledgers, and it cannot be updated or removed. This phenomenon of the Blockchain is said to be immutability discussed earlier.

*(https://miro.medium.com/max/700/1*Vn97Zi2c12AADRfUuanyIw.png)*

Figure 4. Blockchain Network Architecture
(https://www.altoros.com/blog/wp-content/uploads/2017/04/Everledger-Blockchain-IBM-High-Security-Business-Network.png)

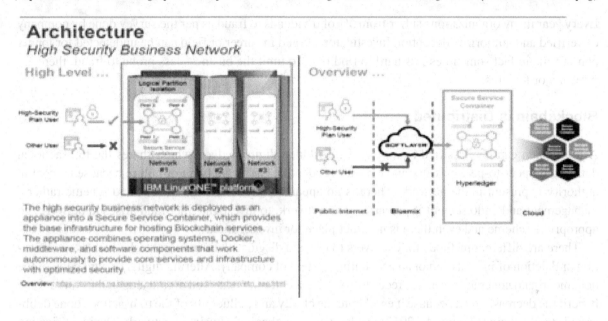

Figure 5. Technical Architecture of Blockchain

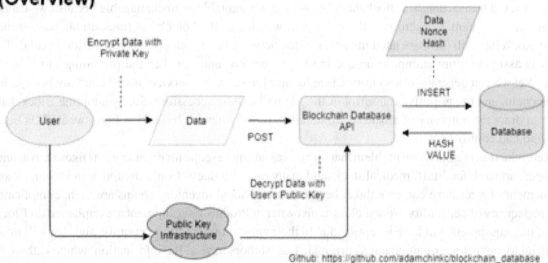

FEATURES OF BLOCKCHAIN

Every year many organizations suffer from 5% of dividends to fraud as per the survey done by company of verified and authorized deception Investigators. Fraud in career or field can be undetected for longer pan of time in fact sometimes it is hard to find out. To limit the business less prone to fraud, there are three major features:

Blockchain is Distributed

A blockchain can be classified as a type of distributed digital ledger, which shares the transactional data among peer-to-peer network and constantly adapted. No single point of failure because no central authority is present in the network. There is no apparent way to enquire about fraud scheme rather a management and endorsement is precarious the network, to investigate the fraud arises in network, no appropriate scheme and even there is no exact place for investigation.

There are different methods for deceivers to use and disguise their immoral tasks such as modification or deletion of information of an accounting system of company. Altering digital or hard copy of the documents and generating crooked records. By using a common or shared digital ledger, the Authors can benefit the decrease fraud because it escalerate the clarity and pellucidity of the transactions done deliberated supply chain (Pflaum, A., 2017) and between members of a business network. The identification of fraud transactions can be done easily because every participant in the network can see the history and transfer of capitals and a member or a group of members in a network controls the majority of network.

Blockchain is Immutable

The registered transactions on Blockchain Network are immutable or unchangeable because we cannot remove or alter them. Consensus is the process in which ahead a "block" of transactions are attached to the blockchain, all the associated members of the network must concede the transaction is valid. The block is assigned a timestamp, insured using Cryptography, and allied to the preceding block in the chain. Yet we can generate a fresh transaction to alter the state of a service, it will candidly be inserted to the chain, and the primitive transcript of the file will still be accessible. So, by adopting Blockchain you can draw the authority of a benefit, comprehensive of where, it has arrive from, where it is been, and who had control of it.

Reproduction is a Universal problem that influences an ample scope for organizations like extravagance of goods, apparel, foodstuff, medical stock, and many more products. Confirmation of the accuracy and endowment of a resource can be a threat because conventional inventory chains are high, complicated and inadequacy of pellucidity. Nonetheless, if an owner or Producer's equipment are implanted on Blockchain, that equipment will have inception due to their constant transaction antiquity, and that will make it crucial to gap off hoax equipment as original. The Authors have al the information, which is there on the Internet and the Authors don not promote other people access on it, whether it may be an email or a Facebook account, or a confidential bank transactions and any other social media. The problem with bringing information on the Internet has a chance of being hacked, duplicated, or penetrated. Immutability is a fundamental phenomenon that Blockchain lead to the table. It anticipates everything that is taped in a ledger from being composed and you no need to worry about your transaction information is safe or not because the way the Blockchain operates it keeps your data safe and secure by attaching to the multiple vulnerabilities. Even any hacker wants to attempted to hack it can't be done because of un-reliability of blockchains. Blockchains ledgers begin with a one or array of transactions, which involves capitals, crypto-currency, data, accord, or values. Once the transaction is verified then it executes and transaction will be recorded. In Blockchain the created object cannot be altered. The effect of network provides immutability in Blockchain. The efficiency of a network is dependent upon the frequency of usage of network. The key feature of Blockchain is based on the ability to be immutable and secure. Let's take a look at how it's changing things in the cyber security world.

Blockchain can be Permissioned

The best deal with confidential data in Businesses cannot tolerate the access of someone to it. So there should ne some way out to safeguard the data from outsiders' and insiders for not corrupting the files of data. In this way, the permissions become major role. But distinct former features we have discussed, not all the Blockchain networks are permissioned. The permissioned networks can be enormous for deceit forestalling because they impede who acquiescing to participate and under what capacity along with their limitation. The contribution by the members of a permissioned network can be started once they are invited and authenticated.

In a permissioned network, management of Identity and controlling network access takes major role. In Linux Foundation the framework of Blockchain is implemented, all the participants issued a crypto-graphic membership cards for their Identity Proof with Hyper ledger Fabric. The assigned membership card permits them to access the transaction that belongs to them. Even prudential users cannot insert a record to the Blockchain without consensus and they cannot damage any records because all the records are encrypted. We cannot neglect any sort of fraud as per operational risks of 2017; it would be very costly and also reduces morale of employee and generate an ambiguous business atmosphere in addition to blunt your business and customer relationships.

SECURITY THROUGH BLOCKCHAIN

A Blockchain network is more secure as its framework, especially while establishing a private Block-chain, you must establish outdo of stage for classification. Still the Blockchain has instinctive resources that support security by soring data in cloud (Park, J., et al., 2017), those with ill intent can manipulate known vulnerabilities in your infrastructure. Exquisitely, you must have groundwork with unified security that can forbid anyone, including core users and supervisors from penetrate confidential data, contradict unauthorized attacks to alter data or functionality in network. Rigorously escort encrypted keys with high-level security standards without any misappropriation. With this competence, your Blockchain network will have the further shelter that required inhibiting attempts from within and without. The Authors can also design absolutely unified industry ready Blockchain framework to promote the evolution, administration, and applications of a multi organizational business network.

As mentioned in previous sections Blockchain is nothing but a sequence of blocks which has transactions as set of records and every block is linked to rest of all other blocks with previous and next hash pointer. It makes it impossible to damage any record by any hackers because they need hash address of that Block along with all other blocks linked to it. This alone might not seem like much of deterrence, but Blockchain has some other essential features, which provides supplementary security.

Figure 6. Architecture for Security

The records on a Blockchain (Aitzhan, N. Z., et al., 2016) are secured through cryptography. All the participants in the network are assigned with private keys with transactions they make and it also requires their won digital signature. If there is any change in records, the digital signature becomes shut-in and concerned authority in the network will get an alarm about fraud attempt. New proclamation is critical to preclude additional contamination. Grievously for enthusiastic hackers, Blockchains are broadcasted and allocated over peer-to-peer networks, which are updated continuously and preserved in synchronized. As a result they are not placed in central position, Blockchians never have single point of failure and information cannot be changed on a single computer. It requires huge amount of computational efficiency to reach each instance of an assured Blockchian and modify them at the same time span. There is some confusion whether small Blockchian networks can easily be accessible to attack or not. The bigger the network is more it is the more challenging it is. By default the Blockchain networks has certain features to protect your data and information in a secured way.

Digital separation has replaced the technique the Authors anticipate about our integrity. From Amazon's "tell it once" payment method through to Facebook's organized as solution with single sign. But many of us are rock the idea of authenticating by own over a relievable online prior of our choosing, which makes our lives easier. Disparity of tendency with an identity circulated by the government, from the date of birth documents to social security cards over driver's licenses and passports, everything is paper based. Many, especially previous generation people prefer birth certificates must hard to trace down and achieve. If any one lost their physical document of birth certificate or any other documents needs a lot of reentry of same information again and again which creates a lot of frustration even people feel to shake their head like anything in a government forms.

Indulge yourself to Blockchain as it is an expeditiously growing science, which basically focus on the essential for belief, performance, and protection in the integrity arena. Blockchain is a mechanism that perch on the cap of Internet and exchange the information immensely effectively through establishment of distributed ledger, which runs beyond the peer-to-peer network. In a Blockchain, applicable branch of the network concede transactions prior to devoted into timely organized blocks of facts and these blocks are constrained composed in a group through isolated benefits, inclusive of hashing using cryptography and consensus algorithms.

The two capable companies have given the demonstration in line with the government of Canada and a chain of banks and tele-communications producers. If this solution is accepted then it will be beneficial for all stakeholders. Every individual will enter the details about themselves only once and after doing this who so ever is interested people has to enter their details only once.

Concurrently, Blockchain identity using a Mobile App based facilitates identity customers to have the equal guarantee as conventional identity issued by the government without the requirement for inconvenience created for documented applications, registrations through online, and entry of data in various places. Concurrently, the confidential services and smart contract empower them to contact required information to authenticate integrity beyond negotiation of the safety and purity of confidential consumer data, the conceivable advantages never block there. Once the label of an identity of Blockchain citizen becomes completely achievable to dream of the world where every citizen is capable of building, controlling and maintaining a complete and credible analysis of their own life travel from their birth to death can be carried through a smart phone. If anyone choses to register their birth through travel records, history of employment, educational certificates uploaded through Blockchain, it creates secured, easy accessible digital identity and also it can be controlled in entire their lives.

It is very early to be sure of Blcokchain technology and still we have to do a lot to bring advanced version of Blockchain for digital identity for reality. Anyhow the people and industries are recovering the full capable of this metamorphic technology the experts need more and more ambitious government about the world must examine the same capability in the integrity scope in Canada and abutment of networks of their own and deal outshine the practice.

DATA SAFETY USING BLOCKCHAIN

To secure transactions distributed ledger technology popular in Blockchain Technology. Recognize and regulation of individual integrity is best of mind, disposed current actions, including the European Union's General Data Protection Regulation. Most of our identity (Liang, G., et al., 2018) is communal without our specific approval, brings reserved in districts the authors are doped of, and when composed amazing obstacles. A Decentralized approach enable us to deal with difficulties such as fraud where people use expiry documents for usage which puts everyone in network risk and it also reduces risk associated with user credentials used for personal interactions and virtual interactions through instruments and it also keeps users at other side to verify very critical to who is and what is at alternative oblique of the cover.

Just imagine loans sanctioned to the people so quickly by the banks by sharing related information by the users without manual verification process would reduce the cost and time and also if you get medical treatment at hospitals with your global identification card also reduces time and to proceed. Through this global identification card you are able to present yourself along with your medical history so doctors can know what exactly is the problem and what medicine to be given.

The Blockchain technology has framed a space to transform bonding between the users and industries are established and driven with various public flaws for identity. Blockchain permits point-to-point digital trade of identity at the peaks of the network, at the equipment. If people would control their identity by themselves, then the scope of digital permit would not have been at that extreme level with public key infrastructure (PKI) associate with certified authorities.

BLOCKCHAIN TECHNOLOGY WITH IoT

Let us consider an IoT network with centralized authority the authors like to call through devices, probably they treat them, as smart using sketches are not permitted to compose protective decisions by themselves without the central authority. In Blockchain model, the entire set of data is accumulated along with each tool and data also depicted and stocked. Prior to any information insertion to the network the hacker has to assemble all necessary resources for DNS attack and it must be confirmed and certified by every node present in the network. Since it permits deposit to be completed without any bank or any negotiator (Zheng, Z. et al., 2017). A Blockchain can be owned in desperate financial benefits like electronic assets, reimbursement, and payment through online. In addition to this it can also used in other fields like IoT, smart investments and services useful for public. Apparently, an IoT (Kumar, N. M., et al., 2018) is no longer conceded to a single node.

In the universe of an IoT, an advanced and it might have imply earlier, is in the amorphous step of growth that might be a good idea for those who can see the capability in merging Blockchain security from grounded. Actually, an IoT produces a rigid threat than the Cryptocurrency in which the distributed network assigned with affecting currency from one unidentified owner to another. There is a necessary need of complex structure to authenticate, protect, and manage all the layers of an entire network. There are many frameworks are built to handle such technical issues and an appropriate framework must be able to identify illegal interruptions and to reduce the spread of malware it has to crumb hacked devices from the network. It would require a protocol to insert and delete equipment from Blockchain without bring out a protective reaction.

In addition, the Blockchain technology must beat a problem such as reasonable result is 51% of attack problem is enforced to tiny, substantially limited to an IoT networks and to obtain the control of a Blockchain expects to compromise a bulk of network equipment a complex task, when the network is spread over a globe, then it inclines and augmented easily when it is directed to a home network. Specialists have resolve to an idea of a dumped on Blockchain converge that promotes greatly more safeguard than centralized version, but doesn't absolutely accommodated aggregation as a developed Blockchain.

The configured Internet is currently not designed to shaft the size and difficulties occurred while handling recent transactions, because it is made up with old technologies where security issues are very huge and happens very frequently. Achieving a Blockchain technology to an IoT directly moderate and subsequently would be a great idea. Bring it to its place and then adjust it subsequently. A defeat to an address the cavernous protective space will convince a global difficulty for millions of householders later.

CYBER SECURITY IN BLOCKCHAIN TECHNOLOGY

The first thing in our mind that "what is the role of cyber security in Blockchain Technology?"

Blockchain technology is creating a path for future. This is beyond panel for abundance organizations depending on immense Cybersecurity conservation. It abolishes flaws and deceptive data and computerizing factual and credible files. This can mark property and it is not sensitive to cyber interventions. The Industries that are associated with Blockchain technology will assure the safety of digital transactions, confidentiality of data and timestamps and it is also a smart choice. Let's see how Blockchain is related to Cybersecurity: the enhancement of Cyber defense is improved using Blockchain technology and it also averts crime and identifies interfere with data. It encrypts data and built it crystalline and agitable.

Cybersecurity (Ahram, T., et al., 2017) outbreaks and data crack have been a reason of main burden for every character. Frequently the hackers abduct confidential information of users such as a PAN number and Aadhar number to employ it for forged transactions. However, blockchain as described above actively verifies and authenticates the identity of a user without expecting any sort of confidential data. Even name of the user is also not required. The Blockchain Technology could play a major role in maintaining Cybersecurity and digital transactions in future.

Figure 7. Security Levers in Blockchain
(https://blog.sodio.tech/wp-content/uploads/2018/06/Secure-Blockchain-based-Cloud-framework.png)

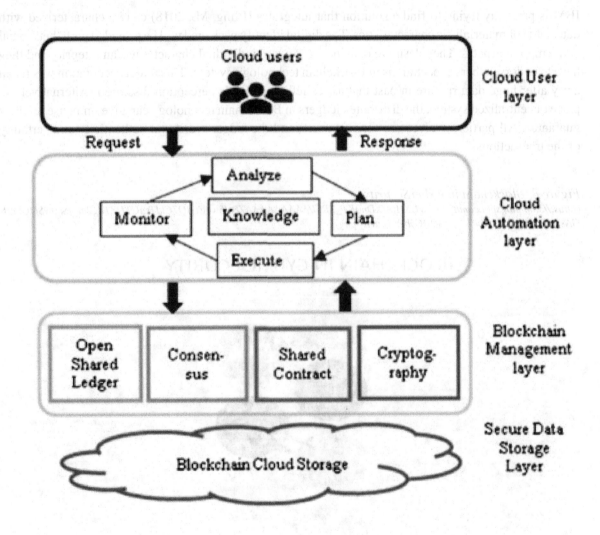

Blockchain guarantees confidence and efficiency between parties, they may use private and public applications. It not only to encrypt data and all given transactions and here everything is decentralized. When a hacker tries to breakdown the data and crucial information this technology alerts an entire system. There is no single point of failure in Blockchian, which can be hacked. Blockchain technology (Shackelford, S. J., et al., 2017) is using Cyber security because it provides an approach to secure everything more than transactional structures. Blockchain (Mylrea, M., et al., 2017) is also currently engaged in prevention of identity theft. The digital identification and actions you are receiving online can be verified by using Blockchain. To reduce the chance of identity theft Blockhain technology provides high-level degree of privacy for Internet users.

DIGITAL IDENTITY USING BLOCKCHAIN TECHNOLOGY

IBM is presently trying to find a solution that integrates (Eling, M., 2018) can be characterized with detectable or materialistic characteristics. The digital identity packaged will be provided with their social and temporal aspects. They desire to convince that every individual character has an integrity and they have to endorse others expectations in Blockchain technology system. This intent acceptation was taken away after huge data rupture in past that arises fellow citizen's perception disclosed. Alternatively in place of centralized system, the distributed ledgers in Blockchain technology can give immense security guarantee. All parties involved are verified users, and the ledgers verify an authenticity and certainty of the transactions.

Figure 8. Blockchain in CyberSecurity
(https://3.bp.blogspot.com/t72wwwUXHfA/XDn0KT_ZR6I/AAAAAAAAZ8/J5wxgTBQ7CkITsaUTUZTdg2cIgfSc0wSQCLcB-GAs/s1600/Blockchain%2Bin%2BCybersecurity.png)

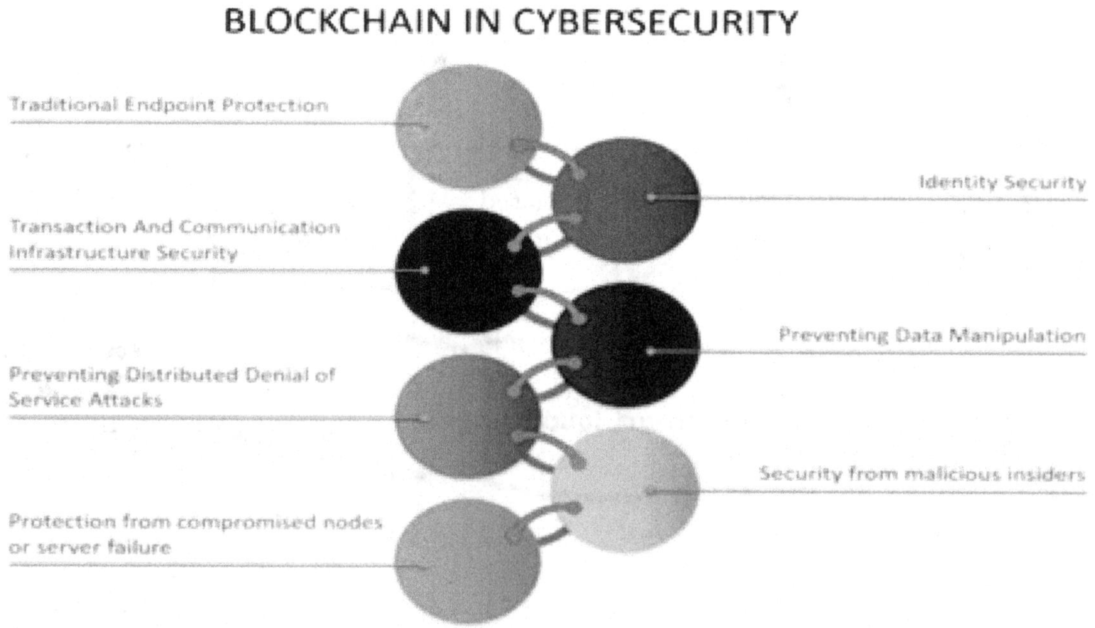

BLOCKCHAIN IN CYBERSECURITY

Traditional Endpoint Protection

Identity Security

Transaction And Communication Infrastructure Security

Preventing Data Manipulation

Preventing Distributed Denial of Service Attacks

Security from malicious insiders

Protection from compromised nodes or server failure

Figure 9. Digital Identity using Blockchain
(https://www.researchgate.net)

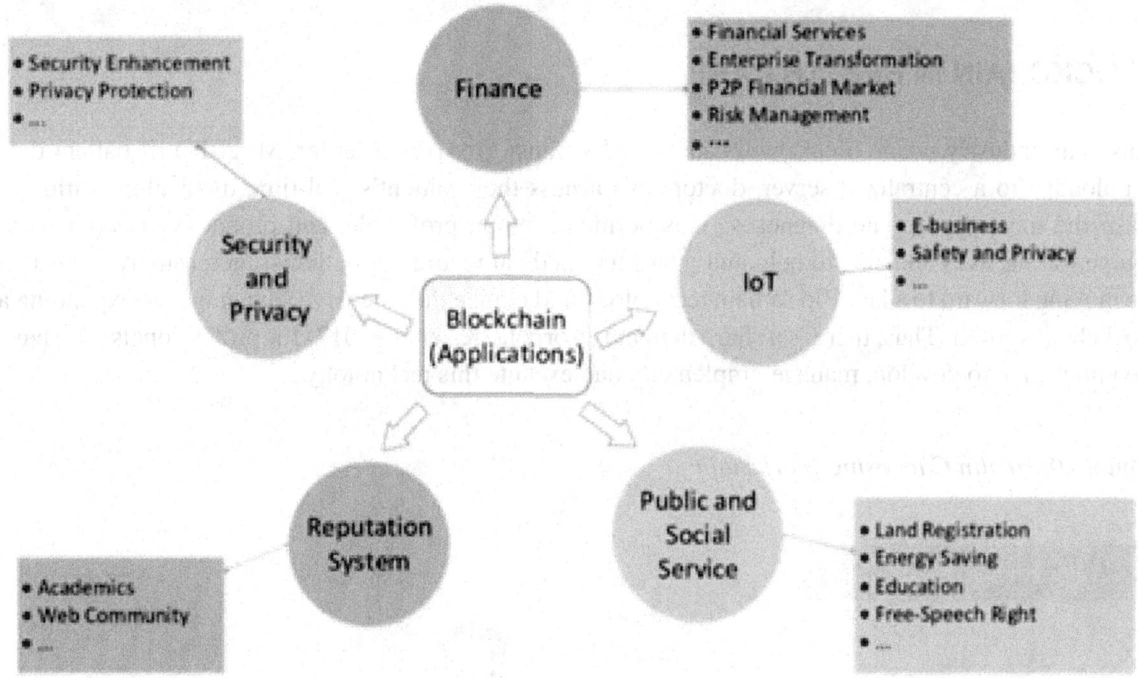

BLOCKCHAIN IN BANKING SECTOR

Currently the usage of Blockchain technology is very slow. As per survey of IBM in 2017, approximately 200 healthcare centers and only 16% of the defendants are conceded to choose Blockchain technology. The promising future that Blockchain (Guo, Y., et al., 2016) influences the healthcare organizations can be fulfilled only if healthcare centers exhibits readiness to accept this technology and accumulate the essential technical framework for it. As of now, authors can say that the acceptability is very slow, but Blockchain will definitely develop a deep-rooted froce on the healthcare industries and may other industries in the future. Since Blockchain's star application is cryptocurrency (Bitcoin) (Vujičić, D., et al., 2018), you must know how the system works. There are numerous platforms such as Coinbase and Coinmama where you can learn how to handle cryptocurrency (7, I. 2016) and digital transactions. You need to register on any of the mentioned platforms that are accessible in your country and then buy coins and start with the process after buying few coins and make your own folder to proceed.

The core objective is to focus to learn process, so we no need to purchase huge amount of coins. Online wallets are the best decision for small transactions, as you persist to make acquires utilizing your wallet, the concept of how digital financial transactions are organized using crypto currencies will constantly become fair choice to you. Just as data structures are a necessary aspect of coding, so it is also a important part of Blockchain technology. It employs a consolidation of data structures and cryptography to develop secure and vigorous surroundings for data. Thus, to incline a Blockchain proficient you must constitute a solid grip on data structures and cryptographic designs and operations consisting hash functions like MD5, CRC32, and SHA1.

BLOCKCHAIN IN HEALTH CARE

This is an industry where blockchain can radically transform lives (Mettler, M. 2016). If patient data is uploaded to a centralized server, doctors can access their patient's real-time medical condition to make the most appropriate diagnoses. This permits prompt, profitable, and productive treatment for compensating lives and also to help and guard the medical records of patients. Increasingly industries are moving forward to adapt Blockchain technology and realize the extensive advantages of expanding a blockchain system. Thus, there is a sharp demand (Korpela, K., et al., 2017) for professionals who have the knowledge to develop, manage, implement, and execute this technology.

Figure 10. Health Care using Blockchain

BLOCKCHAIN IN EDUCATION

Deployment of Blockchain technology in Education sector can give an advantage for verification of academic credentials of students in very secured and effective manner. Manuscripts and other related materials can be uploaded through online system that using Blockchain technology. Even though it is deployed in centrally and it is accessible by all concerned departments and can also be verified easily. Every alteration is recorded and linked with prior entry in the network. In this way no student will get any incorrect or invalid data such unearned degrees since it cannot passed through Blockchain verification process (Cai, Y., et al., 2016). It also provides new designing opportunities for the prominence system and it is also very effective in preclude targeted information such as crucial information like loan application's data where the deceitful information is fact based. Still their capability is bounded in instinctive information fraud like valuation fraud, where the validation of ground-truth is not easy. These systems are efficient in inhibit bad mouthing and conceal attack, but they are restricted in discover poll padding under sable attack, perpetual charges and disguise attack.

SUMMARY

The Blockchain Technology is the fundamental mechanism behind Crypto currencies such as bit-coins, Ethereum and ripple etc. This is a very secured, trusted, efficient technology while dealing with confidentiality of transfer of currency from one place to other. In this chapter we discussed what is Blockchain Technology, how the data can be protected or secured using Blockchain technology, Different types of Blockchain Architectures, Crypto currencies and their applications, various properties of Blockchain Technology, How the Blockchain is associate with IoT and it's benefits along with applications of Blockchain in Health Care, Education, Banking, Cyber security, and digital identification of the user.

REFERENCES

Ahram, T., Sargolzaei, A., Sargolzaei, S., Daniels, J., & Amaba, B. (2017, June). Blockchain technology innovations. In *2017 IEEE Technology & Engineering Management Conference (TEMSCON)* (pp. 137-141). IEEE. doi:10.1109/TEMSCON.2017.7998367

Aitzhan, N. Z., & Svetinovic, D. (2016). Security and privacy in decentralized energy trading through multi-signatures, blockchain and anonymous messaging streams. *IEEE Transactions on Dependable and Secure Computing, 15*(5), 840–852. doi:10.1109/TDSC.2016.2616861

Barbosa, L. S. (2017, November). Digital governance for sustainable development. In *Conference on e-Business, e-Services and e-Society* (pp. 85-93). Springer.

Bazin, R., Schaub, A., Hasan, O., & Brunie, L. (2017, June). Self-reported verifiable reputation with rater privacy. In *IFIP International Conference on Trust Management* (pp. 180-195). Springer.

Brandão, A., São Mamede, H., & Gonçalves, R. (2018, March). Systematic review of the literature, research on blockchain technology as support to the trust model proposed applied to smart places. In *World Conference on Information Systems and Technologies* (pp. 1163-1174). Springer. 10.1007/978-3-319-77703-0_113

Cai, Y., & Zhu, D. (2016). Fraud detections for online businesses: A perspective from blockchain technology. *Financial Innovation, 2*(1), 20. doi:10.118640854-016-0039-4

Calvaresi, D., Dubovitskaya, A., Calbimonte, J. P., Taveter, K., & Schumacher, M. (2018, June). Multi-agent systems and blockchain: Results from a systematic literature review. In *International Conference on Practical Applications of Agents and Multi-Agent Systems* (pp. 110-126). Springer. 10.1007/978-3-319-94580-4_9

Choi, J., & Shin, S. (2016). Propose of smart place IoT systems for strengthen security of the smart grid environment. International Information Institute (Tokyo) Information, 19(5), 1509.

Eling, M., & Lehmann, M. (2018). The impact of digitalization on the insurance value chain and the insurability of risks. *The Geneva Papers on Risk and Insurance. Issues and Practice*, *43*(3), 359–396. doi:10.105741288-017-0073-0

Eyal, I. (2017). Blockchain technology: Transforming libertarian cryptocurrency dreams to finance and banking realities. *Computer*, *50*(9), 38–49. doi:10.1109/MC.2017.3571042

Guo, Y., & Liang, C. (2016). Blockchain application and outlook in the banking industry. *Financial Innovation*, *2*(1), 24. doi:10.118640854-016-0034-9

Hawlitschek, F., Notheisen, B., & Teubner, T. (2018). The limits of trust-free systems: A literature review on blockchain technology and trust in the sharing economy. *Electronic Commerce Research and Applications*, *29*, 50–63. doi:10.1016/j.elerap.2018.03.005

Jaffe, C., Mata, C., & Kamvar, S. (2017, September). Motivating urban cycling through a blockchain-based financial incentives system. In *Proceedings of the 2017 ACM International Joint Conference on Pervasive and Ubiquitous Computing and Proceedings of the 2017 ACM International Symposium on Wearable Computers* (pp. 81-84). ACM. 10.1145/3123024.3123141

Karafiloski, E., & Mishev, A. (2017, July). Blockchain solutions for big data challenges: A literature review. In *IEEE EUROCON 2017-17th International Conference on Smart Technologies* (pp. 763-768). IEEE. 10.1109/EUROCON.2017.8011213

Korpela, K., Hallikas, J., & Dahlberg, T. (2017, January). Digital supply chain transformation toward blockchain integration. *Proceedings of the 50th Hawaii international conference on system sciences*. 10.24251/HICSS.2017.506

Król, M., Reñé, S., Ascigil, O., & Psaras, I. (2018). ChainSoft: Collaborative software development using smart contracts. In *CRYBLOCK 2018-Proceedings of the 1st Workshop on Cryptocurrencies and Blockchains for Distributed Systems, Part of MobiSys 2018* (pp. 1-6). ACM.

Kumar, N. M., & Mallick, P. K. (2018). Blockchain technology for security issues and challenges in IoT. *Procedia Computer Science*, *132*, 1815–1823. doi:10.1016/j.procs.2018.05.140

Liang, G., Weller, S. R., Luo, F., Zhao, J., & Dong, Z. Y. (2018). Distributed blockchain-based data protection framework for modern power systems against cyber attacks. *IEEE Transactions on Smart Grid*, *10*(3), 3162–3173. doi:10.1109/TSG.2018.2819663

Lindman, J., Tuunainen, V. K., & Rossi, M. (2017). *Opportunities and risks of Blockchain Technologies– a research agenda*. Academic Press.

Mettler, M. (2016, September). Blockchain technology in healthcare: The revolution starts here. In *2016 IEEE 18th International Conference on e-Health Networking, Applications and Services (Healthcom)* (pp. 1-3). IEEE.

Mylrea, M., & Gourisetti, S. N. G. (2017, September). Blockchain for smart grid resilience: Exchanging distributed energy at speed, scale and security. In 2017 Resilience Week (RWS) (pp. 18-23). IEEE.

O'Dair, M., & Beaven, Z. (2017). The networked record industry: How blockchain technology could transform the record industry. *Strategic Change*, *26*(5), 471–480. doi:10.1002/jsc.2147

Park, J., & Park, J. (2017). Blockchain security in cloud computing: Use cases, challenges, and solutions. *Symmetry*, *9*(8), 164. doi:10.3390ym9080164

Peters, G. W., & Panayi, E. (2016). Understanding modern banking ledgers through blockchain technologies: Future of transaction processing and smart contracts on the internet of money. In *Banking beyond banks and money* (pp. 239–278). Cham: Springer. doi:10.1007/978-3-319-42448-4_13

Pflaum, A., Bodendorf, F., Prockl, G., & Chen, H. (2017). *Introduction to the digital supply chain of the future: technologies, applications and business models minitrack*. Academic Press.

Seebacher, S., & Schüritz, R. (2017, May). Blockchain technology as an enabler of service systems: A structured literature review. In *International Conference on Exploring Services Science* (pp. 12-23). Springer. 10.1007/978-3-319-56925-3_2

Shackelford, S. J., & Myers, S. (2017). Block-by-block: Leveraging the power of blockchain technology to build trust and promote cyber peace. *Yale JL & Tech.*, *19*, 334.

Vujičić, D., Jagodić, D., & Ranđić, S. (2018, March). Blockchain technology, bitcoin, and Ethereum: A brief overview. In *2018 17th International Symposium INFOTEH-JAHORINA (INFOTEH)* (pp. 1-6). IEEE. 10.1109/INFOTEH.2018.8345547

Yaga, D., Mell, P., Roby, N., & Scarfone, K. (2019). *Blockchain technology overview*. arXiv preprint arXiv:1906.11078

Zhang, N., Zhong, S., & Tian, L. (2017). Using Blockchain to Protect Personal Privacy in the Scenario of Online Taxi-hailing. *International Journal of Computers, Communications & Control*, *12*(6), 886. doi:10.15837/ijccc.2017.6.2886

Zheng, Z., Xie, S., Dai, H., Chen, X., & Wang, H. (2017, June). An overview of blockchain technology: Architecture, consensus, and future trends. In *2017 IEEE International Congress on Big Data (BigData Congress)* (pp. 557-564). IEEE. 10.1109/BigDataCongress.2017.85

This research was previously published in Impact of Digital Transformation on Security Policies and Standards; pages 122-144, copyright year 2020 by Information Science Reference (an imprint of IGI Global).

Chapter 10
Blockchain–Based Data Market (BCBDM) Framework for Security and Privacy:
An Analysis

Shailesh Pancham Khapre
Amity University, Noida, India

Chandramohan Dhasarathan
iD https://orcid.org/0000-0002-5279-950X
Madanapalle Institute of Technology and Science, India

Puviyarasi T.
iD https://orcid.org/0000-0003-3668-3264
Madanapalle Institute of Technology and Science, India

Sam Goundar
iD https://orcid.org/0000-0001-6465-1097
British University Vietnam, Vietnam

ABSTRACT

In the internet era, incalculable data is generated every day. In the process of data sharing, complex issues such as data privacy and ownership are emerging. Blockchain is a decentralized distributed data storage technology. The introduction of blockchain can eliminate the disadvantages of the centralized data market, but at the same time, distributed data markets have created security and privacy issues. It summarizes the industry status and research progress of the domestic and foreign big data trading markets and refines the nature of the blockchain-based big data sharing and circulation platform. Based on these properties, a blockchain-based data market (BCBDM) framework is proposed, and the security and privacy issues as well as corresponding solutions in this framework are analyzed and discussed. Based on this framework, a data market testing system was implemented, and the feasibility and security of the framework were confirmed.

DOI: 10.4018/978-1-6684-7132-6.ch010

INTRODUCTION

The amount of data in today's world is increasing rapidly. Since the establishment of Facebook, it has collected more than 300 PB (petabytes) of personal data, and the scale of this is still expanding. Balazinska et al., Researcher from IBM have suggested that 90% of the data in the world today has been generated in the past two years, and with the emergence of new equipment and technologies, data growth will accelerate further. In the era of big data, data is continuously collected and analyzed, leading to technological innovation and economic growth. Companies and organizations use the data they collect to provide personalized user services, optimize company decision-making processes, and predict future trends. People are concerned about the security of personal data and process of extensive data used (Pang et al., 2017), worrying about whether Internet companies that provide services and collect data will protect users' data privacy, and do people have little control over the data they generate and how they use it (Balazinska et al., 2011). In recent years, many incidents related to violations of user data privacy have been reported. The most famous example is that of Facebook's 50 million user data been leaked, and user privacy has been greatly violated.

To ensure the normal circulation, use of data, and maximize the value of big data, in recent years, many new organizations have emerged regarding personal data sharing and transactions. In addition to the traditional method of data circulation (that is, the widespread data exchange service between companies and users), a big data sharing transaction market has emerged to facilitate data transactions by matching data needs with data sources (Zyskind et al., 2015). These data markets are already of considerable size. These data markets are valued at tens of billions of dollars and continue to grow (Zyskind et al., 2015). In the data market, data holders display their data information to attract potential data consumers; data consumers search and select the data sets they need, and obtain data usage rights by paying a certain fee; the data market gains revenue by facilitating data transactions. However, as the scale of data sharing transactions and the value of data increase, it is expected that fraud and leakage in the process of sharing transactions will gradually increase. The general architecture of a centralized data market is shown in Figure 1. In this architecture, the market platform operated by a centralized company or organization plays a vital role in the system.

The parties involved in the data-market, data buyers and market platforms, can obtain higher profits through collusive fraud, arbitrage purchase strategies and so on. In addition, according to (Zheng et al., 2018), the centralized data transaction model lacks effective information communication channels between data buyers and data sellers, resulting in inefficient data transactions (Goldfeder et al., 2017). Finally, the data market platform has more information advantages, i.e., the market platform knows the data content, but the data buyer cannot know the data content before buying the data, so the market platform can illegally obtain profits by constructing information barriers and controlling information disclosure. The centralized data market as highlighter by (Wang & Krishnamachari, 2019) has some inevitable problems such as data security, data privacy protection and data circulation performance bottlenecks. First of all, the intermediary of data transactions (usually the market platform) must be safe and reliable. The market platform needs to have credibility to ensure that it will not illegally use the data in the transaction and leak the privacy of the data holder (Dziembowski et al., 2018). However, the market platform does have such motive, and even if it uses or sells data illegally, it is generally difficult to pursue this illegal activity. At the same time, the centralized data market can easily become the target of attackers. The user's sensitive information (such as location, chat history, etc.) is stored in a centralized database, and there is a risk of privacy leakage and data loss. Most existing data markets run on centralized servers, and such systems have a single point of failure and a single point of performance bottleneck. Researches designed a centralized system (Missier et al., 2017) have shown that the existing data market will also control the search between buyers and sellers, resulting in inefficient market operation.

In order to avoid the disadvantages of the centralized data market as depicted in Figure.1, a decentralized data market was proposed. The decentralized data market architecture can circumvent the requirement of relying on trusted intermediaries to intervene in data transactions, get rid of single-point failures and single-point performance bottlenecks, and improve transparency and credibility. However, according to (Cao et al., 2016), due to the lack of centralized management in the decentralized data market, its system design and security assurance will be more difficult than the centralized data market. For example, the problem of "double payment" has always been the difficulty of distributed systems. In recent years, blockchain technology has matured, and the decentralized architecture of blockchain can be used as noted by (Subramanian, 2017) in regards to the underlying architecture of the data market to provide good support. Blockchain is a decentralized distributed data storage technology. The introduction of the blockchain layer according to (Mun et al., 2010) in the data market system will enable individual users to directly conclude transactions with data demanders without relying on any third party. This allows, as stated by (Ming Li et al., 2019) users to maintain ownership of the data and ensure the transparency of the transaction process.

Figure 1. Centralized data market architecture

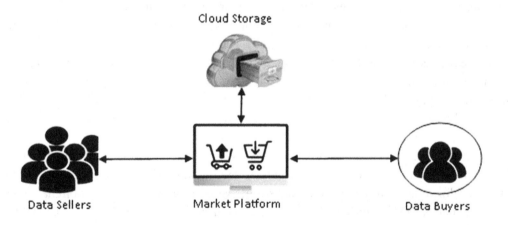

MARKET AND RELATED RESEARCH

Research on Existing Data Trading Market

As data has the function of optimizing decision-making and providing services, various organizations and institutions have begun to pay attention to the circulation and transaction of data. For example, Datashift, Gnip, NTT Data and other companies resell data from social networks such as Twitter, Xignite sells data from the financial industry, Factual is concerned about the transaction of geographic data. Simultaneously, Big-data sharing trading markets have also emerged to facilitate data trading by matching data needs with data sources, such as Infochimps, AWS Data exchange, Qlik Datamarket, Here, etc.

Datacoup is a centralized data market platform that allows users to sell various types of personal data (including financial data and social account data), and its client application allows users to import data from third-party applications (such as Facebook and Twitter). Since Datacoup collects raw data from users, users must completely trust Datacoup in data storage and data management. Similar to Datacoup, People.io is a centralized platform whose biggest feature is that it does not sell personal data directly to other organizations. It uses machine learning algorithms to analyze the user's personal data and then push personalized ads to the user. Although users will not be directly rewarded for providing their personal data, they can earn revenue by receiving personalized advertisements.

The development of the domestic data market is not yet mature, and a complete industrial chain of data circulation and transactions has not yet been formed. For example, there are big data sharing platforms dominated by Internet companies, and most of their data comes from the data collected by their application software, such as Alibaba Cloud. There are also data sharing and transaction platforms such as Data Hall, Sudoku, etc. These platforms collect data from third parties in various ways to realize online transactions of big data resources. In addition, there are government-led big data trading centres, which are mostly government/state-owned enterprises or joint ventures between state-owned enterprises and private enterprises. However, these data trading centres are generally closed, and their specific data market architecture technology is still relatively unknown.

In recent years, the distributed data trading market based on blockchain has attracted great attention from the industry. IOTA is an encrypted "currency" designed specifically for the Internet of Things (IoT), and has used blockchain technology to build a transaction market for IoT data. Similar companies include DataBrokerDAO, Datum, Datapace and Wibson. Some of these companies directly sell their collected data sets, and some collect personal data from the public and sell them to individual users. There are also some examples of using blockchain technology to build data markets. For example, the Shanghai Data Exchange Center uses the alliance chain to store transaction-related information in blockchain nodes to ensure that data transactions are safe, efficient, and credible. Existing blockchain data markets only guarantee certain elements of data market construction, and do not fully consider the goals that should be achieved in constructing a data trading market: decentralization, fairness, privacy, effectiveness, and economic nature. Section 3, will discuss these properties in detail.

Related Research Work

There is also a lot of work in the research community involving blockchain, data markets and related issues. (Wang et al., 2019) discussed the significance of the emerging digital data market and listed research opportunities in this direction. The blockchain has been used to protect the privacy of personal data (Gupta et al., 2019), transforming the blockchain into an automatic access control manager that does not rely on trusted third parties, to clarify the ownership of data and ensure that users control their data, but this work only discusses the storage and sharing of data. In their paper, (Ramachandran et al., 2018) discussed the use of blockchain to share personal health data systems, enabling users to safely control and share their personal health data in a manner consistent with general data protection regulations. Their work focuses on data collection and storage, putting more emphasis on a method to control data quality. To study the issues of fairness, security and privacy in the process of using blockchain (Liu et al., 2019 & Zhou et al., 2018) investigate these issues as concerns to trade physical commodities. The AdChain Registry as observed by (Wright et al., 2008), is an Ethereum-based advertising publisher's registry that provide recommended publishers for advertisers and a set of recommended data sources for specific data buyers. The main consideration of an effective protocol as put forward by (Sharifi et al., 2014) for fair exchange in smart contracts is to focuses on the realization of fairness of digital goods. A Blockchain-Enabled Decentralized Reliable Smart Industrial Internet of Things (BCIIoT) is designed to meet out Industrial Internet of Things (IIoT) by constructing a Smart Factory (Chandramohan & Shanmugam, et al., 2021).

There are many literature on the use of blockchain to build distributed data markets. The researchers (Christidis & Devetsikiotis, 2016) considered the characteristics of the Internet of Things, constructed a decentralized system, and analyzed its performance. The intention was to construct a market for real-time human perception data. However, these systems often do not consider the appropriate pricing mechanism as noted by (Yuan & Wang, 2016). The market still rely on a credible third party in some form, or just stay on the theoretical analysis, there is no complete system (Chanti et al., 2021). Hybrid authentication technique inevitability is taken into consideration (Chandramohan, et al., 2013b), to preserve user privacy and ensuring end point lock for cloud service digital information. The work on the centralized data market by Scott Stornetta. Focuses on the issue of pricing mechanism and has a more detailed design of the data collection, processing, and auction processes. To provide a personal data vault (Rahalkar & Gujar, 2019) proposes a mechanism that provides for managing data policies, allowing individual users to control access and share data at a fine-grained level. Research communities' targets on intelligence perception system built with blockchain (Schuster et al., 2015). The focus on the characteristics and processing methods of picture data in transactions is conducted by (Satoshi Nakamoto et al., 2019). A structured data with critical features is constructed with a blockchain-based data market and introduces a trusted intermediary in the transaction between buyers and sellers, although this makes transactions between buyers and sellers easier (Baumann et al., 2015), but it will also reduce the security of the system a lot. Although the transaction proposed by Buterin et al. still requires the intervention of a third party, it sets up multiple distributed intermediaries to participate in the transaction during the transaction, which limits the intermediary's monopoly ability. The innovation is that its data transmission and payments are carried out off-chain, which can save the expensive storage space of the blockchain. A design of automated pricing negotiation mechanism for the pricing problem in large and small scale industries could be manageable and improved with the blockchain-based data market. Distributed Data Vending (DDV) is a distributed data transaction framework that sells personal medical records. When a data seller wants to sell his medical records, he must upload his encrypted data to a cloud storage service provider and submit his data information to the blockchain smart contract. DDV Zhou et al. still uses third-party cloud storage services to store data from data sellers. Although data has been encrypted before uploading to cloud storage, data buyers and data sellers must still trust third-party cloud services to achieve data durability and data delivery.

Overview of Blockchain

The concept of blockchain was proposed by (W. Scott Stornetta et al., 1991), described a digital architecture system called "blockchain". In 2008, Satoshi Nakamoto proposed Bitcoin as a new type of "digital currency", and the blockchain technology behind it has also received extensive attention in many research fields.

In the blockchain network, all participants are essentially a group of writers who do not trust each other, and they share a data link without a trusted intermediary. In order to prevent the bifurcation phenomenon from erupting in this distributed environment, the blockchain has designed a consensus protocol. Blockchain nodes can provide computing resources as miners to compete for the power to record transactions in the blockchain, and the winners will receive economic incentives. This is a mechanism for blockchain to reach consensus, called Proof of Work (PoW).

Proof of Work makes it theoretically possible for an attacker to break the blockchain system only if he has mastered more than 50% of the computing power of the entire system. However, the consensus protocol has paid the price of consuming massive amounts of computing power and resources. In recent years, the annual global electricity consumption for Bitcoin "mining" has reached 0.13% of the total annual electricity consumption. Each full node must store all transactions to verify the legitimacy of these transactions on the blockchain. In addition, due to the block size limitation and the time interval for generating new blocks, Bitcoin can only process 7 transactions per second, which cannot meet the requirements of processing millions of transactions in real time.

The concept of Ethereum was proposed by (ButerinV et al., 2015), after being inspired by Bitcoin. Its biggest feature is the increased support for smart contracts. It will run a virtual machine in the user's Ethereum node. The smart contract running in it is written in Solidity. The language can support Turing completeness. In order to meet the needs of running in the virtual machine of the user client, the function of Solidity language is designed to be very weak. Solidity only implements a part of the JavaScript function in a special method, making smart contracts more error-prone in Ethereum.

In addition, all calculations related to status updates performed on the Ethereum network need to consume "natural gas" (gas, in Wei units, which is the smallest unit of Ether), which makes complex calculations on the Ethereum network cost-effective.

Blockchain technology provides a new direction for creating a decentralized data market and reducing the role of intermediaries in intervening between trading parties. Blockchain has some characteristics: First, it is decentralized. In a centralized system, each transaction needs to be verified by a central trusted institution, which inevitably increases the cost and performance bottleneck of the central server; second, its transparency with security, transactions can be quickly verified, and honest miners will not be able to recognize invalid transactions. Once a transaction is included in the blockchain, it is almost impossible to delete or roll back the transaction; The third is anonymity. Each user can use their address to interact with the blockchain. At present, many blockchain systems are committed to making the blockchain a completely anonymous system, such as the Monero coin.

Because of these characteristics, blockchain currently has a wide range of application prospects. Applications in different fields (such as IoT, intelligent transportation systems, naming and storage systems, and health record sharing, etc.) all have implementations based on blockchain technology. The underlying technology of the blockchain, the InterPlanetary File System (IPFS) is a content-addressable peer-to-peer hypermedia distribution protocol, which also has wide application value in a distributed system environment.

DESIGN GOALS OF BLOCKCHAIN DATA MARKET

In data transactions, the blockchain system replaces the status of a centralized data market, and buyers and sellers will directly conduct transactions on the execution of smart contracts in the blockchain. The design of the data market based on the blockchain system mainly considers the following questions.

Decentralization: Due to the disadvantages of the centralized data market, many studies have begun to discuss the establishment of a decentralized data transaction system that allows data holders and data demanders to conduct transactions directly through a secure and trusted distributed system. However, many existing related research and system design still rely on trusted third-party entities in some modules, and these third-party entities have the motivation and ability to benefit by disrupting the buyer-seller transaction. Therefore, for the decentralized data market, we believes that a system should be built that does not rely on any trusted third party and only involves data buyers and sellers. The transaction is directly reached by the buyer and the seller, and various security and privacy requirements are realized by the design of the distributed transaction system.

Fairness: Fairness means that the position of buyers and sellers in the entire transaction should be the same, they will reach a consensus on the transaction data and their prices, and they have the ability to stop the transaction at any time. The most basic fairness should be achieved at the end of the smart contract execution, either the buyer gets valid data, the seller gets the payment, or neither the buyer nor the seller get any revenue, it is necessary to prevent data sellers from providing illegal data, data buyers denying data purchase fees and other unfair situations.

Privacy: Privacy requires the system to protect the user's identity privacy and data privacy. Identity privacy is the anonymity of users in the data market. The anonymity of the Bitcoin blockchain is only a pseudonym, due to increasing and authorized agent to protect all users privacy irrespective of users. There are many blockchain systems dedicated to improving their anonymity. Data privacy means that the data can only be used by the user who purchased the data, and the attacker cannot obtain any additional information about the data from the information stored in the blockchain. In many scenarios, data consumers often purchase the right to use a piece of data. In such a system, data privacy requires that data buyers cannot obtain any additional information about the data after using it.

Effectiveness: For all practical systems that are widely implemented, to be able to implement effectively, it is necessary to ensure the participant's experience, which imposes requirements on the execution efficiency and resource consumption of the system. In the blockchain-based data market, it is necessary to consider whether the execution speed of the blockchain system itself can keep up with the needs of big data transactions. Due to the special mechanism of blockchain smart contracts, smart contracts should be avoided as much as possible for complex calculations.

Economic incentives: A major goal of the data market is to seek benefits for all users participating in the system to encourage them to participate in the big data sharing and trading system. The first is that both buyers and sellers will benefit from the transaction. Data sellers can get as much economic benefits as possible by selling their data usage rights, and data buyers can get high-quality data that meets their needs. At the same time, the transaction fee will inspire other participants to do a good job of maintaining the system platform. In the pricing game, some sellers and buyers may collude to capture the interests of other users. Therefore, while providing economic incentives, the data market also needs to ensure that illegal arbitrage and other illegal strategic actions do not occur.

SYSTEM ARCHITECTURE

The blockchain-based data market system designed in this chapter consists of the following three components: a smart contract in the Ethereum blockchain, a client held by system participants, and a peer-to-peer data transmission network. When a data buyer needs some specific data to calculate a specific task (such as the temperature sensor data near the location to calculate the local outdoor temperature), he will use the data filtering module and notify the smart contract. The entire system locates some qualified data through safe calculation. After the interaction between the data buyer and the data seller, the data pricing module determines the sold data and its price. After the payment is completed, the system runs the buyer's calculation task in a safe manner, and returns the result to the buyer. The transaction is completed. In the process of the transaction, the system needs to ensure the design goals mentioned above, and the modules of the system will be described in detail later.

Data Filtering

Data buyers usually do not need all the data of all users, but care about the specific data of specific users. For example, in a crowd sourcing task, a data buyer wants to know the outdoor temperature of a location, he can put forward a restriction: the location of the sensor provided by the seller needs to be within a certain range, and the data provided must also meet certain timeliness. This process is called data screening. Buyers can organize their data needs into a logical expression or a mathematical function and store it in the blockchain for sellers to query and judge.

The filtering conditions of these data are generally relatively simple, so it is not appropriate to upload the buyer's data filtering needs directly to the blockchain, which obviously exposes the privacy of buyers and sellers. According to the form of data filtering, an attacker can easily deduce the buyer's data needs, thereby obtaining the privacy of the buyer and seller. In the above example, if a location in which the buyer is interested is disclosed, the attacker may infer the range of activity of the buyer, and at the same time, the equipment held by the seller near the location is also exposed. Therefore, in order to protect the privacy of system participants, the target data should be screened out while hiding the data screening conditions. The most intuitive solution is function encryption, that is, the user (buyer) who has the decryption key can obtain the function value of the ciphertext data (data filtering function), but will not obtain any information about the plaintext.

In addition, it is sometimes not intuitive to translate buyers' data screening needs into mathematical and logical expressions. Data transactions sometimes also target some unstructured data, for example, buyers need some pictures of "cats". The buyer may be able to judge whether a piece of data is what he wants, but he cannot quantify these needs through simple and appropriate logic .In order to give a logical expression of buyers' screening needs, some complex data processing algorithms need to be run in the system to get the quality of the data and the degree of fit with the screening needs. Since every potential data needs to be calculated, these algorithms should be simplified as much as possible.

Data Storage

Data storage mechanism is a general term used to describe how to push data and where to store it. Mainstream public blockchain limits the number of transactions and the space blocks, which can be the size of the block (Bitcoin) or block consume "natural" upper limit (Ethernet Square). For the data trading market, it is not feasible to store massive amounts of data directly on the blockchain.

Both Quorum and Corda are inspired by the blockchain platform for the financial field. They propose a model that does not store data publicly on the blockchain. Among them, the data is kept off-chain by the participating third parties (financial institutions), and the consensus function aims to ensure that the interacting parties reach an agreement. This method may be practical for financial institutions, but it violates the design goals of decentralization.

Although it is impractical to store complete data in the blockchain, you can upload a "data summary" that is tied to specific data. Therefore, the generally proposed data market is aimed at non-real-time and fault-tolerant transaction modes. These systems can send data to the data backend in a long time interval. This method requires the assistance of the distributed file storage layer. InterPlanetary File System and Swarm are the two main distributed file storage layers. Both of these technologies are peer-to-peer (P2P) technologies with a distributed file transmission system in which files are addressed by the hash value of their content. When the data is successfully stored in IPFS, the user will receive a hash index, which will allow the user to retrieve the file later. This index will replace the data stored in the smart contract, saving the burden of the entire system. These distributed file systems are also open and transparent, and the data stored in them should be encrypted. At the same time, if all users participating in the system maintain an IPFS or Swarm node, the cost is very high, and some system participants can be used as a distributed file storage service provider to charge a certain fee to users who upload data.

Data Pricing

In the data market, a set of data in the form of the sale price and the design has been an active area of research. This chapter considers the design of the pricing mechanism in a game theory environment. Each data holder has a private valuation of their data, that is, the loss of the privacy of the data holder; the data buyer also has an estimate of the data he will purchase, that is, the value of this data to the buyer. Bidders may choose to dishonestly report their valuation of a piece of data. This will bring trouble to the mechanism design of the transaction. The solution in game theory is to design an incentive-compatible mechanism that allows each bidder to get the highest return when reporting its true valuation. Bidders report that their true valuation can make designing a pricing mechanism much easier.

Bundle pricing for multiple copies of related data is also a common problem in data market transactions. Early research usually simply assumed that for data buyers, the expected value of the bundled data is equal to the sum of the individual values of all data. Later research found that data affect each other, and the value of each piece of data depends on the content of the entire transaction data set. The value of the data set comes from the mutual relationship of the data.

Data as a commodity has some unique properties, which make data pricing complex and the need to consider some additional issues. First, the marginal cost of data is extremely low, or there is no marginal cost at all. Marginal cost refers to the cost of copying a commodity after it is produced. The marginal cost of data is basically zero so that once the data buyer obtains the data seller's data, then he can dispose of and sell the data at will. The second is that the value of data and the amount of data are not necessarily related. For example, for someone who needs some pictures of "cats", a bunch of pictures about "dogs" are almost worthless. The third is the quantification of data value. The value of data is difficult to quantify. It is difficult for data holders to estimate the value of data. At the same time, the valuation of different people is also very different.

In response to the characteristics of these data, the data trading model in the data market has also changed. Traditional data markets directly trade user data, and dishonest buyers can resell data sets that they have purchased without the seller's knowledge, thereby gaining benefits. Many works have found that the vast majority of data consumers only need some statistical results or advanced features behind large amounts of data, such as calculating the average of the data set, or training data for machine learning models, rather than the data itself. Therefore, the data market can collect data from data holders and then serve the computing tasks in the hands of data consumers. The buyer provides a specific task whose input is the one-time use right of the multiple pieces of data it purchases, and the output is the result the buyer wants. In this way, the data itself is isolated from the data consumer.

In the above design, the evaluation of the value of data actually becomes the evaluation of the accuracy of the buyer's calculation task or the value of the calculation result to the buyer's value. Although the value of the data itself is difficult to quantify, the improvement in task results is easy to quantify. Because buyers often need data from multiple sellers, it is necessary to distinguish the individual value of each piece of data in the transaction. To calculate the value of data, (Goldfeder & Bonneau et al., 2017), Shapley value can be used to calculate the contribution of a single piece of data. In game theory, calculating the Shapley value is a solution to distribute the benefits and costs fairly to multiple participants in the cooperation. The computational complexity of the Shapley value increases exponentially with the increase in the amount of data, so in practical use, approximate algorithms are often used.

Safe Computing

Blockchain is an open and transparent, decentralized data storage technology. All information entering the blockchain system is public, and the execution of all transactions or scripts is transparent. At the same time, the computing power of blockchain smart contracts is very weak. Due to the block size and limitations, the calculations that can be performed by calling a smart contract are few, but the cost is high. Therefore, no matter whether the task issued by the buyer is directly run in the smart contract (the smart contract can hardly bear such a burden), or delegated to an untrusted individual on the blockchain, it is still unsafe. Similarly, the data screening process and data pricing process also have such problems. Bitcoin, Ethereum and other blockchain public chain nodes have mutual distrust and are completely open and transparent, which has caused new problems in privacy protection.

The goal of this chapter is that in the entire data market system and the transaction process within the market system, the data market does not disclose any additional information about users and their data. There are many ways to perform calculations in the system safely and correctly, while protecting the privacy of all parties. The role of secure computing is to complete various computing tasks while protecting features such as privacy and fairness. Research in different fields can achieve goals in different degrees and angles.

Cryptography is the most intuitive way to achieve secure computing. Secure Multi-Party Computation-MPC (Missier & Bajoudah et al., 2017), is a subfield of cryptography and a direct solution to the problem of secure computing. The goal of MPC is to create a joint calculation method for all parties, while protecting the privacy of these inputs. Unlike traditional encryption methods, cryptography technology ensures the security and accuracy of communication or storage, and this mode of cryptography focuses on protecting the privacy between participants. MPC can now be seen as a practical solution to various real-world problems (especially those that only require simple linear shared secrets), such as distributed voting, private bidding and auctions, shared signature or decryption functions, private information retrieval, etc. Many simple tasks of buyers can be easily performed through MPC. However, the MPC method cannot be used for deep learning tasks. The core of the mainstream MPC framework uses 2 encryption technologies: encryption circuit and inadvertent transmission. MPC converts the buyer's task function into a garbled circuit, which is then sent out inadvertently. In complex and heavy calculation tasks, converting the deep neural network into a garbled circuit will inevitably increase the amount of calculation and lose certain accuracy. At the same time, in MPC, deep learning may lead to unacceptable communication complexity. In addition, homomorphic encryption and zero-knowledge proofs can also be used for simple tasks.

Another method for implementing secure computing is to use trusted hardware, such as a Trusted Execution Environment (TEE). TEE is a general concept, a safe area of the main processor, which guarantees that the codes and data loaded in it are protected in terms of confidentiality and integrity. Assuming that some users have some TEE hardware, these users are regarded as safe users. The seller will send their data to the secure user's TEE device, the buyer's calculation task will be calculated in the TEE, and the result will be returned to the buyer in a safe manner. Only trusted applications running in TEE can access all functions of the device's main processor, peripherals, and memory. Hardware isolation protects data and computing content from user-installed applications running on the main operating system. Typical hardware technologies that support TEE implementation are the Advanced Risc Machines (ARM) Trust Zone and Intel SGX Software Guard eXtensions. SGX is an extension of the Intel architecture and can protect the execution of application programs at the hardware level. For example, SGX can be used to protect buyer data in a cloud computing environment. Examples include VC3 and Haven. The core of SGX technology is to isolate a special area (called "enclave") in the memory, and the designated program can create a "safe area" in this area, and store the key code and data in the "safe area". Only the CPU or the program itself can access the code and data in the "enclave". These existing hardware technologies are claimed to have vulnerabilities. And some open source projects and large companies are also working to make TEE stronger.

Joint learning is a new (Aledhari & Razzak et al., 2020), collaborative machine learning method proposed by Google that does not require centralized training data. Its workflow is: the data seller downloads the current model from the cloud provided by the buyer, improves the model by learning from the seller's data, and then aggregates the changes into a small update. This update of the model is sent to the cloud using encrypted communication, and the updated model in the cloud is immediately aggregated with the updates of other users to improve the shared model. Therefore, all training data is only saved on the seller's device, and there is no separate update stored in the cloud. Joint learning is usually aimed at the situation where a user has multiple data or a data set, and is not applicable to a situation where a single seller only provides a small amount of data. If the seller provides only one piece of data to participate in the training, the malicious buyer may be able to reversely calculate the seller's real data from the model update, and the data training process requires frequent communication, which is very inefficient.

BCBDM SYSTEM IMPLEMENTATION AND VERIFICATION

According to the data market framework designed in Section 4, we implement a data market system based on the Ethereum private chain, including system participants holding desktop application clients, smart contracts in the Ethereum network, and data transmission networks. The desktop client is written in JavaScript, the Ethereum smart contract is written in Solidity, and the data transmission directly uses the IPFS JS interface. The system architecture designed and the interaction between various components are shown in Figure 2.

Figure 2. BCBDM - System architecture and interaction between various components

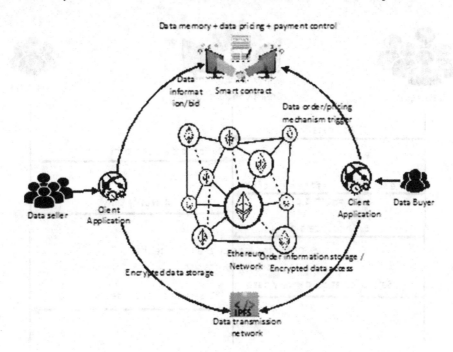

System Implementation Framework

This chapter has implemented a simplified version of the expected system to facilitate the verification and analysis of the correctness and feasibility of the system. It is a simplified system to a buyer and multiple potential sellers to conduct transactions, a buyer only needs one piece of data.

The pricing mechanism uses the second price auction, that is, the data of the transaction adopts the data of the lowest bid by the seller, and the data is paid at the price of the second lowest bid. The buyer's computing task is set to a simple form, and homomorphic encryption or secure multi-party computing can be used to ensure secure computing. We realized two kinds of specific data form transactions in the system, unstructured picture data and structured GPS travel data.

The transaction process of the data market is shown in Figure 3. The data seller adds a new piece of data information in the smart contract, the data buyer adds an order containing the data requirements, and the seller gives a quote after matching the legal data according to the conditions in the order. The system will run the pricing mechanism and calculate the winning data. This data will be used to calculate the buyer's tasks in a secure manner and deliver the data. In the system, the user can perform the following operations.

Register an account. To buy and sell data in the data market, users must first register an Ethereum account, and the client also includes a simple Ethereum account management function. At the same time, the user also needs to register an account in a smart contract hereinafter referred to as Bigdata Data Market (DDM). For example, the user can register an account of a sensor device in the smart contract, which needs to disclose information such as the type and model of the sensor device.

Figure 3. BCBDM Data market transaction process

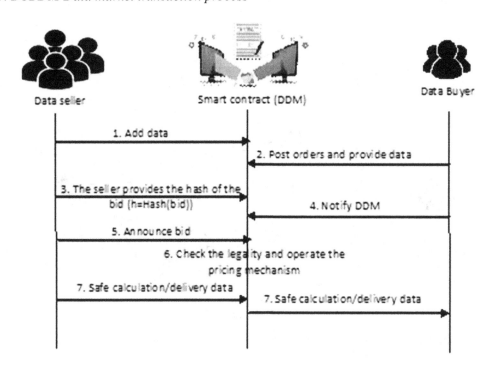

Add data. After generating some data that he wants to sell, the data holder can upload the data to IPFS encrypted, and register this data in the smart contract account, it contains the storage address of the data, the hash value of the data and the registration time. In the BCBDM system design, data buyers are encouraged to set data registration time requirements when adding data orders to purchase data, only data holders who meet the data registration time requirements are eligible to bid for the order to improve the timeliness and reliability of the data.

Release orders. If the data buyer wants to purchase the right to use specific data in the market, then he will add an order in DDM, the order contains the buyer's demand for data (including data type, data selection function, data price limit, data quantity limitation, etc.) and the calculation task of buyers using data.

The data seller provides the hash value of its bid. The data seller selects one or more data that meets the needs of the data buyer, and sets a package price. Due to the completely open and transparent nature of the blockchain, bidding directly in DDM will lead to arbitrage, and sellers of the post-quote can see the bids of other sellers and obtain higher profits by controlling their own bids. We have set a time window in the system, and the seller needs to submit the hash value of his bid within the window, which is equivalent to realizing a sealed auction. At the same time, such a design helps to achieve fairness.

The data buyer informs DDM to obtain the real bid of the market data seller. The data buyer informs DDM to stop accepting users to participate in the transaction and to start accepting users who have already participated in the transaction to disclose their bids. Smart contracts cannot actively execute orders, and need to be triggered by blockchain users. At the same time, data buyers can blacklist some sellers and refuse their bids.

Data sellers publish real bids. The data seller publishes its bid, which needs to match the previous hash value. If the data seller does not announce the real bid within the specified time, indicating that the seller is regrets, the system will reduce the reputation value of the seller as a punishment, and the reputation value of the seller who successfully trades the data will increase. Users with too low reputation value will not be able to participate in the transaction, and the reputation value system can suppress cheating by system participants.

Pricing mechanism, use the classic (Clarke & Groves et al., 2017), Vickrey–Clarke–Groves (VCG) auction mechanism for data selection and price determination. The VCG auction mechanism guarantees authenticity, so each bidder has an incentive to make a real valuation of his personal data.

Safe calculation/delivery data. The system uses homomorphic encryption to calculate the buyer's calculation tasks, and then hands the encrypted result to the data buyer to complete the order. Since secure computing is still at an immature stage, the computational complexity of homomorphic encryption is very high. We have only tested the calculation task of using the additive homomorphic algorithm to calculate buyers. In the future, we will support the other methods according to the secure computing method in Section 4. Data buyers and sellers can also directly trade data, using a hybrid encryption method to encrypt the symmetric key of the data with the public key provided by the buyer. This method can achieve non-communication data transmission in an open and transparent environment.

System Analysis and Verification

We discusse the advantages of the demo system achieved from the design goals of building a blockchain based data market, including fairness, privacy and effectiveness, and also consider the scalability of the system. We found that the system has basically achieved the design goals defined by the blockchain data market, the entire system runs smoothly, the usability is high, and the security and privacy are well guaranteed.

Fairness

Before the transaction result is reached, that is, before the pricing mechanism starts, both parties to the transaction can terminate the transaction. Although this may lead to a reduction in the reputation value of the participants, in the case of "regret" infrequently occurring, the transaction can be terminated at any time. At the same time, after the implementation of the pricing mechanism, due to the characteristics of blockchain and secure computing, neither party to the transaction can prevent the transaction from proceeding. Ethereum transfer and buyer task calculation will be executed, which ensures the non-repudiation of data transactions and guarantees fair transactions.

Privacy

We protect the identity privacy and data privacy of system participants in the system. Identity privacy is achieved based on the anonymous capabilities of the blockchain, while data privacy is fully protected. Data encryption, data selection mechanisms, and security calculations prevent attackers from obtaining any additional information about the data from the execution of transactions. However, the system implemented did not consider exposing the privacy of the seller's pricing of their data. In future work, the privacy of bidding will be considered.

Effectiveness

The operational efficiency of the blockchain has always been criticized. It takes more than ten minutes for a transaction in Bitcoin to be written into the blockchain and the time that this transaction was finally confirmed on the Internet even exceeded one hour. Calculating the data selection function in the client, calculating the buyer's tasks and processing the pictures in a secure manner are relatively time-consuming, which will reduce the user's experience satisfaction with the application. The random click test of the application found that from the perspective of the client user, the average response time of a button is about 4 s, this shows that the current design of the system is not yet able to achieve real-time performance, but it can guarantee the basic use requirements. The system proposed is directly based on Ethereum. To improve the availability of the data market system, a more efficient and lightweight blockchain system can be used.

Table 1. Gas consumption for various operations in the system

Operation	Gas Consumption/Wei
Register an account in a smart contract	110,726
Saving money in smart contracts	27,638
Withdrawing money from smart contracts	35,753
Add an image data order	2,228,844
Add an itinerary data order	715,103
Submit bid to order	29,145
Transfer to other accounts	21,000
Add a trip/picture data	193,852
Computational pricing mechanism	459,230
Average	424,587

Deploying contracts or any type of transaction in the Ethereum blockchain will incur transaction fees. In the Ethereum blockchain, gas is used to estimate costs. Usually, the mining union in the system determines the price for running some instructions, and the initiator of a transaction (such as a data buyer is adding an order to the blockchain and a data seller submitting a bid to the blockchain) needs to specify the maximum gas consumption. Because miners like to deal with transactions that provide high incentives, transactions with lower gas prices can take a long time. However, because the value of personal data is very low, complex calculations in smart contracts will cause the profits of buyers and sellers to decrease linearly. The system proposed guarantees the interests of system participants by reducing the amount of calculation of smart contracts.

Through several tests, we got the average value of gas consumption for various operations in the system (see Table 1). Based on the current price of Ethereum on the Ethereum public chain (each Ethereum price is about US$250), the average consumption of each operation is 424587×10^{10} USD, even if a data buyer needs tens of thousands of data, he needs very little to participate in the system.

There may be a lot of transaction-related information stored in the smart contract. Although the smart contract of Ethereum supports multiple complex data types, the slightly complicated structure in practice will cause the request to be invalid. For example, because the length of the array to be uploaded is very long, and each item is also a very complicated decimal, the 1,024-dimensional array cannot be successfully uploaded to the smart contract at all. Ethereum also has a block gas limit, which is set to 8,000,000 Wei by default, so in fact it is not possible to upload data with too high dimensions (see Table 2). Due to Ethereum's restrictions on the amount of gas in the block, Ethereum is set to a maximum of 8,000,000 Wei by default. If an operation consumes more gas than this value, the operation will be rolled back. Therefore, there is a possibility that the order will be returned in the DDM. The system proposed stores complex data structures (such as data selection functions) in IPFS, and then puts its address in the order and stores it in DDM.

Since data pricing is performed on the Ethereum blockchain through smart contracts, its computational cost cannot be ignored. In order to evaluate the data pricing cost of the system, the gas consumption based on the VCG auction-based data pricing was used to test a large number of sellers' bids. Figure 4 shows the relationship between the gas consumption of VCG data pricing and the number of bids received for data orders. Although the implementation of the data pricing algorithm can be further optimized, when a large number of data sellers bid for the same data order, the data pricing cost will be very high. If the data market based on the Ethereum blockchain is to be realized, the high cost of data pricing will become a major obstacle to the application of the system.

Table 2. Gas consumption under different array lengths

Array length/dimension	Gas Consumption/Wei
50	1466256
100	2228844
125	2542012
150	2885446
175	3243954
200	3632920
225	3991512

Figure 4. The relationship between gas consumption of data pricing and the number of bids received by the order

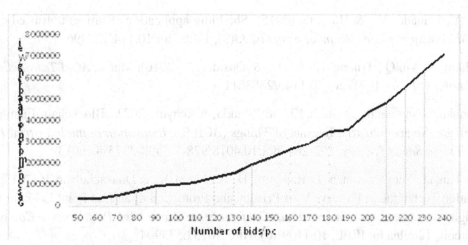

Decentralization and Scalability

Scalability, decentralization and security are the three difficulties aspects which is need to be referred for the inevitable contradictions of the blockchain system. The system is a completely decentralized system and does not depend on any trusted third parties, so scalability and security will be challenged more. In order to ensure security, the system proposed sacrifices scalability, if a support for different data forms, data selling methods and pricing mechanisms is required, then smart contracts need to be rewritten, and compatibility will also have problems, which can be taken into consideration in the construction of the actual data market. In the future deployment of the data market, we will further discuss the trade-offs between scalability, decentralization, and security.

CONCLUSION

Data is an important asset in a data-driven economy, and it has driven the rise of new data trading industries. The data market is an important form of data assetization today. The distributed data market has the privacy protection capabilities and transaction security guarantees that the centralized data market does not have, and has huge market prospects and research prospects. In this chapter, we discuss the characteristics that the future data market should meet, analyze the challenges in the distributed data market based on blockchain, propose preliminary solutions, and discuss the possible future development directions of these technologies. The construction of the actual data market provides reference opinions. Both the data market and the blockchain technology are in the stage of rapid technological development, and researchers need to conduct more in-depth exploration and research based on these issues.

REFERENCES

Balazinska, M., Howe, B., & Suciu, D. (2011). Data markets in the cloud. *Proceedings of the VLDB Endowment International Conference on Very Large Data Bases*, 4(12), 1482–1485. doi:10.14778/3402755.3402801

Baumann, A., Peinado, M., & Hunt, G. (2015). Shielding applications from an untrusted cloud with haven. *ACM Transactions on Computer Systems*, 33(3), 1–26. doi:10.1145/2799647

Cao, T., Pham, T., Vu, Q., Truong, H., Le, D., & Dustdar, S. (2016). Marsa. *ACM Transactions on Internet Technology*, 16(3), 1–21. doi:10.1145/2883611

Chandramohan, Shanmugam, Shailesh, Khapre, Shukla, & Achyut. (2021). Blockchain-Enabled Decentralized Reliable Smart Industrial Internet of Things (BCIIoT). *Innovation in the Industrial Internet of Things (IIoT) and Smart Factory*, 192-204. doi:10.4018/978-1-7998-3375-8.ch013

Chandramohan, D., Vengattaraman, T., Rajaguru, D., Baskaran, R., & Dhavachelvan, P. (2013b). Hybrid Authentication Technique to Preserve User Privacy and Protection as an End Point Lock for the Cloud Service Digital Information. In *International Conference on Green High Performance Computing* (pp. 1-4). Nagercoil, Tamilnadu: IEEE. 10.1109/ICGHPC.2013.6533904

Chanti S., Anwar, T., Chithralekha T., & Uma, V. (2021). Global naming and storage system using blockchain. *Research Anthology on Combating Denial-of-Service Attacks*, 265-281. doi:10.4018/978-1-7998-5348-0.ch014

Christidis, K., & Devetsikiotis, M. (2016). Blockchains and smart contracts for the Internet of things. *IEEE Access: Practical Innovations, Open Solutions, 4*, 2292–2303. doi:10.1109/ACCESS.2016.2566339

Dziembowski, S., Eckey, L., & Faust, S. (2018). FairSwap. *Proceedings of the 2018 ACM SIGSAC Conference on Computer and Communications Security*. 10.1145/3243734.3243857

Goldfeder, S., Bonneau, J., Gennaro, R., & Narayanan, A. (2017). Escrow protocols for cryptocurrencies: How to buy physical goods using bitcoin. *Financial Cryptography and Data Security*, 321-339. doi:10.1007/978-3-319-70972-7_18

Gupta, P., Kanhere, S., & Jurdak, R. (2019). A Decentralized IoT Data Marketplace. *Networking and Internet Architecture, 6*(7), 1-6. arXiv:1906.01799

Li, M., Weng, J., Yang, A., Lu, W., Zhang, Y., Hou, L., Liu, J.-N., Xiang, Y., & De Robert, H. (2019). CrowdBC: A Blockchain-Based Decentralized Framework for Crowdsourcing. *IEEE Transactions on Parallel and Distributed Systems, 30*(6), 1251–1266. doi:10.1109/TPDS.2018.2881735

Liu, K., Qiu, X., Chen, W., Chen, X., & Zheng, Z. (2019). Optimal pricing mechanism for data market in blockchain-enhanced Internet of things. *IEEE Internet of Things Journal, 6*(6), 9748–9761. doi:10.1109/JIOT.2019.2931370

Missier, P., Bajoudah, S., Capossele, A., Gaglione, A., & Nati, M. (2017). Mind my value. *Proceedings of the Seventh International Conference on the Internet of Things*. 10.1145/3131542.3131564

Mun, M., Hao, S., Mishra, N., Shilton, K., Burke, J., Estrin, D., Hansen, M., & Govindan, R. (2010). Personal data vaults. *Proceedings of the 6th International Conference on - Co-NEXT '10*. 10.1145/1921168.1921191

Pang, J. Z., Fu, H., Lee, W. I., & Wierman, A. (2017). The efficiency of open access in platforms for networked cournot markets. *IEEE INFOCOM 2017 - IEEE Conference on Computer Communications*. doi:10.1109/infocom.2017.8057125

Rahalkar, C., & Gujar, D. (2019). Content addressed P2P file system for the web with blockchain-based meta-data integrity. *2019 International Conference on Advances in Computing, Communication and Control (ICAC3)*. doi:10.1109/icac347590.2019.9036792

Ramachandran, G. S., Radhakrishnan, R., & Krishnamachari, B. (2018). Towards a decentralized data marketplace for smart cities. *2018 IEEE International Smart Cities Conference (ISC2)*. doi:10.1109/isc2.2018.8656952

Schuster, F., Costa, M., Fournet, C., Gkantsidis, C., Peinado, M., Mainar-Ruiz, G., & Russinovich, M. (2015). VC3: Trustworthy data analytics in the cloud using SGX. *2015 IEEE Symposium on Security and Privacy*. doi:10.1109/sp.2015.10

Sharifi, L., Freitag, F., & Veiga, L. (2014). Combing smart grid with community clouds: Next generation integrated service platform. *2014 IEEE International Conference on Smart Grid Communications (SmartGridComm)*. doi:10.1109/smartgridcomm.2014.7007685

Subramanian, H. (2017). Decentralized blockchain-based electronic marketplaces. *Communications of the ACM*, *61*(1), 78–84. https://doi.org/10.1145/3158333

Wang, Y. L., & Krishnamachari, B. (2019). Enhancing engagement in token-curated registries via an inflationary mechanism. *2019 IEEE International Conference on Blockchain and Cryptocurrency (ICBC)*. doi:10.1109/bloc.2019.8751443

Wang, Z., Yang, L., Wang, Q., Liu, D., Xu, Z., & Liu, S. (2019). ArtChain: Blockchain-enabled platform for art marketplace. *2019 IEEE International Conference on Blockchain (Blockchain)*. doi:10.1109/blockchain.2019.00068

Wright, C. S. (2008). *Bitcoin: A peer-to-peer electronic cash system*. SSRN Electronic Journal. doi:10.2139/ssrn.3440802

Yuan, Y., & Wang, F. (2016). Towards blockchain-based intelligent transportation systems. *2016 IEEE 19th International Conference on Intelligent Transportation Systems (ITSC)*. doi:10.1109/itsc.2016.7795984

Zheng, X., Mukkamala, R. R., Vatrapu, R., & Ordieres-Mere, J. (2018). Blockchain-based personal health data sharing system using cloud storage. *2018 IEEE 20th International Conference on e-Health Networking, Applications and Services (Healthcom)*. doi:10.1109/healthcom.2018.8531125

Zhou, J., Tang, F., Zhu, H., Nan, N., & Zhou, Z. (2018). Distributed data vending on blockchain. 2018 IEEE International Conference on Internet of Things (iThings) and IEEE Green Computing and Communications (GreenCom) and IEEE Cyber, Physical and Social Computing (CPSCom) and IEEE Smart Data (SmartData). doi:10.1109/cybermatics_2018.2018.00201

Zyskind, G., Nathan, O., & Pentland, A. (2015). Decentralizing privacy: Using blockchain to protect personal data. *2015 IEEE Security and Privacy Workshops*. doi:10.1109/spw.2015.27

Chapter 11

A Reliable Hybrid Blockchain–Based Authentication System for IoT Network

Ambika N.

ⓘ https://orcid.org/0000-0003-4452-5514

Department of Computer Applications, Sivananda Sarma Memorial RV College, Bangalore, India

ABSTRACT

IoT is an assembly of equipment of different calibers and functionality working towards a single goal. A blockchain is a computerized record that contains the whole history of exchanges made on the system. A multi-WSN arrangement model is structured. The hubs of the IoT are isolated into base stations, group heads, and conventional hubs as per their capacities, which encourage the administration and participation of the hubs. A hybrid blockchain model is proposed. To fit the multi-WSN arrange model better, as indicated by the various capacities and energies of various hubs, neighborhood blockchain and open blockchain are sent between group head hubs and base stations individually, and a crossbreed blockchain model is framed. A shared validation plot for IoT hubs is proposed. For group head hubs, the creators utilize the worldwide blockchain for validation, and for customary hubs, they utilize the nearby blockchain for confirmation. The proposal aims in increasing reliability by 1.17% and minimizes sinkhole attack by 2.42% compared to previous contribution.

1. INTRODUCTION

The Internet-of-things known as IoT (Alaba, 2017) (Ambika N., 2019) is a get together of numerous supplies of various gauge and usefulness progressing in the direction of a solitary objective. The gathering point in speaking with one another using the regular stage gave to them. The gadgets in IoT (Khan & Salah, 2018) control distantly to play out the ideal usefulness. The data sharing among the gadgets at that point happens through the system utilizes the standard conventions of correspondence. The brilliant associated devices or ''things'' extend from preliminary wearable accomplices to enormous machines, each containing sensor chips. The surveillance cameras introduced for reconnaissance of an area can be

DOI: 10.4018/978-1-6684-7132-6.ch011

checked distantly anyplace on the planet. Different shrewd gadgets perform assorting functionalities. An example, observing medical procedure (Ambika N., 2020) in clinics, home surveillance (Al-Ali, Zualkernan, Rashid, Gupta, & Alikarar, 2017), recognizing climate conditions, giving following and availability in autos and ID of creatures utilizing biochips are now serving as the network explicit requirements. The information gathered through these gadgets might be handled continuously to improve the effectiveness of the whole framework.

A blockchain (A & K, 2016) is a modernized record that contains the entire history of trades made on the framework. It is a fundamental purpose behind existing clear outcasts from money trades by bringing in trustworthy progressed cash. It is an assortment of associated blocks that are joined by hash regards made after some time. All information on the blockchain is never-ending and can't be changed. It is arranging worldview utilized for revelation, valuation, and move of quanta is the thing that we characterize as blockchain innovation. The innovation has its job in legislative issues, compassionate, social, conservative, and logical areas.

The invention utilizes to reinforce bitcoin. The blockchain is an open record that decentralizes a trust-less framework to move money starting with one point, then onto the next over the web. The innovation intends to take care of the twofold spend issue. The go-between trust is not necessary for the use of the technique. It is a mix of open key cryptography and BitTorrent distributed document sharing. It makes a section of the coin proprietorship affirmed by cryptographic conventions and the mining network. The exchanges that occurred adds to the records. Two components are required – a private key and wallet programming. Utilizing the credentials gives the admittance to the sellers to make exchanges over the web. Wallet programming may record the trading made. The aptitude used in broad daylight record archives includes the report library, the vault of occasions, personalities, and occasions. Any advantage is it controls, follows, and traded. A standard calculation brings innovation into play. The computation acknowledges a document to change over into 64-character code. It guarantees the hash code created can't recover the source record. The exchange utilizes the hash code and timestamp. The source recovers from the proprietor's machine.

The previous contribution (Cui, et al., 2020) uses a hybrid blockchain system. It is a mix of a private and public system. The framework consists of different kinds of devices. Sink nodes gather data for further analysis. Regular devices deployed senses and transmit the processed data to the group heads. The client will be gaining access to the sensed data after authenticating themselves. The sink node and the customers incorporate a public blockchain system. The in-between group heads and regular devices use the local one.

The contribution is an enhancement of the previous suggestion. The nodes use identification and Ethernet address to derive the hashed value. The sink node will be able to map the address of the device to the Ethernet address. Other compromised devices using a similar Ethernet address will come into notice early. The reliability increases by 1.17% in comparison to previous work.

The work divides into seven divisions. The motivation of the proposal is in segment two. The literature survey follows the motive of the contribution. Segment four describes the proposal in detail. The discussion of the analysis of the contribution is in division five. The sixth part discusses future work. The writing concludes in section seven.

2. MOTIVATION

IoT is things made of smart sensors and actuators. These devices are intelligent capable of learning from their experience. These unsupervised devices require security to their network. The previous contribution (Cui, et al., 2020) uses a hybrid blockchain system. It is a mix of private and public blockchain. The framework consists of different kinds of devices. Sink nodes gather data for further analysis. Regular devices deployment senses and transmits the processed data to the group heads. The client will be gaining access to the sensed data after authenticating themselves. The sink node and the customers incorporate the public blockchain system. Local blockchain usage in-between group heads and regular devices.

The adversary can capture the node and make modifications appropriately. A standard device will be unable to detect it at an early stage. Hence reliability is essential for these systems. The proposal is trying to bring trust to the network devices by enhancing reliability and also security.

3. LITERATURE SURVEY

This section discusses the previous contributions towards the domain. A multi-WSN arrangement model (Cui, et al., 2020) is structured. There are numerous hubs in the IoT (Ambika N., 2020). The devices of the IoT isolates into base stations, group heads, and conventional hubs as per their capacities, which encourage the administration and participation of them. To fit the multi-WSN arrange model, better neighborhood blockchain and open-chain are sent between group head hubs and base stations individually, and a crossbreed blockchain model. It suggests a shared validation plot for IoT hubs. To improve the versatility of the IoT confirmation, the authors have received the various leveled blockchain mode. For group head hubs, the creators utilize the worldwide chain for validation. For customary hubs, they use the nearby chain for confirmation.

The general reason for a verification plot is to permit various hubs to convey reliably over a non-confided organizes. In work (Hammi, Hammi, Bellot, & Serhrouchni, 2018), the authors consider a system that claims a lot of things offering and utilizing diverse IoT administrations in an incorporated or an appropriate design. The devices speak with countless different things. Traded messages go through an inconsistent and possibly lossy correspondence organization. The primary objective of our methodology is to make secure virtual zones in IoT situations. Every gadget must discuss just with devices of its zone and thinks about each other gadget as malevolent. It is a structure with a Master of the air pocket that views as an affirmation authority. Some random instruments can be a Master. Besides, each item makes some portion of the framework is called Follower. Every Follower produces an Elliptic Curve (EC) private/open key-pair. Every Follower is given by a structure called a ticket, which speaks to a lightweight testament of 64 pieces.

The contribution presents the out-of-band two-factor confirmation (Wu, Du, Wang, & Lin, 2018) plan to improve the validation and approval measure. The optional validation factor can recognize a home IoT gadget from the pernicious device outside the house, regardless of whether the vindictive instrument imitates the real IoT gadget utilizing the right access token. It solicits the room temperature from the Executor. It can change shading dependent on the current measure. The agent recovers the relationship data of the same from the chain. The agent chooses the related gadget that is in nearness with the unauthenticated device. It sends the activity arrangement to the equivalent. The to-be-authenticated gets and executes the activity arrangement by encoding the succession code to the on/off light switching. The vicinity relative gadget translates the code implanted in the light switching. Vicinity related instrument sends the check result to the chain by summoning the capacity of the Smart Contract on Blockchain. The agent checks chain for the confirmation result through an intelligent contract.

The creators (Huh, Cho, & Kim, 2017) have utilized a couple of IoT gadgets rather than many devices. They have additionally used a cell and three Raspberry Pis. They go about as a meter to monitor power utilization, a climate control system, and light since utilizing genuine gadgets, for example, a climate control frame, would require an excessive amount of overhead. Using a cell phone, the client can set up the arrangement. For instance, a client can set gadgets to turn on vitality sparing mode when power use hits 150 KW. At the point when the client sets up the design through a cell phone, the information sends to the Ethereum arrange. For example, light or forced air systems are recovering estimations of strategy occasionally from Ethereum. Likewise, the meter monitors power use and update it on Ethereum. Accordingly, three unique cycles are going on simultaneously. Ethereum conveyed to the registering stage.

In a multi-hub arrangement (Li, Peng, Deng, & Gai, 2018), the personality data of the gadgets enrolls in the blockchain. Every gadget's ID, open key, a hash of preliminary information, and other data are put away in the blockchain record. Simultaneously, every instrument is a hub in the blockchain arranges, and the agreement system ensures that every hub stores similar data. At whatever point distributed correspondence happens, public-key cryptography utilizes character validation between IoT gadgets. The framework cycle separates into three stages. Everything gadgets require to finish the enrolment in the blockchain before verification. When a device needs to get to the arrangement, it will be confirmed utilizing the enrolment data in the blockchain. After authentication, the gadget checks the honesty of the hash of the primary data to find potential interruption conduct.

The engineering (Almadhoun, Kadadha, Alhemeiri, Alshehhi, & Salah, 2018) is made out of five primary members with admittance to Ethereum contracts through the Internet: admin, end clients, mist hubs, and the cloud workers facilitating IoT information. IoT gadgets do have Ethereum addresses. All different members have of kind Ethereum Address (EA) and interface legitimately with the agreement through an Ethereum customer on account of mist and cloud hubs or through a front-end application/wallet of the Admin and end clients. The Owner of the brilliant agreement can add different clients to be the administrator. The undertaking of the administrators is to oversee the enrolling and de-enlisting of IoT gadgets and haze hubs in the framework. The administrators give consent through the shrewd agreement for end clients to get to IoT gadgets. These consent qualities used by the haze hubs validate clients to get to the IoT gadgets. When the clients are allowed admittance authorization through the intelligent contract, they contact the assigned haze hub liable for dealing with the focused on IoT gadget for verification and access. The keen agreement contains the planning of all the enrolled mist hubs and their related IoT gadgets they oversee. The devices supervise the admittance to IoT gadgets. Each mist hub is regulating and dealing with a gathering of IoT gadgets. Each IoT gadget in the framework plans for one device. The cloud has register and capacity workers total and stores IoT information.

A concentrated keen agreement (Ourad, Belgacem, & Salah, 2018) verifies clients to their particular IoT gadgets. The client authenticates the Ethereum wallet address. If the client is legitimate, the shrewd accord communicates an Access token and the sender's ethereum address. The client and the IoT gadget get the transmitted data from the intelligent contract. The client makes a bundle contains an access token, User IP, Access length, and the ethereum open key. This bundle is marked utilizing the ethereum private key at that point sent with the relating public key. The bundle scrambles whenever needed. Honesty is the thing that is important in this situation marking of the message. When the IoT gadget bundles it confirms its substance. Whenever succeeded, the gadget awards admittance to the client from the sender's IP for the length indicated. Something else, if any of those checks fizzles, the solicitation is dropped.

Toward the beginning of the cycle (Puthal, Mohanty, Nanda, Kougianos, & Das, 2019), singular precipitants/hubs in the system produce exchanges (Trx) with the information and consolidate them into a square. The devices broadcast the squares for additional assessment. The model uses the ElGamal strategy for encryption. Before hub broadcast, the source hub utilizes its private credential to sign and unveils its key, accessible to everybody. It confides instruments inside the system for square approval. With each verification square believed hubs gain trust esteems. It prepares to assess its legitimacy by getting the source hub open key. The mark approves uniquely with the utilization of the credential. In light of the discrete log issue property, one can't process the worth when different qualities are known to them. After mark approval, the believed hub likewise checks the MAC esteem for the second round of assessment. The hubs broadcast the square to the system with PoAh distinguishing proof after confirmation. Following this, device in the system discover the PoAh data from the chain. A singular instrument processes the hash of the square and keeps it to interface the following chain, and the recently figured hash esteem is put away in the current chain to keep up the chain.

The center thought of CertCoin (Jiang, et al., 2019) is to keep up an open record of clients' characters and their related public keys. The framework contains six primary functionalities: enlisting an identification with a relating credential, refreshing the keys, looking through a clue comparing to a given personality, repudiating the open solution comparing to a character, recouping the clue relating to the identification, and mining.

The BATM module (Moinet, Darties, & Baril, 2017) incorporates a trust model called Humanlike Knowledge-based Trust (HKT), given human-like conduct to keep up a notoriety level for every hub. HKT is a trade-off between shared reconnaissances by all devices on the system. It is the nearness of a trusting place. They utilize the payloads contained in the blockchain as a sign of every hub conduct on the system over time. The creators guarantee a hub can't trick others by altering information or professing to be another person. Subsequently, the work assures the dependability of trust assessment without the need for a trusting place. The following advancement will focus on the Network Node trust assessment. The same standards apply to Available administrations, with the distinction that accessible administrations notoriety level is repeated on every hub in the system, subsequently adjusting notoriety level on every device utilizing it. The work performs trust assessment by looking at the current notoriety level of a Network Node to believe him doing certain activities in the network. The contribution uses blockchain-related activities and partners them with a trust level. The level evaluates the base notoriety level for a hub to be trusted to fulfill the result occasion. The work considers two kinds of rules: clocks, key legitimacy breaks, and occasion notoriety factors depicted before.

The cross-area confirmation instrument (Shen, et al., 2020)is running on the head of the blockchain. Personality based Signature (IBS) and Ephemeral Elliptic Curve Diffie-Hellman (ECDHE) credential trade procedures use during the verification and key understanding cycle. In particular, IBS validates gadgets. In IBS-based frameworks, when a device as a petitioner solicitation to be confirmed by another instrument as a verifier, the verifier needs to check the legitimacy of the mark produced by the inquirer utilizing the open key of the inquirer dependent on some fundamental boundaries where the space petitioner lives. A few jobs exist in the proposed instrument, which incorporates IIoT gadgets, Key Generation Center (KGC), Blockchain Agent Server (BAS), and Authentication Agent Server (AAS). They bunch them into various layers by their functionalities. KGC is remembered for the element layer as they are minimal jobs in IBC frameworks. BAS and AAS are two assignment explicit workers presented for specialist missions. The two additional layers incorporate the blockchain layer and the capacity layer. The blockchain layer can be treated as a typical secure channel for area explicit data sharing. Blockchain stores the least data, i.e., area identifier and its coupling esteem comprised of a uniform asset identifier (URI) and hash esteem figured upon the authentic space explicit information. URI focuses on the real stockpiling document situated on the Internet.

IoT gadgets are associated with a passage associates with the blockchain arrangement (Gagneja & Kiefer, 2020). The system administrator confides in a party that has the blockchain on a worker's uses related to processing assets to play out the escalated take a shot for the sake of the IoT gadgets. The blockchain includes squares containing the primary information fields to give a premise to a re-enacted arrange blockchain for IoT. The Sender information field holds the ID of the IoT gadget that is adding the message to the blockchain. The Receiver information field has the open key used to sign communication. This information field is utilized for gadget introduction and shared meeting credential age by the ID of the IoT gadget that is the assigned beneficiary of the message. The Plain Text information field holds messages or directions. The Signature information domain has the mark of the IoT sender utilizing a credential. The information field considers the sharing of open mark confirmation keys with other IoT gadgets uses the blockchain. The Previous Hash information domain uses the past hash-square. The Current information field has the estimation of the current square's hash-value, determined utilizing an SHA work. The Time information category has an hour of square age at a foreordained period. The Proof information subject has the Proof of Work that produces a substantial hash indicated by the blockchain boundaries. The IoT gadgets connect to a door that is associated with a cloud or edge figuring group to do the many hash computations. The blockchain is confirmed utilizing a circle that emphasizes through all squares in the blockchain and checks three conditions for every emphasis. The beginning square sets the blockchain boundaries inside the Plain Text information field.

BCTrust (Tian, Su, & Liang, 2019) is conveyed on the Ethereum blockchain, which gives the best record on the planet, has a network that tails it, and permits to build of an application on it. It guarantees secure exchanges, and, for example, Bitcoin, Ethereum is tried in an enormous scope. In the intelligent contract, just a set of trustful hubs have the composing rights on the blockchain. These favored gadgets are the CPANs of the system. Each CPAN has a couple of private/public keys that permit safely make exchanges with the blockchain. The system has two CPANs and one gadget that has the accompanying qualities: Dresden Elektronik deRFsam3 23M10-R3, have 48 ko of RAM, 256 ko of ROM, and a Cortex-M3 Processor. They sent an Ethereum blockchain duplicate and TestRPC as a customer for associating with the blockchain. The code actualizes using the C language. For associating with the blockchain through TestRPC, they built up an interface that encodes/unravel information to be deciphered per Ethereum. It utilizes JSON RPC for the correspondence, where JSON is a standard printed information arrangement and RPC a far-off methodology call framework. This interface permits programs written in C to speak with TestRPC in a distant strategy call mode, along these lines communicate with the blockchain.

It is a chain-idea (Kim, Kim, & Huh, 2019) dependent on equipment-based and programming-based techniques. The technique for applying the shading range chain to IoT is as per the following: The blockchain utilized in the shading range chain stores the verification status of the gadgets that can get to IoT and works on different workers of the IoT gadget. In the worker, the shading range chain completes the means of affirming the data of the device, putting away the validation condition of the recognized gadget in the blockchain, and checking the verification condition of the put-away gadget. The different gadgets associated with the worker are enrolled in the blockchain through the shading range chain and imparted through the validation step. In the IoT condition, correspondence happens between the worker and the gadget. For secure communication, the worker must confirm that the device confides in an instrument before imparting it. The gadget confirmation measure performs by enlisting the gadget validation status in the shading range chain as follows: as a gadget enrollment technique of the shading range chain, a worker and a gadget create an open key and a private key, for example, an elliptic bend computerized signature calculation (ECDSA)— through a shading range chain for blockchain exchanges. The gadget electronically signs the respective data and the key. It transmits them to the worker, consequently mentioning the enlistment of the device to the shading range chain. The worker thinks about the gotten data with the IoT verification gadget data to affirm that a gadget is a confirmed gadget. A while later, it stores the exchange of proprietorship to the instrument in the blockchain to the worker possessed confirmation token gave by the shading range chain. The put away squares synchronize between the shading range chain workers. If the agreement makes in all workers, the gadget's views as confirmed. An IoT gadget imparts through the confirmation token moved from the worker in the shading range chain. As a gadget validation system of the shading range chain, the device sends carefully marked confirmation data to the worker to speak with the worker. The worker affirms the confirmation status in the shading range chain through the gotten data and checks that it is a verification gadget before playing out the security strategy for secure correspondence. Also, the shading range chain has various validations. The squares production uses the irregular capacity and utilizing the Smart Contract work. It uses a hash convention as opposed to using the current key age convention.

In the proposed framework (Sultana, et al., 2020), various shrewd agreements oversee information and administration sharing among arrange clients. The brilliant accord is Access Control Contract (ACC), Register contract (RC), and Judge Contract (JC). Where ACC deals with the general access control of the framework, the RC enrolls clients (subjects and articles) in the framework. It additionally creates an enlistment table, which stores the data of clients. JC dictates the conduct of the respective. It checks if any misconduct happens. When a subject sends an excessive number of solicitations or drops the created demand, the view is wrong conduct. After the trouble-making conduction, it undergoes the punishment on the subject by the JC. ACC deals with the entrance control between IoT gadgets. At whatever point the respective require any help from the item, it sends a solicitation to the framework. From that point onward, ACC keeps up the entrance control for the subject. It likewise expands the presentation effectiveness of the framework. The object conveys the benchmark structure of numerous ACCs. In this framework, access control is finished by the client rather than the framework itself. The confirmation of clients undergoes finishing by RC by enrolling them in the framework. Making a strategic decision is executed by the JC, which passes judgment on the conduct of clients in the framework. At the point when a subject sends administration demand in the framework. JC checks its doings. It sends a visit, and such a large number of solicitations for help, it is viewed as getting into mischief. Furthermore, if it drops its produced demand, it is otherwise called rowdiness.

4. PROPOSED ARCHITECTURE

The previous contribution (Cui, et al., 2020) uses a hybrid blockchain system. It is a mix of private and public blockchain. The framework consists of different kinds of devices. Sink nodes gather data for further analysis. Regular devices deployment senses and transmits the processed data to the group heads. The client will be gaining access to the sensed data after authenticating themselves. The sink node and the customers incorporate the public blockchain system. Local blockchain usage in-between group heads and regular devices.

The proposed architecture brings reliability compared to. The system uses the following stages –

- Preliminary/Initialization phase – It is the responsibility of the sink node to embed all the credentials into the devices before their deployment. The identities of the instrument are unique. The devices after-deployment transmits the hashed value to the base station for verification. The proposal uses Ethernet details and unique identification to generate the hashed value to enhance trust. The base station will be able to map the Ethernet address to the identity of the devices. In equation (1), the device with identification id_i and Ethernet address Li is hashed using a hashing algorithm and dispatched to the sink node BS.

$$BS \leftarrow hash(id_i \parallel L_i) \tag{1}$$

The other phases are similar to (Cui, et al., 2020). The registration stage consists of group and regular device indexing. The authorization stage is verification between regular devices and customers-regular instruments. The system encompasses the device logout phase.

5. ANALYSIS OF THE WORK

The previous contribution (Cui, et al., 2020) uses Ethernet address to derive the hashed value. This value is verified by the base station. In the proposal, the devices use unique identification and Ethernet address to derive the hashed value. The sinknode will be able to map the unique address to the Ethernet address. This builds in reliability in the system. Other compromised devices using the similar Ethernet address will come into notice early. The work is simulated in NS2. Table 2 provides the parameters used in the study.

Table 1. Parameters used in the simulation

Parameters Used	Description
Dimension of the network	200m * 200m
Number of devices deployed in the network	10
Length of Ethernet address	48 bits
Length of identification	48 bits
Length of hashed value	20 bits
Length of the message	256 bits
Simulation time	60ms

The reliability increases by 1.17% with comparison to previous work (Cui, et al., 2020). The same is represented in the figure 1.

Figure 1. Comparison of Reliability of both systems

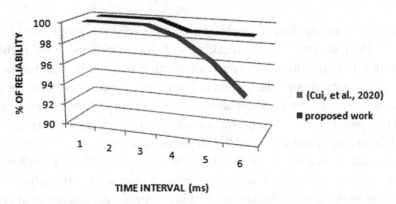

Using the proposal sinkhole attack can be minimized. As the compromised nodes are detected at the early stage, the illegitimate nodes can be detached from the network. The work minimizes sinkhole attack by 2.42% compared to (Cui, et al., 2020). The same is represented in the Figure 2.

Figure 2. Analysis of sinkhole attack

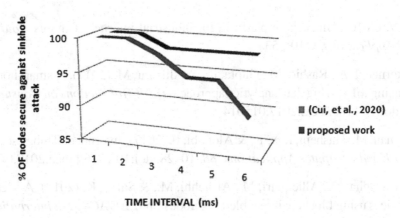

6. FUTURE WORK

In the proposal, the devices use unique identification and Ethernet address to derive the hashed value. The sinknode will be able to map the unique address to the Ethernet address. Other compromised devices using the similar Ethernet address will come into notice early. The reliability increases by 1.17% with comparison to previous work. The work minimizes sinkhole attack by 2.42% compared to (Cui, et al., 2020). The drawbacks of the work –

- Lot of Energy is used implementing public blockchain. This technology is implemented between regular nodes and clients. Some measures can be considered to minimize them.

7. CONCLUSION

IoT is assembly of numerous supplies of various gauge and usefulness progressing in the direction of a solitary objective. The gathering point in speaking with one another using the regular stage gave to them. The gadgets in IoT control distantly to play out the ideal usefulness. The data sharing among the gadgets at that point happens through the system utilizes the standard conventions of correspondence. A blockchain is a modernized record that contains the entire history of trades made on the framework. It is a fundamental purpose behind existing clear outcasts from money trades by bringing in trustworthy progressed cash. It is an assortment of associated blocks that are joined by hash regards that have made after some time. All information on the blockchain is never-ending and can't be changed. It is arranging worldview utilized for revelation, valuation, and move of quanta is the thing that we characterize as blockchain innovation. Both the technologies are combined together to enhance security. In the proposal, the devices use unique identification and Ethernet address to derive the hashed value. The sinknode will be able to map the unique address to the Ethernet address. Other compromised devices using the similar Ethernet address will come into notice early. The reliability increases by 1.17% with comparison to previous work. It minimizes sinkhole attack by 2.42% compared to previous contribution.

REFERENCES

A, B., & K, M. V. (2016). Blockchain platform for industrial internet of things. *Journal of software Engineering and Applications, 9*(10), 533.

Al-Ali, A., Zualkernan, I. A., Rashid, M., Gupta, R., & Alikarar, M. (2017). A smart home energy management system using IoT and big data analytics approach. *IEEE Transactions on Consumer Electronics, 63*(4), 426–434. doi:10.1109/TCE.2017.015014

Alaba, F. A., Othman, M., Hashem, I. A. T., & Alotaibi, F. (2017). Internet of Things security: A survey. *Journal of Network and Computer Applications, 88*, 10–28. doi:10.1016/j.jnca.2017.04.002

Almadhoun, R., Kadadha, M., Alhemeiri, M., Alshehhi, M., & Salah, K. (2018). A user authentication scheme of IoT devices using blockchain-enabled fog nodes. In *IEEE/ACS 15th international conference on computer systems and applications (AICCSA)* (pp. 1-8). Aqaba, Jordan: IEEE.

Ambika, N. (2019). Energy-Perceptive Authentication in Virtual Private Networks Using GPS Data. In Security, Privacy and Trust in the IoT Environment (pp. 25-38). Springer.

Ambika, N. (2020). Encryption of Data in Cloud-Based Industrial IoT Devices. In S. Pal & V. G. Díaz (Eds.), *D.-N. Le, IoT: Security and Privacy Paradigm* (pp. 111–129). CRC Press, Taylor & Francis Group.

Ambika, N. (2020). Methodical IoT-Based Information System in Healthcare. In Smart Medical Data Sensing and IoT Systems Design in Healthcare (pp. 155-177). Bangalore, India: IGI Global.

Balandina, E., Balandin, S., Koucheryavy, Y., & Mouromtsev, D. (2015). IoT use cases in healthcare and tourism. *IEEE 17th Conference on Business Informatics, 2*, 37-44.

Cui, Z., Fei, X. U., Zhang, S., Cai, X., Cao, Y., Zhang, W., & Chen, J. (2020). A hybrid BlockChain-based identity authentication scheme for multi-WSN. *IEEE Transactions on Services Computing, 13*(2), 241–251. doi:10.1109/TSC.2020.2964537

Gagneja, K., & Kiefer, R. (2020). Security Protocol for Internet of Things (IoT): Blockchain-based Implementation and Analysis. In *Sixth International Conference on Mobile And Secure Services (MobiSecServ)* (pp. 1-6). Miami Beach, FL: IEEE.

Hammi, M. T., Hammi, B., Bellot, P., & Serhrouchni, A. (2018). Bubbles of Trust: A decentralized blockchain-based authentication system for IoT. *Computers & Security, 78*, 126–142. doi:10.1016/j.cose.2018.06.004

Huh, S., Cho, S., & Kim, S. (2017). Managing IoT devices using blockchain platform. In *19th international conference on advanced communication technology (ICACT)* (pp. 464-467). Bongpyeong, South Korea: IEEE.

Jiang, W., Li, H., Xu, G., Wen, M., Dong, G., & Lin, X. (2019). PTAS: Privacy-preserving thin-client authentication scheme in blockchain-based PKI. *Future Generation Computer Systems, 96*, 185–195. doi:10.1016/j.future.2019.01.026

Khan, M. A., & Salah, K. (2018). IoT security: Review, blockchain solutions, and open challenges. *Future Generation Computer Systems, 82*, 395–411. doi:10.1016/j.future.2017.11.022

Kim, S. K., Kim, U. M., & Huh, J. H. (2019). A study on improvement of blockchain application to overcome vulnerability of IoT multiplatform security. *Energies, 12*(3), 1–29. doi:10.3390/en12030402

Li, D., Peng, W., Deng, W., & Gai, F. (2018). A blockchain-based authentication and security mechanism for iot. In *27th International Conference on Computer Communication and Networks (ICCCN)* (pp. 1-6). Hangzhou, China: IEEE. 10.1109/ICCCN.2018.8487449

Moinet, A., Darties, B., & Baril, J. L. (2017). Blockchain based trust & authentication for decentralized sensor networks. *IEEE Security & Privacy, Special Issue on Blockchain*, 1-6.

Ourad, A. Z., Belgacem, B., & Salah, K. (2018). Using blockchain for IOT access control and authentication management. In *International Conference on Internet of Things* (pp. 150-164). Santa Barbara, CA: Springer. 10.1007/978-3-319-94370-1_11

Puthal, D., Mohanty, S. P., Nanda, P., Kougianos, E., & Das, G. (2019). Proof-of-authentication for scalable blockchain in resource-constrained distributed systems. In *International Conference on Consumer Electronics (ICCE)* (pp. 1-5). Las Vegas, NV: IEEE. 10.1109/ICCE.2019.8662009

Shen, M., Liu, H., Zhu, L., Xu, K., Yu, H., Du, X., & Guizani, M. (2020). Blockchain-assisted secure device authentication for cross-domain industrial IoT. *IEEE Journal on Selected Areas in Communications, 38*(5), 942–954. doi:10.1109/JSAC.2020.2980916

Sultana, T., Almogren, A., Akbar, M., Zuair, M., Ullah, I., & Javaid, N. (2020). Data sharing system integrating access control mechanism using blockchain-based smart contracts for IoT devices. *Applied Sciences (Basel, Switzerland), 10*(2), 1–21. doi:10.3390/app10020488

Tian, H., Su, Y., & Liang, Z. (2019). *A Provable Secure Server Friendly Two-Party SM2 Singing Protocol for Blockchain IoT. In IEEE Globecom Workshops (GC Wkshps).* IEEE.

Wu, L., Du, X., Wang, W., & Lin, B. (2018). An out-of-band authentication scheme for internet of things using blockchain technology. In *International Conference on Computing, Networking and Communications (ICNC)* (pp. 769-773). Maui, HI: IEEE. 10.1109/ICCNC.2018.8390280

KEY TERMS AND DEFINITIONS

Blockchain: It is a methodology that brings reliability to the network. The hashed code of the previous and present doings is attached to all the transmitted messages. The messages undergo verification for the same.

Internet of Things (IoT): These are unsupervised devices that are created by assembling sensors and actuators.

Sinknode/Base Station: It is a server that is responsible for collecting and assembling the received data. It also embeds credentials, algorithms into the devices. It also transmits necessary data to the devices of the network.

Chapter 12
Towards the Integration of Blockchain and IoT for Security Challenges in IoT:
A Review

K. Dinesh Kumar
https://orcid.org/0000-0003-0843-1561
VIT University, Chennai, India

Venkata Rathnam T.
Annamacharya Institute of Technology and Sciences, Tirupati, India & Jawaharlal Nehru Technological University, Anantapur, India

Venkata Ramana R.
Sri Venkateswara College of Engineering, Tirupati, India & Jawaharlal Nehru Technological University, Anantapur, India

M. Sudhakara
https://orcid.org/0000-0002-2559-4074
VIT University, Chennai, India

Ravi Kumar Poluru
https://orcid.org/0000-0001-8591-5266
VIT University, India

ABSTRACT

Internet of things (IoT) technology plays a vital role in the current technologies because IoT develops a network by integrating different kinds of objects and sensors to create the communication among objects directly without human interaction. With the presence of internet of things technology in our daily comes smart thinking and various advantages. At the same time, secure systems have been a most important concern for the protection of information systems and networks. However, adopting traditional security management systems in the internet of things leads several issues due to the limited privacy and policies like privacy standards, protocol stacks, and authentication rules. Usually, IoT devices has limited network capacities, storage, and computing processors. So they are having more chances to attacks. Data security, privacy, and reliability are three main challenges in the IoT security domain. To address

DOI: 10.4018/978-1-6684-7132-6.ch012

the solutions for the above issues, IoT technology has to provide advanced privacy and policies in this large incoming data source. Blockchain is one of the trending technologies in the privacy management to provide the security. So this chapter is focused on the blockchain technologies which can be able to solve several IoT security issues. This review mainly focused on the state-of-the-art IoT security issues and vulnerabilities by existing review works in the IoT security domains. The taxonomy is presented about security issues in the view of communication, architecture, and applications. Also presented are the challenges of IoT security management systems. The main aim of this chapter is to describe the importance of blockchain technology in IoT security systems. Finally, it highlights the future directions of blockchain technology roles in IoT systems, which can be helpful for further improvements.

INTRODUCTION

The Internet of Things (IoT) has created a remarkable role in all environments of our daily lives. The Internet of Things technology already adopted in several fields to create the flexible environments like automobiles, healthcare, entertainments, sports, industries and homes etc. The adoption of IoT technology in daily activity environments, makes the life comfortable and easy. The main idea of the IoT technology is, all physical objects connected with each other under one network. So that, connected objects analyse the data and makes the proper decisions by sharing the information with each other. The IoT technology transforms these objects as a smart things by using the several technologies like sensors networks, internet protocols, communication technologies, ubiquitous computing, embedded devices and applications. Smart things along with supported technologies perform the tasks while using data analytical models and ubiquitous computing services. The complete concept of the IoT technology is, each and every connected application has to interact with other independent services to make the proper decisions. For example, smart traffic system will enable the vehicles to automatically respond when vehicles met with accidents. To get this potential technology and innovation, the traffic system application need to improve and growth. Additionally, the vehicles need to be manufactured to match the system requirements and robust communication protocols has to be developed for proper communication among different kinds of things. With this vision, traditional devices has become autonomous and smart intelligence and developing technology towards smart cities, smart homes, smart vehicles and smart everything.

The further development of IoT technology is more important to everyday life. This can be rapidly grows the evolution of hardware techniques like increasing the bandwidth by integrating the connected based networks to address issue of underutilization of bandwidth spectrum. The supporting technologies to IoT technology like Cloud computing, Bigdata analytics, Wireless sensor networks and Machine-to-Machine have now developed rapidly as supporting components for the IoT development. On the other hand, the privacy and security issues related to Machine-to-Machine, Cloud computing and Wireless sensors networks remain to increasing in the view of challenges in communication protocols with the IoT. So, the complete architecture of IoT needs to be robust and secured from several attacks which may arise the issues to integrity, privacy and confidentiality of collected data. Still adopting traditional secure paradigms in IoT technology which can lead major issues, because IoT is a collection of heterogeneous devices and several collections of interconnected computer networks. Additionally, the IoT things have sensors which may have limited memory and power. Due to the limited power of sensors, having more chances to get the vulnerable from attackers. In this context, many literature reviews are addressed the security issues in IoT such as author (Alaba et al., 2017) classified the security issues in the view of architecture, application, data, and communication. Authors presented the taxonomy of classification of IoT security issues and also presented attacks on IoT hardware, application components, and networks. In another literature review (Granjal et al., 2015) author presented the analysis of security and privacy issues of IoT protocols. This analysis presented about several privacy key management systems with cryptographic algorithms. In the same way (Yi et al., 2015) and (Wang et al., 2015) authors presented different kinds of security issues for fog computing. Authors (Abduvaliyev et al., 2013), (Butun et al., 2014), and (Mitchell et al., 2014) presented a comparative analysis of intrusion detection system in IoT.

In distributed systems, providing privacy without third-parties is an advanced management that can increase the potential power of IoT based organizations. The IoT technology has taking the advantages of cloud computing and bigdata computing to overcome the limitations. In the same way blockchain technology also increase the potential growth of IoT security systems. Blockchain is a trending technology in security management system which can provide a strong and robust privacy solutions and maximum level of security standards (Banerjee et al., 2018). The developers of blockchain technology argue that this approach is secured by design. In a blockchain technology, not required to store the data with third party organizations. Every record of information is stored in interlocked computers. Now a days, blockchain technology can be used in different applications to authorize, authenticate, and audit data which is collected from different devices. Additionally, blockchain is having decentralization characteristic which can helps to avoid the third party involvement. The main aim of the blockchain technology is, develops a decentralization process as a security measurement to develop a secure index for all transactions in a network. This characteristic helps to improve the IoT security management system.

Many literature reviews addressed the security issues and solutions of IoT security management system, but not completely presented in the view of effective security management system. This chapter presents a complete review on the Internet of Things, IoT security issues and challenges, and blockchain based solutions for IoT security management system. The main contributions of this chapter are:

- A systematic literature review on Internet of Things and Blockchain technologies.
- The taxonomy and classification of security issues in IoT is presented.
- Presented a characteristics of the blockchain based security solutions.
- This chapter focused on the classification of different solutions for the applications of Blockchain technology in an IoT environment.

The rest of the chapter is organized as follows. Section 2 presented about overview of Internet of Things and architecture. In section 3, presented a taxonomy of different kinds of security issues and challenges of IoT security management system. Section 4 describes about blockchain technology and their basic characteristics, whereas, Section 5 presented a different solutions for the application of blockchain in an IoT environment. Future directions for IoT security issues is presented in Section 6. Finally presented a conclusion of this chapter in Section 7.

INTERNET OF THINGS

The Internet of Things term defines the huge category of internet applications and communication protocols developed on top of the interconnected networks whereas billions of things connected under one network (Ammar et al., 2018). Usually the 'Internet of Things' term is a combination of two major parts such as 'Internet' and 'Things'. By this sentence it-self can understand Internet of Things is, each and every object having the capability of connecting to the internet such as sensors, multimedia devices etc., is able to communicate with each other and exchanging the information from anywhere at any time. Ubiquitous computing is the major requirement of IoT and to achieve this, IoT application need to be support all kinds of multimedia devices and communication protocols. Also it requires integration of sensors, edge computing devices like hubs and routers, and multimedia devices. The main idea of this integration of all physical object is exchange the data with each other object so that can make the proper decisions. This integration feature allows managing all connected devices from remote location with less human interactions in connected network infrastructure (Kouicem et al., 2018). The IoT technology transforms these devices from classical to smart by exploring the supporting technologies like communication capabilities, ubiquitous computing, applications, and internet protocols. Figure 1 represents the advanced architecture of IoT where every application is connected with another application in the network. The IoT communication protocols plays a major role in communication among devices to exchange the data and selection of proper function that comply with the different kinds of functionalities of each connected device. In the next level, applications performs the data granularity operations to process the data which is generated from devices for analytics purpose. The IoT structure is a combination of protocols, rules and regulations, performs the analysis of data and exchange information among all connected devices. Based on the survey which is conducted by RnRMarketResearch, the IoT market will be worth nearly $1500 billion by 2020, with Internet of Nano Things. The IoT technology playing a major role in the future technology. In this context, several industries has planned to invest billions of dollars on IoT research. According to the Statista survey, 75.44 billion devices will be connected in worldwide IoT network by 2025. Figure 2 represents the IoT connected devices installed base worldwide from 2015 to 2025.

The IoT architecture could be different from application to application, according to the solution which is intend to build. But, the basic IoT architecture mainly consists of four components, such as Sensors, Gateways, Devices, and Applications. These four components would be used at four stages. At the first stage, data would be collected from different kinds of devices like sensors, actuators, wearable devices, cameras and, multimedia devices. These devices collects the data from the objects or environments and forwards to management services with the help of gateways and networks. These gateways can be Wifi, Ethernet, and WAN networks. Once the data has been aggregated and digitized, it is ready to further processing which performs in-depth analysis. After analysing the data, it is forwarded to cloud based systems or physical datacenters to provide the information to application interfaces. Figure 3 represents the IoT architecture where can see different stages of IoT architecture.

The IoT architecture has another three important aspects such as Wireless sensors networks (WSN's), Addressing, and middleware. The WSN's is the major component in the IoT environment which is collection of sensors networks. These networks have different kinds of sensors, RFID's (Radio frequency identifications), and multimedia devices. These devices exchanges the information together to getting information about temperature, position, and movement etc. WSN's plays a major role to provide useful data and utilized in different areas like environmental services, healthcare, traffic system, government, agriculture and, defence etc. Addressing is the second major aspect of IoT environment. In IoT network each object transforms from classical to smart thing. This transformation creates the smart environment, but identifying the things with unique address is a challenging task for the success of IoT environment. Reliability, scalability, uniqueness and persistence represent challenging features for creation of a unique address for each IoT device. So, IPv6 is the new extension of IPv4 which can solve the some of the device identification issues. Finally, middleware which is third major aspect of IoT environment. In IoT network, connected things has limited processing capabilities and storage. So these middleware services provides the several services like management services, object abstraction, security control, and service composition.

Figure 1. IoT connected network

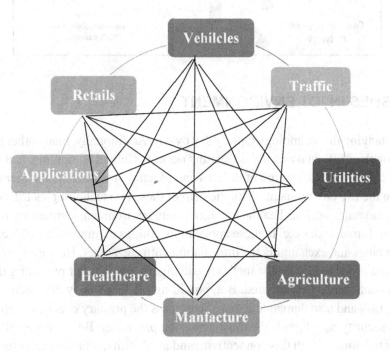

Figure 2. Statista survey on IoT connected devices by 2025.

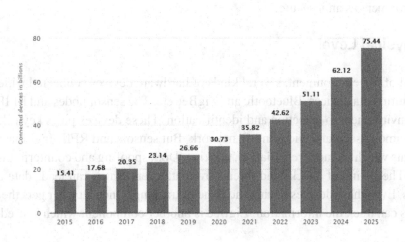

Figure 3. IoT architecture

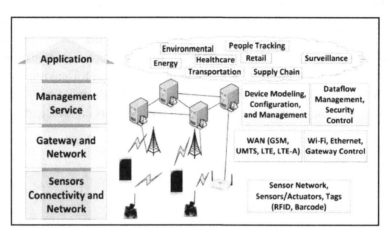

SECURITY ISSUES IN IOT ENVIRONMENT

The IoT concept changing the technology rapidly day by day. Additionally, many other technologies giving support for growth of IoT such as wireless sensors networks, cloud computing, and bigdata analytics etc. (Butun et al., 2014). The automation of devices and Machine-to-Machine another two technologies plays major role in the IoT environment. With the help of these two technologies IoT providing flexible services in several domains such as healthcare, agriculture environments, smart intelligent transportation, smart grids, and smart cities etc. In these applications, things communicate with each other device, including human beings and exchanging the information with each other. Here every transaction of data must be secured and protected by robust methods and algorithms, so that providing the confidence to the users that users data is properly secured. But, providing robust security management to the IoT, is a major challenging task and also demanding task. Security is the primary concern in all networks, but in IoT environments security paradigm is the most important parameter. Because the IoT network built by millions of connected things. With this connectivity and availability, attackers can create many chances to attack the network with malwares (Granjal et al., 2015). Still IoT networks have lots of chances to be affected by several kinds of threats at different levels such as physical level, network level, communication level, and application level (Alaba et al., 2017). So different kinds of attacks at different levels, makes IoT environment as an insecure.

Issues at Physical Level

At physical level of IoT environment, several kinds of hardware devices connected which includes sensors, RFID's, multimedia devices, Bluetooth, and ZigBee etc. The sensor nodes and RFID tags are major devices in IoT environment to detection and identification. These devices plays key role in exchanging the information among several devices in IoT network. But sensors and RFID tags may compromise to attacks and threats which includes repudiation, tracking, DoS, spoofing and counterfeiting etc. (Mitchell & Chen, 2014) These kind of attacks and threats from attackers which can leads data theft issue from sensors and tags. Even these devices having the issue of tracking. Once attacker gets the accessibility of device, attackers can track the information. ZigBee is another component which is used in IoT network frequently to collect the information. It is a one kind of micro controller and protocol. Due to the limited processing power, these devices are having more chances to get attacks and threats. Usually these devices have the information of packets and keys. By getting the accessibility of these devices, attackers can perform hacking, packet manipulation, and key exchange. Bluetooth is the device which is used for data exchange between devices. But few kinds of attacks to Bluetooth devices leads data theft issues and DoS, eavesdropping, Bluesnarfing, and Bluebugging attacks creates more vulnerable to attacks and threats.

Issues at Network Level

At Network level, communication can be done either wired network or wireless networks in IoT environment. In wired network, data can be exchanged by network adapters, routers, and cables between connected IoT devices. This kind of communication completely based on wired network and it develops the reliability, security, and ease of use. But, attackers making the IoT networks as a vulnerable by threats and attacks (Abduvaliyev et al., 2013). Various attacks to wired medium such as extortion hack, data manipulation, equipment hijacking, malicious attacks, and malware signalling systems etc., proven that IoT wired networks also compromises to threats and attacks. On the other hand, wireless medium networks utilizes transmitters, radio communication channels, and receivers to exchange the data in between IoT devices. This wireless connection networks transforms the connectivity from classical connectivity to smart connectivity. However, a wireless network communication channel also compromises to threats and attacks such as data hacking, misconfiguration, DoS attacks, signal loss issues, Man-in-the-Middle attack, protocol tunnelling, and war dialling etc. In IoT networks, security issues at network level makes maximum loss for users. Once data can be hacked from IoT networks, attackers may get the accessibility of entire IoT network. Because, in IoT networks, all applications has the connectivity with each other. So, threats and attacks at network level in IoT networks which leads the several issues (Khan et al., 2018).

Issues at Application Level

In IoT network, several applications have the connectivity with each other and each application have several kinds of supporting IoT devices. The applications in IoT network such as smart grids, smart intelligent transport system, smart cities, smart healthcare, smart agriculture, and smart surveillance etc. Each and every application, have different kinds of connected devices to collect the data from environment. For example, Smart city idea is the new evolution of the technology and includes smart street lights, smart cameras, smart e-governance, smart waste management, and smart water management etc. This kind of environment provides flexible services and makes human lives as an easy and also improves the economic development of city. But, IoT devices in smart city environment are open to several attacks and threats. For example, by data manipulation which is collected by smart cameras from traffic environment, attackers can able to give wrong information to travellers. And also fake disaster detection, DoS attacks, and fake seismic detection creates many issues for human lives (Huckle et al., 2016). Smart grid also one of the good idea of IoT technology. It improves the reliability in smart energy systems. However, smart grid also has possibility to threats and attacks. These attacks in smart grid environments makes maximum loss. For example, malicious attacks in traditional power devices collapse the entire power management system. Smart agriculture is the great idea for farmers, but lack of the knowledge about attacks and threats, farmers may face wrong assumption issues. Another application of IoT environment is smart healthcare management system, it enhance the services for patients. However, smart health cards have the chances to vulnerable. Data manipulations and data misusing of healthcare cards creates several issues. The smart intelligent transport system controls traffic, transportation and smart parking etc. But due to the malware attacks, DoS attacks, and cyber-attacks, attackers get the accessibility of traffic management system.

Additionally, several attacks at other levels makes IoT networks as a vulnerable (Zarpelao et al., 2017). If consider the DoS attacks which makes the IoT devices as a vulnerable to users so that users gets interruptions frequently. These DoS attacks are categorized into several types which includes collision of data, signal jamming, and malware internal attacks. Eavesdropping is another kind of attack, it can be attack on communication channel in either wired network or wireless network. The main aim of this attack is, interruption of communication by extract the data from communication channel. Counterfeiting attack also major concern in security issues in IoT environments. By using this method attacker can do forgery of information, which means attacker can create the duplication of content. Man-in-the-Middle attack is one of the challenging attacks in network environments. By using this approach, attacker can access the data from IoT devices. Figure 4 represents, the taxonomy of security issues in IoT environment. This chapter mainly focused on three levels where can get the several security attacks and threats.

Figure 4. Security issues in IoT environment

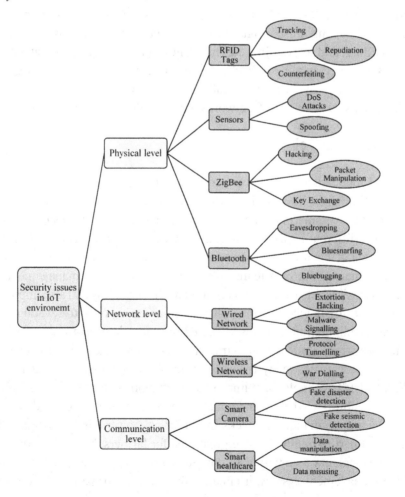

BLOCKCHAIN TECHNOLGY

The Blockchain technology has been rapidly growing in security management system over the past three years (Miraz et al., 2018). As per Statista survey reports, in global market blockchain technologies creates the business worth of $2000 billion by 2020. In next five years, blockchain technology creates huge evolution in security management system. Bitcoin is one of the applications of blockchain technology which transforms the crypto-currency system throughout world. Bitcoin is the digital currency which was developed based on the decentralized management system. In peer-to-peer network, bitcoin transactions can be done by exchanging with public key cryptography. These public keys are will be created based on cryptography rules and can be used for transactions of bitcoins. All these transactions which have done by users, needs to validate and store the information into blockchain. In blockchain, every block acts as a ledger and it stores all the transactions of users. Likewise, every user in peer-to-peer network verifies and stores the information into blockchain. The main advantage of the blockchain technology in crypto-currency system is, avoiding the interactions of third party organizations and their charges for transactions which is done by user. The blockchain technology, also avoids the centralized information storage and centralized control system (Panarello et al., 2018). After that, a transaction based state machine was presented to support the blockchain technologies. Based on these features such as security, privacy, integrity, auditability, system transparency, authorization, and fault tolerance etc., blockchain technology can be adopted in several environments like supply chain management system, agriculture, mobile crowd sensing, smart intelligent transport system, and identity management (Dorri et al., 2016).

In peer-to-peer network, each and every node receives two types of keys such as public key and private key. The public key is used for encryption of message which is sent by users to another user in a network, usually this concept is called encryption method. The private key is used to read a received message which is called decryption method. Likewise, in blockchain technology every node of blockchain has the information of transaction and it has to be sent to every user in blockchain network. To get the information of transaction user needs the private key to authenticate the transaction. Once user receive the information of transaction, that node sends the broadcast message to other users about this transaction. Then users verifies the transaction and stores the information in ledger with previous block of the chain. If validation is not fulfilled, the block will be discarded. The blockchain architecture is mainly composed with a sequence of blocks. These blocks are connected with each other with their hash function values. In ledger, users stores the information of authorized transactions. As shown in the figure 5, every user has a public key and private key. Private key used for signing into blockchain transaction while public key used for represent their address. Once the transaction is validated according to the cryptographic rules, a special node represents as a miners, stores the valid transactions into a time-stamped block. These time-stamped blocks comes back to the blockchain network and it will be verified by hash function value. In this manner, blockchain will be updated with valid transactions (Fernandez-Carames et al., 2018).

The blockchain technology mainly can be categorized into two ways such as either in public manner or in private manner. However, users can able to categorize into several types based on the availability of data and actions can be performed on data (Fernandez-Carames et al., 2018). In public blockchain networks, any user can perform the actions in blockchain network and able to act as a node or miner node. On the other hand in private blockchain networks, the network administrator has to authorize the user to perform the action. But types of blockchain networks are based on decentralized management system. These also provides high level of privacy and security against threats and malicious attacks.

The main differences between public and private is different execution of authorizations of users, ledger maintenance, and protocols. The examples of public blockchain network are Bitcoin, Litecoin, and Ethreum etc., these blockchain networks also called as a permission-less blockchain networks. The private blockchain also called as a permissioned blockchain platform and examples are Corda, Hashgraph, and Ripple or Hyperledger etc.

Figure 5. The working process of blockchain technology

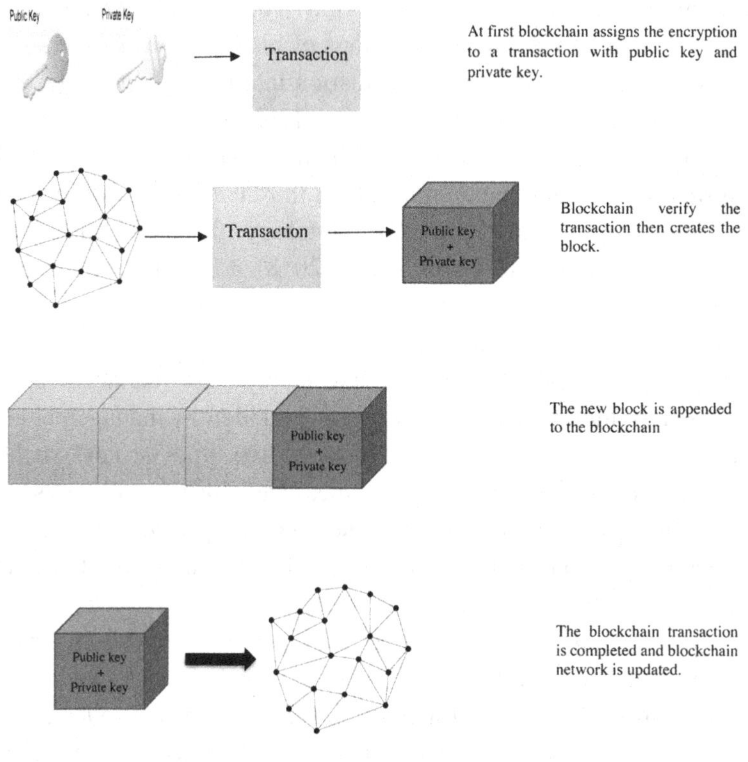

BLOCKCHAIN BASED SOLUTIONS FOR IOT ENVIRONMENT

A shown in the figure 2, IoT devices connectivity will keep on grow and it will reach 75 billion by 2025. In IoT network, each device acts like internet thing and provide the information to other device in a network. With all these connected devices, data generates in huge volume and processing of that data is a challenging task for researchers. On the other hand, security issues for production data also becomes another challenging task (Sfar et al., 2018). Usually, IoT network is a distributed architecture and each node has the possibilities to allow the attacks and threats. Every infected node can collapse the IoT network in fraction of seconds. This kind of centralized environment collapse the entire idea of IoT technology. This problem statement motivated the authors to propose the blockchain based solutions for IoT environment.

The main aim of the blockchain technology is to free users from any kind of third parties those who are regulate and manage the all kind of transactions. This technology plays major role in controlling, managing, and also provides the security and privacy to IoT devices. The blockchain technology provides the key solutions for several security issues in IoT environment (Jesus et al., 2018). An integration of blockchain and IoT technology brings many features in different kinds of environments such as trading, crypto-currency, machine-to-machine transactions, device tracking systems, supply chain management systems, certifications, government records management, and digital identity systems etc. (Panarello et al., 2018). So many industries like IBM working hard to develop blockchain frameworks in IoT industries. The following characteristics of blockchain technology transforms the IoT technology as a more robust.

- The decentralization is one of the primary and main characteristic of the blockchain technology. This feature increase the scalability, reliability, and robustness of the IoT devices. The main advantage of this characteristic is avoids one-to-many or many-to-one traffic flows of network while supporting the participation of all nodes in network. So that, it eliminates network delay issues and issue of a single node of failure.
- The second characteristic of the blockchain technology is anonymity. This feature keeps the IoT devices data as a private. In IoT environment secure of IoT devices data is, most important thing. So anonymity feature does supports to IoT devices, data should be kept private.
- Finally, security is the third characteristic of the blockchain technology. Making the IoT network as a secured from unauthorized users and devices, increase the robustness of the IoT network.

However, integration of these two technologies is not an easy task due to the different challenges like increment of number of nodes and block mining (Reyna et al., 2018). However, the huge efforts of researchers on these challenges, brings the tremendous evolution in technology (Kshetri, 2017). In this context, the following features of the blockchain technology solves the security issues in IoT environment (Khan & Salah, 2017).

Authorization and Authentication

Blockchain technology supports the decentralized management system, so this characteristic can be able to provide the decentralized authorization and authentication rules to IoT devices. So that IoT devices can be able to adopt multi authorization rules for users. Compare with traditional authorization and authentication protocols such as OMA DM, OpenID, LWM2M, OAuth 2.0, and RBAC etc., the blockchain authorization protocols provides secured access protocols to make connection with IoT devices while have less complexity. Additionally, privacy of IoT devices data also increase by accessing blockchain authorization rules and providing the accessibility of data to only authenticated users. These protocols also helps to upgrade, update, reset the IoT devices, allocation of new keys, and change ownership etc.

Address Space

The blockchain technology supports the 160-bit address space and 160-bit hash of the public key which is generated by Elliptic curve digital signature algorithm. With these both features, blockchain technology can able to allocate the addresses for approximately $1.46 * 10^{48}$ IoT devices (Khan & Salah, 2017). Generally, 10^{48} addresses avoids the issues of unique identification. That means when allocating the addresses to IoT devices, verification is not required. At present, Internet assigned numbers authority governance allocating the IPv4 and IPv6 address globally. In future, blockchain technology solves the issues of unique addresses for IoT devices.

Secure Communication

In IoT wired or wireless networks, communication protocols helps to communicate devices with each other. The traditional protocols in IoT networks such as HTTP, CoAP, MQTT, and RPL etc., are not provides robust security and privacy. These protocols integrates with other protocols to provide privacy and secure communication. But, blockchain technology transforms the concept of communication from traditional to advanced secure communication. Blockchain technology provides uniqueness of address and asymmetric key pair to IoT devices. So that, no need to exchange and handle the public key infrastructure certificates unlike in traditional communication. Additionally, IoT devices increases the computing process and memory resources.

Cryptography Algorithms

Due to the limited power of processing capabilities and memory resources, IoT devices not be able to handle the advanced cryptographic rules efficiently. Many cryptography algorithms consuming much power of IoT devices, so that IoT devices regularly gets the issues of shutting down. So, power consumption is one of the main parameter to consider when adopting the cryptography algorithm for IoT devices. Blockchain technology uses sophisticated algorithms for security and privacy while using hash functions. These hash functions are very flexible to implement in IoT devices. For example, SHA-256 is one of the blockchain hash functions which can be used in several IoT devices. Additionally, it also helps to avoid the issues about heavy power consumption of IoT devices.

Identity and Access Management

The identity and access management for IoT devices, is a challenging task due to the ownership of IoT devices. The ownership of IoT devices changes from user to user. Each and every IoT device have some parameters like manufacturer details, device type, serial number, and location etc. In some cases, changes of IoT device parameters, is not possible and creates another kind of issues when users make them as a vulnerable. With the help of blockchain technology, can able to solve these kind of issues easily, and efficiently. Generally, blockchain technology provides secure identity registration, monitoring of nodes, and ownership tracking. So, blockchain technology provide identity registration to IoT connected devices and stores the information about each and every parameter of IoT device into blockchain ledger.

The blockchain technology can be adopted in in several environments and use cases (Ferrag et al., 2018). At first, blockchain technology used for crypto-currency system, and later based on the flexible and secure features this technology providing the services in many fields such as data storage management system, user identity management system, smart intelligent transport management system, smart agriculture, and smart living applications etc. (Fernandez-Carames et al., 2018). In supply management also, blockchain using in IoT environments to transport the goods safely to destination. Likewise, the power management sector also taking the advantages of blockchain to IoT devices by providing smart and intelligent hardware components. Another application is smart health care system, the blockchain technology adding some more features to IoT devices to validate the records of patients. In this context, the following section presents how each IoT application utilizing the blockchain features and giving strengthen to IoT devices (Panarello et al., 2018).

Smart City

The smart city can be able to manage the things with intelligently like mobility, vehicles, surveillance cameras, and environmental resources etc. These things acts as intelligent devices, for example smart surveillance cameras captures the accidents on roads and gives the instructions to traffic management system and emergency management system. This kind of system needs data exchange process among connected IoT devices continuously. So attackers targets the devices to access the information of devices so that, attackers can perform unauthorized actions. The blockchain technology provides the secure solution for this issue. The collected data would be divided into several packets and distributes to connected devices in smart city environment. The blockchain cryptographic methods adds the certification rules to these packets which contains the original data. By adding this rules to packets, packets gets the hash of the collected data from IoT devices. Finally, the owner rebuilds the original data from received packets. For the communication also among IoT devices, blockchain uses Telehash protocol to control the devices from the surveillance cameras to traffic management system. This protocol adds authentication rules to IoT devices, so that they communicate with each other without interaction of central authority.

Smart Healthcare System

The integration of IoT technology and blockchain technology brings the evolution in healthcare system and provides the several flexible services to users. In smart healthcare system, the IoT network architecture builds with several kind of sensors, RFID tags, and routers etc. In healthcare system, record maintenance of patients, data communication from connected devices to computing processors, and monitoring the live conditions of patients etc., are very important things and kept as a private. Once the attacker gets the accessibility of IoT network, attacker may misuse the information of patients. The blockchain gives the solution for this issue by providing the secure communication among IoT devices. For example, IoT devices should authenticate with each other to intercommunication. The protocols like SSL or TLS, should be authenticated by public key infrastructure. Few authors (Biswas & Muthukku-marasamy, 2016) proposed a multilayer blockchain based framework for IoT networks. The aim of the proposed systems is data protection from unauthorized users. This architecture supports three layers for blockchain frameworks, the first layer for data storage based on the blockchain blocks, second layer for secure communication in IoT devices, and third layer for data management with access control system.

Smart Home

The IoT technology giving the automation system ability to devices, to enhance the lifestyle of human lives while providing safety, and flexibility. With this ability people can handle and manage several works from outside the home. However, due to the lack of the knowledge about internal functions of IoT network, consumers may get the issues from attackers. For example, if attacker gets the accessibility of one of the IoT devices from smart home then attacker gets the private and confidential data of consumers. Even Man-in-the-Middle attack can be access the information from home routers and sensors etc. So blockchain provides the solution for these attacks by providing public key infrastructure system.

Author (Dorri et al., 2016) proposed a multi-layer architecture to overcome the security and privacy issues in IoT environment while adopting the blockchain technology. The main aim of the proposed system is providing the availability, confidentiality, integrity, and reliability of data. This framework have three layers such as smart home, network, and cloud storage system. Likewise bitcoin technology, the miner creates the block when new device is added to IoT network. This block contains the information of block header and policy header. At second layer, devices communicate with each other by secure communication protocol. Finally, with the help of secured hash values data could be stored in cloud storage. This framework aims to provide the confidentiality, integrity, and reliability of data. Another integration of IoT and blockchain technology framework (Jentzsch et al., 2018) proved that, blockchain features provides more strength to IoT networks. This framework proposed an automatic authentication technique to smart IoT devices. The main aim of this proposed framework is, providing the possibilities to users to monitor and control the IoT devices and other goods with the help of blockchain rules. This technique allows the external devices into network and authenticating by smart IoT devices. And also used for authorizing the payments without help of intermediate points.

Smart Transactions

At first blockchain technology mainly used for transactions of crypto-currency, now different kinds of fields also trying to adopt the blockchain features in their environment. The blockchain architecture providing the several possibilities to IoT devices, in such way smart devices can able to make the secure and privacy transactions. In this context, (Wilkinson et al., 2014) proposed the framework for secure and privacy transactions. This framework uses p2p protocol to provide private, secure and encrypted cloud storage system. The main of this framework is, allowing the users to give rent their infrastructures to another users by using blockchain features.

FUTURE RESEARCH DIRECTIONS

Presents several advantages of integration of blockchain and IoT, and it helps to many researchers to solve the various security and privacy issues in IoT environment. But, this integration concept needs further investigations to enhance the research directions (Fernandez-Carames et al., 2018). In this context, the following points helps to researchers for further improvements. The future research directions of integration of blockchain technology and IoT are as follows:

- Still many challenges and issues to be addressed in integration of blockchain and IoT, such as cryptographic algorithms enhancement, security, reliability of data, integrity, and scalability etc. These constraints are very important things in the view of blockchain based IoT applications. Additionally, blockchain technology design processes have the limitations in validation protocols, transaction capacity, and implementation of public key infrastructure rules.
- The development of blockchain architecture rules in IoT environments, need to be approval of all management holders to achieve interoperability. And also has to integrated with legacy polices. An international standards also should be support the integration implementations to provide authorization, authentication, protection polices, and access control etc.

- A sophisticated infrastructure will be needed to implement the integration of blockchain and IoT technologies. To fulfil the requirements of IoT security management system by blockchain based rules, infrastructure or framework should be supports control and inter domain rules.
- The IoT network builds with different kinds of devices, architectures, protocols, and several standard rules etc. So, these networks have more chances to become vulnerable, even at single point of failure. Researchers needs to be develop robust standard protocols and cryptographic algorithms.
- Due to the low limited processing power, IoT devices have the chances to become vulnerable. An advanced security algorithms for hardware vulnerabilities, needs to be implement in intermediaries for malfunctioning, verification of packet processing, and routing etc.
- An advanced and robust rules should be provide for supply management methods. The blockchain technology can be used for supply management system. Adopting these rules in IoT environment, blockchain itself may get the challenges such as efficiency, scalability, reliability, regulations, and integration of data.

CONCLUSION

Now a days, IoT technology growing rapidly to provide the flexible services to human lives. This IoT concept brought the evolution in technology. On the other side, IoT devices are becomes vulnerable and losing the capabilities of defending due to the limited processing power and resources. These issues are raising due to the lack of sophisticated standards, secure protocols, and secure software and hardware designs. To resolve these issues, blockchain technology can offer secure standards, secure protocols, and robust cryptographic algorithms to IoT applications. This chapter focused on blockchain based solutions for IoT platforms. At first, presented about IoT technology and IoT architecture. In the next section, presented about several security and privacy issues in IoT platforms. The taxonomy also created to represents about security issues in IoT environment. An examined about blockchain technology and working process, proposed blockchain based solutions for IoT platforms like smart cities, smart healthcare systems, smart home, and smart transactions. Additionally, future research directions were discussed to provide few ideas to developers and researchers for further blockchain based solutions. The main of this chapter is, to provide technological innovation and secure solutions for IoT platforms based on blockchain technology.

REFERENCES

Abduvaliyev, A., Pathan, A. S. K., Zhou, J., Roman, R., & Wong, W. C. (2013). On the vital areas of intrusion detection systems in wireless sensor networks. *IEEE Communications Surveys and Tutorials*, *15*(3), 1223–1237. doi:10.1109/SURV.2012.121912.00006

Alaba, F. A., Othman, M., Hashem, I. A. T., & Alotaibi, F. (2017). Internet of Things security: A survey. *Journal of Network and Computer Applications*, *88*, 10–28. doi:10.1016/j.jnca.2017.04.002

Alvi, S. A., Afzal, B., Shah, G. A., Atzori, L., & Mahmood, W. (2015). Internet of multimedia things: Vision and challenges. *Ad Hoc Networks*, *33*, 87–111. doi:10.1016/j.adhoc.2015.04.006

Ammar, M., Russello, G., & Crispo, B. (2018). Internet of Things: A survey on the security of IoT frameworks. *Journal of Information Security and Applications*, *38*, 8–27. doi:10.1016/j.jisa.2017.11.002

Antonopoulos, A. M. (2014). *Mastering Bitcoin: unlocking digital cryptocurrencies*. O'Reilly Media, Inc.

Banerjee, M., Lee, J., & Choo, K. K. R. (2018). A blockchain future for internet of things security: A position paper. *Digital Communications and Networks*, *4*(3), 149–160. doi:10.1016/j.dcan.2017.10.006

Biswas, K., & Muthukkumarasamy, V. (2016). Securing smart cities using blockchain technology. In *2016 IEEE 18th international conference on high performance computing and communications; IEEE 14th international conference on smart city; IEEE 2nd international conference on data science and systems (HPCC/SmartCity/DSS)* (pp. 1392-1393). IEEE. 10.1109/HPCC-SmartCity-DSS.2016.0198

Botta, A., De Donato, W., Persico, V., & Pescapé, A. (2016). Integration of cloud computing and internet of things: A survey. *Future Generation Computer Systems*, *56*, 684–700. doi:10.1016/j.future.2015.09.021

Butun, I., Morgera, S. D., & Sankar, R. (2014). A survey of intrusion detection systems in wireless sensor networks. *IEEE Communications Surveys and Tutorials*, *16*(1), 266–282. doi:10.1109/SURV.2013.050113.00191

Dorri, A., Kanhere, S. S., & Jurdak, R. (2016). *Blockchain in internet of things: challenges and solutions*. arXiv preprint arXiv:1608.05187

Fernández-Caramés, T. M., & Fraga-Lamas, P. (2018). A Review on the Use of Blockchain for the Internet of Things. *IEEE Access: Practical Innovations, Open Solutions*, *6*, 32979–33001. doi:10.1109/ACCESS.2018.2842685

Ferrag, M. A., Derdour, M., Mukherjee, M., Derhab, A., Maglaras, L., & Janicke, H. (2018). *Blockchain technologies for the internet of things: Research issues and challenges*. IEEE Internet of Things Journal.

Granjal, J., Monteiro, E., & Silva, J. S. (2015). Security for the internet of things: A survey of existing protocols and open research issues. *IEEE Communications Surveys and Tutorials*, *17*(3), 1294–1312. doi:10.1109/COMST.2015.2388550

Huckle, S., Bhattacharya, R., White, M., & Beloff, N. (2016). Internet of things, blockchain and shared economy applications. *Procedia Computer Science*, *98*, 461–466. doi:10.1016/j.procs.2016.09.074

Jentzsch, C., Jentzsch, S., & Tual, S. (2018). *Slock.IT*. Available online: https://slock.it

Jesus, E. F., Chicarino, V. R., de Albuquerque, C. V., & Rocha, A. A. D. A. (2018). A survey of how to use blockchain to secure internet of things and the stalker attack. *Security and Communication Networks*.

Kalra, S., & Sood, S. K. (2015). Secure authentication scheme for IoT and cloud servers. *Pervasive and Mobile Computing*, *24*, 210–223. doi:10.1016/j.pmcj.2015.08.001

Khan, M. A., & Salah, K. (2018). IoT security: Review, blockchain solutions, and open challenges. *Future Generation Computer Systems*, *82*, 395–411. doi:10.1016/j.future.2017.11.022

Kouicem, D. E., Bouabdallah, A., & Lakhlef, H. (2018). Internet of things security: A top-down survey. *Computer Networks*, *141*, 199–221. doi:10.1016/j.comnet.2018.03.012

Kshetri, N. (2017). Blockchain's roles in strengthening cybersecurity and protecting privacy. *Telecommunications Policy, 41*(10), 1027–1038. doi:10.1016/j.telpol.2017.09.003

Kumar, K. D., & Umamaheswari, E. (2017). *An Authenticated, Secure Virtualization Management System in Cloud Computing. Asian Journal of Pharmaceutical and Clinical Research.*

Kumar, K. D., & Umamaheswari, E. (2018). Prediction methods for effective resource provisioning in cloud computing: A Survey. *Multiagent and Grid Systems, 14*(3), 283–305. doi:10.3233/MGS-180292

Kumar, K.D., & Umamaheswari, E. (2018). Efficient Cloud Resource Scaling based on Prediction Approaches. *International Journal of Engineering & Technology, 7*(4.10).

Miraz, M. H., & Ali, M. (2018). *Applications of blockchain technology beyond cryptocurrency.* arXiv preprint arXiv:1801.03528

Mitchell, R., & Chen, R. (2014). A survey of intrusion detection in wireless network applications. *Computer Communications, 42*, 1–23. doi:10.1016/j.comcom.2014.01.012

Panarello, A., Tapas, N., Merlino, G., Longo, F., & Puliafito, A. (2018). Blockchain and iot integration: A systematic survey. *Sensors (Basel), 18*(8), 2575. doi:10.339018082575 PMID:30082633

Reyna, A., Martín, C., Chen, J., Soler, E., & Díaz, M. (2018). On blockchain and its integration with IoT. Challenges and opportunities. *Future Generation Computer Systems, 88*, 173–190. doi:10.1016/j.future.2018.05.046

Sfar, A. R., Natalizio, E., Challal, Y., & Chtourou, Z. (2018). A roadmap for security challenges in the Internet of Things. *Digital Communications and Networks, 4*(2), 118–137. doi:10.1016/j.dcan.2017.04.003

Sicari, S., Rizzardi, A., Grieco, L. A., & Coen-Porisini, A. (2015). Security, privacy and trust in Internet of Things: The road ahead. *Computer Networks, 76*, 146–164. doi:10.1016/j.comnet.2014.11.008

Wang, Y., Uehara, T., & Sasaki, R. (2015). Fog computing: Issues and challenges in security and forensics. In *2015 IEEE 39th Annual Computer Software and Applications Conference* (Vol. 3, pp. 53-59). IEEE.

Weber, R. H. (2015). Internet of things: Privacy issues revisited. *Computer Law & Security Review, 31*(5), 618–627. doi:10.1016/j.clsr.2015.07.002

Wilkinson, S., Boshevski, T., Brandoff, J., & Buterin, V. (2014). *Storj a peer-to-peer cloud storage network.* Academic Press.

Yi, S., Qin, Z., & Li, Q. (2015). Security and privacy issues of fog computing: A survey. *International Conference on Wireless Algorithms, Systems, and Applications,* 685–695. 10.1007/978-3-319-21837-3_67

Zarpelao, B. B., Miani, R. S., Kawakani, C. T., & de Alvarenga, S. C. (2017). A survey of intrusion detection in Internet of Things. *Journal of Network and Computer Applications, 84*, 25–37. doi:10.1016/j.jnca.2017.02.009

This research was previously published in Transforming Businesses With Bitcoin Mining and Blockchain Applications; pages 45-67, copyright year 2020 by Business Science Reference (an imprint of IGI Global).

Chapter 13
Adaptation of Blockchain Architecture to the Internet of Things and Performance Analysis

Mevlut Ersoy
Suleyman Demirel University, Turkey

Asım Sinan Yüksel
Suleyman Demirel University, Turkey

Cihan Yalcin
Suleyman Demirel University, Turkey

ABSTRACT

Internet of Things (IoT) security and privacy criteria are seen as an important challenge due to IoT architecture. In this study, the security of the IoT system that is created with devices integrated into the embedded system by means of various sensors has been ensured by using a single cryptographic structure. The data transmitted between the nodes in the IoT structure is transmitted to the central node using the Blockchain data structure. The transmitted data is verified at central nodes and the energies consumed between nodes during the transmission phase is detected. An infrastructure has been developed for how blockchain technology can be used in the IoT structure. In this study, an experimental environment was developed and comparative analysis were made in terms of energy consumption and data transfer rates.

DOI: 10.4018/978-1-6684-7132-6.ch013

INTRODUCTION

IoT devices consist of different sensors and technologies in today's conditions. They collect data from certain environments, communicate with each other and create information services for the users. Within the context of IoT, an estimated 10-11 billion devices are assumed to be interconnected. These devices do not have autonomous defense skills against malicious approaches. The immature IoT standards are the main reason for this. Besides that, hardware and software modules that are used in IoT devices are non-standardized. Design, development, distribution processes are not hierarchical. Efforts to define a global security mechanism to secure the IoT devices and data transfers have also become a difficult problem to solve due to the diversity of resources on the Internet of Things. To solve this problem, the Internet of Blockchain-Based Things has been developed.

The rapid increase of the network devices and increasing number of cyber-attacks during the data transfer has revealed the necessity to develop solutions for this area. Numerous insecure IoT devices with heterogeneous nature and high computing power make them easy and attractive targets for attackers (Khan & Salah, 2018). The most up-to-date standardization and research activities are aimed at solving various security problems of IoT devices (Khorov et al., 2020). Most connected devices are easily exposed to security threats and attacks such as botnets during data transfer and these threats have proven that these devices have easily exploitable vulnerabilities (Wang et al., 2020). Due to the resource shortage and vulnerability in wireless communication, Advanced security infrastructures are needed for distributed computing systems that do not have a central control unit. (Kumar et al., 2014). The Denial of Service (DoS) and Distributed Denial of Service (DDoS) attacks are the types of attacks that mostly affect wireless networks. There is a lot of work involved to protect against these types of attacks. (Abramov & Herzberg, 2011, Aldaej, 2019). The addition of these protection systems to IoT structures provides significant disadvantages in terms of resource use. For this reason, protection systems added to IoT structures should be in infrastructures to eliminate such disadvantages. Likewise, the blockchain needs to be transformed into a heterogeneous system, such as users and verifiers, with clear role separations (Popov et al., 2019).

Transport and security protocols have great importance that ensure reliable and secure communication. There has been increasing interest to blockchain for security and privacy policies in the Internet of Things (Dorri et al., 2017). Blockchain is a technical framework that allows users to collectively protect the reliable database in a decentralized manner. In a blockchain system, data is generated and saved in units of the nodes. Sequential nodes are combined in a chronological order to create a chained data structure. All user nodes participate in the maintenance, repository, and validity of the data. More than half of users must approve the genesis of the new block. Data is broadcasted to all user nodes to create a network-wide synchronization (Dai et al., 2017). The neighbors of the nodes receive an identity and hash value with this broadcast. More nodes mean receiving higher validation and stronger security as a result. (Akyildiz & Jornet, 2010).The security and end-user privacy issues increase and become stricter in IoT, due to the asymmetric nature of the communications between sensors and the ordinary Internet hosts (Sahraoui & Bilami, 2014). For this reason, the use of blockchain has been proposed to contribute to the security and privacy issues of IoT applications.

In this study, the speed and energy usage of IoT with Blockchain have been analyzed. These analyzes have been compared with the non-blockchain structure in a second experiment under the same circumstances. In the developed experimental environment, Raspberry Pi 3 B + board was used as an embedded system. The IoT infrastructure has been installed with "Docker" in the Rasbian operating system.

The data has been gathered with three different sensors; it was encrypted in the blockchain structure and transferred to neighbor nodes. The data from the previous node has been added to the blockchain structure by validating the hash value and transmitted to the other node. It is ensured that the collected data has been transmitted to the central node in a correct and complete manner. A separate structure without blockchain was established with the same transmission infrastructure and transmission of data to the central node was also provided in this experimental environment.

As a result of the analysis, securely transmitted data with the blockchain structure in the wireless sensor network has been analyzed for energy usage. In these analyzes, it has been determined that less energy is used in WSN structures where blockchain is not used and 17% more energy consumption is realized in data transmissions performed with Proof of Work (PoW) in the blockchain structure. Additionally, IoT and blockchain combination has been considered as a daily life utilization. The research topics and challenges that need to be addressed to provide; reliable, efficient, and scalable IoT security solutions are summarized. The main motivation for this study is to combine the two main technologies and reveal the energy consumption by providing the maximum level of safety.

MATERIALS AND METHODS

The Internet of Things is characterized by small but very frequent volumes of information. Packet transfers in the IoT infrastructure are usually done by the methods required by a certain protocol. Since the packet structures of these protocols are standard, it causes unnecessary packet transfers in the transmission of small-sized data. This will cause unnecessary energy consumption in the IoT infrastructure. The represented network which has embedded devices with objects or sensors that are connected via a private or public network. The devices in IoT can be remotely controlled to perform the requested functionality. Information sharing between smart devices can be done through a network using standard communication protocols. The future importance of IoT is also evident due to applications in daily life. (Khan & Salah, 2018).

Internet of Things

The intensive use of computer networks has resulted in the development of communication systems and protocols, which may meet different needs and applications. The Internet of Things (IoT) is the name given to the entire communication systems that collect data from billions of devices and enable the data to be broadcast over the internet. The purpose of these systems is to provide information to people over the data collected for a particular region. In this way, while improving our lives and working conditions; our homes, vehicles, work areas, and cities can turn into smart interactive spaces. In outdoor and indoor environments, every sector in which there is a human and technology factor is within the scope of the IoT.

The Internet of Things (IoT) is a technology that enables the embedded system devices communicate with each other and exchange data between unique communication channels. The development of IoT is becoming increasingly tailored to the needs of humanity. It is widely used in vehicles, health care, wearable devices, retail sales, logistics, manufacturing, agriculture, utilities, appliances, etc. (Fernández & Fraga, 2018). Internet of Things concept covers the systems that exchange data between them without the need for human interference. An important function of The Internet of Things is to gather data to cause better decision-making or control. The data life cycle includes the following stages: capture, storage, sharing, maintenance, publishing, archiving, and cleanup (Tseng et al., 2020). To meet the expectations, and needs of people through technological devices that are used the Internet connection, these systems gather the data in a certain environment and communicate with each other, and create the information service for the users. The main idea of this notion is to cooperate with the devices using the addressing systems and use the obtained data meaningful way and make it ready for analysis on virtual platforms. The Internet of Things consists of eight main components as shown in Figure 1.

Figure 1. Internet of Things Components (Christoph, 2009)

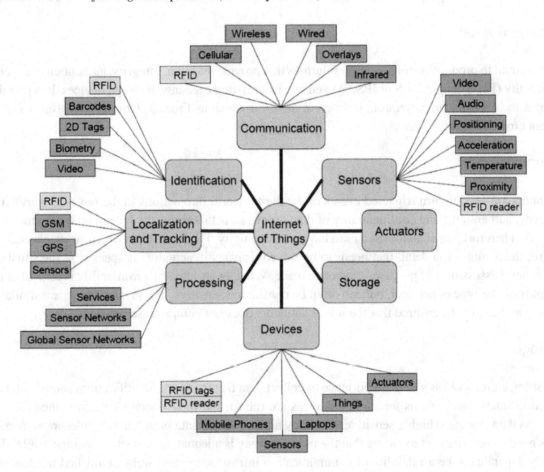

Devices

In the Internet of Things environment, devices are needed to interact with people within the physical world. The integrity of the devices means a tool doesn't contain malware. The originality of a device is often seen as the connecting endpoint. Privacy on a device is the third party's commitment to ensuring that the devices cannot access their internal data. This is normally provided in the case of device integrity. The availability of a device depends on the integrity and reliability of the devices as well as the availability of the communication part connecting the device.

Sensors

Sensors utilized in sensing and perceiving the physical world transfer the data they capture to the digital world. The integrity of the sensor data is a current research goal that must be addressed. Sensor data privacy is a weak need; because the attacker can physically place his own sensor and can detect the same values. Therefore, within the sensor itself, the necessity for sensor privacy is low, and therefore, the need for privacy is based on communication privacy. Stealth in sensors mainly targets the perceived physical world. The availability of sensors mostly depends on the communication infrastructure. Regulations to protect the privacy of people who are currently unaware of the most frequenting sensors need to be done.

Communication

It is essential to produce communication solutions that provide research, integrity, authenticity, and confidentiality (For example; TLS or IPSec) to ensure information exchange between devices. It is possible to meet the need for privacy through different directions such as Freenet, Onion, Thor. Nevertheless, it's not employed by the masses.

Actuators

Actuators are used to turn triggered events in the digital world into actions in the physical world. The integrity, authenticity, and confidentiality of data sent to an actuator mostly depend on communication security. Therefore, the actuator itself must have low sensitivity. The situation in which an attacker cannot control the actuator is a detail that needs to be solved. Privacy in actuators is specific to the situation, so a general assessment of precision cannot be made. Whether an actuator's availability is critical or not depends on the type of actuator, but can often be considered sensitive. The arrangements are similar to sensors and it must be ensured that the use of actuators does not compromise privacy.

Storage

The storage protocol has a great importance to collect data from sensors, identification, and monitoring systems. Safety mechanisms for storage devices are robust, but their operating performance remains poor. As data storage is highly sensitive to privacy and reports of data breaches are widespread, regulations need to be expanded to ensure that the user's privacy is adequately protected. Storage availability mostly depends on the availability of communication infrastructure and well-established mechanisms for storage backup.

Processing

Integrity in data processing is based on the integrity of the device and the integrity of the communication. Besides, the correct design and correct implementation of algorithms for data processing are of great importance. As the machine can often be abiding by actuator actions, it is also a delicate situation in that the actuator can receive incorrect commands. Processing only depends on the originality of the device; hence it depends on the originality of the communication. The nature of confidentiality in the process is not only enthusiastic to the integrity of the device; It also depends on the integrity of the communication in "Case of Distributed Transaction". The processing phase is critical to privacy and storage.

Tracking

Localization and monitoring steps are applied for locating and tracking in the physical world. The integrity of localization and monitoring is essentially based on communication integrity. Also, the integrity of the reference signals used in localization forms various anchor points. Likewise, originality also depends on the communication and device integrity. Privacy and localization, as well as the privacy of tracking data, are of critical importance to ensure the user's privacy. In this context, privacy means that an attacker cannot reveal localization data and therefore basically relies on communication privacy. Privacy in localization data;

- It means that the attacker is not able to reveal the identity of the person or reveal the object to which localization data was attached.
- It means localization and monitoring is not possible without clearing agreement or knowledge.

The availability of localization is important to ensure that reference signals for localization are robust and cannot be manipulated by the attacker.

Identification

Identity enables the data collected from the outside world to be separated by processing, monitoring, storage, and communication between other devices. It shares the same sensitivities as the identification, localization, and tracking clause. The only difference is that it also has high precision in integrity. The attacker can easily manipulate the identification process as well as manipulate the localization process. This is mainly due to an attacker's localization technologies (e.g., GSM) and technological advances (e.g., RFID or biometric) where manipulation is even easier.

From a security perspective, the main disadvantage of IoT applications and platforms is that they rely on a centralized cloud. A decentralized, blockchain-based approach tackles most of the problems associated with the central cloud approach. Some experts point out that blockchain can provide a minimal level of security for IoT devices. There is no single point of failure or vulnerability in the blockchain (Kshetri, 2017).

Internet of Things Management

Node-Red is a web-based visual development tool that is used to connect hardware and API (Application Programming Interface) on the Internet of things applications. The data flow in Node-Red is used with nodes that are interconnected by connection cable tools. The user interface consists of a flow editor with customizable templates. Admins can manage the flows which can be categorized. After a flow is created or modified, the admin saves the stream to the server and begins distributing it back to the Node-Red server (Giang et al., 2015). The flows in the nodes inherit the flow logic from their base class. (Johnston et al., 2004). Furthermore, the nodes are implemented based on observer design patterns. These nodes are subclasses of event organizers API and to maintain their subscriber list, the dataflow spread through to lower nodes. Input nodes can subscribe to external services; they can start "HTTP" requests, listen to data on specified ports, and run them. When the data is processed from an external service with "function," the node calls the "send ()" method with a "JavaScript" object (Blackstock & Lea, 2014).

It is possible to mark the nodes as "Device Nodes", "Server Nodes" or "Mobile Nodes." A server node may require assistance such as; specific programming languages on the platforms, the processing power of a server hosted in the clouds, data storage, or server connectivity outside of the firewall. Node without device ID can be contemplated as mobile node and it can be hosted on the devices or server. It can perform a heuristic scan based on user preferences or determine the best placement of a node. Similarly, a flow pattern can be expanded including different node types. The connections between the nodes and whole local connections work on the same execution engine. However, it can include data transfer between devices/ servers over a local/ wide area network.

Blockchain

Blockchain is a chronological database that operates on a distributed network of multiple nodes or computers that follow the data transactions. It is called "Blockchain" because of the ways in which transactions are recorded and verified. In Blockchain technology, all transactions are verified by all, and cryptographically signed with a hash value (Singh et al., 2020). The Information about a definite number of transactions is organized and encrypted into "blocks". Each new block, node, or computer is validated when a consensus is reached over the network. Blockchain and most distributed ledger technologies concern that contradictions are related to security, privacy, scalability, continuity, and energy consumption. Another approach is to integrate the blockchain with other digital technologies such as the Internet of Things, Artificial Intelligence, Deep Learning, Robotics, or Additive Manufacturing (Lemieux et al., 2019). Distributed Ledger Technology is shown in Figure 2.

Figure 2. Distributed Ledger Technology (Garderen, 2016)

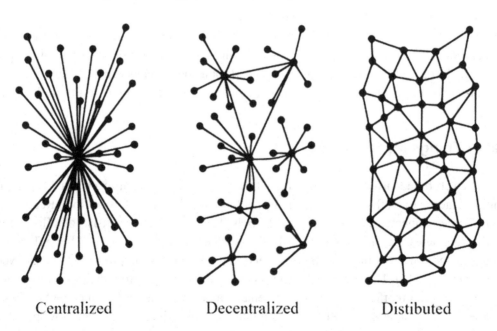

Centralized   Decentralized   Distibuted

Transactions in the blockchain that keep the list of constantly growing transaction records are called, "Block." The first block structure is called the "Genesis Block" shown in Figure 3 (Taş & Kiani, 2018).

Figure 3. Genesis Blog

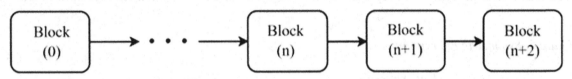

The cryptographic algorithms and/or passwords provide the security and accuracy of the blocks. Each block contains the cryptographic password of the previous block in its content and checks the authenticity of the file. The cryptographic encryption process is called "Cryptographic Hashing" which is a short definition of the "Hash" process. The hash function encodes an entry of any length into a uniform (Uniform String) text string according to the specified algorithm. The generated hash code changes even for each addition of a bit. Thus, a block that is recorded in the distributed ledger and added to the chain becomes unalterable. The block structure is shown in the Figure 4 (Sousa et al., 2018).

Figure 4. Blockchain Structure (Sousa et al., 2018)

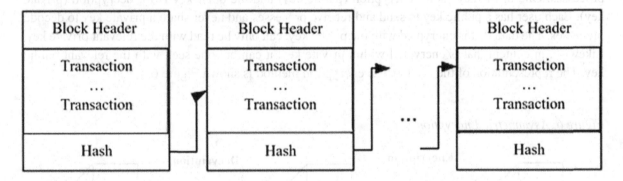

Cryptography

Cryptography is the collection of mathematical methods used to capture personal information and make it unreadable by unwanted parties. Each block has its own unique identity. In case of any retrospective attempt to be made within the block since the generated hash code, it will change itself and not comply with the existing hash code in the next block. Depending on the encryption algorithm, it cannot be returned to the original structure of the data by unwanted people who do not have the spousal key even if the data has been seized. The data can be transformed to the original state only by verifying the unique keys owned by the sender and the recipient.

Symmetric Encryption

In the symmetric encryption algorithms, a single key is used for encryption and decryption processes. Its strength is speed since the encryption and decryption are processed with a single secret key. All of the incoming, sending, and content information can be read if the secret- symmetric key is captured by third parties. Although it is a frequently used method, alter and re-sharing after sending creates a separate burden and cause problems. The representation of the symmetric encryption method is shown Figure 5.

Figure 5. Symmetric Encryption

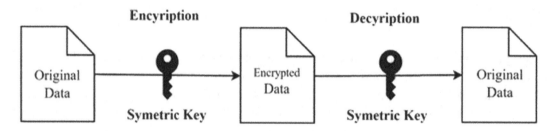

Asymmetric Encryption

In the asymmetric encryption algorithms, two different keys are used for encryption and decryption processes. One of the keys is for encryption (public key) and the other key is for decryption (private key). Each user has a public key to send and receive processes and never share a private key to decode processes. The data that is encrypted with the public key, can only be read with the relevant private key. Likewise, in content that is encrypted with a private key, it can only be seen with the relevant public key. The representation of the asymmetric encryption method is shown Figure 6.

Figure 6. Asymmetric Encryption

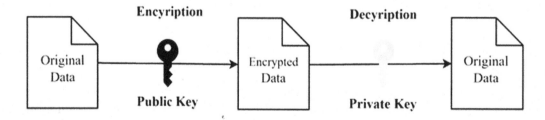

Digital Signing - Authentication

Digital signature (Figure 7) verifies the data integrity, distortion, intervention by third parties, packet loss, and genuinely sent by the expected sender. The hash algorithm is created by the sender (SHA-256) and encrypted with its private key and send to the recipient's public key. By comparing the hash code that is, created by the recipient's hash code of the sender, the recipient can find out whether it came from the right place and the receiver decrypts it with its own private key. If there is a content mismatch when comparing two hash codes (summary value), it is concluded that the user is not the recipient/ sender who created the content and signed the summary value, or it means that the message content was interfered while the data transfer.

Figure 7. Digital Signature-Verification Steps

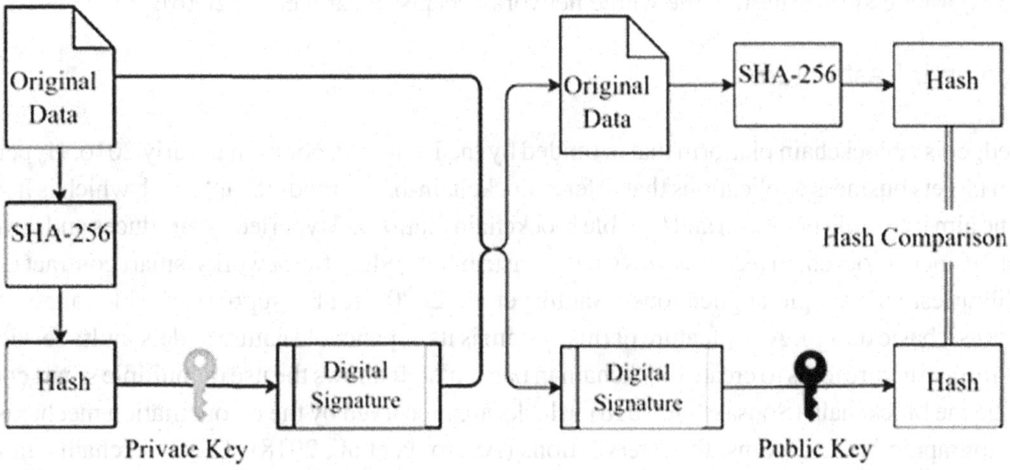

Merkle Tree

The Merkle Tree structure is used for the secure and fast verification in case of exceeding the size of data transfer, and it is a standardized model of major platforms and providers using blockchain. It separates the hash values similar to the tree model in the binary structure and keeps the hashes of the hash values that have been divided into small pieces in order. Each divided data value passes through the hash function to generate its own hashes. This process is directly proportional to the size of the data sent and continues until it is reduced to the maximum data size that can be carried. At this stage, the leaves (Merkle Leaf) combine the hashes of each conjugate that is divided and obtain a new hash. This process continues until it reaches (Merkle Root) the root.

Blockchain Security Services

In order for the attackers to seize the system, they must capture the majority of the nodes in the network. The distributed nature of the nodes greatly reduces this possibility. Hash functions are actively used in the blockchain, and altering a single transaction in the system will require calculating all the blocks in the chain as well. This strives will require tremendous processing power. For each block to be changed in the chain, the other nodes will need to be persuaded and PoW calculations will also need to be performed. This is defined as a 51% attack because all nodes in the network will need to have at least 51% of the mining processing power. Even if this attack is theoretically feasible, in practice it is not within the realm of possibility. (Sousa et al., 2018).

Each computing resource can be thought of as a single transaction manager that can switch between processes and states secured with encryption. When creating a new transaction manager, nodes encode the logic that identifies valid transaction passes and loads them into the blockchain. When creating new transaction manager, nodes encode the logic that identifies valid transaction passes and broadcast into the blockchain. The broadcasted blocks follow the current situation from the transaction manager when a series of valid transitions from the previous block. PoW, consensus algorithms and peer-to-peer protocols protect the state of the machines, the transition logic against malicious attacks, and share this information with all nodes participating in the system. Therefore, nodes can query the state of the machines and obtain a high-precision result that the whole network accepts (Azaria et al., 2016).

Blockchain Infrastructure

Hyperledger is a blockchain platform that is funded by the Linux Corporation in early 2016. Hyperledger platform targets business applications that offer a blockchain-based modular approach which is hosted by IBM. The aim is to build universal and flexible blockchain platform. Hyperledger produces and develops a range of business blockchain technologies such as distributed ledger frameworks, smart contract engines, utility libraries, and sample applications. (Saghiri et al., 2020). It also supports a wide range of smart contracts as a basic design. A key feature of this system is its expandable nature and its multi-services that provide infrastructure tools to create blockchain in particular. It allows the use of multiple smart contracts to manage the blockchain (Sousa et al., 2018). Blocks are preserved by the reconciliation mechanism and the cryptographic hashes against the interventions (Androula et al., 2018). The blockchain can remain attached to the model with or without permission. Without permission, records can be maintained by DLT (Distributed Ledger Technology) decentrally and anonymously. (Cachin, 2016). In an unauthorized chain, anyone can participate without having a specific identity. On the other hand, public blockchains operate between a blockchain among several known and defined participants. An authorized blockchain, the group of assets that does not rely on each other with a common goal (Transactions for Fund, Goods, or Information Exchange), it provides an interaction guarantee of getting a road between (Androula et al., 2018). Consensus-based PoW contains a local currencies for economic incentive (Chain.co, 2014). PoW involves that solving cryptographic puzzle and consumes resources to control the production of new blocks. The Proof of Work task requires miners to find a nonce value to be included in the block so that the hash value of the new block is less than a target value. Also, the difficulty can be adjusted over time to control the block generation rate. After the creation of the generated block, it is published to other nodes. After receiving the new block, the other nodes can validate the PoW by recalculating the hash value and comparing it with the hash value contained in the received block. (Dedeoğlu et al., 2020)

The Fabric Protocol is responsible for creating blocks to the distributed ledger and the services in which block is annexed to the ledger. All these processes are described in the steps below (Figure 8):

Step 1: Clients create a co-mission activity and send message to conjugates for validation. This message is used to call a chain code function. This is done by only if chaincode includes to chaincode ID and timestamps.

Step 2: The approved conjugates are simulating the co-mission actions and sign a compromise agreement. If the client is agreeably authorized, it can process by implementing the access control policies of the chain. After that the transactions are executed according to the current situation. The conjugates transmit the result of this occurrence to the client (it is allowed or rejected to read and write permissions the nodes associated with their current state). This is done with the validator conjugates signature and there is no additional updates are made at this point to ledger.

Step 3: Clients can collect and combine co-mission functions. The clients approves the conjugates signature if the read and write results of the clusters match with conjugates. If these conditions are met, clients create an "envelope" containing an approved literacy permission which includes an approved channel ID and signatures. The channel is the point within the fabric network that provides a special blockchain data section. Each conjugate shares the channel's specific registry that the envelope represents a transaction.

Step 4: The processors suggest co-mission action to broadcast. The service provider does not read the contents of the envelope. It collects the envelopes from all channels in the network only and creates the approved chain blocks which contain these envelopes.

Step 5: The envelope blocks are delivered to conjugates in the channel Envelopes within the blocks are checked and validated whether there is a change in conjugates status for the permission variables to ensure and fulfill approval policies. For this purpose, while the reading set simulates an operation, it contains a series of version keys that allow the reading of the conjugates (Step 2). The hinge on the accomplishment of these confirmations, the motion tender subsumed in the envelopes are marked as valid or invalid.

Step 6: The conjugates enclose the received block to the blockchain of the channel. The permission sets are dedicated to the conjugates current state for each accepted transaction. An event is triggered to broadcast the client that a transaction has been added precisely to the channel's blockchain, and it is decided that the transaction be considered valid or invalid. It is noted that invalid transactions are also added to the ledger, but this does not apply to conjugates. This also brings the advantage of making it possible to detect malicious clients because their actions are also recorded.

Figure 8. Hyperledger Transaction Processing Protocol (Sousa et al., 2018)

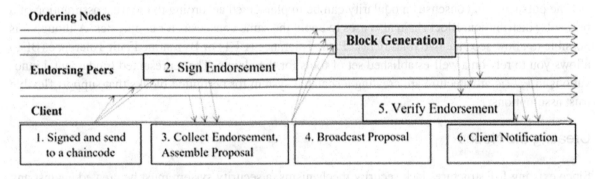

The substantial aspect of the fabric protocol is the verification comparison (step 2) and the verification of validation (step 5) can be done in distinct conjugates. The same operation can also confirm by distinct spouses; it will produce the same output. (Androulaki et al., 2018) The blockchain is similar to a "Reliable" computer service through a distributed protocol operated by connected nodes over the internet. The service represents or creates an asset in which all nodes have some stake. The nodes share the goal of running service, but they don't necessarily trust each other for more. In an unauthorized blockchain, anyone can run a node by spending CPU cycles and it can exhibit an example of "operational security."

On the other hand, the authorized model can typically generate identities and establish a compromise protocol with these nodes.

A Fabric network supports multiple blockchains models that are connected to the same service. In such networks, each blockchain is called a channel and may have different conjugates as its members. The channel can be thought as a part of the blockchain network but the consensus is not coordinated between these channels. The total transaction order is separated from the others in each channel.

Beginning of the Process

Each chain code can define its own permanent entries during the process. The ledger with reading permission also includes a security infrastructure for authentication and authorization because the transaction is applied. It supports registration and transaction authorization through public-key certificates. The privacy of the chain code that occurs through in-band encryption. In simpler terms in order to connect to the network, each conjugate must obtain a registration certificate from the registration system, which is part of the membership services. It is substantial to get necessary transaction certificates and capacitate a peer to be able to connect and operate to network. The chain code that exists for smart contracts is provided with symmetric key encryption. Transactions are executed with a specific key that can be used for all spouses with a registration certificate for blockchain (Cachin, 2016).

Fabrics architecture validates a new execution sequence to distribute entrusted code in an unrelied environment. It divides the process flow into three steps to run in different entities in the system:

Step 1: Take action (process), check the accuracy, confirm.
Step 2: Providing service through a compromise protocol regardless of transaction semantics.
Step 3: To grant transaction confirmation based on trust assumptions that are specific to applications that may affect the time and outcome conditions due to co-time.

The pursuance of consensus modularity can be implemented according to the trust assumption of a particular distribution. Blockchain also uses to apply the same consensus for conjugates. Although it is possible to allow separate two roles; Crash Fault Tolerance (CFT) or Byzantine Fault Tolerance (BFT) allows you to rely on a well-established set of tools for the claims. The represented fundamental innovations in Fabric architecture are creating a scalable system for permitted blocks that support flexible trust assumptions.

Creating the Nodes

Since existing IoT structures lack security mechanisms, a security system must be created against any cyber-attack even in the smallest data communication. In the developed system, blockchain has been used to record the transmission of data distributed between the nodes. These nodes ensure that the data cannot be changed and tampered with. It will not be possible to change or obtain the data recorded from the blockchain structure without seizing all nodes of the chain.

Nodes were created on Raspberry Pi 3B + embedded systems using Node-red and dissociated by different VLANs by setting static IPs. All devices (Raspberry Pi 3B +) were added as peers by creating a Perishable Network in Hyperledger Composer. The sensor data sent over with Node-Red included to the blockchain over IBM Watson. The provided data, read over from the IBM Watson through the Hyperledger Playground interface.

The energies of Raspberry Pi embedded system nodes are provided with an adapter with 5V/2,5A DC features. The wattmeters are connected to the nodes to detect energy expenditures which can be found easily on the market. These Watt Meters were checked in two different experimental groups.

- Data transmission was provided without using blockchain in the first experimental group. It was determined that how much energy was consumed with Raspberry Pi embedded systems and how long the sent data is transmitted.
- The second group was subjected to the same experiments using the blockchain. Tests have been carried out to ensure that the data is going to the correct address, whether the data has been altered or manipulated, and whether the data has been securely transferred to the central node. According to the results obtained; data transfer rates, temperature, and sensor data were analyzed. Additionally, the energy consumptions were compared in the established project.

FINDINGS

In blockchain integrated IoT system; Linux open-source Blockchain Application Hyperledger Fabric and Hyperledger Composer were used. Performance analyses have been made on energy consumption and data transmission speeds. Each device has an enclosure active fans to avoid temperature. GPIO pins, active network connection, embedded lights, and two sensors connected on each device. Also, devices have been sending sensor data every 5 seconds. It should be stated that the sensors which have been used in this context are the general-purpose sensors used in the market.

In Figure 9, "Energy Consumption Without Using Blockchain" shown in blue, and "Energy Consumption With Using Blockchain" shown green below. When the blockchain integration was achieved, integrated fans were embedded on the Raspberry Pi enclosure box to prevent congealment and shutdown due to heating. Upward movements (Peak) of the fans fed from the device's adapter and GPIO pins can be monitored in energy consumption.

Figure 10 shows the energy consumption with and without integration to blockchain. The part indicated by the blue lines is sensor data which is sent periodically to blockchain via Node-Red. The green lines show the sensor data without integrating to blockchain.

The incrementation of power consumption when using blockchain decreased to affordable differences in data transfer analysis when considering the security crisis. Transfer speeds, which differ according to the used smart contracts, provide a solution to the problem of not being preferred due to slowness regarding end-users by using Practical Byzantine Fault Tolerance (PBFT).

CONCLUSION

As the number of interconnected devices on the Internet of Things increases, user's expectations increase accordingly. With the lack of self-defense capability, a rapidly increased number of devices, and immature security standards are becoming harder to establish a security standard on the Internet of Things. On the other hand, blockchain technology which became popular in recent years has brought innovation expectations in this field. Unfortunately, we could not be using this technology efficiently. The idea to combine two major technologies that are expected to affect public, private, and especially academic sectors can eliminate the efficiency and security deficiencies. As long as the technology and intermediary programs that have offered the business markets only by large companies, "structure that is free and easily accessible to users" cannot be reached within this time.

The blockchain that is known as breaking news in the data security sector originally includes the security sectors of the future. The potential security, privacy, and anonymity principles of blockchain when considering the age of speed, will minimize the people's actions which are shifting into multiple efforts on behalf of individuals using this technology. The blockchain's potential has sufficient quality to save users from more than one workload. Besides that using blockchain architecture on the Internet of Things system, the difficulty of meeting the prerequisites, and its presentation on a single platform (Linux) poses a problem for the end-users. The system's hardware infrastructures were created physically and grouped on the Node-Red. Temperature, humidity, motion, proximity, distance sensing, gas, rain, wetness measurement, vibration, and inclination sensors are separately grouped and added to Raspberry Pi 3 B+ cards. It has been observed that when more than two sensors actively provide data to the blockchain, it brings energy-induced long freezes and temperature problems on the processor side on Raspberry Pi cards.

Figure 9. Blockchain Integrated Post-Energy Consumption

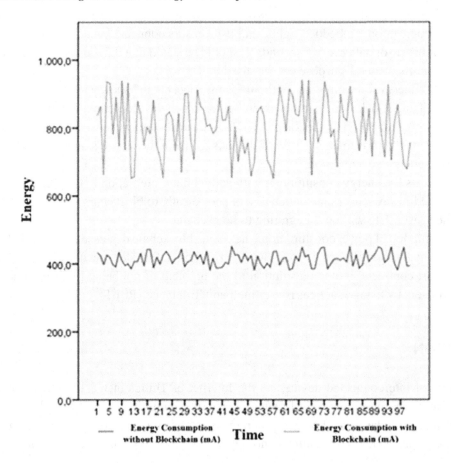

Figure 10. Transfer Speed with and without Blockchain

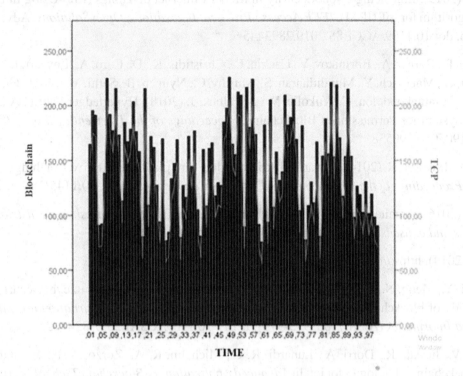

Crypto-based authentication services and key encryption protocols offer significant advantages in terms of security and privacy. As an advantage, blockchain-based cybersecurity systems are much more difficult to seize than other solutions. As the blockchain-based data transfer power increases, insecure data transfer decreases accordingly. Even if the blockchain-based Internet of Things System offers well security solutions for the Internet of Things, blocks and blockchain have no such ability to solve security issues automatically/individually.

This protocol can be spread according to the size of the network and depending on the number of nodes on the network. As the blockchain-based data transfer power increases; insecure data transfer is decreases accordingly. The crypto-based authentication services and key encryption protocols offer well-below cost results when considering the potential damages that security risks can cause. In case of a possible disaster scenario thought; Increased energy consumption has proved to be secure and anonymous data transfer with blockchain cause a tolerable cost.

REFERENCES

Abramov, R., & Herzberg, A. (2011). TCP ack storm DoS attacks. In *IFIP International Information Security Conference* (pp. 29-40). Springer. 10.1007/978-3-642-21424-0_3

Akyildiz, I. F., & Jornet, J. M. (2010). The internet of nano-things. *IEEE Wireless Communications*, *17*(6), 58–63.

Aldaej, A. (2019). Enhancing Cyber Security in Modern Internet of Things (IoT) Using Intrusion Prevention Algorithm for IoT (IPAI). *IEEE Access : Practical Innovations, Open Solutions*. Advance online publication. doi:10.1109/ACCESS.2019.2893445

Androulaki, E., Barger, A., Bortnikov, V., Cachin, C., Christidis, K., De Caro, A., Enyeart, D., Ferris, C., Laventman, G., Manevich, Y., Muralidharan, S., Murthy, C., Nyugen, B., Sethi, M., Singh, G., Smith, K., Sorniotti, A., Stathakopoulou, C., Vukolic, M., ... Yellick, J. (2018). Hyperledger Fabric: A Distributed Operating System for Permissioned Blockchains. *Proceedings of the Thirteenth EuroSys Conference.* 10.1145/3190508.3190538

Blackstock, M., & Lea, R. (2014). Toward a distributed data flow platform for the web of things (distributed node-red). *Proceedings of the 5th International Workshop on Web of Things.* 10.1145/2684432.2684439

Cachin, C. (2016). Architecture of the hyperledger blockchain fabric. In *Workshop on distributed cryptocurrencies and consensus ledgers (Vol. 310,* p. 4). Academic Press.

Chain.co. (2014). https://chain.com/docs/1.2/protocol/papers/whitepaper

Dai, F., Shi, Y., Meng, N., Wei, L., & Ye, Z. (2017, November). From Bitcoin to cybersecurity: A comparative study of blockchain application and security issues. In *2017 4th International Conference on Systems and Informatics (ICSAI)* (pp. 975-979). IEEE. 10.1109/ICSAI.2017.8248427

Dedeoglu, V., Jurdak, R., Dorri, A., Lunardi, R. C., Michelin, R. A., Zorzo, A. F., & Kanhere, S. S. (2020). Blockchain technologies for iot. In *Advanced Applications of Blockchain Technology* (pp. 55–89). Springer.

Dorri, A., Kanhere, S. S., & Jurdak, R. (2017, April). Towards an optimized blockchain for IoT. In *2017 IEEE/ACM Second International Conference on Internet-of-Things Design and Implementation (IoTDI)* (pp. 173-178). IEEE.

Fernández-Caramés, T. M., & Fraga-Lamas, P. (2018). A Review on the Use of Blockchain for the Internet of Things. *IEEE Access : Practical Innovations, Open Solutions, 6*, 32979–33001.

Garderen, P. V. (2016). *Introduction to Blockchain and Recordkeeping, Recordkeeping Roundtable.* http://www.interpares.org/display_file.cfm?doc=ip1_dissemination_ss_van-garderen_rr_2016.pdf

Giang, N. K., Blackstock, M., Lea, R., & Leung, V. C. (2015). Developing iot applications in the fog: A distributed dataflow approach. In *2015 5th International Conference on the Internet of Things (IOT)* (pp. 155-162). IEEE. 10.1109/IOT.2015.7356560

Johnston, W. M., Hanna, J. P., & Millar, R. J. (2004). Advances in dataflow programming languages. *ACM Computing Surveys, 36*(1), 1–34. doi:10.1145/1013208.1013209

Khan, M. A., & Salah, K. (2018). IoT security: Review, blockchain solutions, and open challenges. *Future Generation Computer Systems, 82*, 395–411. doi:10.1016/j.future.2017.11.022

Khorov, E., Lyakhov, A., Ivanov, A., & Akyildiz, I. F. (2020). Modeling of real-time multimedia streaming in Wi-Fi networks with periodic reservations. *IEEE Access : Practical Innovations, Open Solutions, 8*, 55633–55653.

Kshetri, N. (2017). Can blockchain strengthen the internet of things? *IT Professional, 19*(4), 68–72.

Kumar, E. S., Kusuma, S. M., & Kumar, B. V. (2014, April). An intelligent defense mechanism for security in wireless sensor networks. In *2014 International Conference on Communication and Signal Processing* (pp. 275-279). IEEE

Lemieux, V. L., Hofman, D., Batista, D., & Joo, A. (2019). Blockchain technology & recordkeeping. *ARMA International Educational Foundation, May, 30.*

Meghdadi, M., Özdemir, S., & Güler, İ. (2008). Kablosuz Algılayıcı Ağlarında Güvenlik: Sorunlar ve Çözümler. *Bilişim Teknolojileri Dergisi, 1*(1).

Popov, S. (2016). *The tangle.* Academic Press.

Saghiri, A. M. HamlAbadi, K. G., & Vahdati, M. (2020). The internet of things, artificial intelligence, and blockchain: implementation perspectives. In Advanced applications of blockchain technology (pp. 15-54). Springer, Singapore.

Sahraoui, S., & Bilami, A. (2014, May). Compressed and distributed host identity protocol for end-to-end security in the IoT. In *2014 International Conference on Next Generation Networks and Services (NGNS)* (pp. 295-301). IEEE.

Singh, S. K., Rathore, S., & Park, J. H. (2020). Blockiotintelligence: A blockchain-enabled intelligent IoT architecture with artificial intelligence. *Future Generation Computer Systems, 110*, 721–743.

Sousa, J., Bessani, A., & Vukolic, M. (2018). A byzantine fault-tolerant ordering service for the hyperledger fabric blockchain platform. In *2018 48th annual IEEE/IFIP international conference on dependable systems and networks (DSN)* (s. 51-58), IEEE. 10.1109/DSN.2018.00018

Taş, O., & Kiani, F. (2018). Blok zinciri teknolojisine yapılan saldırılar üzerine bir inceleme. *Bilişim Teknolojileri Dergisi, 11*(4), 369–382. doi:10.17671/gazibtd.451695

Wang, Q., Zhu, X., Ni, Y., Gu, L., & Zhu, H. (2020). Blockchain for the IoT and industrial IoT: A review. *Internet of Things, 10*, 100081.

This research was previously published in Blockchain and AI Technology in the Industrial Internet of Things; pages 48-65, copyright year 2021 by Engineering Science Reference (an imprint of IGI Global).

Chapter 14
Blockchain Technology With the Internet of Things in Manufacturing Data Processing Architecture

Kamalendu Pal

ⓘ https://orcid.org/0000-0001-7158-6481

City, University of London, UK

ABSTRACT

Modern manufacturing logistics and supply chain have transformed into highly complex value-creating business networks. It has become increasingly challenging to cross-check the source of raw materials and maintain visibility of products and merchandise while moving through the value chain network. This way, the high complexity of manufacturing business processes and the continuously growing amount of information lead to extraordinary demand to find an appropriate data processing architecture for the global manufacturing industry. The internet of things (IoT) applications can help manufacturing companies track, trace, and monitor products, business activities, and processes within the respective value chain networks. Combining with IoT, blockchain technology can enable a broader range of different application scenarios to improve value chain transparency. This chapter presents a hybrid (i.e., IoT, blockchain, service-oriented computing) data processing architecture for the manufacturing industry.

INTRODUCTION

Modern manufacturing has got a long history of evolution for several hundred years. The first industrial revolution began in the last part of the 18th century (Lukac, 2015). It symbolized production systems powered by water and steam, followed by the second industrial revolution, which started in the early part of the 20th century with the characteristics of mass labour deployment and manufacturing systems based on electrical power. The third industrial revolution began in the early part of the 1970s with automatic production or manufacturing based on electronics and computer data communication technology.

DOI: 10.4018/978-1-6684-7132-6.ch014

The concept of Industry 4.0 was put forward for developing the German economy in 2011 (Pal, 2021). Industry 4.0 is characterized by cyber-physical systems (CPS) production based on heterogeneous data and knowledge integration. It is closely related to IoT, CPS, information and communication technology (ICT), enterprise architecture (EA), and enterprise integration (Pal, 2021).

In a typical manufacturing supply chain, raw materials purchase from suppliers and products manufactured at one or more production plants. Then the product move to intermediate storage (e.g., warehouse, distribution centres) for packing and shipping to retailers or customers. In this way, a manufacturing supply chain consists of business partners in the network, and these are the suppliers, transporters, manufacturers, distributors, retailers, and customers (Pal, 2019) (Pal, 2017). A diagrammatic representation of a manufacturing supply chain is shown in Figure 1.

In this way, a manufacturing supply chain creates a complex network of business processes. Due to globalization and business process decentralization, a manufacturing supply chain's efficient performance needs better visibility - defined as the capability to share on time and accurate data throughout the manufacturing supply chain network and coordination among supply chain business partners. In today's global business environment, companies recognize the strategic importance of well-managed manufacturing supply chains.

Manufacturers are trying to focus on the significance of changes taking place in enterprise integration initiatives (e.g., supply chains), and it is worth reviewing trends in production and operations management. Besides, the global extension of many supply networks means that their members are increasingly geographically dispersed, working across different time zones, many organizational boundaries, numerous types of organizational cultures, and related work practices. These teams are often brought together on short notice and coordinated in nearly real-time to complete a production project or a particular service within limited time and restricted resources. Very often, manufacturing supply chain business partners are engaged in many supply business activities simultaneously. In these situations, communications and real-time coordination between mobile and distributed supply chain members is complex, making the requirement for an efficient communication infrastructure that provides reliable on-demand access to both supply process information and related personnel more accurately.

Figure 1. Diagrammatic representation of a manufacturing supply chain network

Also, the change towards demand-driven production implies that not managing supplies but demands of the customer should trigger and influence the production processes. Consequently, logistics gets a new focus on optimizing the production process in a very dynamic environment. Besides, though there are different solutions and methods for regional business processes minimization (e.g., strategic manufacturing operations scheduling systems, inventory management systems, market trading optimization systems, and so on), generally, these local decisions do not assure the overall business optimization at the global level because of the conflicts between the local goals.

The manufacturing supply chain management (SCM) problem can be defined as the management of relationship across a supply chain network to find the synergy of intra- and inter-company business processes to optimize the overall business operation of the enterprise (e.g., quality assurance, cost minimization, and on-time delivery). The traditional simple integration techniques are not enough to assure global optimization due to their inherent complexity. For example, a researcher (Dreher, 1999) presented a complex VOLKSWAGEN index showing that an automobile is manufactured from 3000 up to more than 20000 parts. Also, researchers (Eschenbacher et al., 2000) shown the complexity of an integrated distributed production planning system for the same supply chain coordinated and controlled centrally would cause a lot of different problems: (i) bottlenecks of centrally control centres of production, (ii) planning in the complete supply chain can be very complex, (iii) confidential internal information must be provided to the individual centre, and (iv) data consistency is a significant issue in decentralized structures.

Manufacturers often use enterprise resource planning (ERP) to integrate procurement, production, distribution, inventory management, and sales systems. ERP evolved from early material requirements planning (MRP) and manufacturing resource planning (MRP II). ERP systems track a range of business resources, including raw materials, manufacturing capacity, inventory, and cash, plus commitments such as sales and purchase orders. Databases in ERP track and share this data across business functions and potentially to outside stakeholders.

Recent inclinations towards the convergence of wireless communications and Internet-based technologies can open new avenues of business operational data collaboration, minimizing the physical dispersion of manufacturing supply chain members. In this way, blockchain, a distributed database (or ledger) of transactions connected into blocks of unique data structure (known as node or block), promises to (i) enhance efficiency, speed, and security of ownership transfer of digital assets (ii) eliminate the requirement for central authorities to certify ownership and help to complete transactions, (iii) minimize administrative expenditure using agreements that can automatically activate, and create trusted actions based on computational algorithms (known as smart contract), and (iv) preventing fraud and corruption by using a transparent and publicly auditable ledger facility.

A significant challenge associated with blockchain adoption is finding out relevant use cases that would benefit from integrating blockchain technology with the Internet of Things (IoT) based information systems in the manufacturing industry. With recent advances in Radio Frequency Identification (RFID) technology, low-cost wireless sensor hardware, and computer network infrastructures, the Internet of Things (IoT) advance has attracted attention in connected manufacturing business activities and sharing operational business information more integrated way.

Spite the vast applicability of IoT-based applications in the manufacturing industry, and there are many challenges for deploying this technology. In the traditional manufacturing supply chain, new orders are sent to suppliers via fax or courier mail. The manufacturing supply chain can be deployed as a resource-interactive network that needs no hands-on operation combined with IoT. Each sensor in the manufacturing supply chain automatically collects the information required and automatically and efficiently performs its flow. However, IoT technology is still at the risk of a single point of failure, and there is a risk of leaking corporate privacy.

Blockchain technology emerges from the early research work of Satoshi Nakamoto (Nakamoto, 2008) on 'Bitcoin', a peer-to-peer (P2P) electronic currency system. This system permitted payments to be directly initiated by one party and send to the other without any intervention of a third-party financial institution (Rana et al., 2019). However, this technology is forming a stepping stone for trusted information exchange among business partners. The blockchain maintains the same ledger by different nodes or members in the blockchain network to complete a trusted transaction. In recent years, prominent public blockchain platforms (e.g., Ethereum, Hyperledger Fabric, Enterprise Operating System (EOS)) help industries to create decentralized applications using smart contract-based blockchain network. In this network, each node on the blockchain is responsible for allocating the ledger copy to all other participating nodes so that the data in the blockchain is tamper-proof.

In this way, blockchain integrated IoT architecture provides advantages of tamper-resistance information-sharing platforms. However, these architectures face many problems. For example, the explosion of data generated by IoT-based systems faces main challenges in data management, data mining, and security problems. Data management challenges are associated with many technology-specific essential issues. IoT sensors, machinery, and special-purpose devices generate huge data that need to process and stored appropriately in the manufacturing industry.

The rest of this chapter is organized as follows. Section 2 describes the overview of manufacturing network data management related technical issues. It also simply explains the paradigms of IoT technology and the blockchain used for business processes automation purposes. Section 3 presents the background knowledge of key technologies for automating the global manufacturing industry. Section 4 describes the challenges for blockchain-based IoT application. Section 5 presents the proposed three-layered framework for an information system. It includes data storage and consolidation policy-related research agendas, and this section also explains the emerging issues in blockchain-based information system's deployment. Section 6 review related research works. Section 7 explains the future research direction. Finally, Section 8 concludes by discussing relevant research issues.

BACKGROUND OF MANUFACTURING NETWORK DATA MANAGEMENT

It has become an important trend for the manufacturing industry to adopt decentralization as a new manufacturing paradigm. At the same time, data analysis advantages give more insights into manufacturing production lines, thus improving its overall productivity. It helps more efficient operations and facilities move from mass to customized production. Also, business processes automation improves the efficiency of industrial production. Detailed information on the constituent parts of manufacturing artefacts and their history are needed to streamline the dedicated manufacturing processes. In this way, digitalization helps to improve the efficiency of manufacturing systems. For example, sub-components of a manufacturing artefact traceability could be done through an RFID code that uses electromagnetic waves to identify and monitor tags attached to objects automatically. Information technology (IT) provides a new way to track the origin and flow of materials; therefore, it helps increase manufacturing operational information transparency. It provides the necessary infrastructure for the customization of product based on user requirements.

Data management challenge relates to many technology-specific essential issues. IoT sensors, machinery, and special-purpose-purpose devices generate massive data that need to be processed and stored in a manufacturing business. Business-specific data centre architecture for information systems also plays a crucial role. Few manufacturing businesses would invest in data storage sufficient to house all the IoT data collected from the network. Consequently, they need to prioritize data for operations or backup based on business uses and value. Data centres architecture are often distributed to improve processing efficiency and response time as IoT devices become more widely used for global business operational facilities.

Data mining applications play an essential role in IoT-based infrastructure. As different data types are available, data consists of traditional discrete data and streaming data generated from digital sensors in manufacturing plants, machinery, vehicles, and shipping packages. These real-time streaming of data provide temperature, humidity, location, and movement-related information of interest items. In this way, in the manufacturing industry, data mining applications provide correctional guidance to facilitate necessary actions.

IoT-based manufacturing chain information system's security is also a major challenging problem. A growing number and type of connected devices are introduced into IoT networks, the potential security threats escalate. Training developers may resolve security challenges to incorporate security solutions (e.g., intrusion prevention systems, firewalls) into products and operational services.

Figure 2. Overview of data management in a blockchain technology

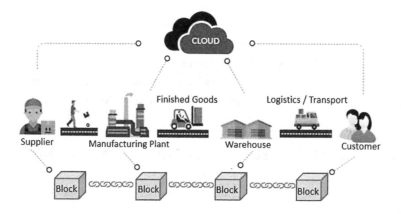

In this way, modern IoT-based infrastructure is often regarded as the catalyst for improving supply chain information sharing ability. Information sharing across manufacturing networks is based on linking unique identifications of objects – tagged using RFID transponders – with records in manufacturing business process-related information. The Electronic Product Code Information Services (EPCIS) plays an essential role in gathering and processing the collected data. IoT technology is used heavily in manufacturing business processes (e.g., inventory management, warehousing, and transportation of products, automatic object tracking) in supply chain management. With access to precise information, manufacturing supply chain operational managers can perform their analysis on a nearly real-time basis and take appropriate strategic decisions.

Despite making to the rapid development of IoT applications, the current IoT-centric architecture has led to many isolated data silos that hinder the full capabilities of appropriate data-driven business information systems. Besides, standalone IoT application systems face security and privacy-related technical issues. Blockchain technology can provide introduced an effective solution to IoT based information systems security. A blockchain enhances IoT devices to send data for inclusion in a shared transaction repository with the tamper-resistant record and enables business partners to access and supply IoT data without central control and management intervention. This chapter presents a blockchain-based design for the IoT applications that secure distributed data management to support transactions services within a multi-party global manufacturing network, as shown in Figure 2.

DECENTRALIZED MANUFACTURING AUTOMATION TECHNOLOGIES

The recent decade has seen the importance of disruptive innovations that have changed many manufacturing (e.g., apparel) business operations. In recent years, manufacturing companies are challenged to accomplish timely and accurate information exchange among the inventory-management applications and across the supply chain tiers. As a response to these challenges, the manufacturing industry initiated the inventory visibility and interoperability research projects, highlighting the requirements to establish interoperable data exchange standards among manufacturing business partners. It provides efficient operations and facilities with the shift from mass to customized production. This section presents some of the critical technologies which help to interoperable data exchange in the manufacturing industry. It includes a brief description of service-oriented computing, IoT based information systems, and an introduction to blockchain technology.

Service-Oriented Computing

Service-oriented computing (SOC) is a vital computing paradigm that utilizes services to support distributed applications' development. Services are self-contained application systems used over industry-specific middleware architectures, capable of describing, publishing, locating, and orchestrating over dedicated data communication networks. These architectures often use in large-scale data centre environment. However, data centres' consolidation and centralization produce a significant problem due to increased distance between customers and relevant services for business. Besides, this arrangement creates different outcomes in high variability in latency and bandwidth related issues. To address this issue, particularly regarding resource-intensive and interactive applications, decentralized SOC architectures, namely cloudlets, have emerged. Cloudlets are small-scale data centres situated near user applications and can mitigate low latency and high bandwidth guarantees. This chapter's research embraces this locality-aware data storage and processing trend and brings it to its full potential with a decentralized access control layer that ensures ownership and data sharing security.

IoT Based Information System

IoT technology's main backbone is a worldwide data communication network of interconnected smart objects. IoT technology's primary purpose is to share information acquired by smart objects, reflecting the manufacturing business activities, transportation, consumption, and other details of the manufacturing industry detail. The gathered information can be used for business-specific applications.

The prompt and effective decision depends on reasoning mechanisms and the quality and quality of business operational data. Every significant manufacturing business has been supported by the advancement of Information Technology (IT) and its applications. For example, the broad adoption of enterprise resource planning (ERP) and industrial business process automation made flexible manufacturing system feasible. It includes computer-aided design, computer-aided product development, and computer-aided process planning made computer integrated manufacturing practice. In developing enterprise information systems (EISs), more and more enterprises rely on IT software service providers to replace or advance their conventional systems. Hence, it makes sense to examine the IT infrastructure changes and evaluate their impacts on the evolution of manufacturing business process automation when a new IT solution (e.g., blockchain technology) becomes influential.

Blockchain Technology

Blockchain technology has attracted wide attention due to cryptocurrencies (e.g., bitcoin) (Nakamoto, 2008).In simple, blockchain is a distributed data structure comprising a chain of blocks. Blockchain technology acts as a distributed global record-keeping digital book (or ledger), which maintains all transactions records. Individually transactions are time-stamped and grouped into blocks where its cryptographic hash function identifies each block. The chain is formed of a linear sequence that each block references the hash of the previous block, creating a chain of blocks known as '*blockchain*'. Technically, a blockchain is managed by a network of nodes, and every node executes and records the transactions. A simple blockchain diagram is shown in Figure 3.

Blockchain technology is considered a strong foundation of research in cryptography, hashing, peer-to-peer (P2P) networks and consensus protocols. The initial excitement about Blockchain technology-enabled P2P transfers of digital currency to anybody in the world, crossing human-created boundaries (such as countries' borders) without intermediaries such as banks. This excitement heightened by realizing that P2P ability can be applied to other, non-crypto currency types of transactions. These transactions involve assets such as titles, deeds, music and art, secret codes, contracts between businesses, autonomous driver decisions, and artefacts resulting from many everyday human endeavours. A transaction record may contain other details based on the blockchain protocol and the application. In simple, a transaction in the blockchain is a transferable activity between different business partners.

A blockchain consists of a set of blocks, as shown in Figure 3, and an individual block encapsulates a hash of the previous block, which is creating a chain of blocks from the first, also called a genesis block the current block, where these blocks consist of transactions. These transactions mean an agreement between two participants, where the value of transfer may be of physical or digital assets, or it could be the completion of a task. The requested transaction is broadcasted to a P2P network consisting of computers, known as nodes, to validate the transfer. A node can be any electronic device (e.g., computer, phone, printer, or even smart machine) in a manufacturing business if connected to the Internet. All nodes have equal importance on a blockchain. Also, each node has a different type of tasks to perform in making a blockchain network. Technically, there are different types of blockchain nodes that have been identified and defined by the research community (Pal, 2020). In a simplistic sense, three types of nodes (i.e., Light Node, Full Node, and Mining or Forging node) are available for commercial information system implementation purpose.

Industry users of the blockchain-based information system network use mining nodes to create new blocks, verified by algorithmic software for their information, and ultimately add them to a distributed P2P network. Blockchain technology uses the consensus algorithm (Ferrag et al., 2018) to add a new block to the network and follow the steps as below:

1. Blockchain network user uses the cryptographic-based private key to sign a transaction and advertises the book to its peers.

2. Blockchain network peers validate the received transaction and advertise it over the blockchain network.
3. Involved users generally verify the transaction to meet a consensus algorithmic digital agreement.
4. The miner nodes add the valid transaction into a time-stamped block and broadcast it again into the blockchain network.
5. Next, verifying the advertised block and matching its hash with the previous block, the block in consideration adds to the blockchain network.

Figure 3. A diagrammatic representation of a blockchain

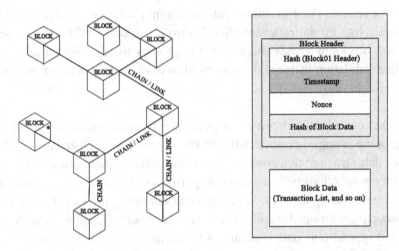

This way, consensus algorithms are one of the most important and revolutionary aspects of blockchain technology. Consensus algorithms use rules and verification methods to validate data that lets the blockchain network included devices agree about adding data to the blockchain network (Bashir, 2017).

One of the benefits of blockchain-based technology is to validate the block trustfulness in a decentralized, trustless business operating environment without the necessity of the trusted third-party authority. In a blockchain-based P2P network environment, it is challenging to reach a *consensus* on a newly generated block as the consensus may favour malicious nodes. This challenge can be mitigated by using dedicated *consensus* algorithms. Typical consensus algorithms are – proof of work (PoW), proof of stake (PoS), and practical byzantine fault tolerance (PBFT) (Bach et al., 2018).

- **Proof of Work (PoW)**: The creation of a newly generated block in a blockchain network is equivalent to the solution of a computationally difficult mathematical problem. The design and development of PoW process are time-consuming and costly, but once solved, other participants in the blockchain network can easily verify the solution. This way, 'Miners' solve a consensus problem, publish the solution to the network, and add the newly created block to the blockchain that will be spread over the chain to be verified by all participating nodes. This process can simultaneously take place in the different areas of the blockchain network. When peers decide to include a new block to the blockchain network, they must cross-check the branch size and choose the most accumulated work (the longest chain) that is considered to be the valid node (Gupta et al., 2018).

- **Proof of Stake (PoS)**: It attempts to create consensus in a different way than PoW. In the PoS, the originator of the next block is selected based on the different randomized combination of miners' resources and the duration that they hold their resources. Contrary to PoW miners that may not have a resource and only attempt to maximize profits by improving computational power, PoS miners defend the blockchain network to protect their wealth and profits. If the stake is higher than the transaction fees, participants can trust them to do their job correctly (Vashchuk & Shuwar, 2018).

- **Practical Byzantine Fault Tolerance (PBFT)**: The basic concept of PBFT originates from a story about a group of generals independently commanding a part of the Byzantine army surrounding a city they wanted to conquer. The most critical thing is that all generals reached a mutual decision to attack or retreat. The Byzantine problem attempt becomes even more complicated when disloyal generals vote for an irrelevant plan (Castro & Liskov, 2002). This consensus algorithm determines new blocks in rounds and selects the sponsor to advertise an uncorroborated block. The transaction validation includes three steps algorithm, and all network nodes vote (Castro & Liskov. 2002) (Joshi et al., 2018).

Classifying blockchains as *public* or *private* helps identify the main characteristics of many blockchain technologies. One of the essential characteristics of blockchain is the 'Distributed Ledger Technology (DLT). A ledge is a data structure that consists of an ordered list of transactions. For example, a ledger may record monetary transactions between business partners or good exchanged among known associate parties for the manufacturing industry. In blockchain technology, the ledger is replicated over all the nodes. Also, transactions are grouped into blocks that are then chained together. Therefore, the distributed ledger is a replicated append-only data structure. A blockchain begins with some initial states, and the ledger records the whole history of update operations made to the states.

In general, blockchain systems make use of cryptographic techniques (Menezes et al., 1997) to ensure the integrity of the ledgers. Integrity in this context means the ability to detect tampering of the blockchain data. This characteristic is crucial in public settings where there is no pre-established trust among business collaborators. However, integrity is also very important in private blockchains because the authenticated nodes can still act maliciously.

Some of the blockchains' promising applications are network monitoring and security services (e.g., including authentication, confidentiality, privacy, integrity, and provenance). All these services are crucial for the distributed applications, primarily due to the large amount of data being processed over the networks. Authentication helps to identify a user uniquely. Confidentiality guarantees that unauthorized users cannot read data. Privacy provides users with the ability to control who can access their data. Provenance allows efficient tracking of the data and resources along with their ownership and utilization. Integrity helps to verify that the data has not been modified or altered. The blockchain network needs to configure and optimize how the system's performance can be swifter if every node does not have to do every operation needed for a transaction on the chain.

Automated Transactions and Smart Contracts

An essential characteristic of blockchain technology is to automate smart contract. In a smart contract, the transactions will be executed only when the predefined conditions are accomplished (Dolgui et al., 2020). The 'contract' is defined in software and stored in the blockchain architecture. Once agreed between the parties, the 'contract' execution is entirely automated, with no need for third-party authorization and no possibility of modification. The steps of a smart contract are shown in Figure 4.

The contract terms agreed upon by manufacturing supply chain network participants are encoded in software written for a blockchain network. The contracts define the statement of obligations, advantages, and penalties, and the terms are enforced when the conditions for execution are satisfied. For example, in a cash-on-delivery smart contract, the contractual business partners realize automatic settlement when the procured items correctly arrive in the warehouse. This high degree of automation makes blockchain technology particularly suitable for multi-tier supplier networks with complex relationships; it is difficult to track the business's status and settle payments in this context.

Figure 4. Concept of blockchain contract

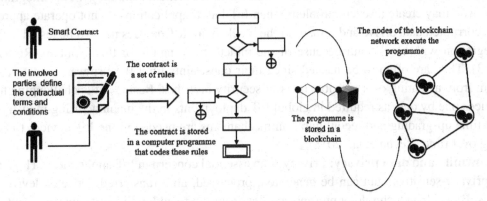

Blockchain technology, at its central, features an immutable distributed ledger, a decentralized network that is cryptographically secured. Blockchain technology can reduce operational costs, create immutable transformation records, and enable transparent ledgers where updates are nearly instantaneous.

Besides, the rapid inclination in the usage of IoT technology applications has led to the emergence of different IoT-based applications in manufacturing network – such as utility monitoring, transportation, and customer service. Some IoT applications also use blockchain-based techniques to incorporate user privacy and security in the development of applications. Despite IoT and blockchain-based applications integration advantages, this combination is not straightforward. The following section presents some of the challenges and the relevant solutions of using the blockchain-based technology that designs for IoT devices.

CHALLENGES FOR BLOCKCHAIN-BASED IoT APPLICATION

This section presents some of the crucial challenges and the related application solutions of deploying blockchain technology, which designs for the devices with permanent storage capability and computing capability on the minimal resources of IoT hardware. Some of the essential integration challenges can be found in the previous research works (Reyna et al., 2018) (Atlam et al., 2018).

Blockchain and IoT Integration Challenges

- **Scalability:** The blockchain size widens with an increasing number of connected devices because it needs to store all the transactional information and validate them. This is a significant integration disadvantage as IoT networks are expected to contain many nodes that can generate big data in real-time. Also, some of the recently implemented blockchain systems can only process a few transactions per second. It is one of the significant disadvantages of IoT (Zheng et al., 2017). To highlight the blockchain scalability issue, researchers reported blockchain storage optimization strategies to resolve the blockchain resource challenge using removing old transaction records (Bruce, 2014). Also, the same researchers worked on redesign blockchain based on IoT limits.

- **Security:** The increasing number of security-related attacks on IoT networks and their ultimate impacts make it essential to secure IoT devices with blockchain technology. This integration characteristic may create a severe problem when IoT-based applications do not operate appropriately and corrupted data arrive and remain in the blockchain. IoT devices need to be tested before their integration with blockchain because of the undetectable nature of this problem (Roman et al., 2013). They are often to be hacked since their constraints limit the firmware updates, stopping them from actuating over possible bugs or security breaches. Besides, it is challenging to update devices one by one, as required in global IoT deployments in the manufacturing industry. Hence, run-time up-grading and reconfiguration mechanisms are needed in the IoT devices to keep running over time (Reyna et al., 2018).

- **Anonymity and data privacy:** Privacy is an essential concern in IoT applications. Huge amounts of privacy-sensitive data can be generated, processed, and transferred between device applications. Blockchain technology presents an ideal solution to address identity management in IoT to protect the person's identity when sending personal data that protect user data privacy. Data privacy in transparent and public blockchain systems has already been discussed in conjunction with some available solutions. The blockchain transactions use particular and even dynamic addresses instead of identities. The user anonymity can be revealed by examing the transactions address advertised to every participant (He et al., 2018). The IoT devices secured data storage and authorization of access are a significant challenge since in order to accomplish it requires integrating security cryptographic solution to the device, considering limited resources.

- **Resource utilization and Consensus:** Trusted authority in centralized architectures make sure consensus integrity, while in the decentralized environment, nodes of the blockchain network need to reach consensus by voting, which is a resource-intensive process. IoT devices are attributed to relatively low computing capabilities and low power consumption, and low-bandwidth wireless connectivity. For example, blockchains that utilize PoW as a consensus mechanism need vast computational power and utilities a considerable amount of energy for the mining process. Computationally complex consensus algorithms are not applicable for IoT scenarios, and the limited resource should be allocated to find a possible agreement. However, PoS is more likely to be used in IoT, but none of these issues has yet been deployed in IoT as a commercial adoption (Atlam et al., 2018) (Danzi et al., 2018).

A distributed and decentralized blockchain architecture can reduce the overall cost of the IoT system in contrast to centralized architectures. However, a decentralized blockchain architecture suffers from a new type of resource-wasting, which poses challenges for its integration with IoT. Resource requirements depend on the blockchain network consensus algorithm. Typically, solutions to this problem are to delegate these tasks to an unconstrained device or another gateway device capable of catering for the functionality. Otherwise, off-chain solutions are also useable in this situation, and off-chain moves information outside the blockchain to minimize the high latency in the blockchain could provide the functionality (Reyna et al., 2018).

- **Smart contracts:** Devices can use smart contract techniques with addresses or guide them as application reaction to listening events. They provide a reliable and secure feature for the IoT, which record and manage their interactions. Working with smart contracts requires using oracles that consist of specific entities that provide real-world data in a trusted manner. Smart contracts should consider the heterogeneity and limitations presented in the IoT. Also, actuation mechanisms directly from smart contracts would help faster reactions with the IoT (Reyna et al., 2018).
- **Predictability:** Devices in manufacturing IoT applications require real-time communication with their operating environment, which means the time used by interactions between things should be predictable. Predictability is even more important for some specific applications based on IoT (Bui & Zorzi, 2011). For example, the transaction finality in blockchain under many consensus mechanisms (e.g., PoW, PoS) is probabilistic, and the confirmation confidence of the transaction in confusion is also probabilistic. It remains a fundamental challenge to incorporate predictability concerns in blockchain architecture (He et al., 2018).
- **Legal issues:** The blockchain integrates different people from many countries without any legal or compliance code to follow, making a severe concern for both manufacturers and service providers. As stated, the lack of regulations for private-key retrieval or reset or transaction reversion mechanisms creates problems. Some IoT applications envision a global, unique blockchain for devices, but it is unclear if this type of network is managed by manufacturers or open to users. In any case, blockchain will require legal regulation. These regulations will influence the future of blockchain and IoT and maybe disrupt the decentralized and accessible nature of blockchain by introducing a controlling, centralized participant such as a country (Governatori et al., 2018).

IoT designers should select a solution based on their restrictions and requirements, the diversity of solutions for blockchain integration with IoT, and different types of IoT devices and their applications. The next section presents the proposed architecture based on IoT, blockchain, and SOC technologies.

PROPOSED ENTERPRISE ARCHITECTURE

This section explains how service-oriented computing (SOC) technology will improve efficiencies, providing new business opportunities, address regulatory requirements, and improve transparency and visibility of global manufacturing activities. The IoT systems allow capturing real-time manufacturing business processes data from the plant-level operational environment. The enterprise architecture for distributed manufacturing (e.g., apparel) supply network used for the current research is shown in Figure 5. The architecture mainly consists of three layers: (i) IoT-based service, (ii) blockchain-based data control, and (iii) data storage and processing part.

IoT-Based Service Layer

The IoT technology development created many opportunities, such as interconnected and interoperable data collection and exchange devices. The data obtained from the IoT devices can make manufacturing more convenient through numerous types of decision-making at all its levels and areas of manufacturing business activities.

Blockchain-Based Data Controlling

The blockchain-based controlling part can potentially improve the IoT technology uses in the manufacturing industry. The manufacturing industry is part of a complex and information-intensive manufacturing supply chain comprising a set of globally connected and distributed organizations, including other critical infrastructures that support word trade, such as transport and international border management.

Figure 5. Enterprise information system architecture for manufacturing (e.g., apparel) business

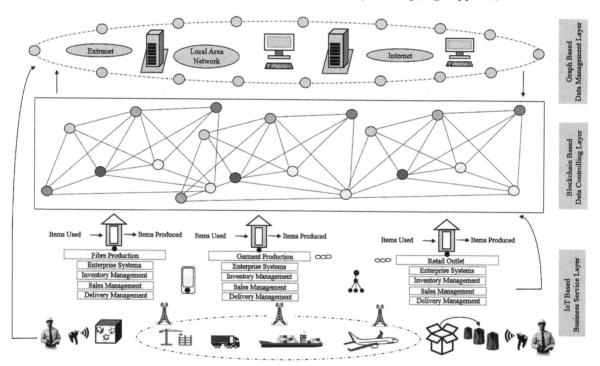

Manufacturing and its supply chain management are regarded as a domain where blockchains are good fits for various reasons. During the product's lifecycle, as it flows down the value chain (from production to consumption), the data produced in each step can be present as a transaction, therefore making a permanent history of the item of interest (i.e., product). Among other things, blockchain technology can effectively contribute to (i) record every single asset (from product to containers) as it flows through the manufacturing chain nodes, (ii) tracking order, receipts, invoices, payments, and any other official documents, and (iii) track digital assets (e.g., certifications, warranties, licenses, copyrights) in a unified way and parcels with physical assets, and others. Moreover, through its decentralized nature, the blockchain can effectively share information regarding the manufacturing step, delivery, maintenance schemes of products between suppliers and vendors, bringing new collaboration opportunities in complex assembly lines.

The challenges in transportation modelling parameters, such as delays in delivery, loss of documentation, unknown source of products, errors, and so on, can be minimized and even avoided by blockchain implementation. The benefits of integrating the manufacturing supply chain with blockchain are enhanced environmental audit-related issues, minimize errors and delays, minimized transport costs, faster issue identification, increased trust (consumer and partner trust) and improved product transport and inventory management.

Data Management Layer

Industries use different blockchain platforms, and different data models are used on the platforms (e.g., Ethereum (Ethereum, 2021) adopted key-value data model, while a few of them, like R3 Corda (Corda, 2021) use relational data model). This characteristic emphasizes that any single blockchain platform not suitable for different types of data used in a wide range of manufacturing supply chain business applications. For example, geolocation data recorded from supply chain transport vehicles may not be efficiently queried using a key-value store. Also, even though blockchain platforms such as Hyperledger Fabric (Hyperledger, 2021) use for a pluggable storage model, service users must decide at development time which storage to use (e.g., either Level DB (Kim, 2016) (key-value store) or CouchDB (CoucDB, 2021) (document store). Thus, special techniques are required for supporting multiple types of data stores such as key-value, document, SQL, and spatial data stores simultaneously in the same blockchain system. In the proposed architecture, a generic graph-database model has been used.

RELATED RESEARCH

Academics and practitioners identified industrial business processes, notably supply chain and logistics management, essential for deploying IoT based information system applications (Atkore, Iera & Morabito, 2018) (Gubbi et al., 2013). IoT-based industrial information systems can enhance enterprise competitiveness through more effective tracking of raw materials' flow, leading to improved business processes' effectiveness and efficiency (Shroud, Ordieres & Miragliotts, 2014).

In the context of globalized business practice, with multiple collaborating-partners based supply chains, IoT-based applications enhance the sharing of more precise and timely information relevant to production, quality control, distribution, and logistics (Chen, Guo & Bao, 2014). However, researchers expressed their concern regarding standalone IoT-based applications and global supply chain management (Pal, 2020). The main concerns were raised on the issues of standalone IoT systems security and privacy.

The research community has proposed different hybrid information system architectures (e.g., IoT with blockchain, cloud-based IoT and blockchain technology). A blockchain enhances IoT-based applications tamper-resistant characteristics. In recent years, different blockchain-based information management systems have been reported by researchers. For example, IBM has developed a new blockchain-based service that is designed to track high-value items through complex supply chains in a secure cloud-based application system (Kim, 2016). Another exemplary industrial application is a fine-wine Provence-tracking service, known as the Chai Wine vault, developed by London-based Company Ever ledger (Finextra, 2016) in a business partnership with fine-wine expert Maureen Downey. Blockchain-based digital identification tools for physical property and packaging have been reported for enhancing high-value parts for supply chain management (Arrear, 2017). An innovative anti-counterfeit application called Block Verify is designed and deployed to track anti-counterfeit products (Hulse apple, 2015) to create a sustainable business world. A start-up company from Finland (i.e., Kouvola) developed a smart tendering application for supply chain management in partnership with IBM. The reported application is built on an automatic blockchain-based smart contract (Banker, 2016). Another blockchain-based smart contract, called SmartLog, launched by Kouvola in recent years (AhIman, 2016).

In recent decades, due to globalization, manufacturing supply chain networks are going through an evolutionary change through the continued digitization of their business practices. These global manufacturing chains evolve into value-creating networks where the value chain becomes an essential source of competitive advantage. At the same time, developments are in progress to integrate blockchain technology with other innovative technological solutions (e.g., IoT-based applications, cloud-based solutions, and fog computing-based automation), leading to novel structures of modern manufacturing supply chains of collaboration and value-enhancing applications for the global apparel business. The reported research in this chapter is one of these value-creating applications, which explains the adoption of IoT-based item description and use in blockchain infrastructure to reap the combined advantages for future-generation apparel supply chain management.

This way, data and organize their transmission both nationally and globally is a requirement. It is still unclear how disparate blockchain technologies and systems will interoperate and integrate with other technological artefacts. This is compounded by unreliable and inefficient transmission standards and protocols that clog the arteries of information sharing between the exchange partners. Besides, an IoT environment is inherently dynamic, unpredictable, and affected by the ever-changing laws and regulations related to security and other interoperability requirements. Such sudden variability and random nature necessitate new laws and regulations in the manufacturing business world. In future, this research will review most of these issues.

FUTURE RESEARCH DIRECTIONS

Blockchain technology with the Internet of Things applications is getting importance in manufacturing industry automation. Besides, data privacy issues remain an essential challenge for regulatory bodies. The European General Data Protection Regulation (GDPR) lay the foundation for users to control their data and information about any devices involved in collecting and processing this data. The main objective is to provide individual entities must have the authoritative power and control over their data assets and to be able to transfer their data without any unmitigated risk. Blockchains gives the advantages of distributed ledger that can securely manage digital transactions, where the centralization of data is not needed. In future, this research will take the initiative that how blockchain technology can be used to develop an audit trail of data generated in IoT devices, providing GDPR rules to be verified on such a trail. This mechanism will help translate such rules into smart contracts to protect personal data transparently and automatically.

CONCLUSION

The economic disturbance caused by the ongoing pandemic due to coronavirus (i.e., COVID-19) are forcing myriad decisions on operation managers in the manufacturing supply chain management (SCM) team. It changes consumer buying patterns – the demand for a stable price, better service levels, which necessitate customer intelligence and varying supply and demand fulfilment related information. The COVID-19 situation has introduced significant stress on manufacturing supply chain networks; competing high street businesses are redesigning their SCM strategies. These strategies heavily depend on real-time information processing power that improves supply chain execution, reduces the operating costs of business, and improve market demand response. The Internet of Things (IoT) technology with blockchain-based information system architecture plays an important role in global manufacturing data sharing purpose.

Companies in the transportation and manufacturing industries can implement decentralized concepts for goods and transport containers tracking. Driven by the requirement for greater transparency in the manufacturing supply chain, which allows traceability from start to finish, comprehensive technical solutions are required. This is often a challenge for information technology (IT) solutions that focus on centralized solutions with complex access rights. Blockchain or derived concepts can remedy because they have already provided industrial solutions, which addressed these issues.

This chapter presents a hybrid enterprise information systems architecture consisting of IoT applications and a blockchain-based distributed ledger to support transaction services within a multi-party global manufacturing business network. The IoT is an intelligent global network of connected objects, which through unique address schemes, can help to collaborate with other business partners to achieve common objectives. The data obtained from the IoT applications along manufacturing business processes can make operational decision-making much more accessible. However, standalone IoT application systems face *security* and *privacy*-related problems. Finally, the chapter presents a research proposal outlining how blockchain technology can impact the IoT system's essential aspects of GDPR related issues and thus provide the foundation for future research challenges.

REFERENCES

AhIman, R. (2016). *Finish city partners with IBM to validate blockchain application in logistics.* https://cointelegraph.com/news/finish-city-partners-with-ibm-to-validate-blockchain-application-in-logistics

Atlam, H. F., Alenezi, A., Alassafi, M. O., & Wills, G. (2018). Blockchain with Internet of Things: Benefits, challenges, and future directions. *International Journal of Intelligent Systems and Applications*, *10*(6), 40–48. doi:10.5815/ijisa.2018.06.05

Atlam, H. F., Alenezi, A., Alassafi, M. O., & Wills, G. (2018). Blockchain with internet of things: Benefits, challenges, and future directions. *International Journal of Intelligent Systems and Applications*, *10*(6), 40–48. doi:10.5815/ijisa.2018.06.05

Bach, L., Mihaljevic, B., & Zagar, M. (2018). Comparative analysis of blockchain consensus algorithms. In *2018 41st International Convention on Information and Communication Technology, Electronics and Microelectronics (MIPRO)*. IEEE.

Banker, S. (2016). *Will blockchain technology revolutionize supply chain applications?* https://logisticsviewpoints.com/2016/06/20/will-block-chain-technology-revolutionize-supply-chain-applications/

Bashir, I. (2017). Mastering Blockchain. Packt Publishing Ltd, 2017.

Bruce, J. (2014). *The mini-blockchain scheme.* Academic Press.

Bui, N., & Zorzi, M. (2011). Health care applications: a solution based on the internet of things. In *Proceedings of the 4th international symposium on applied sciences in biomedical and communication technologies.* ACM.

Castro, M., & Liskov, B. (2002). Practical byzantine fault tolerance and proactive recovery. *ACM Transactions on Computer Systems, 20*(4), 398–461. doi:10.1145/571637.571640

Chen, I., Guo, J., & Bao, F. (2014). Trust management for service composition in SOA-based IoT systems. *Proceedings of the IEEE Wireless Communications and Networking Conference (WCNC),* 3444-3449.

Corda. (2021). https://www.corda.net

CouchDB. (2021). https://www.couchdb.apache.org

Danzi, P., Kalor, A. E., Stefanovic, C., & Popovski, P. (2018). Analysis of the communication traffic for blockchain synchronization of IoT devices. In *2018 IEEE International Conference on Communications (ICC).* IEEE.

Dreher, D. (1999). *Logisttik-Benchmarking in der Automobile-Branche: ein Fuhrungsinstrument zur Steigerung der Wettbewerbsfahigkeit.* Keynote Speech at the International Conference on Advances in Production Management System – Global Production Management, Berlin, Germany.

Eschenbacher, J., Knirsch, P., & Timm, I. J. (2000). Demand Chain Optimization By Using Agent Technology. *Proceedings of the International Conference on Integrated Production Management,* 285-292.

Ethereum. (2021). https://www.ethereum.org

Ferrag, M. A., Derdour, D., Mukherjee, M., Derhab, A., Maglaras, A., & Janicke, H. (2018). Blockchain technologies for the internet of things: Research issues and challenges. *IEEE Internet of Things Journal.*

Finextra. (2016). *Everledger secures the first bottle of wine on the blockchain.* https://www.finextra.com/pressaritcle/67381/everledger-secures-the-first-bottle-of-wine-on-the-blockchain

Governatori, G., Idelberger, F., Milosevic, Z., Riveret, G., Sartor, G., & Xu, X. (2018). On legal contracts, imperative and declarative smart contracts, and blockchain systems. *Artificial Intelligence and Law, 26*(4), 377–409. doi:10.100710506-018-9223-3

Gubbi, J., Buyya, R., Marusic, S., & Palaniswami, M. (2013). Internet of Things (IoT): A vision, architectural elements, and future directions. *Future Generation Computer Systems, 29*(7), 1645–1660. doi:10.1016/j.future.2013.01.010

Gupta, D., Saia, J., & Young, M. (2018). Proof of work without all the work. In *Proceedings of the 19th International Conference on Distributed Computing and Networking.* ACM.

He, Q., Guan, N., Lv, M., & Yi, W. (2018). On the consensus mechanisms of blockchain/dlt for internet of things. In *2018 IEEE 13th International Symposium on Industrial Embedded Systems (SIES)*. IEEE. 10.1109/SIES.2018.8442076

Inera, A. (2017). *Bosch, Cisco, BNY Mellon, other launch new blockchain consortium.* https://www.reuters.com/article/us-blockchain-iot-idUSKBN15B2D7

Joshi, A. P., Han, M., & Wang, Y. (2018). A survey on security and privacy issues of blockchain technology. *Mathematical Foundations of Computing, 1*(2), 121–147. doi:10.3934/mfc.2018007

Kim, N. (2016, July). IBM pushes blockchain into the supply chain. *Wall Street Journal.*

Larimer, D. (2018). *Delegated proof-of-stake consensus.* Academic Press.

Luigi, A., Antonio, I., & Morabito, G. (2010). The Internet of Things: A survey. *Computer Networks, 54*(15), 2787–2805. doi:10.1016/j.comnet.2010.05.010

Lukac, D. (2015). The fourth ICT-based industrial revolution "Industry 4.0"??? HMI and the case of CAE/CAD innovation with EPLAN, in 23rd Telecommunication Forum Telfor (TELFOR), IEEE, 835-838.

Menezes, A. J., van Oorschot, P., & Vanstone, S. A. (1997). *The Handbook of Applied Cryptography.* CRC Press.

Nakamoto, S. (2008). *Bitcoin: A peer-to-peer electronic cash system.* Academic Press.

Pal, K. (2017). Supply Chain Coordination Based on Web Services. In H. K. Chan, N. Subramanian, & M. D. Abdulrahman (Eds.), *Supply Chain Management in the Big Data Era* (pp. 137–171). IGI Global Publication. doi:10.4018/978-1-5225-0956-1.ch009

Pal, K. (2019). Algorithmic Solutions for RFID Tag Anti-Collision Problem in Supply Chain Management. *The 9th International Symposium on Frontiers in Ambient and Mobile Systems (FAMS), 929-934.*

Pal, K. (2020). Internet of Things and Blockchain Technology in Apparel Supply Chain Management. In H. Patel & G. S. Thakur (Eds.), *Blockchain Applications in IoT Security.* IGI Global Publication.

Pal, K. (2021). Applications of Secured Blockchain Technology in Manufacturing Industry. In Blockchain and AI Technology in the Industrial Internet of Things. IGI Global Publication.

Reyna, A., Martin, C., Chen, J., Soler, E., & Diaz, M. (2018). On blockchain and its integration with IoT, Challenges and opportunities. *Future Generation Computer Systems, 28,* 173–190. doi:10.1016/j.future.2018.05.046

Roman, R., Zhou, J., & Lopez, J. (2013). On the features and challenges of security and privacy in distributed internet of things. *Computer Networks, 5710,* 2266–2279.

Shrouf, F., Joaquin, B., Mere, O., & Miragliotta, G. (2014). Smart factories in Industry 4.0: A review of the concept and of energy management approached in production based on the Internet of Things paradigm. *Proceedings of the IEEE International Conference on Industrial Engineering and Engineering Management,* 679-701. 10.1109/IEEM.2014.7058728

Vashchuk, O. & Shuwar, R. (2018). *Pros and cons of consensus algorithm proof of stake. Difference in the network safety in proof of work and proof of stake.* doi:10.1145/3154273.3154333

World Economic Forum. (2015). *Deep shift technology tipping points and societal impact survey report.* http://www3.weforum.org/docs/WEF_GAC15_Technological_Tipping_Points_report_2015.pdf

Zheng, Z., Xie, S., Dai, H., Chen, X., & Wang, H. (2017). An overview of blockchain technology: Architecture, consensus, and future trends. In 2017 IEEE international congress on big data (BigData Congress). IEEE.

KEY TERMS AND DEFINITIONS

Block: A block is a data structure used to communicate incremental changes to the local state of a node. It consists of a list of transactions, a reference to a previous block and a nonce.

Blockchain: In simple, a blockchain is just a data structure that can be shared by different users using computing data communication network (e.g., peer-to-peer or P2P). Blockchain is a distributed data structure comprising a chain of blocks. It can act as a global ledger that maintains records of all transactions on a blockchain network. The transactions are time-stamped and bundled into blocks where each block is identified by its *cryptographic hash.*

Cryptography: Blockchain's transactions achieve validity, trust, and finality based on cryptographic proofs and underlying mathematical computations between various trading partners.

Decentralized Computing Infrastructure: These computing infrastructures feature computing nodes that can make independent processing and computational decisions irrespective of what other peer computing nodes may decide.

Immutability: This term refers to the fact that blockchain transactions cannot be deleted or altered.

Internet of Things (IoT): The internet of things (IoT), also called the internet of everything or the industrial internet, is now a technology paradigm envisioned as a global network of machines and devices capable of interacting with each other. The IoT is recognized as one of the most important areas of future technology and is gaining vast attention from a wide range of industries.

Provenance: In a blockchain ledger, provenance is a way to trace the origin of every transaction such that there is no dispute about the origin and sequence of the transactions in the ledger.

Supply Chain Management: A supply chain consists of a network of *key business processes* and facilities, involving end-users and suppliers that provide products, services, and information. In this chain management, improving the efficiency of the overall chain is an influential factor; and it needs at least four important strategic issues to be considered: supply chain network design, capacity planning, risk assessment and management, and performances monitoring and measurement. Moreover, the details break down of these issues need to consider in the level of individual business processes and sub-processes, and the combined performance of this chain. The coordination of these huge business processes and their performance improvement are the main objectives of a supply chain management system.

Warehouse: A warehouse can also be called a storage area, and it is a commercial building where raw materials or goods are stored by suppliers, exporters, manufacturers, or wholesalers, they are constructed and equipped with tools according to special standards depending on the purpose of their use.

This research was previously published in Enabling Blockchain Technology for Secure Networking and Communications; pages 229-247, copyright year 2021 by Information Science Reference (an imprint of IGI Global).

Chapter 15
Current Trends in Integrating the Blockchain With Cloud– Based Internet of Things

Anchitaalagammai J. V.
Velammal College of Engineering and Technology, India

Kavitha S.
Velammal College of Engineering and Technology, India

Murali S.
Velammal College of Engineering and Technology, India

Hemalatha P. R.
Velammal College of Engineering and Technology, India

Subanachiar T.
Velammal College of Engineering and Technology, India

ABSTRACT

Blockchains are shared, immutable ledgers for recording the history of transactions. They substitute a new generation of transactional applications that establish trust, accountability, and transparency. It enables contract partners to secure a deal without involving a trusted third party. The internet of things (IoT) is rapidly changing our society to a world where every "thing" is connected to the internet, making computing pervasive like never before. It is increasingly becoming a ubiquitous computing service, requiring huge volumes of data storage and processing. The stable growth of the internet of things (IoT) and the blockchain technology popularized by cryptocurrencies has led to efforts to change the centralized nature of the IoT. Adapting the blockchain technology for use in the IoT is one such efforts. This chapter focuses on blockchain-IoT research directions and to provide an overview of the importance of blockchain-based solutions for cloud data manipulation in IoT.

DOI: 10.4018/978-1-6684-7132-6.ch015

I INTRODUCTION

IoT is a network system in both wired and wireless connection that consists of many software and hardware entities such as manufacturing management, energy management, agriculture irrigation, electronic commerce, logistic management, medical and healthcare system, aerospace survey, building and home automation, infrastructure management, large scale deployments and transportation.

There is a need of an advanced prototype for security, which considers the security issues from a holistic perspective comprising the advanced users and their intercommunication with this technology. Internet is primary of IoT hence there can be security loophole. Intercommunication paradigms are developed based on sensing programming for IoT applications, evolving an intercommunication stack to develop the required efficiency and reliability. Securing intercommunication is a crucial issue for all the paradigms that are developing based on sensing programming for IoT applications (Choudhury et al., 2017). Data generated by the IoT devices is massive and therefore, traditional data collection, storage, and processing techniques may not work at this scale. Furthermore, the sheer amount of data can also be used for patterns, behaviors, predictions, and assessment. Additionally, the heterogeneity of the data generated by IoT creates another front for the current data processing mechanisms. Therefore, to harness the value of the IoT-generated data, new mechanisms are needed. If we provide good solution which insures about security of the cloud storage system and communication between IoT device and cloud, then there is no problem to accept cloud storage to store IoT data.

Blockchains, or distributed ledgers for recording transactions, are showing potential for changing how the IoT operates. With the emergence and rapid popularization of the blockchain technology, mainly because of the hype around cryptocurrencies such as Bitcoin (Hussain et al., 2018), people started looking at blockchains as a possible alternative to the centralized solutions. An implicit immutability and decentralization are properties highly desirable in particular IoT scenarios. However, due to certain limitations of blockchains, such as limited scalability, or high computational cost of operating blockchain networks, blockchains are not originally suitable for work with IoT devices. Naturally, research of adapting blockchains for use in the IoT ecosystem has quickly evolved. The chapter the reader to navigate through the blockchain-IoT research directions and to provide an overview of the existing approaches and solutions.

II POTENTIAL ATTACKS IN IOT

A handful of IoT-related attacks seem to receive the most attention in the popular press which few of them are as follows.

1. **Denial of Service (DoS) attacks**: A denial-of-service (DoS) attack deliberately tries to cause a capacity overload in the target system by sending multiple requests. Unlike phishing and brute-force attacks, attackers who implement denial-of-service don't aim to steal critical data. However, DoS can be used to slow down or disable a service to hurt the reputation of a business. For instance, an airline that is attacked using denial-of-service will be unable to process requests for booking a new ticket, checking flight status, and canceling a ticket. In such instances, customers may switch to other airlines for air travel. Similarly, IoT security threats such as denial-of-service attacks can ruin the reputation of businesses and affect their revenue.

Figure 1. Illustration of Cloud based IoT

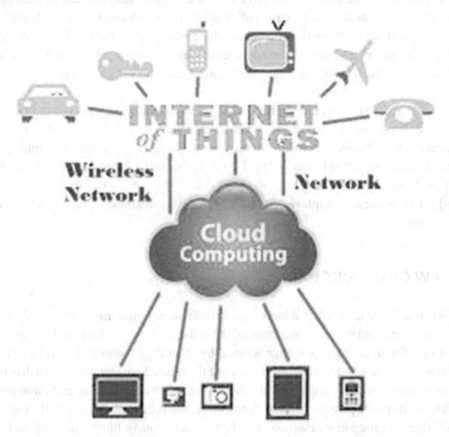

2. **Side-channel attack:** A side-channel attack is the IT equivalent to spotting a liar by their nervous behavior while fibbing rather than what they say. In other words, the attacker can infer which encryption is used without having access to either plain or ciphertext. There are myriad ways this might work. An attacker might study a device's power use or optical or radio emanations. A hacker could even observe the sounds coming from the electronic components within a device and use that information to crack its encryption key.

3. **Pure software attacks:** This category includes malware variants such as viruses and trojans and worms. Also in this category is fuzzing, in which random data is thrown at software to see how it reacts. Distributed Denial of Service (DDoS) attacks can be software-based as well, although they can also occur at lower levels of the OSI Model. One potential example of an IoT-related DDoS risk would be safety-critical information such as warnings of a broken gas line that can go unnoticed through a DDoS attack of IoT sensor networks.

4. **Man-in-the-middle cryptographic attacks:** In a Man-in-the-Middle (MiTM) attack, a hacker breaches the communication channel between two individual systems in an attempt to intercept messages among them. Attackers gain control over their communication and send illegitimate messages to participating systems. Such attacks can be used to hack IoT devices such as smart refrigerators and autonomous vehicles.

5. Identity and data theft

6. Multiple data breaches made headlines in 2018 for compromising the data of millions of people. Confidential information such as personal details, credit and debit card credentials, and email addresses were stolen in these data breaches. Hackers can now attack IoT devices such as smart watches, smart meters, and smart home devices to gain additional data about several users and organizations. By collecting such data, attackers can execute more sophisticated and detailed identity theft.

7. Attackers can also exploit vulnerabilities in IoT devices that are connected to other devices and enterprise systems. For instance, hackers can attack a vulnerable IoT sensor in an organization and gain access to their business network. In this manner, attackers can infiltrate multiple enterprise systems and obtain sensitive business data. Hence, IoT security threats can give rise to data breaches in multiple businesses.

8. **Inside-job:** Here person, employee or staffs who have the knowledge of system can attack the cloud system.

III OVERVIEW OF BLOCKCHAIN

Blockchain is a distributed database that maintains a continuously growing list of records, called blocks, secured from tampering and revision (Nakamoto, 2009). Blockchain was first used to support the digital currency BitCoin (Swan, 2015). It was later adopted by other digital currencies and was the subject of highly publicized successes and failures. At the core of the blockchain technology is a distributed ledger with two types of transactions. A single genesis transaction which creates value and a transfer transaction that transfers value from one party to another. Each transaction is digitally signed by the issuer and posted to the global ledger. A group of transactions are then collected into a block, the block is validated by a third party (a miner) and is locked. This mechanism represents the strength of the blockchain technology. Each block in the chain is immutable since it is linked to its predecessor and any change to any of the blocks invalidates all the blocks downstream in the chain. Each participant in the global network keeps a copy of the ledger and every time a new block is created, it is broadcasted to all the participants that add it to their local copy of the ledger.

Blockchain Types

Blockchains splits into two main categories: public, private and hybrid.

Public blockchains are open blockchains that anyone can join, contribute to, and see its contents. They represent true decentralization and transparency. However, they are generally slower and more expensive to maintain and operate as more difficult consensus mechanisms to prevent Sybil attacks need to be employed.

Private blockchains are valuable for enterprises who want to collaborate and share data, but don't want their sensitive business data visible on a public blockchain. These chains, by their nature, are more centralized; the entities running the chain have significant control over participants and governance structures.

In between the two models stands the hybrid model that combines both the public and private blockchain. For example, selected transactions can be submitted from the private to the public blockchain for open access and secure data provenance.

IV CHALLENGES OF BLOCKCHAIN-IOT INTEGRATION

Blockchain was originally not designed for use in the environment of resource-restricted devices. Certain drawbacks need to be thus first resolved in order to take a full advantage of it.

Throughput and Latency

Compared to centralized solutions, blockchains generally offer lower transaction processing throughput and higher latencies (caused mainly by the blockchain verification process).

Blockchain Size

Depending on the design of the blockchain, all participating nodes need to store some section of the blockchain, if not the whole chain, locally, in order to participate in the validation of blocks. With ever-growing number of participating devices and transactions, the blockchain car reach sizes problematic even for regular computers. For example, the current size of the Bitcoin blockchain is larger than 180GB. For resource-restricted devices, some ways of reducing the blockchain size need to be applied, such as pruning the chain or storing it remotely.

Storage Capacity and Scalability

IoT devices generate lots of data at fast pace. Centralized cloud solutions are usually designed for coping with high storage requirements and can increase their scalability if needed. Availability of data is another important factor of why a centralized cloud is used (for real-time systems, manufactures, etc). Such properties, if not better, need to be ensured in blockchain solutions, as well.

Privacy and Transactional Confidentiality

The drawback of a shared open ledger of transactions is the possibility of corrupted users taking advantage of the available transaction data. Transactions happen in the open and so patterns and connections between nodes can be extracted and used against the users. Also, the content of every transaction is exposed to every node, so private data need to be encrypted or hidden in some other way

Computational Resources

Consensus algorithms are time and resource expensive. Blockchain was designed for an Internet scenario with powerful computers, and this is far from the IoT reality. Blockchain transactions are digitally signed, and therefore devices capable of operating with the currency must be equipped with this functionality. There are several possible solutions to this, e.g., new alternative consensus algorithms could be used, or the signing responsibility could be delegated to an entity capable of such computations. Also, energy efficiency goes hand in hand with resource costliness and the need of nodes to be up and running.

V DIFFERENT CONSENSUS MODELS

Three predominant mechanisms provide consensus in a blockchain:

Byzantine Fault Tolerance (BFT) Algorithms are designed to avoid attacks and software errors that cause faulty nodes to exhibit arbitrary behavior (Byzantine faults). BFT (Lamport et al., 1982) provides consensus despite participation of maliciously misbehaving (Byzantine) nodes. A drawback of this approach, however, is the scalability limit in terms of number of nodes that form the blockchain network (Castro & Liskov, 2002). Alternative approaches to BFT have been proposed, including Practical Byzantine Fault Tolerance (PBFT) (Castro & Liskov, 2002). Examples of blockchain implementations currently exploiting PBFT are Linux Foundation Hyperledger fabric (0.6) and Ripple.

Proof-of-Work (POW), used by Bitcoin and Ethereum, is the widely known mechanism for establishing consensus. In POW, a single node can provide its conclusions to others nodes, which can be in turn validated by the other nodes in the network. A node submitting a generated block, in order to have the consensus reached, must also provide proof of the work it performed, which is a computationally difficult task (a "cryptographically hard puzzle" based on hash functions). POW provides great network stability (Nakamoto, 2008). However, POW is particularly costly because of the computational resources expended. "Miners" are incentivized to participate to earn a cryptomonetary reward, which is granted in return for a successful block generation.

Figure 2. POW consensus mechanism

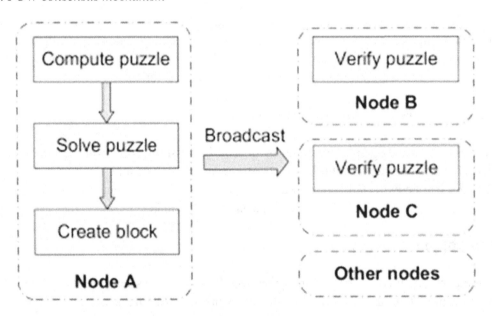

Proof-of-Stake (POS) is similar to POW: nodes are rewarded upon generating a block. However, only a few nodes can participate in this phase (Vasin, 2014). Indeed, the next generator node is picked up deterministically based on the accumulated wealth (i.e., the "Stake"). The mining process for a blockchain based on POS is usually referred to as "forgery" or "minting". The technology that launched PoS was PeerCoin.

VI SELECTION OF BLOCKCHAIN TECHNOLOGY FOR IOT SECURITY

Blockchain technology can help secure IoT devices. IoT devices can be configured either to make use of public blockchain services or to communicate with private blockchain nodes in the cloud over a secure API. Incorporating blockchain technology into the security framework of an IoT system allows IoT devices to securely discover each other, encrypt machine-to-machine transactions using distributed key management techniques, and validate the integrity and authenticity of software image updates, as well as policy updates.

Based on the potential architectural patterns detailed in this report, an IoT device will communicate with a blockchain transaction node via an API, allowing even constrained devices to participate in the blockchain service.

To ensure security, care should be taken during the bootstrapping of an IoT device onto a particular blockchain service. Below is a use case for IoT discovery that supports the enrollment of an IoT device into a transaction node. The IoT device must first be provisioned with credentials that can be used to prove authorization in order to be added to a transaction node. This credential provisioning must be done in a secured environment that safeguards against threats of a particular IoT device ecosystem.

Figure 3. A graphic explanation of how a blockchain works in IoT

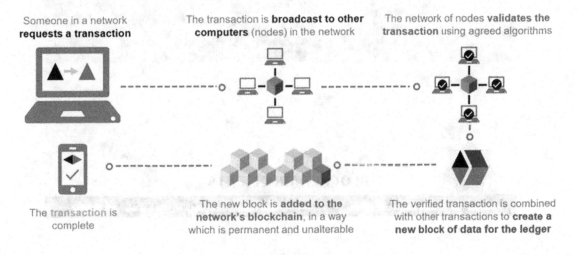

Review of blockchain technology and the market initiatives available to develop it highlights five features to consider when securing the IoT using blockchain technology:

1. Scalable IoT discovery
2. Trusted communication
3. Message authentication/signing
4. IoT configuration and updates
5. Secure firmware image distribution and update

VII THE IOT ARCHITECTURE PATTERN BASED ON A BLOCKCHAIN TECHNOLOGY

The CSA IoT and Blockchain/Distributed Ledger Technology Working Groups propose the following system by which IoT clients within a multi-blockchain service can collaborate.

Figure 4. IoT Architecture Pattern Based on a Blockchain Technology

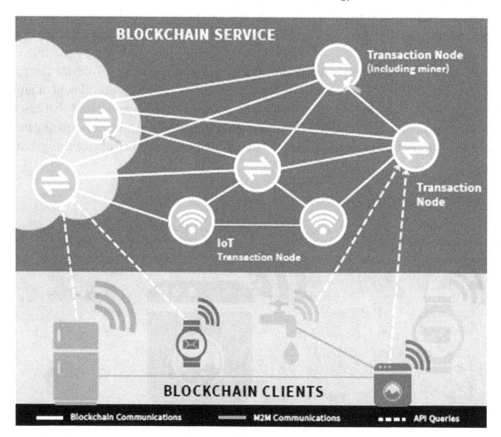

Blockchain Service 1 is a Dedicated Enterprise Implementation:

- Transaction nodes are corporate computers or servers hosted in the cloud.
- IoT blockchain clients are sensors and smart devices deployed within the enterprise area.

Blockchain Service 2 is a Consumer Smart Home:

- Transaction nodes are personal computers and other devices or cloud subscriptions.
- IoT blockchain clients are smart devices, such as refrigerators, temperature sensors and security cameras.

The architecture in which IoT devices are clients of a blockchain service is primarily adopted by current industry efforts for implementing blockchain technology.

Examples of Blockchain Based IoT Projects

There are some examples of companies and projects that are working on blockchain solutions for IoT and supply chains. Below follows a few examples that shows relevant prospects. Table 1 shows some different blockchain technology capabilities with IoT and Blockchain.

A company that has delivered solutions for supply chains involving both blockchain and IoT are Chronicled. This company offers a solution where partners in a supply chain network can cooperate on a blockchain where sensitive information is kept safe. All partners can register events in the supply chain, like data and IoT devices into the Ethereum blockchain ledger. Smart contracts can act as a complement that can supplement traditional business contracts. Trusted parties have access to a shared system with records on an immutable ledger. IoT devices are used for tracking, custody events, money flows and environmental conditions.

Hyperledger Fabric is a project within the Hyperledger framework, originally contributed by IBM. In early 2018, Maersk and IBM announced that they are launching a digital joint venture that is applying this blockchain technology in order to improve global trade and digitalise supply chains. The goal is to offer a platform built on open standards where parts of that platform will use the blockchain ledger. All parties in the supply chain will have access to the platform where they can participate and exchange value. This platform should hopefully address current problems with visibility and documentation.

IOTA is a variant of a public blockchain targeting IoT that uses an invention called "Tangle" at its core, which is a new data structure. Tangle has no blocks, no chain and no miners as a blockchain usually has. Since there are no miners, IOTA needs to achieve consensus in another way and does this by making sure that every participant that wants to make a transaction needs to participate in the consensus by approving the two past transactions. This new architecture means that IOTA has two benefits that are scalability and no transaction fees.

Table 1. Showing essential characteristics for possible Blockchains that might fit for usage within IoT systems

	Bitcoin	Ethereum	IOTA	Hyperledger Fabric
Cryptocurrency	Yes	Yes	Yes	No
Transaction fee	Yes	Yes	No	No
Private/Public	Public	Public (can be Private)	Public	Private
Anonymity	Yes	Yes	Optional	No
Network access	Permissionless	Permissionless	Optional	Permissioned
Decentralised applications	Very limited	Yes, Solidity	Very limited	Yes, Go and Java
Consensus algorithm	PoW	PoW (soon PoS)	Tangle	PBFT
Suitable for IoT	No	Yes (with constraints)	Yes	Yes

Explanation of Terminologies Used in Table 1:

- Cryptocurrency: the electronic currency used by different blockchains.
- Transaction fee: an extra fee (usually very small) for transacting cryptocurrency via blockchains.
- Private/Public: different types of blockchains.
- Anonymity: different blockchains includes anonymity when being a part of the network.
- Network access: if nodes need permission to join the network or if everyone can join (permissionless).
- Decentralised applications: if the blockchain supports applications to be run on the platform (for example smart contracts).
- Consensus algorithm: how trust is created.
- Suitable for IoT: if the particular blockchain is suitable for being used in IoT systems

VI CONCUSION

IoT security and privacy are very importance and play a vital role in the commercialization of the IoT technology. Traditional security and privacy solutions suffer from a number of issues that are related to the dynamic nature of the IoT networks.

Blockchain technology promises to play a major role in addressing these challenges. Throughout this chapter, we have highlighted features to consider when attempting to secure connected devices using blockchain technology. Yet, due to hardware limitations of IoT, we conclude that in a context of several hundred thousand or more IoT devices many of these devices could not serve as transaction nodes (generating transactions, providing consensus, etc.), and thus would fall outside the secure blockchain.

Many devices will benefit from the security and other features offered by blockchain services through APIs from upstream transaction nodes of networks or by specialized intermediaries. Those upstream capabilities can be used to secure IoT devices (configuration and update control, secure firmware update) and communications (IoT discovery, trusted communication, message authentication/signing). We hope this chapter inspires many readers embracing the blockchain opportunity to extend the capabilities of this technology to secure the Internet of Things.

REFERENCES

Castro, M., & Liskov, B. (2002, November). Practical Byzantine fault tolerance and proactive recovery. *ACM Transactions on Computer Systems*, *20*(4), 398–461. doi:10.1145/571637.571640

Choudhury, T., Gupta, A., Pradhan, S., Kumar, P., & Rathore, Y. S. (2017). Privacy and Security of Cloud-Based Internet of Things (IoT). *International Conference on Computational Intelligence and Networks*, 41-45. 10.1109/CINE.2017.28

Hussain, F., Hussain, R., Hassan, S. A., & Hossain, E. (2018). Machine Learning in IoT Security: Current Solutions and Future Challenges. Academic Press.

Lamport, L., Shostak, R., & Pease, M. (1982, July). The Byzantine Generals problem. *ACM Transactions on Programming Languages and Systems*, *4*(3), 382–401. doi:10.1145/357172.357176

Nakamoto. (2009). *Bitcoin: A peer-to-peer electronic cash system.* url:http://www.bitcoin.org/bitcoin.pdf

Nakamoto, S. (2008). *Bitcoin: A peer-to-peer electronic cash system.* https://bitcoin.org/bitcoin.pdf

Nian, L. P., & Chuen, D. (2015). *Introduction to bitcoin, Handbook of Digital Currency: Bitcoin.* Innovation, Financial Instruments, and Big Data.

Swan, M. (2015). *Blockchain: Blueprint for a new economy.* O'Reilly Media, Inc.

Vasin, P. (2014). *Blackcoin's proof-of-stake protocol v2.* https://blackcoin.co/blackcoin-pos-protocol-v2- whitepaper.pdf

Chapter 16
IoT–Fog–Blockchain Framework:
Opportunities and Challenges

Tanweer Alam

(iD) https://orcid.org/0000-0003-2731-4627

Islamic University of Madinah, Saudi Arabia

ABSTRACT

Exploring the unique blockchain-internet of things (IoT) framework may be an attractive structure for enhancing communications efficiency in the 5G networks. The wireless communication would have been the largest research area that allows users to communicate with each other. Nowadays, high-speed, smart, efficient with many technologies, such as low power consumption, and so on, appear to be available to communicate with each other in today's globe. Throughout this framework, the expansion of fog features is enabled for physical objects within IoT. Several of the challenging issues in the field of wireless communications would be to build a new blockchain-based virtualization system across the IoT architecture. The main purpose of this framework is to connect blockchain technology to the IoT and fogging or maintains the IoT cryptography secured when transactions occurred. This strengthens blockchain and fog to build an effective IoT communication system. The recommended method is an important estimation of the extensive work.

INTRODUCTION

The proposed study is a move forward in the area of Internet of Things in 5G diverse systems in which the author proposes a unique blockchain-based virtualization structure of interacting 5G network-connected devices along with the network. That study result would be to introduce a new structure of communications on the IoT. The suggested study utilizes the required study's appropriate as well as effective simulation and could be introduced through an IoT structure. It seems the whole universe is now becoming completely reliant on mobility facilities as well as wireless technology. The Blockchain (BC) throughout the Internet of Things (IoT) has become a novel innovation that behaves on a decentralized, distributed, public as well as a real-time database to collect operations among IoT endpoints (Alam, T., 2019-1). The blockchain is indeed a sequence of blocks, every block is connected to the prior blocks. Every block must have the cryptographically secure key, prior block hash, as well as its information.

DOI: 10.4018/978-1-6684-7132-6.ch016

Figure 1. Blocks in a blockchain

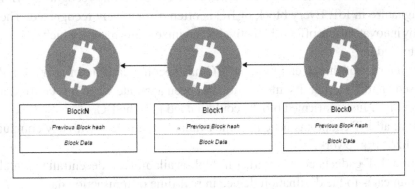

The BC operations will be the fundamental modules that had to transmit information among IoT endpoints. The IoT access points seem to be different kinds of natural however smart devices with integrated detectors, sensors, systems as well as worthy of interacting with several other IoT endpoints (Figure 1). BC's role in IoT would be to have a mechanism for handling protected information records by IoT endpoints (Alam, T., 2019-2). BC seems to be a safe innovation that could be used openly as well as publicly. The Internet of things enables this technology to enable asymmetric cryptography among IoT endpoints in such a diverse system. BC transactions might be monitored as well as traversed through everything accessed to interact throughout the IoT. BC might well enhance interaction protection. The Internet of things has been increasing dramatically throughout the year with its objective in 5G innovations, like Smart Homes as well as Cities, e-Health, distributed intelligence, etc., but has privacy and security obstacles. The protection of confidentiality in connectivity among IoT gadgets paid too much publicity from 2017 to 2019. Many papers were written from 2017 to 2019 in the same field of research. Scott Stornetta wrote an article (Haber, S., & Stornetta, W. S., 1990) on exchanging a report with confidentiality without storing any data about the time-stamping system. A concept of blockchains came, however, in 2008 Satoshi Nakamoto described the first blockchains (Nakamoto, S., 2019). In such a decentralized strategy, the IoT devices have been directly linked. It is therefore much more complicated to be using the conventional current security strategies in the interaction among IoT endpoints. BC is an innovation that provides security in transactions among IoT gadgets. This offers a decentralized, distributed as well as publicly available mutual ledger to collect blocks information which is stored or confirmed in such an IoT system. Its information stored throughout the distributed ledger is immediately attempted to use peer-to-peer configuration. The BC is an innovation at which IoT endpoints handle the transactions in the type of such a block in the blockchain (Figure 2). A blockchain with IoT functions together with its goals that could be summarized:

1) Decentralization structure: Internet of things as well as BC, both approaches would be identical. This structure eliminates the centralized approach or even provides the facility for a decentralized architecture. This enhances the aggregate control system probability of failure or efficiency.

2) Protection: transactions among endpoints were often protected throughout the BC. This is a really different approach to secure interactions. The BC enables IoT gadgets to interact reliably with one another.

3) Identifier: Both connected devices have always been distinctively recognized with such a cryptographic signature in IoT. Every block of BC is often distinctively recognized. Therefore, BC is a trustworthy innovation that offers distinctively recognized information which is accessed throughout a distributed ledger.

4) Accuracy: Internet of things endpoints in BC has become capable of accessing the information being passed on the Internet. Its information has been accurate when it is confirmed by the miners once joining BC. Just confirmed blocks could indeed join the BC.

5) Independent: all IoT endpoints have become available to interact with any computer cluster with a decentralized framework.

6) Optimization: IoT gadgets could interact in high-availability, a decentralized intelligent network that communicates to the destination device in real-time or transaction data.

The Internet of things enables the linked physical objects to exchange their data throughout the diverse system. It could be separated into the following points:

1) Smart Devices: The Internet of things assigns the distinctive identification number to each connected device in the system. These devices could exchange information among the IoT endpoints.

2) Routers: The routers seem to be the machines that operate among physical objects as well as the cloud to make sure that now the link is maintained and therefore that protection has been granted to the network system.

3) Building a network: it would be used to manage the flow of data and also to maintain the quickest route amongst the other IoT endpoints.

4) Cloud: It would be used to store or process information (Computing, F., 2015).

A BC seems to be a chain of certified or cryptographic transaction blocks maintained by the device connected throughout a system. These blocks information is deposited throughout the shared online or transmitted electronically using a ledger. A BC offers secure communication throughout the IoT system. BC might be a confidential, public, and conglomerate of different characteristics (Table 1).

Table 1. Blockchains and its characteristics

BC/ Properties	Efficiency	Decentralized	Accord growth	immovableness	Reading	Determining
Private BC	good	No	yes	Can be	Can be publicly	Only one industry
Public BC	worse	Yes	no	No	publicly	All miners
Consortium BC	good	Sometimes	yes	Can be	Can be publicly	IoT devices

A repository in blockchains is said to have characteristics including a distributed security model, restricted access, higher public access, bottom to top confidentiality or exchangeable identifications, whilst in a central database, the characteristics have become a centralized trust model, low security, low public access, high confidentiality but also un-transferable identifications. A blockchain is now more sophisticated than that of the centrally controlled storage in the above characteristics.

Figure 2. IoT, BC and fogging computations

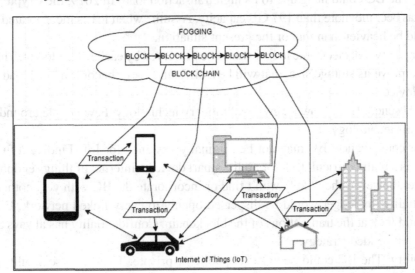

1.1. Opportunities for the Integrated Approach

A BC-IoT interoperability strategy does have many extraordinary possibilities. This unlocks the two new windows next to each other. Several of the possibilities would be characterized as follows:

a) Constructing the trust among parties: due to its highly advanced features, the BC-IoT strategy would develop a relationship amongst the multiple smart devices. Just confirmed gadgets could interact in the system, as well as the miners would first confirm every block of the transaction, then they should join the BC (Bonomi, F., et al., 2012).

b) Lower costs: Such a strategy would lower costs as it interacts effectively without the third party. This removes all third-party nodes among the recipient as well as the sender. This strategy offers full correspondence.

c) Minimize Time: It reduces a huge amount of time. This strategy minimizes the transaction time from weeks to sec.

d) Safety and privacy: It offers privacy and security to gadgets and data.

e) Public services: Such an approach offers wireless devices to social as well as public services. The smart devices could connect among them and exchange information.

f) Investment management: Such an approach safely exchanges money without the need for a third party. This offers quick, safe as well as financial information facilities. This lowered the cost or time of transition.

g) Risk management: Such an approach plays a vital role in examining or reducing the chance of resource or transaction failure.

1.2. Challenges

The IoT-BC might experience several difficulties like scaling, storing, skills and discovery, and so on. The following is also the challenge facing the interoperability strategy:

a) Usability: The BC could hang due to its high transaction load. In 2019, the Cryptocurrency warehousing has become more than 197 GB capacity. Assume when IoT is incorporated into BC so the load would be heavier than that of the present situation.

b) Storing Capacity: An electronic ledger would be preserved by each IoT endpoint. Throughout time, this will improve its storage size, that will be a difficult task or become a huge load on every other wireless device.

c) Abilities Absence: BC is now a new revolutionary technology. Few people around the world understand this technology.

d) Finding or convergence: BC may not be originally designed for IoT. Finding a further gadget in BC or IoT is a really difficult task for all the smart devices. Internet of things endpoints could find one another, however, they likely won't find or incorporate the BC with yet another gadget.

e) Confidentiality: Its ledger would be dispersed openly to every linked network. Every connected device could look at the transactions of the blockchain. Confidentiality has always been a difficult task in the embedded strategy.

f) Compatibility: The BC could be whether public or private. Therefore, scalability around public and private blockchains would also be a difficulty in the BC-IoT strategy.

g) Laws and regulations: An IoT-BC is acting worldwide, and therefore it faces several regulations to implement this strategy worldwide.

1.3. Research Objectives

The objective of the BC-IoT strategy is to bring the new idea where the top innovations incorporate together as well as join a group and facilitate secure communication. This really improves the IoT security and offers secure as well as authentic interaction among physical objects.

2. BACKGROUND

The earlier studies committed to building or optimizing the connectivity structure, however, such a study may not produce its complete structure to IoT-BC communication among smart devices network (Figure 3). This research strategy develops the study in and out of expanding the connectivity of things that utilizing the fog as well as blockchain technology on networking. Exchange information from one specification to the next using wireless communication begins in the form of the radio network packets starting from the 1973 year. A Machine was able to connect with another machine of the same specification. The report published by Statista, The IoT devices will reach in 2025 upto 75.44 billion globally Statista. (2019).

In 2015, Florian Tschorsch and Bjorn Scheuermann introduced the idea of bitcoin systems, blockchain as well as its structure (Tschorsch, F., & Scheuermann, B., 2016). The authors often examine the safety of the blockchain transaction in communication among smart devices. Ali Dorri, Salil S. Kanhere and Raja Jurdak published an article on blockchain technology in IoT in 2016 (Dorri, A., et al., 2016). Throughout this study, the authors presented the structure of blockchain technology for the internet of things to provide secure transactions and use a decentralized strategy. In the article (Samaniego, M., et al., 2016) fog or cloud will be used as the host model to activate the blockchain on the IoT network. In 2016, Boohyung Lee and Jong-Hyuk Lee (Lee, B., & Lee, J. H., 2017) constructed a blockchain structure of transaction safety in IoT systems, such transactions have been fired by IoT-based devices connected. Alexandru Stanciu published an article (Stanciu, A., 2017). In 2017, on blockchain technology which is incorporated with those of the Internet of things nodes to perform the edge resources on IoT network. A convergence structure of the software-defined network (SDN), fog, blockchain, and IoT is intended in the article (Sharma, P. K., Chen, et al., 2017) to promote safety, accessibility, data delivery, elimination end-to-end delay. An IoT Blockchain-based transaction are addressed in paper (Kshetri, N., 2017). The detailed analysis of the safety of information exchanges in the blockchain and its activity in the internet of things is addressed in paper (Kuzmin, A., 2017) and offers a strategy for incorporating all innovations around each other. A paper predicated on the assessment of blocks throughout the Internet of Things blockchains had been released. The blockchains adopted by the internet of things were analyzed and examined by Byzantine-tolerant (Han, R., et al., 2018). A cloud and IoT integration of blockchain technology are described in Song, J. C., et al., 2018). The authors focused on sensor data protection in this article (Panarello, A., et al., 2018). The author discussed the new challenges of integrating blockchains with IoT and cloud. The authors are presented with a fog / edge-based IoT structure that allows the quick response of IoT endpoints to request storage or computing services in the Fog-IoT framework too (Figure 4).

Figure 3. Past, present, and future network

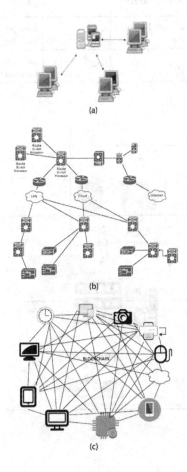

Several consensus algorithms mentioned and compared. The authors discussed the consensus algorithms (Table 2) like Proof-of-Work (PoW), Proof-of-Stake (PoS), Delegated Proof-of-Stake (DPoS), Leased Proof-of-Stake (LPoS), Proof-of-Stake (PET), Practical Byzantine Fault Tolerance (PBFT), Simplified Byzantine Fault Tolerance (SBFT), Delegated Byzantine Fault Tolerance (DBFT), Directed Acyclic Graphs (DAG), Proof-of-Activity (PoA), Proof-of-Importance (PoI), etc.

Table 2. Comparison of the consensus algorithms

Algorithms	Blockchain Platform	Year	Languages	Smart Contracts	Advantages	Disadvantages
PoW	Bitcoin	2009	C++	No	Reduce attacks up to 50 percent	More power consumption and centralized Miners
PoS	NXT	2013	Java	Yes	Efficient energy and decentralized	No stake problem
DPoS	Lisk	2016	JavaScript	No	Effective, efficient and Secure	Partially centralized and double spend attack
LPoS	Waves	2016	Scala	Yes	Realistic use and leasing coins	Decentralization issues
PoET	Hyperledger Sawtooth	2018	Python, JavaScript, Go, C++, and Java	Yes	Inexpensive participation	Specialized hardware requirements and worse for public blockchains
PBFT	Hyperledger Fabric	2015	JavaScript, Python, Java and Go	Yes	Low power Consumption	Sybil Attack
PoWeight	Filecoin	2017	STARK	Yes	Scalability and customizable	Incentivization problem

Figure 4. IoT-Chain

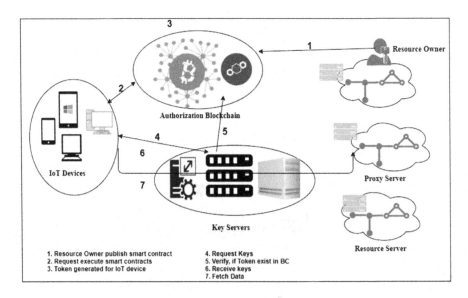

1. Resource Owner publish smart contract
2. Request execute smart contracts
3. Token generated for IoT device
4. Request Keys
5. Verify, if Token exist in BC
6. Receive keys
7. Fetch Data

3. MAIN FOCUS OF THE RESEARCH

The biggest achievement behind this study has been building a structure for communication of things using fog as well as blockchain technology on the Internet. This framework becomes primarily suitable for applications where information becomes regularly conveyed to the connected devices on the internet network. In addition, we used a retransmission strategy, variable packet length, or populated congestion situation to improve the proposed system. A plan of action for this study has been defined. For performance onto the Internet of things, the execution of the IoT-Fog structure to interact safely between IoT devices will be programmed. The whole study would be implemented as a three-layer structure, such layers becoming Fog, Blockchain, and IoT layers. This research supports wireless communication to develop an IoT-Blockchain framework between several gadgets on the IoT. An IoT-Blockchain framework does have the following elements: a) Smart Devices b) Network c) Development tools d) Fog computing with blockchain. BT in IoT provides a mechanism of processing protected information files by IoT endpoints.

BT transactions might be monitored or examined through someone verified to interact throughout the IoT system. An IoT-BT could enhance interaction security. BT's major advantages with IoT are: 1) building trust between IoT public endpoints or minifying the possibility of accidents; 2) minifying transportation costs by communicating directly without third parties; 3) speeding up transactions in real-time. The visualization servers contained efficient services in the fog, the intermediaries are 3rd-party servers that could also store secured information. A token offered by the approved blockchains repository to the smart device does have the power to connect the model, notification key from the use of a key computer, collect information from the fog.

Several smart contracts released in the approved blockchains repository through the visualization servers, intermediaries or fog proprietors. IoT's portable device discovers the smart contacts from within the permitted blockchains repository. Its permitted blockchains repository produces the token to IoT's smart device. A smart device requests the keys in middleware from a key server as well as directs the token with the query. A primary server verifies the token from such an approved blockchain repository or produces a key for each smart device as well as a reaction down to a device. Once again the IoT smart device is permitted to retrieve information from the cloud.

The framework itself has three major components: the IoT nodes, Fog, and blockchain.

The IoT node (IoTN) can be expressed by $\aleph$ th six tuples as follows (Omoniwa, B., et al., 2018):

$$\aleph = \left\{ I_d, S, T, L, S_p, O \right\} \tag{1}$$

where I_d is the unique identification of the IoT node, S is the status of IoT node, T is the type, L is the location, S_p is the specification and O is the application instance.

Every IoT node has a unique identification number (I_d) provided by the IoT office after registering the device to the network. The I_d is generated based on the inherent pattern of the node. The I_d is the prerequisite in IoT nodes network. The Status of the IoT nodes could be inactive or an inactive state. The value of S can be 0 or 1. 0 means node is in an inactive form and 1 means node is inactive form. An IoT node can sense different types of events. Suppose $T_1, T_2, T_3, \ldots, T_n$ are the type of events that are sensed by the IoT node. Then $T = \{T_1, T_2, T_3, \ldots, T_n\}$. The location of the IoT node can be obtained as follows in the x-axis, y-axis, and z-axis during the time t (Maiti, P., et al., 2019):

$$L = \{L_x, L_y, L_z, t\} \tag{2}$$

where L_x, L_y, L_z are the location components of IoT node in x,y, z-axis at the time stamp t.

Packets are transmitted in fog using blockchains node (BCN). Each BCN is also called a block. Every block has its hash code (unique id like a fingerprint), previous block hash code and their own data. The BCN has a connection to exchange information (CEI). Every CEI contains a lot of blocks with its previous blocks hash code and data. These blocks are connected to each other with security through cryptography techniques. The BCNs are similar to the linked list node in the data structure. So, we can say that blockchain is a complex data structure. The blocks are distributing in a decentralized system using the point-to-point topological network. When a new block is created then it moves to the network and visit every connected BCN and checks its authentication. If it is valid then it will connect to the blockchain and its hash will generate only once. This newly generated block stores the hash of the previous block and connects to the chain (Mahishi, A., 2018).

The data transmission among the IoT-devices in the framework can passage from IoT-gateways (IoTG), fog gateways (FGW), blockchain gateway (BCG) or other gateways (OGW). The OGW is the combination of specified gateways other than the IoTG. The IoTG is the collection of gateways among the IoT devices. Suppose that the communication delay among IoT devices is pondered immaterial. Consider $\Omega_1, \Omega_2, \Omega_3$ and Ω_4 are the transmissions delay function among the IoT devices to OGW, OGW to IoTG, IoTG to FGW and FGW to BCG respectively. Suppose $\pounds_1, \pounds_2, \pounds_3$ and $\pounds_4$ are the latencies of OGW, IoTG, FGW, and BCG. Thus, the mean transmission latency can be obtained by the following function (Sarkar, S., & Misra, S., 2016):

$$\sigma = \left(\Omega_1\mu + \Omega_2\theta + \Omega_3\tau + \Omega_4\epsilon\right) + \left(\pounds_1\mu + \pounds_2\theta + \pounds_3\tau + \pounds_4\epsilon\right) \tag{3}$$

where μ, θ, τ and ϵ $(\mu > \theta > \tau > \epsilon)$ are the total data packets sent by IoT devices, OGW, IoTG, and FGW. When data are transmitted from IoT device to the OGW and OGW to the IoTG then it requires energy consumption say $\vartheta1$ and $\vartheta2$ respectively. We consider $\vartheta3$ and $\vartheta4$ are the energy consumption from IoTG to the FGW and FGW to the BCG. Suppose $\omega1, \omega2, \omega3,$ and $\omega4$ are the energies demands to evaluate the unit byte data received from OGW, IoTG, FGW, and BCG respectively. The total value of energy diffusion (φt) in transmission can be obtained by the following formula:

$$\varphi_t = \left[\left\{\vartheta_1\Sigma_{i=1}^x\Sigma_{j=1}^y\gamma_{i,j} + \vartheta_2\Sigma_{i=1}^y\Sigma_{j=1}^z\alpha_{i,j} + \vartheta_3\Sigma_{i=1}^z\Sigma_{j=1}^t\beta_{i,j} + \vartheta_4\Sigma_{i=1}^t\Sigma_{j=1}^w\varepsilon_{i,j}\right\} + \left\{\omega_1\Sigma_{i=1}^x\Sigma_{j=1}^y\gamma_{i,j} + \omega_2\Sigma_{i=1}^y\Sigma_{j=1}^z\alpha_{i,j} + \omega_3\Sigma_{i=1}^z\Sigma_{j=1}^t\beta_{i,j} + \omega_4\Sigma_{i=1}^t\Sigma_{j=1}^w\varepsilon_{i,j}\right\}\right] \tag{4}$$

where $\sum_{j=1}^y\gamma_{i,j}, \sum_{j=1}^z\alpha_{i,j}, \sum_{j=1}^t\beta_{i,j},$ and $\sum_{j=1}^w\varepsilon_{i,j}$ are the total number of bytes transmitted from IoT device to OGW, from OGW to IoTG, from IoTG to FGW and from FGW to BCG at timestamp t.

The total rate of energy consumption ($\delta_{Fog}(t)$) at time-stamp t can calculate as follows:

$$\delta_{Fog}\left(t\right) = \frac{\varphi_t}{t}$$

So:

$$\delta_{Fog}(t) = \frac{\left[\begin{array}{l}\left\{\vartheta_1\sum_{i=1}^{x}\sum_{j=1}^{y}\gamma_{i,j} + \vartheta_2\sum_{i=1}^{y}\sum_{j=1}^{z}\alpha_{i,j} + \vartheta_3\sum_{i=1}^{z}\sum_{j=1}^{t}\beta_{i,j} + \vartheta_4\sum_{i=1}^{t}\sum_{j=1}^{w}\varepsilon_{i,j}\right\} + \\ \left\{\omega_1\sum_{i=1}^{x}\sum_{j=1}^{y}\gamma_{i,j} + \omega_2\sum_{i=1}^{y}\sum_{j=1}^{z}\alpha_{i,j} + \omega_3\sum_{i=1}^{z}\sum_{j=1}^{t}\beta_{i,j} + \omega_4\sum_{i=1}^{t}\sum_{j=1}^{w}\varepsilon_{i,j}\right\}\end{array}\right]}{t} \tag{5}$$

The performance of the proposed system is evaluated through different experiments. Firstly, I have created thousands of blocks with a fixed size by using the open-source software (Node.js). I have created the IoT network, connected with cloud and also, created fog and blockchain.

This suggested structure depicted the use of Fog computing with IoT gadgets onto the edge of the network using blockchain technology to communicate, exchange and share information amongst the IoT endpoints (Figure 5). Transactions in the suggested structure were transferred in the point-to-point network topology. There are some unique IoT endpoints termed as Miners throughout the system. These are usually used to verify network transactions. Whether the transactions are confirmed so they are transformed into the blocks or decided to add to the existing blockchains or transmitted to the channel. Its miners play a vital role in adapting the creation of a new block in the blockchain. Throughout this study, we used many examinations to determine the structure. A hashing algorithm is introduced using the IROHA tool of Hyperledger. A docker-compose is built on the device.

Figure 5. IoT-Fog-Blockchain

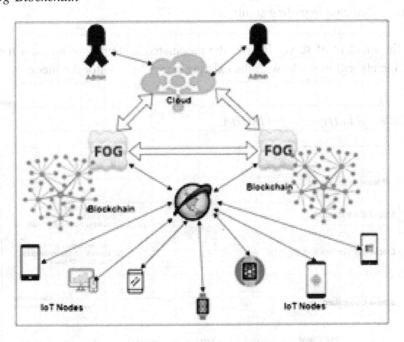

The Icov coverage testing method is used to assess the system spectrum of IoT device coverage (Table 3).

Table 3. Main parameters for performance evaluation

Parameter	Possible Values	Default	Description
COVERAGE		OFF	Allow or deactivate lcov setting for software coverage generation
BENCHMARKING		OFF	Allow or deactivate constructing of the Search Benchmarks library
TESTING	ON/OFF	ON	Allow or deactivate constructing of exams
SWIG_PYTHON		OFF	Allow or deactivate library constructing or Python bindings
SWIG_JAVA		OFF	Allow or deactivate library constructing or Java bindings

A Hyperledger IROHA tool involves several services like decentralized Hyperledger, Proof of Work (PoW) algorithms, P2P system, and so on. Sumeragi in Hyperledger IROHA methodology is introduced in rum blockchains. An IROHA Android and iOS packages need the facility with the blockchain to communicate with the IoT endpoints. According to the Sumeragi algorithm, IoT nodes have requested the transactions or follows the basic steps (Figure 6 and Figure 7):

Step 1: Transmitting: the members confirm, arrange or sign the transactions or send data to the system.
Step 2: Authentication as well as going to sign: this validates, requests or signs the transaction or broadcasts to the peer-to-peer channel's approved IoT endpoint.
Step 3: Committed: Dedicate regarding signing.

Throughout the incident of server failure, the automated system contributes a move named error detection. Also, the algorithm works with the existing server to monitor the inconsistencies.

Figure 6. The Sumeragi in Hyperledger IROHA

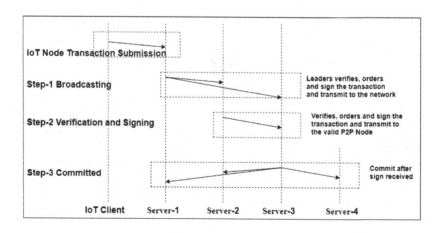

Figure 7. The Sumeragi with errors control in Hyperledger IROHA

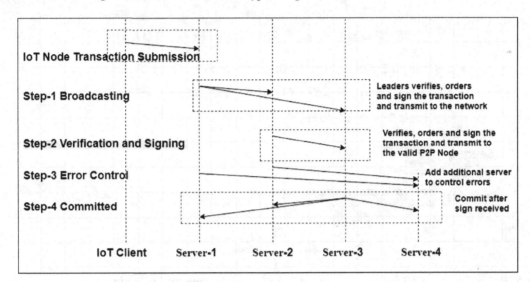

The authors evaluated the performance of 10, 50 and 100 IoT devices using the different experiments (Figure 8, 9, 10 and Table 4, 5, 6).

Figure 8. Ten IoT-nodes evaluation in IoT-Fog-Blockchain

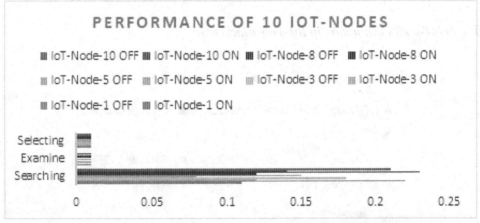

Table 4. Performance of 10 IoT-nodes against searching, examine and selecting

	IoT-Node-1 ON	IoT-Node-1 OFF	IoT-Node-3 ON	IoT-Node-3 OFF	IoT-Node-5 ON	IoT-Node-5 OFF	IoT-Node-8 ON	IoT-Node-8 OFF	IoT-Node-10 ON	IoT-Node-10 OFF
Searching	0.11	0.22	0.12	0.18	0.08	0.15	0.12	0.23	0.14	0.21
Examine	0.01	-	0.01	-	0.01	-	0.01	-	0.01	-
Selecting	0.01	0.01	0.01	0.01	0.01	0.01	0.01	0.01	0.01	0.01

Figure 9. Fifty IoT-nodes evaluation in IoT-Fog-Blockchain

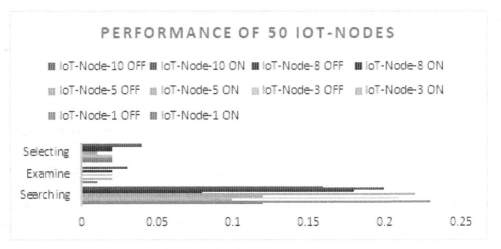

Table 5. Performance of 50 IoT-nodes against searching, examine and selecting

	IoT-Node-1 ON	IoT-Node-1 OFF	IoT-Node-3 ON	IoT-Node-3 OFF	IoT-Node-5 ON	IoT-Node-5 OFF	IoT-Node-8 ON	IoT-Node-8 OFF	IoT-Node-10 ON	IoT-Node-10 OFF
Searching	0.12	0.23	0.10	0.21	0.12	0.22	0.08	0.18	0.20	0.16
Examine	0.01	-	0.02	-	0.02	-	0.02	-	0.03	-
Selecting	0.02	0.02	0.02	0.02	0.01	0.01	0.02	0.02	0.04	0.04

Figure 10. 100 IoT-nodes evaluation in IoT-Fog-Blockchain

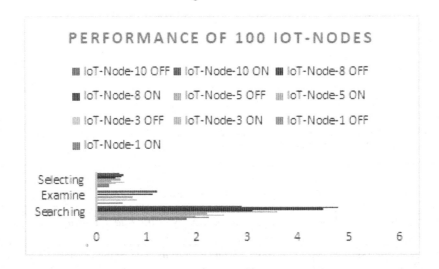

Table 6. Performance of 100 IoT-nodes against searching, examine and selecting

	IoT-Node-1 ON	IoT-Node-1 OFF	IoT-Node-3 ON	IoT-Node-3 OFF	IoT-Node-5 ON	IoT-Node-5 OFF	IoT-Node-8 ON	IoT-Node-8 OFF	IoT-Node-10 ON	IoT-Node-10 OFF
Searching	1.81	2.25	1.97	2.54	2.2	3.6	3.1	4.5	4.8	2.9
Examine	0.53	-	0.81	-	0.72	-	1.13	-	1.22	-
Selecting	0.24	0.25	0.37	0.56	0.29	0.47	0.38	0.5	0.55	0.45

Our proposed system is now ready to evaluate the performance. I found the experimental results positive compared to previous studies. BT is a series of blocks. The size of a block (BS) in blockchain can be obtained by the following formula:

BS (in MB) = HS (in Bytes) + TS (in Bytes) * No of transactions in that block   (6)

where HS is the size of the header.

The Total Mining energy (Te) can be calculated by the sum of all connected IoT nodes mining energy (E):

$$Te = \sum_{i=1}^{n} E(i)$$ (7)

Time (t) taken by a block between interconnected IoT nodes with their bandwidth Bw:

t = BS/ Bw(i,j)   (8)

where Bw(i,j) is the bandwidth between the IoT nodes i,j.

The framework width (Fw) can be obtained by:

Fw=Max(t)   (9)

The hash is the crypto code of the previous block (Hc) that is assigned to every block in the block-chain. The block occurrence (Bo) can be obtained by:

Bo=Te/Hc   (10)

The transactions per second (Ts) held in the blockchain can be obtained by the formula:

Ts=Bo * No of transactions in that block   (11)

The fork in blockchain can happen if the miners received the blocks at the same time. The probability of blockchain fork P(F) can be calculated by the formula:

$$P(F) = 1-(1+Bo*Fw) * e^{-Bo*Fw} \qquad (12)$$

Consider the newly created block BN that is referenced by two previously created blocks. The BN is placed between these two blocks. Consider that the block BN is verified by the miners, the time BN(t) is represented the verification time calculated by the Poisson process μ.

Suppose α be the time taken by the IoT node to compute the transaction process to the fog network. So, the total time taken by each transaction to be visible on the network is α+t. Consider that N is the total number of unverified blocks. The probability of BN in the blockchain of the IoT-Fog framework is calculated by the following formula:

$$P(BN) = N / (N + \mu\alpha) \qquad (13)$$

Consider the 5 IoT nodes connected with the P2P network with the mining energy 500, 1000, 300, 700, and 1500 respectively. They are able to do transactions in the proposed framework. Suppose the size of the header is 100 bytes and the size of the transaction is 500 bytes. The IoT nodes in the framework are five.

Using equation (1), we have calculated the block size:

BS (in MB) = HS (in Bytes) + TS (in Bytes) * No of transactions in that block

BS=100+500*5=2600 MB

By using equation (2), we have calculated the total mining energy:

$$Te = \sum_{i=1}^{n} E(i) = 500+1000+300+700+1500$$

$$= 4000$$

Suppose BS=1 MB= 1,048,576 Bytes.

Total number of transactions in a block = (BS-HS)/TS

= 1,048,576-100/500

= 2096.952

Now, according to Equation (8), we have to calculate the bandwidth of the framework (Table 7).

The IoT-Fog framework is tested using 5 local IoT nodes and 2 remote IoT nodes. The NoSQL database software is used to store the records fetched from blockchain in the fogging by the tool named OPENSHIFT platform. Cloud is created by Amazon. The FogSim software is used to connect the IoT devices to the fogging. The results are found in Figure 11.

Table 7. Bandwidth in the framework device by device

	IoT Node 1	IoT Node 2	IoT Node 3	IoT Node 4	IoT Node 5
IoT Node 1	x	1/8	1/9	1/5	17/86
IoT Node 2	-	x	1/5	15/79	1/9
IoT Node 3	-	-	x	17/71	13/40
IoT Node 4	-	-	-	x	1/9
IoT Node 5	-	-	-	-	x

Figure 11. The performance evaluation of IoT nodes in the IoT-Fog system

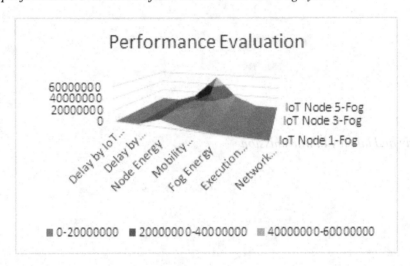

In the blockchain, we need miners for a different experiment. Firstly, I have selected two miners with fixed transactions (suppose 5) and set the fog demands for each miner (ex. 30, 50). Secondly, I have selected three miners with fixed transactions (suppose 5) and set the fog demands for each miner (ex. 30,40,50). If the fog demands are increasing, then the possibility of mining the block by the miner is higher. The computational requirements such as processor usage, Memory usage in blockchain compare to fog and cloud are evaluated (Figure 12, 13 and 14). I found that the processor usage in blockchain was lower than the fog and cloud.

The memory usage depends on the number of blocks and the number of transactions. If a number of blocks in the chain increases, then memory usage also increases. Similarly, if the number of transactions increases then the memory usage also increases.

The author has calculated the transmission delay for synchronization a block in blockchain in this study.

The author has tested the proposed framework using many tests. The summary is displayed in Table 8 and Figure 15 (a), (b), (c), (d).

Figure 12. Computation requirements

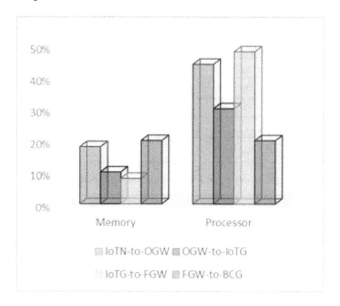

Figure 13. Delay and latency in transmission

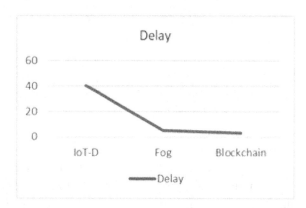

Figure 14. Transmission delay for synchronization a block

Table 8. Energy consumption using different miners

Miners Node	Transmission Delay (MS)	Action Duration (S)	Energy Consumption (KJ)
5	146	301	5.3
5	12	906	5.3
5	100	1220	5.7
10	15	320	12.5
10	12	505	15.8
10	54	230	11.8
50	63	245	20.9
50	43	600	25.5
50	6	309	32.2
100	400	405	35
100	733	506	34.5
100	245	915	36.8

Figure 15. (a) Performance on 5 IoT nodes in IoT-Fog-Blockchain; (b) Performance on 10 IoT nodes in IoT-Fog-Blockchain; (c) Performance on 50 IoT nodes in IoT-Fog-Blockchain; (d) Performance on 100 IoT nodes in IoT-Fog-Blockchain

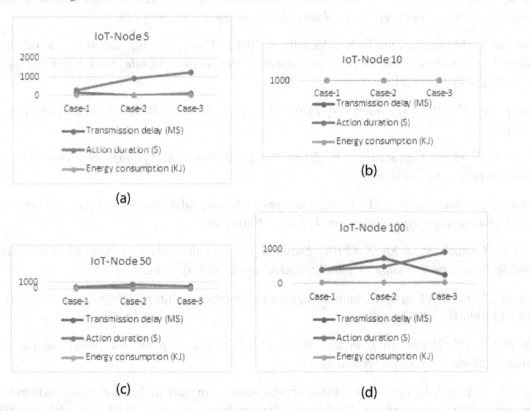

CONCLUSION

The proposed framework is designed and implemented using IoT, fog and blockchain technologies. The proposed framework acted as a combination of the Internet of Things (IoT) and fog computing. The Blockchain is used to create a hyper-distributed public authentic ledger to record the transactions. The research opened a new opportunity in this area. The framework is implemented using a different set of IoT nodes and tested. This study can be a valuable framework to improve the performance of the IoT framework in a heterogeneous environment. This framework is appropriate for providing communication security where huge data is transmitted in a heterogeneous environment in the future. I have tested the system in different scenarios such as memory and processor usage in the integrated system and its impact on the performance of overall the system. We found that the proposed framework, not only increases the throughput but also the direct connection among IoT nodes are eliminated which makes the system far more stable. The outcomes of this research established a new IoT framework with blockchain technology.

REFERENCES

Alam, T. (2019). Blockchain and its Role in the Internet of Things (IoT). International Journal of Scientific Research in Computer Science. *Engineering and Information Technology*, *5*(1), 151–157.

Alam, T. (2019). IoT-Fog: A communication framework using blockchain in the internet of things. *International Journal of Recent Technology and Engineering, 7*(6), 833-838.

Bonomi, F., Milito, R., Zhu, J., & Addepalli, S. (2012). Fog computing and its role in the internet of things. In *Proceedings of the first edition of the MCC workshop on Mobile cloud computing* (pp. 13-16). 10.1145/2342509.2342513

Computing, F. (2015). *The Internet of Things: Extend the Cloud to Where the Things are*. Cisco White Paper.

Dorri, A., Kanhere, S. S., & Jurdak, R. (2016). *Blockchain in internet of things: challenges and solutions*. arXiv preprint arXiv:1608.05187

Haber, S., & Stornetta, W. S. (1990). How to time-stamp a digital document. In *Conference on the Theory and Application of Cryptography* (pp. 437-455). Springer.

Han, R., Gramoli, V., & Xu, X. (2018). *Evaluating blockchains for iot. In 2018 9th IFIP international conference on new technologies, mobility and security (NTMS)*. IEEE.

Kshetri, N. (2017). Can blockchain strengthen the internet of things? *IT Professional, 19*(4), 68–72. doi:10.1109/MITP.2017.3051335

Kuzmin, A. (2017). *Blockchain-based structures for a secure and operate IoT. In 2017 Internet of Things Business Models, Users, and Networks*. IEEE.

Lee, B., & Lee, J. H. (2017). Blockchain-based secure firmware update for embedded devices in an Internet of Things environment. *The Journal of Supercomputing, 73*(3), 1152–1167. doi:10.100711227-016-1870-0

Mahishi, A. (2018). *Build your first blockchain with nodeJS*. https://codingislove.com/simple-blockchain-javascript/

Maiti, P., Shukla, J., Sahoo, B., & Turuk, A. K. (2019). Mathematical modeling of qos-aware fog computing architecture for iot services. In *Emerging Technologies in Data Mining and Information Security* (pp. 13–21). Springer. doi:10.1007/978-981-13-1501-5_2

Nakamoto, S. (2019). *Bitcoin: A peer-to-peer electronic cash system*. Manubot.

Omoniwa, B., Hussain, R., Javed, M. A., Bouk, S. H., & Malik, S. A. (2018). Fog/Edge computing-based IoT (FECIoT): Architecture, applications, and research issues. *IEEE Internet of Things Journal*, 6(3), 4118–4149. doi:10.1109/JIOT.2018.2875544

Panarello, A., Tapas, N., Merlino, G., Longo, F., & Puliafito, A. (2018). Blockchain and iot integration: A systematic survey. *Sensors (Basel)*, 18(8), 2575. doi:10.339018082575 PMID:30082633

Samaniego, M., Jamsrandorj, U., & Deters, R. (2016). *Blockchain as a Service for IoT. In 2016 IEEE international conference on internet of things (iThings) and IEEE green computing and communications (GreenCom) and IEEE cyber, physical and social computing (CPSCom) and IEEE smart data (SmartData)*. IEEE.

Sarkar, S., & Misra, S. (2016). Theoretical modelling of fog computing: A green computing paradigm to support IoT applications. *IET Networks*, 5(2), 23–29. doi:10.1049/iet-net.2015.0034

Sharma, P. K., Chen, M. Y., & Park, J. H. (2017). A software defined fog node based distributed blockchain cloud architecture for IoT. *IEEE Access: Practical Innovations, Open Solutions*, 6, 115–124. doi:10.1109/ACCESS.2017.2757955

Song, J. C., Demir, M. A., Prevost, J. J., & Rad, P. (2018). Blockchain design for trusted decentralized iot networks. In *2018 13th Annual Conference on System of Systems Engineering (SoSE)* (pp. 169-174). IEEE. 10.1109/SYSOSE.2018.8428720

Stanciu, A. (2017). Blockchain based distributed control system for edge computing. In *2017 21st International Conference on Control Systems and Computer Science (CSCS)* (pp. 667-671). IEEE. 10.1109/CSCS.2017.102

Statista. (2019). *Internet of Things (IoT) connected devices installed base worldwide from 2015 to 2025 (in billions)*. https://www.statista.com/statistics/471264/iot-number-of-connected-devices-worldwide/

Tschorsch, F., & Scheuermann, B. (2016). Bitcoin and beyond: A technical survey on decentralized digital currencies. *IEEE Communications Surveys and Tutorials*, 18(3), 2084–2123. doi:10.1109/COMST.2016.2535718

This research was previously published in the International Journal of Fog Computing (IJFC), 3(2); pages 1-20, copyright year 2020 by IGI Publishing (an imprint of IGI Global).

Chapter 17
Blockchain–Empowered Big Data Sharing for Internet of Things

Ting Cai
Sun Yat-sen University, China

Yuxin Wu
Guangdong Baiyun University, China

Hui Lin
Sun Yat-sen University, China

Yu Cai
Chongqing University of Posts and Telecom, China

ABSTRACT

A recent study predicts that by 2025, up to 75 billion internet of things (IoT) devices will be connected to the internet, in which data sharing is increasingly needed by massive IoT applications as a major driver of the IoT market. However, how to meet the interests of all participants in complex multi-party interactive data sharing while providing secure data control and management is the main challenge in building an IoT data sharing ecosystem. In this article, the authors propose a blockchain-empowered data sharing architecture that supports secure data monitoring and manageability in complex multi-party interactions of IoT systems. First, to build trust among different data sharing parties, the authors apply blockchain technologies to IoT data sharing. In particular, on-chain/off-chain collaboration and sharding consensus process are used to improve the efficiency and scalability of the large-scale blockchain-empowered data sharing systems. In order to encourage IoT parties to actively participate in the construction of shared ecology, the authors use an iterative double auction mechanism in the proposed architecture to maximize the social welfare of all parties as a case-study. Finally, simulation results show that the proposed incentive algorithm can optimize data allocations for each party and maximize the social welfare while protecting the privacy of all parties.

DOI: 10.4018/978-1-6684-7132-6.ch017

INTRODUCTION

With the development of 5G and mobile cloud computing, data sharing plays an increasingly important role in IoT development since most IoT applications are deployed upon data sharing (Cao et al., 2019). It is estimated that 5 quintillion bytes of data will be produced by IoT devices and these data will be analyzed and shared among devices, which is producing a large-scale market (Li et al., 2017, Li & Asaeda, 2018). However, the current IoT data market is far from meeting those expectations. One of the main reasons is that the IoT data sharing usually involves multiple parties and so that leads to interest and security problems that make a user reluctant to share data (Barnaghi & Sheth, 2016). More specifically, it is difficult to balance multiple interests due to lack of consensus among participating parties, and on the other hand, there is a lack of secure control and supervision among the complex interactions of multiple parties, so that the privacy of participants cannot be well protected.

Blockchain is an immutable public ledger secured by the participants in a peer-to-peer network. As a major technology behind the emerging cryptocurrencies, it is being popularized and applied rapidly (Dai et al., 2019). Some inherent features of blockchains, such as decentralization, anonymity and automatic performance, make it be an attractive technology for building a shared IoT ecosystem. Consequently, inspired by these advantages, blockchain-based data sharing has been introduced and implemented in the recent research works (Kang et al., 2019, Yu et al., 2018, Xu et al., 2018, Jiang et al., 2018). For example, some proposed a blockchain-based data sharing scheme for the IoV by optimizing consensus management (Kang et al., 2019), and others proposed a new cryptocurrency named LRCoin to enhance the security of data trading in IoT (Yu et al., 2018). Although these approaches have brought blockchain technologies to IoT data sharing, they cannot achieve the efficient and trustable IoT data sharing due to the following challenges:

- **Scalability:** Billions of IoT devices will join the data sharing and they require to trade data in a real time manner. However, most of blockchain systems have the limitations of high latency and low throughput, and scale poorly. Thus, it is important to consider the scalability issues for the blockchain-empowered big data sharing.
- **Traceability:** IoT data sharing usually involves many parties that join the data sharing process and interact with each other to complete the data trading transactions, which makes it difficult to build trust or identify the malicious parties. Thus, a secure monitor and management are needed in IoT systems for a data sharing when involving complex and multiparty interactions.
- **Incentive Mechanism:** The privacy of data sharing participants cannot be well protected in traditional incentive mechanisms. IoT data sharing involves multiple parties and usually lacks of secure control and supervision in the complex interactions, which results in motivation decreases for participating in a data sharing.

To tackle the above research issues, the authors propose a blockchain-empowered big data sharing framework to build a trustable data trading ecosystem. With the proposed architecture, an aggregator manages data in a region area network (RAN) and interacts with the blockchain. Blockchain helps data sharing by working as a trustable data trading platform. In particular, the authors study how to control and manage a secure interaction among multiple parties in IoT systems. Moreover, to scale the blockchain designs, the authors present a sharding consensus to implement the partition of consensus, and use the InterPlanetary File System (IPFS) and Secure Multiparty Computation (SMC) to extend on-chain storages.

Besides, conflicts of interest between multiple stakeholders in data trading decrease the motivation of IoT users to participate in data sharing. In order to encourage the users, the authors propose an iterative double auction mechanism to maximum the overall welfare among multi-parties, while also protect the privacy of data sharing parties. In the proposed mechanism, a data trader only submits bid prices instead of providing private information during trading, and thus the privacy can be well protected. Finally, the authors evaluate the performance of their algorithm via a variety of simulations.

RELATED WORK

Centralized Data Sharing for IoT

As a way to achieve the data sharing in IoT systems, centralized sharing approaches have received a lot of attentions (Li et al., 2017). Some use a lightweight encryption scheme to achieve a data sharing schema between IoT smart devices with the help of cloud-aided edges (Mollah et al., 2017). Others present a practical framework that can provide a secret sharing in IoT-based healthcare systems (Luo et al., 2018). However, the data sharing based on a trusted third party will result in the low efficiency and trust issues.

Blockchain-Based Data Sharing Applications

Recently, the blockchain-based approach is considered to be an effective method to build trustable data sharing (Dai et al., 2019). For example, collaborative edges are leveraged to develop a green blockchain framework for big data sharing in IoT systems (Xu et al., 2018). Some present a multiple blockchain network for the IoT to provide the secure and efficient data interactions (Jiang et al., 2018). Others present a secure, private and light-weight blockchain-based architecture by investigating on a smart home application (Dorri et al., 2016). However, most works simply apply the blockchain directly to IoT systems, ignoring the performance issues of blockchain for big data sharing in the IoT. In this article, the authors present a scalable and manageable blockchain-based framework for the IoT big data sharing. Table 1 illustrates the comparisons among existing techniques and the proposed approach.

Table 1. Comparison of state-of-the-art work

Category	Literature	Scalability	Trust	Traceability	Efficiency	Privacy-Preserving	Decentralization	Latency
Centralized	Mollah (2017), Luo (2018)	Poor	No	No	Low	Support	Low	High
Blockchain-based	Xu (2018), Jiang (2018), Dorri (2016)	Poor	Yes	Yes	Low-Medium	Support	High	Medium
BC-IoT	Our proposal	Good	Yes	Yes	High	Conditional privacy	High	Low

BLOCKCHAIN-EMPOWERED IOT BIG DATA SHARING FRAMEWORK

In this section, the authors propose a secure, scalable, and manageable blockchain-empowered big data sharing architecture, named BC-IoT, to build a data trading ecosystem. The authors first provide an overview of the architecture, and then give the detailed design of relevant components in the BC-IoT.

Overview

The authors depict the proposed architecture for the complex multiparty interactions in an internet of vehicles (IoV) sharing scenario, as shown in Figure 1. The proposed architecture consists of three roles:

- **Asynchronous Consensus Zones:** In order to scalable the blockchain designs and improve the transaction throughput in the proposed architecture, an entire IoT network is divided into multiple RANs according to different geographical locations (e.g., country, nation, and state). Within a Asynchronous Consensus Zones (i.e., RAN), the miners work together to agree on a transaction block and their consensus on data transactions can be processed in parallel.
- **Aggregator:** The aggregator is a RAN leader equipped with high computation and large storage capacity. An IoT user can make a registration and initiate the data transactions through aggregators, where the aggregator is responsible for monitoring the security of data transactions in the region and interacting with the blockchain. Note that, the aggregators in RANs are not fixed but the selected entities from elections according to a Proof of Work (PoW) consensus protocol during each epoch.
- **BC-IoT Chain:** The BC-IoT chain is the core layer that records all data transactions and sharing operations, and ensures the security and trust relationship among IoT users in a data sharing (Chen et. al., 2019). In the proposed architecture, BC-IoT chain is set to check a user identity and transaction authenticity. In particular, it records the IoT network partition information and organizes nodes to track the true identities of malicious traders.

Figure 1. The secure, scalable and manageable blockchain-empowered IoT big data sharing architecture (BC-IoT)

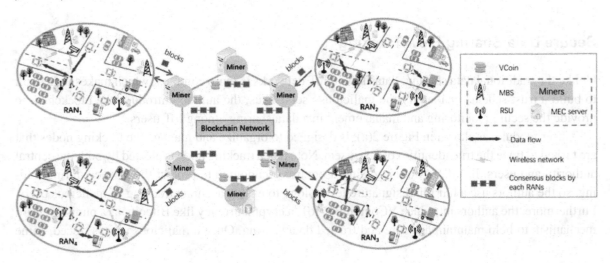

To explain their ideas in a more clear way, the authors next consider an illustrative example of a vehicle-to-vehicle (V2V) data sharing in vehicle networks. Since vehicles may not trust each other, the authors propose to deploy blockchain on the Road Side Unit (RSU) and Macro Base Station (MBS), and thus building a secure and trust data trading environment. However, the blockchain brings high latency and resource consumption to the IoV system, the problem of which becomes more serious as the number of connected vehicles increases. To improve the efficiency and scalability, the authors apply sharding consensus and on-chain/off-chain integration technique in the system. In particular, the proposed scheme also supports the tracking of true identities of malicious vehicles sending fake messages.

Figure 2. The detailed designs of BC-IoT: (a) Relevant components; (b) Extended off-chain storage using the IPFS and SMC

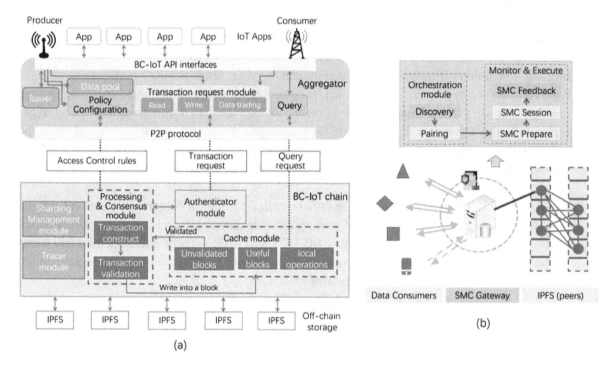

Secure Data Sharing Flow Tracking

Unlike the traditional data sharing, data flow in IoT networks is more complex, which makes it difficult to build a trust schema or identify the malicious users. Thus, the authors introduce the blockchain to provide the secure monitoring and management in a data sharing among IoT users.

Tracer module, as shown in Figure 2(a), is designed to organize and manage the tracking nodes that are tasked to trace the true identities of fake users. Note that a tracking node is elected by both the central authority and users. In IoT networks, trading users use pseudonym to protect the privacy during trading, so the authors use a fair blind signature technology to enable accurate tracking of malicious users. Furthermore, the authors introduce VCoin in BC-IoT, a cryptocurrency like Bitcoin, as a punish-reward mechanism to help maintain a secure and trusted data sharing. Once a malicious user is traced, some punishment (e.g., a certain amount of VCoin) can be imposed on it. In general, their proposal provides a secure supervision by tracking data transactions between the sharing users, which can not only identify malicious users but also protect the privacy of other anonymous users.

Sharding Consensus for Scalability

Applying blockchain to empower the data sharing between multiple users in large-scale IoT networks is challenging. Since most IoT devices have limited resources, it is difficult to support mining that requires a lot of computing power. On the other hand, most IoT applications require low latency, while current blockchain systems have the low throughput. In this case, sharding technique enables a road to scalable the blockchain and provides a promising way to address the aforementioned issues.

A sharding management module is shown in Figure 2(a), which is designed to optimize sharding policies and store related sharding information. The sharding technology can help to scalable blockchain designs and increase the throughput of data transactions for IoT systems. With a sharding, the aggregator in each RAN is set to manage a subset (i.e., shard) of data transactions. In this way, consensus on data transactions generated by the IoT users can be processed in parallel, where miners can agree on blocks of transactions by running consensus protocols (such as PBFT). Then, the blocks generated in every RAN will be sent to accept the final validation of a leader group (i.e., committee, also run by PBFT) organized by aggregators coming from different RANs. Finally, these blocks verified by the commission are added to the blockchain and broadcasted to other users in the network. Due to the number of miners in each RAN is fixed, as more users join in IoT networks, the throughput of data transactions can increase with no additional delays. Thus, the sharding consensus can provide a scalable and efficient approach of implementing big data sharing systems for the IoT.

On-Chain/Off-Chain Collaboration

Data trading in large-scale IoT networks imposes the extremely high storage demands on the proposed blockchain-based structure. However, storing massive trading data on the blockchain is obviously impractical due to its expensive cost. To this end, the IPFS is employed as an off-chain layer to the proposed architecture, providing the IoT users with secure and enlarged storage by collaborating with on-chain storage on the blockchain.

Based on such designs, the operational logging data (e.g, data access and vehicle tracking) are to be recorded on the chain, while the actual IoT data are stored on off-chain. Generally, a data request is treated as a transaction including an identity, a timestamp, and an operation such as $T = (ID, Timestamp, Access \parallel Addr)$. Once the transaction T is validated, an IPFS node at address $Addr$ will send the data to consumers. With such an integrated structure, a user can easily get a data storage address via the blockchain where the pointers to the IPFS nodes are kept on it. Figure 2(a) illustrates the IPFS as an off-chain storage extended to the blockchains, which can be an additional repository to help realize storing a large amount of IoT data.

Secure SMC-Enhanced Data Processing

Transaction data mostly contain a large amount of sensitive user information, but leveraging traditional encryption may cause an encrypted processing problem to a data consumer. For example, a Telematics

Service Provider (TSP) requests a vehicle to share real-time locations and then recommends the nearest gas station to the vehicle. To prevent the privacy disclosure from providing raw data such as the location, the authors introduce Secure Multiparty Computation (SMC) into the IPFS, as shown in Figure 2(b).

The SMC gateway (i.e., a virtual server), acts as an intermediary role in the following two aspects: 1) providing a unified request API for data consumers; and 2) coordinating the IPFS nodes to perform calculations on raw data. With such a design, a TSP can request available metadata related to the location data, which can be computed by a SMC session between the IPFS nodes. Finally, the TSP will receive a result and thus sending GPS coordinates to the target vehicle. Leveraging the IPFS and SMC, the proposed architecture enables an additional secure, decentralized, and off-chain computing layer allowing the multiple untrusted IoT users to share their data without leaking privacy.

ADVANTAGES AND OPEN ISSUES

Advantages

Trustworthiness

Unlike the traditional centralized structure, the proposed architecture utilizes the blockchain to empower the big data sharing in IoT systems. Due to the public ledger and decentralized consensus, blockchain can provide a trustworthy and secure multi-party interactive environment for the IoT users. Moreover, the asymmetric cryptography and digital signature techniques are helpful to authenticate; thus, guaranteeing that there are no cheating transactions in data sharing.

Traceability

The design of the issuer and tracer modules in the proposed architecture can track, record and punish malicious IoT users in data sharing. Assisted by techniques such as the fair blind signature and secret sharing, the authors can accurately trace a malicious data producer, while protecting the privacy of other anonymous IoT users.

Scalability

The proposed architecture is expected to support large-scale data transactions among the expanding IoT nodes by improving the blockchain performance. The proposed architecture contributes in two ways: first, leveraging sharding consensus, it can reduce latency and scale well as the number of traders increases; and second, an integrated on-chain and off-chain storage is presented to reduce the storage costs and expand the capacity of storing data resources for the IoT sharing.

Open Issues

Resource Management

The convergence of computing, communication, cache and control is a big challenge. First of all, the tension between resource-constrained IoT devices and computationally blockchain mining tasks should be considered carefully. Second, the communication issues caused by blockchain-empowered big data trading and interactions involving multiple parties should be well studied. Third, the cache and control in resource-constrained IoT should be investigated to enhance the efficiency of blockchain-empowered big data trading.

Big Data Trading Ecosystem

First of all, using smart contracts, big data trading can be conducted safely and conveniently without third-party control. However, the financial stability of the data trading market should be further explored, especially the price fluctuation is dramatic in many digital commodities (such as CryptoKitties) without any censorship. In addition, how to design incentive mechanisms to motivate different participants and at the same time protect the privacy is another challenge.

CASE STUDY: PRIVACY-PRESERVING INCENTIVE MECHANISM FOR BLOCKCHAIN-EMPOWERED IOT BIG DATA SHARING

To build data trading ecosystem, the active participation of multiple parties involved in an IoT system is indispensable. In this section, the authors focus on a social welfare maximization problem by leveraging an iterative double auction-based incentive mechanism to encourage the user participant in data sharing.

Problem Description

As shown in Figure 3(a), the authors consider an IoV data trading scenario with the proposed architecture. A data consumer first signs up in an issuer and stores data services to the data pool in an aggregator. Then, it broadcasts the data request to public via a transaction request module. Next, the aggregator matches the data trading pair of IoV users and finds the suitable data to meet its requirement. After that, the consumer sends its data demands to a matched producer. If it is validated, the IPFS nodes storing the requested data will send the data to it. Once received, the consumer sends the payment (i.e., VCoins) to a wallet address of the data producer. Finally, the aggregator will record all of generated transactions. After the committee (i.e., a group of pre-selected aggregators) finishing the audit process and reaching the consensus, a block that contains these transactions will be added to the blockchain.

The authors note there is a conflict that the data consumer intends to maximize its utilities, while a data producer wants to minimize the cost. From a social perspective, the aggregator (i.e., a trade matcher) is to maximize social welfare and achieve effective market equilibrium. That is, the aggregator can solve the problem of social welfare maximization (denoted as *SWM*) and thereby optimizing the allocation of data between the producers and consumers.

Figure 3. Case study: (a) A data trading in Internet of vehicles; (b) The scheme of match (Double-Auction)

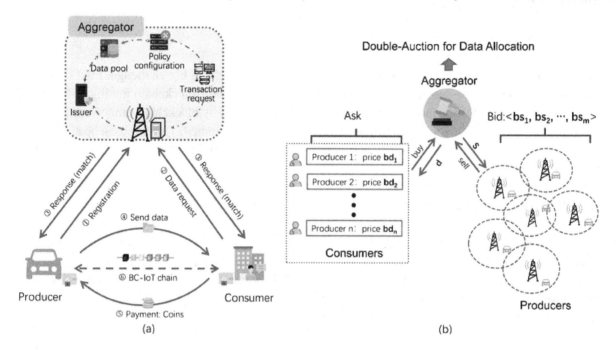

The *Problem SWM* subjects to three constraints: 1) the data amount requested by a consumer is in a limited range of the minimum and maximum demands (i.e., $[D_i^{min}, D_i^{max}]$); 2) the data amount supplied by a producer will not exceed consumer capacity; and 3) the data amount supplied by a producer can satisfy the demand of a consumer. Moreover, the social welfare maximization problem is strictly concave, and where the constraints are compact and convex, so there is a unique optimal solution according to the Karush-Kuhh-Tucker (KKT) conditions.

To obtain the optimal solution, the aggregator needs to get some private information from traders in two parties, such as utility, cost, etc. Therefore, the authors present to use an iterative double auction mechanism to tackle these issues, which can gradually extract the hidden information from traders of both sides to overcome the limitations of complete information requirements.

Iterative Double Auction Algorithm

The authors use Figure 3(b) to depict an iterative double auction scheme, in which one iterative process consists of three basic steps. First, each consumer submits a demand bid for all producers, while every producer submits a supply bid for all consumers. Besides, a consumer C_i needs to submit D_i^{max} and D_i^{min} to the aggregator, where D_i^{max} and D_i^{min} are the maximum and minimum data demand, respectively. And a producer P_j needs to submit a maximum limit of supply, defined as S_j^{max} where there is $S_j^T 1 \leq S_j^{max}$. Second, the aggregator solves an optimal data allocation problem (denoted as *DA*) between two parties based on their submitted bids, and thus computing and announcing new bids to both consumers and producers. Third, all of the consumers and producers need to respectively solve their own problems of utility maximization (i.e., a satisfaction function and the price rule to a consumer; a cost function and the price rule to a producer) to update their optimal bids for the next iteration.

Figure 4. The iterative double auction algorithm

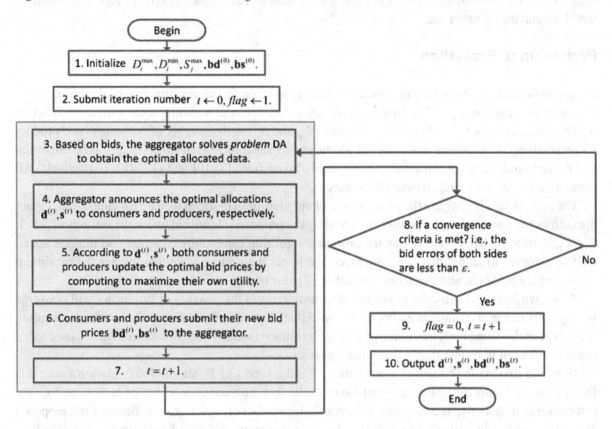

Besides the *problem SWM*, the aggregator is also to solve the following *problem DA*, which aims to allocate the demand and supply and achieve effective market equilibrium:

$$DA : \max_{d_i, S_j} \sum_{i=1}^{N_C} \sum_{j=1}^{N_P} \left(bd_{i,j} \log d_{i,j} - \frac{1}{2} bs_{j,i} s_{j,i}^2 \right)$$

where d_i is the $1 \times N_P$ demand vector of the i-th consumer, S_j is the $1 \times N_C$ supply vector of the j-th provider, $bd_{i,j}$ is the bid price of the i-th consumer interacting with the j-th producer, $bs_{j,i}$ is the bid price of the j-th producer interacting with the i-th consumer, $d_{i,j}$ is the demand amount of the i-th consumer from the j-th producer, and $s_{j,i}$ is the supply amount of the j-th producer to the i-th consumer.

Note that *Problem DA* has the same constraints as *Problem SWM*, and it is also strictly concave and thereby can lead to a unique optimal solution. To ensure that the solutions to *Problem DA* also solves *Problem SWM*, the KKT conditions need to be matched for both *Problem SWM* and *Problem DA* in each case.

In order to extract the hidden information from a trading behavior, it is necessary for an aggregator to design payment rules for consumers and reward rules for producers, and thus both parties are able to submit their bids by price rules. In general, a double auction algorithm requires multiple iterations to attain the effective market equilibrium, as illustrated in Figure 4. The basic idea is to perform multiple iterations on the three basic steps (as defined above) until a convergence criteria is met, that is, $|bd^{(t)} - bd^{(t-1)}| < \varepsilon$ and $|bs^{(t)} - bs^{(t-1)}| < \varepsilon$.

Performance Evaluation

In this section, the authors present simulation results to evaluate the performance of the proposed iterative double auction algorithm. In the experiments, they consider a trading scale with three different $N_C \times N_P$ settings of 5×5, 7×7 and 10×10, where N_C and N_P are the number of consumers and producers respectively. The maximum supplies of producers are randomly taken from [15, 30]. The minimum and maximum demand of consumers are randomly taken from [5, 10] and [12, 18], respectively. All simulation results are averaged over 100 instances.

The authors first investigate the performance of our algorithm in social welfare maximization. Figure 5(a) shows the results of social welfare achieved by the proposed algorithm under the settings of 5×5, 7×7 and 10×10. They observe that the proposed algorithm can rapidly converge and thus the social welfare achieves to an optimal one. Moreover, the larger the trading scale, the greater the maximum social welfare achieves, and the iteration number of convergence increases accordingly.

As shown in Figure 5(b), the payments of consumers and the rewards of producers will converge very quickly to a stable value. In addition, they note that all payments are higher than the corresponding rewards in each trading case, that is, the proposed algorithm is weakly budget balanced since a producer's rewards turns out to be less than a consumer's payment.

Next, the maximum utilities of a consumer C_1 and a producer P_1 are randomly chosen under different cases as Figure 5(c). It is observed from results that the maximum utility of both P_1 and C_1 are fast converge to stability, and they will be larger as the number of traders grows. Besides, the proposed algorithm satisfies incentive compatibility, where the maximum utilities of consumers are higher than that of producers under three test cases.

Figure 5. Performance evaluation of the iterative double auction algorithm: a) Social welfare in three cases; b) The average payment of all consumers and the average reward of all producers; c) The maximum utility of the consumer and producer

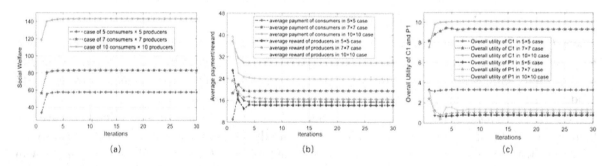

To summary, the authors can observe that:

- The iterative double auction algorithm is efficient, since the social welfare can be maximized quickly. Therefore, the IoT users can work truthfully and obtain their maximum utilities.
- The benefits of an aggregator (i.e., difference between payment and reward) can always be guaranteed under the proposed algorithm. As such, the aggregator (i.e., a miner) will be encouraged to work in a shared IoT system with a certain amount of income, which accordingly empowers the transaction security.
- The proposed algorithm ensures that the utilities of both consumers and producers are non-negative and can increase with transaction scales. Besides, the bid submitted requires only prices without any private information, which improves privacy protection and motivates them to actively participate in the IoT big data sharing.

CONCLUSION

In this article, the authors have proposed a scalable and manageable architecture for IoT big data sharing by integrating the blockchain technology into the IoT. The proposed architecture can support the behavior supervision and privacy protection with a good storage scalability and high consensus efficiency, even if the complex multi-party interactions exist in IoT systems. Finally, the authors have presented an iterative double auction mechanism that can maximize social welfare thereby encouraging the users in an IoT system to participate in the data sharing activities. Simulation results have evaluated the effectiveness of their proposals.

ACKNOWLEDGMENT

This research was supported by the National Key Research and Development Plan (No. 2018YFB1003803); the National Natural Science Foundation of China (No. 61802450, No. 61722214); the Natural Science Foundation of Guangdong (No. 2018A030313005); the Program for Young Innovative Talents Project of Guangdong Province (No. 2019KQNCX226); and the Science and Technology Research Program of Chongqing Municipal Education Commission (No. KJZD-K201802401). The corresponding author is Ting Cai.

REFERENCES

Barnaghi, P., & Sheth, A. (2016). On searching the Internet of Things: Requirements and challenges. *IEEE Intelligent Systems*, *31*(6), 71–75. doi:10.1109/MIS.2016.102

Cai, T., Chen, W., & Yu, Y. (2019). BCSolid: A Blockchain-Based Decentralized Data Storage and Authentication Scheme for Solid. In *International Conference on Blockchain and Trustworthy Systems (Blocksys)* (pp. 676-689). Springer.

Cao, J., Zhang, D., Zhou, H., & Wan, P. J. (2019). Guest Editorial Emerging Computing Offloading for IoTs: Architectures, Technologies, and Applications. *IEEE Internet of Things Journal*, *6*(3), 3987–3993. doi:10.1109/JIOT.2019.2921217

Chen, W., Zhang, Z., Hong, Z., Chen, C., Wu, J., Maharjan, S., Zheng, Z., & Zhang, Y. (2019). Cooperative and distributed computation offloading for blockchain-empowered industrial Internet of Things. *IEEE Internet of Things Journal*, 6(5), 8433–8446. doi:10.1109/JIOT.2019.2918296

Dai, Y., Xu, D., Maharjan, S., Chen, Z., He, Q., & Zhang, Y. (2019). Blockchain and deep reinforcement learning empowered intelligent 5g beyond. *IEEE Network*, 33(3), 10–17. doi:10.1109/MNET.2019.1800376

Dorri, A., Kanhere, S. S., & Jurdak, R. (2016). *Blockchain in internet of things: challenges and solutions*. arXiv preprint arXiv:1608.05187

Jiang, T., Fang, H., & Wang, H. (2018). Blockchain-based Internet of vehicles: Distributed network architecture and performance analysis. *IEEE Internet of Things Journal*, 6(3), 4640–4649. doi:10.1109/JIOT.2018.2874398

Kang, J., Xiong, Z., Niyato, D., Ye, D., Kim, D. I., & Zhao, J. (2019). Towards Secure Blockchain-enabled Internet of Vehicles: Optimizing Consensus Management Using Reputation and Contract Theory. *IEEE Transactions on Vehicular Technology*, 68(3), 2906–2920. doi:10.1109/TVT.2019.2894944

Li, L., Liu, J., Cheng, L., Qiu, S., Wang, W., Zhang, X., & Zhang, Z. (2018). Creditcoin: A privacy-preserving blockchain-based incentive announcement network for communications of smart vehicles. *IEEE Transactions on Intelligent Transportation Systems*, 19(7), 2204–2220. doi:10.1109/TITS.2017.2777990

Li, R., & Asaeda, H. (2018). Secure in-network big data provision with suspension chain model. In *IEEE INFOCOM 2018-IEEE Conference on Computer Communications Workshops (INFOCOM WKSHPS)* (pp. 825-830). IEEE. 10.1109/INFCOMW.2018.8406829

Li, R., Asaeda, H., & Li, J. (2017). A distributed publisher-driven secure data sharing scheme for information-centric IoT. *IEEE Internet of Things Journal*, 4(3), 791–803. doi:10.1109/JIOT.2017.2666799

Luo, E., Bhuiyan, M. Z. A., Wang, G., Rahman, M. A., Wu, J., & Atiquzzaman, M. (2018). Privacyprotector: Privacy-protected patient data collection in IoT-based healthcare systems. *IEEE Communications Magazine*, 56(2), 163–168. doi:10.1109/MCOM.2018.1700364

Mollah, M. B., Azad, M. A. K., & Vasilakos, A. (2017). Secure data sharing and searching at the edge of cloud-assisted internet of things. *IEEE Cloud Computing*, 4(1), 34–42. doi:10.1109/MCC.2017.9

Sun, Y., Song, H., Jara, A. J., & Bie, R. (2016). Internet of things and big data analytics for smart and connected communities. *IEEE Access: Practical Innovations, Open Solutions*, 4, 766–773. doi:10.1109/ACCESS.2016.2529723

Xu, C., Wang, K., Li, P., Guo, S., Luo, J., Ye, B., & Guo, M. (2018). Making big data open in edges: A resource-efficient blockchain-based approach. *IEEE Transactions on Parallel and Distributed Systems*, 30(4), 870–882. doi:10.1109/TPDS.2018.2871449

Yu, Y., Ding, Y., Zhao, Y., Li, Y., Zhao, Y., Du, X., & Guizani, M. (2018). LRCoin: Leakage-resilient cryptocurrency based on bitcoin for data trading in IoT. *IEEE Internet of Things Journal*, 6(3), 4702–4710. doi:10.1109/JIOT.2018.2878406

This research was previously published in the International Journal of Web Services Research (IJWSR), 18(1); pages 58-69, copyright year 2021 by IGI Publishing (an imprint of IGI Global).

Chapter 18
Integrating Blockchain and IoT in Supply Chain Management:
A Framework for Transparency and Traceability

Madumidha S.

Sri Krishna College of Technology, India

SivaRanjani P.

Kongu Engineering College, India

Venmuhilan B.

Sri Krishna College of Technology, India

ABSTRACT

Internet of things(IoT) is the conception of interfacing the devices to the internet to make life more efficient. It comprises the large amount of data in its network where it fails to assure complete security in the network. Blockchain is a distributed ledger where it mainly focuses on the data security. Every block in the blockchain network is connected to its next block, which prevents threats like large data loss. In the area of agri-food supply chain, where IoT plays a very important role, there occurs data integrity issues or data tampering. This can lead to improper supply chain management, timely shortage of goods, food spoilage, etc. So the traceability of agri-food supply chain is necessary to ensure food safety and to increase the trust between all stakeholders and consumers. Many illegal activities can be prevented, and cold chain monitoring can be achieved by bringing in transparency and traceability.

DOI: 10.4018/978-1-6684-7132-6.ch018

INTRODUCTION

The 21st century is all about technology that increases the need for transformation in day-to-day life. People from all over the world are ready to accept the modern tools and technologies by using a remote for controlling devices to voice notes. In the past decade, technologies like Augmented Reality and the Internet of Things played a vital role in humans. Now there is a new addition to the pack called Blockchain Technology (Aung, M. M., & Chang, Y. S.; (2014)). One reason why the modern world is seeing more and more wealth created is that the economics and markets are connected via ever more sophisticated routes of global trade. Whether be it by air, sea, or road, billions worth of goods are being taken from continent to continent every single day, to satisfy demand and meet supply quotas. However, while new methods of storage and route tweaks are still developed to further propel this vital aspect of the global economy, the sheer volume of transport information processed on a daily basis means there is huge inaccuracy of data when trying to monitor an individual product's journey. Major business leaders are dependent on physical supply chains that have long pushed for additional transparency, price-efficiency and data insight, beginning at the creation of a product to its final destination (Storøy, J., Thakur, M., & Olsen, P.; (2013)).

SUPPLY CHAIN MANAGEMENT (SCM)

A supply chain is an entire network of entities, directly or indirectly interlinked and independent in serving the same consumer or customer. It comprises vendors that supply raw material, the producer who convert the material into products, warehouses that store the products, distribution center that deliver to the retailers, and retailers who bring the product to the ultimate user. Figure 1 explains the management of the flow of goods, services, and information involving the storage and movement of raw materials, building products as well as full-fledged finished goods from one point to another are known as supply chain management. Supply chain management includes integrated planning as well as the execution of different processes within the supply chain (Khan, M. A., & Salah, K.; (2018)). These processes include:

- Material flow
- Information flow
- Financial capital flow

Importance of Supply Chain Management

- SCM activities can improve customer service. Effective supply chain management can ensure customer satisfaction by making certain the necessary products are available at the correct location at the right time. By delivering products to consumers on time and providing fast services and support SCM increases customer satisfaction (Mao, D. et al. (2019)).
- SCM decreases overall production costs for the companies. The reduced supply chain costs can greatly increase a business's profits and cash flow.
- SCM can help ensure human survival by improving healthcare, protecting humans from climate extremes and sustaining human life.

- The supply chain is also vital to the delivery of electricity to homes and businesses, providing the energy needed for light, heat, air conditioning, and refrigeration.

Figure 1. Traditional Supply Chain Management

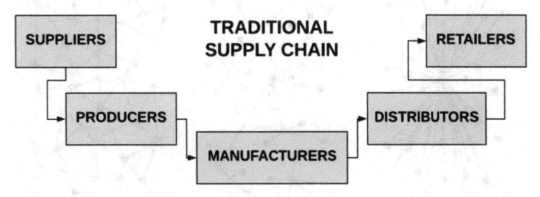

- The main drawbacks of Traditional Supply chain are:
- Product safety cannot be assured at any stage.
- The detailed information about the origin of the product will not be available at the customer end.
- Limited transparency and Lack of traceability (hard to track down).
- Controllability-Lifespan of control.
- Information is stored in Centralized databases.

CENTRALIZED VS DECENTRALIZED

Data Monarchy vs Data Democracy

A centralized System is where the information is stored and maintained in a single centralized server. Figure 2 describes the centralized networks run the very real risk of being attacked, altered or held for ransom. This is because centralized networks store all of their data in one place. By keeping all of your information in one place, it increases its vulnerability to malicious behavior (Peck, M. E. (2017)).

The Disadvantage of a Centralized Database

- Since all the data are stored at the same location, if multiple users try to access it simultaneously it creates a problem. This will reduce the efficiency of the system (Thakur, M., & Hurburgh, C. R. (2009)).
- All the data in the database will be destroyed if there are no data recovery measures in the system when the system fails.
- If the centralized system fails it will stop the entire system from working. This is called a Single point of failure (SPOF).

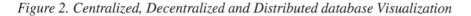

Figure 2. Centralized, Decentralized and Distributed database Visualization

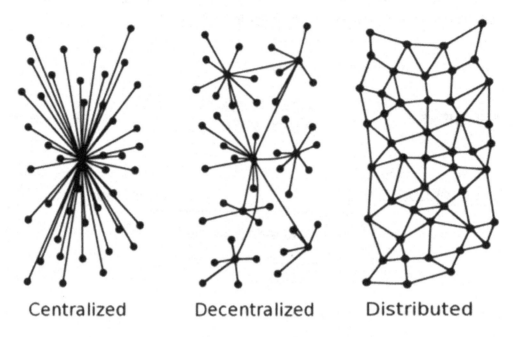

Centralized   Decentralized   Distributed

In a decentralized System, there is no single entity control. A key attribute is that typically no single node will have complete system information (Galvez, J. F., et al., (2018). Here the decisions are not made by the centralized server. Every node makes its own decisions for its behavior and the resulting system behavior is the aggregate response. If parts of a network failure, the rest of the network will still be functional and safe. So, decentralized networks are more secure. This is not just because they use cryptography, but because the information is not all in one place (Madumidha, S et al., (2018), Bogner, A et al., (2016), Tian, F. (2017)). When information is in one place, the system is at a much greater threat to malicious attacks, server failure, and even upgrades will temporarily shut down a centralized server.

Advantage of Decentralized and Distributed System:

- No third party can access the user's information
- No single point of failure
- Transparent-where everyone in the network can see the transaction that has taken place on the network
- Secure
- Cheap transactions globally
- Quick transactions globally

BLOCKCHAIN

A blockchain is a secure, decentralized, immutable public ledger that records every transaction, chronologically, on the network. A linked list of blocks where each block defines a set of transactions. The blockchain is the underlying technology upon which cryptocurrencies and DApps (Decentralised applications that run on a distributed computer system) are built (JoSEP, A. D et al., (2010)). Blockchains update regularly, confirming transactions. Once a transaction has been confirmed and listed in the blockchain, it is impossible to change or tamper with. This makes blockchains extremely secure and highly resistant to fraudulent behavior or human error. Blockchain technology is set to disrupt industries all over the world in the coming years – especially industries where there are a high number of intermediary or third-party companies (Li, D., Kehoe, D., & Drake, P.; (2006)).

Blocks

A collection of data containing multiple transactions over a given period of time on the blockchain network. It contains two parts-the header and the data(the Transactions) (Schneider, M.; (2017), Chinaka, M.; (2016), Lucena, P. et al.; (2018)). The header of a block connects the transactions any change in any transaction will result in a change at the block header. The headers of a subsequent block are connected in a chain-the entire blockchain that needs to be updated if you want to make any change in the blockchain (Holmberg, A., & Åquist, R.; (2018)).

Chain

The cryptographic connection which keeps blocks together using a 'hash' function.

Blockchain is the Combination of Three Technologies

- Cryptography
- P2P Networks(decentralized)
- Game Theory

Cryptography

Cryptography is simply taking unencrypted data or a message, such as a piece of text, and encrypting it using a mathematical algorithm, known as a cipher. For Bitcoin this is SHA-256. In applying this algorithm plain text becomes unreadable without the correct unlocking script (Caro, M. P et al., (2018), Li, C., & Zhang, L. J. (2017)). Asymmetric cryptography is the most secure form of cryptography, which is the form of cryptography that Bitcoin uses. For asymmetric cryptography verification, it needs two keys to do so. This is not the case for symmetrical cryptography. Asymmetric cryptography, therefore, needs a public key and a private key. Asymmetric cryptography is also called "Public-key cryptography". Once a public key is matched to the private key the information, is made intelligible for its owner. Matching the keys is executed with the programmed script. Unlike symmetric key algorithms that rely on one key to both encrypt and decrypt, asymmetric algorithms require a specific key, to perform specific functions. The public key is used to encrypt and the private key is used to decrypt (Zheng, Z.; (2017).

Cryptographic Hash Function

Cryptographic hashing is a fundamental part of blockchain technology and is directly responsible for producing immutability – one of blockchain's most important features. Figure 3 explains about hashing is a computer science term that means taking an input string of any length and producing a fixed-length output. It doesn't matter if the input to a certain hash function is 3 or 100 characters, the output will always be the same length.

Cryptographic hash functions have the following properties:
- Deterministic: No matter how many times you give the function a specific input, it will always have the same output.
- Irreversible: It is impossible to determine an input from the output of the function.
- Collision resistance: No two inputs can ever have the same output.

The cryptographic hashing also enables immutability for blockchain. Every new block of data contains a hash output of all the data in the previous block. A blockchain is made up of a series of blocks with a new block always added to its last. Each block contains zero or more transactions and some additional metadata. Blocks achieve immutability by including the result of the hash function of the previous block.

Figure 3. Cryptographic Hashing Function

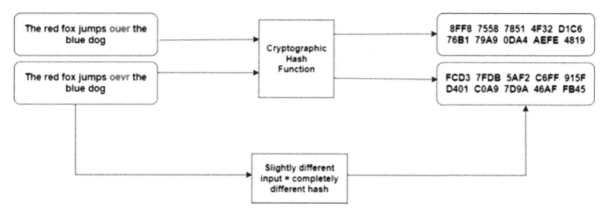

SHA-256

Hash algorithms are computational functions. The input data is condensed to a fixed size. The result is the output called a hash, or a hash value. Hashes identify, compare or run calculations against files and strings of data. To add to an extent blockchain, the program must first solve for the target-hash for it to accept the new block of data. Presently SHA-256 is the most secure hashing function. This function expresses the possible combinations of values that result from the given input data. SHA stands for Secure Hashing Function, and 256 expresses the numerical quantity of the fixed bit length. This means that the target is correct 256 bit, and as mentioned, Bitcoin uses a 65-hexadecimal hash value. Using the SHA-256 function makes it (nearly) impossible to duplicate a hash because there are just too many combinations to try and process. Therefore, this requires a significant amount of computational work; So much so that personal computers no longer mine Bitcoin. Presently miners require Application Specific Integrated Circuits or ASIC. Achieving this target has the probability of 2^256, if you remember your exponents, you will deduce this is an incredibly difficult variable to hit.

Furthermore, using this hash function means that such a hash is intentionally computationally impractical to reverse and as the intentional result that requires a random or brute-force method to solve for the input. Consider the following, if the player has 1 six-sided dice, he has a 1 in 6 chance of rolling a 6. However, the more sides dice has (say 256 sides), his chances of rolling a 6 get a whole lot lower (that's 1 in 256: which is still better than your odds of using brute-force on an extent hash). A hash rate is then the speed at which hashing operations take place during the mining process. If the hash rate gets too high and miners solve the target has too quickly, increasing the potential for a collision, and indicating that the difficulty of the hash needs to be adjusted accordingly. For example, every 10 minutes, at present, new Bitcoin is mined.

Collision Resistance: SHA-256 is collision-resistant because of the large amount of data, so arriving the same target-hash at the same time is nearly impossible. This is also a result of using a target with high min-entropy.

METADATA OF A BLOCK

Figure 4. Blockchain – Metadata of a Block

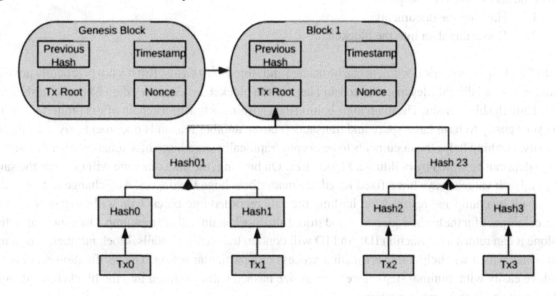

- **Genesis block:**
  - The first block in the blockchain network is known as the 'genesis' block. It is the foundation on which additional blocks are sequentially added to form a chain of blocks. The genesis block is also referred to as block zero.

- **Previous Hash:**
  - This hash address points to the previous block. Every block inherits from the previous block. New block's hash is created by the use of the previous block's hash.
- **Transaction Details:**
  - Details of all the transactions that need to occur.
- **Nonce:**
  - The nonce is abbreviated as "number only used once," in a Bitcoin block is a 32-bit (4-byte). An arbitrary number is given in cryptography to differentiate the block's hash address. Miners (who validates new transactions and record them on the public ledger) adjust the value of the nonce so that the hash of the block will be less than or equal to the current target of the network.
- **Hash Address of the Block:**
  - All of the above (i.e., preceding hash, transaction details, and nonce) are transmitted through a hashing algorithm. The output consists of a 256-bit, 64character length value, which is called the unique 'hash address'. It is referred to as the hash of the block.
- **Timestamp:**
  - Timestamp in the blockchain is used as evidence or proof exists and it keeps proof for notarization. The process will prove that a certain document exists, for some time. Any unauthorized and unauthenticated modification can be detected easily under this and from when the document is being in existence.

This process involves two steps:
1. Hashing the documents.
2. Recording data into the blockchain.

In Blockchain, a single document can be hashed and stored very easily. But it's not practically possible with large-sized digital files to get stored and kept in the blockchain. So every data has to be hashed and stored into the blockchain. The main logic behind data hashing is that blockchain offers limited space and it is very costly to have large space and transaction costs, another reason is document privacy and data security. Hashing helps the documents to be cryptographically stored into blockchain with a timestamp. Large data can be stored by building a Merkle tree. On hashing, the data one time will promise the same output. Hash value always has a fixed length no matter how huge the data is. Any change in hash value will result in a tampered result. After hashing the data recorded into blockchain will especially create a particular space for the hashed document and stored into blockchain with a timestamp. Once the transaction is done it can return a transaction ID. And ID will contain transaction details, block number, timestamp and nonce which will help later verification process of a particular action. The verification process can be done easily with minimal steps since a small size hashed value is stored into the blockchain, it won't take much space and time in retrieving.

- **Merkle Root Tree:**
  - A tree is a computer science term for storing data in a hierarchical tree-like structure where bits of data are called nodes. There is a single root (top) node that has "child" nodes linked under it, which themselves have child nodes, and so on. A Merkle tree (or hash tree) is a tree that uses cryptographic hash functions to store hash outputs instead of raw data in each node.

Each leaf node consists of a cryptographic hash of its original data, and every parent node is a hash of the combination of its child node hashes. Merkle root trees are structures used to validate huge amounts of data efficiently. They cannot only verify that the data received from other peers in a peer-to-peer network like Bitcoin or Ethereum (blockchain-based distributed computing platform) are unaltered but also that the blocks being sent are legitimate. Merkle roots, however, can be understood as the signature of all the transactions included within a single block. In Bitcoin, for example, the Merkle root can be found in the block header (along with the hash of the previous block, the timestamp, and the nonce). Most Merkle Trees are binary, however, there are non-binary Merkle Trees employed by other blockchain platforms. Ethereum is an example of a blockchain that uses non-binary a Merkle Tree.

HOW DO BLOCKCHAINS WORK?

- Figure 5 explain someone requests a transaction or exchange of data or currency.
- The request is shared on the decentralized, peer-to-peer network. The network is made up of independent computers which are called nodes.
- The network of participating nodes validates the transaction using the required computing algorithms.
- Transactions include any of the following: cryptocurrencies, smart-contracts, records, among others.
- To make new blocks cryptographic algorithms are applied. The block of data includes the original transaction. Once it is added to the blockchain the block cannot be altered.
- After the network verifies the transaction, the miner adds a new block to the digital ledger. The new block is combined with the other blocks of data.
- The transaction is complete. This means the data is successfully transferred to its new owner, (in the case of a cryptocurrency). Otherwise, there is just a new block of data on the chain.

Figure 5. Blockchain Process

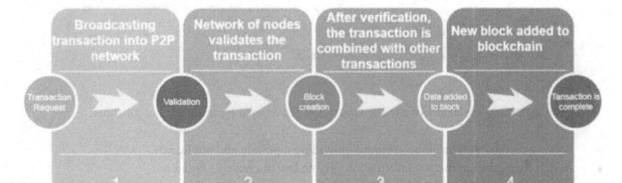

Digital Signature:

Digital signatures are one amongst the most aspects of guaranteeing security and integrity of the info that's recorded onto a blockchain. They are a standard part of blockchain protocols that are used for securing transactions and blocks of transactions, conveyance of information, contract management and the other cases where identifying and preventing any external tampering is very important. Digital signatures utilize Asymmetric cryptography that means that info is often shared with anyone, through the employment of a public key.

Figure 6. Digital Signature Signing and Verification

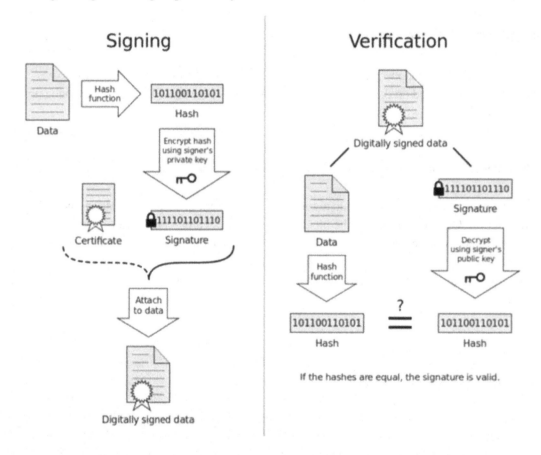

Digital signatures are distinctive to the signer and are created by utilizing 3 algorithms:

- A key generation algorithmic program, providing a private and public key.
- A signing algorithm merges information private key to create a signature.
- An algorithm that verifies signatures and determines whether the message is authentic or not based on the message, the public key, and signature.

The key options of these algorithms are:

- Making it impossible to figure out the private key based on the public key or info that it has encrypted.
- Ensuring the authenticity of a signature based on the message and also the private key, verified through public key

PEER-TO-PEER NETWORK - DECENTRALIZED & DISTRIBUTED NETWORK

Figure 7. Peer to Peer Network

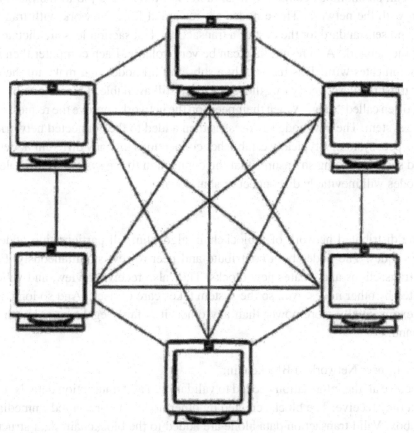

Every node of the network in Figure 7 is a client as well as server, holding identical copies of the application state. The process is by design very democratic, not only because it relies on multiple participants, but because there are few benefits to undermining the system. If a proposed block does not meet the parameters of the consensus, it will not be approved and added to the chain.

Features of Peer-to-Peer Networks

- Each peer is equal in authority.
- Peers give computing resources to the network to use the network.
- Sometimes peers are referred to as nodes. Generally, running a node puts the user in control of his network data.
- No single party owns or controls the network.
- Each user is essentially a server.
- It's almost impossible to hack because the network is distributed across many different computers.
- The more users, the more powerful the network becomes.

Each node is an autonomous computer. It is, therefore, the node's job to maintain connection and communication with the network. These nodes are rewarded for their work with transaction fees. At present, there is no set standard for the cost of a transaction. Transaction fees are dictated by the supply and demand of the network. As a result, they can be very volatile. Each computer then maintains a list of peers it communicates with. This list is only a subset of all nodes that make up the entire network. Each computer must regularly verify that those peers are still available. This is done by sending peers a small message, often called "ping." When their peers on the network approve the request other computers are added to the system. The new node's address is then added to the connected network. When a node joins the peer-to-peer system, it typically establishes connections to many different nodes for the sake of redundancy and security. Doing so ensures that the connection to the system as a whole is maintained, as individual nodes will inevitably disconnect or shut down.

- Peer control:
  - In the distributed network of a blockchain-algorithm, all participating nodes supervise all other nodes. The nodes both contribute and peer-review simultaneously. Each node verifies transactions and creates new blocks. They also receive, review, and validate the blocks created by other nodes. And so the system takes care of itself. And so long as no individual has exponentially more power than any other, it is fairly egalitarian, but driven by market demand.

Working of peer-to-peer Network in Blockchain:

All nodes receive all the information needed to validate and add transaction data. Nodes process new transaction data they receive. The blocks created by other nodes are processed immediately on arrival at the node's inbox. Valid transaction data alone are added to the blockchain-data-structure. All nodes take part in a race for solving the hash puzzle. Due to the nature of the hash puzzle, it is unpredictable which node will solve it first. They are informed when a node solves the hash puzzle of a new block. All nodes receive the newly created block and recognize the winner of the race for solving the hash puzzle. The nodes of the system review and verify newly created blocks and ensure that only correct blocks are accepted. They add new blocks to their copy of the blockchain-data-structure and hence grow the transaction history. The collectively maintained transaction history is kept free of invalid transactions and hence maintains integrity. No transaction data will be added twice. No valid transaction will get lost even if previously processed blocks are reprocessed. The system can perform ex-post validity checks on the transaction history and correct it retrospectively. Nodes have an incentive to process transactions and to create new blocks quickly. They also have an incentive to inform all other nodes about a new block because earning a reward depends on having transactions examined and accepted by all other nodes. Nodes have an incentive to work correctly, to avoid accepting any invalid transaction data or producing invalid blocks. Nodes have an incentive to review and revalidate blocks and transactions in a retrospective way.

GAME THEORY

Game Theory is the study of strategic decision making. Nodes of P2P network validates transactions by consensus, following economic incentive mechanisms like Proof of Work or Proof of Stake, etc.

Consensus Mechanism:

- The blockchain-algorithm is a sequence of programmed instructions that govern how nodes process new transaction data and blocks. This is known as the "consensus mechanism".
- The validity of each block is evaluated based on two distinct groups of validation rules:
  ◦ Validation of the transaction data
  ◦ Validation of the block headers
- The validation rules for block headers are based on the formal and semantic correctness of the block headers. That means that there is no ambiguity of the data in the block header. This is crucial, as it is part of the validation process; invalid data will stop the transaction.
- A central element of validating block headers is the verification of the proof of work or the hash puzzle respectively. Only blocks whose headers contain a correct solution of its hash puzzle are processed further. Every block whose header fails the verification of its proof of work is discarded immediately.

Blockchain miners try to solve a mathematical puzzle, which is referred to as a proof of work problem and so on. Whoever solves it first gets a reward. In Blockchain technology, the process of adding transactional details to the present digital/public ledger is called 'mining.' Mining involves generating the hash of a block transaction, which is tough to forge, which ensures the safety of the entire Blockchain without needing a central system.

Proof of Work:

The miners figure out a series of cryptographic puzzles to 'mine' a block so that it can be added to the chain. This procedure requires a massive amount of energy from the individual and an equally large amount of computational usages. It should be noted that the puzzles have been purposefully designed to be hard, as well as taxing on the system. When a miner ends up solving a puzzle, they present their mined block to the network for authentication. Verifying whether or not the presented block belongs to the chain is a fairly uncomplicated task.

Proof of Stake:

Proof of stake makes the mining process into virtual and will employ validators as replacements for miners. This is how this particular procedure will work: The validators will need to lock up a portion of their coins as stake. Following this, they will proceed to start validating the blocks, meaning that when they uncover a block that they believe can be added to the chain, they will verify it by placing a bet on it. When the block get conjoined validators will then be given a reward that is correspondent to their bets.

Some other consensus mechanisms are proof of Burn, Delegated proof of stake, delegated Byzantine fault tolerance, proof of elapsed time, proof of capacity, proof of Activity and so on.

Other components of Blockchain:

- **Node:**
  ○ A copy of the ledger operated by a member of the blockchain network
- **Coin:**
  ○ The purpose of a coin is to act like money – to allow transactions of products and services to occur. Depending on the coin, it is a store of value, unit of account or medium of transfer
- **Token:**
  ○ A means of payment, but it has some added layer of functionality. Holders of tokens often get value from them beyond speculative returns, such as being able to vote on certain business decisions or technical changes, earn dividend payments for holding or staking tokens, or to get discounts on, or access to, services.
- **Cryptocurrencies:**
  ○ They are secured digital currencies using cryptography and built using blockchain technology. Ex.bitcoin
- **DApps:**
  ○ DApps are 'Decentralised Applications'. Applications, like Bitcoin or Ethereum, Hyperledger that are built on a decentralized blockchain.

Blockchain Platforms

- **Bitcoin:**
  ○ Bitcoin was launched in 2009. It is the most famous blockchain network that offers cryptocurrency transactions. The bitcoin blockchain has a 1MB block limit. It takes 10 minutes to mine, or create, a new block on the bitcoin blockchain.
- **Ethereum:**
  ○ Ethereum was launched in 2015. It is an open-source blockchain platform. It does not have any block limit. It introduces smart contracts for decentralized applications (Dapps). Ethereum can serve as both a public and private blockchain network. The number of transactions that are put into a block is decided by the validators. Each block is mined in 12-14 seconds and the number of transactions per second is around 15.
- **Hyperledger:**
  ○ It is mainly designed for enterprise applications. It is an open-source, private blockchain network.

SUPPLY CHAIN INTEGRATION

Supply chain processes and records are other areas that can gain from blockchain applications and a shared ledger. Now IBM is working on blockchain solutions to supply chain problems. Because blockchain relies on a shared immutable ledger, record management and traceability can be significantly improved. Food distributors are one of the main industries that are invested in blockchain and supply chain. Food distribution has the most opportunity to gain from blockchain applications. Currently records keeping and tracing product is error-prone and time-consuming because many processes have yet to be digitized. That means that keeping track of the movement of a product, for instance, food is very difficult. Not only does this pose concerns for efficiency, but it creates a serious issue for health concerns. The distributor must work quickly to isolate the spoiled food as well as alert the public once a food item is recalled. However, if all levels and handlers of a product are recorded on a shared network, it is very easy to isolate where the tainted food came from. They will also be able to isolate where and when the product was purchased. Currently, we must trust food labels alone. However, if blockchain were incorporated into supply chain processes, consumers could learn all about the processes of their products.

Use of Smart Contracts:

A Traditional contract is not efficient for blockchain technology. The traditional supply chain consists of a large number of paper documents which result in a lack of transparency. Smart contracts are a type of self-executing contract with the terms of agreement residing in the lines of code. To be more specific, these agreement terms are those that are between a buyer and a seller. Both the code and the agreements exist across a distributed and decentralized blockchain network. Figure 8, these contracts allow for the execution of transactions and agreements among dissimilar, anonymous parties. On top of that, it is without a need for a central authority, a legal system, or any external enforcement. They essentially make all transactions traceable, transparent, and above all else, irreversible. The primary goal of these contracts is to boost the overall transparency of the transaction. All the while it reduces fees and eases any potential for conflict over a lack of performance. Unlike traditional contracts, however, smart contracts have absolutely no room for interpretation. This is due to all of the terms being predetermined and conditions executed automatically. Every smart contract is assigned with a unique address of 20 bytes. The contract code can never be changed once the contract is deployed into the blockchain, the user can only send a transaction to the contract's address. This transaction will be executed by every consensus node in the network to reach a consensus on its output.

- The benefits of using a smart contract include:
  - Turning legal obligations into more of an automated process
  - Guaranteeing a higher-level degree of security for parties involved in a contract
  - Reducing the conventional reliance on intermediates and any other form of middlemen
  - Lowering transaction costs

Figure 8. Smart Contract Flow Diagram

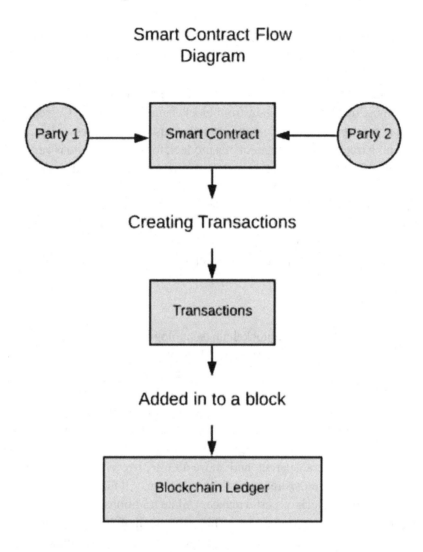

METHODS OF TOKEN IN BLOCKCHAIN

The Ethereum Platform is an open-source project that determines with two networks. One is a user account, which controls in a private key and address. Second is a Smart Contract account that is controlled by code which is built inside. The code is compiled and ran using Ethereum Virtual Machines (EVM), which runs on individual nodes. The interaction between contracts is called transactions. The transactions update the state of smart contracts allowing for the state to be changed and viewed transparently from interacting with individual smart contracts. On top of the Ethereum network, the "Producer-Consumer" Network is built to globally access real-time transaction execution.

- Token: The Ethereum ecosystem follows Ethereum Request for Comments (ERC) feedback system among users. ERC – 20 is a token framework that is used to build a digital token on the Ethereum network. Provider-Consumer exploits the ERC-721 proposal to track and create assets that will provide asset and non-fungible token standard. This standard helps in integrating with Provider-Consumer with the current Ethereum Platform. All the digital assets are created on its own with the help of the ERC-721 standard.
- Steps in transferring an asset
  ○ Using a phone app
  ○ IoT devise that triggers a transaction
- The tokens in Ethereum blockchain provide security that is approved in the ERC-20 contract. The Provider-Consumer software assigns private keys to execute the whole transaction process. To operate on different phones ERC-721 contracts are used. It also provides a level of abstraction for IoT devices and users.

INTERNET OF THINGS

Internet of Things (IoT), makes communication between objects possible. The Internet of things is the concept of connecting the devices to the internet to make it more efficient. IoT plays an important role in tracking goods and sensing food spoilage. The benefit of machines having IP addresses is an overall increase in effectiveness and efficiency. Rather than waiting on a human to notice that the dishwasher is leaking, the system itself acknowledges the malfunction and can even manage its repair. By enabling machine communication we will continue to see a significant improvement in manufacturing and distribution, as it is a more effective check of the system. Issues are noted and returned to the manufacturer to implement the improvement. For example, smart thermostats regulate temperature more effectively than a human, and as we move towards automated vehicles, we will also see greater communication between traffic infrastructure and the vehicles themselves. Naturally, the IoT requires shared data so that machine communication is executed effectively. The needs of the human user are then tracked by the machine and sent to the manufacturer.

Gas and Payment:

Ether is a cryptocurrency of Ethereum which is used for the transaction. Gas is the unit used to measure the fees required for a particular computation. With every transaction, a sender sets a gas limit and gas price. Gas price is the amount of Ether in which the user willing to spend on every unit of gas, and "gwei" is the unit that is applied to measure gas. The smallest unit of Ether is "Wei", where 10^{18} Wei =1 Ether. One gwei is 1,000,000,000 Wei. gas limit represents the maximum amount of Wei that the sender is willing to pay for executing a transaction. For example, let's say the sender sets the gas limit to 50,000 and a gas price to 20 gwei. This implies that the sender is willing to spend at most 50,000 x 20 gwei = 1,000,000,000,000,000 Wei = 0.001 Ether to execute that transaction.All the money spent on gas by the sender is sent to the miner's address. Not only is the gas used to pay for computation steps, but it is also used to pay for storage usage. Imposing fees prevents users from overtaxing the network.

Blockchain in supply chain overall process:

- Figure 9 explains the Provider-Consumer Solution provides blockchain a most efficient structure of a database having a public ledger that includes digital information on the products, people, or events that can be accessed or inspected by many users. With the help of blockchain, there is a chance to
    - Increase Transparency
    - Reduce Error
    - Prevents product delays
    - Eliminate unethical and illegal activities
    - Better management
    - Increase the trust between consumer and supplier
- The customer demands are increasing every day and to meet that we need an improved supply chain. Also for a better marketing environment, we can make use of Blockchain technology in supply chains.
- Ether:

Ether is not meant to be a unit of currency on a peer-to-peer payment network; rather, it acts as the "fuel" or "gas" that powers the Ethereum network. Ethereum is an open-source platform that runs smart contracts. Smart contracts are self-executing when certain conditions are met. The smart contract execution requires computational resources that must be paid for in some way: this is where ether comes in. Ether is the crypto-fuel or currency allowing smart contracts to run. It provides the reward for nodes to validate blocks on the Ethereum blockchain, which contains the smart contract code. 5 ethers are created whenever the block is validated and awarded to the successful node. A new block is generated roughly every 15–17 seconds.

- The **timestamp** plays a vital role in the supply chain given various time-based competitive issues, such as lead time, delivery, and food spoilage concerns. The timestamp is also expository to traceability and information transparency
- The supplier uploads the data about the food product like its harvested date, price. The Food product is then tagged with RFID chip. The tags are placed on any items, ranging from individual parts to delivery labels. Inside the RFID tag, it consists of a microchip and antennae. Identifying information Special printers are used to print the tags which wirelessly load the identifying information to the tags. The information on the tags can be used for multiple tasks. When RFID scanners scan the item, information is read from the tag which could include some necessary information that could be very effective in maintaining Supply chain such as:
    - ID number
    - Serial numbers for individual product
    - Location logs
    - Bin location of a product
    - Order status
    - Its components

- The information can be updated and sent through any RFID receiver and the information is not limited to just holding the ID and serial numbers. The information that RFID can provide will be matched with the system. To track shipment and stock locations automatically as the product moves through warehouses and Trucks. Implementation of RFID to these systems can ensure that both correct products and the correct qualities of the product are collected at both points, thereby eliminating errors. Coupled with the IoT the product information can be tracked at all stages of shipment and storage, increasing accuracy, efficiency, and accountability.

Figure 9. Supply Chain Process using RFID

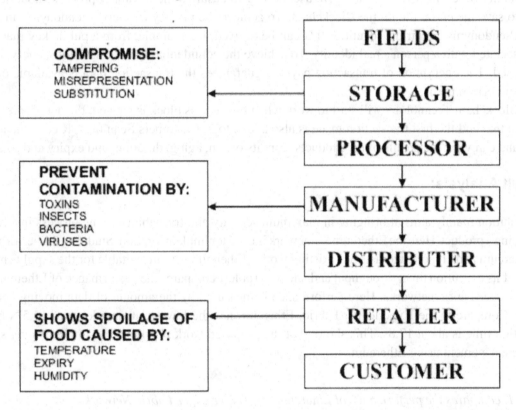

- The fully utilized RFID-enabled supply chain network can determine the product's location.
- After RFID tags are attached by the supplier, then the producer gets information about the food product and adds QR code to packaging.
- Then the product moves from producer to distributor, in which the distributor automatically receives a notification about the receipt of food products. Then Distributors choose suiting 3PL (Third Party Logistics) based on fully available data on the customer, delivery date and other user information. Then 3PL (distribution, warehouse and fulfillment services) is informed about the origin and destination of food products. It flexibly optimizes network flows. Now the retailer runs a machine learning-based forecasting and also provides an app for end customers.

- The product information will remain the same. Then the product is ready for sale, it moves to market by retailers. The store has full transparency in delivery time. They adopt orders, promos, etc. accordingly. All these transactions take place in a Smart Contract. Now at each process involved in the production, each organization scans the RFID and updates the details using a mobile app to the blocks which are stored in the cloud. So the cloud also plays a major role in storing blocks. The verification, validation, transactions, etc., all are done through the app or website. A mobile app and a website serve as a platform for communication.
- Data Protection: Ethereum Blockchain platform ensures that the user's data is encrypted which means it is a difficult task to modify data. You can also save a cryptographic signature of a file on the Blockchain. This would give users a way to ensure a file is tamper-proof without needing to save the entire file on the Blockchain. To achieve the privacy of users, pseudonyms are used. Pseudonyms are virtual identities that can be derived, for example, from a public key that is associated with a person's real identity. To achieve the confidentiality of transactions, encryption is used. The encryption of transaction payload guarantees the transaction data is available only to authorized parties.
- Blockchain Technology will start to work when the genesis block is created, the details are stored in that and the first transaction made is also added to it. Customers Scan the QR code via an app and can view the details of the products from its origin, aging, duration, and expiry and so on.

Result Analysis:

The solution mainly aims at bringing in maximum security and traceability in the process involved in supplying a product. Here the Ethereum framework is used for implementation. Studying the performance of Ethereum and Hyperledger Fabric (existing work), Ethereum is more suitable for the supply chain in terms of its execution time, throughput and latency. Table 1 compares the performance of Ethereum and Hyperledger Fabric networks. Here performance is measured by the amount of data moving between nodes. Compare to the Hyperledger Fabric, Ethereum has the lowest latency delay of 14.55s but its execution time is about 17.8s. This shows that the proposed work is efficient in implementing supply chain management using Ethereum.

Table 1. compares the performance of Ethereum and Hyperledger Fabric Networks

Parameters	Ethereum	Hyperledger Fabric
Execution time	17.8	20
CPU Load (in percentage)	46.78	18.32
Latency (in seconds)	14.55	17.46

Benefits of Blockchain in the Supply Chain:

- The reduction of error-prone paperwork.
- Improved accuracy through automation.
- Increased accountability through distributed networks.

- Immutable public ledgers.
- Improved production and manufacturing.
  - ◦ Automating the purchase process:
- With blockchains, automatic contracts (smart contracts) can be set up. Once the users agreed conditions are met, these smart contracts automatically execute their terms– shipment authorization, service payment, etc.
  - ◦ Improving transaction flow:
- Validation times for transactions between producers and clients (like signatures, orders, payments, contracts, etc.) are drastically reduced. It provides virtual real-time management of flows and relationships with business partners.
  - ◦ Being more reactive:
- Blockchains can help you detect fraud by identifying problems from the very start of the transaction (inconsistencies with validation, suspicious identity of a party, etc.). An alert is instantly sent when it comes to product recovery.
  - ◦ Securing the supply chain:
- Imputing a tag(RFID) to each product recorded in a blockchain enables provider to secure his supply chain. Origin, place of storage, property certificates, records, authenticity: all the necessary information is in a single ledger(public ledger in the blockchain)
  - ◦ Ensuring integral traceability:
- Blockchains ensure the traceability of flows and goods by recording all transactions made by users. These records are indestructible and constitute tamper-proof evidence that guarantees the integrity of information.
  - ◦ Streamlining internal documents:
- The validity of data shared among participants of the network prevents the creation of multiple versions of a document. Each party involved in the transaction thus has access to the same data.

CONCLUSION

Blockchain shows a significant scope to benefit today's today's supply chain. Currently, blockchain is actively improving a multitude of issues, including, maintaining and developing cryptocurrencies, eliminating middle-men, increasing data protection through cryptographic processes, decreasing error-prone records, and developing self-executing smart-contracts. Although blockchains alone will not be able to tackle all the challenges of the supply chain and logistics, they will contribute to securing transactions, fighting fraud and limiting errors. For now, it is not possible to handle data from large infrastructures that need to be processed by the millisecond. Only single or double-digit transactions can be processed per second by the blocks in a blockchain, but these results may be improved in the future. As proof, Walmart and some multinational food retailers came together to work with IBM on developing a blockchain dedicated to their activity. In the future, we are more likely to see a decrease in centralized servers and an increase in decentralized networks. That means that users will have more access to better information.

REFERENCES

Armbrust, M., Fox, A., Griffith, R., Joseph, A. D., Katz, R., Konwinski, A., Lee, G., Patterson, D., Rabkin, A., Stoica, I., & Zaharia, M.JoSEP. (2010). A view of cloud computing. *Communications of the ACM*, *53*(4), 50–58. doi:10.1145/1721654.1721672

Aung, M. M., & Chang, Y. S. (2014). Traceability in a food supply chain: Safety and quality perspectives. *Food Control*, *39*, 172–184. doi:10.1016/j.foodcont.2013.11.007

Bogner, A., Chanson, M., & Meeuw, A. (2016, November). A decentralized sharing app running a smart contract on the ethereum blockchain. In *Proceedings of the 6th International Conference on the Internet of Things* (pp. 177-178). ACM.

Caro, M. P., Ali, M. S., Vecchio, M., & Giaffreda, R. (2018, May). Blockchain-based traceability in Agri-Food supply chain management: A practical implementation. In *2018 IoT Vertical and Topical Summit on Agriculture-Tuscany (IOT Tuscany)* (pp. 1-4). IEEE.

Chinaka, M. (2016). *Blockchain technology-Applications in improving financial inclusion in developing economies: a Case study for small scale agriculture in Africa* (Ph.D. dissertation). Sloan School Manage., Massachusetts Inst. Technol., Cambridge, MA, USA.

Galvez, J. F., Mejuto, J. C., & Simal-Gandara, J. (2018). Future challenges on the use of blockchain for food traceability analysis. *Trends in Analytical Chemistry*, *107*, 222–232. doi:10.1016/j.trac.2018.08.011

Holmberg, A., & Åquist, R. (2018). *Blockchain technology in food supply chains: A case study of the possibilities and challenges with the implementation of a blockchain technology supported framework for traceability* (M.S. thesis). Fac. Health, Science Technology, Karlstad Univ., Karlstad, Sweden.

Khan, M. A., & Salah, K. (2018). IoT security: Review, blockchain solutions, and open challenges. *Future Generation Computer Systems*, *82*, 395–411. doi:10.1016/j.future.2017.11.022

Li, C., & Zhang, L. J. (2017, June). A blockchain-based new secure multi-layer network model for the Internet of Things. In *2017 IEEE International Congress on the Internet of Things (ICIOT)* (pp. 33-41). IEEE. 10.1109/IEEE.ICIOT.2017.34

Li, D., Kehoe, D., & Drake, P. (2006). Dynamic planning with wireless product identification technology in food supply chains. *International Journal of Advanced Manufacturing Technology*, *30*(9-10), 938–944. doi:10.100700170-005-0066-1

Lucena, P., Binotto, A. P., Momo, F. S., & Kim, H. (2018). *A case study for grain quality assurance tracking based on a blockchain business network*. Available: https://arxiv.org/abs/1803.07877

Madumidha, S., SivaRanjani, P., Rajesh, S., & Sivakumar, S. (2018). Blockchain security for Internet of Things: A literature survey. *International Journal of Pure and Applied Mathematics*, *119*(16), 3677–3686.

Mao, D., Hao, Z., Wang, F., & Li, H. (2019). Novel Automatic Food Trading System Using Consortium Blockchain. *Arabian Journal for Science and Engineering*, *44*(4), 3439–3455. doi:10.100713369-018-3537-z

Peck, M. E. (2017). Blockchains: How they work and why they'll change the world. *IEEE Spectrum*, *54*(10), 26–35. doi:10.1109/MSPEC.2017.8048836

Schneider, M. (2017). *Design and prototypical implementation of a blockchain-based system for the agriculture sector* (M.S. thesis). Fac. Bus., Econ. Inform., Univ. Zurich, Zürich, Switzerland.

Storøy, J., Thakur, M., & Olsen, P. (2013). The TraceFood Framework–Principles and guidelines for implementing traceability in food value chains. *Journal of Food Engineering*, *115*(1), 41–48. doi:10.1016/j.jfoodeng.2012.09.018

Thakur, M., & Hurburgh, C. R. (2009). Framework for implementing a traceability system in the bulk grain supply chain. *Journal of Food Engineering*, *95*(4), 617–626. doi:10.1016/j.jfoodeng.2009.06.028

Tian, F. (2017, June). A supply chain traceability system for food safety based on HACCP, Blockchain & Internet of things. In *2017 International Conference on Service Systems and Service Management* (pp. 1-6). IEEE.

Zheng, Z., Xie, S., Dai, H., Chen, X., & Wang, H. (2017, June). An overview of blockchain technology: Architecture, consensus, and future trends. In *2017 IEEE International Congress on Big Data (BigData Congress)* (pp. 557-564). IEEE.

This research was previously published in Large-Scale Data Streaming, Processing, and Blockchain Security; pages 203-229, copyright year 2021 by Information Science Reference (an imprint of IGI Global).

Chapter 19
Cloud–Centric Blockchain Public Key Infrastructure for Big Data Applications

Brian Tuan Khieu
San Jose State University, USA

Melody Moh
🆔 https://orcid.org/0000-0002-8313-6645
San Jose State University, USA

ABSTRACT

A cloud-based public key infrastructure (PKI) utilizing blockchain technology is proposed. Big data ecosystems have scalable and resilient needs that current PKI cannot satisfy. Enhancements include using blockchains to establish persistent access to certificate data and certificate revocation lists, decoupling of data from certificate authority, and hosting it on a cloud provider to tap into its traffic security measures. Instead of holding data within the transaction data fields, certificate data and status were embedded into smart contracts. The tests revealed a significant performance increase over that of both traditional and the version that stored data within blocks. The proposed method reduced the mining data size, and lowered the mining time to 6.6% of the time used for the block data storage method. Also, the mining gas cost per certificate was consequently cut by 87%. In summary, completely decoupling the certificate authority portion of a PKI and storing certificate data inside smart contracts yields a sizable performance boost while decreasing the attack surface.

INTRODUCTION

Verification of one's identity continues to be the cornerstone upon which any interactions or transactions between two parties lie. One key method of verifying one's identity is through using public and private keys, which are cryptographically related strings that can be used to lock and unlock files. If a public key is used to lock a file, only its corresponding private key can be used to unlock it and vice-versa. People

DOI: 10.4018/978-1-6684-7132-6.ch019

could use a public key to lock or encrypt a file, and they would be sure that the only person who could unlock it would be whoever held the matching private key. However, the issue after the establishment of public and private keys was identifying whether or not someone's private key and persona were appropriately matched. Malicious actors could claim to be another party and attempt to associate their own public key with the false persona in an attempt to redirect and steal sensitive information. Thus, public key infrastructure (PKI) was born in order to properly associate online identities with the correct public keys so that any online communication could be trusted to involve the correct parties.

However, with the pervasiveness and expansion of the Internet of Things, there comes new challenges for securing and authenticating the heavy flow of data generated by IoT devices. PKI's age has shown, and it has been unable to keep up with the demands of the IoT and Big Data era (Claeys, Rousseau, & Tourancheau, 2017). Big Data ecosystems require solutions that are scalable and resilient, two attributes that fail to be applied to traditional PKIs. Thus, in order to further secure the internet, a new method for identity verification over the web needs to be realized. The main issue with the currently outdated PKI lies with the Certificate Authority (CA) portion of the PKI (Doukas, Maglogiannis, Koufi, Malamateniou, & Vassilacopoulos, 2012; Gupta & Garg, 2015). CAs are the authorizing parties within a PKI; they validate and associate online personas with public keys by distributing and revoking digital certificates. These digital certificates act as ID cards for anyone that communicates over the internet, and they give a degree of assurance that the party one is communicating with is actually who they say they are. As of now, these CAs are the main points of failure within a PKI system; once any one CA is compromised, the whole PKI crumbles (Zhou, Cao, Dong, &Vasilakos, 2017). Furthermore, it is currently extremely difficult for a traditional CA to revoke an old identity. However, there are newer iterations of PKI that attempt to overcome these shortcomings; one of which is called Web of Trust (WoT). Another promising new solution marries the traditional PKI system with that of cloud and blockchain technology to overcome the weaknesses of the past (Tewari, Hughes, Weber, & Barry, 2018). Both of these systems are new ways of verifying identities that can pave the way towards a safer and more secure internet.

In this chapter, we explore the current state of PKI and its new incarnations that attempt to address the limitations of traditional systems. By doing so, we aim to answer the following questions: "How can new technologies such as blockchain be leveraged to improve traditional PKIs" and "What are the pros and cons of using one new solution over another". This chapter is extended from a conference paper which reported preliminary results (Khieu & Moh, 2019).

This chapter is organized in the following manner. First, it will establish background information surrounding the project and then cover research related to this area with a specific focus on other implementations of different PKIs. Afterwards, the methodology and reasoning behind our solution to the issues with the PKI model will be detailed. Subsequently, the chapter will cover the test results and performance comparisons between the different PKI models including our solution. Finally, the chapter will conclude with a summary and areas for future work.

RESEARCH OBJECTIVE

The objective of this research is to test and implement a Cloud-based blockchain PKI system, CBPKI, to provide Big Data applications with a scalable and persistent identity management system. In addition, the goal is to determine whether such a system can outperform traditional PKI models using metrics such as complete revocation time.

PUBLIC KEY INFRASTRUCTURE

A public and private key are two mathematically and cryptographically linked strings of characters. The two of them together form a key pair; an operation conducted using one can be reversed using the other half of the key pair. In practice, encrypting a document with a public key ensures that the only feasible method of decrypting said document is by using the corresponding private key. As their names imply, a public key is the public portion of a key pair while the private key is the private portion. Key pairs help ensure the privacy and integrity of online communications.

A public key infrastructure is a system that authenticates devices and handles digital certificates; digital certificates are essentially virtual ID cards designated by the PKI to associate an identity with a public key. By relying on a public key infrastructure, users trust that any party with a digital certificate distributed by the PKI is accurate. Once a certificate is retired or deemed to be compromised, the public key infrastructure will revoke that certificate to protect other users from communicating with anything that tries to use the revoked certificate. Currently, PKIs revolve around a Certificate authority (CA) to administer and revoke certificates using the X.509 standard.

Certificate authorities certify and issue these certificates to requesting users. Since they are central to the security provided by PKIs, they often must endure more attacks. Once a certificate authority is compromised, the integrity and authenticity of every certificate within the ecosystem comes under question.

WEB OF TRUST

As Chen, Le and Wei (2009) explain, WoT is a new system that attempts to validate one's identity and corresponding public key in a different way from how traditional PKI systems do. In order to avoid the single point of failure of PKIs, it mimics human society and its network of authenticating statements by the individuals; trust between parties is generated through past interactions with other parties. Certificate Authorities are not needed or used by WoT systems since they disperse the role of authenticator and validator to all of the user in the system. The basis for WoT is comprised of three rules: When two parties interact, they generate "trust information" (Chen et al., 2009). Secondly, every party knows what information belongs to them. And finally, every party must provide "trust" feedback to everyone else. These tenets form a model in which users are able to make decisions on whether to trust others.

In the research conducted by Bakar, Ismail, Ahmad and Manan (2010), it is stressed that WoT relies on a decentralized nature of authenticating users and they push for a trust scoring process for WoTs. The researchers postulate that this decentralization property allows the systems to overcome the past issues of traditional PKIs. With users providing trust scores for each other, there is no longer a need for a CA to dispense certificates. Instead, each user acts as a fraction of a CA, and only when enough pieces are put together is something allowed to be verified and used. Thus, according to the research by Bakar et al. (2010), the single point of failure in PKIs, the CA, is completely removed as a factor in WoT systems. However, this avoidance of a need for a CA comes at a cost as stated by the two papers referenced above.

While WoT systems lack the weak spot that traditional PKIs possess, the study conducted by Alexopoulos, Daubert, Mühlhäuser, and Habib (2017) criticizes the WoT model and conclude that the decentralized nature of the model negatively impacts its ease of setup and limits its applicable areas. By its very nature, WoT systems require further assistance in the setup phase than other PKIs (Alexopoulos et al., 2017). Not only does it require a sizable amount of users to be effective, it also needs enough of a history of interactions to generate meaningful trust scores. Furthermore, this process is not automatable, because the system is based on activity from real users. WoT complicates the initial setup, because it requires a number of real people to manually validate other real people until it can successfully run on its own. In addition to the effects on its setup, WoT cannot be applied to every use case due to its decentralized nature (Bakar et al., 2010). For example, systems that require a strict hierarchy of users, e.g. government agencies, do not have time for nor wish for the trust building process. If a system cannot handle the initial setup requirement of having enough users validate both each other and enough new users, then WoT should not be applied to it. In the case of Big Data applications and ecosystems, the Web of Trust model fails to properly meet the needs of the two. The setup requirements are too burdensome, and while WoT can eventually scale properly, the need for cross-verification would be another bottleneck on the ecosystem,

BLOCKCHAIN PKI

Blockchain technology is a relatively new invention; it revolves around the usage of a public immutable ledger called a blockchain. Multiple parties on a network encode transactions into this ledger after going conducting a verification process. In a blockchain network, every party holds essentially the same power to verify new transactions that wish to be recorded onto the public ledger. The whole system is decentralized, and the users act as a self-policing force to ensure the integrity of every transaction that is embedded into the public ledger.

Within a blockchain network, miners, nodes that hold a current version of the ledger, compete with one another in an attempt to be the first to mine a new block on the ledger. They do so to receive transaction fees for their services rendered. Once a block has been mined, the data will be publicly accessible on the blockchain network.

Closely associated with blockchains, smart contracts are digital contracts typically hosted on an electronic public ledger. It comprises of an agreement between two parties and facilitates the completion of said agreement. The smart contract allows money to be deposited within it for holding and future disbursement upon successful completion of the aforementioned agreement between both parties. If a party does not abide by the terms, the money the contract holds will automatically refund the held deposit and self-terminate. Smart contracts are self-executing and can be used in a large variety of applications from legal processes to residential leases.

Tewari et al. (2018) emphasized the viability of integrating current iterations of both PKIs and blockchains. In order to shore up the current weakness of PKIs, the group implemented a blockchain PKI management framework by developing a hybrid x.509 certificate that included details such as the blockchain name and hashing algorithm used. The system relied upon a Restful service as a communication medium; users could request certificates or certificate revocation lists (CRL) from the framework. Upon receiving a request for a new certificate, the framework would generate a hybrid certificate, send the requesting user a copy of it, and finally embed the certificate into a smart contract for storage in the Ethereum blockchain (Tewari et al., 2018). This approach fused many aspects of both blockchain technology and traditional PKIs; this lends itself an increased ease of usage and compatibility due to the usage of pre-existing technologies.

Along similar lines, Alexopoulos, Daubert, Mühlhäuser, and Habib (2017) highlighted the importance of establishing perpetual access to the new PKI framework in order to avoid certain attacks. In their study, they also utilized blockchain technologies to circumvent the issues with CAs. The authors note that the CAs of old could be blocked by Denial of Service (DOS) attacks that would prevent the distribution of CRLs (Alexopoulos et al., 2017). Since internet entities rely on checking these CRLs for whether a given certificate is still valid, the denial of access to them would allow faulty or compromised certificates to be accepted. Because of the decentralized and immutable nature of blockchain ledgers, they can be used to easily distribute the lists of certificates a Certificate Authority has created as well as its CRL. This makes DOS attacks ineffective versus this new PKI model; there will also be ensured access to the PKI due to the distributed nature of the blockchain (Tewari et al., 2018; Alexopoulos et al., 2017). However, these benefits of integrated blockchain PKIs come at the cost of limitations created through integration; one such limit is that CRLs can often exceed the size of a block which poses an issue for access to said CRLs.

Conversely to the previous approach by the two groups, Chen, Yao, Yuan, He, Ji, and Du (2018) decided to completely overhaul the PKI model and developed a service that heavily utilizes blockchain technology and concepts. CertChain is a new PKI scheme that aims to overcome the issues with past implementations of blockchain based PKIs. Specifically, past implementations possessed three issues: Centralized nodes could overpower other nodes and thus control a larger share of the blockchain. When checking the history of operations on a certificate, the entire blockchain would need to be traversed in order to find said info. And finally, block size limits would often break up CRLs whose size could reach 76MB. Unfortunately, for each of these issues, Tewari et al. and Alexopolous et al. chose to leave these issues as future concerns and did not implement safe guards versus them (Tewari et al., 2018; Alexopoulos et al., 2017).

Throughout their study, Chen et al. (2018) develop solutions for the problems with the integrated approach taken by Tewari et al. (2018) and Alexopolous et al. (2017) in order to create a more robust blockchain PKI. J. Chen et al. addresses the first issue of centralization through dispersing the trust within the system by use of a distributed dependability-rank based protocol (Chen et al., 2018). Essentially, an incentive mechanism was put in place to determine whether or not a CA would be made leader of a block like that of a centralized node in typical blockchains. Each CA would be given a dependability rank that would move up or down depending on the CA's good or bad behavior. On the other hand, the approach Tewari et al. and Alexopolous et al. took relies on the infeasibility of aggregating that much control over the network of nodes (Tewari et al., 2018; Alexopoulos et al., 2017). Rather than build in a safeguard like how J. Chen et al. does, they prefer to pay the sacrifice of provable security for the convenience of integration (Tewari et al., 2018; Alexopoulos et al., 2017; Chen et al., 2018). Regarding the second issue of traversal, this was solved through the proposal and development of a new data structure called CertOper while this issue goes unaddressed by Tewari et al. and Alexopolous et al. (Tewari et al., 2018; Alexopoulos et al., 2017). This data structure would be stored in a block and allow for operations such as efficient query and forward traceability (Chen et al. 2018). And finally, the issue of block size limits for CRLs was solved through the usage of Dual counting bloom filter, a method that efficiently stores data space wise and eliminates false positives that may come up during queries (Chen et al., 2018). And in regards to the existing integrated versions of blockchain PKIs, they also fail to address this issue (Tewari et al., 2018; Alexopoulos et al., 2017). CertChain builds upon the idea of blockchain based PKIs by overhauling previous hybridized systems in order to overcome the inherent issues with the fusion approach. Unfortunately, while it is faster and more robust in its security, it will be quite expensive to implement and maintain. The second problem, the issue of traversal, places an unnecessary bottleneck on the verification process of a certificate; this hindrance prevents blockchain PKIs from fully addressing the needs of Big Data applications and ecosystems.

REAL WORLD STATUS OF PKI

Current traditional PKIs are unable to keep up with the demands of new applications; in one survey, over 60% of respondents stated that their current PKI system was unable to handle new apps regardless of what the software was based in (Grimm 2016). Some companies have already taken steps towards basing their PKI in the cloud; others use newer versions such as the Web of Trust (WoT) approach. However, the WoT version generally lacks speed due to its manual nature of authenticating new users even though it is quite strong in its security.

The literature notes that WoT systems are currently used in several applications when they fit the use case, but blockchain based PKIs lack the same amount of adoption. Bakar et al. notes that while WoT is not applicable to every situation, it lends itself well to systems that are also decentralized in nature and can tolerate the manual addition and validation of new users. Currently, WoT is used in Peer to Peer (P2P) file-sharing networks and is embedded in some email clients (Bakar et al., 2010). Despite its manual nature, WoT has been adopted by some niche applications, but this manual nature and large setup requirements hold it back from being properly applied to Big Data applications. Blockchain based PKIs have not been as widely adopted primarily due to the lack of commercial offerings. This new iteration of a PKI has not fully left the research and development phase of its life cycle. However, it has further reaching consequences than that of WoT systems; it possesses more viability in replacing traditional PKIs than WoT systems do (Alexopoulos et al., 2017). And while there may not be any commercially available blockchain based PKIs available, Tewari et al. stresses that they can be implemented if one is willing to bear both the cost of development as well as that of encoding certificates into a blockchain (Tewari et al., 2018).

SECURITY OF CLOUD AND IOT

Past work in the area of cloud computing and IoT note the inherent security issues with both and attempt to rectify them in a variety of manners. In regards to IoT, these problems result from the computing limitations of the devices which prevents full-fledged security solutions from being applied to them. Stergiou, Psannis, Kim, and Gupta (2018) surveyed the literature surrounding cloud and IoT technology and identified limitations such as that regarding the security of a cloud service provider to customer relationship. The customer must surrender any potentially sensitive and damaging information to the provider by use of the service and trust that the provider has undertaken proper measures to protect said information. With the integration of cloud and IoT, issues arise regarding the storage location of sensitive data and lack of trust in service-level agreements. The group developed a new hybridized Advanced Encryption Standard (AES) platform composed of both IoT and cloud technologies to rectify some of these limitations (Stergiou et al., 2018). Similarly, Tewari and Gupta addressed the security issues regarding IoT resulting from the limited resources of its devices (2016). Their approach differed by use of an ultra-lightweight solution consisting of only bitwise operations for mutual authenitication between RFID tags and readers. Due to lack of computationally intensive operations, this method would be more readily usuable directly by the IoT sensors themselves.

Furthermore, the literature highlights the need for a proper management system in IoT and Big Data ecosystems and proposes several solutions. In one paper, the authors proposed that all data from IoT devices in a smart building be relayed to a cloud server with the additional ability to control such sensors remotely (Plageras, Psannis, Stergiou, Wang, & Gupta, 2017). This system aimed to provide proper monitoring of sensors and optimization of energy efficiency within a cloud environment. Contrastingly, another approach took techniques applied to Wireless Sensor Networks (WSN) to develop a new solution, an Efficient Algorithm for Media-based Surveillance Systems (EAMSuS) to provide privacy and security for IoT networks (Memos, Psannis, Ishibashi, Kim, & Gupta, 2017). WSN techniques were paired with High Efficiency Video Encoding (HEVC) compression and one-time pads in order to cover the privacy and security weaknesses of a one-to-one adaptation of WSN techniques to IoT ecosystems.

SUMMARY OF THE LITERATURE

The literature identifies that researchers have developed two key methods for solving the issues with traditional PKIs. D. Chen et al. and Bakar et al. developed and tested WoT systems; these systems avoid incorporating the CAs, the single point of failure of past PKIs, by offloading the validation and addition of new users through a community based trust model (Chen et al., 2009; Bakar et al., 2010). Alternatively, Tewari et al. (2018) developed a blockchain based PKI that demonstrated its practicality and compatibility with current technologies while also improving and protecting CAs. Chen et al. (2018) took the scheme further and developed a new system that overcomes the issues plaguing existing blockchain based PKI models. In summary, while PKIs have become outdated, there are two models that improve upon and may ultimately replace traditional PKIs to pave the way for a safer, more secure internet. However, there are still areas that require more development and research to increase the viability of replacing traditional PKIs. And even then, both solutions do not completely satisfy the needs of current Big Data applications in terms of scalability and persistence.

Additionally, the literature notes the inherent weaknesses in the security of IoT environments due to the computational limitations of the sensor devices. Stergiou et al. developed a hybrid cloud and IoT AES system to address the weaknesses of both cloud and IoT systems with the strengths of the other (2018). Conversely, another approach minimized the need for heavy computation through simplifying authentication down to bitwise operations (Tewari & Gupta, 2017). Several management systems were also proposed for IoT and Big Data environments. One revolved around the use of a cloud server to provide remote monitoring and control of sensors (Plageras et al., 2017). Another proposed the usage of WSN techniques paired with HEVC and one-time pads for proper application to IoT networks (Memos et al., 2017).

RELATED RESEARCH

Several other public key infrastructure models also utilize blockchain technology. These other models do closely resemble our proposed model, but we have made significant departures from their approaches.

X509Cloud, the model proposed by Tewari et al. (2018) emphasized the storage, retrieval, and revocation of certificates. In order to circumvent the associated maintenance costs of verifying identities, the model aims for mutual authentication between users and the organizations. The framework connects a cloud service to a Bitcoin inspired blockchain protocol that is used to store in newly created certificates. This approach differs from CBPKI in that instead of storing the entire certificate itself within a blockchain, mine holds all relevant certificate data within a smart contract.

A paper authored by Alexopolous et al. (2017) analyzed the merits of integrating open distributed ledgers (ODLs). Alexopolous et al. (2017) developed a formally defined trust management model for use with ODLs; these ODLs are the ledgers that blockchain technologies have implemented and center around. The paper also provided an analysis of common attacks versus typical trust management systems and detailed how the use of ODLs assisted in mitigating or even preventing the harm. This mathematical model was used in part as a blueprint for the implementation of CBPKI. It also inspired further modifications in an effort to circumvent the common denial-of-Service attack.

Conversely, to the previous approach by the two groups, Chen et al. (2018) overhauled the PKI model and developed a service that heavily utilizes blockchain technology and concepts. The proposed model, CertChain, does not simply embed certificates inside of a blockchain. Instead, CertChain uses a newly created data structure, CertOper, to aid in both the storage of certificates within a blockchain and traversal along a blockchain. Also, it modified certificate authorities into miners belonging to the CertChain blockchain network. CBPKI does not go as far as CertChain does in terms of using a newly developed blockchain system specifically designed to fix the power centralization and block traversal issues. Rather, CBPKI uses the pre-existing blockchain Ethereum to store certificate data. However, CertChain directly inspired the use of smart contracts to store certificate data to address the traversal issue, and the usage of smart contracts is addressed in section 10.1.1.

These projects inspired CBPKI, but they differ from it in some significant aspects. While CBPKI utilizes blockchain technology to store data, it does not store the certificate itself; rather, it holds certificate data such its validity and expiration date within a blockchain. In addition, our proposed model altered the certificate authority portion of a PKI by hosting it as a stateless web app on a cloud provider.

PROPOSED SOLUTION AND METHODOLOGY

The following sections detail our newly proposed model for a PKI system that utilizes blockchain and cloud technologies, and they are organized as follows. Firstly, the model itself and the enhancements are explained in the next section. Afterwards, implementation details are covered, and the final section discusses the differences CBPKI possesses compare to models from related works.

Model

CBPKI consists of a stateless certificate authority that stores certificate data on the Ethereum network, a blockchain network that allows unlimited processing potential for smart contracts. The certificate authority is implemented as a Restful API; upon receiving a certificate service request posted to it, the CA generates a new certificate. Shortly following, the new certificate is embedded into a blockchain whose address is listed on the certificate itself. A python script is used to check for the certificate's appearance within the blockchain. Upon revocation of a certificate, the certificate is similarly embedded within a different blockchain for further verification purposes. Figure 1 below displays the overall flow of the generation and verification of a certificate using CBPKI.

Figure 1. CBPKI process of certificate generation and verification

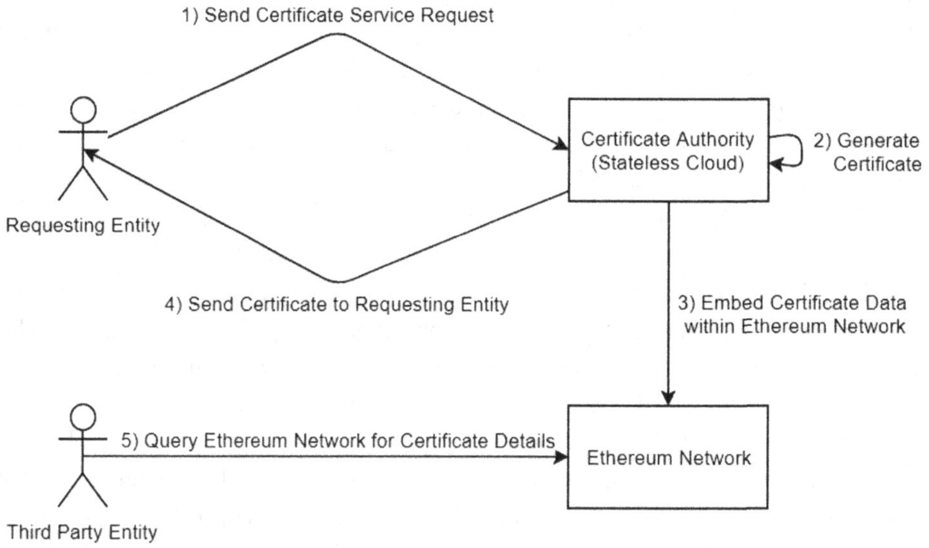

Enhancements

One specific enhancements over past PKI models is the transformation of the certificate authority into a stateless web service hosted on the cloud. The conversion of the certificate authority into a stateless protocol hosted on a cloud platform significantly reduces the size of the viable attack surface. Since coveted data is no longer stored within the CA itself, it also lowers the value of targeting the certificate authority for attacks. In addition, stateless web services are more conducive to relying on the protections offered by cloud platforms. For example, Amazon offers a web traffic monitoring service named AWS Shield to secure stateless web services. In addition, hosting the CA on a cloud platform with auto-scaling mitigates the common Denial-of-Service attack; with auto-scaling, more resources are automatically provisioned to the certificate authority so it can handle the flood of requests during a DOS attack.

The second enhancement made by CBPKI is the use of smart contracts as a storage device on the blockchain network. In general, the use of blockchains in PKI systems allows persistent certificate revocation list access and further circumvention of DOS attacks. Using smart contracts to store certificate data instead of using block transaction data fields yields the additional benefits of lowered mining times and operating costs. Also, CBPKI removes the need for CRLs due to the storage of certificate validity within the smart contracts. This allows for direct verification of a certificate as opposed to traversing a blockchain for a certificate's status thus making our solution better fit the needs of Big Data applications.

Implementation

As noted earlier, CBPKI builds on the works of Tewari et al. (2018), Alexopolous et al. (2017), and Chen et al. (2018). Three different PKIs were built for testing and comparison purposes: a traditional PKI and two Cloud Based PKIs utilizing blockchain technology. Both the traditional PKI and the Cloud PKIs used a remote CA in order to standardize the experiment. The overarching approach is as follows:

1. Implement a Restful API using Python and Django to act as a CA. Allow for the traditional CA to service queries for its certificate revocation lists (CRL).
2. Connect the Certificate Authority to the Ethereum Test Net Ropsten. Associate a cryptocurrency wallet with the CA in order to pay for the associated cost of embedding a certificate
3. For one of the blockchain PKIs, hash a X.509 certificate and embed it into the transaction data field of a block and send it to be mined in Ropsten. Similarly for the new approach, set up a smart contract in which to embed the hash of an X.509 certificate and send it to be mined in Ropsten. In both cases, the X.509 certificate requires the address of where it is stored within Ethereum.
4. Implement certificate verification methods for the Blockchain PKIs. This involves searching for the hash of a certificate within a blockchain or pulling certificate information from the smart contract.

Distinct Features

The modifications to the approach created by Tewari et al. (2018) and Alexopolous et al. (2017) center around the hosting of the CA on the cloud as well as the embedding of certificate data in smart contracts. Both research groups utilized a Restful API implementation of a CA in order to accept and service requests for certificates. However, they did not host the CA in the Cloud; conversely, CBPKI's hosting of the CA within a cloud service such as Amazon Web Services (AWS) allows for some added security benefits. For one, AWS offers web traffic monitoring and filtering of requests to a web app. In addition, Denial of Service attacks are mitigated since AWS with its auto-scaling feature will simply continue to provision more resources in order to meet the increased demand. This change allows for CBPKI to scale properly with any changes in demand by Big Data applications.

CBPKI also drew upon the hybridized certificate implementation from Tewari et al. (2018) and Alexopolous et al. (2017); the modified certificates possess information regarding where pertinent certificate or CA information is stored in the blockchain network. In addition to the hosting of the CA on a cloud service, our proposed solution differs from the two referenced papers' approach in how certificate data is stored within the blockchain network. Instead of storing the revocation list data within a block's transaction data field, our new approach stores said data within smart contracts. This has the added benefit of lower gas cost to be mined as well as quicker mining speed as opposed to the block approach. Also of note is that this method addresses the traversal issue with the approach of Tewari et al. (2018) and Alexopolous et al. (2017) as put forth by Chen et al. (2018). Instead of having to traverse the blockchain in search of a revoked certificate, the certificate itself would contain the direct address of where to access the smart contract that contains all of the relevant data regarding said certificate. Since smart contracts can update its data fields, the CA can simply update the status of a certificate to revoked; this removes the need for CRLs and eliminates the traversal issue certificate data will be directly accessible. Note that in order to use this PKI system, one needs to simply implement a quick verification script that matches the hash of the certificate on hand with that stored within the smart contract. This use of smart contracts helps our solution better fit the needs of Big Data applications in both terms of scalability and persistence. For one, it avoids the need for a traversal along the blockchain in order to verify the certificate. And secondly, there should be minimal persistent access issues to the data required for verification since said data is being held in a distributed network with no single point of failure.

PERFORMANCE AND RESULTS

This section consists of the performance and results from the experiments conducted on the CBPKI model. Three different models were used for testing, and these models consisted of one traditional PKI and two variants of the CBPKI model. The section is organized as follows. First, the experimental settings subsection details the environment and testing methods used for each model. Then, the results subsection summarizes the outcomes of the tests. And finally, the last subsection evaluates each model's level of security compared to one another.

Experimental Settings

The experiments conducted on our proposed work revolved around access times and the costs associated with operating different models. Our proposed model utilized many different software tools, and two different variants were used alongside one another for the tests. As mentioned earlier, three models in total were subjected to the same conditions, and their performance was evaluated based on three metrics relating to speed, time, and cost where applicable.

Implementation and Resources

The following software resources are required for the implementation of our project: Python Programming language, Python Packages Cryptography, Hashlib, and Web3.py, Heroku, Django web framework, Django API TastyPie, Solidity Smart Contract programming language, X.509 certificates, Ethereum Test Net Ropsten, MetaMask, Ethereum IDE Remix, Etherscan, and the Infura Ethereum API. Django and the API Tastypie were used to implement the CA as a Restful API; these two technologies were available at no cost. Django web apps can be hosted by use of Heroku, a cloud platform as a service, and Heroku could also be used at no cost by use of its free tier. The Solidity smart contract programming language is available at solidity.readthedocs.io. In addition, the Python programming language is also available at python.org, and the X.509 certificates being used can be imported by installing the pyca/cryptography package for python with pip. Also, the Hashlib python package, which is used to hash certificates, and Web3.py, which handles connections to the Ethereum network, are available through pip. Ethereum Test Net Ropsten is a test blockchain network for the cryptocurrency Ethereum. MetaMask is a free Ethereum wallet which is used to pay for the gas required to mine blocks or smart contracts. Ethereum IDE Remix is a free IDE for Ethereum smart contracts used to create and deploy said smart contracts. Also, Etherscan is a website that can monitor transactions, smart contracts, and wallets. Finally, Infura is a blockchain API that allows a connection between the Ethereum network and a python script. Below in Table 1 is a compilation of all software tools used along with their associated costs.

Table 1. Software tools used and associated costs

Software Tool	Cost
Python Programing Language	Free
Python Package: Cryptography	Free
Python Package: Hashlib	Free
Python Package:Web3.py	Free
Heroku Cloud Platform	Free Tier Used
Django Web Framework	Free
Django API: TastyPie	Free
X.509 Certificates	Free
Ethereum Test Net Ropsten	Free
Ethereum IDE Remix	Free
Etherscan	Free
Infura Blockchain API	Free
Solidity Smart Contract Programming Language	Free

Experimental Settings

Every test run used the same settings amongst each model; fifty runs were conducted for each model type. Across different models, the most similar conditions as possible to one another were used; each PKI model would be loaded with the same initial dataset of a 2 MB large certificate history list. This history list consisted of details regarding old certificates the CA had distributed in the past. Each model was also paired with a certificate revocation list that was 1MB big; this CRL comprised of half of the distributed certificates within the certificate history list. The traditional model stored the both the history and revocation lists within cloud platform. Instead, the CBPKI block storage version held the data from both lists within two separate blockchains while the smart contract version used smart contracts as storage devices.

Experimental Settings

The metrics used for judgment of both the traditional PKI and the CBPKIs will be revocation status access time. Certificate revocation status time within this chapter is defined as the time it takes for a given certificate's status to be verified. In addition, the two CBPKIs will have additional metrics regarding mining time of certificate data and gas costs of mining certificate data in their different storage methods. Mining time is the time it takes for the data storage method to be mined and thus publicly accessible on the blockchain network. Mining gas costs are the amount of gas or money required in order to pay miners to service the mining request.

PKI Models

During the experiments, three PKI models were used; these models were the traditional version, CBPKI block storage version, and the CBPKI smart contract version. The traditional version is hosted on a cloud service to limit variables, but it still holds all certificate data and certificate revocation lists together with its certificate authority. The two CBPKI models instead use a stateless CA hosted in the cloud while holding certificate data within the Ethereum blockchain network. However, they differ distinctly in how they store said data. The block storage version stores the certificate itself within the transaction data field while the smart contract version merely stores a hash of the certificate along with key certificate data inside smart contracts.

Results

Overall, there is a notable improvement in each area for the Cloud PKI implementation using smart contracts to store certificate data. While both CBPKIs allow for faster CRL retrieval than that of the traditional PKI, Table 2 shows that the smart contract version is faster than the block storage version. This is mostly likely due to how the block storage version requires a traversal across the blockchain in order to find the specific certificate while the smart contract version simply pulls the relevant validity data directly from the smart contract.

Table 2. Certificate revocation status access times (ms)

Model	Mean
Traditional	208.52
Block Storage	142.97
Smart Contract	129.34

Regarding the mining times, there is a significant speedup when using smart contracts as displayed in Table 3. Smart contracts are smaller and thus do not need as many resources to complete mining when compared to blocks. According to the monitoring done by Etherscan, most of the time used for mining the block was spent waiting to be serviced. Mining times are highly dependent on network congestion which helps explain the variance between different run times.

Table 3. Mining timings per certificate (ms)

Model	Mean
Block Storage	325.60
Smart Contract	21.36

The final category of tests centered on the mining gas cost to embed certificate data into the Ethereum network. As the Table 4 shows, the average cost of mining a smart contract is greatly reduced in comparison to that of an entire block. This average reduction of about $5 gives significant savings in the operational costs of a PKI utilizing blockchain technology. However, it pales in comparison to the traditional PKI since there is a negligible cost associated with storing a certificate in a database.

Table 4. Mining gas cost per certificate ($)

Model	Mean
Block Storage	5.97
Smart Contract	0.79

Security Analysis and Qualitative Comparison

The various public key infrastructure models covered in this chapter possess clear benefits and tradeoffs. Traditional models retain the discussed failings of certificate authorities; their large attack surface size makes them vulnerable and a target for infiltration and disruption. The weaknesses of these traditional models are well known which thus makes them quite susceptible to any attacks launched by malicious actors. However, they are cheap to operate in terms of issuing certificates, and apart from hosting and electricity costs, there is a negligible cost per certificate issuance. The CBPKIs both decrease this attack surface size significantly, and by making the CA stateless, they are able to piggyback on a cloud platform's security measures. But as noted in table 5 below, this comes at a significant operating cost.

Using blockchain technology as a storage device for certificates and certificate data does not come for free. Amongst the two CBPKI models, the smart contract variant outperformed the corresponding block storage version in every metric used. The smart contract version has the additional benefit of not requiring CRLs which has resulted in measurable performance boosts over the block storage version. Table 6 highlights the inherent tradeoffs between the two approaches. It is important to note that the smart contract version does not necessarily possess immutability. Depending on the implementation, the smart contract data fields could be subject to malicious alteration. While the code behind the smart contract itself is immutable, the data it holds does not possess this attribute. Thus, even though the block storage method may be more costly and slower to use than the smart contract CBPKI model, the block storage model is more secure since its records are immutable. Another thing of note is that one must be careful in programming a smart contract; since the code itself is immutable, a bugged smart contract can run forever on the network.

Table 5. Qualitative comparison of PKI models

PKI Model	Certificate Issuance Cost	CA Attack Surface Size
Traditional	Low	High
CBPKI Block Storage	High	Low
CBPKI Smart Contract	Medium	Low

Table 6. Qualitative comparison of CBPKI variants

PKI Model	CRL Size	Immutable Records
Block Storage	High	Yes
Smart Contract	Low	No

CONCLUSION

Traditional PKIs contain issues regarding its certificate authorities that inhibit their ability to properly meet the demands of Big Data ecosystems. These issues can be addressed by usage of integrating current PKIs with existing blockchain and cloud technologies. Offloading the certificate authority to the cloud allows the PKI to tap into existing security measures against common attacks such as Denial of Service. In addition, storing certificate data in the blockchain enables persistent CRL and certificate data access while avoiding potential caching issues and DOS attacks. The aforementioned qualities provide an advantage for our CBPKI model over past models in fitting the needs, scalability and availability, of Big Data applications and ecosystems.

The results of the conducted tests reflect a significant performance increase of blockchain PKIs over traditional PKIs. Furthermore, the proposed solution of storing certificate data in smart contracts also outperformed the block storage version in terms of CRL access time, mining speed, and mining cost. However, this mining cost is a large source of the operational costs associated with blockchain PKIs, something that traditional PKIs don't possess.

Areas for further research are based on the study conducted by Chen et al. (2018). As noted earlier, the group of researchers highlighted three specific issues regarding the approach taken by Tewari et al. (2018) and Alexopolous et al. (2017). Additional study could be conducted in trying to resolve these issues without having to completely overhaul the PKI system as done by Chen et al. (2018). In addition, since there is a significant operating cost associated with storing certificate data on a blockchain network, further study in the reduction of this cost is also warranted.

Additional areas for future work involve the cloud portion of the CBPKI model. Routing requests for certificates through a cloud service opens up a plethora of possibilities for the application of cloud and alternative services. One such possibility is to further merge the CBPKI model with a machine learning model to automatically verify and revoke faulty certificates, potentially before the certificate has even been issued.

REFERENCES

Alexopoulos, N., Daubert, J., Mühlhäuser, M., & Habib, S. M. (2017). Beyond the Hype: On Using Blockchains in Trust Management for Authentication. *2017 IEEE Trustcom/BigDataSE/ICESS*.

Bakar, A. A., Ismail, R., Ahmad, A. R., & Manan, J. A. (2010). Trust Formation Based on Subjective Logic and PGP Web-of-Trust for Information Sharing in Mobile Ad Hoc Networks. *2010 IEEE Second International Conference on Social Computing*. 10.1109/SocialCom.2010.149

Chen, D., Le, J., & Wei, J. (2009). A Peer-to-Peer Access Control Management Based on Web of Trust. *2009 International Conference on Future Computer and Communication.* 10.1109/ICFCC.2009.77

Chen, J., Yao, S., Yuan, Q., He, K., Ji, S., & Du, R. (2018). CertChain: Public and Efficient Certificate Audit Based on Blockchain for TLS Connections. *IEEE INFOCOM 2018.*

Claeys, T., Rousseau, F., & Tourancheau, B. (2017). Securing Complex IoT Platforms with Token Based Access Control and Authenticated Key Establishment. *2017 International Workshop on Secure Internet of Things (SIoT).* 10.1109/SIoT.2017.00006

Doukas, C., Maglogiannis, I., Koufi, V., Malamateniou, F., & Vassilacopoulos, G. (2012). Enabling data protection through PKI encryption in IoT m-Health devices. *2012 IEEE 12th International Conference on Bioinformatics & Bioengineering (BIBE).*

Grimm, J. (2016). PKI: Crumbling under the pressure. *Network Security, 2016*(5), 5–7. doi:10.1016/S1353-4858(16)30046-0

Gupta, R., & Garg, R. (2015). Mobile Applications Modelling and Security Handling in Cloud-Centric Internet of Things. *2015 Second International Conference on Advances in Computing and Communication Engineering.*

Tewari, H., Hughes, A., Weber, S., & Barry, T. (2018). A blockchain-based PKI management framework. *NOMS 2018 - 2018 IEEE/IFIP Network Operations and Management Symposium.*

Zhou, J., Cao, Z., Dong, X., & Vasilakos, A. V. (2017, January). Security and Privacy for Cloud-Based IoT:Challenges. *IEEE Communications Magazine, 55*(1), 26–33. doi:10.1109/MCOM.2017.1600363CM

This research was previously published in Security, Privacy, and Forensics Issues in Big Data; pages 125-140, copyright year 2020 by Information Science Reference (an imprint of IGI Global).

Chapter 20
A Novel Intrusion Detection System for Internet of Things Network Security

Arun Kumar Bediya
Jamia Millia Islamia University, India

Rajendra Kumar
Jamia Millia Islamia University, India

ABSTRACT

Internet of things (IoT) comprises a developing ecosystem of responsive and interconnected devices, sensors, networks, and software. The internet of things keeps on extending with the number of its different equipment segments for smart cities, healthcare, smart homes, assisted living, smart vehicles, transportation, framework, and many more are the areas where the internet of things benefits human lives. IoT networks are meant to be monitored on real-time events, and if these devices get attacked, it can have an unfavorable effect on the system. This paper discussed many possible attacks at IoT networks and distributed denial of service (DDoS) attack is one of the most dangerous among them. Blockchain technology can be utilized to develop a framework to protect IoT systems; blockchain is a new technology used for cryptocurrency transactions. This paper proposed BIoTIDS an intrusion detection system for the IoT network using blockchain. BIoTIDS is able to detect an intruder in the IoT network and also able to identify DDoS attacks in IoT networks.

INTRODUCTION

The Internet of Things (IoT) technology and IoT devices are widening at a swift pace, many reports speculate that IoT devices will expand to 26 billion by 2020, Currently, it is numerous times that was evaluated total devices in 2009 and it is undeniably more than the 7.3 billion cell phones, PCs and tablets that are dependent upon to being used by 2020 (Middleton, Kjeldsen, & Tully, 2013).

DOI: 10.4018/978-1-6684-7132-6.ch020

The IoT can be defined as "an overall system of interconnected objects", these objects must have three characteristics, a unique identity by which it can be addressed, it can be accessed using the internet or smart interface, and lastly it must be self-organized and repairable. IoT is a combination of hardware and software, where hardware may consist of sensor nodes, Radio Frequency Identification (RFID), low energy Bluetooth devices, Near Field Communication (NFC) and many more. The software provides middleware, information queries, data repository, and data retrieval and exchange. All WSN devices turn on the IoT component when it is supervised using the internet and significant security issues happen just when nodes are associated with the internet. This acquires many concerns identified with privacy and security, standardization and power management (Billure, Tayur, & Mahesh, 2015; "Internet of Things,"). Internet of things architecture comprises of three layer perception layer, network layer, and application layer. At perception layer sensors and actuators perform the collecting of data from the environment and prepare data to propagate towards the network layer. At network layer transmission of data from one device to another device is the primary task performed by this layer. Gateways, cloud computing devices, Routers, Switches are connected at this layer and use 3G, 4G, Wi-Fi, and Bluetooth networks. Finally providing smart surroundings is the primary task of the application layer. Data integrity, data authenticity, and data confidentiality are ensured at the application layer(Bediya & Kumar, 2019). Distributed denial of service (DDoS) attack is possible at each layer of IoT thus it is important to secure IoT networks with DDoS. DDoS detection, identification, and countermeasure have become a critical demand to secure IoT devices (Vlajic & Zhou, 2018; Zargar, Joshi, & Tipper, 2013).

Computer systems infected by malicious programs and remotely controlled by hackers are botnets (Choi, Lee, & Kim, 2009; Cooke, Jahanian, & McPherson, 2005). Botnets are generally utilized by unauthorized users to perform activities such as monetary frauds, illegal access to computer machines, and leak information (Mahjabin, Xiao, Sun, & Jiang, 2017). Botnets are a serious issue to computer networks and currently, IoT devices and networks do not have sufficient security mechanisms but have weak configuration and obtained hard coded credentials. Finally, the IoT system becomes easy targets for attackers that have such vulnerabilities (Aldaej, 2019). Research shows that approximately 16-25% of computers linked with the internet are active participants of botnets (AsSadhan, Moura, Lapsley, Jones, & Strayer, 2009; Kambourakis, Kolias, & Stavrou, 2017; Sturgeon, 2007).

Blockchain addresses the issue of centralized DDoS mitigation frameworks by presenting a distributed database that depends on a peer to peer network, giving a significant level of assurance and reliability. Exactly when another block is gathered by a node, it is imparted to the remainder of the nodes in the system. Each node that has obtained a block verifies it and communicates it further. Only leaders (miners) are allowed to add the block in the blockchain. These leaders are chosen arbitrarily by determining consensus algorithms liable to the methodology of the Proof of Work concept. Once a block is included in a blockchain it becomes irrevocable and cannot be removed or modified (Bano, Al-Bassam, & Danezis, 2017). Public and private are two types of blockchain. Public and private are the two kinds of blockchain. Public blockchain nodes can add or leave the network but in private blockchain nodes are planned and fixed. Ethereum that adopts the PoW consensus is a Public blockchain where each transaction has cost estimated in terms of "Gas". Bitcoin is another famous variant of Public blockchain. The private blockchain is also recognized as a permission blockchain. Ripple and Hyper ledger are Private blockchain variants (Fernández-Caramés & Fraga-Lamas, 2018). This paper proposing DDoS detection techniques on the Internet of Things networks using the blockchain concept. The motive of the presented paper is to constitute a secure and trusted environment by providing intrusion detection systems using blockchain technology. DDoS attack fundamental structure is presented in Figure 1, it contains four different components and three distinct phases. The attacker is the first component, various masters or handlers are the second component, slaves or zombies are third component, and the last component is the machine which is the target or victim.

During the first phase or primary phase, the attacker pays a great deal of its time to develop a group of malicious machines i.e. masters or handlers, these handler machines as they delegate and command other different attacking machines. The group of master army formation is generally a computerized process where a ceaseless examination is accomplished to search for machines having security-related vulnerabilities. The attacker installs a malicious program in these master machines to add more machines to form an attacking army. The attacker is able to control slave machines through master machines, as slave machines are controlled by the master machine. In the second phase, if the sufficient machines are added in the attacking army, this army is called a botnet (Liu, Xiao, Ghaboosi, Deng, & Zhang, 2009). The attacker begins the circulation of data, code and commands to master machines and further master machines send this information to prepare for the attack on the victim machine. In the third and last phase, the attacker instructs the attacker army to start and execute the attack. This attack is in a distributed manner and all attackers send a huge volume of traffic packet on the victim that turns into a flood at victim machine. In such attacks attacker use spoofed IP address so that it is unable to track that which machine is transmitting such data packets. The attacker hides itself using a spoof IP address. Figure 1 shows the basic architecture of the DDoS attack. There are various types of DDoS attacks among them the primary type are bandwidth depletion attack, resource depletion attack, infrastructure attack, and zero-day attack. Further, it is classified in various types of attack as shown in Figure 2.

The Main Contributions of this Research Paper

Proposing the intrusion detection method by in the IoT network by analyzing traffic patterns of the network represented as Method 1.

Proposing the DDoS attack detection method in the IoT network using traffic pattern analysis represented as Method 2.

BIoTIDS framework that extending security level of the IoT network by utilizing blockchain as database to store transaction records of the IoT network, and ensuring the security of the network data.

The paper is organized into four sections. Section II discussed the background and related work that summarize blockchain, IoT attacks, Intrusion detection, Low Power IoT devices, and Goldfinger attack. Section III described the proposed BIoTIDS, IDS framework model based on blockchain for IoT networks. In section IV authors briefly discuss the need for BIoTIDS, finding and discussion. Section V describes the purpose of BIoTIDS framework, its importance, and concludes the difficulties and future scope.

Figure 1. Fundamental Architecture of DDoS Botnet Attack

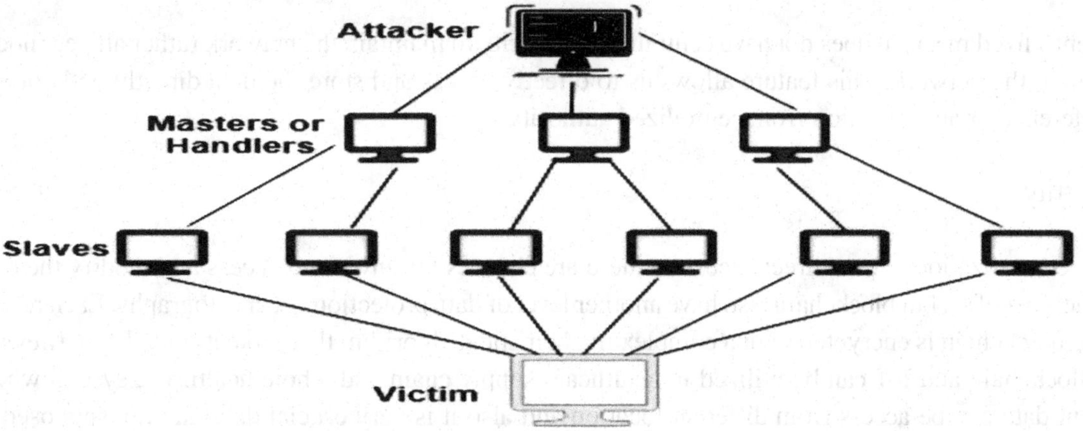

BACKGROUND AND RELATED WORK

Blockchain

Blockchain is absolutely an indigenous invented by Satoshi Nakamoto. Blockchain is an internet database and decentralized ledger over many computers that are associated with each other in the P2P network, each of which is called 'nodes' that consists of all transaction records, which occur between P2P following the consensus protocol. Distributed ledger runs over the web with the help of cryptographically secure hash functions. Consensus protocol provides append-only, immutable and tamper-proof transactions among peers. The transactions can be recorded in blockchain without trusting the third party. It is a strategy for recording information between two parties efficiently in an open environment and in a verifiable way. It knows who possesses what at a specific time and monitors transactions continuously. When the transaction occurs, it guarantees that there is only one single proprietor of anything or property and no twofold use are going on in the network (Jain & Jain, 2020; Lingareddy & Krishnamoorthy, 2020). There are many features that makes blockchain technology reliable, transparent and secured technology that can be utilized for various purposes, in our framework we have utilized it for security purpose so as the data produced by IoT network devices can be secured by any kind of counterfeiting . Some of features of blockchain are as follow:

Immutability

Among various features of blockchain immutability is the key feature of blockchain, Immutability means that the data or records cannot be changed. In a connected network, IoT devices process transactions in the blockchain that leads to an immutable transactional database towards authentication concern.

Decentralization

Decentralized means it does not have centralized authority to maintain the network rather all peer nodes maintain the network. This feature allows us to directly access and store the data directly without any interference or authorization from centralized authority.

Security

As decentralization allows direct access so there are chances for anyone to access and modify the data for their benefits, but blockchain also have another level of data protection i.e. cryptography. Each record in the blockchain is encrypted with a complex mathematical algorithm that protects data like a firewall.

Blockchain and IoT can be utilized in healthcare supply chain and whole healthcare system where patient data can be access from different location and also it is very crucial data that not supposed to be altered and lost. There is huge opportunities to unwind these technology to support efficiency, transparency, security and effectiveness in the field of healthcare system (Jayaraman, Saleh, & King, 2019; Wickramasinghe, 2020). (Kuppusamy, 2020) Explore the adaption of blockchain for smart education system. Author elaborated how the blockchain is helpful to manage student's records, awards and qualification, other properties and payment system in this era of digitization.

Blockchain saves each transaction record made on the network. Rather than keeping a common central database as a bank or third party or government database, it maintains distributed ledger across the network of nodes (Singh, Singh, & Kim, 2018). Blockchain technology is expanding at a rapid pace for the last four years.

Blockchain technologies have the ability to trace, organize, follow up all transactions, store data and transactions at the large scale of devices, also it enables the formation of programs that does not require centralized control. Blockchain is contemplated as the fundamental contribution of Bitcoin since it tackled enduring financial issues known as Double Spend problem. The Bitcoin recommended its solution comprised in searching for the node that mined the maximum and added the legitimate transactions in the blockchain. Though the primary motive of blockchain was developed as a mechanism for a cryptocurrency, it is not compulsory that blockchain can only be useful in developing cryptocurrency but this technology can be utilized in any decentralized applications (Raval, 2016). As the name signifies blockchain is the chain of blocks that are connected by cryptographic hashes. The blocks are in the order of timestamp. To use blockchain it is mandatory to create a peer to peer network where all nodes must be intent to use blockchain. In a blockchain, each node in the network has two keys, public key, and private key. Like cryptography techniques, the public key is utilized by different nodes to encrypt the message sent to another hub and private key empowers node to peruse encoded messages. The private key is used to signed blockchain transactions and pubic key as utilized as a unique key. Therefore only the user's maintains validated private key can decrypt the message that is encrypted by the corresponding public key.

IoT Security Attacks

Figure 2 shows the classification of DDoS attacks. There are various security threats, vulnerabilities, and security issues are recognized in IoT networks (Bediya, 2019; Gandhi, 2018; Maleh, 2018 ;). Some of the major security issues are described briefly below.

Distribute Denial of Service (DDoS)

It is the attack that disturbs the normal traffic of targeted machine or servers of the network with huge traffic or create flood of traffic. It is the most widely recognized attack for wireless sensors network and nodes connected with IoT network. It causes waste of network assets and frames the service out of reach from authorized users.

Node Capture

Capturing the node or device physically an attacker can control, leak all information, obtain security keys including group key, matching key, radio key, etc. after that impact the protection of the whole framework.

Addition of Fake Nodes

New node inclusion to the system can be done by attackers, and feed fake data or code. This can stop the system for transmitting real data by keeping busy with limited energy sources, it can harm the energy source sleep, control it or can destroy the entire network.

Impersonation

Authentication in the dispersed condition is extremely troublesome to the perceptual node; taking into consideration that malicious node utilizes a fake identity to perform malicious or conspiracy attacks.

Software Vulnerabilities

Hackers can find out software vulnerabilities like buffer overflow vulnerabilities exist in the software due to non-standard code development by software developers. It can be exploited to carry their purposes. User privacy can be compromised in data communication. Existing data processing algorithms and data protection mechanisms are not ideal and this can cause loss of information and disastrous vandalism.

Intrusion Detection Techniques

An Intrusion detection system IDS is a technique that can be applied to a network of devices for detecting and monitoring transmission data packets. The motive of IDS is collecting information of a threat, taking appropriate steps when threat is detected and keeping records of all such events in the network (Becker & Vester, 2017). IDSs are categorized into two types namely Network-Based Intrusion Detection System (NIDS) and another as Host Base intrusion Detection System (HIDS) depending on the monitory technique of the network system. HIDS works for a specific machine and monitors intrusions for a single machine whereas NIDS runs on a distributed network and it monitors overall network traffic and detects intrusion on the network. NIDS sensors can be placed anywhere on the network. These are two basic intrusion detection techniques. It can be named as misuse detection and anomaly detection. A combination of HIDS and NIDS is known as the Hybrid system and is now a current trend (Can & Sahingoz, 2015).

Figure 2. DDoS attack classification

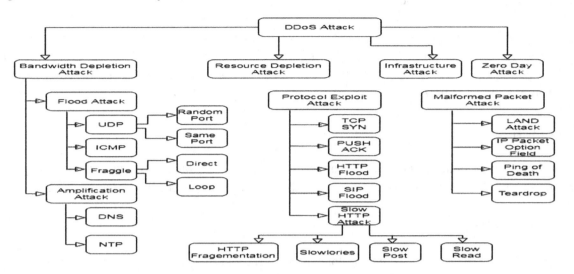

Host-Based Intrusion Detection (Nobakht, Sivaraman, & Boreli, 2016)

Host-based intrusion detection and mitigation framework of IoT-IDM for smart home IoT network using OpenFlow SDN. This framework detects an attack on smart devices in the home network and to countermeasure, it triggers defensive action against the identified attack.

This framework is able to work remotely which means end-users need not have knowledge of security but a third party can manage its security needs like Security as Service (SaaS). Also, this framework works on low energy with less computational overhead on the home routers. It monitors the traffic of specific hosts with filters to reduce the traffic volume and detects the malicious activities of a single host. After detecting the attack IoT-IDM framework is supposed to provide suitable action and send details to connecting router/switches to prevent attacks from specific hosts to protect victim IoT devices.

Network Time Protocol Based Detection (Kawamura, Fukushi, Hirano, Fujita, & Hamamoto, 2017)

In this technique, the local clock (system clock) plays an important role. A local clock is important for all nodes connected to the internet. There are various reasons that slow down and speed up from the correct time and therefore it is rectified and synched by synchronized services. When a network node receives a large amount of packet from DDoS attack, lots of interrupts happen in continuous manners and that leads to local clocks fluctuating from the actual time. The coefficient of variance is computed to identify and detect DDoS attacks on the network.

There are other intrusion detection systems for IoT networks proposed in (Meng, Li, Su, Zhou, & Lu, 2017) and (Meng, 2018) and used Bayesian method framework for intrusion detection system in which each packet is supposed to be individual and distinct from their source.

Low Power IoT Devices

In (Buccafurri, Lax, Nicolazzo, & Nocera, 2017), the author discussed an elective method to execute an open record defeating the restrictions of IoT device constraint. A chain is manufactured by utilizing the SHA-256 algorithm with length k. The created chain is utilized to record each activity. The value of k constrains the biggest size of the block that needs to be confirmed before approving a provided message. In Mobius, an IoT platform server Etherium can be utilized as a database server (Jeon, Kim, & Kim, 2018).

An event of a virtual machine would be executed by each node of IoT, which permits the node to use and exercise its blockchain. To empower low power devices, to configure IoT gateway as blockchain node, activity based communication mechanism, blockchain based infrastructure access by resource-constrained IoT devices a Proof of Work concept can be utilized (Özyılmaz & Yurdakul, 2017).

Significance of Blockchain in IoT Applications

There are a lot of dimensions in the real world where IoT applications can utilize blockchain technology. Blockchain also have features such as immutability, decentralization and security features that are discussed in section II. These features enable blockchain significant to be utilized in IoT networks. Also there are many security issues that can be handled by blockchain in IoT network. Combination of IoT and blockchain is able to provide secured, transparent, directly accessible and reliable system (Chander, 2020). Some of the applicable areas where blockchain can be beneficial in the IoT network are described below.

Financial Transaction

There may be a system required for IoT applications that performs all financial transactions with other parties. Although financial transactions can still continue using traditional payment systems, they apply some transaction fees and it is required to trust banks or intermediaries. But using blockchain in these IoT system third parties will no longer required that also remove the third parties charges for transaction. Hence blockchain can play important role in IoT system of financial transaction.

Distributed System

IoT applications may need a distributed system where there is should not be a trusted centralized system available. Blockchain complete this need for IoT network and it has feature to support distributed system. Though certain private agencies, companies, banks or government agencies on that user still blindly trust but there are lots of chances that centralized authority is being attacked by hacker and overall system can be broken or misused.

Peer to Peer Exchange

Peer level exchanges and communication are required in IoT applications such as intelligent swarm and fog computing. These IoT applications can avail peer to peer feature by using blockchain. Though in IoT system, gateway is used for most of the communication that route data from nodes to destination remote server and peer level communication at nodes is not frequent.

IoT Network Solutions by Blockchain

We have seen how blockchain is significant technology for IoT network. Here we discuss what solutions and features blockchain provide to IoT network. Blockchain has the ability to resolve various problems and issues that are encounter by IoT systems (Fernández-Caramés & Fraga-Lamas, 2018). Blockchain provide major features like immutability, decentralization and more security to IoT networks that are also discussed in background section. There are some more including these solutions that blockchain endows to IoT systems. The IoT network issues that approached using blockchain technology are described below.

Server Cost and Its Capacity

IoT network comprises of many computers nodes that may communicate to each other and it may require storing transaction in the database. Currently for these tasks a centralized server and storage servers are required that increase the cost of the network. As blockchain works on decentralized networks model so there is no extra servers are required.

Deficient Architecture

In blockchain devices validity is verified and the transaction is digitally signed and cryptographically verified. Thus nodes that verify transactions and validity checkers can be removed from the network that makes IoT architecture more efficient in terms of cost and time.

Server Spare Time and Insufficiency of Services

There is not a single point of malfunctioning because in the blockchain same records are managed by different and distributed systems. This save network transition time and lesser time consumption empowers network devices to perform more services.

Manipulation

Records cannot be manipulated until the attacker owns the higher computational power of the systems. Computation cost and time consumption in manipulation of records can be minimized using blockchain. Thus it also saves energy and power consumption of low power devices connected to IoT network.

PROPOSED BIOTIDS FRAMEWORK

In the IoT network, there is a possibility that nodes having low energy, low processing power and less memory to store data. There are many chances that attacker attacks on the IoT system, and inject malicious codes that make devices busy to do unnecessary tasks or attackers send a huge volume of traffic packet on the victim machine that turns into a flood at victim machine and victim machine does not able to do the actual tasks that are meant to be perform. IoT device have low processing power and its power can be consumed by performing malicious tasks. That also wastes the device energy and memory capacity. Hence it is very important to identify these types of attacks on the system or network.

BIoTIDS Architecture

Proposed framework BIoTIDS is able to detect intrusion in the system and capable to identify attacks by the attacker. BIoTIDS framework shown in Figure 3 and Figure 4 have the following components.

IoT Network

IoT network can be comprises of various computer machines and sensors nodes. It is the main system that is needed to keep safe from intruder and prevent from any attacks such as DDoS attack. IoT network nodes have very low energy, processing power and memory.

Intrusion Detection System (IDS)

This component of the framework has the feature of monitoring and analyzing the pattern of the sender's machines. It fetch previous patterns of the sender machine, if the pattern match it send to store the transaction but if the pattern does not match, It send the alarm to network administrator.

Blockchain Manager

The functionality of blockchain manager is to receive the transactions, add the properties of the sender node with the transaction and create a block. Finally it adds the created block in the blockchain. Blockchain manager also sends the patterns to IDS each time when a new transaction received at IDS node.

Blockchain

Proposed framework utilized blockchain to store the blocks that has transaction details and properties of the sender's node. The purpose of using blockchain in the framework is to ensure the security of the transaction. Blockchain has the feature that data or transaction stored in it is not modifiable i.e. it is immutable in nature. If any data modified maliciously then other peer verify and revert the modified data.

BIoTIDS Functionality

To describe the systematic functionality of BIoTIDS in the case when the IoT network is injected with malicious code that sends huge traffic through the IoT node toward the database. Figure 3 and Figure 4 shows workflow diagram of BIoTIDS for different proposed methods and also described in the following steps.

1. Each node of IoT network can send the transactions to store it in the blockchain database. The transaction can also be of request to the database such as storing previous state of the node, received packets from other nodes, sending acknowledgement etc.

2. If it is first transaction of the node, IDS send it to blockchain manager to store the transaction and pattern of the sender machine that are the properties such as resource requested, request time, node location, total request from the node and average request time of node as a block of blockchain database.

3. If it is not the first transaction then IDS fetch the sender's machine recent patterns and match it with currently received pattern. This pattern matching is done with the help of proposed two methods that are described in next section. If a previous pattern does not match with the current pattern, IDS send alert or alarm to the network administrator. These pattern matching can be done using proposed methods.

BIoTIDS is able to detect an intrusion using method 1 and it is also able to detect DDoS attack in the network using method 2. In the proposed model when a new request generated in the IoT network, it is sent for pattern matching that is based on previous data. New pattern stored as a block in the blockchain, this block stores various information of a new pattern such as resource requested, request time, node location, total request from the node and average request time of node and many more. All collective data form a pattern of data. Blockchain store all previous requests received. Each node in the network matches their pattern with the peer node and monitors its pattern.

Method 1: Once a new pattern arrives, IDS matches the new pattern with other existing previous patterns. If pattern matched it is sent to blockchain manager to store a block in the pattern blockchain system, and thus a new block is added in the blockchain as described in Figure 3. Pseudocode for this method is described below.

If IDS found that the pattern does not match with the previous pattern data stored in the form of the block then IDS declares a new pattern request as an intrusion in the IoT network. There are two options for the decision on a new pattern request arrival. First, if new data attributes matched with past pattern then it is not an intrusion and sent to store in blockchain, second if attributes do not match than calculate past pattern standard deviation (PSD) and mean value (M). If a new pattern standard deviation (NSD) is larger than the sum of mean plus three times PSD value than it is declared as an intrusion but if it is lesser than it is declared as the new pattern and sent to store in blockchain.

Method 2: The average request interval l is the request frequency time from a single node for a fixed time interval. Average request interval l is maintained in a block against each node. For example, if the value of l is 30 seconds for a particular node N, it means N sends requests for the database query in an average of 30 seconds. These 30 seconds will be average request time for node N. Pseudocode for this method is described below.

Figure 4 shows once a new request is received from a node, IDS fetch requested node average request time l and its threshold time t. Threshold time t can be different for each. If IDS found the value of average request time l is less than its threshold average request time t then IDS send a new request to blockchain manager and it stores the new request as a block in the blockchain. Instead, if IDS found the value of l is less than t then IDS sends alert to IoT network manager that the IoT network is node is attacked by DDoS attack. Algorithm 2 describes that each time average request interval l for each node has to be calculated. The basic principle is when the system starts receiving requests in m time from node N.

Algorithm 1. *Pseudo-code for Intrusion Detection System (IDS) for IoT Network using Blockchain*

```
Input: past pattern data, new
pattern data
Output:    true    or    false
(Intrusion found)

function
CheckIntrusion(pastpatterns,
newpattern)
{
    past_pattern_request =
    pastpatterns.getrequest(ne
    wpattern.time);
    if (past_pattern_request
    contains newpattern )
    {
        return true;
    }
    else
    {
      psd =
calcultedStandardDeviation(pa
stpatterns)
      nsd =
calcultedStandardDeviation(ne
wpatterns)
      M  = mean(pastpatterns,
newpatterns);
if (nsd > M+3*psd){
   return true; }
else {
 return false;}


    }
}
```

If value of m is less than l. The value of l will also be decreased in the same proportion. If system reduces the value of l and it reaches to less than t then the requested node N is supposed to be infected by DDoS attack. After that IDS will send alert to IoT network administrator that node N is inform regarding DDoS attack. Further administrator can take an appropriate action for particular node that can be blocking of this device for sending new database query requests or remove this node connectivity from the network until it is not repaired or virus free.

Algorithm 2. *Pseudo-code for DDoS Attack Intrusion Detection System (IDS) for IoT Network using Blockchain*

```
Input: past pattern data, new
pattern data
Output: true or false (DDoS
attack)

Function
isDdosAttack(pastpatterns,
newpattern){
if(l<t )
{
  l =
pastpatterns.getrequest(newpatt
ern.Id);
  l = (l+m)/totalrequests;
  return false;
}
else {
  return false;}
}
```

Figure 3. Proposed BIoTIDS for Intrusion Detection in IoT Network Based on Blockchain

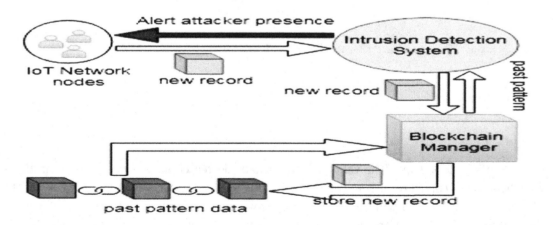

Figure 4. Proposed BIoTIDS Workflow to Detect DDoS Attack in IoT Network Based on Blockchain

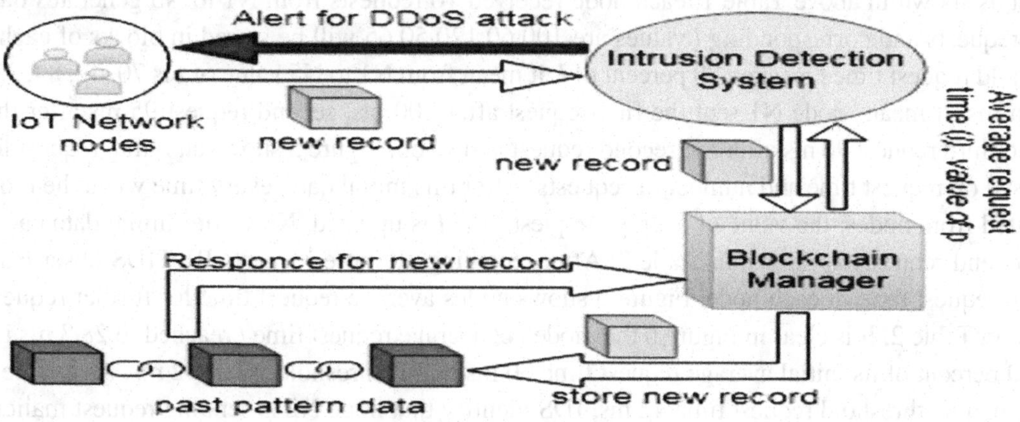

DISCUSSION AND FINDINGS

IoT networks are vulnerable in some aspects of security, many issues have discussed in section II, and thus the security of IoT network is very critical. Attack detection systems can secure IoT network from these attacks. DDoS attacks in IoT networks are needed to be taken very seriously, as DDoS has taken place in the largest attacks that happened in 2019. Mirai attack is the biggest example of a DDoS attack (Ikeda, 2020). Thus it is necessary to build a security framework that can be able to secure the IoT network from such a malicious attack. In this paper, the BIoTIDS attack detection framework is proposed that is a blockchain-based intrusion detection system for the IoT network. The BIoTIDS presented two methods where Method 1 can detect an intrusion in the IoT network and Method 2 that can detect DDoS attacks in the IoT network. To evaluate BIoTIDS functionality of DDoS attack detection, we have examines frameworks Method 2, where we have taken an example of an IoT network that having five nodes in the network.

Table 1. Initial data for different nodes

Request time/ Node	N1	N2	N3	N4	N5
R1	100	65	120	40	70
R2	95	55	110	50	72
R3	90	65	130	55	65
R4	110	55	125	45	68
R5	105	60	116	58	63
R6	90	58	110	46	70
R7	95	62	118	48	72
R8	105	65	122	52	62
R9	110	57	132	52	50
R10	100	58	117	54	58
Avg. Request Time (l)	100	60	120	50	65

In normal case (when no attack on network) for initial data we took 5 nodes N1-N5 and their first 10 request as shown in above Table 1, each node received 10 requests from N1 to N5 generates database query requests and corresponding l values are 100,60,120,50,65 will be stored in blocks of each node. Threshold request time t is taken 70 percent of l, it mean from N1 to N5 value of t is 70, 42, 84, 35, 45.5 each in ms. It means node N1 sent the first request after 100 ms, second request 95 ms after the first request, third request 90 ms after the second request and so on. Figure 5 shows an initial request for N1-N5 based on request time and number of requests. After this initial data, every time when the request is generated from nodes, the value of average request time l is updated. Now after initial data each node further send requests as shown in Table 2. After receiving 10 more requests BIoTIDS observed every average request time of each node. Figure 6 shows nodes average request time for further requests described in Table 2, It is clear in Figure 6 that node N2 average request time l reached to 28.3 ms i.e. less than 70 percent of its initial average request time 60 ms that is threshold value 42 ms. As l value of N2 is less than its threshold request time 42 ms, IDS identify that node N2 is sending request maliciously, more frequent than its normal behavior and it send alert to IoT network administrator that node N2 is infected or attacked by DDoS as it is behaving abnormally. IoT network administrator can remove N2 from the network or halt all operations and requests from N2 until it is not repaired. In this case only one node was infected and it is detected by BIoTIDS but if more than one node gets infected then also BIoTIDS is able to detect at the same time. Thus we can see that BIoTIDS framework is able to identify the attack on IoT network hence in this manner proposed framework work according to as per design.

Figure 5. Initial request pattern

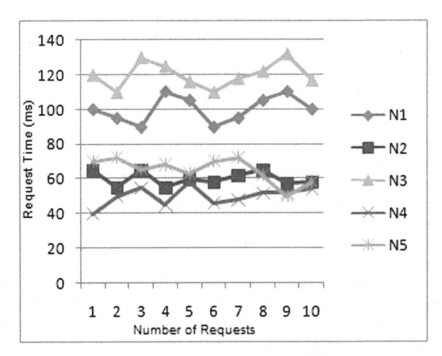

Table 2. Evaluation data for each node

Request time/ Node	N1	N2	N3	N4	N5
R1	102	30	120	62	80
R2	108	30	140	65	72
R3	118	28	100	50	50
R4	116	20	128	52	48
R5	92	10	102	48	60
R6	124	12	118	52	66
R7	98	20	136	48	40
R8	102	12	140	42	42
R9	106	15	80	40	80
R10	112	16	70	48	88
Avg. Request Time (l)	103.9	39.65	116.7	50.35	63.8

Figure 6. Evaluation of BIoTIDS Framework

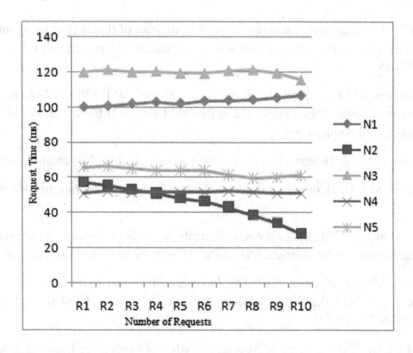

CONCLUSION AND FUTURE WORK

Internet of things networks may have low power, low computational power devices. DDoS is the most popular and most harmful threat to an IoT network system, IoT network cannot be unaffected from it. To overcome this problem authors utilized the blockchain technology mechanism to build an intrusion detection system. Each block contains IoT node requests data. This paper presented an intrusion detection system that works for the internet of things network. Our proposed BIoTIDS presented two methods one for intrusion detection and another for DDoS attack detection.

Algorithms for both methods also described. The first algorithms uses standard deviation and mean values while the second algorithm uses average request time values. Both algorithms can be used with present BIoTIDS, It can identify intrusion effectively. Blockchain technique is efficient to store data patterns of IoT nodes requests. Though there is a computation overhead on IDS to calculate PSD, *M, l* and *p*, etc. But still, it efficient to secure the internet of things network system. For future work, it can also use a machine learning algorithm for IDS to identify intrusion and DDoS attacks in the IoT network. A smart IDS evolution is required for IoT networks.

ACKNOWLEDGMENT

This work is supported by Visvesvaraya PhD scheme, MeitY, Govt. of India. 'MEITY-PHD-2216.

REFERENCES

Aldaej, A. (2019). Enhancing cyber security in modern internet of things (iot) using intrusion prevention algorithm for iot (ipai). *IEEE Access : Practical Innovations, Open Solutions*, 1. doi:10.1109/ACCESS.2019.2893445

AsSadhan, B., Moura, J.M.F., Lapsley, D., Jones, C., & Strayer, W.T. (2009). *Detecting botnets using command and control traffic.* Paper presented at the 2009 Eighth IEEE International Symposium on Network Computing and Applications.

Bano, S., Al-Bassam, M., & Danezis, G. (2017). The road to scalable blockchain designs. *USENIX.*

Becker, J., & Vester, M. (2017). *Intrusion Detection System Framework for Internet of Things.* Academic Press.

Bediya, A. K., & Kumar, R. (2019). A Layer-wise Security Analysis for Internet of Things Network: Challenges and Countermeasures. *International Journal of Management, IT and Engineering*, 9(6), 118–133.

Billure, R., Tayur, V. M., & Mahesh, V. (2015). *Internet of Things-a study on the security challenges.* Paper presented at the 2015 IEEE International Advance Computing Conference (IACC). 10.1109/IADCC.2015.7154707

Buccafurri, F., Lax, G., Nicolazzo, S., & Nocera, A. (2017). Overcoming limits of blockchain for IoT applications. *Proceedings of the 12th International Conference on Availability, Reliability and Security.* 10.1145/3098954.3098983

Can, O., & Sahingoz, O. K. (2015). *A survey of intrusion detection systems in wireless sensor networks.* Paper presented at the 2015 6th international conference on modeling, simulation, and applied optimization (ICMSAO). 10.1109/ICMSAO.2015.7152200

Chander, B. (2020). *Blockchain Technology Integration in IoT and Applications. In Security and Privacy Issues in Sensor Networks and IoT.* IGI Global.

Choi, H., Lee, H., & Kim, H. (2009). BotGAD: detecting botnets by capturing group activities in network traffic. *Proceedings of the Fourth International ICST Conference on COMmunication System softWAre and middlewaRE*. 10.1145/1621890.1621893

Cooke, E., Jahanian, F., & McPherson, D. (2005). The Zombie Roundup: Understanding, Detecting, and Disrupting Botnets. *SRUTI*, *5*, 6–6.

Fernández-Caramés, T. M., & Fraga-Lamas, P. (2018). A Review on the Use of Blockchain for the Internet of Things. *IEEE Access : Practical Innovations, Open Solutions*, *6*, 32979–33001. doi:10.1109/ACCESS.2018.2842685

Gandhi, U. D., Kumar, P. M., Varatharajan, R., Manogaran, G., Sundarasekar, R., & Kadu, S. (2018). HIoTPOT: Surveillance on IoT devices against recent threats. *Wireless Personal Communications*, *103*(2), 1179–1194. doi:10.100711277-018-5307-3

Ikeda, S. (2020). *IoT-Based DDoS Attacks Are Growing and Making Use of Common Vulnerabilities. Internet of Things.* http//internetofthingsagenda.techtarget.com/definition/Internet-of-Things-IoT

Jain, J. K., & Jain, V. (2020). *A Novel Survey on Blockchain for Internet of Things. In Transforming Businesses With Bitcoin Mining and Blockchain Applications.* IGI Global.

Jayaraman, R., Saleh, K., & King, N. (2019). Improving Opportunities in healthcare supply chain processes via the Internet of Things and Blockchain Technology. *International Journal of Healthcare Information Systems and Informatics*, *14*(2), 49–65. doi:10.4018/IJHISI.2019040104

Jeon, J. H., Kim, K.-H., & Kim, J.-H. (2018). *Block chain based data security enhanced IoT server platform.* Paper presented at the 2018 International Conference on Information Networking (ICOIN). 10.1109/ICOIN.2018.8343262

Kambourakis, G., Kolias, C., & Stavrou, A. (2017). *The mirai botnet and the iot zombie armies.* Paper presented at the MILCOM 2017-2017 IEEE Military Communications Conference (MILCOM). 10.1109/MILCOM.2017.8170867

Kawamura, T., Fukushi, M., Hirano, Y., Fujita, Y., & Hamamoto, Y. (2017). *An NTP-based detection module for DDoS attacks on IoT.* Paper presented at the 2017 IEEE International Conference on Consumer Electronics-Taiwan (ICCE-TW). 10.1109/ICCE-China.2017.7990972

Kuppusamy, P. (2020). *Blockchain Architecture Stack to Smart Education. In Digital Transformation and Innovative Services for Business and Learning.* IGI Global.

Lingareddy, L., & Krishnamoorthy, P. (2020). *Blockchain Technology and Its Applications. In Impact of Digital Transformation on Security Policies and Standards.* IGI Global.

Liu, J., Xiao, Y., Ghaboosi, K., Deng, H., & Zhang, J. (2009). Botnet: Classification, attacks, detection, tracing, and preventive measures. *EURASIP Journal on Wireless Communications and Networking*, *2009*(1), 692654. doi:10.1155/2009/692654

Mahjabin, T., Xiao, Y., Sun, G., & Jiang, W. (2017). A survey of distributed denial-of-service attack, prevention, and mitigation techniques. *International Journal of Distributed Sensor Networks*, *13*(12), 1550147717741463. doi:10.1177/1550147717741463

Maleh, Y., Ezzati, A., & Belaissaoui, M. (2018). *Security and Privacy in Smart Sensor Networks*. IGI Global. doi:10.4018/978-1-5225-5736-4

Meng, W. (2018). Intrusion detection in the era of IoT: Building trust via traffic filtering and sampling. *Computer*, *51*(7), 36–43. doi:10.1109/MC.2018.3011034

Meng, W., Li, W., Su, C., Zhou, J., & Lu, R. (2017). Enhancing trust management for wireless intrusion detection via traffic sampling in the era of big data. *IEEE Access : Practical Innovations, Open Solutions*, *6*, 7234–7243. doi:10.1109/ACCESS.2017.2772294

Middleton, P., Kjeldsen, P., & Tully, J. (2013). *Forecast: The internet of things, worldwide, 2013*. Gartner Research.

Nakamoto, S., & Bitcoin, A. (2008). A peer-to-peer electronic cash system. *Bitcoin*. https://bitcoin. org/ bitcoin. pdf

Nobakht, M., Sivaraman, V., & Boreli, R. (2016). *A host-based intrusion detection and mitigation framework for smart home IoT using OpenFlow*. Paper presented at the 2016 11th International conference on availability, reliability and security (ARES). 10.1109/ARES.2016.64

Özyılmaz, K. R., & Yurdakul, A. (2017). *Work-in-progress: integrating low-power IoT devices to a blockchain-based infrastructure*. Paper presented at the 2017 International Conference on Embedded Software (EMSOFT).

Raval, S. (2016). *Decentralized applications: harnessing Bitcoin's blockchain technology*. O'Reilly Media, Inc.

Singh, M., Singh, A., & Kim, S. (2018). *Blockchain: A game changer for securing IoT data*. Paper presented at the 2018 IEEE 4th World Forum on Internet of Things (WF-IoT). 10.1109/WF-IoT.2018.8355182

Sturgeon, W. (2007). Net pioneer predicts overwhelming botnet surge. *ZDNet News*, (January), 29.

Vlajic, N., & Zhou, D. (2018). IoT as a land of opportunity for DDoS hackers. *Computer*, *51*(7), 26–34. doi:10.1109/MC.2018.3011046

Wickramasinghe, N. (2020). *Blockchain in Healthcare: A Primer. In Handbook of Research on Optimizing Healthcare Management Techniques*. IGI Global. doi:10.4018/978-1-7998-1371-2.ch015

Zargar, S. T., Joshi, J., & Tipper, D. (2013). A survey of defense mechanisms against distributed denial of service (DDoS) flooding attacks. *IEEE Communications Surveys and Tutorials*, *15*(4), 2046–2069. doi:10.1109/SURV.2013.031413.00127

Zheng, Z., Xie, S., Dai, H.-N., Chen, X., & Wang, H. (2018). Blockchain challenges and opportunities: A survey. *International Journal of Web and Grid Services*, *14*(4), 352–375. doi:10.1504/IJWGS.2018.095647

This research was previously published in the Journal of Information Technology Research (JITR), 14(3); pages 20-37, copyright year 2021 by IGI Publishing (an imprint of IGI Global).

Chapter 21
Information Sharing for Manufacturing Supply Chain Management Based on Blockchain Technology

Kamalendu Pal

(iD) https://orcid.org/0000-0001-7158-6481

City, University of London, UK

ABSTRACT

Internet of Things (IoT) and blockchain technology-based information system (IS) can be used to improve tracking of goods and services in offering and build a collaborative operating environment among the business-partners of the manufacturing industry. In this process IS architecture plays an important role in storing, processing, and distributing data. Despite contributing to the rapid development of IoT applications, the current IoT-centric architecture has led to a myriad of isolated data silos that hinder the full potential of holistic data-driven decision-support applications with the IoT because of technical issues (e.g., standalone IoT applications suffer from security and privacy-related problems). This chapter presents a proof of concept of a hybrid enterprise information system architecture, which consists of IoT-based applications and a blockchain-oriented distributed-ledger system to support-transaction services within a multiparty global manufacturing (e.g., textile and clothing business) network.

INTRODUCTION

In recent decades, many global manufacturing industries, such as automotive, pharmaceutical, apparel, consumer electronics, started to operate globally in extending the geographical boundaries of their business operations. At the same time, global manufacturing business today appreciates the value and consequence of building an effective supply chain as part of organizational proliferation and profitability. A manufacturing supply chain is a cooperative business network of facilities and distribution options that

DOI: 10.4018/978-1-6684-7132-6.ch021

perform the functions of material procurement, the transformation of these materials into intermediate and finished products, and distribution of these finished products to customers (Pal, 2017). Supply Chain Management (SCM) aims at improving the allocation, management and control of logistical resources and their operational issues.

The operational structure of the manufacturing supply chain can vary from industry to industry. For example, there are a handful of computer manufacturers, but only a few microchips sellers dominate at their tier in personal computer manufacturing supply chain networks. The automotive industry has few final-stage assemblers, but many manufacturers for most parts. In recent year aircraft manufacturing giant – Boeing need to resynchronize its supply chain, and decisions made now by tier-three and tier-four suppliers will affect Boeing's 2021 production rate. Yet uncertainty makes decision-making difficult for owners and executives in the supply chain. This results in 'mixed supply-based' approach in the manufacturing industry. The actual application of a mixed supply-based approach has been established in the textile and clothing industry. Thus, rather than contracting either cost-effective overseas manufacturers or responsive domestic suppliers, the mixed supply-based approach can be used to optimize the manufacturing supply requirements and supplier selection is often driven by corporate policy and market demand.

Much manufacturing company product and service operates in supply chain networks that interconnect hundreds of suppliers, wholesalers, logistics service providers, and distribution channels with physical operations located around different continents. The operational environment in which global manufacturing businesses are collaborating with their suppliers and customers have recognized interoperability of information systems as importance. The need to address this change becomes even more important when considering that new paradigms such as the Internet of Things (IoT) and its ability to capture real-time information from different aspects of manufacturing business processes by using RFID tags and sensors-based data communication networks. In this process enterprise information system architecture plays an important role in storing, processing, distributing data and relevant information.

Despite the growing potential to apply IoT in manufacturing supply chain management systems, there are many challenges need to be resolved. For instance, IoT-related technical issues experienced when operating at the whole manufacturing business level, such as security, authenticity, confidentiality, and privacy of all business-partners. From an IoT vulnerability perspective, practitioners and academics consider security to be the most important issue. Existing security solutions are not well suited because current IoT devices may consume a significant amount of energy and may have significant information processing overhead. Also, problems such as counterfeiting, physical tampering, hacking, data theft might raise trust concerns among manufacturing supply chain business partners.

Appropriate protection must be developed to leverage the value and enhance the trust of connected IoT devices in manufacturing supply chains. For example, blockchain technology now offers several potential solutions to address known issues related to IoT. A blockchain is a distributed network for orchestrating transactions, value, and assets between peers, without the assistance of intermediaries. It also commonly referred to as a 'ledger' that records the transaction. Another way to view a blockchain is as a configuration of multiple technologies, tools and methods that address specific problems. With the adopting of blockchain technology, manufacturing businesses aim to enhance information transparency and improve trust in their supply chains while supporting the interoperability among the networked supply chain exchange partners. As a result, it has gained considerable attention from academics, practitioners, manufacturers who seek to combine IoT with other technologies. At the same time, developments are in progress to integrate blockchain technology with IoT solutions, leading to novel structure of modern manufacturing supply chains, a new partnerships, as well as new way of collaboration and value creation across manufacturing networks.

This chapter presents how manufacturing companies can leverage IoT in combination with blockchain technology to streamline their manufacturing supply chains business processes. When combined, these enabling technologies will help global manufacturing companies to overcome problems related to data acquisition and integrity, address security challenges, mitigate traceability concerns, and reduce information asymmetry. In the following sections, the chapter reviews IoT-based information system in the context of an apparel manufacturing supply chain business case and present an architecture to store data and process these data in a service oriented platform to get nearly real-time information for operational decision making purpose.

The rest of this chapter is organized as follows. Section 2 uses a simple apparel manufacturing supply chain business case. Section 3 describes the background knowledge about the global textile industry. It also explains different paradigms of the ICT world, which are used for business processes automation. Section 4 presents the proposed three-layer framework for an information system. Section 5 explains the emerging issue in blockchain based information system's deployment. Section 6 reviews related research works. Section 7 provides an overview of future research directions. Finally, Section 8 concludes the chapter by discussing relevant research challenges.

OVERVIEW OF APPAREL MANUFACTURING SUPPLY CHAIN

Textile and clothing industries are an integral part of the world economy and society. In a global economy privileged access to natural resources, capital, trained human resources, and even access to markets are not enough to gain a competitive advantage for any apparel enterprise. Moreover, the future of world textile manufacturing, in a vision of 'Gandhian Engineering' based economy (Prahalad & Mashelkar, 2010) needs cost-effective production methods to cater the constantly evolving demands of its customers. In this way, a profound globalization effect is currently shaping the future of global apparel manufacturing industry. In a typical apparel manufacturing chain, raw materials are purchased from suppliers and products are manufactured at one or more production plants (Pal, 2019). Then they are transported to intermediated storage facilities (e.g. warehouse, distribution centres) for packing, loading and shipping to retailers or customers. In this way, an apparel manufacturing supply chain consists of business entities in the chain and these are suppliers, manufacturers, distributors, retailers, and customers (Pal, 2017). In many industries (e.g. apparel), manufacturing and logistics supply chains are challenged by their increasing complexity and the need for higher flexibility to meeting individual customer requirements (Pal, 2020).

Based on mandatory national and international policies, transparency in the textile and clothing industry is often limited to the *'made in'* label. Since this tag usually refers to the last, most important aspect of the clothing production process, it may lose sight of important steps taking place before that point. While the garment industry has been under a microscope in recent years, especially when it comes to 'fast fashion', shoppers are becoming increasingly conscious and want to know more about where their products come from. As conscious customers demand sustainability and integrity on large scale, new transparency solutions are gaining attraction all along the textile supply chain, ideally from farm to retail. Transparency-enabling systems – besides promoting a fairer and cleaner fashion industry – represent also a tool that helps brands to combat the proliferation of counterfeit goods, recognized by Apparel Fashion Business as one of the biggest threats to the global fashion industry.

Secured traceability implies not only the ability to identify, capture, and share required information on product transformation throughout the supply chain, but also the ability to ensure the security of the traceability data. Due to information asymmetry and lack of transparency, textile and clothing industries often face challenges in implementing and maintaining enough traceability. The supply chain actors find it difficult to identify and track the suppliers and sub-suppliers involved. Additionally, the opaque and largely untraceable structure of the supply chain has enabled the easy intrusion of counterfeits. Hence, a secured traceability system is imperative to ensure that the required traceability data are captured and shared among supply chain actors, thereby allowing the tracking and tracing of the products in the supply chain. Further, a secured traceability system helps organizations in various decision-making processes and protects customers from counterfeits.

In this way, product and service provision is getting importance in the apparel industry. Flexibility and adaptability are the crucial characteristics of today's short-lived fashion clothing, where fashion trends and customer demands change in the blink of an eye. Moreover, there exists another layer of complexity in current apparel manufacturing network, which is attributed to the geographical separation of the contributing suppliers and manufactures; and efficient information sharing mechanism within the business partners along the global supply chain operations. In this way, sharing, storing and processing of apparel supply chain data requires secure information systems architecture. Apparel manufacturing supply network data could be analyzed for locating the areas with problems so that proper operating instructions could be provided by the logistics controlling management teams.

Modern information and communication technologies (ICTs) often regarded as the catalyst to improve supply chain information sharing ability. Information sharing across textile manufacturing networks is based on linking unique identifications of objects – tagged using RFID transponders or barcodes – with records in supply chain database management systems. In this process, Electronic Product Code Information Services (EPCIS) is the most relevant industry standard. Internet of Things (IoT) is one of the most promising technological innovations, is used now-a-days in apparel manufacturing. In simple, RFID tags, sensor technology, and relevant data communication networking provision form the concept of IoT. The IoT is a concept in which the digital world of information technology integrates seamlessly with the real world of things. This real-world becomes easily accessible through modern computers and data communication networked devices in the apparel manufacturing business. In recent decades, IoT technology is used heavily in apparel manufacturing business processes - inventory management, warehousing, and transportation of products, automatic object tracking and supply chain management. With access to precise information, apparel supply chain operational managers can perform their analysis on a nearly real-time basis and can take appropriate strategic decisions.

Despite contributing to the rapid development of IoT applications, the current IoT-centric architecture has led into a myriad of isolated data silos that hinders the full potential of holistic data-driven business applications with the IoT. Moreover, standalone IoT application systems face security and privacy related problems. The blockchain technology has introduced an effective solution to the IoT based information systems security. A blockchain enhance IoT devices to send data for inclusion in a shared transaction repository with the tamper-resistant record and enables business partners to access and supply IoT data without the intervention of central control and management. This chapter presents a blockchain-based design for the IoT applications that brings secure distributed data management to support transactions services within a multi-party global apparel business network, as shown in Figure 1.

Figure 1. RFID tagging level at different stages in the apparel manufacturing network

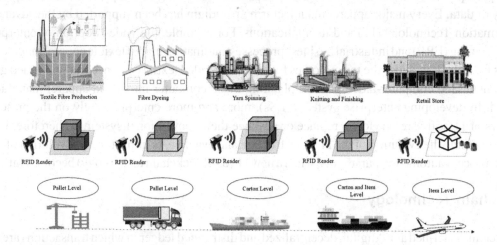

BACKGROUND INFORMATION

In recent decades, it has become a significant tendency for the apparel industry to adopt decentralization as a new manufacturing paradigm. At the same time, advantages in data analysis give more insights into apparel production lines, thus improving its overall productivity. This enables more efficient operations and facilitates the shift from mass to customized production. This section presents a brief review of important aspects of service-oriented computing, the IoT based information system, and provide an introduction on the blockchain technology.

Service Oriented Computing

Service oriented computing platforms are mainly hosted in large-scale data centre environments that are empowered by the data communication networks. The consolidation and centralization of data centres, however, yield an increased distance between clients and services. This arrangement creates different outcomes in high variability in latency and bandwidth. To address this issue, particularly with regards to resource-intensive and interactive applications, decentralized service-oriented computing architectures, namely cloudlets, have emerged. Cloudlets are small-scale data centres that are situated nearer to users and can mitigate low latency and high bandwidth guarantees. This research embraces this locality-aware data storage and processing trend and brings it to its full potential with decentralized access control layer which ensures ownership and secure sharing of data.

IoT Ecosystems

The Internet of Things (IoT) is a smart worldwide network of interconnected objects, which through unique address schemes can interact with each other and cooperate with their neighbours to reach common goals. The primary purpose of the IoT is to share information acquired by objects, which reflects the manufacture, transportation, consumption and other details of textile and clothing industries detail. The gathered information can be used for effective operational decision making.

The prompt and effective decision not only depend on reasoning techniques but also the quality and quantity of data. Every major apparel manufacturing paradigm has been supported by the advancement of Information Technology (IT) and its applications. For example, the wide adoption of enterprise resource planning (ERP) and industrial business processes automation made flexible apparel manufacturing systems feasible. It includes the technologies for computer-aided textile design, computer-aided garment development, and computer-aided process planning made computer integrated apparel manufacturing practical. In developing enterprise systems (ESs), more and more enterprises rely on the professional providers of IT software service to replace or advance their conventional systems. Therefore, it makes sense to examine the evolution of the IT infrastructure and evaluate its impact on the evolution of apparel business process automation paradigms, when a new IT (e.g. blockchain technology) becomes influential.

Blockchain Technology

A blockchain is defined as a "digital, decentralized and distributed ledger in which transactions are logged and added in chronological order to create permanent and tamperproof records". Essentially, it is a novel mechanism for storing, securing and sharing data between multiple nodes in a network. A blockchain breaks away from the traditional centralized approach by managing chain data across a distributed and interlinked network of nodes. The main characteristics of blockchains are shared recordkeeping, immutability, decentralization, distributed trust, multiple-party consensus, independent validation, tamper evidence, and tamper resistance. The term blockchain gained its popularity as the output of a combination of configured technologies, tools and methods underpinning the cryptocurrency - Bitcoin. Bitcoin is a decentralized digital currency based on an open system of computer networks and online communication protocols and was the first successful application built on an online blockchain.

Blockchains can be configured to encrypt and store on-chain or off-chain data and record timestamped transactions. Furthermore, they can automate agreements through the utilization of smart contracts to run procedures based upon a set of conditions, terms, and rules that participants in the system have agreed upon. A blockchain platform can support multi-party exchange relationships in global supply chains by authenticating participant identities, authorizing their access and enhancing recordkeeping of transactions. This capability is possible by cryptographic mechanisms and recursive hashing of blocks. Each block contains a header and a body, the former of which contains the hash of the previous block, thus connecting the individual blocks. Any attempt to tamper with a block necessitates that the headers of previous and consecutive blocks be changed accordingly to avoid detection, and it gets progressively more difficult to tamper with as the chain gets longer. Since their pervasiveness and distributed nature characterize IoT networks, a centralized approach to collecting, storing, and analyzing all relevant supply chain data may cause delays and lead to a situation often referred to a single point of failure. A blockchain, therefore, has the potential to address the challenges mentioned above and provide supply chain exchange partners with trust based on decentralization. The lack of centralized controls in blockchains ensures a high-level of scalability and robustness by using resources of all involved nodes and eliminating many-to-one traffic flows.

Blockchain is a distributed data structure comprising a chain of blocks. Blockchain acts as a distributed database or a global ledger that maintains records of all transactions on a blockchain network. The transactions are time-stamped and bundled into blocks where each block is identified by its cryptographic hash. The blocks form a linear sequence where each block references the hash of the previous block, forming a chain of blocks called the '*blockchain*'. A blockchain is maintained by a network of nodes and every node executes and records the same transactions. The blockchain is replicated among the nodes in the blockchain network. Any node in the network can read the transactions. Figure 2 shows the structure of a blockchain.

Figure 2. A simple blockchain structure

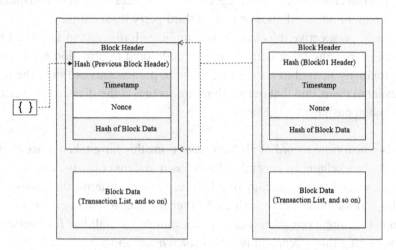

Blockchain technology, at its core, features an immutable distributed ledger, a decentralized network that is cryptographically secured. Blockchain architecture gives participants the ability to share a ledger, through peer-to-peer replication, which is updated every time a block of the transaction is agreed to be committed.

The technology can reduce operational costs and friction, create immutable transformation records, and enable transparent ledgers where updates are nearly instantaneous. It may also dramatically change the way workflow and business procedures are designed inside an enterprise and open-up new opportunities for innovation and growth.

Figure 3. Structural parts of a blockchain

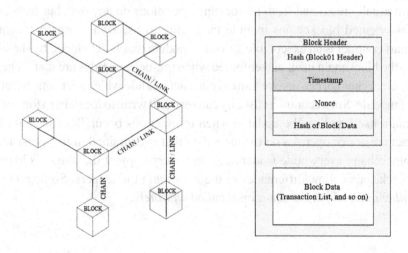

Blockchain technology can be viewed from a business, legal and technical perspective:

- From a business perspective, blockchain is an exchange network that facilitates the transfer of value, assets, or other entities between willing and mutually agreeing participants, ensuring privacy and control of data to stakeholders.
- From a legal perspective, blockchain ledger transactions are validated, indisputable transactions, which do not require intermediaries or trusted third-party legal entities.
- From a technical perspective, blockchain is a replicated, distributed ledger of transactions with ledger entries referencing other data stores (for additional information related to ledger transactions). Cryptography is used to ensure that network participants see only the parts of the ledger that are relevant to them, and that transactions are secure, authenticated and verifiable, in the context of permission business blockchains.

A blockchain is a historical record of all the transactions that have taken place in the network since the beginning of the blockchain. In general, a blockchain system consists of several **nodes**, as shown in Figure 4, each of which has a local copy of a **ledger**. In most systems, the nodes belong to different organizations. The nodes communicate with each other in order to gain agreement on the contents of the ledger and do not require a central authority to coordinate and validate transactions.

The process of gaining this agreement is called *consensus*, and there are a few different algorithms that have been developed for this purpose. Users send transaction requests to the blockchain in order to perform the operations the chain is designed to provide. Once a transaction is completed, a record of the transaction is added to one or more of the ledgers and can never be altered or removed. This property of the blockchain is called *immutability*.

Cryptography is used to secure the blockchain itself and the communications between the elements of the blockchain system. It ensures that the ledger cannot be altered, except by the addition of new transactions. Cryptography provides integrity on messages from users or between nodes and ensures operations are only performed by authorized entities.

The authority to perform transactions on a blockchain can use one of two models, *permissioned* or *permissionless*. In a permissioned blockchain, users must be enrolled in the blockchain before they can perform transactions. The enrollment process gives the user credentials that are used to identify the user when he or she performs transactions. In a permissionless blockchain, any person can perform transactions, but they are usually restricted from performing operations on any data but their own.

Most business-oriented blockchains include the ability to use *smart contracts*, sometimes called *chaincode*. A smart contract is an executable software module that is developed by the blockchain owners, installed into the blockchain itself and enforced when pre-defined rules are met. When a user sends a transaction to the blockchain, it can invoke a smart contract module which performs functions defined by the creator of that module. Smart contracts usually can read and write to local data stores which is separate from the blockchain itself and can be updated when transactions occur. The business logic contained in a smart contract creates or operates on business data that is contained in this persistence data store.

In a simple blockchain, every node is identical, and every copy of the ledger is identical. However, more complex blockchains allow differences in the nodes and the ledgers. Some blockchains support the concept of *subchains*, which are sometimes called *channels*.

Figure 4. Components of a generalized blockchain

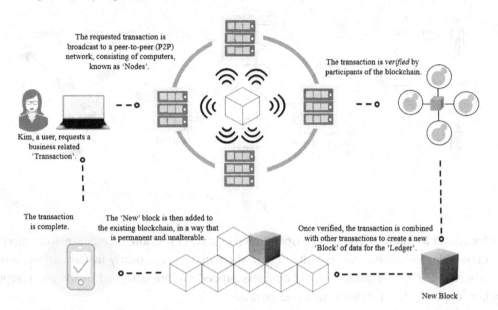

Subchains are logically separate chains that occupy the same physical blockchain. Each subchain may be owned by a different entity and may be accessible to a different set of users. Nodes may be set up so that some nodes participate in certain subchains and not in other subchains. The result of this configuration is that the ledger on some nodes will contain transactions for that subchain while the ledgers on other nodes will not. Another variation on the basic blockchain is one in which nodes are assigned specific purposes instead of being identical in their function. This configuration may be used to optimize performance since the system can be faster if every node does not have to perform every operation required for a transaction on the chain.

Automated Transactions and Smart Contracts

An important character of blockchain technology is its automated smart contract. In a smart contract, the transactions will execute only when the predefined conditions are met. This possibility widely known as a "Smart Contract" creates the option of automated financial transactions. The "contract" is defined in software and stored in the blockchain. Once agreed between the parties, the execution of the "contract" is entirely automated, with no need for third-party authority and no possibility of modification. The steps of a smart contract are shown in Figure 5.

Blockchain is one of the most hyped innovation these days, and it has been gaining a lot of attention as an information technology to be widely adopted in various areas (e.g. automated payments, trace and track transactions, information sharing among business partners) in the global manufacturing business. Since its inception in 2008 (Nakamoto, 2008), blockchain continued to emerge as a disruptive innovation that will revolutionize the way business community interact, automate different types of information exchange in the context of global supply chain management.

Figure 5. Concept of blockchain contract

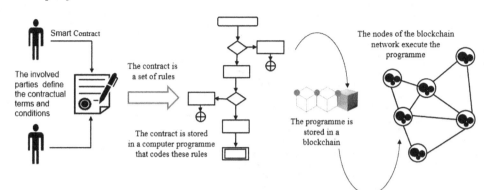

The blockchain technology can reduce operational costs and friction, create transformation records that are immutable, and enable transparent ledgers where updates are nearly instantaneous. It may also dramatically change the way workflow and business procedures are designed inside an enterprise and open-up new opportunities for innovation and growth.

One of blockchain's direct benefits is that it provides a possible solution to identity management. Blockchain can be used in a manufacturing supply chain network to know who is performing what actions. Moreover, the time and location of the actions can be determined.

Blockchain provides a valid and effective measurement of outcomes and performance of key supply chain management business activities. Once the inputs tracking data are on a blockchain ledger, they are immutable. Other suppliers in the supply chain network can also track shipments, deliveries, and progress. In this way, blockchain produces trust among suppliers. By getting rid of middleman auditors, the efficiency of business processes can be improved, and costs can be reduced. Individual suppliers can perform their checks and balances on a nearly real-time basis.

Blockchain also enhances the ability of an accurate way of measuring product quality during transportation. For example, by analyzing data on the travel path and duration, stakeholders in a manufacturing supply chain can know whether the product was in a wrong place or whether it remained in a location for too long. Blockchain can provide traceability history of a product and by doing this counterfeit product can be traced with ease. In this way, the blockchain-based information system may give the customers confidence that the product is genuine and of high quality and make them significantly more willing to purchase the manufactured item.

Academics and practitioners have advocated blockchain as the biggest innovation in computer science (Tapscott, 2016). The World Economic Forum (WEF, 2015) proposes blockchain to be among six computing "mega-trends" that are likely to shape the world in the coming decades. It is worth to consider the industrial advantages of blockchain application in key manufacturing supply chain activities. Researchers have begun to grapple with this nascent trend of blockchain deployment in different organizational objectives, and particularly the use of various information system architectures using blockchain technology in conjunction with other information technologies (IoT, Service Oriented Computing, and so on) for manufacturing business process automation.

ENTERPRISE INFORMATION SYSTEM ARCHITECTURE

Service oriented computing (SOC), and IoT applications are key technologies that will have a huge impact in the next decades for apparel manufacturing supply chain management. This section describes how SOC technology will improve efficiencies, providing new business opportunities, address regulatory requirements, and improve transparency and visibility of global apparel manufacturing activities.

The IoT systems allow capturing real-time manufacturing business processes data from plant-level operational environment. The enterprise architecture for distributed apparel manufacturing supply network used for current research is shown in Figure. 6. This architecture mainly consists of three layers: (i) IoT-based service, (ii) blockchain-based data controlling, and (iii) data storage and processing part.

Figure 6. Enterprise information system architecture for an apparel business

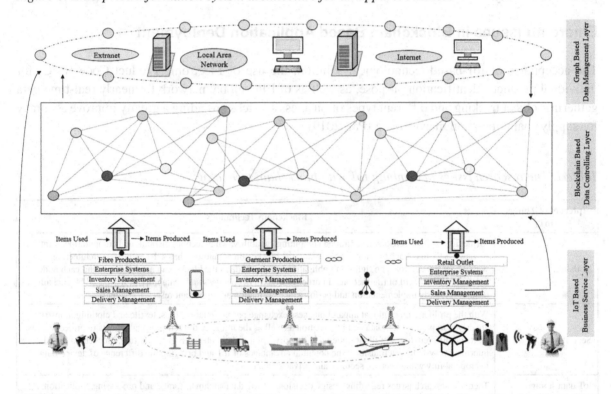

IoT-based Service Layer

The development of the IoT has created many devices, such as sensors, interconnected and interoperable devices for data collection and exchange. The data obtained from the IoT can make apparel manufacturing more convenient through numerous types of decision-making at all its levels and areas of apparel business activities.

Blockchain-based Data Controlling

The blockchain-based controlling part is a distributed database, which record transactions occurred in each period in blocks, chained using of cryptographic hashes. The reliability of such a structure comes from the fact that every transaction is approved by a consensus of the majority of nodes acting in the system. This prevents any single node or small group of nodes from tampering with data and ensures all and only valid transactions are recorded.

Data Storage and Processing

Apparel manufacturing and distribution chain nodes register as semantic-enabled agents in the blockchain. Tagged objects are registered as assets in the blockchain supported graph-based data storage and processing facility.

Emerging Issues in Blockchain Based Application Deployment

The acceptance of IoT-based technological solution, the use of Electronic Product Code (EPC) for individual products identification purpose, as well as of EPC global network for nearly real-time data gathering, object tracking and different types of business services providing a greatly improve accuracy for supply chain operation management (Pal, 2019).

Table 1. The research issues of combing IoT with blockchain technology

Internet of Things (IoT)	Blockchain Technology
Scalability	IoT devices such as sensors have limited computing capability, which is both difficult and computation point of view costly to enhance performance. Again, the blockchain technology has a decentralized architecture without central control. The rights and obligations of any node in the blockchain are the same, and each node has a complete record of transactions. In order to assess effectiveness and scalability of IoT-based blockchain technology, early implementation and performance evaluation are important research challenge.
Security	With the proliferation of global apparel business exchange partner relationships, textile and clothing industries are driven to protect their data and information as well as the integrity of their physical objects to protect against theft and different types of illicit trade including diversion and counterfeiting. In addition, blockchain-based information systems can transform the potential advantages of IoT and bridging the difference of device-data interoperability while keeping security and privacy intact.
IoT data storage	There are research issues regarding design decisions of IoT data streams, storage and processing applications.

Blockchain-based technologies allow for the decentralized aggregation of vast amounts of data generated from IoT devices and ensure that benefits are shared more equitably across supply chain exchange partners. Some of the research issues (e.g. scalability, security, and traceability) are highlighted in Table 1.

Blockchain facilitates machine-to-machine interaction where sensors and IoT devices attached to machinery will be synchronized, resulting in high flexibility and collaboration with exchange partners. The importance of this new capability lies in the secure communication, confidentiality, and integrity of the exchange transactions. Users can transact with the machine directly and engage in on-demand manufacturing services by sending transactions to a registered machine. Blockchain-based distributed ledgers that harness smart contracts enable the embedding of business logic covering a wide range of purposes such as payment conditions, product acceptance, smart inventory replacement, predictive maintenance, and repairs.

By combining blockchain technology and IoT, business information exchange partners gain new and timely insights into their supply chain in real-time with more precise and reliable information about key processes, events, and product attributes – such as quality, performance and availability. This fusion of IoT and blockchain technology can help to enhance end-to-end traceability and enable rapid recall capabilities of unsafe goods. As a result, exchange partners will be informed about the products, potential risks, and the preventative and corrective actions needed for sustaining enough flow of safe products to the final consumers.

RELATED RESEARCH WORKS

Academics and practitioners identified industrial business processes, particularly supply chain and logistics management, are important areas for deploying IoT based information system applications (Atkore, Iera & Morabito, 2018) (Gubbi et al., 2013). IoT based industrial information systems can enhance the competitiveness of enterprise through more effective tracking of the flow of raw materials, leading to improve the effectiveness and efficiencies of business processes (Shroud, Ordieres & Miragliotts, 2014). In the context of globalized business practice, with multiple collaborating-partners based supply chains, IoT-based applications enhance to facilitate the sharing of more precise and timely information relevant to production, quality control, distribution and logistics (Chen, Guo & Bao, 2014). However, researchers expressed their concern regarding standalone IoT-based applications along with global supply chain management (Pal, 2020). The main concerns were raised on the issues of standalone IoT systems security and privacy.

Different hybrid information system architectures (e.g. IoT with blockchain, cloud based IoT and blockchain technology) have been proposed by the research community. A blockchain enhances IoT-based applications tamper-resistant characteristics. In recent years, different blockchain-based information management systems have been reported by researchers. For example, IBM has developed a new blockchain-based service that is designed to track high-value items through complex supply chains in a secure cloud-based application system (Kim, 2016). Another exemplary industrial application is a fine-wine Provence-tracking service, known as the Chai Wine vault, developed by London-based Company Ever ledger (Finextra, 2016) in business-partnership with fine-wine expert Maureen Downey. Blockchain-based digital identification tools for physical property and packaging have been reported for enhancing high-value parts for supply chain management (Arrear, 2017). An innovative anti-counterfeit application, called Block Verify, is designed and deployed for tracking anti-counterfeit products (Hulse apple, 2015) to create a sustainable business world. A start-up company from Finland (i.e. Kouvola) in partnership with IBM, developed a smart tendering application for the supply chain management. The reported application is built on an automatic blockchain-based smart contract (Banker, 2016). Another blockchain-based smart contract, called SmartLog, the application was launched by Kouvola in recent years (AhIman, 2016).

In recent decades, due to globalization manufacturing supply chain networks are going through an evolutionary change through continued digitization of its business practices. These global manufacturing chains are evolving into value-creating networks where the value chain itself turns into an important source of competitive advantage. At the same time, developments are in progress to integrate blockchain technology with other innovative technological solutions (e.g. IoT-based applications, cloud-based solutions, and fog computing-based automation), leading to novel structures of modern apparel manufacturing supply chains, new types partnerships, holistic mechanisms of collaboration and value enhancing applications for the global apparel business. The reported research in this chapter is one of these values creating applications, which explains the adoption of IoT-based item description and use in blockchain infrastructure, in order to reap the combined advantages for future-generation apparel business supply chain management.

FUTURE RESEARCH DIRECTIONS

Beyond geographical boundaries, the combination of blockchain with IoT can be delayed by both regulatory uncertainties and the lack of industry standards. Although blockchain technology could enhance peer-to-peer connectivity between supply chain exchange partners, the integration of blockchain and IoT challenges some of the institutional assumptions common in international business. Indeed, harmonization (or 'equivalency' between sovereign states) of data protection laws remains a problem, while stronger industry self-regulation to govern and control the access to data and organize their transmission both nationally and globally is a requirement. It is still unclear how disparate blockchain technologies and systems will interoperate with each other and integrate with other technological artefacts. This is compounded by the existence of unreliable and inefficient transmission standards and protocols that clog the arteries of information sharing between the exchange partners. Additionally, an IoT environment is inherently dynamic, unpredictable and affected by the ever-changing laws and regulations related to security and other interoperability requirements. Such sudden variability and chaotic nature necessitate new laws and regulations in the manufacturing business world. In future, this research will review most of these challenges and will try bringing together potential solutions for naïve manufacturing operational managers.

CONCLUSION

Today's textile and clothing supply chain face significant volatility, uncertainty and complexity imposed by a dynamic operating environment. Changes in customer buying pattern – the demand for lower price, higher service levels, mobile commerce and so on – necessitate customer intelligence and varying fulfilment models. These have introduced significant stress on apparel manufacturing supply chain networks, compelling clothing businesses to revisit their supply chain design strategies. It includes the deployment of appropriate information systems that enhance supply chain execution. In such scenarios, enterprise information systems architecture plays a very important role.

This chapter presents a hybrid enterprise information systems architecture, which consists of IoT applications and a blockchain-based distributed ledger to support transaction services within-in a multi-party global apparel business network. The IoT is a smart worldwide network of interconnected objects, which through unique address schemes can interact with each other and cooperate with their neighbour to reach common goals. The data obtained from the IoT applications along apparel business processes can make operational decision-making much easier. However, standalone IoT application systems face security and privacy related problems.

Security and business organizational issues tend to enhance the need to build an apparel manufacturing supply chain management system leveraging blockchain ledger technology. Regardless of the particularities of the specific textile manufacturing supply chain related application, blockchain can offer a wide range of advantages. By registering and documenting a product's (e.g. cotton, fibre, textile cloths) lifecycle across the manufacturing supply chain nodes increases the transparency and the trust of the participating business-partners. Finally, the chapter presents the research proposition outlining how blockchain technology can impact important aspects of the IoT system and thus provide the foundation for future research challenges.

REFERENCES

AhIman. (2016). *Finish city partners with IBM to validate blockchain application in logistics*. https://cointelegraph.com/news/finish-city-partners-with-ibm-to-validate-blockchain-application-in-logistics

Atzori, L., Iera, A., & Morabito, G. (2010). The Internet of Things: A survey. *Computer Networks*, *54*(15), 2787–2805. doi:10.1016/j.comnet.2010.05.010

Banker, S. (2016). *Will blockchain technology revolutionize supply chain applications?* https://logisticsviewpoints.com/2016/06/20/will-block-chain-technology-revolutionize-supply-chain-applications/

Chen, I.-R., Guo, J., & Bao, F. (2014). Trust management for service composition in SOA-based IoT systems. *Proceedings of the IEEE Wireless Communications and Networking Conference (WCNC)*, 3444-3449.

Finextra. (2016). *Everledger secures the first bottle of wine on the blockchain*. https://www.finextra.com/pressaritcle/67381/everledger-secures-the-first-bottle-of-wine-on-the-blockchain

Gubbi, J., Buyya, R., Marusic, S., & Palaniswami, M. (2013). Internet of Things (IoT): A vision, architectural elements, and future directions. *Future Generation Computer Systems*, *29*(7), 1645–1660. doi:10.1016/j.future.2013.01.010

Hulseapple, C. (2015). *Block Verify uses blockchains to end counterfeiting and making world more honest*. https://cointelegraph.com/news/block-verify-uses-blockchains-to-end-counterfeiting-and-make-world-more-honest

Inera, A. (2017). *Bosch, Cisco, BNY Mellon, other launch new blockchain consortium*. https://www.reuters.com/article/us-blockchain-iot-idUSKBN15B2D7

Kim, N. (2016, July). IBM pushes blockchain into the supply chain. *Wall Street Journal*.

Nakamoto. (2008). *Bitcoin: A peer-to-peer electronic cash system*. Academic Press.

Pal, K. (2017). Supply Chain Coordination Based on Web Services. In H. K. Chan, N. Subramanian, & M. D. Abdulrahman (Eds.), *Supply Chain Management in the Big Data Era* (pp. 137–171). Hershey, PA: IGI Global Publication. doi:10.4018/978-1-5225-0956-1.ch009

Pal, K. (2019). Algorithmic Solutions for RFID Tag Anti-Collision Problem in Supply Chain Management. *Procedia Computer Science*, 929-934.

Pal, K. (2020). Internet of Things and Blockchain Technology in Apparel Supply Chain Management. In H. Patel & G. S. Thakur (Eds.), *Blockchain Applications in IoT Security*. Hershey, PA: IGI Global Publication.

Prahalad, C. K., & Mashelkar, R. A. (2010). Innovation's Holy Grail. *Harvard Business Review, July-August Issue*, 88(7/8), 132–141.

Shrouf, Mere, & Miragliotta. (2014). Smart factories in Industry 4.0: A review of the concept and of energy management approached in production based on the Internet of Things paradigm. *Proceedings of the IEEE International Conference on Industrial Engineering and Engineering Management*, 679-701.

Tapscott, D. (2016). *How will blockchain change banking? How won't it?* https://www.huffingtonpost.com/don.tapscott/how-will-blockchain-change_b_9998348.html

World Economic Forum. (2015). *Deep shift technology tipping points and societal impact survey report.* http://www3.weforum.org/docs/WEF_GAC15_Technological_Tipping_Points_report_2015.pdf

KEY TERMS AND DEFINITIONS

Block: A block is a data structure used to communicate incremental changes to the local state of a node. It consists of a list of transactions, a reference to a previous block and a nonce.

Blockchain: In simple, a blockchain is just a data structure that can be shared by different users using computing data communication network (e.g., peer-to-peer or P2P). Blockchain is a distributed data structure comprising a chain of blocks. It can act as a global ledger that maintains records of all transactions on a blockchain network. The transactions are time stamped and bundled into blocks where each block is identified by its *cryptographic hash*.

Cryptography: Blockchain's transactions achieve validity, trust, and finality based on cryptographic proofs and underlying mathematical computations between various trading partners.

Decentralized Computing Infrastructure: These computing infrastructures feature computing nodes that can make independent processing and computational decisions irrespective of what other peer computing nodes may decide.

Immutability: This term refers to the fact that blockchain transactions cannot be deleted or altered.

Internet of Things (IoT): The internet of things (IoT), also called the Internet of Everything or the Industrial Internet, is now technology paradigm envisioned as a global network of machines and devices capable of interacting with each other. The IoT is recognized as one of the most important areas of future technology and is gaining vast attention from a wide range of industries.

Provenance: In a blockchain ledger, provenance is a way to trace the origin of every transaction such that there is no dispute about the origin and sequence of the transactions in the ledger.

Supply Chain Management: A supply chain consists of a network of *key business processes* and facilities, involving end users and suppliers that provide products, services and information. In this chain management, improving the efficiency of the overall chain is an influential factor; and it needs at least four important strategic issues to be considered: supply chain network design, capacity planning, risk assessment and management, and performances monitoring and measurement. Moreover, the details break down of these issues need to consider in the level of individual business processes and sub-processes; and the combined performance of this chain. The coordination of these huge business processes and their performance improvement are the main objectives of a supply chain management system.

Warehouse: A warehouse can also be called storage area and it is a commercial building where raw materials or goods are stored by suppliers, exporters, manufacturers, or wholesalers, they are constructed and equipped with tools according to special standards depending on the purpose of their use.

Chapter 22
Developing Smart Buildings Using Blockchain, Internet of Things, and Building Information Modeling

Konstantina Siountri
University of Piraeus, Greece & University of the Aegean, Greece

Emmanouil Skondras
University of Piraeus, Greece

Dimitrios D. Vergados
University of Piraeus, Greece

ABSTRACT

Building information modeling (BIM) is a revolutionary technology that provides all the necessary mechanisms to achieve end-to-end communication, data exchange and information sharing between project actors, leading to smarter outcomes for communities and more efficient projects for AEC service providers. 3D models generated in the context of engaging in the BIM process and as-delivered physical assets through building management systems (BMS) adopt Internet of Things (IoT) architectures and services. However, the orchestration of IoT devices in a highly modular environment with many moving parts and inter-dependencies between the stakeholders of this environment, lead to many security issues. This article focuses on applying novel technologies in the construction industry, such as BIM, IoT, and Blockchain, but also on examining their interconnection and interoperability on a proposed system architecture on a case of a building (museum), where efficient security, management and monitoring are considered crucial factors for the unobstructed operation of the organization that hosts.

DOI: 10.4018/978-1-6684-7132-6.ch022

INTRODUCTION

The expansion of Information and Communication Technologies (ICT) has been proved to transform urban life, to build powerful, intelligent and smart industrial systems and applications, enabling people to improve their quality of life within the city environment. As a direct result of the digital revolution, current urban plans are transforming the vision of sustainable cities, which must meet not only economic and environmental indicators' requirements, but also make current technological developments easy to use and accessible to their residents.

The application of Internet of Things (IoT) and Digital Technologies in Smart Cities environment has been increased, providing new challenges in the new digital ecosystem (Ahlgren, Hidell, & Ngai, 2016), aiming to provide interconnection of smart devices, collect and process data from different environments and provide products and services to end users, application groups and sectors i.e. farms, government, transportation, health, cultural management etc. (Mehmood, Ahmad, Yaqoob, Adnane, Imran, & Guizani, 2017). Smart cities have been equipped with IoT platforms and various electronic devices, applying machine learning and AI algorithms and therefore becoming smarter and more efficient than before (Arasteh et al., 2016). However, building is the key element of a city and therefore remains the key element in a smart city ecosystem.

The Architecture, Engineering and Construction (AEC) industry has not embraced digital transformation with the same enthusiasm as other industries (e.g. such as manufacture industry). In the building sector, AEC industry consists of a high number of stakeholders that have been used to operate in the same way for decades and yet have not embraced digital transformation with the same enthusiasm as other industries (e.g. such as manufacture industry, aerospace industry or financial industry) (Woodhead, Stephenson, & Morrey, 2018). In fact, AEC is one of the least digitalized sectors and for many Economic Analysts this relates to the flat or falling productivity rates (E.U.B.I.M. Taskgroup, 2017). Nevertheless, the construction sector is strategically important to economies in terms of output and job creation. The European construction sector output of €1.3tn4 (trillion) is approximately 9% of the region's GDP and it employs over 18 million people. The failure to recognize the need to transform will put eventually at risk the sustainability of the "change resistant" construction companies.

To address this problem, during the last years, the construction industry is trying to transform by emerging technologies with great potential for the development of ICT, enabling new players to adapt and to take advantage of the opportunities that are emerging. Building Information Modeling (BIM) is a revolutionary technology that is characterized as the opportunity of the Architecture -Engineering - Construction (AEC) industry to move to the new digital era, with potential to reduce cost, project delivery time and increase productivity, as it provides automation capabilities for more integrated communication, data exchange and sharing between project actors within a virtual 3D environment (Gu, N., & London, K., 2010).

Beyond the smart devices and services that has been developed in a smart city, the documentation of the characteristics of a building, through Building Information Modeling (BIM) in combination with the collected data from smart devices and the intelligent applications developed, will be the basis of the IoT platforms and the provided services in the integrated digital ecosystem. The designed virtual models (produced by a BIM – Building Information Modeling – process) and as-delivered physical assets (monitored in real-time, i.e. through BMS – Building Management Systems) (Pasini et al., 2016) could adopt an IoT framework, which consists in a data model for network of equipment, sensors (building automation), wearables.

This convergence could improve a data-driven asset management, by enriching building information in operation and provide better services to users. However, there is a need to ensure predefined conditions, in order to reduce the probability of fraudulent activity throughout this supply chain. Although the communication infrastructure provides the desirable QoS (i.e. through the expansion of fiber optics networks, development of broadband wireless networks, wireless sensor networks (WSNs), 5G network technologies, modern short-range communication etc.), the application of the Blockchain will help to address the security issues in the BIM - IoT architecture (Akpakwu et al., 2017).

This study focuses on applying novel technologies in the construction industry such as the BIM, the IoT and the Blockchain, but also on examining their interconnection and interoperability. It is destined to enable new opportunities to new coming players in this industry, by allowing them to adapt and take advantage of the full potential that the construction sector can offer.

To this end, in the light of the already discussed obstacles and dilemmas that emerge in the construction sector, in this paper we are going to propose a system architecture that utilizes the Blockchain technology as a means to securely adapt in a BIM-based architecture coupled with an IoT. On the grounds of implementing the Blockchain technology in this system architecture, we delve into a use case on a museum building. Due to the special nature of museums (storage and protection of invaluable artifacts), where security, management and monitoring is of high importance, we are scrutinizing the scope of combining these three technologies, but also discuss on the overall performance of such a system architecture. In view of a growing trend of adopting the BIM technology worldwide that leads to the so-called city information modeling (CIM) (Correa, 2015), we will describe how the proposed architecture can serve the model of a Smart City.

The remainder of the paper is organized as follows: Firstly, the convergence of BIM, IoT and the Building as a Services (BaaS) model is described. Furthermore, the convergence of BIM and Blockchain technologies is mentioned. Subsequently, the proposed system architecture is presented, while a case study of a smart BIM-based museum is considered. Finally, the conclusions of the discussed work are described.

BIM, IOT AND BUILDING AS A SERVICE (BAAS) MODEL

Building Information Modeling (BIM)

Several definitions have been proposed for the BIM in the literature (Sanhudo et al., 2018; Volk, Stengel, & Schultmann, 2014). Indicatively, BIM is described as "a process involving the generation and management of digital representations of physical and functional characteristics of places" and the International Standardization Organization (ISO) as a "process or method of managing information related to facilities and projects to coordinate multiple inputs and outputs, using shared digital representations of physical and functional characteristics of any built object" (ISO, 2012).

The National Building Information Modeling Standards (NBIMS) committee of USA defines BIM as follows: "BIM is a digital representation of physical and functional characteristics of a facility. A BIM is a shared knowledge resource for information about a facility forming a reliable basis for decisions during its life cycle; defined as existing from earliest conception to demolition. A basic premise of BIM is collaboration by different stakeholders at different phases of the life cycle of a facility to insert, extract, update or modify information in the BIM to support and reflect the roles of that stakeholder" (National Institute of Building Sciences, 2015).

Although the concept of Building Information Modeling (BIM) is not new, as it has existed since the 1970s (Eastman, 1974), the last years several national-level initiatives around the world (Governments and public procurers) encourage the adoption of BIM technologies. For example, the European Commission through the EU BIM Task Group undertook the initiative to "encourage the common use of BIM, as 'digital construction', in public works with the common aim of improving value for public money, quality of the public estate and for the sustainable competitiveness of industry" (E.U.B.I.M. Taskgroup, 2017). This global trend is growing, indicating that BIM proves to be a real game changer bringing profound digital dividend and economic growth to the construction sector (around 15–25% savings to the global infrastructure market by 2025) (World Economic Forum, 2016).

BIM technology leads to accurate digital representation of constructions (any kind of constructions such us buildings, bridges, pipeline networks, etc.) by upgrading the computer aided design (CAD) systems into a project folder that includes many useful information for the entire life cycle of the project. The correct implementation and full exploitation of the BIM technology leads to the integrated design and implementation of construction projects with the direct result of higher quality results at a lower cost and in a shorter time.

In practice, BIM has rapidly grown from being a 3D model with three primary spatial dimensions (width, height, and depth) to a 4D BIM, where time (construction scheduling information) is added, and 5D BIM where cost information is linked to it (Gopalakrishnan, Agrawal, & Choudhary, 2017). The BIM model contains also non-geometric information, such as material for building components, i.e. weight, price, procedures, scale and size (Succar, 2009). It offers real-time data sharing and collaborative decision making the amongst various stakeholders, improves visualizations and simulations (i.e. early virtual prototyping etc.), reduces material and time waste and reduces costs due to better construction outcomes and higher predictability of performance.

The main components of BIM are the following:

- Visualization. It involves the 3D presentation of the construction projects through photorealistic design, allowing the use of technologies such as of virtual reality and augmented reality.
- Coordinated design. It concerns the possibility of simultaneous modifications (plans, facades, sections) and implementation of alternative scenarios when changes are required either in the design phase or during the construction or the operation of a built asset.
- Building object properties. It concerns the registration of all the characteristics of the building elements.
- Specifications. It concerns the interconnection of building elements with their specifications (eg technical, economic, environmental, legal, operational etc.).
- Information coordination. It concerns the interconnection of the design phase with the applicable regulations and implementation standards.
- Information flow. It refers to the possibility of extracting information into open standard formats to allow for the interoperability of software concerning building modeling.

The Levels of development (LoD) may vary, depending on the characteristics of the building, the objectives of the study, e.g. a simplified model with low geometric accuracy and a small amount of information can correspond to LoD 200. A model closest to reality but with a large deviation between virtual and real model may correspond to LoD 300. A detailed BIM model reproducing as much as possible more geometric abnormalities of the building and enriched by the maximum available information may correspond to LoD 400. LOD 500 is a field verified representation (i.e., as-built) in terms of size, shape, location, quantity, and orientation.

The data exchange is possible by shared neutral exchange formats, such as Industry Foundation Classes (IFC). IFC is "a common data schema developed by building SMART, recognized as ISO standard, which makes it possible to hold and exchange relevant data and information between project team members within a BIM environment and across BIM tools and platforms commonly used for design, construction, procurement, maintenance and operations" (BuildingSMART, 2011).

BIM and IoT

As the world experiences rapid urbanization, population growth and rapidly-ageing population (almost a quarter of our population being older than 60 within the next 30 years), cities have become the focal point for much of the research into the flow of information between the operational and capital asset construction workflows. Communities that meet the needs of citizens using a strategy that includes consuming, analyzing and using information about the natural and built environments in the decision-making process are termed smart communities.

An "as built - BIM model" that has been created according to several uses upon-agreed and various phases of the building process can lead to the life-long monitoring system of a construction, the Building Management System (BMS) (Pasini, Ventura, Rinaldi, Bellagente, Flammini, & Ciribini, 2016). Building Management Systems (BMS), also known as Building Automation Systems (BAS), are already known as network systems installed to control the functionality of individual pieces of building equipment.

Figure 1. The Building Management System (BMS)

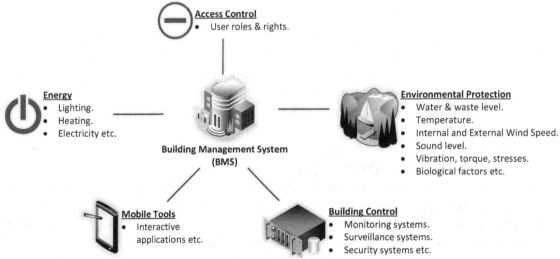

With the integration of BIM models, the quantity and the quality of information of each construction is expanded, making its monitoring more efficient. In Figure 1, a BMS architecture is presented where the system elements, such as the energy management, the access control, the environment protection, the building control, the mobile applications that are intended for the users are integrated on a 3D model of a building.

The utilization of BIM is going to grow bigger or become a formal licensing procedure in the future, which is destined to enable and control the digital model of each building and provide accountability about errors and inaccuracies. Taking responsibility for retrieving, storing, distributing or updating the relative information and ensuring its accuracy entails a great deal of risk (Azhar, S., Khalfan, M., & Maqsood, T., 2012).

Whilst a suggested development of BIM seems to be CIM - City Information Modeling that encompass an entire city (Figure 2), with the integration of Geographical Information Systems (GIS) and BIM, the framework concerning the storage and the processing of the upcoming big volume of BIM's data, is an important issue that needs to be taken into deep consideration. Cloud based solutions (Chen, Chang, & Lin, 2016; Gopalakrishnan, Agrawal, & Choudhary, 2017) seem to be an answer, but questions arise about the nature of this service, whether it is going to be governmental or private cloud.

Figure 2. The connection between Building Information Modeling (BIM) and City Information Modeling (CIM)

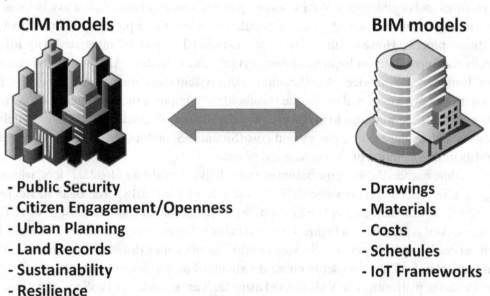

BIM and CIM tools are connected directly with the vision of Smart Cities planning and management, as CIM models can also join different systems and stakeholders and enables simulations that could help cities monitor water, energy, utilities, traffic, congestion, impact of natural disasters such as earthquakes or hurricanes, flood control, etc. (Figure 3), with data collected from IoT devices (Mahamadu, Mahdjoubi, & Booth, 2013). It may also provide spatial information about planning and investment, to help communities find ways to accommodate change and growth, while maintaining the health of citizens, business and environment.

Figure 3. The factors of the City Information Modeling (CIM)

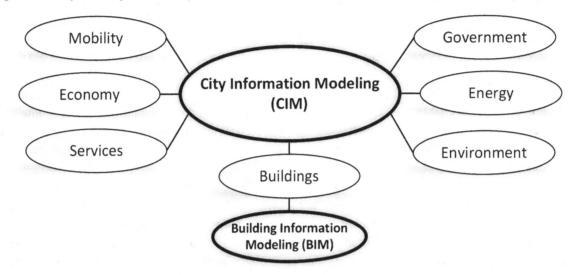

The Building as a Service (BaaS) Model

Nowadays, firms and organizations of AEC industry that design and build capital assets focus more on the ability to stay within the budgetary and schedule requirements on projects, without involving into the operational process. However, the delivery of "as-built BIM models" integrated with IoT technology unlocks the opportunity to implement new services and is leading AEC to new business models providing 'Buildings as a Service'. A collaborative data system that comes from a 3D geometry model with data retrieved by sensors will enable the stakeholders to improve the user interaction with services or facilities, to visualize warnings to maximize the performance of technological systems, define more efficiently control strategies, save energy and cost (Siountri, Skondras, & Vergados, 2018) and make future profits of the operation of the constructed projects.

This procedure enables the implementation of a new delivery model for cloud services, which is called Buildings as a Service (BaaS) (Woodhead, Stephenson, & Morrey, 2018). The BaaS model provides a fully visualized environment for implementation, deployment, maintenance and usage of ICT services into buildings. As it is presented in Figure 4, BaaS combines Infrastructure as a Service (IaaS), Platform as a Service (PaaS) and Software as a Service (SaaS) functionalities (Siountri, Skondras, & Vergados, 2018). In particular, IaaS lets the user to create a virtualized infrastructure consisted of several Virtual Machines (VMs) or platforms. The VMs created using IaaS are provided as PaaS to software developers along with the specific usage rights.

Subsequently, PaaS provides the appropriate components for the design, development and deployment of SaaS services. Also, SaaS provides cloud services to end-users. SaaS users cannot configure the source code of their services or control the underlying cloud infrastructure, since they are tasks accomplished from PaaS and IaaS, respectively.

Figure 4. The Building as a Service (BaaS) model architecture

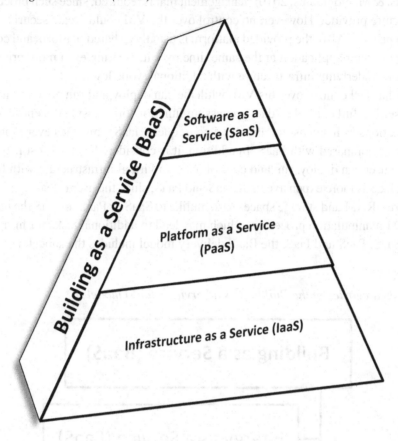

In general, the determination of the advantages and the disadvantages of each one of the SaaS, PaaS and IaaS delivery models is very useful, in order to provide a complete view of their functionalities. SaaS is the most cost-effective delivery model, since the user leases only the software that he uses and not the resources that host it. In addition, SaaS services are easy in use, as well as can be rapidly provided on-demand because they are already deployed to the cloud by their provider. Also, the user does not have to worry about the services management, as this is a provider's responsibility. On the other hand, user has no control neither over the application implementation and parameterization, nor on data processing functionalities. Also, the user has limited control over application deployment and upgrade processes, while integration with other user's software or systems is difficult, since such integration must be supported by the service provider.

PaaS is less cost effective in comparison to SaaS, while at the same time it is more cost effective than IaaS, as the user is leasing only the software platform (e.g. an Operating System installation) and not the entire infrastructure that hosts the platform. Unlike SaaS, user can deploy his own applications to run on the underlying platform and, thus, he has full control over the software that he runs. Therefore, the user has also full control over the rights of the users accessing his software as well as over the data processing functionalities inside his applications. Furthermore, the integration between user applications as well as with external systems can be done in application level, since user has full control over his applications source code. Also, another PaaS advantage is the minimal Virtual Machine (VM)

(Doukas, Pliakas, & Maglogiannis, 2010) management that is required, since such processes are handled by the infrastructure provider. However, no control over the VM could create security risks in terms of application data privacy. Also, the provided platform is usually a shared platform and could coexist with other users running their application at the same time over it, creating even more privacy risks as well as overloading the underlying infrastructure with additional workflows.

In IaaS, user has full control over his VM, while he can deploy and run anything he wants inside it. Furthermore, user has full control of data processing functionalities inside the entire VM and not only inside his applications as happens in PaaS. As a consequent, IaaS simplifies ever more the integration with other systems compared with PaaS. In addition, it is considered as the most privacy aware cloud service since the user can deploy, run and control his own virtual infrastructure with full control to his VMs. However, IaaS is more expensive than SaaS and PaaS, since the user is leasing physical resources, such as CPU cores, RAM and storage space. Also, unlike to SaaS or PaaS, in IaaS the user is responsible for the entire VM manipulation processes, which may lead to additional tasks for him.

Integrating SaaS, PaaS and IaaS, the BaaS delivery model includes the subcategories in Figure 5.

Figure 5. The subcategories of the Building as a Service (BaaS) model

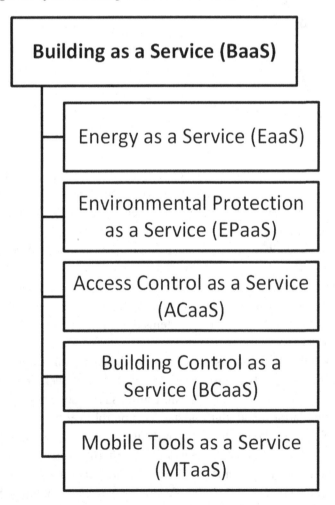

- Energy as a Service (EaaS): EaaS provides cloud services for the manipulation of the energy consumption of a building. The end-users of EaaS can configure factors that affect energy requirements of a building, including the lighting, the heating and the electricity.
- Environmental Protection as a Service (EPaaS): EPaaS provides the necessary cloud services in order to monitor the environmental conditions and factors that affect the condition of users and objects (equipment, facilities, furniture etc.) inside the building. Such factors include humidity level, waste level, temperature, sound level, vibration, torque, biological pollutants, as well as internal and external wind.
- Access Control as a Service (ACaaS): ACaaS defines the distinct user roles and the levels of accessibility in spaces, facilities and information. Each user obtains access to specific parts of a building, while at the same time he/she has specific and well-defined rights.
- Building Control as a Service (BCaaS): The BCaaS model provides the surveillance and security control of a building against human invasion, terrorism or natural disasters. Cameras, sensors and actuators can be used as auxiliary equipment. Indicatively, a cloud infrastructure can collect information about emergency situations and broadcast warning messages to administrators or users.
- Mobile Tools as a Service (MTaaS): The MTaaS model defines that users are registered to a centralized cloud manager, such as a Software Defines Network (SDN) controller (Fahmin et al., 2018; Huang et al., 2017; Yousaf et al., 2017). Subsequently, each user can retrieve data or interact with multimedia material about a specific geographic area or object of a building.

BIM and Blockchain

BIM modeling promotes collaboration, information sharing and data management between various stakeholders through a common working platform. The openness and high decentralization create uncertainties and therefore many security challenges and vulnerabilities arise (Mathews, Robles, & Bowe, 2017). These concerns are resulted by: a) data leaks and intellectual theft, b) the determination of roles and access privileges of each project member according to the level of Development (LOD) (Fathi et al., 2012) and c) the accountability about risks and errors in the processes.

The convergence of Cloud Computing, IoT and BIM leads to security dilemmas and considerations. In view of the multi-dimensional nature of security concerns, Blockchain is a possible solution to eliminate trust issues (Li, Greenwood, & Kassem, 2018), allowing security experts to immediately pinpoint where problems and deviations from normal behavior occurred in the BIM supply chain but also in the management and operation of the IoT architectural elements. Due to the usage of chain of blocks in the role of the distributed ledger and a highly effective consensus algorithm facilitating the synchronization of information amongst the stakeholders, this technology can be utilized for many purposes in the Building and Construction sector.

Thus, the integration of Blockchain in the processes of BIM, promise a completely secure and private environment to conduct business with full governance over the process. This technology enables proof-of-ownership (rights issues), proof-of-provenance (record keeping through a traceable immutable ledger) and reduction in human errors and deviations. It can either serve as an immutable way to store information and utilize it as a log, or it can be the origin system, where the deployment of smart contracts will be facilitated.

Moreover, as BIM-related data is expected to be stored over cloud storage for maintenance purposes in an accessible repository during the life cycle of a facility (Eastman, Teicholz, Sacks, & Liston, 2011) in a smart city content. By integrating multiple BIM models in a BMS, several security challenges arise. Given that the BIM model contains information both about the building architecture, but also its digital character, such the deployed communication and computer networks and devices at the edge such as sensors and actuators, it is critical to maintain control and governance over the sharing of this information. Therefore, appropriate security measures should be orchestrated, such as authorization and authentication mechanisms, end-to-end monitoring of communication amongst the sensors, IoT devices and the backbone infrastructure, perimeter defense systems on the backend infrastructure. Due to the heterogeneity of the network architecture and the complexity and variety of the communication protocols, the security measures are not compatibility amongst themselves all the time. Therefore, the blockchain technology is ideal for dealing with the issues of heterogeneity (Ammar, Russello, & Crispo, 2018).

Since utilizing BIM models in the construction, emerges the need for classification of information, partitioning and risk management, only among the right privileged stakeholders. The AEC companies and the City Urban Services (CUM) shouldn't have access to the data and assets management of a private property or a governmental institution during its life cycle. Therefore, the Blockchain is a necessity in keeping track that the privileges are assigned properly to the authorized individuals but also that they are enforced properly. This technology adds a complementary layer of security enabling control over the security processes and immediate response in the event of breach. Moreover, one major characteristic of the Blockchain paradigm is that tampering with its data isn't feasible. Therefore, transparency and verifiability are enabled improving the security level (Panarello, Tapas, Merlino, Longo, & Puliafito, 2018).

In our approach, Blockchain is considered to serve as a monitoring mechanism, collecting information about the activity of each sensor and system but also monitoring the actions that each individual implemented on the system such as accessing the system or processing the collected data. However, the Blockchain can serve many purposes concerning the security aspects such as monitoring mechanism but also as the base system deploying smart contracts for the purposes of construction among the stakeholders.

THE PROPOSED SYSTEM ARCHITECTURE

The proposed system architecture combines BIM, IoT and Blockchain, is related with the evolving role of smart buildings in an IoT environment and allows the efficient management of information of the building's components either regarding their structure or its users' behavior (access, movement, reaction, etc.). The use of Blockchain provides an additional layer of data security. Furthermore, the proposed scheme is generic and can be applied in various buildings' categories, public or private (e.g. museums, hospitals, ministries, industrial buildings, commercial buildings, institutions etc.) that are directly connected with services and human activities and are related with sensitive personal data i.e. patients, or valuable information about business or national interest. BIM and Blockchain technologies could prevent the unauthorized access to spaces or information and enable the secure storage and the management of data relating to building's operation, improving the provided IoT services.

As a use case, we consider a museum building, which by nature, is very sensitive from its construction up until its daily operation. This is happening due to the content of a museum, its exhibits. The operation and maintenance of a museum is of high importance due to the exhibition of tangible and intangible evidence of humans and their history. The exhibitions' environment is the building, where the storage, documentation and preservation of monumental objects takes place (Lewis, 2016).

Nowadays, museums require multiple administrative roles on the exhibition areas, the objects exposed in them, the security and the convenience of the visitors, the financial management of the tickets and the profits from museum shops, the workshops, the laboratories and the storage areas, which usually contain numerous artifacts of equal cultural value with the ones being exposed to public.

Finally, the museum's employees working for the management, protection, conservation and enhancement of spaces and exhibits play a critical role in guaranteeing the smooth and seamless operation of the organization.

The safekeeping and security of exhibit collections is the top priority of museums, which, unfortunately, sometimes isn't fulfilled. Failure of the top priority is occurred because of theft (i.e. the robbery of paintings valued at $500 million by Isabella Stewart Gardner Museum in 1990) or due to natural disasters (i.e. fire that destroyed the Brazilian National Museum in 2018).

Preventive Maintenance should consider the following threats (Michalski & Boylan, 2004):

1. Natural Factor: earthquakes, fire, floods, etc.
2. Environmental Factor: humidity, temperature, infrared radiation, atmospheric pollution, internal wind, level of sound, etc.
3. Biological Factor: action of microorganisms, plants, animals, insects, etc.
4. Human Activity: unauthorized access, false or inefficient documentation vandalism, bad cleaning processes, theft, warfare, etc.
5. Factors of deterioration of the building, damages, defective construction materials.

As far as it concerns the documentation of the collection, the data is relating with: i) the information of acquisition (valid title of ownership), ii) the id catalogue of the collection items (full identification and description, provenance, condition, treatment), iii) the location tracking of each item inside the museum (between the spaces of exhibition, the laboratories and the storage room), iv) the monitoring of the personnel access on the items and v) the procedures of loan to other museums (ICOM, 2014).

In a "smart museum", the correlation of content, time, space and human interaction is of great importance and the real-time monitoring of these events interacting along with fast response in case of a breach, can guarantee the security and safety of the museum's exhibits collection.

We have already mentioned that a virtual replica of a building during the construction process could be a useful management tool during its life cycle operating period. Moreover, BIM models could enable Public Services having access to city's building structural models, in order to face more efficiently natural disasters (i.e. fire, earthquakes, etc.) or control the energy consumption and the environmental footprint of its built stock. Since these models contain sensitive information about the buildings of a city, which can relate to constructional issues of buildings and urban planning, they should be stored to a Governmental Cloud. Although the system infrastructure of a Governmental Cloud is similar to other types of Cloud (e.g. Private Clouds), its administration mechanisms are considered as more appropriate for hosting data about buildings or critical infrastructures of a city. Specifically, a Governmental Cloud can ensure the privacy, the confidentiality and the integrity of the stored data, with respect to the security policies set by the administration of a city, preventing the exposure of sensitive information to malicious or unauthorized users. Furthermore, it should be noted that the security policies of a Governmental Cloud can continuously be updated considering the current legislation guidelines of a city, while this fact cannot be guaranteed in cases where non-Governmental Clouds are used.

Between BIM and BMS models, Blockchain technology could control the data access of a building (Figure 6). This system could allow the updates of information (i.e. in cases of renovations or reconstruction), but it could not allow unauthorized users retrieve information concerning the operation of a building (i.e. retrieve information about the position of sensors or cameras). An IoT platform could collect data a) of the behavior of museum users (personnel, visitors, administrators), b) of every action that happens to museum objects (devices, artifacts) and c) of the performance of every building component.

Figure 6. The proposed system architecture: The convergence of BIM, IoT and Blockchain

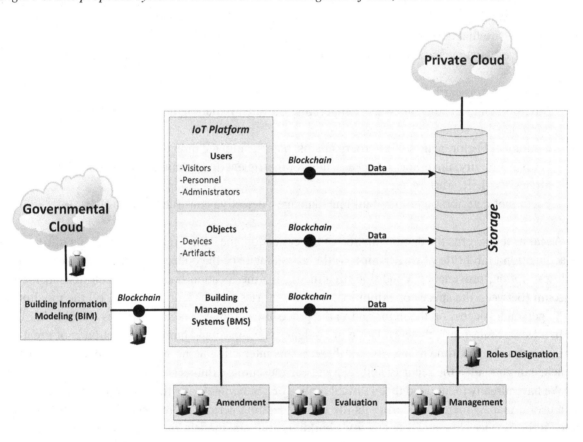

All this information could be retrieved from IoT systems and be recorded in a Blockchain (ICOM, 2014), before it is stored in a private cloud. The management and evaluation of data could be accessible only by the responsible administrators of the museum to move to the necessary amendments, systems adjustments, artifacts and personnel re-organization. This constant cycle of feedback and evaluation could help the administrators of a "smart" museum automatically identify anomalies in the process and could guarantee the safety of the exhibits and the services provided to users.

In our days, we consider smart devices and services as part of a smart city environment. Therefore, the BIM and CIM data can improve the IoT services and the Blockchain technology can assure the data integrity, preventing unauthorized users to retrieve information concerning the operation of a building, either private (private properties, firms, banks etc.) or public.

CONCLUSION

Smart communities need to be able to continuously adapt to provide the services that enhance quality life. Many of them realize that a more streamlined flow of information between operational and construction life cycle data will allow them to more accurately plan, fund and maintain community infrastructure assets. Based on this consideration, in this paper, the integration of Building Information Modeling (BIM) with Internet of Things (IoT) and Blockchain technologies has been analyzed, as they are considered as complementary developments that could collaborate enabling the secure storage and the management of data relating to building's operation, improving the provided IoT services. The use case of this architecture in a smart museum was analyzed due to its special characteristics. However, the proposed system architecture can be applied in several categories of public (e.g. hospitals, ministries) or private buildings, where efficiency of structures, safety of humans and assets, along with and the security of personal data is of a high importance. Thus, the convergence of BIM, IoT and Blockchain introduces an innovative application of the IoT and Blockchain in the AEC industry.

ACKNOWLEDGMENT

The publication of this paper has been partly supported by the University of Piraeus Research Center (UPRC).

REFERENCES

Ahlgren, B., Hidell, M., & Ngai, E. C. H. (2016). Internet of things for smart cities: Interoperability and open data. *IEEE Internet Computing*, 20(6), 52–56. doi:10.1109/MIC.2016.124

Akpakwu, G. A., Silva, B. J., Hancke, G. P., & Abu-Mahfouz, A. M. (2017). A survey on 5G networks for the Internet of Things: Communication technologies and challenges. *IEEE Access: Practical Innovations, Open Solutions*, 6, 3619–3647. doi:10.1109/ACCESS.2017.2779844

Ammar, M., Russello, G., & Crispo, B. (2018). Internet of Things: A survey on the security of IoT frameworks. *Journal of Information Security and Applications*, 38, 8–27. doi:10.1016/j.jisa.2017.11.002

Arasteh, H., Hosseinnezhad, V., Loia, V., Tommasetti, A., Troisi, O., Shafie-Khah, M., & Siano, P. (2016, June). Iot-based smart cities: a survey. *Proceedings of the 2016 IEEE 16th International Conference on Environment and Electrical Engineering (EEEIC)* (pp. 1-6). IEEE. doi:10.1109/EEEIC.2016.7555867

Azhar, S., Khalfan, M., & Maqsood, T. (2012). Building information modelling (BIM): Now and beyond. *Construction Economics and Building*, 12(4), 15–28. doi:10.5130/AJCEB.v12i4.3032

BuildingSMART (2011). Open Standards.

Chen, H. M., Chang, K. C., & Lin, T. H. (2016). A cloud-based system framework for performing online viewing, storage, and analysis on big data of massive BIMs. *Automation in Construction*, 71, 34–48. doi:10.1016/j.autcon.2016.03.002

Correa, F. R. (2015). Is BIM Big Enough to Take Advantage of Big Data Analytics? *Proceedings of the International Symposium on Automation and Robotics in Construction* (Vol. 32). IAARC Publications.

Doukas, C., Pliakas, T., & Maglogiannis, I. (2010). *Mobile healthcare information management utilizing Cloud Computing and Android OS. Proceedings of the 2010 Annual International Conference of the IEEE Engineering in Medicine and Biology* (pp. 1037–1040). IEEE; . doi:10.1109/IEMBS.2010.5628061

Eastman, C. (1974). An Outline of the Building Description System.

Eastman, C., Teicholz, P., Sacks, R., & Liston, K. (2011). *BIM handbook: A guide to building information modeling for owners, managers, designers, engineers and contractors*. John Wiley & Sons.

Fahmin, A., Lai, Y. C., Hossain, M. S., & Lin, Y. D. (2018). Performance modeling and comparison of NFV integrated with SDN: Under or aside? *Journal of Network and Computer Applications*, *113*, 119–129. doi:10.1016/j.jnca.2018.04.003

Fathi, M. S., Abedi, M., Rambat, S., Rawai, S., & Zakiyudin, M. Z. (2012). Context-aware cloud computing for construction collaboration. *Journal of Cloud Computing*, (1).

Gopalakrishnan, K., Agrawal, A., & Choudhary, A. (2017). Big Data in Building Information Modeling Research: Survey and Exploratory Text Mining. *MOJ Civil Eng.*, *3*(6).

Gu, N., & London, K. (2010). Understanding and facilitating BIM adoption in the AEC industry. *Automation in Construction*, *19*(8), 988–999. doi:10.1016/j.autcon.2010.09.002

Heiskanen, A. (2017). The technology of trust: How the Internet of Things and blockchain could usher in a new era of construction productivity. Construction Research and Innovation, 8(2), 66–70. doi:10.1 080/20450249.2017.1337349

Huang, C. M., Chiang, M. S., Dao, D. T., Pai, H. M., Xu, S., & Zhou, H. (2017). Vehicle-to-Infrastructure (V2I) offloading from cellular network to 802.11 p Wi-Fi network based on the Software-Defined Network (SDN) architecture. Vehicular Communications, 9, 288–300. doi:10.1016/j.vehcom.2017.03.003

ICOM. (2014). *Environmental Guidelines ICOM-CC and IIC Declaration. International committee for Documentation*. Standards-Guidelines.

ISO. (2012). Framework for building information modelling (BIM) guidance, ISO/TS 12911:2012.

Lewis, G. (2016). The ICOM Code of Ethics for Museums: Background and objectives. In Museums, Ethics and Cultural Heritage (pp. 67-75). Routledge.

Li, J., Greenwood, D., & Kassem, M. (2018). *Blockchain in the built environment: analysing current applications and developing an emergent framework*. Diamond Congress Ltd.

Mahamadu, A. M., Mahdjoubi, L., & Booth, C. (2013, December). Challenges to BIM-cloud integration: Implication of security issues on secure collaboration. *Proceedings of the 2013 IEEE 5th International Conference on Cloud Computing Technology and Science* (Vol. 2, pp. 209-214). IEEE.

Mathews, M., Robles, D., & Bowe, B. (2017). BIM+ blockchain: A solution to the trust problem in collaboration?

Mehmood, Y., Ahmad, F., Yaqoob, I., Adnane, A., Imran, M., & Guizani, S. (2017). Internet-of-things-based smart cities: Recent advances and challenges. *IEEE Communications Magazine*, *55*(9), 16–24.

Michalski, S., & Boylan, P. J. (2004). Care and preservation of collections. In *Running a museum: a practical handbook* (pp. 51–90). Academic Press.

National Institute of Building Sciences. (2015). *National Building Information Modeling Standard*. NBIMS.

Panarello, A., Tapas, N., Merlino, G., Longo, F., & Puliafito, A. (2018). Blockchain and iot integration: A systematic survey. *Sensors (Basel)*, *18*(8), 2575. doi:10.339018082575

Pasini, D., Ventura, S. M., Rinaldi, S., Bellagente, P., Flammini, A., & Ciribini, A. L. C. (2016). Exploiting Internet of Things and building information modeling framework for management of cognitive buildings. *Proceedings of the 2016 IEEE International Smart Cities Conference (ISC2)*. IEEE. doi:10.1109/ISC2.2016.7580817

Redmond, A., Hore, A., Alshawi, M., & West, R. (2012). Exploring how information exchanges can be enhanced through Cloud BIM. *Automation in Construction*, *24*, 175–183. doi:10.1016/j.autcon.2012.02.003

Sanhudo, L., Ramos, N. M., Martins, J. P., Almeida, R. M., Barreira, E., Simões, M. L., & Cardoso, V. (2018). Building information modeling for energy retrofitting–A review. *Renewable & Sustainable Energy Reviews*, *89*, 249–260. doi:10.1016/j.rser.2018.03.064

Siountri, K., Skondras, E., & Vergados, D. D. (2018, October). A Delivery Model for Cultural Heritage Services in Smart Cities Environments. *Proceedings of the Euro-Mediterranean Conference* (pp. 279-288). Cham: Springer. doi:10.1007/978-3-030-01765-1_31

Succar, B. (2009). Building information modelling framework: A research and delivery foundation for industry stakeholders. *Automation in Construction*, *18*(3), 357–375. doi:10.1016/j.autcon.2008.10.003

Taskgroup, E. U. B. I. M. (2017). *Handbook for the introduction of building information modelling by the European public sector*. Academic Press.

Volk, R., Stengel, J., & Schultmann, F. (2014). Building Information Modeling (BIM) for existing buildings—Literature review and future needs. *Automation in Construction*, *38*, 109–127. doi:10.1016/j.autcon.2013.10.023

Woodhead, R., Stephenson, P., & Morrey, D. (2018). Digital construction: From point solutions to IoT ecosystem. *Automation in Construction*, *93*, 35–46. doi:10.1016/j.autcon.2018.05.004

World Economic Forum. (2016). Shaping the Future of Construction.

Yousaf, F. Z., Bredel, M., Schaller, S., & Schneider, F. (2017). NFV and SDN—Key technology enablers for 5G networks. *IEEE Journal on Selected Areas in Communications*, *35*(11), 2468–2478. doi:10.1109/JSAC.2017.2760418

This research was previously published in the International Journal of Interdisciplinary Telecommunications and Networking (IJITN), 12(3); pages 1-15, copyright year 2020 by IGI Publishing (an imprint of IGI Global).

Chapter 23

Composite Identity of Things (CIDoT) on Permissioned Blockchain Network for Identity Management of IoT Devices

Anang Hudaya Muhamad Amin
ⓘ https://orcid.org/0000-0002-2010-9789
Higher Colleges of Technology, UAE

Nabih T. J. Abdelmajid
Higher Colleges of Technology, UAE

Fred N. Kiwanuka
Higher Colleges of Technology, UAE

Saif Hamad AlKaabi
Higher Colleges of Technology, UAE

Sultan Khalid Abdulqader Rashed Ahli
Higher Colleges of Technology, UAE

ABSTRACT

Internet of things (IoT) is in the forefront of many existing smart applications, including autonomous systems and green technology. IoT devices have been commonly used in the monitoring of energy efficiency and process automation. As the application spreads across different kinds of applications and technology, a large number of IoT devices need to be managed and configured, as they are capable of generating massive amount of sensory data. Looking from this perspective, there is a need for a proper mechanism to identify each IoT devices within the system and their respective applications. Participation of these IoT devices in complex systems requires a tamper-proof identity to be generated and stored for the purpose of device identification and verification. This chapter presents a comprehensive approach on identity management of IoT devices using a composite identity of things (CIDoT) with permissioned blockchain implementation. The proposed approach described in this chapter takes into account both physical and logical domains in generating the composite identity.

DOI: 10.4018/978-1-6684-7132-6.ch023

1. INTRODUCTION

The rapid growth in the development of Internet-of-Things (IoT) has led to an increase in its utilization for smart applications. In green technology, IoT is becoming a forefront in the monitoring of energy efficiency and process automation. In a complex monitoring systems such as smart building and smart factory, large number of IoT devices need to be managed and configured. In addition, these devices are used in different kinds of integrated applications that could generate massive amount of sensory data. As such, there is a need for a proper mechanism to identify each IoT devices within the system and their respective applications. Participation of these IoT devices in complex-systems requires a tamper-proof identity to be generated and stored for the purpose of device identification. In addition, having an effective identity management mechanism of IoT devices would enable us to eliminate the possibility of identity spoofing and presence of rogue devices in the system. This perhaps could be achieved through integrating multiple information that defines the physical and logical identity of the devices.

With the advent in the field of process automation, Industrial process control and monitoring is a vital task that has been carried out by networks of Internet-of-Things (IoT). Critical event such as a surge in the electrical current or sudden increase in the temperature of boiler could be detected and monitored seamlessly. Rapid growth in the utilization of IoT in smart applications have continuously expand the IoT deployment in large-scale networks.

Sustainability is the key consideration for IoT deployments in smart applications. According to Mahadi et al. (Abu Hassan et al., 2018), there are four important factors that influence the sustainability of IoT usage in smart applications, namely performance expectancy, effort expectancy, social influence, and facilitating conditions. These four factors are derived from the Unified Theory of Acceptance and Use of Technology (UTAUT), as described in (Venkatesh et al., 2003).

There are numerous examples of IoT implementations for smart applications, including the works by Jain et. al. (Jain et al., 2019) in smart foundry and Catarinucci et. al. (Catarinucci et al., 2015) in their works on IoT-aware smart healthcare system. Apart from these initiatives, there are a number of IoT deployments focusing on enhancing and improving existing green technology applications. These can be seen from the works carried out by Garcia et. al. (Garcia et al., 2018) in wireless sensor network (WSN) based monitoring scheme for green technology, and IoT-based smart agriculture by Gondchawar and Kawitkar (Gondchawar & Kawitkar, 2016).

Our particular interest in IoT deployment for smart applications is in the smart building monitoring and management. Smart building usually comprises of different types of IoT devices and different kinds of applications. Rapid advances in different kinds of technology, including IoT, data analytics, and machine learning has risen up the demands for smart-building applications. There are different types of smart building applications ranging from smart office, smart library, smart home, and smart facilities. The benefits of having smart systems in building and infrastructure management is such that it helps in ensuring reduction in the amount of wasted energy used, as well as improved resource utilization.

Smart building applications typically consist of five components as described by Qolomany et. al (Qolomany et al., 2019). Figure 1 shows the composition of these components, which include sensors and actuators, smart control devices, software platform, networking and communication, and HVAC system. Integration of these components is essential in ensuring smooth execution of the applications.

An important aspect of smart building management is to ensure the safety and security of interconnected devices, users, and the applications. Security is an important aspect in smart building applications as its breach impact to the physical objects tend to be at a larger scale since it can directly affects our physical environment. For instance, if a hacker can hack into the smart air-conditioning device, they can simply manipulate the temperature control for the building. Some of the important works in ensuring the safety and security of IoT devices in smart building applications can be seen through the works of Bandara et al. (Bandara et al., 2016) and Hernandez-Ramos et al. (Hernández-Ramos et al., 2015) on secure access control framework for API-enabled devices.

Apart from access control, another important security measure to be considered is the identity management of IoT devices in smart building applications. Device identity plays an important role in ensuring the system is secure from identity spoofing and the existence of rouge devices as described by Zhang et al (Zhang et al., 2015). With increasing number of devices that take part in smart building systems, the need for a tamper-proof identity management is essential. In addition, our hypothesis is such that device identity management should also incorporate information related to different kinds of applications commonly accessing the devices, as well as the information on users accessing data from these devices. With this composite information, the device identity could be further strengthened by adding multiple contextual information into it.

In this chapter, we present a comprehensive approach on identity management of IoT devices using a composite Identity-of-Things (CIDoT) with permissioned blockchain implementation. Our proposed approach takes into account both physical and logical domains in generating the composite identity. The logical domain also include the respective application that utilizes the IoT device, either for sensory data acquisition or process automation. We propose the use of permissioned blockchain for identity storage and verification, which enables the identity to be immutable. For simulation purposes, we will demonstrate the use of CIDoT in the smart building application. The proposed identity management would enable the system owner to acquire a holistic view of the IoT device identity from the infrastructure and application perspectives.

Figure 1. Smart building components

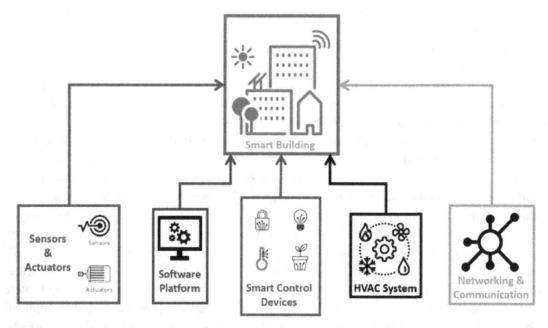

The outline of this chapter is as follows: Section 2 will present some of the reviews on the current works related to IoT device identity. Section 3 will be focusing on the theoretical foundation for composite identity for devices, from the context of smart building applications. In section 4, we delve into the possibility of incorporating IoT data in a blockchain network, by looking into some existing works in IoT-blockchain implementations. We will also explore the potential of blockchain for IoT identity management. Section 5 presents the proposed framework for composite identity-of-things on IoT-Blockchain network for smart building applications. Discussions on the underlying structure of the proposed framework will be presented. Finally, Section 6 provides a conclusion for this chapter.

2. IOT AND IDENTITY

IoT network usually comprises of different types of sensors and processing devices that are connected over a communication network. A typical structure of IoT network comprises of heterogeneous devices as described by Sethi and Sarangi (Sethi & Sarangi, 2017) can be visually represented as layers as shown in Figure 2.

Figure 2. Layered representation of IoT Network

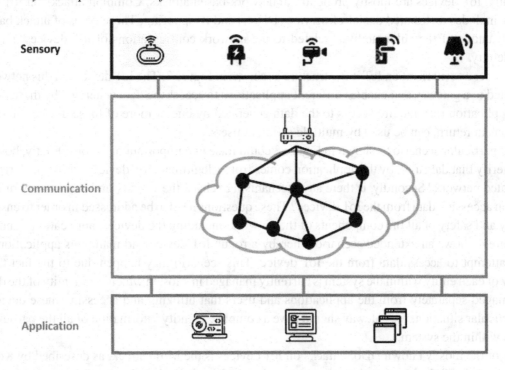

The sensory layer is basically the physical layer, which contains sensors used to sense and gather information about the environment. The communication layer is responsible for connecting to other smart things, network devices, and servers. Finally, the application layer deals with the process of delivering application specific services to the user.

The existence and introduction of IoT devices enables seamless integration between physical and cyber world (Wang, 2018). In this particular circumstance, it makes the physical world easier to be attacked through the cyber world. A malicious instruction or execution of code from the cyber world can cause serious damage in the physical world, and thus, IoT security issues should be handled carefully and effectively. Tackling security issues related to IoT devices requires specific measures, due to several distinct properties such as resource-constrained end-devices, high privacy requirements, heterogeneous devices and communications, and trust management.

An important security aspect in relations to IoT devices is their identity. With common heterogeneity and mobility features of IoT devices, identity requires a more dynamic management approach. According to Mahalle et. al. (Mahalle et al., 2010), with IoT devices, addressing identity problem requires changes to the architecture for naming, addressing, and discovery. These changes are essential as to be capable of managing different forms of communications and systems integration. The term Identity-of-Things (IDoT) as discussed by Lam and Chi (Lam & Chi, 2016), basically extends the functionality of existing identity and access management (IAM) models by considering logical and physical identity of devices based upon several distinctive attributes and different kinds of authentication approaches.

2.1. Attacks on IoT Device Identity

Generally, IoT devices are mostly prone to the network-based attacks. Common attacks on IoT device identity includes distributed denial-of-service (DDoS) and IP spoofing. These types of attack basically take advantage of the vulnerabilities related to the network configurations of ioT devices, including their identity.

Consider a scenario of an IoT infrastructure as shown in Figure 3. The IoT devices in this network are connected to a gateway that enables different applications to access the data generated by these devices. Each application may require access to the data generated by one or more of these devices. These applications in return, can be used by multiple different users.

This particular scenario as shown in Figure 3 could raise two important questions: Firstly, how users could verify that data used by the application comes from a legitimate IoT devices within the large-scale distributed network? Secondly, is there any mechanism to check the validity and authenticity of the application accessing data from the IoT devices? These questions need to be addressed in order to ensure the security and safety of all the components of the network, including the devices, applications, and users.

Figure 4 shows an extended scenario whereby a rogue IoT device and malicious application exist, which attempt to access data from the IoT device. This scenario may happen due to the fact that the identity of each entity within the system is currently managed in silos, in which the identity of the devices are managed separately from the applications and users that utilizing and accessing these devices. In this particular situation, the gateway should have a complete identity information of all the participating entities within the system.

One of the mostly known DDoS attacks on IoT devices is the Mirai attack, as described by Kolias et al (Kolias et al., 2017). Mirai exploits the insecure IoT devices through their open Telnet ports. It scanned big blocks of the internet for open Telnet ports, then uses default username/password combinations in attempt to log in. The attack was able to amass a botnet army. Figure 5 shows the Mirai attack mechanism.

Figure 3. Common infrastructure for IoT system with connected devices, applications, and users

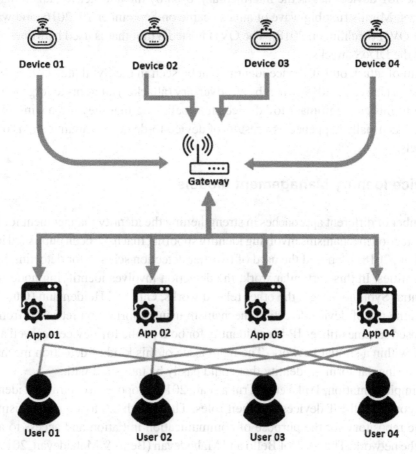

Figure 4. Presence of rouge device and malicious application that can compromise the IoT network and related applications

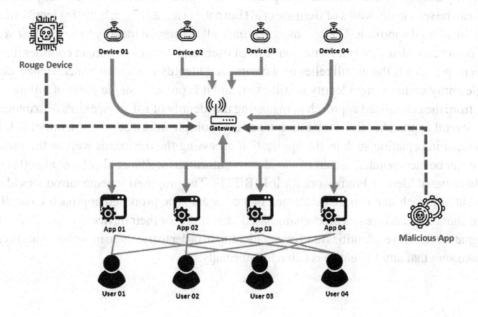

In this attack, IoT devices act as the intermediary, used by the attacker to launch massive attack on a particular target. Mirai's first big wave of attacks came on September 19, 2016, and was used against the French host OVH (Fruhlinger, 2018). The OVH hosted a tool that is used by Minecraft server hosts to fight against the DDoS attacks.

Another form of attack on IoT device identity can be seen in the Sybil attack. A Sybil attack as described by Jan et. al (Jan et al., 2015) whereby an adversary (attacker) attempts to forge multiple identities at a given time to mislead legitimate IoT devices into believing that they are having many neighbors. This kind of attacks usually happened as a results of device-to-device communications over error-prone wireless channels.

2.2. IoT Device Identity Management Models

There are a number of different approaches in strengthening the identity management for IoT devices, as well as attack detection mechanisms involving identity spoofing that have been published in the literature. Jan et al (Jan et al., 2018) proposed the used of two-tier detection scheme for detecting Sybil nodes and their forged identities. In this particular work, the detection involves identifying nodes that exert high energy as potential Sybil nodes. On the other related works, Guo and Heidemann (Guo & Heidemann, 2018) proposed the use of device detection mechanism using information retrieved from the IP traffic flow. The proposed scheme utilizes IP-based identity for both public IoT devices, as well as other devices that are located within a similar network. The main issue of this kind of detection mechanisms is such that it relies on a singular form of identity that could easily be tampered with.

In different implementation, Trnka et al (Trnka et al., 2018) proposed a centralized identity repository that hold the records of all IoT devices and their roles. The OAuth 2.0 token mechanism was used and governed by the repository for the purpose of communication initiation and access to all the services offered within the network. The work of Bello and Mahadevan (Bello & Mahadevan, 2019) is also focusing on centralized conceptual cloud-based identity management framework, which is based on a cloud management model for IoT device identity.

An identity management model that incorporates both logical (application/user) and physical (device) identities can be seen in the works of Bernabe et al (Bernabé et al., 2017) on holistic identity management using a claims-based approach. The proposed approach allows partial identity to be used for verification, allowing personally identifiable information (PII) of users and devices to remain confidential. A limitation of such approach is that it still relies on a centralized identity credential issuer. Hence, dependency on a single entity in managing identity is still exist, and it is prone to single point of failure.

Apart from the centralized approach in managing the identity of IoT devices in a distributed network, there are several approaches that look into integrating multiple information as identity for IoT devices. The additional information such as the application accessing the device, as well as the user/owner of the device can be incorporated as part of the identity information. Zhu et al (Zhu et al., 2017) proposed a Blockchain-based Identity Framework for IoT (BIFIT). The proposed scheme introduces identity self-management approach that can be performed by end users. The proposed approach basically extracts the device signatures and creates blockchain-based identifiers for their device owners. It also correlates device signature (low level identities) and owner identity in order to use them in authentication credentials and to make sure that any IoT entity is behaving normally.

In this chapter, we will explore the possibility of creating and using a composite identity as the identity model for IoT devices in a distributed network. The hypothesis is such that adding more information will basically strengthen the identity credentials for IoT devices. In the following section, we will describe the theoretical foundation for the proposed composite identity of IoT devices.

3. COMPOSITE IDENTITY: A THEORETICAL PERSPECTIVE

The notion of composite identity is increasingly adapted by different kinds of applications that usually being deployed in a distributed network. For instance, Singi et al (Singi et al., 2019) introduces the composite identity framework for global distributed software delivery. The common hypothesis of the use of composite identity in identifying object or element is such that it strengthens the identity against potential attacks like identity spoofing and forged identity.

Our definition of composite identity is a composition of multiple identity elements that builds up a single main identity of a particular IoT device. Composite identity basically incorporates multiple identifiable information that distinctively represent a device and its related applications or operations. Having composite identity enables clear verification and authentication of devices, similar to how individuals are verified using multiple identity elements (ID card and fingerprint). Figure 5 shows the composite identity for IoT devices.

The composite identity *ID* for a given device *x* can be represented in the following equation:

$$ID_x = \{\alpha_n\}; \ 1 \leq n \leq m \tag{1}$$

Whereby α_n is an identity element within the m composition.

Collectively, for a system with *X* number of devices x_i where $1 \leq i \leq X$, there exists (n) composite identities each with a unique identifier ID_x. The composite identity is defined by a set of *m* identity elements αn as defined in Equation 2.

$$x_i \leftarrow ID_i \leftarrow \alpha_{in}; \ \text{for} \ 1 \leq n \leq m, \ 1 \leq i \leq X \tag{2}$$

From this representation, we can observe that there are two important factors that contribute to the size of the composite identity, namely the number of IoT devices and the number of identity elements that are incorporated into the device identity. Figure 6 and 7 shows the projected growth in terms of the size of the identity with increasing number of identity elements and the number of IoT devices within the network.

A definition of composite identity is basically a combination of different identity elements that builds up a single main identity of a particular IoT device. Composite identity can provide a complete view of known identity including its applications and operations by incorporating multiple identifiable information that clearly represent a device. By implementing composite identity, we enables clear verification of devices, in a similar way on how individuals are verified using multiple identity elements (ID card and fingerprint).

In considering the identity elements for composite identity, two important domains are taken into account as previously shown in Figure 5, namely device and application domains. Each domain consists of a number of identity elements. Note that both logical and physical identity are being considered. For example, in the device domain, we considered both device addresses (IP address – logical) and MAC address – physical) as identity elements in the composite identity. On the application domain, the application identifier, such as the software license and the user ID can be used as the identity elements in the composition.

Based on the projected trends, one of the key important issue to be considered in implementing composite identity for IoT devices is the network storage capacity to accommodate huge amount of identity elements for all the devices within the network. To address this particular issue, we propose the use of distributed storage in a form of distributed ledger within a permissioned blockchain network.

Blockchain is a distributed ledger technology that enables secure and tamper-proof data transactions through its smart contract implementations. In the following section, we will further discuss the implementation of blockchain network for distributed data storage in IoT network. We will delve into the possibility of implementing a permissioned blockchain scheme for IoT device identity management.

Figure 5. Identity elements that comprise the composite identity for IoT device.

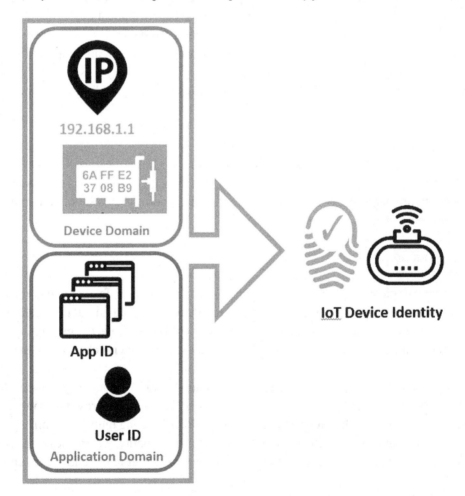

Figure 6. Growth trend in the number of identity element data per network for increasing number of devices in a network

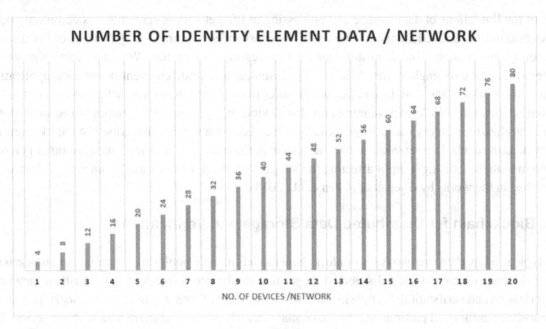

Figure 7. Growth trend for the number of identity elements per network with increasing number of identity elements per identity for the entire network

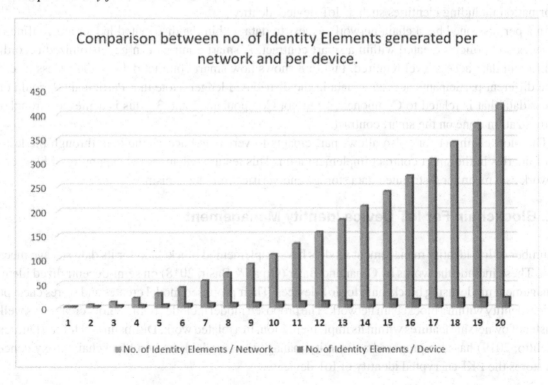

4. IOT AND BLOCKCHAIN

One of the limitations of data storage and processing in IoT network is such that it is commonly being conducted in a centralized manner. A typical IoT network infrastructure usually consists of IoT devices, a gateway, and a centralized repository for data processing and storage. With this particular system design, it is prone to single point-of-failure. For instance, a centralized event monitoring application, such as the works of Jan et al. (Jan et al., 2018) suffer from several drawbacks when applied to the IoT-related applications. With massive number of IoT devices in a network, the amount of transmitted data to a centralized repository can be significantly increased. As a result connection bottleneck from IoT network to the central server could cause the system performance to be deteriorated. Another potential problem with the existing setup is affecting the integrity of event data obtained from the IoT devices, as described in the works by Chen et al (Chen et al., 2018).

4.1. Blockchain for Distributed Data Storage and Verification

In a typical setup, there are two types of blockchain models namely public and permissioned blockchain. Public blockchain consists of a distributed ledger that can be accessible by anyone, without any prior authorization and verification. Permissioned blockchain on the other hand, is a form of blockchain model comprises of authorized participants that can collaboratively access and share data within a secure data network. The benefit of implementing permissioned blockchain for distributed data storage and verification is that it allows data to be shared and replicated in a secure form with consensus, provenance, immutability, and finality (Andolfatto, 2018). Consequently, this model can be useful in securing critical information including identities such as IoT device identity.

In a permissioned blockchain network, access to data within the distributed ledger are confined by the rules and policies created within a smart contract. A smart contract can be customized according to different data access level required. Figure 8 shows how smart contract defines the access level for three different participants accessing data in the distributed ledger. Note that Participant A could only access data that is related to Component 1 but not Components 2 and 3. This is achieved through the customization done on the smart contract.

The blockchain network also allows participants to verify and access the data through predefined set of queries in the smart contract implementation. This feature enhances the capability of blockchain network as a mean for distributed data storage and verification mechanism.

4.2. Blockchain For IoT Device Identity Management

A number of IoT identity management models have implemented blockchain for its data storage mechanism. These include the works by Omar and Basir (Omar & Basir, 2018) on semi-decentralized identity management model using blockchain for IoT devices. Their proposed model creates and stores encrypted device identity within a blockchain network. The proposed model includes both identity creation as well as transfer of ownership features within its implementation. In a related work, Dittmann and Jelitto(Dittmann & Jelitto, 2019) has also proposed an identity management model based on blockchain proxy concept that stores the PKI-encrypted identity of IoT devices.

Figure 8. Smart contract defines the access to data that resides on the distributed ledger within the blockchain network

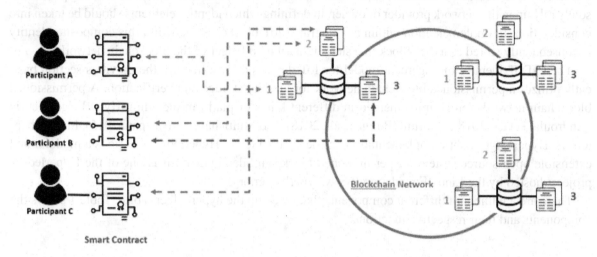

Beside identity management, implementation of blockchain can also be seen in the access control management for IoT devices. Xu et al (Xu et al., 2018) has proposed a blockchain-enabled decentralized capability-based access control for IoT devices. The implementation model being proposed includes a robust identity-based capability token management strategy that utilizes a smart contract for registration, propagation and revocation of the access authorization. In another related work, Guin et al (Guin et al., 2018) has also proposed the use of blockchain network to authenticate resource-constrained IoT devices using identities generated by SRAM-based physically unclonable functions (PUFs) in order to minimize the impact of the attacks conducted by rogue devices.

The related works discussed in this section have so far been focusing on the IoT device identity management, without extending its consideration on the applications and the users that utilizing these devices. It is also important to take into account these factors as they are highly related to the IoT devices being used in the network. In addition, both logical and physical identity of IoT devices, incorporating the

User and/or application information that are linked to these devices should be considered. With such approach, we expand the spectrum of identity information of IoT devices, to include both device and application domains.

In the next section, the composite identity-of-things with an integrated blockchain network for IoT device identity management will be further discussed and explored. A typical setup for identity management using permissioned blockchain on smart home application will be reviewed.

5. COMPOSITE IDENTITY-OF-THINGS (CIDOT) FRAMEWORK ON IOT-BLOCKCHAIN NETWORK

Identity of IoT device typically being set up using either the logical or physical identification of the particular device. The dependency for single identification element for IoT devices as discussed in Section 2, may leads towards potential breach of confidentiality and eventually capable of bringing down the entire device network, through the network attacks such as the Sybil and Mirai attacks (See Section 2.1).

Composite identity of IoT device is mainly composed of a set of logical and physical identity elements, including MAC address, IP address, application ID, device type, and device owner. The composition is solely rely upon the network provider or owner, in defining which identity elements should be taken into consideration. In implementation within an integrated IoT-blockchain network, this composite identity is consequently stored as a data block in a shared distributed ledger of the blockchain network.

The CIDoT identity management model for IoT devices as described in the previous section basically utilizes a permissioned blockchain network for identity storage and verification. A permissioned blockchain network can be implemented in different kinds of platform including Hyperledger Fabric (Androulaki et al., 2018), Quorum (Baliga et al., 2018), and Multichain (Greenspan, 2015). In this chapter, the Hyperledger Fabric implementation has been considered. Hyperledger Fabric is a modular and extensible open-source system for permissioned blockchain deployment. It is one of the Hyperledger projects hosted by the Linux Foundation (www.hyperledger.org).

There are a number of different components that made up the hyperledger fabric. Table 1 shows the components and their respective functions.

Table 1. Hyperledger Fabric components and their functions

Component	Function
Distributed Ledger	Distributed database that contains data and related transactions.
Peers	Network services that maintain the ledger and execute smart contracts.
Ordering Service	Manage transaction sequence and distributes blocks to peers.
Smart Contract	Transaction logic whose output agreed upon by the peers.
Consensus	The process by which agreement is obtained on the peer network.

The permissioned blockchain model for distributed identity management requires the use of blockchain proxy that handles the device identity records to be stored and verified on blockchain network, as proposed in (Dittmann & Jelitto, 2019). Figure 9 shows the system view of the identity management model for IoT devices. In ensuring the authenticity of data stored in the blockchain network, a PKI certificate authority (CA) is registered with the blockchain that acts as identity provider trusted by the participating peers. The CA is responsible to issue an identity certificate to each blockchain proxy which uses the certified private key to sign the blockchain transactions. The choice of CA is depending upon the decision made by the network owner/provider. Hyperledger Fabric also come with its own CA as the certificate authority that issues certificates to the blockchain proxy. The blockchain proxy could represent the network owner/provider that owns the IoT devices. Also note that the identity elements that made up the composite identity come from two main sources, namely the IoT devices, and the related application systems that linked up to the network.

In Figure 9, it is also shown that the blockchain proxy will hold its security credential in its wallet, which is used to verify its identity to the blockchain network. The proxy has a responsibility to submit the transaction to the blockchain peer. The blockchain transaction in this system model is implemented in the form of smart contract, which can be executed by the blockchain peer, in order to commit it to the ledger.

Figure 9. System view of the CIDoT identity management model for IoT devices with permissioned blockchain network

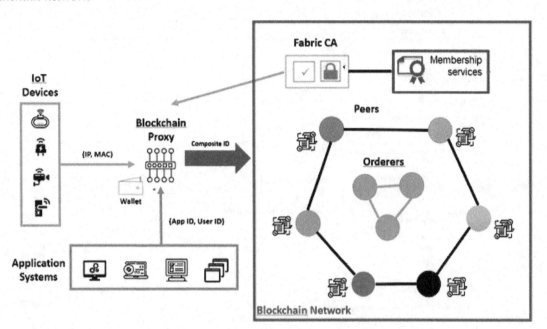

5.1. Smart Contract for Identity Data Access and Verification

An important component in Hyperledger Fabric implementation is chaincode. Chaincode is a program written in programming language such as javascript, java, and Go, which contain the list of smart contract transactions for storing and updating data on distributed ledger. Figure 10 shows a chaincode, consists of a number of smart contract code written in Javascript that can be used to access the composite identity data in the CIDoT implementation.

The chaincode as shown in Figure 10, includes two smart contracts, namely **queryDev()** that is used to query for an identity information of a particular device; and **createDev()**, that is used to create a device identity information. In order to access these smart contracts, the user application requires access to them. Figure 11 shows a Javascript code used to access the smart contracts.

The Javascript code shown in Figure 11, basically used to execute the smart contract **queryDev()** with input parameter: **DEV4**. Also note that in order to execute this smart contract, the user is verified against the credentials stored in the wallet.

5.2. System Flow

Figure 12 illustrates the process flow for the composite identity creation and storage in a permissioned blockchain network.

The composite identity is created by the blockchain proxy, based on the received identity elements from the IoT device and the organization/user that runs the application. This identity will then be stored as data block in Blockchain network. This is achieved via smart contract configuration made by the blockchain proxy.

Figure 10. A snapshot of the CIDoT chaincode that consists of two smart contract codes to access data stored in the blockchain network

```
/*
 * SPDX-License-Identifier: Apache-2.0
 * This is the chaincode code written in Node.js programming language for the CIdoT Application.

 * Last revision: 13th of March 2020
 */

'use strict';

const { Contract } = require('fabric-contract-api');

class CidotData extends Contract {

    async queryDev(ctx, devNumber) {
        const devAsBytes = await ctx.stub.getState(devNumber); // get the device from chaincode state
        if (!devAsBytes || devAsBytes.length === 0) {
            throw new Error('${devNumber} does not exist');
        }
        console.log(devAsBytes.toString());
        return devAsBytes.toString();
    }

    async createDev(ctx, devNumber, macAdd, app, ipAdd, owner) {
        console.info('============= START : Create Device ===========');

        const dev = {
            ipAdd,
            docType: 'dev',
            macAdd,
            app,
            owner,
        };

        await ctx.stub.putState(devNumber, Buffer.from(JSON.stringify(dev)));
        console.info('============= END : Create Device ===========');
    }
}

module.exports = CidotData;
```

Figure 11. A snapshot of the CIDoT user application code written in Javascript to execute the smart contracts in Figure 10

```
/*
 * SPDX-License-Identifier: Apache-2.0
 * This is the application code written in Node.js programming language for the CIdOT Application.
 * to access the smart contract included in the chaincode.
 * Date created: 12th of March 2020
 * Last revision: 13th of March 2020
 *
 */
'use strict';

const { Gateway, Wallets } = require('fabric-network');
const path = require('path');
const fs = require('fs');

async function main() {
    try {
        // load the network configuration
        const ccpPath = path.resolve(__dirname, '..', '..', 'first-network', 'connection-org1.json');
        const ccp = JSON.parse(fs.readFileSync(ccpPath, 'utf8'));

        // Create a new file system based wallet for managing identities.
        const walletPath = path.join(process.cwd(), 'wallet');
        const wallet = await Wallets.newFileSystemWallet(walletPath);
        console.log('Wallet path: ${walletPath}');
        const identity = await wallet.get('user1');
        if (!identity) {
            console.log('An identity for the user "user1" does not exist in the wallet');
            console.log('Run the registerUser.js application before retrying');
            return;
        }

        // Create a new gateway for connecting to our peer node.
        const gateway = new Gateway();
        await gateway.connect(ccp, { wallet, identity: 'user1', discovery: { enabled: true, asLocalhost: true } });

        // Get the network (channel) our contract is deployed to.
        const network = await gateway.getNetwork('mychannel');

        // Get the contract from the network.
        const contract = network.getContract('cidot');

        // Evaluate the specified transaction.
        const result = await contract.evaluateTransaction('queryDev', 'DEV4');
        console.log('Transaction has been evaluated, result is: ${result.toString()}');

    } catch (error) {
        console.error('Failed to evaluate transaction: ${error}');
        process.exit(1);
    }
}

main();
```

Figure 12. System flow for the composite identity creation and storage on the permissioned blockchain network

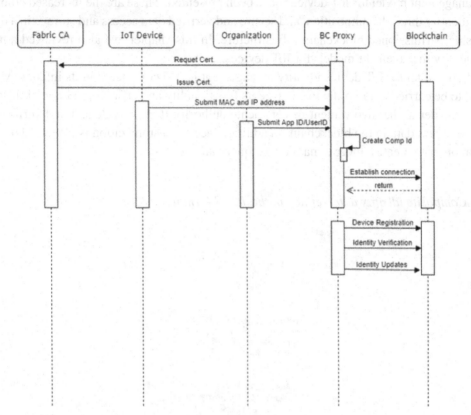

5.3. Application Design

Smart building application as described in the Introduction section, typically consists of a number of IoT devices that are used to monitor the conditions of the building. The implementation of composite identity management (CIDoT) of the IoT devices basically follows the system model as shown in the previous section. Figure 13 shows a typical composite identity data stored in JSON format within the Hyperledger Fabric permissioned blockchain.

With implementation of data format such as JSON, data can be retrieved by different applications more dynamically and being independent of the programming platform.

6. CONCLUSION

This chapter presents an alternative approach towards enhancing the identity of IoT devices in a distributed network using a composite identity design within an integrated IoT-permissioned blockchain network. IoT device is an important component that builds up smart applications, including smart building management system and other green systems. The composite Identity-of-Things (CIDoT) model could help in providing another layer of defense for the IoT network against the network-based attacks such as the presence of rogue devices, as well as the botnet attacks. Two important enhancement towards existing identity management model for IoT devices have been presented. These are the increased complexity of the device identity through composition, and secure and verified data access and storage in a distributed network using permissioned blockchain infrastructure. In this chapter, we also reviewed a number of different identity management models for IoT devices.

The CIDoT model for IoT device identity management is still considered in its infancy. More detail works need to be carried out in order to enhance its functionality and efficiency. Some of the important aspects to consider is the involvement of certificate authority (CA) to delegate and verify the proxy certificate to access data in the blockchain. In addition, access customization is also need to be further explored, in order to create a more dynamic data query and access.

Figure 13. Composite identity data defined in the JSON format

```
const devapp = [
    {
        ipAdd: '192.168.1.1',
        macAdd: 'FA:DF:0F:D5:3E:1A',
        app: 'Matlab',
        owner: 'Tomoko',
    },
    {
        ipAdd: '192.168.1.2',
        macAdd: 'EB:E0:1E:C4:4F:2B',
        app: 'SensorAnalytics',
        owner: 'Brad',
    },
    {
        ipAdd: '192.168.1.3',
        macAdd: 'DC:F1:2D:B3:50:3C',
        app: 'TensorFlow',
        owner: 'Jin Soo',
    },
    {
        ipAdd: '192.168.1.4',
        macAdd: 'CD:02:3C:A2:61:4D',
        app: 'Matlab',
        owner: 'Max',
    },
    {
        ipAdd: '192.168.1.5',
        macAdd: 'BE:13:4B:91:72:5E',
        app: 'SensorAnalytics',
        owner: 'Adriana',
    },
    {
        ipAdd: '192.168.1.6',
        macAdd: 'AF:24:5A:80:83:6F',
        app: 'TensorFlow',
        owner: 'Michel',
    },
    {
        ipAdd: '192.168.1.7',
        macAdd: '90:35:69:7F:94:70',
        app: 'Matlab',
        owner: 'Aarav',
    },
    {
        ipAdd: '192.168.1.10',
        macAdd: '63:68:96:4C:C7:A3',
        app: 'TensorFlow',
        owner: 'Shotaro',
    },
];
```

REFERENCES

Abu Hassan, M., Kudus, N., Sidek, S., Mohamed, S., & Aripin, M. A. (2018). Factors That Influence The Sustainability Of IoT Usage For Smart Living. *International Journal of Pure and Applied Mathematics*, *119*, 573–587.

Andolfatto, D. (2018). Blockchain: What it is, what it does, and why you probably don't need one. *Review - Federal Reserve Bank of St. Louis*, *100*(2), 87–95. doi:10.20955/r.2018.87-95

Androulaki, E., Barger, A., Bortnikov, V., Cachin, C., Christidis, K., De Caro, A., Enyeart, D., Ferris, C., Laventman, G., Manevich, Y., & Muralidharan, S. (2018, April). Hyperledger fabric: a distributed operating system for permissioned blockchains. In *Proceedings of the Thirteenth EuroSys Conference* (pp. 1-15). 10.1145/3190508.3190538

Baliga, A., Subhod, I., Kamat, P., & Chatterjee, S. (2018). *Performance evaluation of the quorum blockchain platform*. arXiv preprint arXiv:1809.03421.

Bandara, S., Yashiro, T., Koshizuka, N., & Sakamura, K. (2016, August). Access control framework for api-enabled devices in smart buildings. In *2016 22nd Asia-Pacific Conference on Communications (APCC)* (pp. 210-217). IEEE. 10.1109/APCC.2016.7581479

Bello, A. & Mahadevan, V. (2019). A cloud based conceptual identity management model for secured Internet of Things operation. *Journal of Cyber Security and Mobility*, 53-74.

Bernabé, J. B., Ramos, J. L. H., & Gómez-Skarmeta, A. F. (2017). Holistic Privacy-Preserving Identity Management System for the Internet of Things. *Mobile Information Systems*, *2017*, 6384186–1. doi:10.1155/2017/6384186

Catarinucci, L., De Donno, D., Mainetti, L., Palano, L., Patrono, L., Stefanizzi, M. L., & Tarricone, L. (2015). An IoT-aware architecture for smart healthcare systems. *IEEE Internet of Things Journal*, *2*(6), 515–526. doi:10.1109/JIOT.2015.2417684

Chen, Y. J., Wang, L. C., & Wang, S. (2018). Stochastic Blockchain for IoT Data Integrity. *IEEE Transactions on Network Science and Engineering*.

Dittmann, G., & Jelitto, J. (2019, June). A Blockchain Proxy for Lightweight IoT Devices. In *2019 Crypto Valley Conference on Blockchain Technology (CVCBT)* (pp. 82-85). IEEE. 10.1109/CVCBT.2019.00015

Fruhlinger, J. (2018). *The Mirai botnet explained: How teen scammers and CCTV cameras almost brought down the internet*. CSO Online. Disponible en: https://www.csoonline.com/article/3258748/security/the-mirai-botnet-explainedhow-teen-scammers-and-cctv-cameras-almost-brought-down-the-internet.html

Garcia, G. T., Sanchez, V. M., Marin, C. N. L., Cortez, J. I., Acevedo, C. A. R., Gonzalez, G. S. A., Ameca, J. L. H., & Garcia, M. D. C. M. (2018). Wireless sensor network for monitoring physical variables applied to green technology (IoT green technology). *European Journal of Electrical Engineering and Computer Science*, *2*(2). Advance online publication. doi:10.24018/ejece.2018.2.2.15

Gondchawar, N., & Kawitkar, R. S. (2016). IoT based smart agriculture. *International Journal of Advanced Research in Computer and Communication Engineering*, *5*(6), 838–842.

Greenspan, G. (2015). *Multichain private blockchain-white paper.*

Guin, U., Cui, P., & Skjellum, A. (2018, July). Ensuring proof-of-authenticity of IoT edge devices using blockchain technology. In *2018 IEEE International Conference on Internet of Things (iThings) and IEEE Green Computing and Communications (GreenCom) and IEEE Cyber, Physical and Social Computing (CPSCom) and IEEE Smart Data (SmartData)* (pp. 1042-1049). IEEE. 10.1109/Cybermatics_2018.2018.00193

Guo, H., & Heidemann, J. (2018, August). IP-based IoT device detection. In *Proceedings of the 2018 Workshop on IoT Security and Privacy* (pp. 36-42). 10.1145/3229565.3229572

Hernández-Ramos, J. L., Moreno, M. V., Bernabé, J. B., Carrillo, D. G., & Skarmeta, A. F. (2015). SAFIR: Secure access framework for IoT-enabled services on smart buildings. *Journal of Computer and System Sciences, 81*(8), 1452–1463. doi:10.1016/j.jcss.2014.12.021

Jain, R. K., Banerjee, P., Baksi, D., & Samanta, S. K. (2019, July). IoT Based Interface Device for Automatic Molding Machine towards SMART FOUNDRY-2020. In *2019 10th International Conference on Computing, Communication and Networking Technologies (ICCCNT)* (pp. 1-6). IEEE.

Jan, M.A., Nanda, P., He, X., & Liu, R.P. (2015, August). A sybil attack detection scheme for a centralized clustering-based hierarchical network. In *2015 IEEE Trustcom/BigDataSE/ISPA* (Vol. 1, pp. 318-325). IEEE.

Jan, M. A., Nanda, P., He, X., & Liu, R. P. (2018). A Sybil attack detection scheme for a forest wildfire monitoring application. *Future Generation Computer Systems, 80*, 613–626. doi:10.1016/j.future.2016.05.034

Kolias, C., Kambourakis, G., Stavrou, A., & Voas, J. (2017). DDoS in the IoT: Mirai and other botnets. *Computer, 50*(7), 80–84. doi:10.1109/MC.2017.201

Lam, K. Y., & Chi, C. H. (2016, November). Identity in the Internet-of-Things (IoT): New challenges and opportunities. In *International Conference on Information and Communications Security* (pp. 18-26). Springer. 10.1007/978-3-319-50011-9_2

Mahalle, P., Babar, S., Prasad, N. R., & Prasad, R. (2010, July). Identity management framework towards internet of things (IoT): Roadmap and key challenges. In *International Conference on Network Security and Applications* (pp. 430-439). Springer. 10.1007/978-3-642-14478-3_43

Omar, A. S., & Basir, O. (2018, July). Identity management in IoT networks using Blockchain and Smart Contracts. In *2018 IEEE International Conference on Internet of Things (iThings) and IEEE Green Computing and Communications (GreenCom) and IEEE Cyber, Physical and Social Computing (CPSCom) and IEEE Smart Data (SmartData)* (pp. 994-1000). IEEE. 10.1109/Cybermatics_2018.2018.00187

Qolomany, B., Al-Fuqaha, A., Gupta, A., Benhaddou, D., Alwajidi, S., Qadir, J., & Fong, A. C. (2019). Leveraging machine learning and big data for smart buildings: A comprehensive survey. *IEEE Access: Practical Innovations, Open Solutions, 7*, 90316–90356. doi:10.1109/ACCESS.2019.2926642

Sethi, P., & Sarangi, S. R. (2017). Internet of things: Architectures, protocols, and applications. *Journal of Electrical and Computer Engineering, 2017*, 2017. doi:10.1155/2017/9324035

Singi, K., Kaulgud, V., Bose, R. J. C., & Podder, S. (2019, May). ShIFt-Software Identity Framework for Global Software Delivery. In *2019 ACM/IEEE 14th International Conference on Global Software Engineering (ICGSE)* (pp. 122-128). IEEE. 10.1109/ICGSE.2019.00032

Trnka, M., Cerny, T., & Stickney, N. (2018). Survey of Authentication and Authorization for the Internet of Things. *Security and Communication Networks*, *2018*. doi:10.1155/2018/4351603

Venkatesh, V., Morris, M. G., Gordon, B., & Davis, F. D. (2003, September). User acceptance of information technology: Toward a unified view. *Management Information Systems Quarterly*, *27*(3), 425–478. doi:10.2307/30036540

Wang, Z. (2018). A privacy-preserving and accountable authentication protocol for IoT end-devices with weaker identity. *Future Generation Computer Systems*, *82*, 342–348. doi:10.1016/j.future.2017.09.042

Xu, R., Chen, Y., Blasch, E., & Chen, G. (2018, July). Blendcac: A blockchain-enabled decentralized capability-based access control for iots. In *2018 IEEE International Conference on Internet of Things (iThings) and IEEE Green Computing and Communications (GreenCom) and IEEE Cyber, Physical and Social Computing (CPSCom) and IEEE Smart Data (SmartData)* (pp. 1027-1034). IEEE. 10.1109/Cybermatics_2018.2018.00191

Zhang, Z. K., Cho, M. C. Y., & Shieh, S. (2015, April). Emerging security threats and countermeasures in IoT. In *Proceedings of the 10th ACM Symposium on Information, Computer and Communications Security* (pp. 1-6). 10.1145/2714576.2737091

Zhu, X., Badr, Y., Pacheco, J., & Hariri, S. (2017, September). Autonomic identity framework for the internet of things. In *2017 International Conference on Cloud and Autonomic Computing (ICCAC)* (pp. 69-79). IEEE. 10.1109/ICCAC.2017.14

This research was previously published in Role of IoT in Green Energy Systems; pages 59-80, copyright year 2021 by Engineering Science Reference (an imprint of IGI Global).

Chapter 24
Privacy Preserving Data Mining as Proof of Useful Work:
Exploring an AI/Blockchain Design

Hjalmar K. Turesson
York University, Canada

Henry Kim
blockchain.lab, York University, Canada

Marek Laskowski
blockchain.lab, York University, Canada

Alexandra Roatis
Aion Network, Canada

ABSTRACT

Blockchains rely on a consensus among participants to achieve decentralization and security. However, reaching consensus in an online, digital world where identities are not tied to physical users is a challenging problem. Proof-of-work provides a solution by linking representation to a valuable, physical resource. While this has worked well, it uses a tremendous amount of specialized hardware and energy, with no utility beyond blockchain security. Here, the authors propose an alternative consensus scheme that directs the computational resources to the optimization of machine learning (ML) models – a task with more general utility. This is achieved by a hybrid consensus scheme relying on three parties: data providers, miners, and a committee. The data provider makes data available and provides payment in return for the best model, miners compete about the payment and access to the committee by producing ML optimized models, and the committee controls the ML competition.

DOI: 10.4018/978-1-6684-7132-6.ch024

INTRODUCTION

Bitcoin (Nakamoto, 2009) presented a workable solution to the problem of double spending of electronic cash without a controlling central entity such as a bank. Launched in 2009, the Bitcoin network implements a peer-to-peer network of computers that maintains a distributed ledger, tracking all the network participants' cryptocurrency balances. In an open network of pseudonymous participants, reaching consensus about what transactions to include in the ledger is challenging – a simple voting scheme won't work since an individual can get an unfair influence by pretending to be an arbitrarily large number of individuals in a "Sybil attack" (Douceur, 2002). For Bitcoin, Sybil-resistance was achieved by requiring participants to expend real-world resources for a chance to append new transactions to the ledger, a scheme known as Proof-of-Work (PoW) (Back, 2002; Nakamoto, 2009; Dwork & Naor, 1993).

BACKGROUND

PoW "proves" that the important task of appending the next block to the ledger is given to someone – a miner – who is "rich" enough that they cannot be corrupted to tolerate a Sybil attack. Wealth is proxied by the miner's access to resources; for Bitcoin, that is the abundant amount of electricity and computational resources required to solve a very difficult mathematical puzzle before others do. However, for every block, it follows that the vast amounts of energy expended by the winning miner and the numerous losing miners are wasted (Vries, 2018; O'Dwyer & Malone 2014; Budish 2018). There have been some attempts at ameliorating this shortcoming by instead securing the blockchain with useful work via a Proof-of-Useful-Work (PoUW) scheme. PoW requires miners to collective expend vast computational resources to solve a mathematical problem whose solution has no other purpose. PoUW entails solving a mathematical problem whose solution is useful to a third-party external to the blockchain. Early examples were Primecoin (King, 2013), where the work required was to search for chains of prime numbers, and Permacoin (Miller et al., 2014), intended to direct mining resources to distributed storage of archival data. However, these efforts have failed to reach wide adoption possibly due to the limited utility of the work performed. More recent efforts have attempted to solve the orthogonal vectors problem useful for graph theory analysis (Ball et al., 2017) or perform computational tasks for executing Software Guard eXtensions (SGX) instructions on Intel chips (Zhang et al., 2017).

Here we take a different approach and focus on a specific, but common, task: privacy-preserving data mining. Our approach also results in work towards providing a dual-purpose scheme that is useful for domains of blockchain (consensus mechanism) and AI (data mining).

WHY PRIVACY-PRESERVING DATA MINING

The application of machine learning (ML) to important problems in medicine and finance often results in an apparent contradiction: Training the models requires access to large and varied data sets under industry or regulatory expectation that security and privacy will be preserved, even though the size and scope of the data collected makes it attractive to hackers and increases likelihood of malicious or even unintended privacy breaches. Recent news reports have highlighted data security and privacy failures (Armeding, 2018; Cameron, 2017; Subramanian & Malladi, 2020). To mitigate this seeming contradiction and limit data leaks, a popular scheme obfuscates the raw data and applies machine learning on the transformed data, enabling data-driven discovery ("mining") of insights while ensuring that the data remain private. This scheme which preserves privacy yet maintains data utility and modeling accuracy is called privacy-preserving data mining (Thuraisingham, 2005).

Given the popularity of AI (Siau & Wang, 2020; Wang & Siau, 2019), it is attractive to conceptualize a blockchain's proof-of-work mathematical problem as a data mining problem. However, proof-of-work is most compelling for blockchain use cases in which the proof of access to resources is a proxy for proof of incorruptibility amongst untrusted potential validators (Nakamoto, 2018). Bitcoin and Ethereum are blockchain networks that exemplify this "trustless," "permissionless" context. Clearly, raw, un-obfuscated data cannot be provided to third party validators (cryptocurrency miners) to do data mining on such open blockchains; miners may be trusted to do transparent, straightforward validation, but they cannot be trusted with raw data. Hence, our PoUW solves a privacy-preserving data mining problem, not a generic data mining problem using raw data.

Given a training data set of numerical features and a categorical or continuous target (output variable) associated with each example, the PoUW task can be set up as an ML competition, where miners compete to predict the targets given some inputs. The miner that best predicts the test targets wins. A standard ML competition relies on a trusted party, the organizer, who has full access to the data set and withholds a subset of the targets from the competitors. The organizer releases two sets of data to the competitors: a complete set of inputs-target pairs for model training (the training data) and a partial set consisting of only inputs, the test data inputs. During an initial training phase, the competitors train their ML models and submit their predictions based on test data inputs. Once this phase is over and submission can no longer be made, the organizer compares the submissions to the test targets and assigns the competitor with the best predictions the winner. However, without the trusted organizer, the correct input-target mapping would be publicly available and hence no training would be required for a perfect score. Thus, for a permissionless blockchain, the trusted organizer has to be replaced by a secure and trustless mechanism. We demonstrate that this can be accomplished using a hybrid consensus scheme.

Another challenge when using ML as a PoUW is that the difficulty cannot be set in advance. In most PoW blockchains, the average block interval is adjusted via an adaptive parameter, the difficulty (Mingxiao et al., 2017). This acts as a threshold where the first miner to exceed it wins. Should the mining power increase or decrease over time, the difficulty threshold is adjusted accordingly to maintain the average time it takes to cross it. Thus, the difficulty provides a known relationship to the amount of computation required, and by corollary, to the rate of block generation (Zheng et al., 2017). In contrast, for our PoUW, the amount of work depends on unknown factors. How much computation is needed to train a model to reach some set level of performance depends crucially on the data set. On one hand, given a simple, low-dimensional training set good performance can be reached with a trivial amount of computation, while on the other hand, training a model on high-dimensional image or audio data may take weeks on high-end hardware Without advance knowledge of the dimensionality and probability distributions in the data, there is no way of reliably estimating how much computation is required. Consequently, the block interval cannot be controlled by the ML equivalent of a difficulty parameter. Though we list our contribution below, our work does not overcome this general constraint for ML on PoUW.

A number of proposals for hybrid consensus where the scheme is combined with a classic consensus scheme (Pease, Shostak & Lamport, 1980; Castro & Liskov 1999) have been made. In these, PoW is used to select members of a consensus group privileged to write blocks (Bentov et al., 2014; Decker, Seidel & Wattenhofer, 2016; Kokoris-Kogias et al., 2016; Pass & Shi, 2016; Duong, Fan, & Zhou, 2016), resulting in a permissionless blockchain capable of greater block rates than blockchains based on Nakamoto consensus (i.e. Bitcoin-style consensus) (Eyal et al., 2016; Pass & Shi, 2016).

Our Contributions

Our novel Proof-of-Useful-Work for privacy-preserving data mining builds on ByzCoin (Kokoris-Kogias et al., 2016), bitcoinNG (Eyal et al., 2016), and ML competitions. Data privacy is achieved with a geometric data perturbation, a perturbation method that preserves privacy while still allowing for efficient model learning by several common ML algorithms. This work addresses two key challenges for blockchain consensus schemes and privacy-preserving data mining. First, it provides a way of decreasing the energy waste inherent to Nakamoto consensus-based blockchains. Second, it lays the groundwork for a decentralized two-sided market for machine learning models.

The advantages of this strategy are threefold: (1) it decreases the energy waste, (2) it provides a decentralized market for machine learning models, and (3) it harnesses the full computational potential of blockchain networks. Furthermore, our work is an exemplar for how the two emerging technologies of AI and blockchain can be combined to offer business and societal value. Of the six classes of useful applications that integrate AI and blockchain (Dinh and Thai, 2018), our work contributes synergistically to the areas of *Decentralized Computing for AI* and *Privacy Preserving Personalization*. That is, for example, AI developers can make use of GPU's that operate to solve PoUW problems with data secured via the blockchain, where the data has been transformed via AI techniques to preserve privacy and personalization. As Dinh and Thai write, "Despite rapid development, both AI and blockchain have a long road ahead of them." As exploratory as our research is, we put forth that our work could be one of the early cobblestones laid for that road.

Overview of the Proposed Framework

Our PoUW mechanism can be used with some version of a classical consensus protocol for a permissionless blockchain. Classical consensus protocols require a fixed size committee of known members that together collect transactions from users, append them block-wise to the blockchain, and ensure that the chain will have only one history that cannot be deleted or rewritten (Castro & Liskov, 1999; Bano et al., 2017). Ours is a scheme by which miners can perform useful work that allows them to join a fixed size committee of members participating in the consensus protocol. With this goal, we follow the hybrid consensus protocols (Pass & Shi, 2016; Kokoris-Kogias et al., 2016; Duong, Fan, & Zhou, 2016; Bentov et al., 2014; Decker, Seidel & Wattenhofer 2016) where PoW is utilized to dynamically select committee members. A blockchain that employs our scheme is composed of two parallel chains: one made up of long-interval PoUW-mined keyblocks, and the second, made up of short interval transaction blocks produced by a fixed size committee executing a classical, PoW consensus protocol (see Figure 1). Unlike other works, our work entails ML model training that requires the committee to time the generation of keyblocks in addition to agreeing upon transaction blocks.

Once a fixed-size committee is in place several consensus protocols could serve the purpose of producing the transaction blocks (Pass & Shi, 2016; Duong, Fan & Zhou, 2016; Bentov et al., 2014; Decker, Seidel & Wattenhofer 2016; Castro & Liskov, 1999).

Figure 1. Hybrid blockchain
kb$_i$ is keyblock i; tb$_j$ is transaction block j and Tx pool is the transaction pool. Full arrows indicate block linkage by hashes.

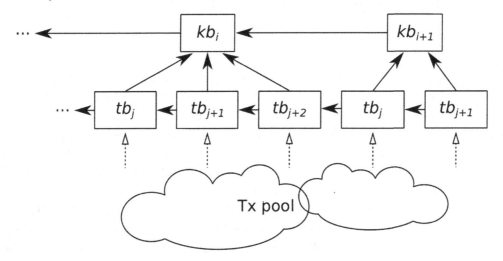

Our scheme rests on the actions of four parties: (1) data providers, (2) miners, (3) the committee and (4) non-committee nodes. In short, the data provider provides data, pre-processes and makes it publicly available. Critical to the pre-processing is splitting the data set into a test set and a training set, where the test targets are kept secret during the competition period. The miners train ML models on the training data and submit their predictions of the test data. The winning miner writes a keyblock and gets to join the committee. The committee generates transaction blocks and signs miner submissions, thereby controlling the timing of keyblocks. Finally, the non-committee nodes accept transaction blocks signed by the committee and the keyblock with the winning proof made up of the test targets and the best predictions.

Cryptography

We rely on four cryptographic tools: digital signatures, a hash function H, an encryption-decryption function E and a threshold cryptosystem.

In a threshold cryptosystem, n parties share a secret key, out of which a subset of size t is required for its use. Specifically, in a (t,n) threshold cryptosystem, n parties set up a group public key and each party retains an individual share of the secret key. With this setup, t of the n parties are required for creating a signature that validates against the group public key or decrypting a ciphertext encrypted by that key (Libert, Joye & Yung 2014; Boneh, Lynn & Shacham, 2004). A signature that validates against the public key thus represents a cryptographic proof of agreement by at least t committee members. The group keys are set up at the beginning of each round by running a distributed key generation protocol (Hanke, Movahedi & Williams, 2018).

The Blockchain

Members pass through the committee in a first-in, first-out queue. I.e. the leaving member is the one that has been a committee member longest. The selection of m is discussed in Future directions. Λ (lambda) is similar to the minimum block-depth to consider a transaction final in bitcoin (around 6 in bitcoin).

Since, a miner joins the committee by a Nakamoto-style PoUW there is a probability that a better keyblock will be found and thus another miner nominated to enter the committee. By, requiring a λ blocks before a miner can enter the committee the selection of members becomes irreversible in the same way that a bitcoin transaction becomes irreversible by waiting for λ blocks of confirmations.

The blockchain is composed of two parallel chains of: keyblocks and transaction blocks (see Figure 1). Keyblocks are mined and they provide access to the committee. By winning a keyblock, a miner becomes a committee member for a fixed number m of keyblocks. In our design, we assume that m is a parameter that is manually tuned; we deem the analysis of m on system performance to be beyond scope for this paper.

As a new member enters the committee another member is selected to leave based on a First-In, First-Out (FIFO) queueing method. The implication of FIFO use is that it signals that committee member tenure is determined fairly. This keeps m constant. The committee members' public keys are recorded in the keyblocks from $kb_{h-\lambda-m}$ to $kb_{h-\lambda}$, where kb is a keyblock, h is the current blockheight, and λ is a non-negative integer that serves as a security parameter. λ is similar to the minimum block-depth to consider a transaction final in bitcoin (around 6 in bitcoin). Since a miner joins the committee by a Nakamoto-style PoUW, there is a probability that a better keyblock will be found and thus another miner would be nominated to enter the committee. By requiring λ blocks before a miner can enter the committee, the selection of members becomes irreversible in the same way that a bitcoin transaction becomes irreversible by waiting for λ blocks of confirmations.

New keyblocks are mined with a fixed time interval controlled by the committee. To ensure that all miners compete on the same data set, each keyblock is tied to a specific data set by the inclusion of a hash of the data set (e.g. an IPFS hash) in the previous keyblock (see Figure 2). This data set is mined by the miners, who submit their hashed test target predictions included in proposals for the next keyblock. The winning miner gets to append the next keyblock, and joins the committee once the keyblock has become part of the stable chain – i.e. after λ blocks. The accepted block is the best predictions of the test targets and needs to be signed by the committee. Thus, the keyblock contains six parts:

1. A hash of the test set predictions;
2. Test targets;
3. A committee signature proving a timely submission;
4. A hash of the data set for the next keyblock;
5. A transaction of the reward from the data provider to the winning miner;
6. A hash of the previous block.

The Data Providers

In preparation for a future keyblock round, the data provider releases the data set that it wants modeled. To this end, the data provider has to perform two tasks. First the data must be pre-processed and released to the network, and second, the data provider has to commit to payment in exchange for the winning model.

In order to maintain data privacy and not leak information about the input-target mappings, the raw data has to be obfuscated. There are multiple approaches to this and among them is homomorphic encryption of the data. However, although promising, this is currently not viable for practical ML on relatively large data sets (Mendes & Vilela, 2017; Armknecht et al., 2015). Instead, we opt for a geometric data perturbation (GDP) that allows for ML on cleartext data, while still maintaining data privacy and mitigating information leakage (Chen & Liu, 2011). Cleartext data is obfuscated, but not encrypted – obfuscating the vector [1, 2, 3] might result in another vector of readable values [4.5, 3.2221, 103.01]. In contrast, encrypting [1, 2, 3] results in gibberish[1].

Many ML algorithms rely on multidimensional geometric relationships to learn a model of the data. GDP preserves this information, which allows the following algorithms to learn well on the perturbed data while maintaining privacy when the unperturbed data is made publicly available: SVM classifiers kernels, linear classifiers, linear regression, regression trees, neural networks, and all Euclidean distance–based clustering to. GDP achieves this by a sequence of random geometric transformations including multiplicative transformation by R translation transformation by ψ and a distance perturbation by Δ (Chen & Liu, 2011). $G(X)=RX+\psi+\Delta$ where G is the geometric perturbation function and X is the input data array. The requirements on the data are these: the data set X is a numerical set with examples (records) in rows and attributes (features) in columns, and each row belongs to a predefined class indicated by the class label y. Of course, the major disadvantage of GDP is that it cannot process high volumes of data efficiently.

In this mode, prior knowledge about the input-target mapping in the original data set cannot inform the learning of the model of the perturbed data set. Beyond maintaining privacy, this also ensures that a model trained on the perturbed data is only useful to a party with access to the perturbation matrices ($PM=[R,\psi,\Delta]$). However, up until the end of the submission period, the perturbation matrices need to be inaccessible to the data provider. If the provider has full insight into the input-target mapping of the test set, it can take advantage of this by proposing a keyblock with perfect predictions in order to join the committee.

To keep the perturbation matrices secret to all parties during the submission period, they are twice encrypted ($EPM \leftarrow E(E(PM,pk_{dp}),pk_{C})$) – first, by the data provider's public key, and second, by the committee's public key. This ensures that the perturbation matrices are ultimately only accessible to the data provider but first after they are released by the committee. Similarly, the test targets are also encrypted by the committee's public key in order to keep them secret until the committee has stopped signing the submissions, thus giving the committee control in the release of the test targets.

The intermediate steps of the pre-processing must be kept secret from all parties including the data provider. For this reason, the pre-processing must be executed by verifiable computation, a way of having an untrusted party execute some code with a trusted (verifiable) result. An untrusted party is an entity tasked to perform a computation who does not hold privileged security permissions such as public/private keys or read/write access. Verifiable computation is a kind of cryptography where even untrusted parties can verify the result of a computation – i.e. verify that a computation has been executed correctly. In this case, it is important to prove that the data obfuscation has been done correctly.

This means that anyone independent of whether they are to be trusted or not should be able to run the data obfuscation. And by verifiable computation they can prove that it was done correctly. I.e. there is no need to trust since we can verify.

There are multiple proof-based verifiable computation schemes, all with different strengths and weaknesses but their basic structure is common. A worker performs a computation and returns proof that the client (or verifier) can use to quickly verify that the computation was executed correctly along with the results of the computation. If the proof is validated, the client accepts the results; if not, the client can reject with a high probability that the computations were incorrectly executed. Verifiable computation schemes are much slower than native execution and generally are too slow for practical use (Walfish and Blumberg 2013). However, this computation is only performed for the keyblocks (not transaction blocks) (see Figure 1). Keyblocks are generated at a rate much slower than execution times of verifiable computation algorithms. Thus, there is latitude to select among multiple schemes in our work. The requirements that need to be fulfilled within the chosen scheme are the following: (1) Non-interactive, publicly verifiable proof that the pre-processing was correctly executed; (2) the proof needs to be zero-knowledge, that is, it can be verified without access to the pre-processing arguments, thus maintaining data privacy; and (3) a relatively small proof that can be included in a key block. In addition, the same pre-processing function will be used repeatedly (but with new arguments) for all data sets, which favors schemes with a relatively high initial setup cost whose cost basis can be amortized across repeated use.

The pre-processing function F takes the original data *Data* and u, the concatenation of the data provider's public key pk_{dp} and the committee's public keys pk_C ($u \leftarrow pk_{dp} \| pk_C$) as arguments. The original data is kept private by the data provider. The function F perturbs, shuffles, and splits the data, and then encrypts and hashes the test targets y_{test}. It returns the perturbed training inputs X^p_{train} training targets y_{train} perturbed test inputs X^p_{test} a hash of the test targets $Hy_{test} \leftarrow H(y_{test})$ and the test targets encrypted by the committee's public key $Ey_{test} \leftarrow E(y_{test}, pk_C)$ and *EPM*:

$$\left(X^p_{train}, y_{train}, X^p_{test}, Hy_{test}, Ey_{test}, EPM \right) \leftarrow F\left(Data, u \right)$$

For brevity, we give the complete output of F the label F_{out}.

A key generation algorithm, KeyGen takes as arguments the function F and security parameter k and returns a public evaluation key pk_E and a public verification key pk_V (Walfish & Blumberg, 2013; Parno et al., 2013):

$$(pk_E, pk_V) \leftarrow \text{KeyGen}(F, k)$$

The two keys, pk_E and pk_V are included in the blockchain's genesis block.

The worker algorithm executed by the data provider takes the public evaluation key pk_E the data *Data*, and the concatenation of data provider's and committee's public keys u as arguments. It returns F_{out} and π_{out} a proof of F_{out} is correctness:

$$(F_{out}, \pi_{out}) \leftarrow \text{Compute}(pk_E, Data, u)$$

Given the verification key pk_V the deterministic verification algorithm returns 1 if the computation was correctly executed, and 0 otherwise:

$$\{0, 1\} \leftarrow \text{Verify}(pk_V, u, F_{out}, \pi_{out})$$

Given these constraints, we use the Pinocchio heuristic (Parno et al., 2013) for best fit.

HD^{i+2} is the hash of dataset 2 steps ahead of the current keyblock i. The miners need to know which dataset to mine for the next keyblock (which doesn't exist yet), thus, a has of that dataset is included in the previous keybloack. To make the data set available to the miners it can be uploaded to IPFS (Benet, 2104) from where miners can individually access it. Alternatively, the data can reside on blockchain services that are provided complementarily via AWS, Microsoft Azure, or IBM Cloud platforms. We recognize that data processing off-premises may alter some of our analysis, but we made the design choice that a more involved addressing of this matter was beyond scope of this paper.

Figure 2. Keyblocks

kb_i is keyblock i; λ is a security parameter, HDi^{+2} is the hash of the test targets for data set i+2; dp is the data provider, $\textbf{Ey}_{test}^{i+2}$ is the encrypted test targets for keyblock i+2. $\textbf{pk}_{i-\lambda}$ and $\textbf{sk}_{i-\lambda}$ are the public and secret keys for committee $\textbf{C}_{i-\lambda}$ respectively

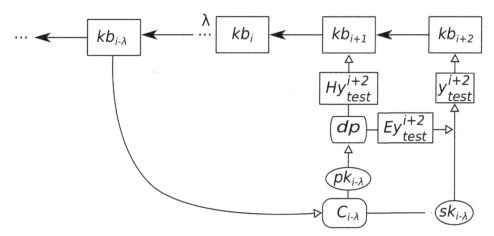

The Miners

In contrast to most hashing based PoW's where miners work on different instances of the same computational challenge – i.e. a partial inversion of a hash function – the PoUW proposed here provides a new challenge with each keyblock round.

In each keyblock round, the miners train ML models and commit to proposals for the next keyblock that includes their test target predictions. Instead of submitting their entire prediction set, miners commit to the predictions by submitting a hash of the predictions plus a nonce. This mitigates the risk that a miner's predictions are resubmitted (i.e. stolen) by someone else. Submissions are signed by the committee up until a deadline after which the committee decrypts the encrypted test targets, enabling the verifiers to evaluate a prediction score (e.g. F1-score) by comparing the test targets to the submitted predictions. The keyblock with the highest prediction score is accepted and the miner producing it joins the committee after an additional λ keyblocks.

Multiple data providers may simultaneously release data sets. Based on their payment commitments, the miner winning a round selects the next round's data set by including a hash of the selected data set in the proposed keyblock. This ties the next keyblock to the data set (see Figure 2). Data providers that expect a greater value from a model would thus commit to a greater payment. This creates a long-term incentive for miners to not only win the keyblocks but also to produce models useful to the data providers.

The Committee

The committee is made up of m committee members who all gained membership by winning at least one keyblock. The committee has two tasks: (1) generate transaction blocks and (2) control the period over which the miners can submit predictions. Transaction blocks are generated according to a classical consensus protocol[2]. To control the mining period, the committee members must do two things: sign the miners' keyblock proposal; and then end the submission period, thus stopping the signing and decrypting the test targets (see Figure 2). Committee members perform these tasks with a key pair derived from threshold cryptography, where each member has a share of the secret key sk_c and a signature that validates against the public key pk_c once t of m committee members have signed.

Verifiers

Finally, nodes external to the committee, that is, verifiers, accept and propagate the block with the best prediction score.

Simulation

Our proposal hinges on the viability of using test set targets, predictions, and a performance score to capture the quality of the predictions as a Proof-of-Useful-Work. A concern is that two or more miners will produce predictions resulting in the highest performance scores. In such a case it is unclear who should receive the reward. We had not provided a mechanism for breaking such tie between multiple top miners. We addressed this issue in two parts. First, we performed a Monte Carlo simulation to estimate the probability of multiple simultaneous winners, p_{multi} (see Figure 2), and second, we modeled the operation of the blockchain with a mechanism to break ties added. We add this model to our design.

The probability of multiple simultaneous winners, p_{multi}, depends on three factors: the number of miners (more miners leads to a greater p_{multi}), the size of the test set (smaller test set increases p_{multi}) and how difficult the task is (the easier the ML task is the greater p_{multi}). In order to explore these factors we simulated the mining of 86,400 keyblocks. Assuming a keyblock interval of one hour, this corresponds to around 10 years of operation. For each 86,400 block simulation we explored three different test set sizes (100, 10,000, and 100,000) all with eight equally distributed classes, four different difficulties (i.e. average error rate; 0.05, 0.1, 0.2, and 0.4), and two different numbers of concurrent miners (100 and 1000). The results can be seen in Figure 3. It is apparent that across conditions there are non-zero probabilities of two or more miner simultaneously producing predictions resulting in the top performance score. In addition, as discussed above, in real world circumstances, there is no way to control the difficulty of the data set. This is a vulnerability where a data provider could upload a data set where all miners can get a perfect score for malicious reasons. Thus, based on this argument and the simulation results presented in Figure 3, the performance score alone is not sufficient to decide on who will receive the reward. It is necessary to introduce something that can break any tie that might arise.

To break ties, we introduced the following rule:

Tie-break Rule: *When a tie arises (i.e. there are more than one top score), the top scoring miners' addresses are hashed, and reward goes to the miner with the greatest hash.*

Figure 3. Monte Carlo simulation of the probability of multiple miners submitting the best predictions for the same keyblock (p_{multi}). Difficulty is a parameter that models the average error rate on a data set.

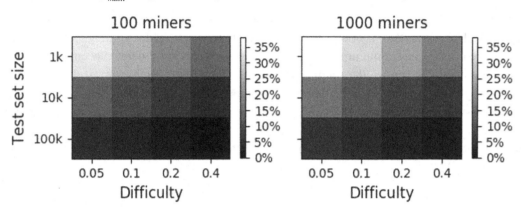

To test the viability of this, we modeled the proposed system using cadCAD (cadcad.org), a Python package for simulation of complex systems.

System Modeling

Recall that the blockchain is separated into two chains – a chain of keyblocks and another or transaction blocks – where appending a block to the former gives access to participate in the latter. For the question at hand the process of generating transaction blocks could be ignored, and thus, we only modeled the key chain.

We modeled the following components: data providers, miners and the committee:

1. **gen_kb_offer()**: This function returns a kb_offer, a dictionary holding a randomly drawn reward value, a random hash (e.g. an IPFS hash) referencing a data set, and a partial reward transaction.
2. **provide_data()**: This function calls gen_kb_offer() 100 times, simulating 100 data providers.
3. **propose_kb()**: This function simulates the action a single miner takes to propose a key block. It randomly selects a kb_offer among the 100 returned by provide_data(). The selection is weighted by the size of the reward, making a kb_offer with a higher reward more likely to be selected. Then, the hash of the data set from the selected kb_offer is added to the keyblock as well as the reward transaction and the predictions. Please note that the reward offered and the data set hash both relate to mining required for the next keyblock, while the reward transaction and predictions relate to the current block.
4. **mine()**: This function calls propose_kb() one time per miner.
5. **score_predictions()**: This function simulates the action of the committee and takes as input the proposed keyblocks and returns a performance score (accuracy) for each.
6. **select_next_kb()**: This function returns the winning keyblock given the prediction scores. In case of a tie, it is broken by comparing the hashes of the top miners' addresses.

With the above function we simulated the generation 172,800 keyblocks, which is around 20 years of operation assuming a one hour keyblock interval. Data providers ($n = 100$) generated keyblock offers containing a hash to the data set (e.g. an ipfs hash), a reward for next keyblock and a reward transaction for the current keyblock. Miners ($n = 1000$) select the keyblock offers based on the offered reward size and generate keyblock proposals containing test set predictions. The committee members receive the keyblock proposals calculate the performance score and in case of a tie, breaks it by comparing hashes of the top miners' addresses. The winning keyblock is appended to the keychain and the miners begin work on the data set linked to that keyblock.

The simulation showed that our scheme converges upon one miner being rewarded with a keyblock under all instances when the Tie-break Rule is applied. This address the key concern that the system loses significant credibility if ties are permitted and the winner is chosen haphazardly.

RELATED WORKS

There are a handful of projects working on different ideas involving blockchain and privacy-preserving computation and data mining.

Enigma

Enigma is a peer-to-peer project aiming to become a decentralized platform for general privacy-preserving computation and data storage. The Enigma project relies on an external blockchain, like Ethereum, to record, organize and reimburse certain events while storage and computation are done in a privacy-preserving manner off-chain with the help of encryption, distributed hash tables and secure multi-party computation. The Enigma project differs from our proposal in that it aims to support general privacy-preserving computation through multi-party computation (MPC) (Zyskind, Nathan & Pentland, 2015), not specifically privacy-preserving ML. MPC provides high security guarantees but, similarly to homomorphic encryption, doesn't scale well for big ML tasks (Chen, Pastro & Raykova, 2019).

OpenMined

OpenMined is an open-source community directly aimed at developing a platform for secure, privacy-preserving ML. They are building a toolset allowing ML models to be trained anonymously and in insecure environments, where the model is private to the ML practitioner, and the data stays private to the individuals from whom it originates. They rely on homomorphic encryption and multi-party computation for model privacy and federated learning for data privacy (OpenMined, 2018).

The scheme starts with an ML practitioner creating a model, specifying which type of data to train it on, and committing to a bounty for the trained model. This model is then encrypted/shared and submitted to a network where the members anonymously download and locally train the model if they have the correct type of data. The updated models are uploaded to the network and members get compensated in proportion to how much they contributed to improving the performance of the final model. Upon reaching a performance criterion, training stops, and the original model creator can decrypt and use the model. With this scheme, the data scientist maintains full ownership of the model while still getting it trained without having access to the training data, and the data holders get paid for their contribution while maintaining full ownership over their data (OpenMined, 2018). This strategy is like that of the Enigma project but uniquely focuses on privacy-preserving ML. It does differ from our proposal in that we instead propose a model trained on plaintext and transformed data. This also guarantees model privacy albeit indirectly since the model outputs will be useless to anyone without the decryption key.

TrueBit

TrueBit is a protocol designed to bring scalable – but not necessarily privacy-preserving – computation to smart contract platforms. It is being developed for Ethereum but should in principle be adaptable to any smart contract platform. It works by setting up opposing financial incentives for both performing the actual computations and for checking those computations. A verification game is run in order to settle disputes between the two parties. Like above-mentioned projects, scalability is achieved by outsourcing the computation to off-chain parties, and only performing small tasks in a contract (Teutsch, 2017).

However, the verification game is still rather inefficient, which means that the security of TrueBit computations degrades with increasing complexity and data. Thus, for tasks relying on great amounts of data, for example, ML tasks, TrueBit as currently proposed is probably not sufficient (Teutsch, 2017), requiring either successful optimization or another strategy altogether.

The Golem Project

The Golem project is also aiming to create a market for computation where parties can pay for and get paid for computation. Like the other projects, computation should be done off-chain, and only book-keeping tasks and reimbursement will be handled on-chain. Their goal is for a great variety of tasks to run on the Golem network, but currently, it is only possible to run video rendering and some proof of concept ML tasks (Golem, 2016). The exact scheme by which security will be ensured has not been specified, but TrueBit provides a possible mechanism by which to implement Golem (Teutsch, 2017; Golem, 2016). The Golem project differs from our proposal in that it is not privacy oriented.

The DanKu Contract

Algorithmia has developed a smart contract for the Ethereum blockchain with the goal of establishing an automated marketplace for machine learning models.

The scheme is structured like an ML competition, where a data provider commits to pay for a trained model and makes training data available via a smart contract. Miners submit trained models to the same contract and after some period of time the test data is released and an evaluation function (in the contract) evaluates the submissions. The best submission receives the payment (Kurtulmus & Daniel, 2018).

While the proposal is interesting and relatively uncomplicated, it results in quite a lot of on-chain data storage and computation. For example, to secure against manipulation by the data provider, sha3-hashed data groups must be uploaded to the contract, and thus, stored on-chain (Kurtulmus & Daniel, 2018). Assuming a data set of 10,000 exemplars and data group size of five exemplars, this corresponds to 2,000 256-bit sha3 hashes, totaling 64 kB. On the Ethereum platform, given 625,000 gas per 1 kB[3], this is five times above the Ethereum block gas limit of around 8 million[4]. Similarly, the evaluation function requires a forward pass of the trained models to be run in the contract that results in a severe limit to the complexity of the model. This will likely lead block miners to reject large data sets and complex models, limiting the usefulness of the DanKu contract. Additional complications arise since the Ethereum Virtual Machine doesn't have a complete math library, so it does not support floating point operations that are useful for DanKu.

Numer.ai

Numer.ai is an open ML competition on obfuscated financial data, and winners are rewarded with an ERC20 token. The data set is in plain text but obfuscated to protect it and make it useful only to Numer.ai. The submitted predictions are used to guide a hedge fund. However, apart from payout with an ERC20-token, this is not a decentralized blockchain project, but a normal hedge fund with outsourced management (Craibet al., 2017).

CONCLUSION

Incentives

Our proposal does not rely on a block reward to incentivize miners. Instead, it is fully reliant on fees. Miners and committee members receive payments for the services they perform. Committee members receive fees for the transactions they add to the blockchain, whereas miners train ML models for data providers and are paid via an on-chain contract. How much depends on the value of the model to the data provider. Thus, beyond simply winning the block, it is in the miners' long-term interest to provide good models to data providers. It is worth noting that after the block is won the resulting model is valuable only to the party with access to the perturbation matrices PM– the data provider. Thus, there is no incentive to steal or withhold the model from the data provider, since the model is useless to everyone else.

For the timing of the submission deadline, the data provider, the miners, and the committee have opposing incentives. It is in the data provider's interest that the submission deadline is as late as possible since then more work will be performed for the reward it pays. The miners, on the other hand, are motivated to perform as little work as possible (i.e. short deadline) for the same reward, whereas the committee reaps transaction fees up until the deadline and are thus interested in a long deadline. However, only the committee controls when the deadline falls; the other parties' motivations are ignored. The committee's incentive to extend the deadline can be curtailed by fixing the number of transaction blocks that can be produced between two keyblocks. This removes the possibility for committee members to earn more transaction fees by delaying the deadline and processing more transaction blocks. A more detailed exploration regarding submission deadlines is worthwhile for future work off our research.

Attacks

Committee members could collude in order to stay in the committee. Together, t of m colluding members could decrypt Ey_{test} and thus make perfect predictions without training any model. For comparison, miners in a PoW blockchain have a similar incentive to collude in order to execute a majority attack. However, combination of two factors help to mitigate this attack. First, miners depend on the cryptocurrency to not lose value (i.e. they hold and expect to win more cryptocurrency), and second, any such an attack is detectable since the resulting blockchain fork can be observed. The value of the cryptocurrency would likely be negatively impacted if a majority attack was detected. Thus, security is provided by transparency and the long-term economic incentives of miners.

Our proposal depends on data providers finding trained models sufficiently valuable to pay for them. Should they not, then they will stop providing payments and data and the network will grind to a halt. In this respect, the committee members' long-term economic incentives are similar to those of PoW miners, that is, they are incentivized to not negatively impact the value of the cryptocurrency. However, for the analogy to be complete, it is important to consider whether collusion would be detectable. The data provider is the only party who can directly detect whether a model has been trained or not by assessing how well it generalizes to new data. A data provider receiving a model that doesn't generalize to new data is unlikely to pay for yet another model. Similarly, a putative data provider that doesn't believe it will receive a useful model in return for payment is also unlikely to provide data. Thus, despite committee collusion not being publicly observable (e.g. in the form of a fork), it is still indirectly observable via the data providers. The result of committee collusion would negatively impact the value of the native cryptocurrency, and for this reason, go against the incentives of the committee members.

Future Directions

A difficult problem is that should t of m committee members be Byzantine (i.e. not following protocol), they can completely control the committee, and can maintain that control for an indefinite number of keyblocks without much effort. This contrasts with a PoW blockchain where a majority attach requires constant effort. However, the risk of collusion decreases with the number of committee members m and the size of t. Thus, it is of greatest importance to identify the compatible classical consensus protocol that allows for the greatest number of committee members, that is, highest possible node decentralization. While a large m is desirable, classical consensus protocols have tends to have a high communication complexity, severely limiting it's size (Castro & Liskov, 1999). The critical importance of the parameter m requires careful consideration; however, this task falls outside of the scope of this work and is deferred to later studies. In similar vein, we address that the focus of this paper is to elucidate a blockchain system design, where the story is strengthened by what is admitted coarse simulation. We believe that our simulation achieves its intended purpose, though we believe that a more systematic simulation of our design is another venue for further enquiry.

Another concern is Denial-of-Service (DoS) attacks by miners. A miner can cheaply submit a large number of keyblock proposals since proposals that do not reflect any model optimization are cheap to produce. Until the submission period is over and the test targets y_{test} are released, the committee cannot evaluate the quality of a given submission. This makes it possible for a miner to perform a DoS attack overwhelming the committee's capacity to sign keyblock proposals. This attack vector might be mitigated by requiring miners to deposit cryptocurrency and returning it only to well-behaving miners. However, further consideration of this is deferred to future work.

Finally, the committee selection suffers from a cold start problem. The selection of the first committee poses a problem since the proposed scheme requires an existing committee in order to update the committee. There are alternative ways to select the initial committee, and we will briefly outline two here. First, the initial committee could simply be made up of a group of participants that in random order exit the committee as new members enter by winning the mining competition. This requires a benevolent group but is otherwise not too different from how Bitcoin started with Satoshi Nakamoto as the sole miner during the first year. Another approach entails beginning with a standard PoW, adding one member for each keyblock until the committee is full, and thereafter switching to PoUW. This circumvents the reliance on the benevolence of the initial members, but somewhat delays the initialization of the PoUW and creates a few additional complications.

REFERENCES

Armknecht, F., Boyd, C., Carr, C., Gjøsteen, K., Jäschke, A., Reuter, C. A., & Strand, M. (2015). A Guide to Fully Homomorphic Encryption. *IACR Cryptology ePrint Archive, 2015*, 1192.

Back, A. (2002, September 2). *Hashcash-a denial of service counter-measure*. Hashcash.org.

Ball, M., Rosen, A., Sabin, M., & Vasudevan, P. N. (2017). Proofs of Useful Work. *IACR Cryptology ePrint Archive, 2017*, 203.

Bano, S., Sonnino, A., Al-Bassam, M., Azouvi, S., McCorry, P., Meiklejohn, S., & Danezis, G. (2017). *Consensus in the age of blockchains*. arXiv preprint arXiv:1711.03936

Benet, J. (2014). *IPFS-content addressed, versioned, p2p file system*. arXiv preprint arXiv:1407.3561

Bentov, I., Lee, C., Mizrahi, A., & Rosenfeld, M. (2014). Proof of Activity: Extending Bitcoin's Proof of Work via Proof of Stake. *IACR Cryptology ePrint Archive, 2014*, 452.

Boneh, D., Lynn, B., & Shacham, H. (2004). Short signatures from the Weil pairing. *Journal of Cryptology, 17*(4), 297–319. doi:10.100700145-004-0314-9

Budish, E. (2018). The economic limits of bitcoin and the blockchain (No. w24717). National Bureau of Economic Research.

Cameron, D. (2017, December 27). The Great Data Breach. *Disasters*, 2017.

Castro, M., & Liskov, B. (1999, February). Practical Byzantine fault tolerance. In OSDI (Vol. 99, No. 1999, pp. 173-186). Academic Press.

Chen, K., & Liu, L. (2011). Geometric data perturbation for privacy preserving outsourced data mining. *Knowledge and Information Systems, 29*(3), 657–695. doi:10.100710115-010-0362-4

Chen, V., Pastro, V., & Raykova, M. (2019). *Secure computation for machine learning with SPDZ*. arXiv preprint arXiv:1901.00329

Craib, R., Bradway, G., Dunn, X., & Krug, J. (2017). Numeraire: A Cryptographic Token for Coordinating Machine Intelligence and Preventing Overfitting. *Retrieved, 23*, 2018.

De Vries, A. (2018). Bitcoin's growing energy problem. *Joule, 2*(5), 801–805. doi:10.1016/j.joule.2018.04.016

Decker, C., Seidel, J., & Wattenhofer, R. (2016, January). Bitcoin meets strong consistency. In *Proceedings of the 17th International Conference on Distributed Computing and Networking* (p. 13). ACM.

Dinh, T. N., & Thai, M. T. (2018). AI and Blockchain: A Disruptive Integration. *IEEE Computer, 51*(9), 48–53. doi:10.1109/MC.2018.3620971

Douceur, J. R. (2002, March). The sybil attack. In *International workshop on peer-to-peer systems* (pp. 251-260). Springer. 10.1007/3-540-45748-8_24

Duong, T., Fan, L., & Zhou, H. S. (2016). *2-hop blockchain: Combining proof-of-work and proof-of-stake securely.* https://eprint. iacr. Org/2016/716

Dwork, C., & Naor, M. (1992, August). Pricing via processing or combatting junk mail. In *Annual International Cryptology Conference* (pp. 139-147). Springer.

Eyal, I., Gencer, A. E., Sirer, E. G., & Van Renesse, R. (2016). Bitcoin-ng: A scalable blockchain protocol. In *13th {USENIX} Symposium on Networked Systems Design and Implementation ({NSDI} 16)* (pp. 45-59). USENIX.

Golem. (2016, November). *The Golem project – crowdfunding white paper.* https://golem.network/crowdfunding/Golemwhitepaper.pdf

Hanke, T., Movahedi, M., & Williams, D. (2018). *Dfinity technology overview series, consensus system.* arXiv preprint arXiv:1805.04548

King, S. (2013). *Primecoin: Cryptocurrency with prime number proof-of-work.* Academic Press.

Kogias, E. K., Jovanovic, P., Gailly, N., Khoffi, I., Gasser, L., & Ford, B. (2016). Enhancing bitcoin security and performance with strong consistency via collective signing. In *25th {USENIX} Security Symposium ({USENIX} Security 16)* (pp. 279-296). USENIX.

Kurtulmus, A. B., & Daniel, K. (2018). *Trustless machine learning contracts; evaluating and exchanging machine learning models on the ethereum blockchain.* arXiv preprint arXiv:1802.10185

Libert, B., Joye, M., & Yung, M. (2016). Born and raised distributively: Fully distributed non-interactive adaptively-secure threshold signatures with short shares. *Theoretical Computer Science, 645,* 1–24. doi:10.1016/j.tcs.2016.02.031

Mendes, R., & Vilela, J. P. (2017). Privacy-preserving data mining: Methods, metrics, and applications. *IEEE Access: Practical Innovations, Open Solutions, 5,* 10562–10582. doi:10.1109/ACCESS.2017.2706947

Miller, A., Juels, A., Shi, E., Parno, B., & Katz, J. (2014, May). Permacoin: Repurposing bitcoin work for data preservation. In *2014 IEEE Symposium on Security and Privacy* (pp. 475-490). IEEE. 10.1109/SP.2014.37

Mingxiao, D., Xiaofeng, M., Zhe, Z., Xiangwei, W., & Qijun, C. (2017, October). A review on consensus algorithm of blockchain. In *2017 IEEE International Conference on Systems, Man, and Cybernetics (SMC)* (pp. 2567-2572). IEEE. 10.1109/SMC.2017.8123011

Nakamoto, S. (2008). *Bitcoin: A peer-to-peer electronic cash system.* Bitcoin.org

O'Dwyer, K. J., & Malone, D. (2014, June). Bitcoin mining and its energy footprint. In *25th IET Irish Signals & Systems Conference 2014 and 2014 China-Ireland International Conference on Information and Communities Technologies.* 10.1049/cp.2014.0699

OpenMined. (2018). *OpenMined Building Safe Artificial Intelligence.* www.openmined.org

Parno, B., Howell, J., Gentry, C., & Raykova, M. (2013, May). Pinocchio: Nearly practical verifiable computation. In *2013 IEEE Symposium on Security and Privacy* (pp. 238-252). IEEE. 10.1109/SP.2013.47

Pass, R., & Shi, E. (2017, October). Hybrid consensus: Efficient consensus in the permissionless model. In *31st International Symposium on Distributed Computing (DISC 2017)*. Schloss Dagstuhl-Leibniz-Zentrum fuer Informatik.

Pease, M., Shostak, R., & Lamport, L. (1980). Reaching agreement in the presence of faults. *Journal of the Association for Computing Machinery*, *27*(2), 228–234. doi:10.1145/322186.322188

Siau, K., & Wang, W. (2020). Reaching agreement in the presence of faults. *Journal of Database Management*, *31*(2), 74–87. doi:10.4018/JDM.2020040105

Subramanian, H., & Malladi, S. (2020). Bug Bounty Marketplaces and Enabling Responsible Vulnerability Disclosure: An Empirical Analysis. *Journal of Database Management*, *31*(1), 38–63. doi:10.4018/JDM.2020010103

Teutsch, J., & Reitwießner, C. (2019). *A scalable verification solution for blockchains.* arXiv preprint arXiv:1908.04756

Thuraisingham. (2005). Privacy-Preserving Data Mining: Development and Directions. *Journal of Database Management, 16*(1), 75-87.

Walsh, M., & Blumberg, A. J. (2013). Verifying computations without reexecuting them: from theoretical possibility to near practicality. In *Electronic Colloquium on Computational Complexity* (Vol. 2). Revision.

Wang, W., & Siau, K. (2019). Artificial Intelligence, Machine Learning, Automation, Robotics, Future of Work and Future of Humanity: A Review and Research Agenda. *Journal of Database Management*, *30*(1), 61–79. doi:10.4018/JDM.2019010104

Zhang, F., Eyal, I., Escriva, R., Juels, A., & Van Renesse, R. (2017). {REM}: Resource-Efficient Mining for Blockchains. In *26th {USENIX} Security Symposium ({USENIX} Security 17)* (pp. 1427-1444). USENIX.

Zheng, Z., Xie, S., Dai, H., Chen, X., & Wang, H. (2017, June). An overview of blockchain technology: Architecture, consensus, and future trends. In *2017 IEEE International Congress on Big Data (BigData Congress)* (pp. 557-564). IEEE. 10.1109/BigDataCongress.2017.85

Zyskind, G., Nathan, O., & Pentland, A. (2015). *Enigma: Decentralized computation platform with guaranteed privacy.* arXiv preprint arXiv:1506.03471

ENDNOTES

1   The result under an actual encryption scheme] starts like this: <8c>^M^D ^C^B<91>…
2   In order to keep the manuscript as simple and short as possible, I have left out the exact type of Classical consensus protocol, since various such protocols could be used as long as the conditions provided by the PoUW holds true.
3   https://ethgasstation.info/index.php
4   https://ethstats.net/

This research was previously published in the Journal of Database Management (JDM), 32(1); pages 69-85, copyright year 2021 by IGI Publishing (an imprint of IGI Global).

Index

A

B

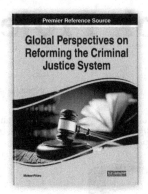

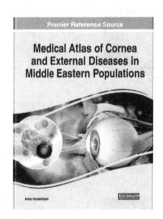

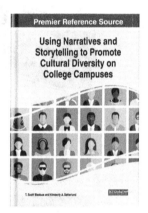

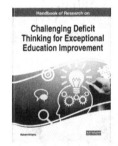

Printed in the United States
by Baker & Taylor Publisher Services